# 1988
# Yearbook
# of Science
# and the
# Future

1988

# Yearbook
# of Science
# and the
# Future

Encyclopædia

Britannica, Inc.

Chicago
Auckland
Geneva
London
Manila
Paris
Rome
Seoul
Sydney
Tokyo
Toronto

# 1988

# Yearbook of Science and the Future

The University of Chicago
The Yearbook of Science and the Future is published with the editorial advice of the faculties of the University of Chicago.

# Contents

## Feature Articles

# Europe's Growing Power in Space

## by Reimar Lüst

*Little more than a decade old, Europe's first fully integrated space program is rapidly expanding its expertise and competitiveness in every sector of space activity.*

The launch of the first Soviet and U.S. satellites in the late 1950s gave the world a psychological and political shock. Although at that time some of the larger European countries, notably the United Kingdom and France, could make a limited response, it was clear that no European country on its own could rival the superpowers. By the 1960s the concept of a united European space research program was being put forward as the only way in which Europe could hope to play a significant role in the exploration and exploitation of space.

Unity among such diverse cultures and languages was not an easy goal, and it was not until 1975 that Europe could boast that a single organization—the European Space Agency (ESA)—had been forged to express its ambitions in space. Before that time Europe had two separate bodies interested in space, the European Space Research Organization (ESRO) and the European Launcher Development Organization (ELDO), which had had rather different fortunes since their establishment in 1964. In bringing these two entities together the eleven member states that signed the ESA Convention—Belgium, Denmark, France, West Germany, Ireland, Italy, Spain, Switzerland, Sweden, the U.K., and The Netherlands—gave themselves a means to voice European views in the councils of the space powers. Austria and Norway were admitted to full membership in January 1987, at which time Finland became an associate member. Canada acquired a "special status" in ESA following the signing of a cooperation agreement in 1981.

## ESRO

The scientists, who were mainly responsible for persuading European governments to set up ESRO, had from the outset the belief that all satellite projects and the teams that monitored, designed, built, tested, and operated the satellites should be truly international. The result was a successful series of scientific sounding-rocket payloads and satellites, the data from which added greatly to human knowledge about the near-Earth space environment and more distant reaches of space.

ESA

*Sounding rocket carrying a short-duration experiment to the upper atmosphere lifts off from Kiruna, Sweden. In the middle and late 1960s ESRO, a predecessor of the European Space Agency, launched about 100 sounding rockets from diverse locations around the world.*

**REIMAR LÜST** *is Director General of the European Space Agency.*

*(Overleaf) Alain Nogues—Sygma*

Sounding rockets are designed primarily for experiments of short duration (normally a few minutes) within the upper atmosphere at heights of typically 160 kilometers (100 miles) but occasionally as high as 320–480 kilometers (200–300 miles). Many sounding-rocket experiments measure, directly or indirectly, the temperature, pressure, density, composition, structure, and movement of the upper regions of the atmosphere and the ionosphere. In the rocket's few minutes of flight the instruments can analyze the radiation from the Sun and from space beyond the solar system and can provide information on the way such radiation acts and interacts with the Earth's atmosphere. More recently, sounding-rocket payloads have carried materials sciences experiments to be done under low-gravity conditions in the fields of fluid physics, metallic dispersions, crystal growth, and furnace operation. By late 1968 ESRO had launched about 100 sounding rockets from such diverse sites as Kiruna, Sweden; Andøya, Norway; Sardinia; Woomera, Australia; and Greece. Its direct involvement in sounding-rocket experiments ended in the early 1970s.

Four years after it was founded, ESRO was ready with three scientific satellites, all placed in orbit in 1968 by U.S. launchers. ESRO 2 spent three years studying cosmic rays and solar X-rays; ESRO 1A sent back data on the aurora, other polar phenomena, and the ionosphere between October 1968 and June 1970; and HEOS 1 provided nearly seven years' data on the interplanetary medium and the bow shock. Another four satellites were launched before ESRO merged into ESA in 1975. (*See* table on page 11.)

The meteorologic and communications satellites launched by the U.S. in the 1960s interested a number of European countries, which consequently began working to expand ESRO from a purely scientific research organization to encompass and emphasize applications satellites. As the budget was proving inadequate even for scientific work by the beginning of the 1970s, the member nations of ESRO decided that the time was ripe to reorient the objectives of the organization. While electing to continue an obligatory science program on a reduced basis (a new satellite approximately every two years but no sounding rockets), they also budgeted funds for applications satellites. Three applications satellite programs were approved from the outset: Aerosat for aeronautical navigation, Meteosat for meteorology, and the Orbital Test Satellite (OTS) for telecommunications. Furthermore, the organization was given a coordinating and concerting role covering all space programs of the member states.

ESRO's members were also becoming increasingly aware of the political, economic, and technological advantages of having a major stake in the growing exploration and exploitation of space. Meeting at minister level, the countries decided to embark on three new programs. One, the space laboratory Spacelab, constituted Europe's contributions to the U.S. post-Apollo program. The second was the maritime navigation satellite MAROTS. The third, the Ariane launcher, was to replace ELDO's then current launcher project, Europa III. This last decision reflected the will to establish a single European space agency.

Photos, ESA

*Early scientific satellites launched for ESRO include ESRO 2 (far left) and HEOS 1 (left). The former spent three years studying cosmic rays and solar X-rays, while the latter sent to Earth nearly seven years of information on the interplanetary medium and the bow shock.*

## ELDO

By the early 1960s several European countries had their own small rocket launcher programs. Nevertheless, their political leaders realized that if Europe were to compete seriously in space matters, it could not continue to rely on launch opportunities provided by other countries. The solution, which came into existence in 1964, was ELDO. Australia, Belgium, France, West Germany, Italy, The Netherlands, and the U.K. were its member states, while Denmark and Switzerland were granted observer status on its council. ELDO established its headquarters in Paris and was granted the use of several national installations, particularly the

| ESA/ESRO Scientific Spacecraft Launched (to 1985) | | | |
|---|---|---|---|
| spacecraft | launch date | end of useful life | mission |
| ESRO 2 | 5/17/68 | 5/9/71 | cosmic rays, solar X-rays |
| ESRO 1A | 10/3/68 | 6/26/70 | auroral and polar cap phenomena, ionosphere |
| HEOS 1 | 12/5/68 | 10/28/75 | interplanetary medium, bow shock |
| ESRO 1B | 10/1/69 | 11/23/69 | same as ESRO 1A |
| HEOS 2 | 1/31/72 | 8/2/74 | polar magnetosphere, interplanetary medium |
| TD 1A | 3/12/72 | 5/4/74 | astronomy (UV, X- and gamma-ray) |
| ESRO 4 | 11/26/72 | 4/15/74 | neutral atmosphere, ionosphere, auroral particles |
| COS B | 8/9/75 | 4/25/82 | gamma-ray astronomy |
| GEOS 1 | 4/20/77 | 6/23/78 | dynamics of the magnetosphere |
| ISSE 2 | 10/22/77 | 9/87* | Sun/Earth relations and magnetosphere |
| IUE | 1/26/78 | beyond 1990* | ultraviolet astronomy |
| GEOS 2 | 7/24/78 | 10/85 | magnetospheric fields, waves and particles |
| Exosat | 5/26/83 | 4/9/86 | X-ray astronomy |
| Giotto | 7/2/85 | † | encounter with Halley's Comet |
| *anticipated    †may be retargeted to another comet | | | |

*The European Space Research and Technology Centre (above), located in Noordwijk, The Netherlands, houses most of ESA's project teams, technology support engineers, the space science department, and extensive testing and laboratory facilities. ESTEC technicians (opposite page, top) prepare to test a fairing for the Ariane 4 launcher. Mission control specialists (opposite page, bottom) staff the main control room of the European Space Operations Centre at Darmstadt, West Germany, from which ESA satellites are monitored and maneuvered.*

Woomera firing range in Australia, until it decided in 1966 to build its own launching base at the French space center in Kourou, French Guiana.

ELDO did not have the same opportunity as ESRO to develop a flexible approach or program. The technical and financial decisions had been made in advance by the founding governments, which had distributed responsibilities among themselves. To make use of existing development work, ELDO's initial objective was to construct a heavy spacecraft launcher called Europa I using the U.K. Blue Streak rocket as its first stage and the French Coralie as the second stage. The third stage was to be designed and developed in West Germany. Almost immediately it was realized that a more powerful launcher was needed, and Europa II, which would be capable of placing a 200-kilogram satellite in geostationary orbit, was authorized (one kilogram is about 2.2 pounds). Unfortunately, the management structure, wherein different countries were responsible for each stage of the launcher, led to technical problems, and by 1972 it was realized that a complete organizational overhaul was necessary. By then some countries were disenchanted with the idea of a European launcher, and Europa III, which was to supercede the earlier models, was abandoned. Because a launcher was included in the proposed single space agency that would become ESA, the demise of ELDO as a separate organization was hastened.

## ESA

Although countries found it difficult to agree on a common policy, by 1972 they had settled on a single agency with the task of integrating national and European space programs. Three years later the European Space Agency was formally established.

12

The agency's policy-making body is the ESA Council, composed of representatives of the member nations. The Council makes decisions on the policy to be followed by the agency and on scientific, technical, administrative, and financial matters, each nation having one vote (none in the case of an optional program in which it is not participating). The level of the agency's resources for its mandatory activities covering a five-year period is determined by a unanimous decision of all members. Other decisions are taken on either a simple or a two-thirds majority vote.

The ESA convention established a Science Programme Committee, which deals with and decides on matters related to the mandatory science program. The Council may also establish such other subordinate bodies as program boards to assist in decision-making on individual programs. Delegates from the member nations sit on all such committees and program boards.

The chief executive and legal representative of ESA is the director general, who is appointed by the Council for a defined period. He is assisted by an inspector general and the directors of administration, the European Space Research and Technology Centre (ESTEC), operations, space transportation systems, space stations and platforms, science, Earth observation and microgravity, and the telecommunications program. Together they oversee the work of about 1,250 scientific and technical staff members and 350 others.

Paris is home to ESA's head office, where the director general and most of the directors and their immediate staff officers are located. The agency also maintains three major establishments. ESTEC is located in Noordwijk, The Netherlands. It houses most of the project teams, the space science department, and the technology support engineers and has extensive testing and laboratory facilities. The European Space Opera-

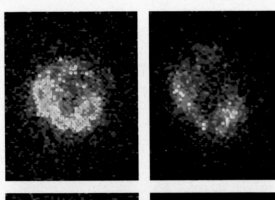
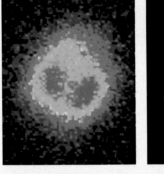
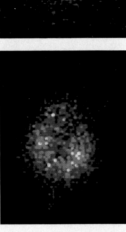

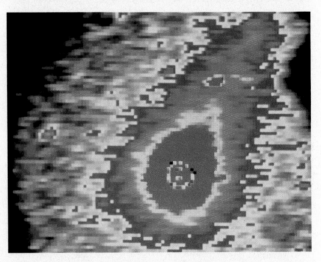

*The 300-year-old supernova remnant Cas A (four photos at top left) was one of the X-ray sources imaged by ESA's Exosat spacecraft (top right). The highly successful International Ultraviolet Explorer (left), an ESA-NASA-U.K. venture, observed solar-system objects, including Comet Bradfield (above), as well as distant stars and supernovas.*

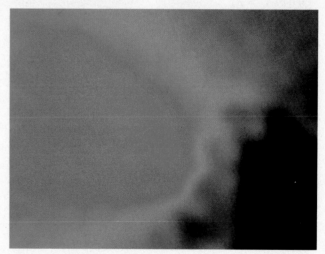

Imagery of the Earth's weather (top left) from Meteosat 2 (top right, piggybacked on an Indian telecommunications satellite before launch) has become a staple of European weather forecasts. Nucleus of Halley's Comet (above) was photographed with the Halley Multicolor Camera aboard ESA's Giotto spacecraft (left).

tions Centre (ESOC), in Darmstadt, West Germany, houses the major control centers from which ESA satellites are monitored and maneuvered and the data retrieval systems that receive scientific and technical information from satellites. ESOC sits at the hub of a worldwide network of tracking and monitoring stations. ESRIN, located in Frascati, Italy, comprises two distinct operations—the ESA Information Retrieval Service, which is host to numerous data bases used by European space industry and institutes, and Earthnet, which receives and processes Earth observation images from U.S. satellites. It will provide a similar service for images for the remote-sensing satellite ERS 1 when it becomes operational in 1989.

## Scientific achievements

Despite a dwindling budget in real terms, the list of ESA/ESRO scientific satellite successes is impressive. Lack of abundant launch opportunities encouraged scientists and engineers to build spacecraft and instruments to a very high standard. As a result the lifetime of many satellites greatly exceeded initial expectations (*see* table on page 11).

The scientific instruments flown on these missions fall into three main categories. In the first are those that make on-site measurements; for example, magnetometers orbiting in planetary magnetospheres or plasma detectors monitoring the solar wind in interplanetary space. In the second are such remote-sensing instruments as telescopes that collect and analyze radiation from distant stars, including radiation of wavelengths that cannot penetrate the Earth's atmosphere to reach ground-based instruments. In the third category are instruments that take advantage of the so-called microgravity environment experienced in spaceflight.

Europe's early satellites revealed much about the way in which cosmic rays and charged solar particles reach the Earth. Satellites placed in highly eccentric orbits added greatly to knowledge of the interplanetary magnetic field, the solar cycle, and the activity around the shock wave that occurs where the Earth presents a barrier to the supersonic solar wind. The TD 1A satellite, launched in 1972, was the first ESRO mission carrying telescopes beyond the atmosphere to view the stars.

ESA joined the National Aeronautics and Space Administration (NASA) and the U.K. to build and operate the International Ultraviolet Explorer (IUE). ESA contributed the spacecraft's solar panels and a ground station at Villafranca, Spain. Although intended for 24 months of operation at its launch in 1978, the satellite is still functioning well after more than nine years. The range of astronomical subjects it has studied has been large, but three are of particular significance. First, IUE has examined several supernovas, the explosive death of massive stars, immediately after their discovery. Second, in observing the normal mass loss from stars as they burn, IUE has dramatically altered previous ideas on this phenomenon. Finally, from its measurements of the atmospheres, coronas, and winds in cool stars, a broad theme has been established in which magnetic fields control the structures and energy balance of the stars' outer atmospheres.

16

The nature of gamma rays from interstellar regions is such that new methods of detection had to be designed. COS B, launched in 1975 and intended for a two-year observation life, gave a nearly flawless performance for six and a half years. It demonstrated that most of the gamma radiation arriving near the Earth originates in our own Galaxy. Orbited in 1983, Exosat has given European astronomers a rich harvest of new data about highly condensed, X-ray-emitting objects in the universe ranging from white dwarfs and neutron stars to radiation-swallowing black holes.

For many the return of Halley's Comet after 76 years was a disappointing spectacle to the naked eye. For astronomers it was an exciting key event, for five spacecraft from Europe, Japan, and the Soviet Union encountered the comet in the spring of 1986. On March 14 ESA's space probe Giotto passed within 600 kilometers (370 miles) of Halley, giving mankind its first pictures of the solid body at the comet's heart.

Scientists now know that the nucleus is shaped like a peanut shell, about 15–16 kilometers (9–10 miles) long and 8–10 kilometers (5–6 miles) across. It is thought that its surface is covered by a thin insulating layer of very black, porous, refractory substance. The nucleus has been found to rotate, although the actual rotation period is still in dispute. Direct photographic observation has shown that the comet sheds its mass in jets of dust and gas that emanate from the sunlit side. Water vapor proved to be the dominant parent molecule in the coma. Yet other data have given insight into the composition of the comet, which probably contains matter unchanged since the birth of the solar system.

ESA

*Ulysses, awaiting launch from a U.S. space shuttle, is intended to study the interplanetary medium in three dimensions. It will be the first space probe to leave the plane of the solar system and observe the Sun above its poles.*

*ESA's Spacelab module (above) rests in the cargo bay of an orbiting space shuttle. View of Spacelab 2 hardware in the shuttle's cargo bay (above right) includes components of the instrument pointing system (visible at center).*

Still waiting for launch aboard a space shuttle is the 2.4-meter (95-inch) Hubble Space Telescope. NASA's orbiting observatory will be a strong force in astronomy, and ESA has a 15% share, having contributed the solar arrays and the Faint Object Camera (FOC) with its associated photon detector assembly. The FOC will observe the most remote parts of the universe and consequently the earliest phases of its evolution.

Two other scientific satellites in the development stage are Hipparcos, due for launch in 1988 or 1989, and the Infrared Space Observatory (ISO), which should be launched in 1992. Hipparcos is a space astrometry mission that will measure the position and proper motion of 100,000 selected stars with the highest accuracy so far achieved and so lead to a much greater knowledge of the internal structure and evolution of stars. ISO will allow a thousandfold increase in sensitivity over ground-based or balloon-borne infrared instruments. It will play a key role in observing distant galaxies and the birth of stars.

Like the Hubble Space Telescope, the space probe Ulysses awaits the new launch schedule following the explosion of the space shuttle *Challenger* in 1986. Ulysses will be the first man-made object to leave the ecliptic plane and to observe the Sun above its poles. Its objectives are to study the interplanetary medium in three dimensions, in particular the solar wind; the interplanetary magnetic field, gas, and dust; and galactic cosmic rays, all as a function of the distance above the ecliptic plane.

## Telecommunications satellites

The earliest exploitation of satellites for telecommunications purposes came with the establishment of high-capacity intercontinental links in the

18

1960s, in particular for transmitting television programs. Concurrently a quiet revolution was taking place in the development of semiconductors, integrated circuits, computers, and satellites so that new applications for telecommunications satellites emerged: electronic mail, videotext, videophones, telex, data transmissions, high-speed telecopying, and video-conference facilities.

In July 1970 the decision was taken to establish ECS, the European telecommunications satellite program. By 1972 approval was given to construct an Orbital Test Satellite (OTS) to test the ECS design and to validate transmission techniques and on-board technology. This was followed by MAROTS, a maritime verison of OTS for communications experiments with ships at sea. OTS, designed for three years' service, operated from 1978 to 1984 before giving way to the first ECS operational satellite launched in June 1983.

The national postal, telephone, and telegraph services of the European countries realized that to make the most of the satellite systems they would need a single organization through which they could negotiate with ESA and run the day-to-day operations of the systems. For this purpose they set up Eutelsat, to which ECS satellites would be handed over for operational control after the initial test period. The first ECS satellite is now dedicated almost exclusively to the distribution of television programs to cable networks, but thanks to experiments carried out on OTS and to the development of small ground stations, later versions of ECS are equipped for multiservices; that is, specialized services between small stations installed on company sites or in their immediate vicinity. Currently two ECS satellites are operational, and two others await launch by Ariane vehicles. The Olympus satellite, due for launch in 1988, is intended to expand Europe's experience with broadcasting satellites, worldwide networks for teleconferences, and satellite links in

*ESA scientist-astronaut Ulf Merbold carries out a materials sciences experiment during Spacelab's maiden flight in 1983. The many studies conducted aboard this and subsequent Spacelab flights paved the way for a future program of microgravity research.*

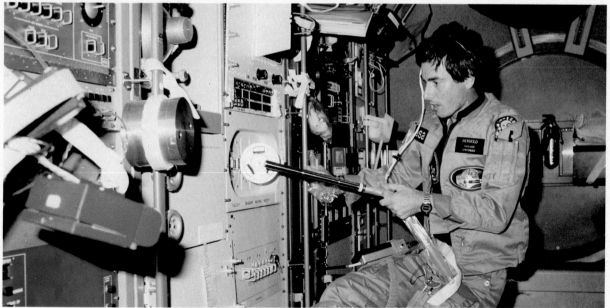

NASA

the retrieval and transfer of information, preparatory to the next generation of operational satellites.

Meanwhile, the MAROTS concept evolved into MARECS, as the international body Inmarsat requested an operational satellite in orbit over the Atlantic. In 1981 ESA launched MARECS A and transferred it to Inmarsat. MARECS B2 has since been launched and handed over as well.

## Earth observation satellites

Earth observation has become an important space application. Meteorologic satellites are now essential for daily weather forecasting and for predicting such hazards as severe storms and floods. Remote-sensing satellites assist in crop-yield forecasts, water resource management, monitoring of forests, prospecting for minerals and oil, geodetic mapping, environmental control, monitoring of icebergs, and control of land use—all services for which a high potential demand exists. In the future even earthquake prediction by satellite may become possible.

An early priority of ESA was to test the viability of a Europe-wide meteorologic service using satellite data. In 1977 the first Meteosat satellite was launched, followed in 1981 by Meteosat 2. For many years the images from those satellites have been familiar to television viewers across Europe as the basis for their weather forecasts. The satellites not only disseminate the images, acquired every 30 minutes in the visible and infrared regions of the spectrum, but also collect and disseminate data from international data-collection platforms on land and sea and in the air.

The success of this "preoperational" Meteosat program paved the way for an operational version, which was established in 1983 and which will have three new working satellites in orbit by 1990. Eumetsat, an

An unmanned free-flying platform for experiments, the European Retrievable Carrier (Eureca) will be placed in orbit by space shuttle and then retrieved and returned to Earth after several months of in-space operation.

ESA

organization representing the European national meteorologic offices, has been set up on lines similar to those of Eutelsat.

Remote sensing in Europe has also widened in scope with the decision to build and operate ERS 1, which is discussed below.

## Spacelab

Spacelab brought a new dimension to transatlantic cooperation in manned spaceflight. Both NASA and ESA had recognized the need for a "shirt-sleeve" laboratory in space in which scientists could work and which would allow investigators on the ground to participate actively in space experiments via communications links. ESA's pressurized Spacelab module, which was designed to fit in the cargo bay of a shuttle orbiter, gives that facility to shuttle missions. As part of the Spacelab concept ESA also designed and constructed pallets that can be used in several configurations to carry unmanned payloads like telescopes and sensors in the cargo bay of an orbiter. A final element is the instrument pointing system (IPS). Located on the pallets, IPS improves the shuttle crew's control over the pointing of such instruments as telescopes, which require more accurate bearings than the orbiter can provide.

Spacelab made its maiden flight in late 1983 on board the shuttle *Columbia*. Its crew included the first ESA scientist-astronaut, Ulf Merbold, who acted as a payload specialist responsible for carrying out and controlling a number of in-space experiments. The mission proved a great success, as did subsequent Spacelab flights. Among the many experiments flown were several microgravity studies in the life sciences and materials sciences, paving the way for a more concerted program of microgravity experiments for the future. West Germany made use of Spacelab to fly a national mission, called D-1, and a further mission is planned. NASA bought a second Spacelab module from European industry to increase the frequency with which it could be flown.

The success of Spacelab prompted Europe to continue its development of space transportation systems by designing and constructing the European Retrievable Carrier (Eureca). An unmanned free flyer, Eureca will take experiments into space on the space shuttle. Once the shuttle is in orbit, Eureca will be released into space to support the operation of its on-board experiments for several months until it is retrieved by the shuttle and returned to Earth.

## Ariane: Europe's launch vehicle

Ariane's rise to a place of eminence among space launchers has been a very real indication that the lessons of ELDO were learned and applied. All stages of its design and construction followed an integrated approach. The initial objective was to develop a launcher capable of placing a 1,500-kilogram satellite in geosynchronous transfer orbit, a figure later increased to 1,845 kilograms. The basic Ariane configuration consists of three stages and a fairing, or shell, in which the satellites are seated.

Economic considerations, competition from other launchers, and demands from users to provide launchers for increasingly heavy satellites

ESA

*An Ariane 3 carrying two telecommunications payloads—ESA's ECS 2 and the French Telecom 7A—lifts off from Kourou, French Guiana, in August 1984.*

led ESA to develop more powerful members of the Ariane family. Ariane 2 was designed to place a payload of more than 2,000 kilograms in transfer orbit, and Ariane 3 (Ariane 2 plus two strap-on solid boosters) can take a payload of more than 2,500 kilograms or two payloads of approximately 1,200 kilograms each. Satellites for direct broadcasting and comparable heavyweight payloads call for capabilities beyond those of Ariane 3. To meet these demands, Ariane 4 is being constructed to take payloads as high as 4,300 kilograms while having the flexibility to offer six different configurations to potential users.

The launch site at Kourou, French Guiana, has been considerably enlarged and a second launch pad constructed to allow more frequent launches. The European governments, while leaving ESA in control of future launcher development, have set up a special company, Arianespace, to market Ariane launch services to the world.

### Securing ESA's future

By the end of ESA's first decade of existence, it was necessary to reassess its position politically, technically, scientifically, and financially. The ministers responsible for space activities in their respective countries therefore met in early 1985 to approve a comprehensive and coherent plan that would take the European space program into the 21st century. From the outcome of the meeting it was clear that the member states possessed a genuine and strong political will to achieve a program that would be a powerful tool for negotiation with other major space powers. The ministers also indicated that they sought to expand Europe's autonomous capability and competitiveness in all sectors of space activity.

### Space sciences

In the realm of the space sciences an expanded budget will support a four-part program of flight opportunities destined to enable European space researchers to consolidate the continent's standing in the scientific world. The first part, a solar-terrestrial program, is aimed at exploring solar, heliospheric, and space plasma physics. Its two component projects are the Solar and Heliospheric Observatory (SOHO), which will be placed between the Sun and Earth at a distance of 1.5 million kilometers (930,000 miles) from the Earth to make high-resolution measurements of the solar spectrum, vibrations in the Sun (helioseismology), and the solar wind; and Cluster, consisting of four spacecraft equipped to make field and plasma measurements of the Earth's magnetosphere. The remaining three parts comprise a mission to one or more asteroids or comets, which would include bringing back material; a mission for X-ray spectroscopic studies in which a space observatory carrying several telescopes would probe the evolution of large- and small-scale structures of the universe; and a spectroscopy mission in the far-infrared/submillimeter wavelengths, by which the physics and chemistry of the cool universe could be studied.

Additional elements would include a number of medium-size missions (about $200 million) rather like Giotto, Ulysses, and Hipparcos. Among

*Ministers of ESA's member nations meet in Rome in early 1985 to discuss ways to assure the continued vitality of Europe's space program.*

ESA

22

*As ESA's first remote-sensing satellite, ERS 1 will explore the numerous scientific and commercial applications of remote-sensing data from coastal, oceanic, and ice-covered regions of the Earth. Current plans call for launch in 1989.*

the possibilities being considered are planetary orbiters, solar telescopes, plasma and auroral projects, ultraviolet spectroscopy, and stellar seismology missions. There is also room for smaller missions ($100 million), which would normally be missions of opportunity and participation in projects of other agencies; for example, a Titan probe as Europe's part of a NASA/ESA Saturn-Titan mission.

## Earth observation

Long-term objectives of ESA's Earth observation program are fivefold: to prepare by the mid-1990s operational satellite systems for ocean, ice, coastal zone, and meteorologic applications; to develop a second-generation meteorologic satellite that would continue the Meteosat system; to begin developing experimental/preoperational satellites for land applications, with emphasis on all-weather microwave instrumentation; to provide research tools for monitoring geodynamic phenomena (solid-Earth research); and to prepare potential future missions by means of advanced system and instrument studies. Funding for this program, at around $190 million a year, initially is being concentrated on the European Remote Sensing Satellite (ERS 1) project.

The sea covers the largest part of the globe and provides a livelihood or means of transport for many people. For a continent such as Europe the effect of ice is also crucial. Consequently, for its first remote-sensing satellite ESA has chosen an ocean and ice mission. In its role as an experimental/preoperational system ERS 1 will define, develop, and exploit the coastal, ocean, and ice applications of remote-sensing data and increase the scientific understanding of coastal zones and global

23

ocean processes. The commercial application of such data is relevant to offshore oil activities, ship navigation, fisheries, and oil pollution monitoring. ERS 1 is planned for launch in 1989. A second flight model with a similar mission might be launched in 1992 or 1993 to provide users with five to six years of continuous data. By 1996 an operational system based on the first two missions should be ready.

The object of a second-generation Meteosat is to provide improved profiles of such quantities as temperature and water vapor and high-resolution data for timely forecasting and regional applications. For continuity with the present Meteosat program, it would be necessary to launch the first second-generation satellite by the end of 1994. To complement Meteosat's geostationary coverage and to provide coverage of polar regions, a polar-orbiting satellite is contemplated. The possible use of a polar platform as part of a permanent in-orbit installation is discussed below.

ESA's future land-applications plan includes Advanced Land 1, an experimental/preoperational system that would define, develop, and exploit land applications of advanced all-weather remote-sensing data acquired from microwave instrumentation while improving Europe's ability to manage its land-based activities and resources. Applications include agriculture, forestry, land-use management, water resources and land surface processes, geology, cartography, and environmental monitoring.

Several solid-Earth projects will contribute to understanding the physical forces and processes that are active in the planet's interior and responsible for catastrophic events on the surface. The Precise Orbit Positioning Satellite (Popsat) would be designed to observe geophysical phenomena and monitor their dynamic behavior in earthquake prediction research. First launch may be in 1992 or 1993 and a second one perhaps five years later. A geopotential satellite mission would aid in understanding the line structure of the Earth's gravity field and allow inference of such crustal features as lithosphere structure and mantle convection. Also being considered is a spaceborne laser ranging mission that would monitor local or regional deformations in seismic areas by means of a two-color laser system.

## Microgravity experiments

Life sciences and materials sciences, the newest fields to be included in in-space payloads, have received more consideration since the success of Spacelab. Europe recognizes important roles not only for Spacelab and Eureca but also for a space station in microgravity research and development. The overall objective of ESA's microgravity program is to prepare for the future use of microgravity in space and therefore, as a first phase, to promote fundamental materials- and life-sciences research and to establish a data base upon which future researchers and industry can draw.

One microgravity project, Biorack, is a multiuser facility for experiments in cell and developmental biology, botany, and radiobiology and is specifically designed to operate in Spacelab's low-gravity environment. Main elements are thermal conditioning units (including incubators)

24

and a glove box housed in a standard equipment rack. The incubators contain centrifuges to simulate Earth-gravity conditions for experimental controls.

Another facility, the Improved Fluid-Physics Module (IFPM), establishes a "floating zone" of liquid in the microgravity environment. It allows mechanical, thermal, and electrical stimuli to be applied to the liquid, the behavior of which can then be observed and recorded. Results from the fluid-physics modules flown in previous Spacelab missions are already providing valuable insight into basic phenomena in a number of fields, from crystallization to life sciences.

The Space Sled is a life-sciences facility for Spacelab designed to determine human response mechanisms to controlled linear accelerations in weightlessness. A major goal is to evaluate responses of the central and peripheral neurosensory systems, which have evolved in Earth's gravitational field. The test subject, a Spacelab crew member, is secured in a seat which can be locked in any of three mutually orthogonal positions and to which various patterns of linear acceleration are applied.

As in any new field, considerable basic research is necessary before potential applications become crystallized. Those involved in this early phase of the microgravity program are hopeful that it will lead to discoveries and improvements of direct benefit to life on Earth. The growth of more perfect crystals for electronic components, improved metallurgical processes leading to new or better alloys, a deeper understanding of the human body and thus of preventive medicine, and greater insight into such biologic processes as plant growth are but some of the avenues to be explored.

*Preparations for future Spacelab flights include astronaut training on Biorack (below left), a facility designed for microgravity research in the life sciences. Main elements are thermal conditioning units with incubators and a glove box. The Space Sled (below), another future Spacelab facility, will assess responses of the human neurosensory system to controlled linear accelerations in weightlessness.*

Photos, ESA

## Telecommunications

ESA's future telecommunications program is built on past achievements and centers on the development and in-orbit testing of advanced payload systems at an average yearly expenditure of $170 million. One element in the program is the Advanced Orbital Test System (AOTS), a major demonstration mission that is foreseen for 1993 or beyond. A preliminary definition of the system could be a cluster of two satellites with intersatellite links and having the capability of performing rendezvous maneuvers and possibly docking experiments, plus a multifrequency and multiservice payload capable of a high level of on-board processing and carrying large reconfigurable antennas and possibly frequency-sensitive subreflectors.

Another element, a permanent space communications installation, would begin with DRS 1, a two-satellite working data relay system starting operation before the mid-1990s. The spacecraft would use radio-frequency links with ground stations and be interlinked with light beams. A second-generation system, DRS 2, could be introduced in the late 1990s.

ESA's objective in the field of navigation satellites is to promote establishment of a worldwide demonstration/preoperational system consisting of a number of spacecraft and Earth stations. Europe's contribution could include as many as six satellites or piggyback payloads and one main Earth station.

Other telecommunications packages will also be developed in such fields as propagation, data collection, search and rescue, polar communications, navigation, and UHF broadcasting.

## Permanent installations in space

In 1984 U.S. Pres. Ronald Reagan invited Europe to participate in a program centered on the construction of a permanent, manned space station in Earth orbit in the 1990s. As of early 1987 the precise details of the partnership had not been settled, but ESA had agreed to conduct preliminary design studies of a polar-orbiting platform, to be used primarily for Earth observation, and a permanently attached pressurized laboratory module. ESA also decided to conduct preliminary design of a man-tended free flyer (MTFF) comprising a pressurized module and resource module, the main purpose of which would be to carry internationally sponsored experiments in the materials sciences, life sciences, and fluid physics that require a long-duration, undisturbed microgravity environment.

ESA also has begun studying a co-orbiting platform based on an enhanced version of Eureca. This platform initially would be returned to Earth for servicing but later could be serviced in space when the space station becomes operational.

A strong element in the program is the need to ensure that all relevant fields of space science and applications benefit effectively. The specific roles to be played by Europe will depend on a final decision, but should a suitable partnership with the U.S. not be possible, Europe may opt for some type of autonomous in-orbit station.

*The Vulcain, a cryogenically fueled engine capable of 100 tons thrust, is part of a completely new technology being developed for the Ariane 5 launcher.*

ESA

26

*Hermes, a small spaceplane resembling the shuttle, has been put forward by France as a possible manned space transportation system. Hermes could be orbited from ESA's Kourou space pad atop the new Ariane 5 launcher.*

## Space transportation systems

The Ariane 4 launcher exploits the basic Ariane 1 technology as far as is economically possible. For the next generation of launchers, Ariane 5, a completely new technology is being developed, one that features a large, cryogenically fueled engine (the Vulcain) of 100 tons thrust and large solid boosters. This design should be significantly more reliable and cost-effective than earlier Arianes in placing satellites in either geostationary orbit or low Earth orbit. Its larger fairing diameter of 4.5 meters (14.8 feet) would allow wider payloads. Moreover, it eventually would be capable of orbiting a manned spaceplane (about 15 tons in low Earth orbit for the Hermes concept). Ariane 5 should be ready in 1995, with total development costs assessed at around $2.6 billion.

France has put forward the idea of a small spaceplane, Hermes, that could be launched by Ariane 5. The ESA council has agreed to "Europeanize," that is, bring under ESA's general program, the preparatory work for Hermes. Several other projects to put humans in space are being considered in Europe. The U.K., for example, is working on a single-stage horizontal takeoff and landing vehicle called HOTOL, which if successful could obviate the need for specially constructed launcher sites and revolutionize launch methods. West Germany is considering a two-stage system called Sänger after a famous German engineer, the first stage having common features with a global hypersonic aircraft and the second stage being a rocket plane. All these future systems are still in the intensive study phase, and it is likely that a choice for development will be made around 1990.

# GAIA
## A Goddess
## of the Earth?

*by Stephen H. Schneider*

**A controversial hypothesis
suggests that life on Earth has
long controlled the temperature
and composition of the planet's
atmosphere for its own benefit.**

It often seems obvious that life on Earth lives at the mercy of powerful nonbiologic forces like volcanic eruptions, severe storms, droughts, climatic changes, and even drifting continents. But cell by cell, plant by plant, and animal by animal, life has also been working to change its own physical and chemical environment. Over the long run of geologic time, life may even control these powerful nonliving forces for its own good— at least that is the daring view of British physicist James E. Lovelock and American microbiologist Lynn Margulis. Together they conceived the Gaia hypothesis, describing it as follows:

The Gaia hypothesis states that the lower atmosphere of the earth is an integral, regulated, and necessary part of life itself. For hundreds of millions of years, life has controlled the temperature, the chemical composition, the oxidizing ability, and the acidity of the earth's atmosphere. (*Natural History,* June–July 1976, p. 86)

Or, as Lovelock once put it,

In other words, the air we breathe can be thought of like the fur of a cat and the shell of a snail, not living but made by living cells so as to protect them against an unfavourable environment. As usual, with unfashionable ideas or concepts, it was very difficult to find any journal prepared to publish it. (*Co-Evolution Quarterly,* Spring 1980, p. 28)

As the latter quote suggests, the Gaia hypothesis is interesting not only as a novel scientific proposition but as a case study of the sociology of science and the process by which new ideas are formed and received by the scientific community and the public. Lovelock was not unaware of the skepticism that Gaian thinking would receive from some Earth scientists, to many of whom life on the planet is primarily passive, responding to inexorable inorganic forces and in return modifying the local environment and to some extent the chemical environment, for example, by photosynthetically taking up carbon dioxide and then putting back oxygen. But few would have agreed that the influence of life is so effective and directed that it actually controls the environment for its own purposes. Indeed, that is the essence of the controversy surrounding Gaia: whether environmental self-control exists and whether it is in a sense a "conscious" act of life processes. The former makes fascinating scientific debate, while the latter has strong religious implications. Nevertheless, Lovelock has argued that "whether or not the hypothesis is right or wrong is less important than is the fact that it is the kind of refracting glass through which the world can be seen differently" (*Co-Evolution Quarterly,* Spring 1980, p. 28). Let us look then through Lovelock's glass and examine some of the scientific ideas and arguments surrounding the Gaia hypothesis.

*STEPHEN H. SCHNEIDER is a Senior Scientist at the National Center for Atmospheric Research, Boulder, Colorado, and coauthor of* The Coevolution of Climate and Life.

*Illustrations by Jane Meredith*

## A scientist apart

James Lovelock is not the garden-variety scientist. He is not affiliated with a university, a national laboratory, or a large corporation but does most of his work in a home laboratory in the green rolling hills of Cornwall, England. He has not always been financially secure. Once he recounted that in the 1950s, when on a long visit with his family to

Harvard Medical School, where he was expected to survive on $3,000 per year, he sold his rare blood every few weeks at $50 a pint to keep the family in food.

But like life on Earth, Lovelock has always managed to survive, playing the role of what he calls an "independent scientist." Nevertheless, this has involved some concessions out of financial necessity. "The artist all too often finds no market for work he likes to do and is consequently obliged to produce 'potboilers' to survive," writes Lovelock. "So it is with independent scientists—except that our 'potboilers' are inventions. I have made about thirty of these; which from time to time were patented and sold and the proceeds used to sustain the family and the laboratory" (*Co-Evolution Quarterly*, Spring 1980, p. 28). One of them, from the 1950s, was a device so sensitive that it could detect trace chemicals in the atmosphere in exceedingly minute quantities. This instrument helped provide background information about environmental pesticides that Rachel Carson used in writing *Silent Spring*. It is also the basis of the explosive "sniffers" used in airports and has been employed to measure chlorofluorocarbons and other gases that might threaten the ozone layer or affect climate through the so-called greenhouse effect.

## The birth of an idea

Perhaps only such an individual as Lovelock, reluctant to compromise with conventions either social or scientific, can dream up an idea as simple and as radical as the Gaia hypothesis. But it did not come in a flash accompanied by an Archimedean "Eureka!" Like nature itself the Gaia hypothesis gradually evolved, under the influence of encounters with scientists having very different backgrounds.

In the 1960s Lovelock served as a consultant to NASA, using his background as an instrument designer and his knowledge of human physiology from his work at medical schools to examine the possibility of finding life on Mars when the Viking spacecraft landed there in 1976. NASA's scientists were busily designing instruments that would analyze chemicals in the soil, looking for compounds of possible biologic origin. Lovelock, working with biologist Diane Hitchcock, took an opposing view: not only were such experiments likely to fail but there also was a more certain way of telling whether life existed on Mars without even having to go there. Such an alternative angle came from a "systems view" of the planet, while also suggesting that organic and inorganic processes are not independently evolving. Lovelock somewhat sarcastically recalls his impression of work at NASA on the biologic detection experiment:

Here I discovered an extraordinary dichotomy. Seen at first hand, the engineering and physical sciences of the NASA institution was often so competent as to achieve an exquisite beauty of its own. By contrast (with some very noticeable exceptions), the quality of the life sciences was primitive and steeped in ignorance. It was almost as if a group of the finest engineers were asked to design an automatic roving vehicle which could cross the Sahara Desert. When they had done this they were then required to design an automatic fishing rod and line to mount on the vehicle to catch the fish that swam among the sand dunes. (*Co-Evolution Quarterly*, Spring 1980, p. 26)

31

In essence, Lovelock believed NASA would not find life on Mars because observations from Earth had already revealed enough about the Martian atmosphere to make the probability of life extremely small. Since the living beings of any planet are obliged to use available materials as both a source of nutrients and a sink for their wastes, if they exist in any significant number they are bound eventually to alter the composition of the atmosphere. On Earth, for example, such gases as methane and ammonia abound even though chemical processes exist that would transform them to carbon dioxide and other molecules. These gases persist in the Earth's atmosphere because they are continuously regenerated by bacteria and other organisms. Since telescopes and spectroscopes show the Martian atmosphere to have a relative paucity of these and other gases—oxygen and nitrogen, for example—that would be products of life, Lovelock doubted that Martian life existed. This chain of reasoning, however, rests on the assumption that life on Mars would have the same biochemical properties as life on Earth, an assumption impossible to test without a direct trip.

Lovelock's work at NASA eventually led him to his most important association, with Lynn Margulis of Boston University. Margulis, in addition to her contributions in microbiology, is an interdisciplinary scientist, combining knowledge from geology, botany, molecular biology, cell biology, zoology, and genetics in a search for symbiotic relationships—like Gaia. Together, they postulated the Earth to be a self-regulating system of the biota and the environment, with the capacity to maintain both the climate and chemical composition of the atmosphere in a state favorable to life. The innovative and controversial part of their hypothesis is that somehow life maintains control mechanisms for its own good—a process that has variously been termed homeostasis, negative feedback, or cybernetic control. Or as Lovelock once quipped, "We call it the 'Gaia Hypothesis' after the classical Greek word for our Mother Earth. It is a more convenient term than biological cybernetic system with homeostatic tendencies" (*The Atmosphere: Endangered and Endangering*, Fogarty International Center Proceedings number 39, U.S. Government Printing Office, p. 115).

Lovelock reached the idea from the metaphor of human physiology. For example, a special "thermostat" in the brain maintains the body at a nearly constant temperature despite wide variations in external conditions. A temperature rise of just a few degrees usually means that the body is sick with fever; a drop of a few degrees means that it is perilously close to death. This homeostatic control system is well known to physiologists even though the detailed mechanisms of its regulation are not yet fully understood. Why then, Lovelock and Margulis ask, could not the Earth be viewed as a whole physiological system (in what Lovelock has called the new science of "geophysiology") whereby complex but not yet well-understood mechanisms maintain a stable environment beneficial for life on the planet? Just as the brain's thermostat directs the body to conserve heat in a cold environment and to dissipate heat in a warm environment, why cannot the Earth have its own internal feedback

32

control system? The Gaia hypothesis simply states that such mechanisms of physical and chemical control exist in the totality of life on Earth.

## Regulation of atmospheric oxygen

What are some principal scientific arguments for life's self-control of its environment? One involves the Earth's oxygen, the gas that combines with other chemical elements to liberate energy, which is used to drive the metabolic processes of most current forms of life. Oxygen emanates slowly from inside the Earth in volcanoes, but usually it is combined with such other elements as carbon (carbon dioxide, or $CO_2$, for example, is the most abundant gas on our apparently lifeless sister planets Mars and Venus). Oxygen is also present in water, another compound undoubtedly emitted from the Earth's interior as it cooled some four billion years ago. Since there was initially little free oxygen in the atmosphere, there was very little material capable of filtering out the Sun's ultraviolet radiation. Solar ultraviolet is effective in breaking up the water molecule into hydrogen and oxygen atoms. Hydrogen, being a small and light element, could then be heated in the upper atmosphere to speeds high enough to escape the Earth altogether. Oxygen would be left behind.

Could such a mechanism have filled the Earth's atmosphere with oxygen even in the absence of life? Although it might have contributed in a small way, two arguments suggest that it was not sufficient to account for the present atmospheric oxygen level of 21%. First, when water vapor moves upward in the atmosphere—from higher pressure to lower pressure—it expands. From the laws of thermodynamics, any expanding gas must cool. Some four billion years ago the Earth's temperature appears to have been just cold enough so that as water vapor rose and expanded it

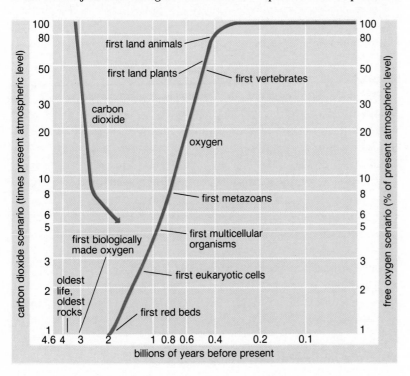

*Since the origin of the Earth some 4.6 billion years ago, the oxygen content of the atmosphere has increased and the carbon dioxide content decreased. Two scenarios are plotted at left, but considerable uncertainty exists about the precision with which such scenarios can be known. Although life appears to have been making oxygen more than three billion years ago, about a billion years passed before appreciable amounts of free oxygen appeared in the atmosphere and more than another billion years before atmospheric oxygen began approaching its present level. Another uncertainty—and topic for debate—concerns the relative importance of biological and inorganic processes in shaping these scenarios. Likely dates for some key events in Earth history are indicated on the diagram.*

Adapted from "The Biosphere," Preston Cloud. Copyright © September 1983 by Scientific American, Inc. All rights reserved.

cooled sufficiently to condense into liquid and fall back as rain or snow. In other words, most of the water vapor on Earth never rose high enough in the atmosphere to be dissociated by ultraviolet light, as it probably did on warmer Venus, but fell back to fill up the oceans. By contrast, no such "cold trap" operated on Venus, where most of the water vapor dissociated and where the oxygen that was left behind then combined with minerals in the crust.

A second argument against a nonbiologic origin for today's high atmospheric oxygen level has to do with the fact that there have always been many minerals in the Earth's crust in a reduced state, or capable of combining with oxygen. As oxygen is liberated into the environment, it ultimately reacts with minerals like elemental iron and copper, oxidizing them to metal oxides; hence, the reason automobiles rust and bronze statues tarnish. Yet, in spite of this ever present oxygen sink, evidence from geologic sediments suggests that the oxygen level on Earth has been near its present value for something like the last half billion to one billion years—the time over which most complex multicellular life evolved. It is extraordinarily improbable, Lovelock has argued, that this reactive gas could have been maintained so long at such a high level without continuous input from photosynthesizing life forms like cyanobacteria (blue-green algae) and green plants.

On the other hand, if atmospheric oxygen had risen much beyond 30% in the past half billion years, there would have been disastrous fires any time a lightning stroke occurred, even in wet, humid vegetation. What then could have kept the oxygen level from rising as a result of overly abundant life? One possible answer, proposed by Lovelock and Margulis, is the biologic production of methane by bacteria. Methane is short-lived in the atmosphere, combining with oxygen to form carbon dioxide. Perhaps that mechanism is a biologic sink for oxygen and has been Gaia's way of maintaining reasonable constancy of this vital element.

## Regulation of global temperature

Consider another argument for planetwide environmental self-control, this time the control of climate. It is widely believed that the Sun has been heating up since its formation many billions of years ago. This is not idle speculation but based on the known principles of nuclear physics, in which the hydrogen in the Sun fuses to helium. This process inevitably requires the Sun to emit more heat over time. Calculations suggest that some four billion years ago, when primitive life first appeared on Earth, the Sun was perhaps 25% less luminous than it is today. Current climatic theories often suggest that such a low solar energy output would have made the early Earth a frozen ball. Yet sedimentary rocks that could have been formed only by flowing water have been dated as far back as 3.8 billion years ago. Therefore, at least some parts of the Earth had both life and liquid water when the Sun was perhaps only 75% as powerful as today.

Known as the faint early Sun paradox, this problem was given a plausible explanation by U.S. astronomer Carl Sagan in 1971. He and a

34

colleague suggested that the gases methane and ammonia, then thought to be important components of the early atmosphere, are efficient absorbers of infrared radiation and would thus have served as a heat trap, preventing the loss of energy from the Earth to space through the greenhouse effect. In other words, these gases provided a "supergreenhouse" effect that kept the Earth's temperatures equable while the Sun was still relatively faint. Today, although $CO_2$ has replaced methane and ammonia as the best candidate for a supergreenhouse effect in the early atmosphere, the basic idea is still attractive. Lovelock and Margulis have argued that both the emission and the removal of such greenhouse gases as carbon dioxide, ammonia, and water vapor by life are part of the Gaian temperature-control mechanism.

But why has the planet not subsequently overheated, since over the past four billion years the Sun has increased its luminosity by 25%? Lovelock and Margulis turn to Gaia again, noting that life in the oceans in the form of tiny organisms called phytoplankton incorporates carbon dioxide into calcium carbonate skeletons. Thus, as the Earth warmed, the phytoplankton flourished and took up $CO_2$ more efficiently. When

*The role of biological processes in regulating the physical and chemical environment is central to the Gaia hypothesis. According to James Lovelock and Lynn Margulis, "For hundreds of millions of years, life has controlled the temperature, the chemical composition, the oxidizing ability, and the acidity of the Earth's atmosphere."*

35

they died and sank to the bottom of the ocean, they removed $CO_2$ from the system. Moreover, as the planet warmed, the oceans would lose more water to evaporation and rainfall would increase, creating more runoff from the land. In that runoff are nutrients that feed the phytoplankton and dissolved carbon compounds that form during the weathering process. In the Gaian view the net loss of $CO_2$ is just enough to compensate for the warming Sun.

### Reaction to Gaia

Ironically, when the Gaia hypothesis was first introduced, it was embraced not by the scientific establishment (which virtually ignored it) but by the ecology zealots—people looking for "oneness" in nature, for which Gaia provided a marvelous symbol. Gaia also appealed to the polluting industries, which applauded the idea of a magical control system in nature that would allow mankind to pollute with impunity and would still keep the planet fit for life.

Lovelock himself had a number of debates with environmental scientists over just this point. In 1975 the late anthropologist Margaret Mead held a conference in North Carolina at the National Institute of Environmental Health Sciences entitled "The Atmosphere: Endangered and Endangering." She saw the atmosphere as a great symbol of global unity that might help the highly fractionated political factions on Earth to recognize their interconnectedness. At that time controversy was raging over whether chlorofluorocarbons—spray-can propellants and refrigerants— released to the atmosphere could deplete the ozone shield that protects life on Earth from solar ultraviolet and its effects: sunburn and skin cancer in humans, blindness in some insects, and genetic damage in many life forms. But if there were homeostatic control, then perhaps such a danger would not be as serious as some environmentalists were claiming.

At the conference Lovelock said,

Without in any way wishing to deny its importance to us as a species, to the planet as a whole it [pollution] may be much less important than we think. We tend to forget that pollution is a way of life of many natural species and was so long before we appeared on the scene. . . . Our capacity to pollute on a planetary scale seems rather trivial by comparison and the system does seem to be robust and capable of withstanding major perturbations. The doomsters' cliche "and we'll destroy all life on Earth" seems rather an exaggeration when applied to an affair such as the depletion of the ozone layer by a few percent. (*The Atmosphere: Endangered and Endangering*, p. 119)

A large debate then broke out. Climatologist Stephen Schneider of the National Center for Atmospheric Research, Boulder, Colorado, and energy analyst John Holdren from the University of California at Berkeley countered that although they agreed that no human intervention, probably not even nuclear war, could remotely be powerful enough to threaten all life on Earth, when one is dealing with human beings, of which five billion are locked precariously into national boundaries and a billion or so are living at the limits of malnutrition, even slight disturbances in the environmental systems that produce food and recycle wastes can

36

be catastrophic to humans or other species. While not a threat to the survivability of the entire biosphere, changes of 5 or 10% in the carrying capacity of the Earth for human beings, they argued, must be viewed as having social and political consequences on a global scale.

Lovelock responded by agreeing that, from the point of view of humans, pollution could be an enormous problem but that if one approached environmental problems from a perspective in which nature exerted feedback on the system, one might very well propose different solutions from what hitherto had been offered. As the report of that conference demonstrates, what emerged was not a scientific debate answerable by experiments and hypothesis testing but rather a fundamental value conflict rooted in how one feels about taking chances with the future of the planet:

A crucial exchange, perhaps the fundamental problem confronted by the conference, occurred when a participant suggested that we should convey to the public the conclusion that "we don't know enough, we are trying to learn more, let's hang on tight while we can." Immediately came the response, "No, let's hedge against the worst." (*The Atmosphere: Endangered and Endangering*, p. 123)

Even today that philosophical dilemma applies to such environmental questions as the greenhouse effect, ozone depletion, acid rain, and toxic-wastes disposal, for it is extremely unlikely that scientific assessment can possibly answer all questions relevant to enlightened policy-making before the planet performs the experiments on Laboratory Earth, with human beings and every other living thing along for the ride. Other than that debate very little serious discussion of Gaia took place in the scientific establishment for nearly a decade.

Scientific indifference to the Gaia hypothesis, fortunately, has been substantially decreasing in the 1980s. The subject has been featured on popular television programs produced by the BBC and Boston's WGBH and in the award-winning television series "Planet Earth," coproduced by WQED, Pittsburgh, Pennsylvania, and the U.S. National Academy of Sciences. Moreover, a major international scientific meeting on the Gaia hypothesis is scheduled to take place in 1988. Serious scientific consideration of any idea, even such a radical one as Gaia, is certainly to be welcomed, for the very basis of the scientific method is to propose ideas, formulate testable hypotheses, perform those tests, and reevaluate the ideas in light of what is learned. However, in the process of critical analysis, which is the primary activity of most scientists, brilliant and beautiful ideas do get ground down, and some tumble altogether. When the two pro-Gaia arguments advanced above—the regulation of atmospheric oxygen and of climate—are given scientific scrutiny, some alternate inorganic ways to explain the same phenomena suggest themselves.

## Oxygen: another look

The first argument calls attention to the relative constancy of atmospheric oxygen over the past half billion years to make a case for biologic homeostasis. But where was this self-control in earlier times? More than three billion years ago one-celled cyanobacteria began producing oxygen.

Why then did it take another two billion years or more for oxygen levels to build to near their present amounts?

One explanation is inorganic. In the Earth's rock record are many formations known as red beds. They represent the conversion of a reduced form of iron, probably the compound FeO, to the oxidized form $Fe_2O_3$. Life dwelled largely in the oceans for most of its tenure on Earth and thus put its photosynthetic oxygen into the water. Why did the oxygen not immediately leave the oceans and enter in the atmosphere? The red beds may be part of the answer, for they appear to be the product of the removal of oxygen by a simple chemical process and subsequent deposition as geologic sediments. Only about two billion years later, when all the reduced iron was used up, was oxygen free to build in substantial amounts in the atmosphere.

To be sure, no one disputes the significant role of life in producing oxygen, but the time at which it appeared in abundant amounts in the atmosphere may have been controlled by inorganic phenomena related to the availability of readily oxidizable materials in the environment. Moreover, when oxygen eventually did build up, it was hardly welcome

38

news to the major forms of life then living on Earth—anaerobic bacteria, to most of which oxygen was poisonous. The oxygen rise forced them to take refuge in reasonably oxygen-free spaces—the bottoms of swamps, lakes, and oceans and, later on, the guts of termites or the polyps of coral reefs. This has led critics of Gaia to raise a question about biological control. Why, if it was in the interests of the early biota to control their environment, would they produce oxygen, a poison for themselves?

One possible answer is that, until the oxygen built up and, subsequently, an ozone shield was allowed to develop (since ozone cannot be formed until oxygen exists in the atmosphere), harmful ultraviolet radiation would bombard the land, making it difficult for life to come ashore. In other words, one form of life gave its all so that new forms could evolve, many of which are now on Earth. While one could argue that this is biological control at a planetary scale, it certainly would be no boon for the species doing the work. Evolutionary biologist Richard Dawkins, a Gaia critic, said of this idea,

At the level of the individual organism, I'm quite happy to say that the function of a bird's wing is to keep the bird up, the function of a bird's eye is to form a well-focused image and so on. I'm quite happy with that kind of purposeful language because that's at the right level in the hierarchy of life. What I am not happy about is to talk about the function of a particular gas in the regulation of the biosphere because it implies that individual organisms that are manufacturing that gas are doing so for the good of the biosphere. It further implies that if it were bad for them as individuals, they might still do it because that's the only way the biosphere will persist and the real danger is that people will think, will assume that individual organisms will sacrifice themselves for the benefit of the entire system and that's wrong and it's dangerously wrong in the sense that it's very widely believed among laymen and even among professionals. ("Goddess of the Earth," from the "Nova" television series, 1986)

To that Lovelock responded,

In the early days when it was a bit poetic, one thought of life as optimizing conditions on Earth for its survival. Now that I understand the theory behind Gaia very much more than I did then, I recognize that this is not so, that it's nothing as highly contrived or complicated as that. There's no foresight or planning involved on the part of life in regulating the planet. It's just a kind of automatic process. ("Goddess of the Earth," from the "Nova" television series, 1986)

Thus, Lovelock's recent thinking suggests no "religion," no purposefulness on the part of life, one of the aspects that made Gaia somewhat anathema to conventional science. On the other hand, his response still does not answer the criticism that it is hardly homeostatic or self-optimizing for species to poison themselves unless one also argues that, whether by accident or design, some forms of life sacrifice for the good of the overall biosphere.

## Climate revisited

The second argument for the Gaia hypothesis deals with the control of climate through temperature regulation by control of greenhouse gases. For the Earth to maintain a reasonably stable climate as the Sun increased its energy output over the past few billion years, Lovelock and Margulis hypothesized that the carbonate-secreting plankton absorbed the greenhouse gas $CO_2$. Several possible problems exist with this mechanism. First, phytoplankton, although biologically primitive compared with such species as trees, are still much more sophisticated than cyanobacteria and other bacteria, which appear to have been the only living things for nearly the first three billion years. Indeed, cells with nuclei, so-called eukaryotes, which include the phytoplankton, evolved only some billion years ago. Thus, phytoplankton as it exists today could not have been the primary carbon sink during the three billion-year period in which simpler life dominated and the Sun was continuing to heat up. Perhaps bacteria participated in such a $CO_2$-removing process, but the mechanisms as well as any quantitative assessment of the magnitudes have yet to be shown.

More serious a criticism is the assertion that temperature control through $CO_2$ removal could be accomplished inorganically. Working together at the University of Michigan, geochemists James Walker, Paul Hays, and James Kasting developed an elaborate feedback control similar to the Gaian idea but based on a nonliving mechanism. Instead of removing the $CO_2$ in the form of calcium carbonate skeletons, they postulate an inorganic competitor that involves the weathering of silicate minerals in the rocks on land. In the inorganic model it is assumed that as the Sun heats up, climate becomes warmer and rains increase. Since carbon dioxide in the air dissolves in raindrops to form weak carbonic acid, the more it rains, the more $CO_2$ will be dissolved. This rain dissolves minerals, part of the well-known weathering process. The weak carbonic acid combines with calcium silicate in rocks to form sediments containing carbon compounds. As the Sun heated up, this mechanism would remove carbon dioxide and reduce its greenhouse effect.

Lovelock, aware of the inorganic competition, has reworked it to include life in the feedback mechanism:

The Gaian variant of Walker's model assumes that the biota are actively engaged in the process of weathering and the rate of this process is directly related to the biomass of the planet. If conditions are too cold, the rate of weathering declines, and as a consequence of the constant input of $CO_2$ by degassing from the Earth's interior, the $CO_2$ partial pressure rises. ("Geophysiology: A New Look at Earth Science," in *The Geophysiology of Amazonia, Vegetation and Climate Interactions*, R. E. Dickinson, ed., Wiley, New York, 1987, pp. 11–23)

Unfortunately, no evidence, empirical or theoretical, is yet sufficient to resolve the conflict between the organic and inorganic competitors.

Moreover, frequent statements made by Gaian supporters that the Earth's temperature has been reasonably "constant" since the planet's inception cannot be supported or denied from paleoclimatic evidence. Of course, direct temperature measurements have been made only for the past few hundred years. Nevertheless, fossils of the many life forms that have existed can give a rough "proxy thermometer" from which one can estimate past conditions. For example, looking at the sediments can reveal the distribution of warm- and cold-loving species. There also exist chemical fingerprints such as the ratio of various stable isotopes of oxygen, whose incorporation into the shells of clams or the skeletons of plankton, for example, tell something about temperature conditions when the animals secreted their shells. Thus, science has something like a half billion years' worth of evidence from which to draw crude, but not wildly speculative, ideas about the mean temperature of the Earth. Before that, some geochemical evidence provides a very rough range in which temperatures had to be, but that range is so liberal as to stretch from an average planetary temperature near freezing to temperatures presently experienced in the Sahara Desert. Therefore, one of the most tenuous aspects of the entire argument over the faint early Sun paradox and Gaian climate control has to do with the question of how warm or cold the Earth had to be when life first got a toehold on the planet.

It is not necessary to assume that the mean temperature was within a few degrees of the present temperature, for there is no evidence from four billion years ago to suggest that life was widespread around the planet. It is possible that the planet was quite cold by present Earth standards and that life existed only in warm, tropical regions in limited domains or even in areas heated by upwelling lava or other flows from the interior. On the other hand, it is also plausible that the temperature was so hot that life existed only in the polar regions. Today there is no way to resolve to much better than plus or minus 20° C (36° F) what the mean temperature of the Earth was three billion to four billion years ago. For more recent geologic history the evidence gets more abundant; by a billion years ago the record of life is sufficient to suggest that the Earth's temperature was probably not more than 10°–15° warmer or a few degrees cooler on average than it is today. Although this comparatively narrow range is suggestive of some partial climate-control mechanisms, it is not known whether such partial control was from organic processes, inorganic processes, or—more likely—both.

## Strengths and weaknesses

The Gaia hypothesis is a profound concept, for which Lovelock and Margulis deserve significant recognition. The idea that climate and life mutually influence each other provides an important counterpoint to the parochial view of the world as physical environment dominating life, the predominant paradigm in the natural sciences for many decades. Nevertheless, to say that climate and life "grew up together" and mutually influenced each other—the concept of coevolution—is not to say that life somehow self-optimizes its environment. It is the latter idea on which much more elaboration is needed. The early physical environment largely carved out the ecological niches in which early life forms had to live. Life then altered these constraints on itself by changing the composition of the atmosphere. To be sure, this changed the competitive balance of species and forced evolutionary change—indeed, coevolutionary change—within organic and inorganic parts of the environment. But "optimization" is not nearly as apparent. If one simply defines optimization in terms of the best current adaptations to the current environment, then life might be optimizing itself. But what about the losers? To them the current environment has not been optimized.

41

A principal confusion with the idea of the self-regulation of life on a global scale arises in defining what "life" means in this context. Is "life" the maintenance of the stability (*i.e.*, the survival) of extant species for the longest period of time? Is "life" the maintenance of the maximum biomass, the sum total weight of living organisms? Is "life" the maintenance of the maximum diversity of species? All of these seem legitimate definitions, yet to "optimize" each one is probably inconsistent.

To consider a specific example, at the end of the Pleistocene epoch some 10,000 years ago, when the last ice age receded, the carbon dioxide content of the atmosphere was perhaps a third less than it is today. This implies that the weakened greenhouse effect made that age even colder than it otherwise would have been. A principal explanation for the decrease in $CO_2$ has to do with the biochemistry of the oceans, perhaps a planktonic response to altered nutrient availability. In other words, life in the sea seems to have been altering the chemical composition of the atmosphere, the climate, and its own environment. (Lovelock believes $CO_2$ concentration in the atmosphere to be an inverse measure of the biomass.) Yet it is hard to imagine how making an ice age even colder could be any general statement of homeostatic or self-regulation by life. The preponderance of evidence suggests that biomass on land was reduced relative to today by at least 10–20% at the peak of the last ice age. Since the vast bulk of living biomass is on land, this terrestrial loss far outweighed any gain marine life may have made from increasing its uptake of $CO_2$.

*For some scientists the Gaia hypothesis has made its most important contribution in stressing the important role of feedback mechanisms between organic and inorganic components of the Earth. In particular Gaia has challenged scientists to see the planet at a geophysiological level of organization rather than as a simple hierarchical structure.*

42

For some scientists Lovelock and Margulis's major contribution has been to stress the very important role of feedback mechanisms between organic and inorganic components of the Earth. In particular, they have challenged scientists to view the Earth at a geophysiological level of organization. Gaian supporters believe, rightly, that a whole-system view should be as legitimate a scientific pursuit as the more traditional reductionist views. But, in fact, there already exists a rich tradition in the philosophy of science that deals with issues of levels of organization. Moreover, the organizational level at which complex systems can be viewed most profitably cannot be determined without detailed empirical investigation. Some may prefer the traditional "bottom-up" approach, starting with subatomic particles or cells and working toward larger structures such as organs or coupled systems. Others may prefer a "top-down" approach, believing that systems are more efficiently studied at higher levels and that details should be predicted from that level. Both approaches appear valuable, especially for a science that is developing, if only to see which one yields more understanding and insight. In this context the Gaian scientists' call for a geophysiological approach to the interaction among organic and inorganic components of Earth is both welcome and overdue. But it does not mean that one should accept the proposition that such an interaction is always self-regulatory for life.

Feedback can be a two-way street. Its interactive processes can not only stabilize but also destabilize, like the ice age case mentioned above. Although life and the environment have coevolved, their interactions may not always have been optimum to all forms of life or even to the overall biomass. Such interactions simply lead to mutual change, some beneficial and some detrimental for some forms of life at some times. That alone is enough to encourage looking beyond the confines of biology, climatology, geophysics, chemistry, and other narrow disciplines to view the organic and inorganic parts of the planet as coupled systems. Nevertheless, it seems to be speculation at best and environmental brinksmanship at worst to believe that somehow, through self-regulation, Gaia will protect the planet from the negative consequences of all human activity.

To some the idea of planetary-scale homeostasis, the principal intellectual thrust behind the Gaia hypothesis, is more like religion than science. As religion Gaia can be deep, beautiful, and fascinating. As science, it is in need of more explicit formulation, so that empirical testing can be designed. Brilliant ideas are what drive future understanding, regardless of whether the initial formulations emerge intact. Only time—and serious scientific study—will tell how Gaia will fare in the future history of the Earth sciences.

# Superstrings

## by Frank E. Close

*Treating elementary particles as tiny strings residing in a ten-dimensional universe may wrap up our present understanding of force and matter into a "theory of everything."*

North, east, and upward. We are trapped in a three-dimensional universe that is evolving in the fourth dimension of time. What would a five- or six-dimensional universe be like? Does it even make sense to contemplate? We are so used to the status quo that we can hardly imagine things otherwise, but need it be this way? Why do we live in four dimensions?

An ultimate theory of the universe ought to answer this last question. It is one of the simplest questions to pose and yet one of the most difficult to tackle. It is not at all clear how to begin investigating it, let alone finding an answer. But in the past few years theoretical physicists have become excited by an idea called superstring theory, which is sketching out a new picture of space and time at unimaginably short distances and intervals. This theory may hold the first clues bearing on the question of our four dimensions, though at present it is still far from being understood.

Moreover, superstrings promise to overthrow our worldview in no less profound a way than did the arrival of quantum theory and general relativity earlier this century. Indeed, superstring theory subsumes both of these great pillars of 20th-century physics and modifies them. It is little surprise, therefore, that one noted scientist has described superstring theory as potentially the greatest development in theoretical physics in 50 years.

Within its four-dimensional skeleton the universe is the way that it is because of the varieties of fundamental particles that it contains and the nature of the forces acting upon them. It is very important, therefore, to understand this menu before grappling with the ultimate questions. This has been the strategy of the branch of science known as high-energy physics, or particle physics, wherein huge accelerators speed up bits of atoms and collide them, re-creating conditions similar to those that existed soon after the big bang of creation. In the past decade these experiments have given profound insights into the origins of matter and perhaps even of the universe.

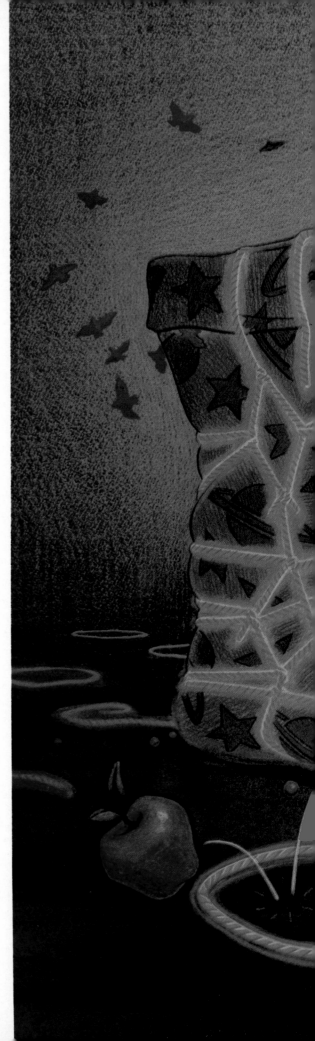

Particle physicists believe that they are near to formulating a grand unified theory of forces and matter. Yet for many years they have also been uncomfortably aware that their great paradigms, quantum theory and general relativity, are incompatible. Superstrings appear to solve these major problems and promise an ultimate "theory of everything." Although we are still a long way from such a goal, if indeed it is possible in principle, the excitement is intense, and many scientists feel that we are witnessing the birth of a new paradigm.

## Quantum theory

The immediate senses are aware of structures larger than about a tenth of a millimeter (four thousandths of an inch), simple microscopes extending that awareness to the dimensions of microbes. Until the end of the last century, "classical physics" sufficed to describe the known phenomena in this macroscopic universe. But hints of profound novelties occurring at short distances were already reaching the senses. Hot bodies emit electromagnetic radiation, and the standard theory made a nonsensical prediction—that the ultraviolet energy radiated by a hot body is very high and that the total energy is infinite. In reality, no such thing happens. The paradox, called the ultraviolet catastrophe, signaled a major failing of the existing worldview.

The great German physicist Max Planck found the solution when he formulated quantum theory, which extended physics into the realm of microscopic distances—that is, atomic scale and smaller. On such a short distance scale, high-energy radiation like ultraviolet light behaves according to a "new" physics, and Planck's quantum theory implied that classical laws have to be modified for microscopic phenomena. Matter is made of atoms, which are extended objects about a ten-billionth of a meter ($10^{-10}$ meter) in diameter, with a detailed inner structure. These tiny entities radiate energy in a way rather different from that predicted by classical theory. Once scientists appreciated the essential role of quantum theory at microscopic distances, the ultraviolet catastrophe vanished.

Quantum theory gave rise to a different worldview than hitherto. In quantum theory there is a fundamental uncertainty principle, an intrinsic unknowability in that we cannot measure both the position and the momentum or energy of a system to infinite precision. The more precisely a position measurement is made, the less precisely the momentum and energy of that system is knowable. This is imperceptible for macroscopic objects but more and more striking for phenomena at atomic and subatomic scales of length.

At very short distances even the energy that pervades so-called empty space is subject to great uncertainties and can fluctuate enormously in magnitude. Because energy and mass are equivalent ($E = mc^2$, as Einstein stated), these fluctuations can be interpreted as particles and antiparticles materializing transiently out of the vacuum. For distances less than a ten-trillionth of a meter ($10^{-13}$ meter), the energy fluctuations can be greater than twice the mass of an electron at rest. In these circumstances an electron and positron (the antimatter counterpart of an electron) can

***FRANK E. CLOSE*** *is Senior Principal Scientist at Rutherford Appleton Laboratory, Oxfordshire, England, and Professor of Physics, Queen Mary College, University of London.*

*Illustrations by Alex O'Neal*

appear fleetingly, until they meet and mutually annihilate. As a result, it is no longer possible to say that a system contains a fixed number of particles; electrons and positrons are continuously coming and going on brief time scales. Nor is the vacuum a void. Empty space seethes with an infinite number of particles and antiparticles.

Standard quantum theory, essential in every theoretician's toolkit, underwrites our theories of three fundamental forces acting on and within individual atoms. These are the electromagnetic force, which holds the electrons in the atomic periphery; the strong force that binds the atomic nucleus; and the weak force responsible for beta decay and the interactions of ghostly neutral particles called neutrinos. Together they are thought to control all phenomena other than those due to the fourth great force—gravity. This force, known the longest, is in fact the least well understood. Superstring theory is exciting in large part because it is the first to offer the promise of including gravity naturally in a unified theory of all forces and matter in the universe.

## General relativity

Physicists rarely invoke general relativity and quantum theory in the same breath. The two pillars of modern physics apply to very different situations, where they have never been found wanting. Whereas quantum theory describes the motion and behavior of individual atoms and microscopic phenomena, general relativity describes bulk matter—not just falling apples but the motions of planets and galaxies and the evolution of the entire universe—and it makes profound statements about the relation between gravity and the curvature of space and time.

From a pragmatic point of view, general relativity does quite well without quantum theory, and vice versa. When physicists deal with objects that are interacting gravitationally, they do not need microscopic descriptions. Conversely, when they study the interactions of atoms and subatomic particles, the gravitational force between these entities at the energies available on Earth is too feeble to detect.

Three centuries ago Isaac Newton gave the first quantitative description of nature's forces with his celebrated theory of gravity. Although the force of gravity between atoms at earthly energies is feeble, all particles of matter do attract one another gravitationally, with the result that the collective effects of many particles, such as those the Earth comprises, produce discernible effects, holding us on the ground and keeping the Moon in its orbit.

When objects are moving very fast, the effects of gravity differ from those described by Newton's theory. One example is seen in the rotation of the elliptic orbit of the planet Mercury, whose perihelion (point of closest approach to the Sun) advances faster than predicted by Newton's theory. Einstein's theory of general relativity subsumes Newton's theory and to date agrees with all observations of gravitational phenomena.

General relativity predicts that gravity can deflect light. If enough mass is concentrated in a small region, the resulting gravitational forces may be so powerful that they entrap light, resulting in a black hole. In

*Radio map of "twin quasars" amply demonstrates the relation between gravity and the curvature of space and time predicted by general relativity. The two images in the upper and lower central region are actually of a single object, quasar 0957 + 561, whose radiation has been deflected by the gravitational field of a galaxy (the faint patch just above the lower image) lying along the line of sight to the quasar. Were the intervening body sufficiently massive, it might bend passing radiation sharply toward itself and entrap it, becoming a black hole. Whereas general relativity successfully describes the motion and behavior of bulk matter and its gravitational interaction with radiation, it comes into conflict with quantum theory at microscopic scales of length. There the two theories together imply the existence of minuscule, fleeting black holes and the breakdown of the very concepts of space and time in which quantum theory must operate.*

Observations made by Perry E. Greenfield, David H. Roberts, and Bernard F. Burke; The National Radio Astronomy Observatory, operated by Associated Universities, Inc., under contract with the National Science Foundation

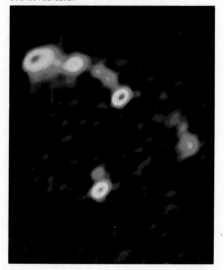

the vicinity of a black hole, familiar notions of space and time begin to break down. Space-time curls up on itself; time, in a sense, stands still. It is here that the conflict with quantum theory appears.

## Incompatibility

As mentioned above, quantum theory implies that there are fluctuations in energy taking place within extremely short distances and times. If at $10^{-13}$ meter electrons and positrons are continuously bubbling in and out of existence, at distances less than ten trillionths of a trillionth of a trillionth of a meter ($10^{-35}$ meter) the energy fluctuations are so great that particles ten million trillion ($10^{19}$) times as massive as a proton can form and annihilate. According to general relativity such large masses within these minute distances are black holes. So, together, the two theories imply that very small black holes are coming and going, their gravity distorting the environment so much that our notion of space and time fails.

The problem is that quantum theories of force fields are built on the assumption that it makes sense to talk about space and time at all scales of length. The swarm of microscopic black holes spawned from the marriage of general relativity and quantum theory counters that assumption. Even if we ignore these conceptual conflicts and attempt to calculate numbers, we find nonsensical results. Quantities that in reality must be finite—for example, the gravitational force between two electrons $10^{-24}$ meter apart—turn out in the theories to be infinite.

It is not new for infinities to appear as the answers in quantum theory calculations. They occur frequently in quantum electrodynamics, the quantum field theory of the electromagnetic force, but are "harmless" in that they can be removed by a well-defined mathematical technique called renormalization. Unfortunately, general relativity implies that gravity's strength increases at high energy, and this turns out to undermine the technique. The unwanted infinities remain, reminiscent of the ultraviolet catastrophe that heralded the birth of quantum theory. Some new ingredient or new theory is called for, incorporating general relativity and quantum theory. Before a look at what superstring theory appears to have achieved in this regard, it will be helpful to make a voyage into matter and review the developments that led to the superstring idea.

## Grand unified theories

A hundred years ago many people doubted that atoms existed. Those who believed in them assumed that they were minute particles, the ultimate seeds of matter. All of the interactions of matter were thought to take place by means of four fundamental forces: gravitation, electricity, magnetism, and short-range molecular forces, the last one being responsible for such everyday phenomena as the adhesion of jam to toast. A series of remarkable discoveries then led to the realization that electricity and magnetism are actually two manifestations of the same basic force, now called the electromagnetic force.

Next, when atomic structure was investigated, the electrically neutral atom proved to contain charged constituents: the positive nucleus and

48

negative electrons. Only then did it become clear that the short-range molecular forces were actually merely complicated residual effects of the powerful electromagnetic forces at work between the charged constituents inside the neutral atoms. Thus physics was left with only two basic forces: gravitation and electromagnetism. Of the original four one had been "lost" to unification, and the other had been declared "not fundamental" as a result of understanding atomic structure.

Soon scientists questioned how the atomic nucleus could exist, several positively charged particles (protons) being crammed together in defiance of the rule "Like charges repel." The answer to this paradox: a strong attractive force at work in the nucleus. And what about the radioactive decays of nuclei? These were shown to be caused by another, more feeble force that became known as the weak force.

Once again physicists had four fundamental forces. Then in the 1960s the proton and neutron were found to consist of more basic particles called quarks. The strong force was realized to be a complicated residual effect of a yet more powerful force acting on the quarks, a force tantalizingly like the electromagnetic force in origin. This force is generated by so-called color charges carried by quarks (the whimsical name does not refer to real colors), and its quantum field theory came to be called quantum chromodynamics by analogy with quantum electrodynamics. The weak force, which also shows similarities with the electromagnetic force, recently was united successfully with quantum electrodynamics.

Quantum theories define the fundamental particles of matter, such as electrons and quarks, in terms of such properties as mass, charge, momentum, and certain other, less concrete concepts. These basic properties are often expressed in the form of quantum numbers having integer or fractional values. All matter particles, for example, have an intrinsic angular momentum, or spin, with the common magnitude $\frac{1}{2}$.

The forces are carried between matter particles by particle-like bundles of radiation called force, or field, particles. The carrier of electromagnetic radiation is called the photon. The weak force is mediated by the neutral Z and electrically charged W particles (whose discovery in 1983 clinched the proof that the theory uniting weak and electromagnetic interactions was correct). Analogously, the strong, or color, force between quarks involves particles called gluons. Like matter particles, force particles are also distinguished by quantum properties. In contrast to the matter particles whose spins are $\frac{1}{2}$, the force carriers have spin 1.

Particles whose spin is a half integer are called fermions; those with integer spin are bosons. Thus the particles that comprise matter are all fermions; the carriers of the forces are all bosons.

The ways that quantum properties can be grouped to define the different types of matter and force particles and their relationships are governed by underlying symmetries. Mathematically these symmetries are describable with the aid of a branch of mathematics called group theory. Group theory classifies families of symmetry transformations like rotations and permutations and provides a kind of catalog of symmetries having generic names like $SU(2)$, $O(3)$, and $E_8$. Ordinary rotations, such

49

as the ways a cube can be rotated around an axis so as to leave it seemingly unchanged from its original position, form an O(3) group.

Less than 20 years ago quantum electrodynamics was the only successful theory of a fundamental force field. An important ingredient in the theory is a mathematical symmetry in its equations that—like the ways for rotating a cube while conserving its appearance—describes all the ways for particles to interact electromagnetically while conserving their fundamental quantum properties. Quantum electrodynamics envisions space-time as a set of points. At each point such quantities as electric charge are described by a pair of numbers (complex numbers) as if they were vectors in some fictional space. One number represents the size, or length, of the vector; the other its orientation. Physical measurements reveal the size, but the orientation is unobservable. The equations of quantum electrodynamics must remain unchanged if the orientations change by rotation. Mathematically this rotational symmetry is called a U(1) symmetry. For it to occur it is necessary that a massless field particle having spin 1 exist—exactly the properties of the photon carrier of the electromagnetic force.

In the early 1970s excitement mounted as a series of experimental discoveries showed that the weak and strong forces can be described by analogous, but rather richer, rotational symmetries: SU(2) for the weak force and SU(3) for the color force between quarks. At about the same time, physicists began appreciating the role of broken symmetries in nature, in particular that systems exhibiting symmetry at high temperatures (high energies) can "hide" their symmetry at lower energies. For example, at high temperatures the tiny atomic magnets in a lump of iron are pointed every which way; on a microscopic scale the laws governing the magnetic force are spherically symmetric, and no one direction is preferred over any other. But at low temperatures a phase transition occurs, and the iron becomes magnetized macroscopically in one direction; the symmetry of the microscopic laws becomes hidden. The phenomenon of hidden or "spontaneously broken" symmetry is characteristic of systems containing many particles and, as was said above,

*According to current theory, nature at its most fundamental level comprises 12 elementary matter particles and 4 forces. Matter particles are defined and distinguished by such quantum properties as mass, electric charge, and spin; each of the six quarks is further differentiated into three subtypes, or colors, by a quantum property called color charge. All matter particles are fermions, having a half-integer spin. The four forces that govern the interactions between matter particles vary greatly in range and strength. Each force is mediated by its own carrier particle, which is also defined by quantum properties. All force carriers possess an integer spin and are thus classified as bosons. The ways in which quantum properties can be grouped to account for the different matter and force particles are governed by underlying symmetries that can be described mathematically with the aid of group theory.*

| fermion matter particles (spin ½) | | | | | | forces and their boson (integer spin) carriers | | | | | | | |
|---|---|---|---|---|---|---|---|---|---|---|---|---|---|
| leptons | | | quarks | | | force | range | strength at $10^{-13}$ cm compared with strong force | carrier | rest mass MeV/$c^2$ | spin | electric charge | remarks |
| name | rest mass MeV/$c^2$ | electric charge | name | rest mass MeV/$c^2$ | electric charge | | | | | | | | |
| electron neutrino | c. 0 | 0 | up | 310 | ⅔ | gravity | infinite | $10^{-38}$ | graviton | 0 | 2 | 0 | conjectured |
| electron | 0.511 | −1 | down | 310 | −⅓ | electro-magnetism | infinite | $10^{-2}$ | photon | 0 | 1 | 0 | observed |
| muon neutrino | c. 0 | 0 | charm | 1,500 | ⅔ | weak | <$10^{-16}$ cm | $10^{-13}$ | intermediate bosons W⁺ | 81 | 1 | +1 | observed |
| muon | 106.6 | −1 | strange | 505 | −⅓ | | | | W⁻ | 81 | 1 | −1 | observed |
| tau neutrino | < 164 | 0 | top/ truth | > 22,500 (hypo-thetical) | ⅔ | | | | Z⁰ | 93 | 1 | 0 | observed |
| tau | 1,784 | −1 | bottom/ beauty | c. 5,000 | −⅓ | strong | <$10^{-13}$ cm | 1 | gluon | 0 | 1 | 0 | permanently confined |

quantum theory implies that the vacuum is a many-particle system. This allows the possibility that there are fundamental symmetries at work in particle physics, manifest at high energies but hidden at the low energies of present-day experiments.

Today we know that this is so. The SU(2) symmetry that marries the weak interaction with its U(1) electromagnetic cousin is hidden at low energies because the force carriers, the W and Z particles, have enormous masses—unlike the massless photon. The symmetry becomes apparent above a thousand trillion ($10^{15}$) degrees, recently attained at the CERN proton-antiproton collider in Geneva. There the long-sought W and Z were produced in the laboratory along with photons as the symmetry between the weak and electromagnetic forces was restored for the first time on Earth as they were at the start of the universe.

At low energies the electromagnetic and weak forces appear as two distinct phenomena; above $10^{15}$ degrees they are revealed as a single "electroweak" force. Theorists believe that at temperatures above $10^{30}$ degrees there exists a grand symmetry uniting the electroweak and strong forces. Such temperatures were reached only in the first $10^{-35}$ second after the big bang. Because these early moments appear to have had a profound effect on the subsequent history of the universe, high-energy particle physics bears crucially on cosmology.

A central problem in building a grand unified theory is identifying what symmetry nature uses at high energies, what mathematical group the theory belongs to. There are many large groups that contain the smaller U(1), SU(2), and SU(3) groups that are descriptive at low energies. Although theorists offer arguments for preferring some groups over others, most find this multiplicity of choices unsettling because it signals that the ultimate description of nature is still obscure. One key ingredient on which everyone agrees, however, is that an ultimate theory must include "supersymmetry"—a symmetry that unites bosons of integer spins and fermions of half-integer spins—in order to realize the conditions of the present universe from the symmetric conditions of the big bang.

Yet another feature of the low-energy hidden symmetry must be incorporated in a successful final theory. In the real world the mirror images of natural processes can usually also occur. Billiard balls rebound to the right from a pool table cushion as well as they do to the left. For processes controlled by the weak interaction, such as the ejection of a beta particle in a nuclear decay, this is not so. There is a slight but natural handedness in nature, called chirality from the Greek word for "hand." The problem is that quantum field theories that incorporate the necessary chirality tend to violate sacred conservation laws such as that of electric charge. These violations, termed chiral anomalies, render the theories inconsistent. Part of the excitement of superstring theory is that it avoids the chiral anomalies in an almost unique way.

## Superstrings

Quantum theory is formulated on the assumption that space-time and the fundamental bosons and fermions therein can be adequately represented

51

by a set of dimensionless points. On the other hand, according to general relativity space-time at distances of $10^{-35}$ meter is distorted like a discrete foam. In superstring theory these descriptions, though valid enough in their own worlds, are shown to be only approximations to a more basic and profound description that takes account of structure on the most microscopic scale. In this theory the basic particles are not points but extremely short, one-dimensional strings.

Although some of the elements of superstring theory can be traced back to the 1920s, its promising form originated with Michael Green of Queen Mary College, London, and John Schwarz of the California Institute of Technology in 1984. Their theory involves two kinds of strings: open and closed. An open string can be pictured as a curve having a length less than $10^{-35}$ meter and a variable shape but no thickness. A closed string, like a snake biting its tail, is an open string bent and connected at the ends to form a loop.

Strings can vibrate in ways analogous to the familiar vibrations of violin strings. Quantum theory constrains the energy and angular momentum of these vibrational modes, and the resulting set of states are what the gross senses perceive as particles with various masses and spins. Strings can also interact in ways that correspond to the observed interaction of particles. A particle collision can be pictured as two open or closed strings touching and joining briefly before parting company. One string breaking into two strings describes a particle decay, while the fusion of strings describes two particles meeting to produce a third particle.

The "super" in superstring theory comes from the demand that supersymmetry be incorporated—a demand that at first looks unfulfillable. Consistency with quantum theory and relativity constrains the theory

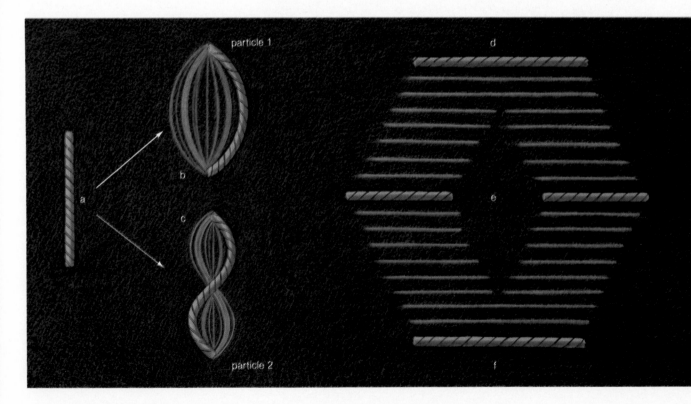

very tightly, so much so that a nonsensical conclusion results: The allowed string vibrations describe not only objects with the properties of subatomic particles but also objects that have a negative probability of occurring. These objects are called ghosts, and because no one can make sense of them, there is general agreement that any true theory of nature must be free of them. The occurrence of ghosts has undermined several attempts to build grand unified theories. But the bizarre property of superstring theory is that it contains a natural ghostbuster—if space-time has ten dimensions!

For there to be any sense to superstring theory, it appears that there must have been ten dimensions in the heat of the big bang, and as the universe cooled a phase transition caused six of them to become hidden from view. We may picture them as curled-up, embryonic dimensions, existing within distances of less than $10^{-35}$ meter and unresolved by our macroscopic senses. In a simple two-dimensional analogy, a garden hose viewed from a distance looks like a one-dimensional line. But when it is seen more closely at better resolution, its curved surface extending in two other dimensions becomes apparent. Similarly, in superstring theory the size of the six curled-up dimensions is similar to the length of the strings. We appear to live in three spatial dimensions, unaware of the others, in the same sense we perceive particles as points instead of tiny strings.

## Toward compatibility and unification

This intrinsic structure of space-time at scales of $10^{-35}$ meter appears to allow the successful fusion of general relativity and quantum theory. The pathological infinities that beset quantum gravity in a space-time consisting of points vanish in string theory because strings interact in a

*In superstring theory particles are regarded not as points but as one-dimensional strings less than $10^{-35}$ meter long. Strings can vibrate, each vibrational mode being identifiable with a different subatomic particle. For example, a string (a) vibrating in one mode (b) corresponds to particle 1; the same string vibrating in a second mode (c) corresponds to particle 2. Strings also can interact in ways identifiable with observed particle interactions. A string breaking into two strings (d to e) describes a particle decay. Two strings combining into one (e to f) describes the fusion of two particles into a third particle. In its original form superstring theory involves both open and closed strings; a later version, the heterotic theory, uses closed strings alone. An open string has two free ends (as in g), whereas a closed string is like an open string bent (h) and connected at the ends to form a loop (i). In an example of a closed string interaction, two loops (j) fuse into a single loop (k).*

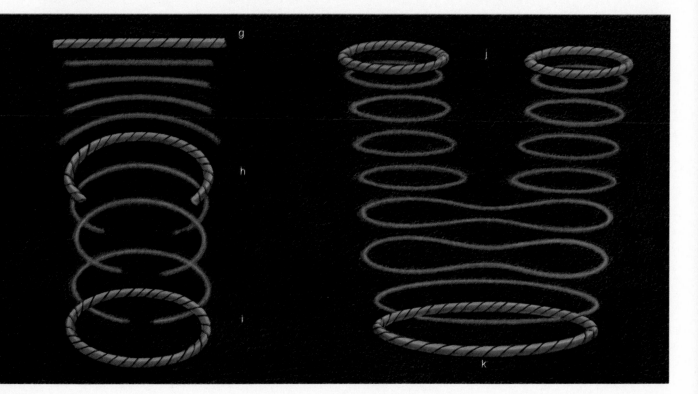

different way than do point particles. When two closed strings interact, for example, there is no single point of interaction any more than the legs of a pair of trousers join at a single point. The junction is smeared out, and what was infinite becomes finite, at least in all cases so far calculated. Theorists are currently trying to prove that string interactions remove all unwanted infinities. Superstring theory seems to be saying that space-time is better represented as strings than as points and that ten is a "natural" number of dimensions for the universe to have. On the other hand, it has not revealed why six dimensions should remain curled up after the big bang while four develop macroscopically.

Some quantum properties of particles, such as electric charge, have no obvious connection to space and time yet must be included in any realistic theory of force and matter. The way that Green and Schwarz incorporated them was to consider a huge family of open and closed strings that could be transformed into one another according to the rules of group theory. The different strings then correspond to sets of particles whose members are identical in all respects but for their electric charges and related properties. Further excitement arose when they accomplished this while not only avoiding the unwanted chiral anomalies but also finding that only one group seemed to do the job—one known as SO(32). This was the first time in the search for a unified theory that a unique mathematical structure had been imposed on the theories,

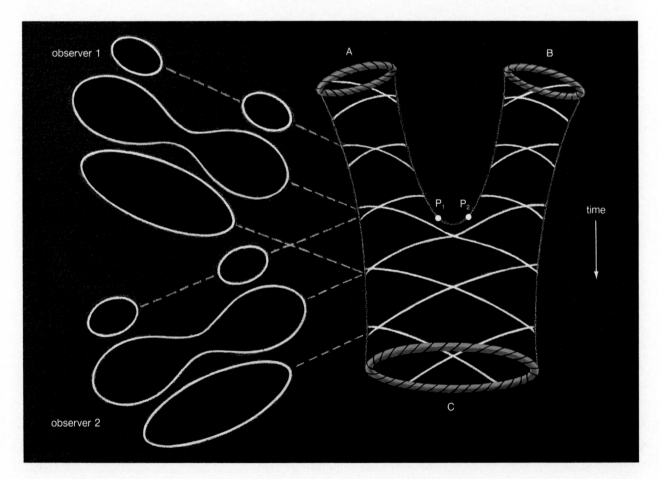

as if the universe itself actually required this structure and no other. They also noticed that the absence of anomalies required a detailed interdependency of the gravitational and the other forces described by the theory, making unification of the forces both a profound and necessary ingredient in superstring theory.

In the course of their research Green and Schwarz found that another mathematical group, $E_8 \times E_8$, would make the anomalies disappear. Unfortunately, it could not be applied to a theory involving open strings, whose free ends were thought necessary for particles to carry electric charge, color charge, and some other quantum properties. This inadequacy was disappointing because the known particles and the separate

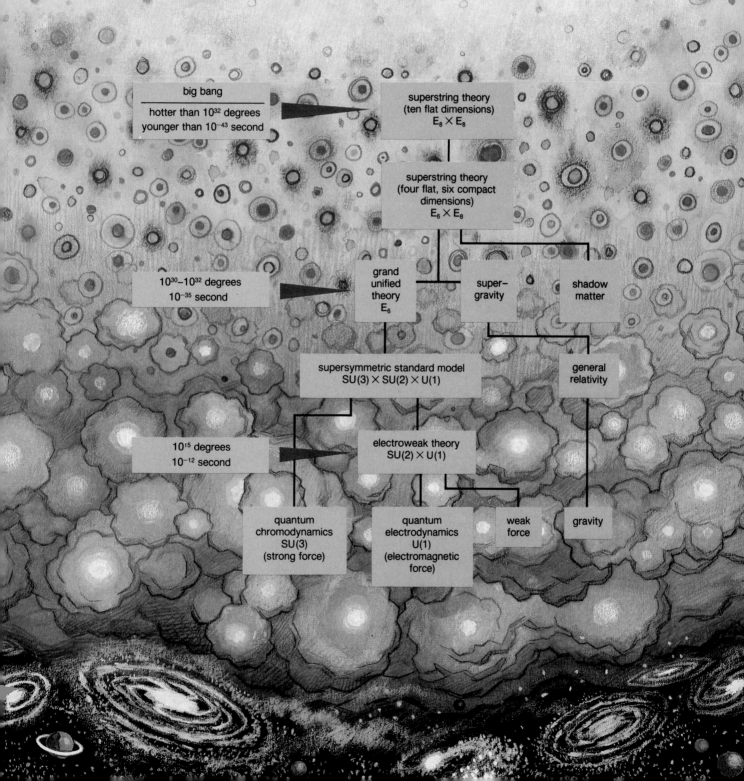

forces manifested at the relatively low energies currently accessible respect the mathematical groups SU(3), SU(2), and U(1), which emerge rather naturally from a $E_8 \times E_8$ structure; by contrast, an SO(32) structure does so only when "forced" with extra assumptions. Moreover, apart from the fact that the absence of anomalies in our universe required one to impose their absence in theory making, there was no natural reason within Green and Schwarz's theory why this should be so.

Then, in 1985, David Gross and three collaborators at Princeton University (known as the Princeton string quartet) showed that it indeed is possible to construct a string theory that involves only closed strings and an $E_8 \times E_8$ structure and that, moreover, naturally has no anomalies. Because this theory borrows various desirable features from the Green-Schwarz theory to make a vigorous hybrid, it is known as the heterotic string version.

The heterotic string is a closed-string loop that contains two sets of ripples, or traveling waves, moving in opposite directions. So complex and independent are these ripples that they occupy different dimensional spaces: those moving clockwise occupy 10 dimensions, while those moving counterclockwise occupy 26 dimensions. When the Princeton group mathematically curled up 16 of the 26 dimensions of the counterclockwise vibrations so that the whole string is in 10 dimensions, they found that the group structure $E_8 \times E_8$ emerged naturally and that the quantum properties that had needed the free ends of open strings now resided in a smeared-out fashion over the entire loop. Although heterotic strings introduce exciting features, the initial asymmetric formulation, with some waves in 26 dimensions and others in 10, suggests that we are still only glimpsing the outline of an ultimately elegant theory.

## The tasks ahead

One goal of current research is to find a formulation of the theory without its disturbing asymmetries, from which it is certain that profound insights will emerge. Another is to correlate the theory completely with the spectrum of particles and effects observed at the low energies of the present universe. In its present state superstring theory is little more than a mass of mathematics that looks excitingly plausible as a theory of nature, at least at high energy. For it to be accepted it will have to yield detailed solutions that predict what is actually seen today.

The known group structures of the strong and electroweak forces are contained within a single $E_8$ group. Physicists hope eventually to understand how this relates to curling up six of the ten dimensions. Perhaps then they will have the first clues as to why the universe is four-dimensional on the everyday, macroscopic level.

A separate puzzle concerns the necessity of the $E_8 \times E_8$ group in the theory, which taken literally requires that there are two $E_8$ structures to the universe. If one of them contains the forces and matter that we are made of and that build the stars whose light we see, then what of the other $E_8$ component? If the theory is right it seems to imply that a "shadow universe" exists in parallel with the familiar one. It has matter

and forces of its own but does not share the electromagnetic, weak, and strong forces of ours. Thus we cannot see or interact with it other than by means of gravity, which is common to both.

It is tantalizing that the motions of galaxies and other cosmological phenomena do suggest that there is considerable "dark" matter in the universe. It does not shine on us but tugs incessantly on the matter that we do see. It would indeed be astonishing if a theory that began as a quest for quantized gravity should lead to the discovery of an entire second universe.

For further discussion of grand unified theories, symmetry breaking, and the interrelationship of cosmology and particle physics, see *1986 Yearbook of Science and the Future* Feature Article: THE INFLATIONARY UNIVERSE.

FOR ADDITIONAL READING

Frank Close, *The Cosmic Onion: Quarks and the Nature of the Universe* (American Institute of Physics, 1986).

F. Close, M. Marten, and C. Sutton, *The Particle Explosion* (Oxford University Press, 1987).

Michael Green, "Superstrings," *Scientific American* (September 1986, pp. 48–60).

*If superstring theory is correct, it seems to imply the existence of a parallel shadow universe, having matter and forces of its own but invisible to us. Although this universe today would probably be in a form far less dramatic and more plausible than depicted above, its presence could have profoundly affected the early evolution of our own universe and the large-scale structure presently observed.*

# Exploring the Planets

*by Ronald Greeley
and Jeffrey M. Moore*

**Space probes to the planets and their satellites are providing a wealth of information about these bodies, revealing differences and similarities among them.**

Two revelations in the Earth sciences during the past 25 years have altered the perception of planets and how they evolve. The first was the realization that the rigid, outer part of the Earth is segmented into "plates" that are constantly in motion. The theory of plate tectonics that was derived from this discovery has provided a unifying theme for understanding much of the geologic evolution of the Earth. The second revelation resulted from the exploration of the Solar System. Beginning in the 1960s data returned from space probes have enabled scientists to study the geology of planets and satellites. As a result, knowledge of geologic processes is no longer limited to the Earth but now embraces nearly the entire family of planetary objects.

Although exploration of the Solar System has only just begun, analyses of spacecraft data reveal both differences and similarities among the planets and satellites. The new discipline that has emerged from these studies, comparative planetology, seeks to understand these differences and similarities, especially when assessed against the new understanding of the geologic evolution of Earth provided by the theory of plate tectonics.

## Planetary evolution

Geologic histories have been constructed for most of the solid-surface planets and satellites in the Solar System, although the level of understanding is far from uniform because exploration is incomplete. Much of the knowledge of planetary geology and geophysics is derived from remote sensing of planetary surfaces combined with data on planetary bulk properties. The bulk properties (such as planet composition and size) are important factors, as they govern the amount of energy available to melt or deform planetary interiors. This energy, in turn, controls many of the processes that shape planetary surfaces, such as volcanism and tectonism.

Planetary composition is partly a function of distance from the Sun at the time of Solar System formation. The inner planets—Mercury,

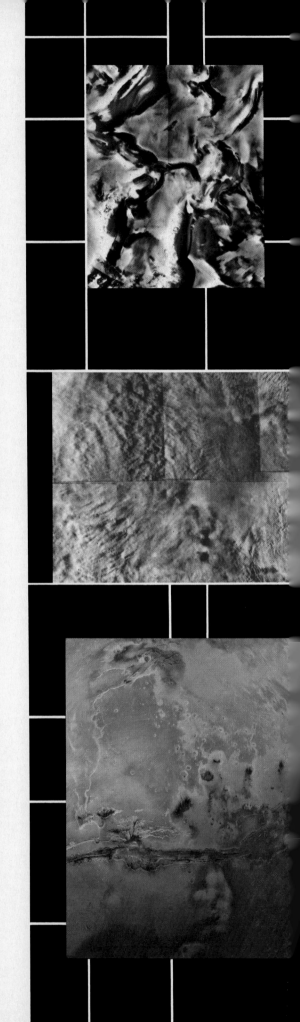

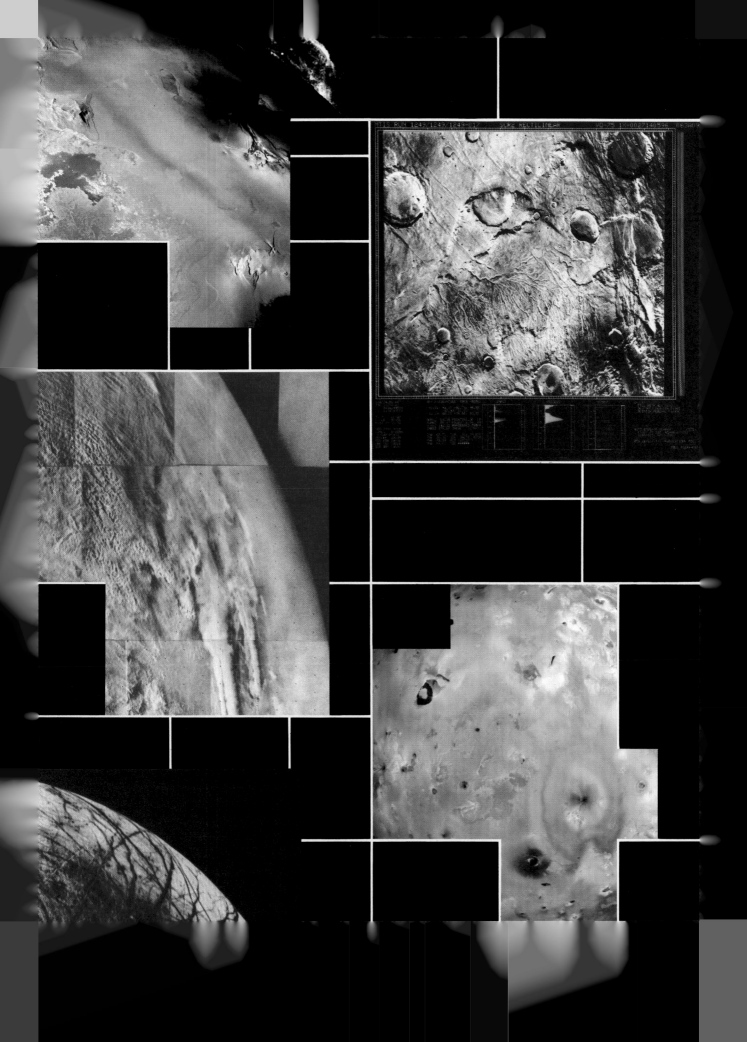

*RONALD GREELEY is Professor of Geology and JEFFREY M. MOORE is a Graduate Research Associate in the Department of Geology at Arizona State University, Tempe.*

Venus, Earth, and Mars, along with the Earth's Moon—all orbit within a few hundred million kilometers of the Sun. (One kilometer is about 0.62 miles.) They are composed principally of silicate compounds and metal alloys, all of which have high melting points. Beyond the asteroid belt lie the giant gas planets, such as Jupiter and Saturn. Although these objects are not of direct geologic interest because they lack solid surfaces, their satellites are solid-surface objects amenable to geologic study. For simplicity, satellites are now typically included as "planets" in the geologic context. Some objects, such as Jupiter's moon Io, consist mostly of silicate materials. However, most of the satellites of the outer planets are composed largely of materials that melt at comparatively low temperatures, such as water ice. Thus, planets display a wide variety of bulk compositions, from rocky objects with high melting temperatures through intermediate forms composed of both rocky materials and ice to easily melted icy satellites.

Prior to the Voyager mission through the outer Solar System, it was generally assumed that the amount of heat generated in a planet or satellite is a function of its size. In most models of Solar-System formation, large objects were thought to possess more radioactive materials and thus be capable of producing more heat. This hypothesis certainly appeared to be true for the inner planets; the Earth is the largest of the terrestrial planets and is extremely active both tectonically and volcanically. In contrast, the Earth's Moon is much smaller and has been relatively inactive for more than a billion years.

The relationship between planetary size and activity was explained by noting that large bodies have a lower ratio of surface area to volume than do small bodies. Radioactive decay produces heat in amounts approximately proportional to an object's volume. This heat must be radiated to space through a surface that increases by the square of the radius, whereas the volume increase is cubed. Thus, a planet with twice the radius of another will produce two times as much heat per unit of surface area, other factors being held constant. While basically correct, this model does not account for energy produced from other sources. For example, scientists at the U.S. National Aeronautics and Space Administration's (NASA's) Ames Research Center calculated the amount of heat that would be generated within Io as a consequence of tidal forces among the satellites and Jupiter. In effect, Io is first pulled inward toward Jupiter and then outward by the outer, neighboring satellites. It was predicted that substantial heat would be produced in this fashion and that Io would experience active volcanism. When Voyager 1 arrived at Jupiter in 1979, images of Io revealed some half dozen active volcanoes spewing gas and ash hundreds of kilometers above the surface. The tidal distortions within Io create so much frictional heating that it is one of the most active bodies in the Solar System despite its small size.

Therefore, not only is size important in considering heat production within planetary objects but the orbital and gravitational interactions with neighboring bodies must also be assessed. In addition to the encounter with Io, Voyager's journey past Saturn and Uranus revealed their icy

*(Opposite page, top) Ash and gases from the volcano Pele rise more than 200 kilometers (125 miles) above the surface of Io, a moon of Jupiter. Fallout deposits from the eruption covered an area the size of Alaska. In spite of its small size Io is active volcanically because substantial heat is generated when it is first pulled inward toward Jupiter and then outward toward the outer moons. The picture is a mosaic of eight high-resolution photographs taken by Voyager 1 in 1979. Impact basin measuring some 900 kilometers (560 miles) in diameter and having several concentric rings is revealed on the Earth's Moon (opposite page, bottom). Such basins are among the largest impact scars found on planets and their satellites. Generally those bodies having many large craters are very old—on the order of four billion years.*

Courtesy, Alfred McEwen, Arizona State University and the U.S. Geological Survey, Flagstaff, Arizona

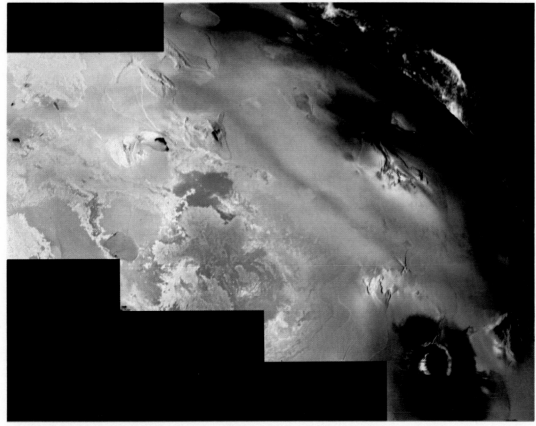

satellites for the first time. Many of those objects are 500 to 1,000 kilometers in diameter—less than half the size of the Earth's Moon—and show evidence that their surfaces have been covered by internally generated materials. Heat, probably produced by tidal flexing similar to that on Io, is believed to have mobilized ices in the interiors of these satellites, causing them to erupt and flow across the surface as a form of volcanism. The interiors of these satellites may include frozen water-ammonia or other similar mixtures that have relatively low melting temperatures, potentially leading to eruptions even for modest amounts of heat.

Planetary size, composition, and the gravitational interaction among satellites and their parent planets thus are major factors controlling planetary evolution. The interplay of these factors varies considerably and has produced an enormous diversity of planetary landscapes.

### Planetary processes

The appearance of a planet's surface is the result of many geologic processes operating over long periods of time. There are four primary processes in planetary evolution: impact cratering, which results from the collision of planetary objects; volcanic processes, involving eruptions of magma onto the surface; tectonism, involving deformation of the lithosphere (the solid part of the object); and gradation, which includes the erosion, transportation, and deposition of surface materials by agents

NASA

61

such as wind and water. Each process produces specific landforms, some of which indicate the process involved in their formation. Learning to recognize these landforms is one of the primary goals of planetary geology, for it is through this recognition that geologic histories can be derived for planetary objects.

Cratered terrains dominate most planetary surfaces. Impact craters range in size from more than 1,000 kilometers in diameter to tiny pits only a few micrometers across. They form when one planetary object strikes another, excavating a hole. Typical impact velocities exceed ten kilometers per second and thus can transfer tremendous energies to the object being struck. High shock stresses occur within a fraction of a second after impact and typically convert both the impacting object and the surface being struck into vapor, melt, and shock-deformed rocks. Material thrown from the crater, called ejecta, is distributed radially from the crater.

Surfaces of airless objects, such as the Moon, are exposed to the steady impact bombardment of objects of all sizes and develop a layer of fragments called the regolith. The process of regolith formation "softens" the surface and is responsible for its smooth appearance on the Moon. The jagged terrain portrayed in the renditions of the Moon by early artists attests to the fact that surface degradation by cratering and regolith formation was unanticipated prior to the space age.

Through geologic time the number of impact craters increases on planetary surfaces. Thus, by the comparison of the number of impact craters on one surface with that on another, difference in crater distributions can be used to infer relative ages. Moreover, if the frequency of crater formation is known, then the actual age of the surface can be estimated. Generally, planetary surfaces having many large (more than 100 kilometers in diameter) craters are very old—probably on the order of four billion years. Because the Solar System itself is only four and one-half billion years old, these surfaces are considered to date from the very early period of Solar System history. Conversely, sparsely cratered landscapes on airless planets suggest more recent processes, such as resurfacing by lava flows.

The question then arises as to whether impact craters are found on Earth. The answer is yes, but compared with the heavily cratered surfaces seen on the Moon and elsewhere in the Solar System, the approximately 200 impact scars identified on Earth would appear to be an anomalously low number. However, because much of the Earth's surface has been recycled by crustal plate tectonics and modified by erosion, most of the impact craters have been destroyed or obliterated. Thus, most impact scars on Earth are found on the oldest parts of the continents.

On the Earth impact cratering may have played a role in changing the evolutionary path of life. Studies carried out during the past several years have uncovered evidence that an impact on the Earth 65 million years ago led to global environmental change and the extinction of many life-forms. The evidence for the impact is found within a thin layer of clay at the stratigraphic boundary of the Cretaceous and Tertiary periods. Abnormally high amounts of rare metals associated with meteorites, glassy droplets of impact melt, and impact-shocked quartz in the clay are attributed to a large impact with an extraterrestrial body. The impact is believed to have ejected material high into the atmosphere and led to drastic changes in the environment that caused the extinctions of many species, including the dinosaurs, and the rise of new species. Although the link to mass extinctions is not accepted by all researchers, evidence is compelling that a major impact event did occur on the Earth at the end of the Cretaceous Period.

The recognition of impact craters and an understanding of the mechanics of cratering as a geologic process are among the most important areas of study in comparative planetary science. With further exploration of the Solar System, knowledge of crater formation as a function of planetary size and composition becomes necessary for the interpretation of planetary surface history. Equally important is the recent realization that impact events may have played a role in the evolution of life on Earth.

## Volcanic processes

Volcanic processes involve the generation of magma in the interior of planets and its eruption onto their surfaces. Volcanic features, such as lava flows, provide direct clues to the thermal history of the planets on which they are found. The form of volcanoes and volcanic terrains results from many complex factors, including planetary environment and the properties of the magma.

Planetary factors governing volcanism include the presence or absence of an atmosphere and gravitational acceleration. For example, eruptions of cinders on the Earth typically produce steep-sided cones because at-

*Portrayal of the Earth's surface reveals features associated with plate tectonics. These include mid-oceanic ridges, where new crust is formed from the eruption of lava as plates diverge. Off the west coast of South America is a deep trench that has formed in an area of plate convergence, where the edge of one plate has been thrust below that of another.*

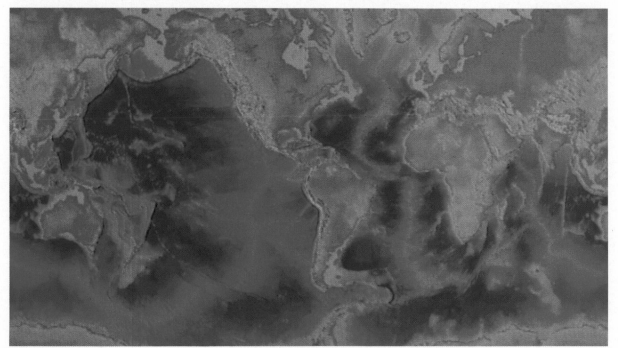

Margo H. Edwards and Raymond E. Arvidson, Washington University, St. Louis, and James R. Heirtzler, Woods Hole Oceanographic Institution

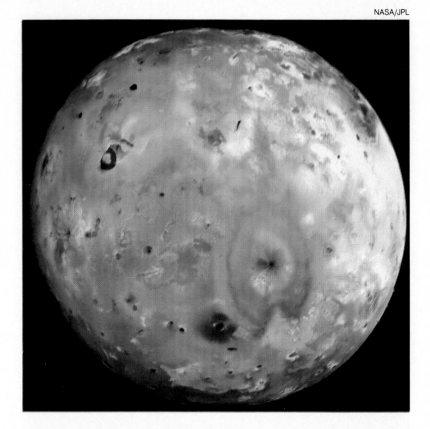

mospheric drag and the high gravitational acceleration cause the ejected cinders to fall close to the vent. In contrast, cinder cones on the Moon are low and widespread because the cinders are thrown farther from the vent in the low-gravity, airless lunar environment.

Properties of the magma, such as viscosity, are important in governing the form of volcanoes. Very fluid lavas spread out easily, leading to the formation of volcanic plains such as those seen as the dark areas of the Moon. In contrast, high-viscosity lavas form thick, stubby flows that accumulate into dome-shaped volcanoes. The gas content of the magma is also important. For example, the amount of gas in the magma controls the explosivity of the eruption. On the Earth vigorous explosive eruptions resulting from the rapid release of gas have produced ash deposits that cover thousands of square kilometers. Explosively produced ash also blankets vast parts of Io. Conversely, explosive volcanism may not occur on Venus. It has been proposed that the extremely dense atmosphere on that planet would prevent the rapid degassing of magma as it reaches the surface.

On the Earth volcanism is prevalent along tectonic plate boundaries and over "hot spots." Where plates diverge, enormous floods of very fluid lava may erupt, forming new crust. Where plates converge, older crust may be subducted below the surface, melted, and erupted back to the surface. Other areas beneath the uppermost crust appear to be zones of long-term heat production and magma formation. Called "hot spots," these are sites of active volcanoes, some of which may be pro-

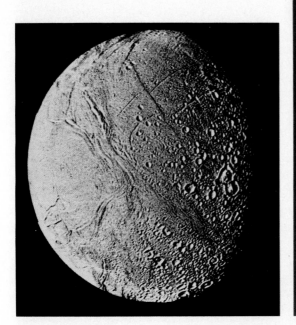

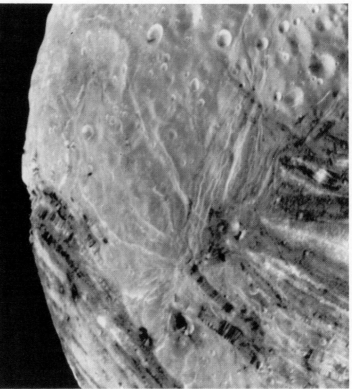

duced in an assembly-line fashion as a crustal plate slides over the hot spot. This mechanism has been proposed for the Hawaiian chain of island volcanoes.

Volcanic plains formed by flood eruptions of high-temperature, fluid, iron-rich lavas dominate the terrestrial planets. On Earth most of the ocean basins are floored with vast lava plains. Similarly, the dark regions on the Moon are low-lying areas flooded by lava. More than half the surface of Mars and much of the plains on Mercury appear to be covered by lava flows. In all of these cases most of the lavas appear to have reached the surface through large fissures. On Earth the fissures are often associated with plate tectonism; on the Moon and Mercury most of the fissures formed as a consequence of crustal fracturing by large impacts.

The three largest terrestrial planets (Earth, Venus, and Mars) all exhibit volcanoes produced from central vents, such as shield volcanoes. The discovery by Mariner 9 of Olympus Mons and the other volcanoes on Mars provided the first clear evidence that volcanism was important on that planet. As on Mars, the largest mountains on Earth and possibly Venus are also shield volcanoes composed of thousands of individual lava flows. Some Martian shield volcanoes are more than 500 kilometers across and 20 kilometers high, making them nearly ten times the size of the largest volcano on Earth, Mauna Loa. The enormous size of the Martian features is thought to result from a continuous supply of magma from a "hot spot" for hundreds of millions or even billions of years.

Io, the only object other than the Earth known to have active volca-

*Jupiter's moon Io (opposite page), Saturn's moon Enceladus (above left), and Uranus's moon Miranda (above) all show evidence of extensive resurfacing. This reflects vigorous internal heating, a surprising discovery on Enceladus and Miranda because they are relatively small (500 and 484 kilometers [310 and 300 miles] in diameter, respectively).*

Photos, NASA/JPL

65

Photos, NASA/JPL

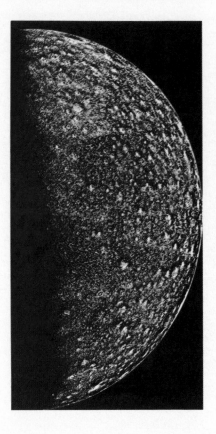

noes, is almost completely covered by volcanic deposits, including plains composed of lava flows and ash. In addition, shield volcanoes have been identified from long, radial flows emanating from central calderas. The volcanic vents are much more randomly distributed on Io than on the terrestrial planets, suggesting a different heat source.

Volcanism has reshaped the surfaces of nearly all solid-surface objects in the Solar System. Even relatively small and inactive bodies such as the Moon reveal large areas covered by volcanic materials. Some of the outer planet satellites show surfaces that may be covered by the icy equivalent of lava flows. Thus, understanding volcanism in its varied forms is critical in determining the geologic evolution of the planets.

### Tectonic processes

Tectonic deformation of the Earth's crust can be recognized by folded and faulted rocks. Geologists have long understood that these local features can be related to the type of deformation, such as tension or compression of the crust. Insight into deformation on larger scales, however, was not gained until the concept of global plate tectonics was formulated in the 1960s.

The types of tectonic structures and the timing of their formation are closely linked to the thermal evolution and interior properties of planetary objects. Many objects, especially the smaller satellites, reveal little evidence of tectonic deformation. Unlike Earth, these so-called one-plate planets have thick lithospheres that formed early and preserved

*Callisto (above), a moon of Jupiter, has a diameter of 4,820 kilometers (2,990 miles) and thus is one of the largest satellites in the Solar System. Composed of half water-ice and half silicate rock, it shows little evidence of resurfacing and therefore is not active internally. Mimas (above right) is an icy moon of Saturn that has preserved the record of its early intense cratering, revealing that it also has not been resurfaced.*

66

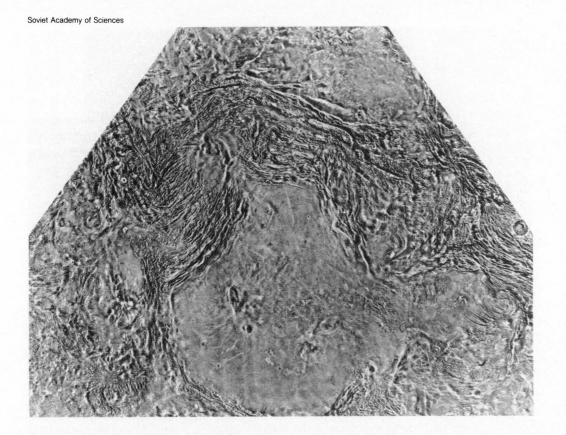

the record of intense impact cratering. Tectonism on such bodies is expressed primarily by vertical movements, forming features such as extensional faults and grabens (depressed segments of crust bounded on at least two sides by faults).

In contrast to one-plate planets, the Earth has a lithosphere that is highly mobile and exhibits extensive lateral movement. This activity creates a variety of landforms, including mountain ranges formed where two plates converge and systems of transform faults where two plates slide past one another. Enormous rift valleys can form where plates are pulled apart. Such sites, called spreading centers, are zones where lava flows produce new crust. In other areas old crust is carried beneath overriding plates, creating narrow, deep trenches. Formation of new crust and destruction of old crust occurs at a rate of more than ten centimeters (four inches) per year in some areas. This rate is so rapid that over geologic time there can be a renewal of much of the Earth's surface in only a few hundred million years.

The patterns formed by tectonic features on the Earth provide a key to interpreting internal processes and constitute an important model for comparison with other planets. Because Venus is similar to the Earth in size, mass, and, presumably, composition, it is the most likely candidate for Earthlike tectonism. Most data about the planet are from the Soviet Venera and the United States Pioneer-Venus missions. The Venera series includes both orbiting spacecraft and surface landers. Of particular importance are the images returned by the Venera 15 and 16 orbiters.

*Mosaic of images of Venus obtained by a Soviet probe reveals a smooth-surfaced plateau surrounded by mountains. This terrain is similar to the Tibetan Plateau and Himalaya Mountains on Earth, a region that was formed by plate tectonic processes.*

67

Because Venus is perpetually shrouded by clouds, its surface can be "seen" from orbit only by means of radar imaging systems. Venera 15 and 16 radar images, taken in the mid-1980s for the northern hemisphere, reveal features as small as two kilometers across. In combination with topographic data from the Pioneer-Venus spacecraft, these images are providing the first clues to the diversity of the Venusian surface.

Scientists have speculated as to whether the exploration of Venus has shown the planet to have Earthlike tectonism. The answer is perhaps. Lakshmi Planum is a continent-sized plateau on Venus bounded on three sides by mountain ranges more than ten kilometers high. In some respects the plateau and the mountain ranges resemble the Tibetan Plateau and Himalaya Mountains on Earth, which were produced by the collision of two crustal plates. Other parts of Venus show ridges and valleys that intersect at angles to form chevron patterns. Although other modes of formation have been proposed, in some respects the Venus terrain resembles landforms created at spreading-plate centers on Earth. Thus, although several terrains might have formed by plate tectonism, unequivocal evidence for Earthlike plate processes on Venus has not yet been found.

The geologically most vigorous planets and satellites, such as Earth and Io, display tectonism associated with hot spots where heat is conducted through a crust. Some areas on Venus may indicate hot spots associated with mantle convection. Gravity data acquired from orbit over these areas indicate a thin lithosphere. One such area, Beta Regio, appears to be a large volcanic center similar to some of the hot-spot rift valleys in eastern Africa. The crust in Beta Regio has been extensively fractured into branching rift valleys hundreds of kilometers long, two kilometers deep, and as wide as 350 kilometers. Superposed on this landscape are volcanolike isolated mountains more than 100 kilometers across.

The most dominant tectonic feature on Mars is the Tharsis bulge. This broad, gentle swelling in the Martian crust rises 10–11 kilometers. Superposed on the bulge are numerous volcanoes, fractures, and craters. Two origins have been proposed for the Tharsis bulge. The first suggests that the crust was uplifted by mantle convection. Alternatively, the bulge is simply a thick accumulation of lava flows and other volcanic products. Analyses of geophysical data on the Martian lithosphere and geologic studies both support the latter hypothesis.

Nearly one-third of the Martian surface is affected by fractures related to the Tharsis bulge. Valles Marineris is a canyon system that cuts into the flank of the bulge and extends more than 4,000 kilometers eastward. Ridges similar to those on the lunar lowlands occur on lava plains surrounding Tharsis. The ridges and the canyon system can be related to the enormous weight imposed on the crust by the accumulation of lava flows. Models suggest that the strain associated with the weight was relieved through fracturing and faulting to produce features seen around the bulge. Tectonism, thus, is important in the evolution of all internally active planets and satellites. The extent of tectonic modification is directly related to the energy production of each body.

## Gradational processes

Gradation is a complex process that begins with weathering and erosion, continues with transport of the weathered debris, and ends with deposition. Thus, gradation is a leveling process in which high areas are worn down by erosion and low areas are filled by deposition. The driving force of gradation is gravity, either working alone, as in some landslides, or else operating through the agents of running water, glaciers, or wind. Even though gradation tends to be more important on planets having atmospheres, it operates on all planets in one form or another. For example, landslides are seen even on airless bodies such as the Moon.

Running water is an effective agent of gradation. The discovery of water-cut channels on Mars in the early 1970s came as a surprise because the present Martian environment precludes the existence of liquid water. Several types of water-cut channels were found, and geologic studies show that one type or another formed throughout much of Martian history. Some channels appear to have originated from catastrophic floods, similar to those that occurred in Washington State in association with the sudden release of glacial water. Others form valley networks that might indicate the collection of surface water into tributary systems.

Sand and dust storms occur frequently on the Earth. Any planetary object having an atmosphere and loose particles on the surface may

*Mosaic composed of 102 separate images obtained by a Viking Orbiter covers almost an entire hemisphere of Mars. At the center is the 4,000–kilometer (2,485-mile)-long Valles Marineris canyon system, which was formed by tectonic action. Three volcanoes lie to the west. To the north in the Lunae Planum/Chryse Planitia region are outflow channels that may have been shaped by the action of ice or wind.*

69

experience aeolian, or wind, processes. Low-density atmospheres, as on Mars, require very high wind speeds to move grains. Conversely, in the high-density atmosphere of Venus, particles move under very gentle winds. The extent of aeolian processes on other planets was not fully appreciated until Mariner 9 and the Viking missions revealed numerous aeolian features on Mars, including sand dunes. Global dust storms sweep Mars nearly every year, making aeolian activity the dominant process on that planet. Windblown sediments form a mantle over much of Mars, including the polar regions, where light and dark deposits are considered to be layers of ice and dust. The most abundant aeolian features are elongate streaks found in association with craters and hills. Some streaks change their appearance within a few weeks, while others remain unaltered for months. These features are considered to form by erosion and deposition of windblown particles, and so they reveal the directions of prevailing surface winds.

Soviet landers measured wind speeds on the surface of Venus that are within the range needed to move particles, and some Venera images included features suggestive of aeolian processes. Radar data acquired from orbit also indicated areas that might be blanketed by sediment, perhaps of aeolian origin. Thus, wind presumably does play some role in shaping the surface of Venus, although the extent to which it does so remains uncertain.

The study of landforms developed by gradation provides clues to climate history. For example, one can consider the channels formed by

*Landforms on Mars that were shaped by the wind include (top center) parallel ridges called yardangs, found on eroded surfaces and oriented with the prevailing winds; at the bottom left are sand dunes, which are located on smooth surfaces, downwind of the yardangs. Because of the planet's low-density atmosphere, very high winds are needed to move particles of sand across its surface.*

water on Mars. Most valley networks in the Martian highlands are old, suggesting that the atmosphere of Mars was warmer and denser than it is today. Some investigators suggest that rainfall played a role in the early history of Mars. The Martian climate later changed to produce a colder environment and a less dense atmosphere. The question then arises as to whether this change was unique to Mars or whether it occurred in response to some event or events that affected not only Mars but other planets as well, including Earth. Venus also raises questions of climate history. Data from the U.S. Pioneer-Venus probe indicate that Venus may have released enough water in its evolution to have formed Earth-sized oceans. It is a matter of debate as to whether the water was immediately converted to oxygen and hydrogen as it was released from the interior or if oceans once existed and were later evaporated. Although connections of climate histories for Earth, Mars, and Venus have not been made, comparisons among all the terrestrial planets remain an item of intense study by climatologists.

## Conclusion

The exploration of the Solar System has now spanned nearly a generation, producing many stunning discoveries and a wealth of new information. Dozens of spacecraft, both manned and unmanned, have transformed the view of the planets from fuzzy telescopic dots to crisp objects for geologic study. More important, the Earth now can be perceived and appreciated as a member of a diverse family of Solar System objects.

The exploration of the Solar System has yielded new insights into the evolution of the planetary bodies. The Earthlike planets of the inner Solar System are seen to be essentially similar rocky objects with landforms that can be recognized and understood from observations and experience on the Earth. By contrast, the Voyager surveys of the icy satellites of the outer planets have confronted planetary scientists with new challenges. In recent years an understanding of geologic processes on these satellites has begun to emerge.

The exploration of the Solar System represents a triumph of imagination and will. The events of the last generation are perhaps too recent for full appreciation. However, the scientific significance of these voyages of discovery has been nothing less than revolutionary in providing new views of the Solar System and in providing a new perspective on our own planet, Earth.

*Features on Ariel, a moon of Uranus, show that the satellite has undergone extensive resurfacing. During the last twenty years spacecraft, both manned and unmanned, have provided a wealth of new information about the Solar System.*

NASA/JPL

FOR ADDITIONAL READING

J. Kelly Beatty, Brian O'Leary, and A. Chaikin, *The New Solar System* (Cambridge University Press, 1981).

Ronald Greeley, *Planetary Landscapes* (Allen & Unwin, 1985).

William K. Hartmann, *Moons and Planets,* 2nd ed. (Wadsworth Publishing Co., 1983).

Bruce C. Murray, Michael C. Malin, and Ronald Greeley, *Earthlike Planets* (W. H. Freeman and Co., 1981).

Bruce C. Murray, ed., *The Planets* (W. H. Freeman and Co., 1983).

# FOR FLAVOR,

## *A Dash of Chemistry*

### by Gary A. Reineccius

More than 10,000 different chemicals contribute to the aroma and taste of foods. What they are, how they form, and what each lends to a food's appeal is required knowledge for the specialists who create artificial and natural flavors for the food industry.

Even the simplest of organisms respond to chemicals in their environment. Flagellated bacteria, for example, will swim toward the chemicals characteristic of their food. Although this detection ability initially may have assisted primitive life in finding food, in humans the chemical senses—taste and smell—now serve more important physiological, safety, and pleasurable functions.

Physiological functions include stimulation of the secretion of saliva and other digestive actions. Studies have shown that people better utilize the nutrients in their diet if they receive odor and taste stimuli provided by food.

The role of chemical senses in protection is obvious. Taste and odor have been called the "gatekeepers of the alimentary system." Foods that are spoiled or unsafe are often readily detected by taste or odor before they are swallowed.

Many people most value the chemical senses for the daily pleasure they give. In their delight over a first morning cup of coffee, a fresh croissant, a soft, fragrant brie cheese, or a helping of rich ice cream, they are responding to what is collectively called the flavor of food.

### The flavor senses

The perception of flavor is generally broken up into three categories—taste, odor, and trigeminal responses—according to the sensory organs involved. Traditionally the taste response is further divided into salty, sour, sweet, and bitter components. The taste response comes entirely from cells located in taste buds on the top and sides of the tongue and going down the back of the throat. Individual taste cells end in hairlike processes called microvilli that project from a pore on the surface of the taste bud (*see* Figure 1, page 75).

The taste cells do not contact food components directly but rather do so through the microvilli. Substances can be tasted only when they are in solution as separate molecules or ions. If they are not in solution when taken into the mouth, they must first dissolve in saliva before they can interact with the microvilli. Each taste cell will generally respond to more than one of the four basic taste stimuli. The actual mechanism of creat-

*GARY A. REINECCIUS is Professor in the Department of Food Science and Nutrition, University of Minnesota.*

*Illustrations by Anne Hoyer Becker*

73

ing a response—an electrical discharge generated in the taste cells and carried by nerve fibers to the brain—differs for each of the basic tastes.

The saltiness of ordinary table salt (NaCl) and virtually all salty foods is a person's perception of the sodium ion ($Na^+$). The chloride ion ($Cl^-$) of salt produces no response at all. The taste receptor for sodium is a sodium-transport pathway; $Na^+$ passes through the microvilli and actually enters the taste cell to generate a signal. The ammonium ion ($NH_4^+$) and the positive ions of potassium, calcium, lithium, and magnesium can also stimulate a response similar to saltiness.

Sour taste comes from positively charged hydrogen ions ($H^+$). In solution an acid molecule will dissociate into a base ion and $H^+$. The acetic acid ($H_3CCOOH$) in vinegar, for example, is ionized into $H^+$ and $H_3CCOO^-$. Like sodium, the hydrogen ion may enter the cell to produce a response, but the issue has not been settled. Although the hydrogen ion is the main determinant of sourness, the rest of the acid molecule can modulate the intensity and quality of the response.

The sweetness receptor is likely a protein on the microvilli that changes shape when it contacts something sweet. As the protein reconfigures, it initiates an electrical discharge. The key to the sweetness of a substance appears to be the physical structure of its molecule; that is, certain features of the molecule must be properly arranged in three-dimensional space in order to elicit a sweet response.

Bitterness is an especially interesting but poorly characterized taste. There appears to be little chemical or structural similarity among bitter substances. Many bitter compounds are alkaloids, which are often toxic. Accordingly, some scientists have suggested that the instinctive dislike of bitter substances is a protective evolutionary response. By contrast, the enjoyment of bitterness is a learned response, one that typically occurs during early adulthood. People are most sensitive to bitterness in the back of the mouth and are less likely to taste a bitter substance with the front of the tongue.

The sense of taste is highly functional at birth. Studies have demonstrated clearly that newborns and infants respond positively to sweet substances: Both will drink more of a sugar-water solution than water alone and will respond to changes in concentration of sugar solutions. It is reasonable to suppose that the ability to recognize sweet substances (which usually have a high calorie content) is valuable to survival of the species. Likewise, the recognition and rejection of bitter, often toxic substances is a survival mechanism.

Smell is a much more sensitive and discriminating chemical sense than taste. It has been estimated that a human being can distinguish among more than 10,000 different odors. To be detected as an odor, a material must be in gaseous form; that is, dispersed in the air as separate molecules.

The smell response comes from the olfactory region in the nasal passages (*see* Figure 2, page 76). As air is drawn in, it passes the tubinate bones, which act as baffles, creating turbulence and warming the incoming air. The turbulence enhances the probability that any odor molecules

74

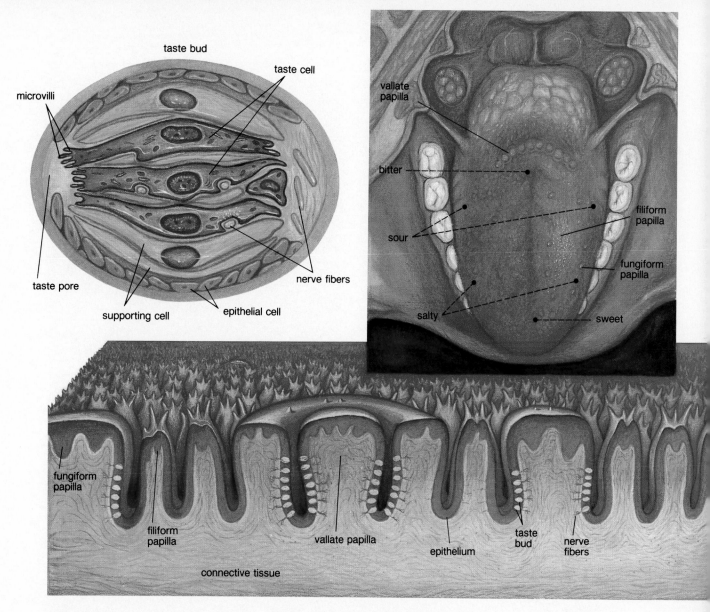

in the air will come in contact with the olfactory area, two membranous patches each having roughly the area of a fingertip and located on either side of the inner nose. A more detailed view of the olfactory area is also shown in Figure 2. The odor receptors are olfactory cells embedded in the epithelial membrane. To react with these cells odor molecules must make a short journey through an overlying layer of mucus. Although the actual mechanism of odor response has not been completely resolved, it is postulated that the response pattern of the olfactory nerve cells to a given odorant is matched by the brain to an event or an object previously associated with that odor.

Contrary to the sense of taste, the sense of smell shows substantial development and refinement after birth. This is somewhat surprising, considering that baby animals depend on smell for such functions as nursing, home orientation, emotional calming, food recognition and weaning, and contact behaviors like huddling and identification of individuals and kin. Much of the work in olfactory development has been done on ro-

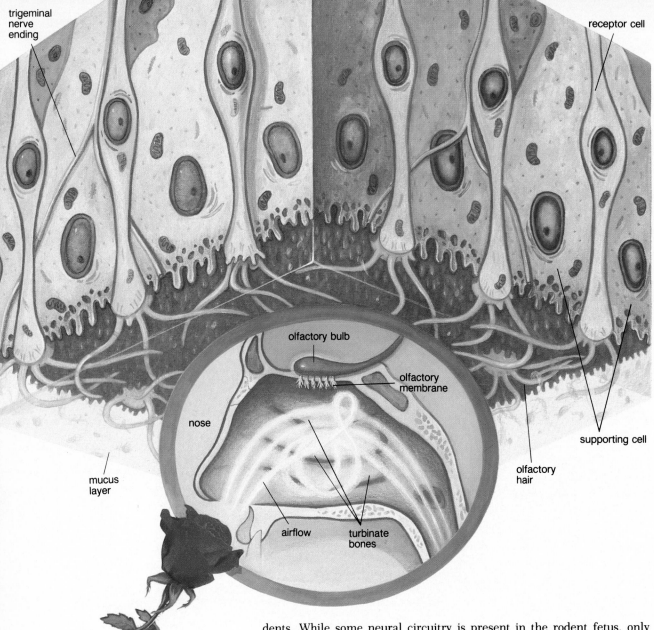

trigeminal nerve ending

receptor cell

olfactory bulb

olfactory membrane

nose

supporting cell

olfactory hair

mucus layer

airflow

turbinate bones

dents. While some neural circuitry is present in the rodent fetus, only about 1% is complete before birth. Human newborns are somewhat more advanced; ample evidence exists that within hours of birth they can detect some odors. Nevertheless, the olfactory system continues developing rapidly after birth.

Although infants can smell various odors, they do not have the strong reactions to pleasantness and unpleasantness that adults exhibit. In a classic study children were presented with the odors of sweat, feces, and amyl acetate (a pleasant fruity odor). Children younger than five years of age generally did not appear to find one odor more pleasant than another. Between the ages of five and six, reactions were mixed, and after age six the adult pattern emerged.

The trigeminal response to flavor includes the burn of red peppers and horseradish and the cooling of mint and menthol. The trigeminal receptors are simply free nerve endings in the mouth and olfactory area that respond to certain chemicals. Because they do not end at the tissue surface but are slightly recessed, they respond less quickly and sensitively than smell or taste receptors. People who eat peppery foods know that the burning comes on slowly and builds up. For the same reason the response is not readily removed, say, by simply rinsing out the mouth.

While people are probably more familiar with the oral trigeminal response, certain foods (*e.g.*, carbonated beverages, vinegar, horseradish, mustard, and some spices) elicit a harsh, pungent response in the olfactory region. The flavor chemicals responsible for this stimulation are quite different from those that warm the mouth. They must be very volatile and readily pass into the nasal cavity (*e.g.*, carbon dioxide, ammonia, acetic acid, and isothiocyanate). By contrast, those substances that stimulate the mouth trigeminally are relatively large nonvolatile molecules such as those found in pepper (capsaicins) and ginger (gingerone).

The overall perception of flavor then is a complex sensation. Several hundred different stimuli may be sensed and processed by the brain to arrive at the final assessment of a "good cup of coffee." Even the taste sensors on the tongue contribute a variety of sensations. Acid is not simply "sour" but a particular sour nuance given by a particular acid or blend of acids. The malic acid found in such fruits as apples gives a different taste from the citric acid that predominates in citrus fruits. Likewise, the sugars in a particular food each have a distinct sweet character. Although sucrose has long been the standard of sweetness, many foods today, particularly carbonated beverages, are sweetened with fructose syrups. Fructose has a different sweetness character that is perceived more rapidly and that lingers longer in the mouth. Corn syrups have their own unique sweetness, often being characterized as honey- or caramel-like. The artificial sweeteners also create different sensations of sweetness. Saccharin, for instance, is very rapidly perceived and leaves many people with a bitter aftertaste. Similar statements could be made about bitter and salty sensations. Thus, even taste, which seems to be very simple, does in fact have its subtleties.

## Fruit and vegetable flavors

Flavor in plant foods arises most often as the result of degradation of the plant's major chemical building blocks—its fats, proteins, and carbohydrates. While the plant is growing, thousands of chemical reactions are proceeding, providing the materials needed for growth and maintenance. Enzymes facilitate these reactions, which otherwise would be too slow to sustain the plant. When the plant dies or is harvested or when its fruit ripens, most of these enzyme systems remain active. Enzymes that were initially involved in synthesizing fats, proteins, or carbohydrates now may operate in reverse to break down these same materials. Enzymes and their substrates (the substances upon which the enzymes act), once separated in an orderly manner in the living cell, may now contact each other and undergo many reactions that were not previously possible. An end result of this enzymatic reaction is food flavor.

Fruits and vegetables differ greatly in how and when flavor is formed. In the case of fruits, flavor appears during a brief ripening period. At

*Figure 2 (opposite page). Responding to odors is the responsibility of a pair of membranous patches located high in the inner nose (bottom). As air passes through the nose it is warmed and stirred by the turbinate bones, increasing the chance that any odor molecules in the air will contact the olfactory membranes. The odor receptors are olfactory cells buried among the supporting tissue of the membranes (top). At the membrane surface each olfactory cell swells into a knob from which project several olfactory hairs. To reach the hairs, odor molecules must travel through an overlying layer of protective mucus. The harsh pungent response elicited in the nose by such foods as horseradish and mustard comes from the stimulation of trigeminal receptors, free nerve endings in the olfactory membrane that are sensitive to various chemicals.*

77

*Flavor in fruit is formed during a brief ripening period, during which the enzyme systems that were originally active in synthesizing various chemical components for the growing plant operate in reverse to break down these same materials. As ripening proceeds, fruit tissues soften and the surface often changes color. Although fat is present in fruit in only small amounts, it breaks down into many important flavors.*

this time plant respiration increases greatly, tissues soften owing to the loss of cellular integrity, and the surface often changes color. Although fruits have little fat, it is the fat that breaks down into many important flavors. For peaches and pears several lactones make up the characteristic flavor. Lactones are cyclic (ring-containing) molecules, many of which have pleasant fruity or flowery odors. A person smelling or tasting γ-undecalactone alone would identify it as peachy—a poor peach but yet a peach.

Nature does not use just one flavor chemical, however, but a host of well-balanced notes. For example, more than 150 volatile chemicals have been isolated and identified in peaches; a few of the more important contributors to peach odor and their odor characters are listed in Table I. Note that although the lactones give the peach a peachy note, other compounds are responsible for its fresh, green, and pitty characters. The absence of this flavor symphony is apparent in the taste of a cheap artificial flavor. As is discussed below, artificial flavors are most often a simple blend of 10–20 compounds. It is impractical, as well as impossible, to make an artifical flavor with 200–300 compounds. Natural flavors are nearly always smoother, deeper, and more complete and well rounded than the artificial counterpart.

Vegetable flavors are quite different from fruit flavors. Vegetables, with few exceptions, are totally devoid of their characteristic flavor until

| Table I. Most Significant Flavor Compounds in Peaches | |
|---|---|
| compound | flavor character |
| γ-undecalactone | sweet, fruity, peachy |
| γ-dodecalactone | fatty, buttery, peachy |
| δ-dodecalactone | strong, fresh fruit, peachy |
| γ- and δ-decalactone | fruity, peachy |
| ethyl cinnamate | cinnamonlike, honey, peach/apricot |
| cis-3-hexen-1-ol | intense "green" odor, leafy, cut grass |
| methyl salicylate | wintergreen (main flavor in root beer) |
| linalool | floral |
| ethyl butyrate | fruity with pineapple undertone |
| benzaldehyde | almond |

78

*An onion has little odor until its tissue is cut, bitten, or damaged in some other way. Then, very rapidly, enzymes mix with precursor molecules to generate the vegetable's potent flavor and eye-irritating ability.*

they suffer tissue damage. Such damage might come from cutting the vegetable with a knife, grating it, biting it, or cooking it. Only when cellular disruption allows enzymes to mix with the flavor precursors does flavor develop. These precursors in themselves are not volatile and hence would elicit little flavor response. When attacked by enzymes in the vegetable cells, however, they are rapidly cleaved into volatile, flavorful fragments. It may come as a surprise that an onion has little odor or character until it is cut. Then, very rapidly, a potent flavor is formed that brings tears to the eyes. The compound responsible for irritating the eyes, thiopropanal-*s*-oxide, is unstable. Shortly after it is formed, it starts to decompose to pyruvic acid, sulfur, and carbon dioxide.

The fact that onion flavor appears only after cellular disruption can be used to make chopping onions more agreeable. If onions are kept refrigerated until ready to be sliced or diced, the cold temperatures will slow down the flavor-forming reactions enough for the cook to escape much of the usual torture.

The compounds that lend vegetables their flavors are different from those of fruits, and sulfur-containing molecules figure very heavily. If one consciously smells cooked cabbage, cauliflower, brussels sprouts, and

| Table II. Characteristic Flavor Compounds in Vegetables | |
|---|---|
| compound | raw vegetable |
| 2-isobutyl-3-methoxypyrazine | green pepper |
| 2,5-dihydro-3,4-dimethylthiophen-2-one (sulfur-containing) | leek |
| nona-*E,Z*-2,6-dienal | cucumber |
| 3-methylsulfinylpropylisothiocyanate (sulfur-containing) | cabbage |
| 1-hexen-3-one | artichoke |
| oct-*Z*-5-en-2-one | dried beans |
| methyl-1,2-dithiolane-4-carboxylate (sulfur-containing) | asparagus |
| hex-*Z*-3-enal | peas |

*The complex flavor of a fried hamburger derives primarily from the heat-induced reactions of proteins and sugars. At least 800 volatile contributors to flavor have been identified in cooked meats.*

onions, one will detect a common note, which comes from sulfur compounds. Yet slightly different flavor components and their blends give each of these vegetables a distinct odor character. Characteristic flavor compounds for several vegetables are listed in Table II on page 79.

## Heated-food flavors

A broad group of foods take on their characteristic flavors after being heated. Examples include bread, coffee, tea, chocolate, meats, pastries, and maple syrups. As is commonly known, the flavor of these foods develops almost entirely during baking, roasting, boiling, or frying. Unroasted coffee or cocoa, for instance, has only a sour, bitter, fermented flavor, while their roasted versions boast well-rounded, exceptionally pleasing tastes and odors. The flavor of such foods derives primarily from the reaction of proteins and indigenous sugars. From as few as 30–40 reactants (proteins, acids, and sugars) come flavors of complex compositions. To date more than 800 volatile chemicals have been identified in cooked meats and about the same number in the aromas of chocolate and coffee.

It is of interest that for coffee, chocolate, and bread, no individual compound or even a small number of individual compounds are known to approach the main flavor character of these foods. Their flavor instead is due to a blend of numerous chemicals. As an illustration, the flavor from chocolate has been isolated, separated by gas chromatography into individual flavor chemicals (*see* Figure 3), and then characterized by a person smelling the separated components. Each peak on the chromatogram represents an individual flavor component. The area of each peak is proportional to the concentration of that chemical. Checking the

| | | | |
|---|---|---|---|
| 1 | beany | 27 | musty |
| 2 | bready | 28 | nutty |
| 3 | buttery | 29 | oily |
| 4 | butterscotch | 30 | oxidized (heated oil) |
| 5 | caramel | 31 | oxidized (stale potato chips) |
| 6 | cereal | | |
| 7 | chemical | | |
| 8 | chemical (solvent) | 32 | peanuts |
| 9 | cherry almond | 33 | pecans |
| 10 | clove | 34 | pine tree |
| 11 | coconut | 35 | plastic |
| 12 | corn | 36 | popcorn |
| 13 | earthy | 37 | pumpkin |
| 14 | earthy potato | 38 | pungent |
| 15 | eggy | 39 | roasted |
| 16 | fatty | 40 | rotten |
| 17 | fecal | 41 | sharp |
| 18 | fermented | 42 | soapy |
| 19 | floral | 43 | soapy (detergent) |
| 20 | fruity | | |
| 21 | green grass | 44 | sour |
| 22 | green, leafy | 45 | spicy |
| 23 | heavy resin | 46 | vegetable |
| 24 | hot oil | 47 | walnuts |
| 25 | mothballs | | |
| 26 | mushroom | | |

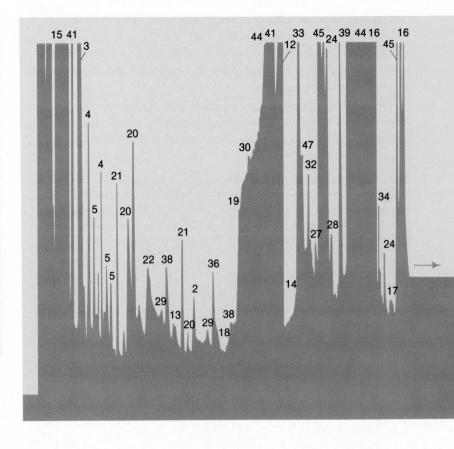

chromatogram shows it to be devoid of peaks identified as chocolate-like in character. It is, in fact, the sum of all of these nonchocolate flavors that ultimately gives chocolate.

While the flavor of bread comes primarily from heating, for yeast-leavened bread the initial fermentation process also plays a significant role. The contribution of fermentation is readily seen when one compares the flavors of a yeast-leavened biscuit and a baking-powder biscuit. The former has a slightly acidic, richer aroma and taste. Although the primary product of yeast fermentation is carbon dioxide gas, numerous low-molecular-weight compounds are also formed. Some of these compounds contribute directly to flavor; others undergo further chemical reaction during baking. Together they build a very complex aroma.

Some heated foods like roasted nuts owe their basic flavors to single compounds. Almond, for example, derives its characteristic flavor from 5-methylthiophen-2-carboxaldehyde; peanuts, from 2,5-dimethylpyrazine; and hazelnuts, from methylthiomethylpyrazine.

Heated foods typically obtain their flavors from a broad group of chemicals called heterocyclics. Heterocyclics are ring-containing carbon compounds that incorporate such atoms as sulfur, oxygen, or nitrogen or some combination of them in the ring. While heterocyclics are occasionally found in nonheated foods, they are extremely important to the flavor of roasted, toasted, baked, or broiled foods. (*See* Table III, page 83.)

## Fermented foods

Such foods as beer, wine, sausages, and cheese provide another variety of flavors for enjoyment. These fermented products obtain their charac-

University of Minnesota, St. Paul; photo, Sara J. Risch

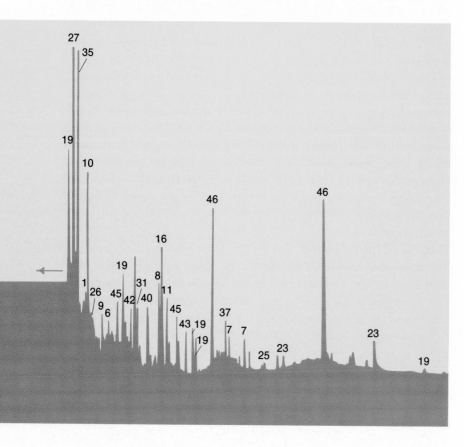

*Figure 3. Chromatogram (opposite page and this page, bottom) records the composition of chocolate flavor that has been isolated and separated into flavor chemicals. Each peak represents an individual component, while the area under the peak is proportional to the concentration of that chemical (flat peaks resulted when concentrations exceeded the range of the chart recorder). The odor of each chemical, characterized by the author as it emerged from the gas chromatograph (above), is identified by number in the legend on the opposite page. Significantly, no single peak in the chromatogram is chocolate-like in flavor. It is rather the sum of all the nonchocolate flavors that gives chocolate its distinctive flavor.*

*Although the rich aroma and taste of yeast-leavened bread comes primarily from baking, the fermentation process also contributes significantly in the form of numerous low-molecular-weight compounds.*

teristic flavors directly or indirectly from the growth of microorganisms: yeasts (*e.g.*, wine), bacteria (many cheeses), or molds (blue cheese). Flavor is formed in these products by way of two major mechanisms.

The first directly involves activity of the microorganisms in the food. Microorganisms obtain energy to grow and multiply from various food constituents (*e.g.*, the sugars in plant materials or milk). In order to extract this energy, they convert the energy source enzymatically into smaller molecules. These metabolic by-products accumulate in the food, contibuting a unique flavor that depends on the energy source used and the metabolism of the microorganisms involved. Flavor compounds coming from this metabolic activity are generally highly oxidized substances of low molecular weight. Examples include grain alcohol (ethanol), short-chain esters, acetaldehyde, diacetyl, acetic acid, propionic acid, and lactic acid. Acetaldehyde is important to the flavor of yogurt, while diacetyl is the major flavor compound in buttermilk. Short-chain esters carry the flavor of beer.

The second flavor-producing mechanism in fermented products involves changes in the food once the microorganisms have died. These changes are induced not by life processes but rather by residual microbial enzymes liberated from the dead microbial cells. Consequently, they occur only during storage or aging of the fermented foods. This mechanism of flavor formation plays its most important role in aged cheeses. Although a freshly made cheddar cheese curd has a definite fermented flavor, it is rubbery and squeaks when bitten. Once this curd has been formed into blocks and starts aging, many changes occur. The bacterial starter culture used in the initial fermentation (*Streptococcus lactis*) dies off, primarily because the organisms have used up all the sugar in the milk. As the organisms die, their cell walls rupture and release the cellular constituents into the cheese curd. Among the constituents are a number of viable enzymes, which then start to act on the cheese.

The two most significant enzyme systems for flavor development in aged cheese are the lipases and proteases. Lipases attack the fat in the cheese and break down some of it into free fatty acids, which add a unique tart taste. Similarly, proteases attack the milk protein, converting some of it into free amino acids and peptides. These molecules give a meaty, brothy background flavor to the cheese. Protein breakdown also changes the rubbery texture into a softer, more pastelike consistency. The longer a cheese is aged, the greater will be the extent of fat and protein degradation.

### The task of identification

The number of chemicals responsible for flavor is considerable. More than 4,300 different, naturally occurring, volatile flavor compounds have been identified to date, a tally that includes only those chemicals contributing to the aroma of a food—not to its taste or its trigeminal effect. Scientists estimate that at least 10,000 different chemicals in foods contribute to aroma. The identification of these compounds is a challenge. One major problem is that some compounds need be present in only vanishingly small amounts to elicit a sensory response. A food may contain as little as one part in a hundred trillion ($10^{14}$) of a chemical, and yet that chemical can be very significant to flavor. One part in a hundred trillion is equivalent to one drop in three billion gallons of water. This amazing sensitivity of the human nose puts the analytical instrumentation available to the flavor chemist to shame.

## Flavor making for the food industry

Consumers rarely deal with—or are even aware of—the people who prepare flavors for processed foods. The flavor industry sells its products, natural and artificial flavors, to the food manufacturer (*e.g.*, General Foods, Unilever, Nestle, Pillsbury, or Quaker Oats), which then takes the credit when its foods are a tasty success or suffers the loss when they fail to catch on. The flavor companies generally remain offstage.

The flavor industry is small, comprising about 900 companies worldwide with total annual sales of less than $2 billion. To put that sales figure into perspective, $2 billion is less than half the annual sales of such U.S. food companies as Pillsbury or General Mills. The four largest flavor companies—International Flavors and Fragrances, U.S.; Givaudan, Switzerland; PPF-Naarden, England; and Haarmann and Reimer, West Germany—account for approximately 30% of the total sales. The remaining 70% is divided among 15–20 intermediate-sized companies (another 25% of total sales) and a host of small companies. Flavor production is very similar to that of a typical chemical-manufacturing facility. Compounds are synthesized and flavor fractions isolated and refined for use in foods. The typical flavor company will have on hand nearly 3,000 different materials. Some are pure compounds and spice extracts, while others, like cinnamon bark and clove buds, are exotic materials from around the world.

The flavorist is the person who "creates" a flavor. He (or she) often, but not always, has a college degree in a scientific area. Although it may seem obvious that the flavorist must have an unusually good sense of taste and smell, that is not necessarily true. He has simply learned to use these senses to their fullest. He has also spent perhaps five or ten years developing a memory for odors and tastes. He will consciously smell and record every odor that passes, whether at work, in the park, or in the subway. The flavorist must remember the odor and taste properties of several hundred chemicals. To describe odors he needs a vocabulary that he derives by being conscious of the world around him. He typically will have in excess of 1,400 pure compounds in his laboratory. When the natural extracts of spices, herbs, citrus, and other materials are added, the selection may well exceed 2,000 items.

When the flavorist is given an assignment—for example, to create an artificial, slightly underripe, seedy, wild strawberry flavor for a gelatin dessert—he first will attempt to find the real food counterpart. This may mean a trip to the local fruit stand for domestic, farm-grown strawberries or sending an order to France for imported wild strawberries. The flavorist now has a target, the natural product. Next he searches the

| Table III. Important Flavor Compounds in Some Heated Foods | |
|---|---|
| compound | food |
| 2,4,5-trithiahexane | cooked cabbage |
| 2-ethyl-3,6-dimethylpyrazine | potato chips |
| 2-acetyl-2-thiazoline | bread |
| 2,5-dimethyl-3-furanthiol | roasted meat |
| 2-acetylthiazole | crackers |

scientific literature to see what compounds have been found in the wild strawberry. Checking the Weurman list, a technical publication issued by the Central Institute for Nutrition and Food Research in The Netherlands that lists all of the flavor compounds indentified in each food, he notes that nature uses 184 chemicals to make a strawberry flavor. Cost of production dictates that this number be reduced. Many of the naturally occurring compounds make only minor contributions to flavor. Also, many of them are not permitted to be added to foods because they are known to be toxic or because insufficient safety information is available.

With these limitations in mind, the flavorist then gathers those compounds he believes to be most significant and makes dilute solutions of each. Each solution is tasted, and notes are taken on its taste and at what concentration the compound might be used in strawberry flavor; this process further narrows the choices. Ideally, the flavorist would like to use no more than 20 compounds. From the reduced list, combinations of flavor chemicals are tasted and evaluated for a slightly underripe, seedy, wild strawberry flavor. After a few days of full-time effort, the flavorist settles on a product that he hopes will please his client and ultimately be a success in the marketplace.

The process of creating a natural flavor is somewhat different and much more difficult than creating an artificial flavor. When the flavorist gets such an assignment, say, the flavor for a strawberry beverage, he can work only with natural products; e.g., spice oils, fruit juice, fruit concentrates, various fruit essences, and the like. While the only true way to a strawberry beverage is to use strawberry juice, the juice is too expensive and often is not available. About three times as much natural strawberry flavoring is sold as there are strawberries in the world (the case is even worse for grapes, for which the ratio is ten to one). So both economics and supply point out that natural juices usually cannot be used to provide flavor. Instead, real juice is used only as a base, which does little more than provide color, while other natural products are added to supply the flavor. These substances might be extracts of roots (orrisroot is raspberry in character), floral essences, essential oils (oil of tagetes—from a marigold—is somewhat applelike), absolutes (e.g., alcoholic extracts of currants), or oleoresins (e.g., solvent extracts of clove). Careful blending of numerous natural products usually yields a flavoring of acceptable strength and character.

Nevertheless, no plant is strawberry flavored except strawberry. All other natural flavoring materials have their own unique flavor. Furthermore, many of these essences and extracts are only pale reflections of the flavor of their natural sources (mints and citrus being notable exceptions). Artificial flavors, by contrast, are quite often vastly superior in strength and character to the natural flavorings commercially available. They are most often the identical compounds used by nature to make a flavoring. Yet, because they are synthesized in a laboratory, current U.S. food laws do not consider them natural. To make a natural flavor one must blend materials that are not strawberry. This requirement can produce flavorings so inferior that, were it not for the color of the prod-

Making and evaluating a new flavor for the food industry (opposite page) is a multistep, cooperative effort. The flavorist, or flavor chemist, who actually creates the flavor has access to hundreds of pure compounds and extracts in the laboratory (top left). Using a knowledge of chemistry and a well-developed memory and vocabulary for odors and tastes, the flavorist mixes various combinations of ingredients in the search for the one that best approximates the target flavor (top right). Assisting the flavorist, the chromatographer reconstructs gas chromatography data stored in computer memory on compounds that have been identified in foods (center right). In a test kitchen of the flavor company (bottom left), the food technologist prepares a finished product that subsequently will be judged by other technologists serving as panelists (bottom right).

Courtesy, Food Materials Corporation, Chicago, Illinois; photos, Cameramann International, Ltd.

85

uct and the label describing what to expect, the consumer would likely be unable to identify them. It would make an interesting experiment to prepare a series of naturally fruit-flavored gelatin desserts or carbonated beverages and ask people to guess the flavor while blindfolded.

In addition to "artificial" and "natural" flavors, many countries (excluding the U.S.) have a third category: the Nature Identical System (NIS). NIS flavors can contain synthetic versions of the same compounds that are found in the food itself to duplicate a natural product unless a compound is known to be toxic. This gives the flavorist much more freedom to create a good-quality flavoring without its being labeled artificial. There is considerable logic to this system since it is hard to rationalize how a strawberry flavor created with synthetic chemicals is any different from the identical chemicals made by a plant.

Browning flavors, those which approximate the taste of such foods as meat, chocolate, coffee, tea, or bread, are generally "created" in a different manner. These flavorings are called reaction products because they are formed by heating various mixtures of sugars and amino acids, which react to reproduce the intended flavor. There is, for example, no meat in a bouillon cube. The proper mixing and heating of a simple sugar (*e.g.*, ribose) and an amino acid (*e.g.*, cysteine) generate the meaty flavor. Additional ingredients are put into a reaction product to provide certain flavor notes. Monosodium glutamate (MSG) may be supplied to give body or richness to a soup reaction product. Adding a fat prior to heating the reaction mixture will lend the flavor the character of a particular kind of animal: mutton tallow for a mutton meat flavor or fish oil for a roasted or baked fish note. As mentioned above, the characteristic flavors of many heated foods depend on dozens or hundreds of compounds, making them difficult to reproduce with simple blends. The flavorist finds it easier to react a few ingredients, using heat, to develop the desired flavor.

The flavorist is indeed both a chemist and an artist. His chemistry controls the reactions causing flavor formation, while his artistry imitates nature much the same as a rendered still life. The flavorist's media are chemical compounds, and his target is the product of hundreds of stimuli assembled and evaluated by the brain.

## The safety of flavorings

In most parts of the world, people believe that natural products are safe and nutritious. It is almost a sacrilege to deny the purity of nature. Yet a quick look at the effects of hemlock tea, some members of the mushroom family, or even green potatoes proves without question that nature makes some of the most deadly poisons known. While one may argue that people have learned through time what is safe to eat, that is not necessarily true. They may know what foods will kill them quickly but not what foods have a long-term detrimental effect. Closely examined, virtually any food will prove to contain toxic substances. The spice saffron, for instance, contains the chemical saffrole, a known carcinogen. Pepper contains substances that have been shown to induce skin cancer in rats. Carrots contain myristicin, also a carcinogen. Cabbage and other

86

members of the Brassica family contain goitrogens, compounds that interfere with the functioning of the thyroid gland. Surprisingly large books are devoted to elucidating the toxic chemicals in supposedly pure and safe natural foods.

By comparison, what can be said about artificial flavorings? These mixtures generally comprise 10–20 pure compounds, all of which have been evaluated for toxicity (as allergens, mutagens, carcinogens, etc.) by means of animal testing. In the U.S. they have been judged by the Food and Drug Administration (FDA) to be safe for consumption as food flavorants. Because they are identical in all respects to those supplied by nature for those same flavors, their use to flavor foods seems logical. Artificial flavor chemicals are also self-limiting in usage level. The flavor manufacturer cannot arbitrarily put 10 or 20 times the normal amount of a particular flavor compound into a flavoring and have it go unnoticed. For a natural-tasting flavor, both the compounds and their proportions must be those found naturally.

From the chemist's viewpoint the difference between a natural and an artificial flavor is one of complexity; the artificial flavor is simpler in composition. Among the missing ingredients are natural substances that have been shown to be toxic. A good example is smoke flavor. Natural smoke, coming from the home grill or the commercial smoking operation, contains significant benzopyrenes, which are known to cause cancer in animals. Artificial smoke flavor excludes benzopyrenes and includes only effective, safe flavor compounds. Chocolate provides another example. Only 225 of the 835 flavor compounds found in chocolate are permitted by the FDA to be added to foods. The rest are compounds either known to be toxic (*e.g.*, pyridine) or insufficiently studied to be permitted for use in foods. From the standpoint of safety alone, consuming a few safety-tested flavor compounds in an artificial flavor thus seems preferable to consuming a host of chemicals of either known toxicity or unknown safety in a natural product.

Realistically, however, in a world in which eating natural foods is as fundamental as the maintenance of life itself, the choice the consumer should be pondering is whether the naturally or artificially flavored product has the best flavor and is the best value. Natural flavorings are more expensive than their artificial counterparts and are certainly no safer. Are they worth the higher price?

# IRRADIATING FOOD

## by Noel D. Vietmeyer

Food can be preserved for long periods of time by treating it with radiation. However, considerable controversy surrounds the use of this technique.

Imagine strawberries that stay fresh for a month, roast beef dinners that stay moist and succulent for years, and hot dogs with no chemical preservatives that can be kept on the kitchen shelf for decades. Such possibilities are part of the promise of food irradiation.

After more than four decades of research this 20th-century nuclear technology seems poised to join conventional food-preservation processes such as pasteurization, canning, freezing, curing, vacuum packing, and the use of chemical fumigants and preservatives. Since 1983 the U.S. Food and Drug Administration (FDA) has issued limited approvals for the irradiation of foods as diverse as spices, pork, fruits, and vegetables.

Proponents of food irradiation say that this official recognition of the method's safety is the start of a technological revolution that will change the way people handle foods. According to them refrigeration will become less important in warehouses, trucks, supermarkets, and the home; fresh seafood and other highly perishable foods will be available in places that now only can get such food frozen; and scores of different new and exotic fruits will come flooding into supermarkets.

On the other hand, opponents say that this controversial technology is dangerous and must be stopped before it adds an unnecessary new nuclear hazard to modern life. Moreover, observers in the business world point out that irradiated foods face so many uncertainties and challenges in the marketplace—consumer acceptance, economic feasibility, and market development, for instance—that the process may never attain more than a minor role in practice.

*NOEL D. VIETMEYER is a Professional Associate with the National Research Council in Washington, D.C.*

*Illustration by Constantino Mitchell*

Although the future of food irradiation is unclear, the technology's promise is enticing and potentially vast. Living things exist in a swarm of bacteria, parasites, and pests, and today heat, cold, or chemicals are used to keep them from contaminating foods. These physical and chemical methods of food preservation contribute vitally to the way in which people live. They make it possible to ship perishable foods around the world. Indeed, food preservation is so important that it is a cornerstone of industrial civilization, allowing cities to be thousands of miles away from the farms that supply their food.

However, today's food-preservation methods collectively have their limitations. Each year, for instance, more than four million people in the United States get food poisoning, and several thousand of these victims die. Studies by the Federal Centers for Disease Control show that in a typical year salmonella causes 2,000 deaths, campylobacteria causes 2,100 deaths, other enteric diseases cause 2,000 deaths, and trichinosis—a disease produced by the parasite found in pork—causes 1,000 deaths. The U.S. Department of Agriculture (USDA) has estimated that food poisoning from pork and chicken alone costs the nation more than $1 billion annually in medical expenses and lost wages.

And beyond the serious food poisoning, there are between 24 million and 81 million cases of less serious food-borne diarrheal disease each year. According to the estimates of Douglas Archer and John Kvenberg of the FDA's Division of Microbiology, this causes an economic loss of between $5 billion and $17 billion annually as a result of medical expenses and lost productivity on the job.

## Origins

The concept of practical food irradiation grew out of the atomic energy program of World War II. Researchers and politicians at first had high hopes that it would be accepted and would transform food handling throughout the world. But in 1958 these hopes were dashed when the United States Congress declared food irradiation to be not a process but an "additive." As a result, each separate irradiated food had to be tested exhaustively and proved safe, as if radiation were a chemical pesticide. Consequently, almost all scientists and corporations lost interest in the process. Only the United States Army and a few die-hard scientists continued working in food-irradiation research in North America.

Irradiating food for commercial purposes proceeded in almost 30 European and other countries, but even there work remained at a low level because in the United States—the originator of the technology—food irradiation was illegal. South Africa and The Netherlands established notable food-irradiation industries, although both remained quite small. South Africa, for instance, sells irradiated papaya to parts of Europe.

In the early 1980s, however, interest in food irradiation began rising again in the United States. This happened because irradiation is an alternative to chemical preservatives, several of which were banned from use in foods because of fears that they cause cancer. These bans threatened to disrupt or destroy large sections of the produce industry.

*Examples of traditional methods of food preservation include drying (of cod, left) and a combination of salting and drying (of strips of smoked salmon, below). Microorganisms can not grow well in food that has been dehydrated.*

The renewed interest was also spurred by the increasing public health threats from food-borne diseases. During recent years there had been a resurgence of microbial contamination and in the number and severity of food-borne-disease outbreaks. In addition, certain strains of salmonella and campylobacteria had become resistant to antibiotics.

## The food-irradiation process

Most food irradiation is achieved with gamma rays, a penetrating form of radiation similar to X-rays but more powerful. The electromagnetic energy in the streams of such waves breaks the bonds of life, disrupting the bodies of insects and the cells of microorganisms—even those hidden deep inside the food. The food itself is not made radioactive in any way. (Just as teeth are not left radioactive after an X-ray.)

Although most of the radiation passes through the food, some is absorbed. The absorbed energy "strips" electrons from the atoms and molecules it impacts, and this "ionization" process produces free radicals that are extremely reactive chemically. By combining with nearby DNA (deoxyribonucleic acid) enzymes and other cellular components vital to the functioning of the cell, they disrupt the processes necessary for cells to divide and grow and function.

The extent of the effects depends on the organism. Little radiation is required to affect sophisticated organisms like insects; a lot is required to affect bacteria and viruses. The results also depend on the dose delivered. Low doses—below 1,000 grays—cause living cells of complex organisms to stop dividing. (In the International System of units, the measure of absorbed dose of radiation is known as the gray. One gray is one joule of energy absorbed per kilogram. The older system of units, still widely used, was based on the rad; 100 rads equal one gray.) Thus, fruits slow down their ripening; insects stop growing and reproducing; and living plant cells—such as found in seeds or the "eyes" of potatoes—die. (This process can also be used to inhibit the sprouting of potatoes and onions.) In addition, trichina worms lurking in a pork chop are sterilized so that they cannot lay eggs in the intestines of someone who eats them. (Larvae hatching from those eggs cause the severe gastrointestinal distress of trichinosis.)

Medium doses—between 1,000 and 3,000 grays—kill complex organisms such as the larvae and adults of parasites and insects, and they inhibit the growth and reproduction of most simple organisms such as fungi and bacteria. By reducing the number of molds and microbes that cause decay, such doses often double or triple the shelf life of such foods as chicken and red meat—the most expensive items in the average consumer's diet and those that spoil the quickest. In addition, these doses sharply reduce the number of toxic microorganisms, such as salmonella and campylobacteria, that pose public health threats.

*In a typical radiation treatment plant, food is placed on a conveyor belt and then carried into a shielded concrete room that contains a source of gamma rays. While the food is moving around it, the energy source is raised from a protective tank of water and releases a shower of radiation.*

Reprinted with permission from "Food Irradiation," Pamela S. Zurer, *Chemical & Engineering News*, vol. 64, no. 18, pp. 46–56, May 5, 1986. Copyright 1986 American Chemical Society

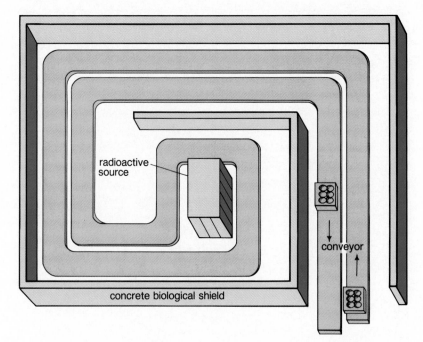

radioactive source

conveyor

concrete biological shield

High doses—more than 10,000 grays—eliminate all organisms, including viruses. This produces sterile food that can be stored indefinitely without refrigeration.

In an irradiation facility food is loaded on a conveyor belt that carries it into a shielded concrete room containing a source of gamma rays. The glowing radiation source is raised from a protective tank of water, and its electromagnetic energy showers the food. Usually the food is contained in its normal shipping cartons piled up on pallets. The conveyor belt moves the pallets around the source so that the food is dosed evenly on all sides.

The food is usually already in its final packaging so that it is protected from later exposure to the air and recontamination from microbes. Gamma rays penetrate glass bottles, metal cans, plastic containers, foil pouches, and other standard packaging. One problem with glass is that some forms are discolored when subjected to irradiation. (This is actually an inexpensive way to tint glass; bottles of some well-known men's colognes get their amber hue not from dyes but from an irradiator.)

The normal source of the gamma rays is cobalt-60. A potential alternative is cesium-137, which is being promoted partly because it is a waste product of nuclear weapons production and its storage is becoming a problem. Also being considered are particle accelerators that bombard food with streams of electrons and are not radioactive at all.

Irradiation is sometimes described as a "cold" process because the food usually stays cool. Therein lies one advantage over canning and other conventional food-preservation methods. Without heat the food remains virtually unchanged from its normal state. It loses little of its natural flavor, odor, or texture. And irradiation also can penetrate packaging materials—plastic foil, for instance—that cannot be heated.

In principle, irradiation works for all types of foods: meat, seafood, breads, desserts, fruits, and vegetables—cooked or uncooked. However, some foods are particularly sensitive. Cucumbers, for instance, become soft when irradiated; citrus fruits and bell peppers can turn mushy and

*Computer (opposite page, top) monitors materials as they move through a radiation treatment plant, noting their weight and the amount of radiation that they receive. The materials, generally hospital supplies and food, are contained in their normal shipping cartons piled up on pallets (above left). The source of the radiation is usually cobalt-60, shown above after being raised from its protective tank of water.*

93

*After four weeks in the refrigerator strawberries that had been irradiated (above left) showed no signs of spoilage, while those that had not received radiation had become moldy. (Right) The potatoes on the left were irradiated, while those on the right were not treated and had begun to sprout after two months.*

brown; and dairy products develop off-flavors. Such adverse effects can be reduced by chilling or freezing the food before it is irradiated.

Irradiating foods is not simple in practice. Achieving the proper dose is a complex operational challenge. Each type of food requires its own level. And each batch must be stacked and moved so that all parts of it receive at least the minimum exposure while none receives more than the amount that would destroy its flavor, texture, or nutritional value or that would exceed the maximum legal dose.

Irradiation is not a panacea against spoilage either. Food rots not only because of living contaminants. It decays because of three intercoordinated attacks: its own enzymes break down its tissues from within; air oxidizes its molecules from without; and microbes and insects degrade it as they feed and grow. Irradiation works only on the microbes, insects, and other living things; it has no effect on enzymes or oxidation. But enzymes and oxidation are the easiest problems to overcome by conventional means: heating the food briefly (blanching) denatures the enzymes and halts their assault; vacuum packing in airtight containers (such as plastic packs, pouches, and sealed bottles) blocks oxidation.

## The approval process

Because the 1958 law listed irradiation as a food additive, each proposed new use must be approved by the FDA. Obtaining such approval is a complicated procedure that takes years and is fraught with uncertainty. Processors must conduct exhaustive laboratory tests to prove that irradiation is safe for each food item they propose to treat in that way.

Despite such difficulties, the FDA recently began authorizing the irradiation of some foods. In 1983 it approved the use of irradiation to kill insects in spices such as black pepper. In 1984 the agency approved the low-dose irradiation of pork for trichina control. In early 1986 it approved the medium-dose irradiation of fruits and vegetables for insect disinfestation.

Approval from the FDA is a critical step toward receiving the necessary authorization from the USDA that permits legal use. It is, therefore, the key to commercialization. The 1983 FDA authorization for spices led to the first tentative commercial steps for irradiation of widely consumed foods in the United States. Dried spices, many of which come from tropical countries where sanitation and handling procedures are poor, are a common source of intestinal disease. Because they are dry, they are less susceptible to degradation or radiation-induced hazard even at elevated doses. As of 1986 approximately 1% of the spices sold in the United States—usually spices being used in processed foods such as frozen pizzas—were being decontaminated by irradiation.

The 1986 FDA authorizations for fruits and vegetables were more significant. They have begun to stimulate increased commercial activity. A handful of companies are already in the food-irradiation business. Food-irradiation facilities now operate in New Jersey, Virginia, North Carolina, and Arkansas. In April 1986 a new one was dedicated on the New Jersey docks to process fruits and vegetables arriving in the United States from such countries as Haiti and Chile. Another is expected to be built in Hawaii so that tropical fruits can be shipped to the mainland states without fear of introducing fruit flies. Others are being planned for construction in Africa, Asia, and Eastern Europe.

## Safety

The first study of food-irradiation safety was conducted in 1943 by researchers at the Massachusetts Institute of Technology. It involved irradiation-sterilized hamburger meat and was done at the request of the

| Some foods that can be irradiated | | |
| --- | --- | --- |
| **food** | **purpose** | **dose** |
| potatoes | inhibition of sprouting | 50–150 grays |
| wheat flour, grains | disinfestation | 200–1,000 grays |
| fresh fruits and vegetables | disinfestation; extension of shelf life | 250–1,000 grays |
| mushrooms | inhibition of cap opening; fresh appearance | 60–1,000 grays |
| tropical fruits | retardation of ripening | 250–1,000 grays |
| strawberries, small fruits | control of fungus | 1,750–2,250 grays |
| cod, ocean perch | extension of shelf life | 1,750–2,250 grays |
| crab | extension of shelf life | 2,000–3,000 grays |
| chicken | extension of shelf life; reduction of pathogens | 3,000–7,000 grays |
| portion controlled ham (refrigerated storage) | extension of shelf life; reduction of pathogens | 2,000–7,000 grays |
| prime beef cuts (refrigerated storage) | extension (doubling) of shelf life | 2,000–7,000 grays |
| frozen shrimp, frog legs (imported) | eradication of salmonella | 5,000 grays |
| spices | sterilization | 10,000 grays |
| meats, poultry, and fish | sterilization | 25,000–50,000 grays |

Source: Stephanie R. Arnold, *National Food Review*, vol. 20 (February 1983).

U.S. Army. (The Army was trying to find ways to deliver better food to World War II troops on the front lines.) Since those experiments were done, more than 400 others have fed irradiated foods to animals at research centers and universities throughout the world. Overall, these demonstrate that at low doses there is virtually no loss in vitamins and other nutrients. Even at the highest doses nutritional losses are far less than occur in canned or highly cooked foods.

In 1979 a panel representing the World Health Organization, the Food and Agriculture Organization of the United Nations, and the International Atomic Energy Agency reviewed these studies. It reported that "the irradiation of any food commodity up to an average overall dose of [10,000 grays] presents no toxicological hazard." The report also stated that "irradiation of foods up to an overall average dose of [10,000 grays] introduces no special nutritional or microbiological problems."

The current FDA regulations allow only one-tenth of that amount. They apply to doses up to 1,000 grays that can extend the shelf life of fruits and vegetables but do not sterilize meat. Canada, a leader in food irradiation, has proposed permitting foods to be irradiated with up to 10,000 grays, but the FDA is awaiting more data on the safety of the process before authorizing higher doses.

The reasons for the FDA's caution are that safety studies are complex and difficult to define and that some of their results may not be obvious for decades. In addition, a few of the earlier tests were ambiguous, inconclusive, and even seriously flawed. This allows both proponents and opponents to read their own interpretations into the results.

Ionizing radiation creates traces of compounds that are not normally in food. Current concern over the safety of irradiated foods centers on these "unique radiolytic products" (URPs). URPs are not radioactive, and so far none has been found to be toxic in the trace amounts found in irradiated foods. Researchers have found that other processes, such as cooking, also create most or all of the same compounds.

*Sacks of imported paprika await irradiation at a facility in Arkansas. In 1983 the U.S. Food and Drug Administration authorized the irradiation of some varieties of spices, many of which come from tropical countries where sanitation is poor.*

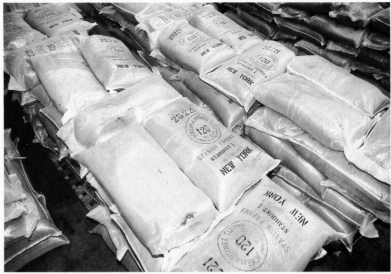

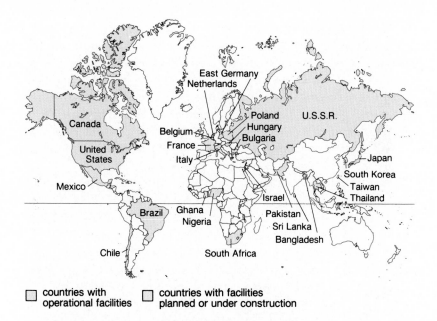

☐ countries with
operational facilities

☐ countries with facilities
planned or under construction

Unlike chemical additives, URPs cannot be concentrated in the diets of laboratory animals. This makes it difficult to pin down any of their possible adverse effects. However, URPs occur in amounts below the levels normally considered to be any hazard to health, and vacuum packaging or freezing the food during irradiation drastically reduces their formation.

Botulism is another food safety issue raised by the prospect of food irradiation. The *Clostridium botulinum* bacterium forms spores that produce the toxin responsible for botulism, a disease that causes paralysis. Such spores are much more resistant to radiation than are the normal microbes that cause food to spoil. Researchers, therefore, are concerned that destruction of the spoilage bacteria by irradiation would allow food to smell fresh and yet still contain the dangerous botulism spores.

The proliferation of nuclear technologies is another concern. In a food irradiator there is no danger of a meltdown or explosion, but if food is to be widely irradiated, critics say, there will have to be many more sources of radiation scattered throughout the nation and the world. The operation of those and the shipment and storage of radiation source materials and wastes could be a public hazard.

Proponents see this as of no concern. Cobalt-60 is a man-made radioisotope that has been used for more than 30 years in hospitals and medical centers for radiation therapy of cancer without an accident involving radiation exposure or a release of radioactive material. It is a solid that is encased in metal tubes for easy handling and storage. Cobalt-60 radiation is already widely used in industry. More than 100 industrial irradiators operating worldwide use cobalt-60 to sterilize dozens of types of medical disposables such as needles, surgical masks and gowns, tampons, and bandages. In addition, some use radiation to treat insulation on wire and cable, to cross-link plastic food wrap, and to vulcanize sheet rubber. In the United States these facilities are licensed, regulated, and inspected for safety by the Nuclear Regulatory Commission.

*Many nations throughout the world have begun operating irradiation facilities, while others plan to do so in the near future.*

Reprinted with permission from "Food Irradiation," Pamela S. Zurer, *Chemical & Engineering News*, vol. 64, no. 18, pp. 46–56, May 5, 1986. Copyright 1986 American Chemical Society.

97

## A food handling revolution?

Many observers say that, in principle, food irradiation has enormous commercial potential. Some foresee a $1 billion business in the United States by 1995, accompanied by fundamental changes in the way food is handled. Consumers, they say, will have foods that will last indefinitely without refrigeration. Meats can be stored on the shelf for years. Fruits will keep for months. The use of refrigerated warehouses and trucks and home refrigerators will decline. In principle, all this will bring savings in energy and an increase in the variety of foods available.

However, this food revolution could arrive only if the FDA approves high-dose food irradiation. A petition for this was filed in 1981, and a decision on it by the FDA is likely in the near future. If the petition is approved, it will allow companies to sterilize foods completely.

For more than a decade one company has been preparing such germ-free meals for hospital patients who must remain in a sterile environment as well as for astronauts in space. After the joint U.S. and Soviet space rendezvous in 1975, a Soviet cosmonaut said that his most memorable moment was "the medium-rare filet mignon!" The Soviet space program uses heat to sterilize meat, and so for cosmonauts a rare steak is impossible.

Given FDA approval, this company is prepared to sell beef scallopine, sweet-and-sour pork, teriyaki steak, scallops, and shrimp in supermarkets from coast to coast. It plans advertising campaigns on television and in magazines. It will promote its meals for use when the power goes off. It will target, for example, campers, sailors, athletes, and hunters, who will be able to eat their favorite foods no matter where they go. And it will encourage travelers to carry food in their suitcases so that they can have their own favorite meals no matter where they are.

Irradiated foods have particular promise for institutional feeding programs—prepared meals can be shipped and stored, soft and moist, at room temperatures without spoiling. Hospitals, prisons, and school cafe-

*Food that had been irradiated one month earlier and not refrigerated since that time shows no signs of decay. Such meals can be shipped or stored at room temperature without spoiling and thus can be carried easily by travelers or kept in large quantities for institutional feeding.*

terias could serve meals with little or no on-the-spot preparation. The United States military by itself represents a huge market.

The great humanitarian promise for food irradiation could be in the third world, where up to 50% of the crops grown are lost to spoilage. Irradiation could save some of that. It could also allow countries of Africa, Asia, and Latin America to export a wealth of exotic-tasting tropical fruits that are now banned from the United States and Europe because of the possibility of introducing fruit flies.

## The future

There are still many uncertainties, however. The public has a deep-seated fear of radioactivity, and whether food irradiation companies can overcome the widespread perception that irradiated food itself poses a threat is not certain. Already a small but vocal group of consumer activists is mounting a campaign to ban all food irradiation. Much of their criticism derives from emotional opposition to nuclear technologies of any type.

Against the backdrop of these critics, the fledgling industry must convince the public that irradiating food is safe. Proponents say that their surveys indicate that the public is less afraid of nuclear food preservation than of chemical additives or food poisoning, but many companies are already afraid to use irradiation because they fear that the public image of their corporations may be damaged.

The question of consumer acceptance is crucial. Right or wrong, in many people's minds the term radiation raises the specter of nuclear weapons and nuclear power and all the accompanying fears and controversies. Recent FDA rulings have required that foods carry a label bearing a logo and the words "treated with irradiation." This may cause public revulsion. The label also must include the international symbol designating irradiated foods, a circle with a stylized flower inside it.

If food irradiation surmounts the hurdles of FDA approval and public acceptance, it still faces the challenge of economic viability. The economic benefits of irradiation depend on such variables as the volume of food processed through each radiation facility, handling and shipping procedures, marketing tactics, and costs compared with other preservation methods. Questions still need to be answered, too, about where the irradiation facilities would be located in relation to the growers, the logistics of labeling, and the funding of any necessary research.

Many researchers and entrepreneurs are optimistic that all the uncertainties can be resolved. Some think that irradiation will be the greatest advance in food preservation ever achieved—a revolution in food distribution! Others are far from sure, concluding that it may take a whole generation for such a change to be accepted, the same amount of time that it took for canning and then freezing to catch on.

One thing does seem certain. Because of irradiation at least a few foods will be around a long, long time. Archaeologists digging into our ruins far into the future will be able to see, smell, and taste the fruits, vegetables, meats, and prepared meals we have today. Through irradiation, food can achieve immortality.

# AGRITECHNOLOGY

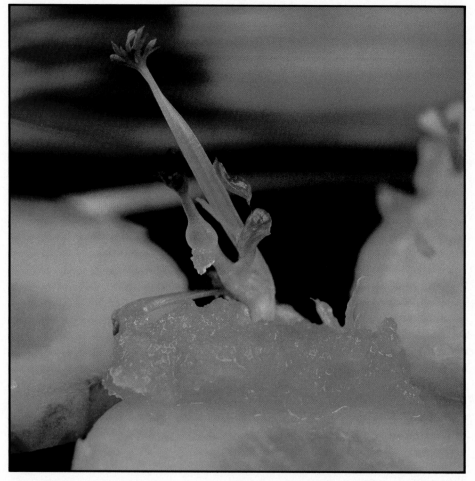

# BUILDING A BETTER PLANT

**by Ricki Lewis**  Wielding the latest biotechnological tools, agricultural scientists are delving inside plant cells to produce crops with qualities never before seen in nature.

Six thousand years ago Indians living in Mexico began to tranform a wild grass into a bountiful crop by selecting the hardiest seeds each season and sowing them the next. Since that time the corn, or maize, plant (*Zea mays*) has been a prominent target of agricultural manipulation, which has ranged from traditional breeding strategies to modern biotechnology.

Sixty centuries after the Mexican Indians introduced corn, the crop caught the attention of Charles Darwin, who noticed that plants with unrelated parents had plumper and more numerous kernels than plants resulting from self-fertilization. In the early 20th century the U.S. botanist George Shull applied the laws of inheritance to Darwin's observations and developed hybrid corn, which revolutionized agriculture by producing vigorous, high-yield crops capable of thriving under a variety of soil and climatic conditions. From 1933 to 1944 the fraction of the U.S. corn belt planted in hybrid varieties rose from 1 to 88%.

Instead of relying on the combinations of characteristics provided by nature, modern agritechnologists—those who are applying the latest biotechnological advances to agriculture—actually delve inside cells to coax certain traits into existence. How surprised would those early Indian farmers be to know that corn cells have already been manipulated to give rise to plants having butter-flavored kernels, carrying bacteria that manufacture insecticide for them, or containing high-quality protein not found in the garden-variety plant.

The new agritechnology has an international flavor, with research groups scattered as widely as California, London, Shanghai, and Australia. Its effect on agriculture promises to be as profound and revolutionary as hybridization studies were earlier. It is estimated that by 1995, 5% of the U.S. agricultural industry will consist of products of biotechnology—a figure that is certain to rise in succeeding years.

Agritechnology introduces qualities that will appeal to farmers, food processors, and consumers alike. It can improve such agronomic characteristics as

*RICKI LEWIS is a Lecturer at the State University of New York at Albany and a science writer.*

*Illustrations by Anne Hoyer Becker; (overleaf) © Dan McCoy—Rainbow*

adaptability, yield, and resistance to disease and pesticides; make anatomical alterations that ease harvesting; increase nutritional content; and fine-tune sweetness, acidity, texture, flavor, and size and shape to consumer preferences. A recent boon to the food processor, for example, is the new high-solids tomato, which hastens the journey from field to soup can.

Agritechnology is also a time and space saver. Altering plants at the subcellular level shrinks the time needed to develop new varieties from the decade or more of conventional breeding to a season or two. Successful new crops begin as tiny plantlets that are first observed in a greenhouse and then transplanted to the field only if they survive.

## Old and new ways to a better plant

The steps of traditional breeding and biotechnology are similar. First, an interesting trait is identified and bred into, or engineered into, a plant whose other characteristics comprise an economically sound package; for example, promoting larger fruit size in a plant that can withstand temperature extremes and resist pests. The new variety is then tested in several different habitats and during different seasons to determine the conditions under which it grows best. Finally, it is distributed to growers.

Traditional plant breeding introduces new varieties by a sexual route. Pollen carrying the genes for traits in male sex cells fertilizes ovules that bear egg cells carrying a different combination of traits. Because each sex cell brings with it a different genetic package, offspring from a single cross tend to express different combinations of the parents' traits. This is the reason that siblings are not identical; it is also the reason that a vigorous crop one season may produce some small seeds and plants the next.

Unlike traditional breeding, biotechnology goes beneath the organismal level of reproduction to the level of the cell, the basic unit of life. Rather than beginning with sperm and eggs, which have a half set of genetic instructions each, most biotechnologies begin with somatic, or body, cells. Somatic cells, which form a nonsexual part of the plant such as the leaf or stem, have a complete set of genetic instructions. Plants regenerated from somatic cells do not have the unpredictable mixture of characteristics found in sexual reproduction. Consequently, biotechnology promises the dual ability to introduce a countless number of new varieties and to assure consistency in crop quality from season to season.

## Journey through a plant cell

Understanding agritechnology requires some knowledge of the insides of a cell. A typical plant cell is boxlike in shape and so small that a thousand of them lined up would span the width of a person's little finger. A plant cell is bounded by an outer rigid cell wall, which hugs the more fluid cell membrane just within. These two barriers control the kind and amount of substances that enter and leave the cell. Within the cell membrane is a moving, jellylike substance called cytoplasm, which includes a variety of structures called organelles.

*A plant cell (opposite page, center) is typically boxlike in shape. Its outer wall and cell membrane enclose a variety of structures termed organelles immersed in a jellylike cytoplasm. Most of the cell's genetic material is found in the nucleus, usually as extended threads of DNA molecules. When the cell is about to divide, its DNA wraps into very compact supercoiled bundles called chromosomes. The DNA of a chromosome (top and right) is divided into functional units called genes, each gene comprising paired strands made up of four different nucleotide building blocks. The specific sequence of nucleotides in a gene serve as instructions for the cell's synthesis machinery, which uses the information to assemble the amino acids present in the cell into proteins.*

102

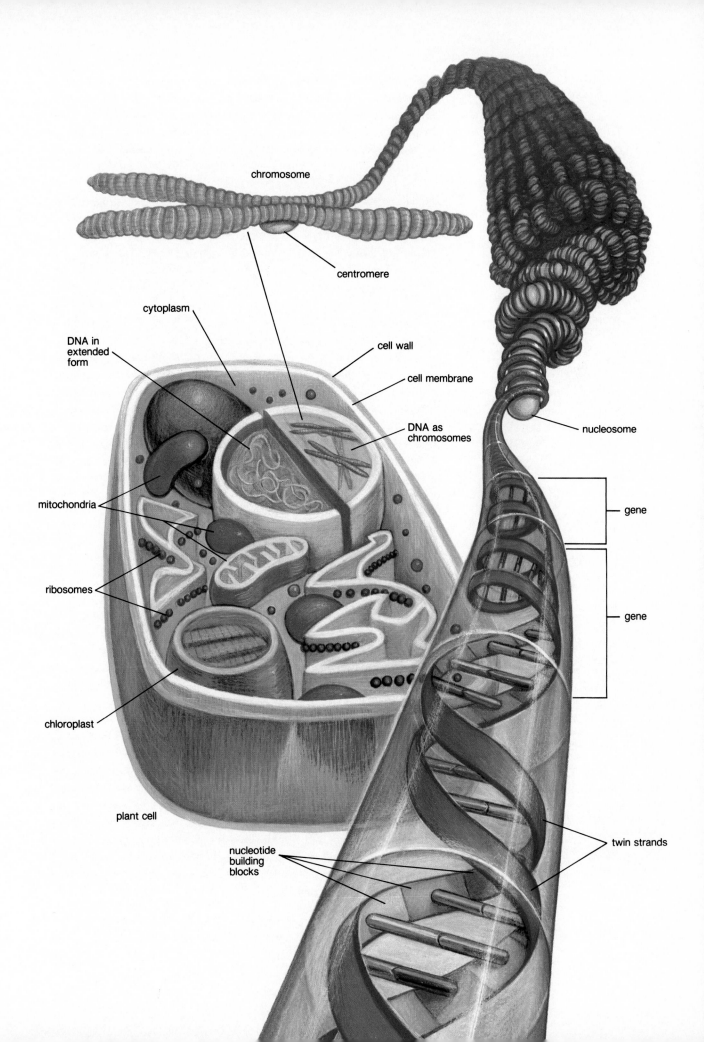

chromosome

centromere

cytoplasm

DNA in
extended
form

cell wall

cell membrane

DNA as
chromosomes

nucleosome

mitochondria

gene

gene

ribosomes

chloroplast

plant cell

twin strands

nucleotide
building
blocks

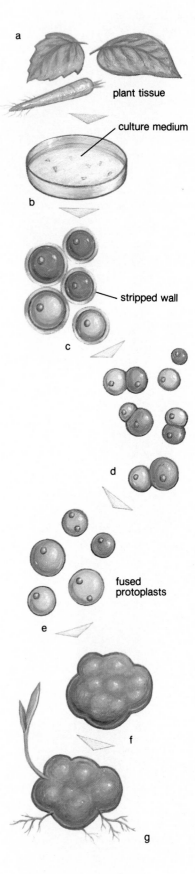

a

plant tissue

culture medium

b

stripped wall

c

d

fused
protoplasts

e

f

g

In addition to cytoplasm the cell houses a roundish structure called the nucleus. This is the genetic headquarters, containing long filaments of the chemical deoxyribonucleic acid (DNA) that organize into rod-shaped chromosomes when the cell is about to divide. Each species has a characteristic number of chromosomes, and within an organism each somatic cell contains complete genetic instructions.

The DNA of a chromosome is divided into functional units called genes, each of which is built of a long string of four different DNA building blocks called nucleotides. The sequence of building blocks in a particular gene spells out a unique message to some of the cell's organelles, which use the sequence information to assemble amino acids floating around in the cell into proteins. A gene, therefore, specifies the construction of a particular protein. The proteins made by a cell, reflecting which of its genes are active, or being expressed, establish its identity and specialty; for example, as part of a rosebush or cedar and as part of its leaf, stem, or root.

Genetic material is found in two other places in a plant cell besides the nucleus, in the organelles known as chloroplasts and mitochondria. The roundish, green chloroplasts trap energy from sunlight and convert it to chemical energy needed by the plant (and the organisms that eat it). The footprint-shaped mitochondria house the chemical reactions of cellular metabolism. Chloroplasts and mitochondria are thought to have descended from once free-living simple cells that were swallowed up by more advanced cells. The organelles came to depend upon genes in the nuclei of their host cells but retained some DNA from their evolutionary past.

Biotechnology can alter plant functions at any of several levels of cell organization: the individual cell, its organelles, and the genes within its nucleus. Each of these approaches is examined below.

## Protoplast fusion: the best of two cells

Protoplast fusion creates new types of plants by combining cells from different types of plants and then regenerating a hybrid from the fused cell. A protoplast is simply a plant cell whose cell wall has been removed by treatment with digestive enzymes. Two protoplasts may join on their own, or they can be encouraged to do so by exposure to polyethylene glycol or a brief jolt of electricity.

A single gram (about 1/28 of an ounce) of plant tissue can yield as many as four million protoplasts, each of which is a potential new plant either by itself or when fused with another protoplast. Some of the botanical creations of protoplast fusion, called somatic hybrids, are interesting if not always useful. A pomato plant, resulting from a tomato protoplast fused with a potato protoplast, produced both types of vegetables, but they were small and seed quality was poor. The same fate befell a parsley-carrot union. Less useful still was a fusion of radish and cabbage; ironically, the not-very-tasty plant grew radish leaves and cabbage roots. Protoplast fusion has been more successful when the parent cells have come from closely related species. For example, when a protoplast from

104

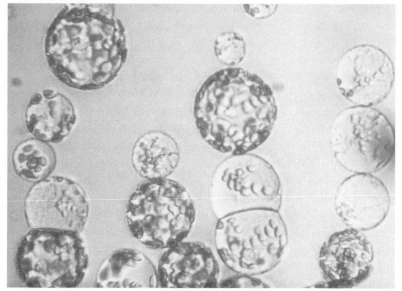

*Protoplasts—plant cells stripped of their cell walls—fuse to create hybrid cells having new mixtures of traits.*

a potato plant that is killed by the herbicide triazine was fused with a protoplast from the wild black nightshade, a relative that is resistant to the herbicide, the resultant potato plant could be grown in soil treated with triazine for weed control.

Protoplast fusion has limitations. Bringing together quantities of two cell types typically gives a mixed bag of results: single cells, fused cells of the same species, and the sought-after fused cells of two different types. Only some of the fusion products go on to divide and develop into plants, however, and there is no guarantee that such plants will have useful combinations of traits. Crops that can form fused protoplasts and regenerate plants include endive, clover, millet, alfalfa, carrot, cassava, sunflower, citrus, cabbage, rapeseed, and asparagus. At present, the high cost of development is holding back commercial application of the technique.

## Cell culture for uniformity: artificial seeds, clonal propagation

A fascinating thing happens when protoplasts or tiny pieces of plant tissue (explants) are nurtured in a dish with nutrients and plant hormones. After a few days the cells lose the special characteristics of the tissues from which they were taken and form a white lump called a callus. The lump grows, its cells dividing, for a few weeks. Then certain cells of the callus form either a tiny plantlet with shoots and roots or a tiny embryo. Researchers do not understand how or why this happens, and it is apparently a phenomenon unique to plants. (In humans it would be the equivalent of a cultured skin cell, for example, multiplying into a blob of unspecialized tissue and then sprouting tiny humans or human embryos.) Somehow, unlike the original cells, in which only a subset of genes is expressed (the genes that make a cell part of a leaf, for example), the callus cells are unspecialized. All of its genes are capable of expression, much like those of a fertilized egg.

*Protoplast fusion (opposite page) combines the contents of two different kinds of plant cells to create new plant types. Tissues from different plants (a) are placed in tissue culture (b). By means of enzymes the cell walls are dissolved (c), leaving protoplasts. Protoplasts from two plant types are mixed and encouraged to fuse (d). Among the fusion products (e) are hybrid protoplasts carrying the contents of both cell types. These are selected and grown into undifferentiated tissue called callus (f), which then goes on to regenerate plants with useful combinations of traits (g).*

The embryos and plantlets that form from callus can be valuable for either their uniformity or their occasional variation, depending on the goal of the biotechnologist. Nutrient and hormone surroundings can be manipulated to favor identical or different regenerated embryos or plantlets.

Artificial seed technology relies on genetically identical, somatically derived embryos grown from callus. A natural seed is a plant embryo and its food supply, packaged in a protective shell. An artificial seed is much the same, built of a somatic embryo suspended in a transparent polysaccharide gel containing nutrients and hormones and given protection and shape by an outer biodegradable polymer. Biotechnologists can actually improve upon nature with artificial seed technology by packaging the embryo with pesticides, fertilizer, nitrogen-fixing bacteria, and even microscopic parasite-destroying worms. Plant Genetics, Inc., of Davis, California, has been a leader in developing artificial seeds.

The advantage of artificial seeds for the farmer is their guarantee of a uniform crop, one in which plants mature at the same rate, for example, cutting costs at harvest time. Uniformity is possible because the embryos are genetically identical. By contrast, the embryos of seeds obtained from sexual reproduction contain unpredictable mixtures of parental traits. To date, artificial seed technology has been most successful for celery, lettuce, cotton, and alfalfa, and future prospects include rice, corn, and sugar pine trees. It will still be a few years, however, before artificial seeds are sprouting in the farmer's field.

Uniform plants are also the goal of clonal propagation, in which cells or protoplasts are cultured in larger bioreactors, and then individual cells

*Cloning of carrot plants in the laboratory is illustrated in the sequence of photos below. (Top left) Sections of carrot root are cored, and thin slices (explants) of the corings are placed in a culture dish containing nutrients and a hormone that stimulates callus formation. After a few days the carrot root cells lose their specific characteristics and form an undifferentated, growing lump of callus (top right; at five weeks). After about three months the callus begins producing differentiated tissue (bottom left), which is transferred to another medium to encourage growth of shoots and roots. Eventually the new carrot plantlets are strong enough to be moved from their sterile medium into regular potted soil (bottom right).*

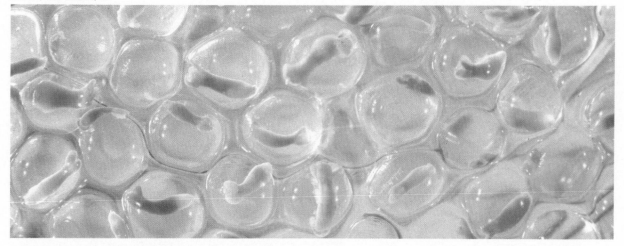

are grown into identical plants (clones). Clonal propagation offers a way to grow such valuable trees as oil palm, redwoods, and chestnuts rapidly and inexpensively and is also suitable for asparagus, carrot, potato, and strawberry. Clonally propagated oil palm, orchids, and potatoes are already being grown commercially.

## Cell culture for variety: somaclonal variation

Embryos and plantlets have been grown from callus since the 1950s. Recently, what was once regarded as a liability—the occasional appearance of new variants when uniformity was sought—has been turned into an entirely new technology called somaclonal variation. In 1981 P. J. Larkin and W. R. Scowcroft of the Commonwealth Scientific and Industrial Research Organization in Canberra, Australia, suggested that the changeling plants that sometimes arose in cell culture could be a source of agriculturally useful variants.

The suggestion produced results in 1983 when William Sharp and David Evans of DNA Plant Technology in Cinnaminson, New Jersey, took a run-of-the-mill medium-sized red tomato, chopped up bits of leaf tissue, grew them into callus, and regenerated 230 plantlets. After growth to adulthood 13 of the plants were markedly different from the original tomato plant; one variant, for instance, had tangerine-colored fruits; two others lacked a joint between the stem and the tomato, making harvesting easier; and two others had a high solids content, of interest to the canning industry. The new varieties were called somaclonal variants because they were derived from a single somatic cell and were therefore clones of it and each other.

The tomato experiment was astounding because one would have to look through millions of naturally grown tomato plants to find 13 genetic variants. Apparently something about the culturing process uncovers inherited variation present in the original explant or protoplast. It may be that a genetic variant that would not be noticeable if it existed only in one leaf cell among thousands becomes obvious when the cell that contains it gives rise to an entire new plant.

*Experimental artificial seeds (above) consist of somatically derived alfalfa embryos encapsulated in a calcium alginate gel. As supplied to growers, the gel package would also include nutrients, hormones, pesticides, and other components needed for embryo-to-plant development.*

107

Agricultural Research Service, USDA

*Clonal propagation of such plants as strawberry (above) offers farmers the advantages of an entire crop that shares the same genetic instructions.*

Pioneered on the tomato, somaclonal variation is being applied to corn, potatoes, wheat, bananas, oil palm, and sugarcane. The technology makes it possible to alter or add traits one at a time to an existing genetic background. In addition, it tends to introduce only biologically useful variants; a genetic change for the worse would result in a callus cell or plantlet that would not be healthy enough to develop further. In the future, researchers hope to find ways to predict whether certain callus cells will yield useful variants as adult plants, thus skipping the stages of greenhouse growth and field testing. Presently somaclonal variants of carrots and celery are in the test-marketing stage.

Whereas somaclonal variation uses somatic cells, sex cells can also be used to grow callus, from which plantlets can be coaxed, in a process called gametoclonal variation. A plantlet regenerated from a sex cell has only one copy of each chromosome in its cells and therefore cannot reproduce. To get around this drawback, gametoclonally derived plantlets are exposed to the drug colchicine, which causes each chromosome to make a duplicate of itself. The cells of the plant thereby become absolutely pure, with each gene present in two identical forms. Such a feat would take at least five or six years by conventional breeding; with cell culture it takes a year or two. New wheat variants having altered height, seed structure, and disease resistances have been derived from gametoclonal variation.

### Boosting natural variation: mutant selection

Researchers can choose specific characteristics of new plant variants arising in cell cultures by exposing cells or protoplasts to noxious substances and then selecting only those cells that survive. If such a cell can regenerate a plant, then that plant and its progeny may also be resistant. Many companies are turning to this technique of mutant selection to tailor seeds that are resistant to certain herbicides. For example, workers at Molecular Genetics in Minnetonka, Minnesota, recently treated corn cell cultures with American Cyanamid's imidazolinone herbicide. The cells that survived the treatment were grown into corn plants, some of which were resistant to the herbicide and passed on the resistance. In the near future American Cyanamid should be able to sell its herbicide along with seed biologically guaranteed not to be harmed by it.

leaf (differentiated tissue)

a

b

hormones and nutrients

c

callus (undifferentiated tissue)

d

embryos

e

artificial seeds

f

g

h

*New high-solids tomato (left), the product of somaclonal variation, has proved of interest to the canned-food industry. The same technique has also yielded varieties showing increased fruit size and pigmentation (above right) compared with the existing variety from which they were derived (above left).*

## Altering organelles

At the subcellular level biotechnologists can devise combinations of nuclei, cytoplasms, and organelles not known in nature to mold interesting new variants. The stars of organelle manipulation are the chloroplasts and mitochondria, whose genes confer such traits as male sterility (important in setting up crosses), herbicide resistance, and increased efficiency in obtaining and using energy.

Cybridization is a technique that produces a plant cell having cytoplasm derived from two cells but containing a single nucleus. Just prior to the fusion of two protoplasts, the nucleus of one is intentionally destroyed by radiation. Researchers then select fused cells that contain one nucleus and the desired combinations of organelles. In another approach scientists isolate individual chloroplasts or mitochondria and surround them in a fatty bubble called a liposome, which transports its contents across the cell membrane into a selected cell. Introducing a chloroplast in this manner creates a "chlybrid" cell; sending in a mitochondrion produces a "mibrid."

## Within the nucleus: recombinant DNA technology

In recombinant DNA technology, or gene splicing, single genes are transferred from a cell of one type of organism to a cell of another. If the recipient cell is a plant and can be regenerated, the resulting plant should possess the trait controlled by the transplanted gene. The technology works because all organisms share the same genetic language. A gene from a bean plant would make its protein even if it was in a sunflower, a feat that already has been accomplished to boost the protein quality of sunflower seeds.

*New plants grown from cell culture can be valuable for either their uniformity or their occasional variation, depending on the goal of biotechnological research. In somatic embryogenesis plant cells are cultured into callus (a–c), which is then manipulated with nutrients and hormones to form genetically identical plant embryos (d). The embryos, which can be packaged in a protective shell as artificial seeds (e), guarantee a uniform, consistent crop (f). In somaclonal variation, wherein the culture medium is manipulated to encourage variety, the callus is regenerated into plants (g), some of which exhibit new traits (h).*

109

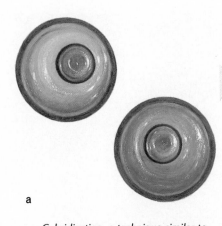
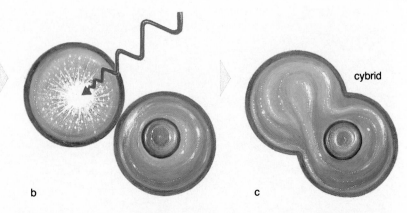

a                b                c        cybrid

*Cybridization, a technique similar to protoplast fusion, produces a plant cell having cytoplasm and organelles derived from two cells but containing only one nucleus. Just before two protoplasts are fused (a), the nucleus of one is destroyed by radiation (b). The fusion product (c) is called a cybrid.*

Recombinant DNA technology in plants is mechanically challenging. The first step is to identify and isolate an interesting gene. Bacteria are often the source of such genes, which can confer on plants built-in resistances to disease, insecticides, herbicides, and environmental extremes. The gene of interest is obtained by treating the donor DNA with a restriction enzyme, a natural product that normally cuts up the DNA of viruses that infect bacteria. Today several types of restriction enzymes are commercially available. Each type cuts DNA at a specific sequence of its nucleotide building blocks. Molecular biologists have several ways to "screen" the gene-sized pieces of DNA that result for the gene they want.

In the next step researchers depend on a transport system, called a vector, to get the desired gene into the recipient cell. A vector may be a small virus or a circular, nonchromosomal piece of DNA called a plasmid that occurs naturally in some cells. The vector is treated with the same restriction enzyme used to isolate the donor gene. Because a single type of enzyme cuts all DNA at the same sequence, the donor and vector DNAs are left with complementary ends that attract one another. When cut donor DNA is mixed with cut vector DNA, some of the original vector

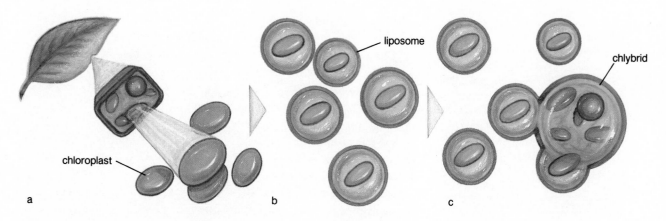

chloroplast

liposome

chlybrid

a                                        b                                        c

re-forms with one or more copies of the donor gene incorporated into the molecule. The actual recombinant DNA molecule, then, is a vector containing a piece of foreign DNA.

The next and hardest requirement is to send the vector and its stowaway gene into the nucleus of a plant cell of the recipient species. For dicots—plants whose seedlings have two leaves, such as potatoes, tomatoes, alfalfa, tobacco, soy, and petunias—foreign genes are introduced on a Ti (tumor-inducing) plasmid, found in the microorganism *Agrobacterium tumefaciens*. In its natural state the Ti plasmid invades plant cells and causes a cancerlike growth called crown gall disease. But the tumor-causing DNA sequence of the plasmid can be chemically removed without impairing its ability to enter a plant-cell nucleus, taking with it whatever genes the agritechnologist has attached.

Genetic engineering of the monocots—plants whose seedlings have a single leaf, such as the cereals—lags behind that of the dicots because many naturally occurring plasmids cannot enter monocot cells. One solution is to use monocot protoplasts, because removing the cell wall makes the cell membrane more likely to admit foreign DNA. In a technique

*Such organelles as chloroplasts can be isolated from the cells of their parent plant (a) and surrounded in liposomes, microscopic spheres of fatty molecules (b). When mixed with protoplasts of selected cells, the liposomes fuse with the cell membrane (c), delivering their contents to the cellular interior and creating "chlybrid" cells. Mitochondria introduced in this way produce "mibrid" cells.*

*Rice plants (opposite page) are grown from cultured sex cells in a process known as gametoclonal variation. Inset depicts various stages of the process: Pollen-bearing anthers cut from rice plants are placed in culture (left), where the pollen grains form callus (center) and eventually produce plantlets (right). When strong enough, the plantlets are moved to pots (main photo) and examined for beneficial variants. (This page) Corn on the left, developed by mutant selection to resist the herbicide imidazolinone, is compared with a nonresistant strain after treatment of the field with herbicide.*

(Opposite page) photos, © Dan McCoy—Rainbow; (this page) courtesy, Pioneer Hi-Bred International; photo, Curt Maas

*Identifying the appropriate gene from an organism with a useful trait and moving it into a target plant is the goal of recombinant DNA technology, or gene splicing. In the form of the procedure diagramed below, a DNA fragment carrying the desired gene—for example, one conferring resistance to a particular herbicide—is isolated from its source, which is generally another plant or a microorganism. Next, the fragment is spliced into the naturally infectious Ti plasmid (found in the tumor-causing bacterium Agrobacterium tumifaciens) from which the tumor-inducing genes have been removed. The plasmid incorporating the foreign DNA is then allowed to invade the protoplast of the recipient plant, where it enters the nucleus and becomes integrated into the plant's genetic material. Finally, by means of cell culture, the protoplast is regenerated into a mature plant that expresses the desired trait.*

called electroporation a brief jolt of electricity opens up transient holes in the cell membrane that permit entry of foreign DNA. Genetic material can also be injected into the cell with microscopic needles or sent across the cell membrane within liposomes. For these methods to work, however, the foreign DNA must still make its way to the nucleus, where it can be expressed and transmitted when the cell divides.

Whichever way a foreign gene enters a plant cell, the procedure is useless unless a mature plant can be regenerated from the engineered cell and shown to have the desired characteristic. At Stanford University, for example, corn protoplasts have been engineered to resist a particular antibiotic, but the altered protoplasts can be grown only into callus, not a corn plant. On the other hand British, French, and Japanese scientists have reported the successful regeneration of rice plants from nonengineered protoplasts, a significant step toward introducing new genes in this important monocot. Regenerating a plant is not the end of the road either; the transferred gene must be expressed in the appropriate tissue at the right time in development, and the characteristic must be passed to future generations.

Once these technological hurdles have been overcome, the power and possibilities of plant genetic engineering are enormous. Already some interesting new plants have debuted. Tobacco given a gene from the bacterium *Bacillus thuringiensis* manufactures a bacterial protein that is toxic to many plant-killing caterpillars. Corn, too, will benefit from *B. thuringiensis*. Researchers have transferred the bacterial toxin gene to a bacterium, *Pseudomonas fluorescens*, that lives in corn roots. When corn seeds are coated with the engineered *P. fluorescens*, the bacteria colonize the roots after seed germination and churn out the *B. thuringiensis* protein, which kills caterpillars that arrive to munch on the roots. Likewise, engineered, plant-colonizing bacteria carrying foreign genes for herbicides are being developed for coating the seeds of crop plants.

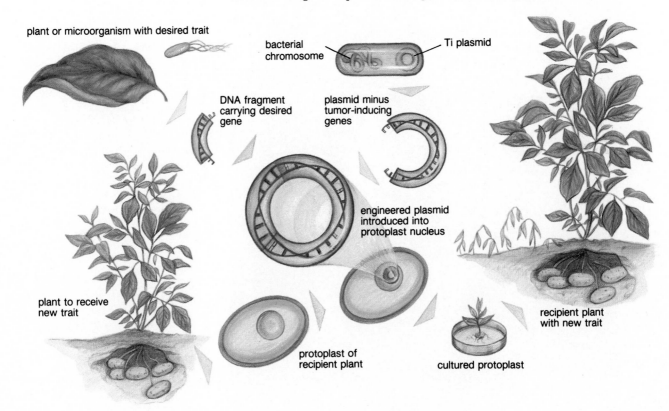

plant or microorganism with desired trait

bacterial chromosome

Ti plasmid

DNA fragment carrying desired gene

plasmid minus tumor-inducing genes

engineered plasmid introduced into protoplast nucleus

plant to receive new trait

recipient plant with new trait

protoplast of recipient plant

cultured protoplast

Someday scientists expect to genetically engineer crop plants to "fix" nitrogen from its inaccessible atmospheric form ($N_2$) to a biologically useful form such as nitrate ($NO_3$) or ammonia ($NH_3$), a job presently accomplished at great expense by the fertilizer industry. Biotechnologists are modeling experiments on the legumes—for example, alfalfa, soy, and clover—which obtain usable nitrogen from *Rhizobia* bacteria that colonize their roots. Genetic engineering can attack the nitrogen-fixation problem in several ways—by increasing the efficiency of *Rhizobia* in its natural legume hosts, by expanding the number of different crops that *Rhizobia* can colonize, and, ultimately, by moving the bacterial genes for nitrogen fixation directly into crop plants.

## Combining technologies

Despite its precision, recombinant DNA technology depends on cellular methods to regenerate plants. An exciting example of how these approaches are used together is the design of a crop that is resistant to the herbicide used to protect it.

The traditional route to herbicide resistance was to look for a resistant weed that is related to a crop plant. The hardy weed and its domesticated cousin were then crossbred until a variant arose that retained the desired qualities of each parent plant. If a herbicide-resistant crop could not be bred, then the herbicide was simply not used.

Today, instead of changing herbicides to fit crops (the "spray and pray" approach), biotechnologists are altering crops to fit herbicides. As discussed above, mutant selection is one way—simply culture cells in the presence of the herbicide and regenerate plants from the surviving cells. The recombinant DNA route to herbicide resistance focuses on identifying that part of the crop plant's physiology that is damaged by the herbicide and then finding a gene (from any organism) that might enable the plant to prevent or undo whatever damage the herbicide does.

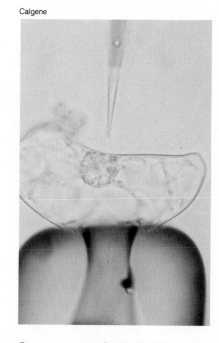

*One way to move foreign DNA into a plant cell nucleus is by direct injection with a microscopic glass needle.*

*The potential of plant genetic engineering is demonstrated in a comparison of two tobacco plants wounded and infected with Agrobacterium tumifaciens. The plant on the right, whose cells have been endowed with a specific microbial gene by means of gene splicing, totally resists the infection, whereas the unmodified plant on the left shows the tumor mass characteristic of crown gall disease.*

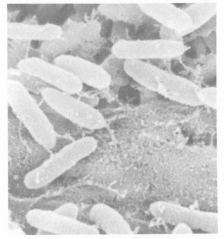

*Genetically engineered bacterium* Pseudomonas fluorescens, *shown colonizing corn roots, carries a foreign gene for a protein that is toxic to several kinds of root-eating caterpillar. When corn seeds are coated with the modified bacterium, the microbe colonizes the roots of the emerging plants and protects the crop from insect attack.*

Consider the herbicide glyphosate, sold by Monsanto as Roundup and said to "kill anything green." It inhibits the enzyme EPSP synthase, which a plant cell uses to manufacture three essential amino acids. As of late 1986, two biotechnology approaches had rendered certain plants resistant to glyphosate. Researchers at Monsanto in St. Louis, Missouri, found a viral gene that enables petunias, tobacco, and tomato plants to overproduce EPSP synthase sufficiently to counteract the effect of the herbicide. The viral gene is hooked to another gene for a "chloroplast transit peptide," which delivers the excess EPSP synthase just where it is needed—to the chloroplast. Researchers at Calgene, Davis, California, circumvented glyphosate's toxicity another way. They found a gene in the bacterium *Salmonella typhimurium* that manufactures an EPSP synthase that works even in the presence of glyphosate. They used a plasmid to move the gene into cells of tobacco and regenerated plants.

## Beyond the laboratory

A biotechnologically manipulated plant is under its creator's control when on a shelf in a laboratory or greenhouse. The same plant growing in a field is quite another story, because it can interact with other species. Field-testing a plant that manufactures its own insecticide is far more complex than field-testing a chemical insecticide.

But field-testing is the essential next step for the new products of agritechnology, and it is already a reality. In late 1985 the U.S. Environmental Protection Agency (EPA) approved the first "deliberate release" of a genetically engineered organism into the environment, an "ice-minus" bacterium that prevents frost formation on strawberries. As of late 1986 the University of California was scheduled to test 2,400 plants on ⅕ of an acre. The first field test of a genetically engineered plant, a disease-resistant tobacco developed at Agracetus in Middleton, Wisconsin, began in May 1986. Later in the year another tobacco, engineered by Ciba-Geigy for herbicide resistance, was planted outdoors in North

Carolina. By the end of 1986 nearly 100 other products of biotechnology were awaiting the final hurdle of the field test.

Regulatory agencies approving field tests of a genetically engineered organism have several concerns: How long will the plant or bacterium survive? How quickly does it multiply? How far can it travel? And, most importantly, what are its effects on the living and nonliving environment? A potential problem is that such organisms can pass on their new talents—such as herbicide or insecticide resistance—to neighboring weeds. In one case researchers in the EPA's Microbial Ecology and Biotechnology Branch suggested an ingenious safeguard against this threat. To seed-coat bacteria that have been engineered to manufacture pesticides, they would add a "suicide plasmid." Crop seeds would be coated with the bacterium and with a chemical that turns the bacterium on. By the time the chemical degraded or washed away, the seedling's roots would be well established. In the chemical's absence the suicide plasmid would turn on, producing enzymes that cut up the DNA of the bacterium. The engineered bacteria would be around only long enough to do their job and then destroyed to prevent them from transferring the resistance to weeds.

## Legalities

Not all problems concerning agritechnology are biologic. Researchers are sculpting corn that has an amino-acid profile not seen in nature, sunflowers that churn out bean proteins, and tobacco that makes its own pesticides. At what point does a biologically altered plant become a new variety, qualified for patent protection? It often depends upon the country in which the plant is developed.

U.S. patent laws have gradually changed to help the biotechnologist. Modifications started in 1930 with the Plant Patent Act covering asexually produced plants. In 1970 the Plant Variety Protection Act broadened patents to cover single, novel varieties of sexually reproducing plants but did not include seeds. The criteria for patentability were the same as for any invention—it must be novel, useful, and not obvious. At the time, however, no one realized that crops would soon be alterable in a gene-by-gene fashion.

A landmark in U.S. patent law came in 1980 after General Electric researcher Ananda Chakrabarty had transferred four different plasmids into one bacterial cell, a combination not seen in nature. A Supreme Court decision on his work ruled that novel life forms could be patented, and this ruling extends to all parts of a plant. A recent example of a plant patent is one granted to Molecular Genetics's high-tryptophan corn plants, seeds, and tissue cultures.

European patent laws are more stringent. In 1961, 17 nations conceived the International Union for the Protection of New Varieties of Plants, which allowed breeders ownership of varieties they created, irrespective of who owned the parent stock. Twelve years later the European Patent Convention made it even more difficult to obtain a patent by barring patents on animals, plants, or "essentially biological processes for the production of plants or animals."

Agracetus

The first field test of a genetically engineered plant, a crown-gall-resistant tobacco, took place in Wisconsin in 1986.

Petunias and tobacco (opposite page, bottom) were both genetically engineered to resist the herbicide glyphosate, but in different ways. Gylphosate kills plants by suppressing the activity of an essential enzyme, EPSP synthase. In the photo on the left, the petunias in the back row were given a viral gene that allows them to overproduce the enzyme sufficiently to counteract the effect of a commercial glyphosate spray; by contrast, the unmodified petunias in the front row show no resistance to the spray. In the photo on the right, the glyphosate-sprayed tobacco plants in the center row carry a bacterial gene for a form of EPSP synthase that operates even in the presence of glyphosate. In the left row are engineered tobacco plants that were not sprayed; in the right row are unmodified tobacco plants that have succumbed to glyphosate spray.

115

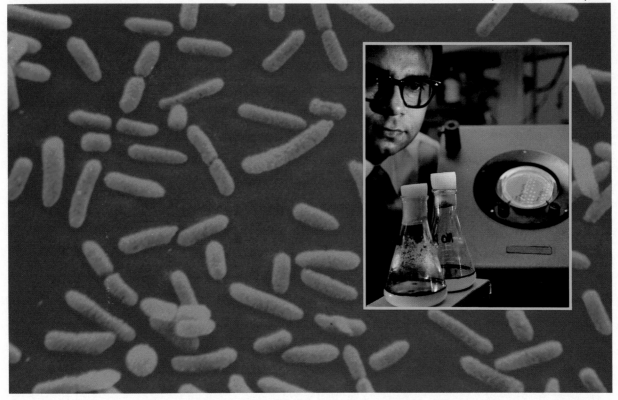

Photos, General Electric Research and Development Center, Schenectady, N. Y.

*A bacterium genetically tailored to digest oil slicks efficiently was the subject of a landmark U.S. Supreme Court ruling in 1980 that made man-made microorganisms patentable. Ananda Chakrabarty (inset), its inventor, had combined genetic material from four different strains of Pseudomonas bacteria.*

*Infamous corn leaf blight of 1970 devastated most of the main producing areas of the U.S. because of a lack of genetic diversity among the hybrid varieties in use at the time. Many societies have learned the same lesson in the same way—that relying on a few crop varieties can spell disaster.*

Agricultural Research Service, USDA

Today in Europe, opinion is divided on just what should and should not be patented. The Organization for Economic Cooperation and Development (OECD), an international body devoted to promoting economic growth and world trade, argues for increased patent protection of genetically engineered plants. But another group, the International Coalition for Development Action (ICDA), feels that patents on genetically engineered organisms would put control of crop plants almost entirely in the hands of multinational seed companies, whose well-funded research and development efforts would snatch up all of the patents. ICDA claims that this situation would hurt third world nations, where many potentially valuable natural plant varieties exist. They strongly support the original 1961 law protecting breeders.

## Food for the future

As biotechnologists manipulate plant cells, organelles, and genes to fashion new varieties, another breed of plant scientist faces an equally important and complementary task, that of cataloging and preserving naturally occurring plants that have potential value as crops or sources of new genes.

Many societies have learned the hard way that relying on a few crop varieties, no matter how successful they are, can be disastrous. When a fungal blight devastated Ireland's potato crop in the mid-1840s, the country experienced widespread famine. The mistake was repeated in 1970 when corn kernels turned to dust and leaves and stalks fell to the

116

ground from Florida to the Midwest—victim, like Ireland's potatoes, to a fungus infection. Perhaps surprisingly, the answer to the problem of genetic uniformity can be found operating not in a modern laboratory but among Kampuchean rice farmers, who plant each field with five to seven unrelated varieties. If foul weather or a new pest should attack, at least some of their rice survives—biologic insurance through diversity.

Today germplasm banks for storing seeds to help preserve genetic diversity of crop plants have been established in some countries and are being promoted worldwide. Consider again rice, a staple of the less developed nations that feeds more than 2.3 billion people each year. Fossils indicate that rice has been around for at least 130 million years. It appears to have been cultivated in China some 7,000 years ago, and by 300 BC it was a food throughout Asia. It is only in the past few centuries that rice has found its way onto the tables of the New World.

As migrating peoples took their native rices with them, the forces of natural selection molded the plants into varieties adapted to a wide range of environments, from deep salty water to the driest of drylands. From the 1930s to the 1950s many nations collected hundreds of native rice varieties, growing small amounts of each every season just to keep the collections going.

But in the 1960s highly productive newcomers, the semidwarf rices, literally took over, accounting for nearly all of China's crop and almost half of the rices of many other Asian nations. To offset a potential disaster due to reliance on a few types of rice, the International Rice Research Institute (IRRI) in the Philippines was founded in 1961. It soon became a clearinghouse for the world's rice varieties, cold-storing the seeds of 12,000 natural variants by 1970 and of more than 70,000 by 1983. Today the IRRI and the many nations contributing to it have provided three priceless services to humanity: the salvation of rice from a "genetic wipeout" caused by reliance on a few types, the return of endangered or extinct varieties to their native lands, and, perhaps most importantly, a supply of genetic material for biotechnologists to fashion rices in the years to come. In the vaults of the IRRI and of the world's other germplasm banks reside, literally, the seeds for our future.

Photos, The International Rice Research Institute, P. O. Box 933, Manila, Philippines

Technicians of the International Rice Research Institute in the Philippines sort rice seed prior to sealing under vacuum in aluminum cans (top). After careful cleaning, hand selection, fumigation, and drying, seeds are canned and maintained in short-, medium-, and long-term storerooms for later regeneration. In the long-term storeroom (above) thousands of natural rice variants from all over the world are preserved at −10° C (14° F) and 30% relative humidity. Under these conditions the seed is expected to remain viable for more than 75 years.

FOR ADDITIONAL READING

Jack Doyle, *Altered Harvest: Agriculture, Genetics, and the Fate of the World's Food Supply* (Viking, 1986).

David A. Evans and William R. Sharp, "Applications of Somaclonal Variation," *Bio/Technology* (June 1986, pp. 528–532).

Michael Hansen *et al.*, "Plant Breeding and Biotechnology," *BioScience* (January 1986, pp. 29–39).

Ricki Lewis, "Building a Better Tomato," *High Technology* (May 1986, pp. 46–53).

Julie Ann Miller, "Somaclonal Variation," *Science News* (Aug. 24, 1985, pp. 120–121).

Keith Redenbaugh *et al.*, "Somatic Seeds: Encapsulation of Asexual Plant Embryos," *Bio/Technology* (September 1986, pp. 797–801).

117

# The Problem of Salt in Agriculture

## by James D. Rhoades

*For centuries irrigation has increased the salinity of soil, reducing the fertility of such land. The problem has become worse in recent years, and effective control measures must be developed.*

Irrigation is an ancient practice that predates recorded history. While only about 15% of the world's farmland is irrigated, it contributes about 35–40% of the total supply of food and fiber, and it stabilizes production against the vagaries of weather. Inevitably, however, irrigation leads to the salination of soils and waters. The salt contained in the irrigation water tends to be left behind in the soil as the pure water passes back to the atmosphere through the processes of evaporation and plant transpiration (the passage of watery vapor through membranes or pores). Typically, excess water is applied to the land or enters it by seepage from delivery canals. These waters percolate through the soil and underlying strata and flow to and cause waterlogging in land of low elevation. In turn, saline soils are formed in such land through the process of evaporation.

The salt problem in irrigated agriculture is not new. The rise and fall of the Mesopotamian civilization nearly six thousand to seven thousand years ago has been attributed to the development of irrigated agriculture and to its subsequent failure as a result of rising water tables and soil salination. In the American Southwest the decline of ancient Indian civilizations centuries ago is also attributed to salination of land and water. Today salinity seriously affects productivity on about 20 million hectares (one hectare equals 2.47 acres) of the world's irrigated land. It threatens the economy of many arid countries, such as Egypt, Iraq, and Pakistan, where irrigation is the backbone of agriculture. In the United States an estimated 30% of all irrigated land suffers from reductions in yield caused by salt. Salinity also constitutes the most serious water-quality problem in many rivers and groundwater systems that are located in arid and semiarid regions. The problems of soil salination, waterlogging, and water pollution are increasing as irrigation is being expanded and as less suitable waters and soils are being used to meet the ever increasing need for food in the world.

Surviving the salinity threat requires that the seriousness of the problem be widely recognized, that the processes contributing to salination be understood, and that effective control measures be developed and

**J. D. RHOADES** is a Research Leader at the U.S. Salinity Laboratory, Riverside, California, and Adjunct Professor of Soil Science at the University of California at Riverside.

(Overleaf) Salt builds up on the banks of an irrigation canal in Colorado. Irrigation inevitably leads to the salination of soil and water. Photograph, Soil Conservation Service; photography by Tim McCabe

implemented that will sustain the viability of irrigated agriculture. Considerable advancement has been made in the development of control methods in recent years, but information gaps continue to exist, and new and improved technologies are still needed. This necessitates the continuation and expansion of research and development. The causes of salination, the extent of the problem, practices used to control salinity, and research opportunities and needs are discussed in this article.

## Effects of salt on plants and soils

Salt-affected soils are those that are of reduced value for agriculture because of their content (or the past effects) of salts, consisting mainly of sodium, magnesium, calcium, chlorides, and sulfates and secondarily of potassium, bicarbonates, carbonates, nitrates, and boron. Saline soils contain excessive amounts of soluble salts for the practical and normal production of most agricultural crops. Soluble salts exert both general and specific effects on plants, both of which influence crop yield. Excess salinity in the crop root zone causes a general reduction in growth rate. In addition, certain salt constituents are specifically toxic to some plants. For example, boron is highly toxic to many crops when present in the soil solution at concentrations of only a few parts per million. In some woody crops sodium and chloride may accumulate in the tissue over time to toxic levels. These toxicity problems are, however, much less prevalent than is the general salinity problem.

Salts also may reduce the suitability of the soil as a medium for plant growth. The suitability of soils for cropping depends appreciably on the readiness with which they conduct water and air (permeability) and on their aggregate properties (structure), which control the friability (ease with which crumbled) of the seedbed (tilth). In contrast to saline soils, which are well aggregated and whose tillage properties and permeability to water and air are equal to or higher than those of similar nonsaline soils, sodic soils have reduced permeabilities and poor tilth. Sodic soils are those that contain excessive adsorbed sodium, given the electrolyte concentration (salinity) of the infiltrating water; this combination causes the breakdown of soil structure and loss of permeability. Sodic soils are less extensive than saline soils.

## Sources of salt and causes of salt-affected soils

The original sources of salts are the dissolved products of mineral weathering, emanations from volcanic eruptions, discharges from deep thermal sources, and the primary ocean. These salts have been redistributed over time. Winds blowing over the oceans pick up salt particles, which originate at the sea surface as spray, and carry many of them onto the land, where they are mixed with other salts derived from weathering products and sedimentary sources.

As a result of specific local conditions of climate, topography, geologic history, land use, or the nature of the sediment or soil, salts have accumulated in certain locations in amounts many times higher than the average concentration. In landscapes with good rainfall and effective

120

drainage systems, soluble salts are transported by flowing surface waters and groundwaters eventually to the sea. During this migration their concentration and composition undergo many changes as a result of their different mobilities and their varying affinities to form or interact with compounds they meet in their path. The migration and redistribution takes place essentially exclusively through the agency of water, which acts both as solvent and as transporting vehicle. But in many parts of the world with internal or ineffective drainage, the salts accumulate in relatively low-lying regions such as valley basins or upland depressions. Such obvious areas of accumulation account for only a fraction of the salts in the landscape. Much salt is stored in subsoils and deeper substrata of the hydrogeologic system as well as in groundwaters. In some

*Salt in the soil kills alfalfa in California (top) and stunts corn in Colorado (left and above). The salt consists primarily of sodium, magnesium, calcium, chlorides, and sulfates.*

121

regions marine incursions in the past have left buried saline sediments in the landscape; often these underlie irrigation projects or rain-fed agricultural lands. Such salt reservoirs may be returned to circulation after a change in the local topographical or climatic conditions or through the actions of humans.

Salt-affected soils occur mostly in regions having an arid or semi-arid climate; that is, where evapotranspiration (the combined effects of evaporation and plant transpiration) exceeds rainfall and, therefore, where leaching (dissolving out by the action of a percolating liquid) and transportation of salts to the oceans are not so nearly complete as in humid regions. Such soils also usually occur in relatively low-lying places that receive water by gravitational flow from higher locations. Sodic soils usually occur in slightly elevated areas that receive salt inputs from the upward, capillary (caused by surface tension) flow of soil water and are often found adjacent to saline and periodically waterlogged areas; sodium accumulates there because of its comparatively high solubility and mobility. These slightly elevated areas are periodically leached by rain or snowfall, which, at least temporarily, reduces the concentration of soluble salts in them.

Restricted drainage usually contributes to the salination of soils and may involve low permeability of the soil or the presence of a high groundwater table. High groundwater tables often are related to topographic position. The drainage of waters from the higher lands of valleys and basins may raise the groundwater level so that it is near the soil surface in the lower lands. Low permeability of the soil causes poor drainage by impeding the downward movement of water.

While salt-affected soils occur extensively under natural conditions, the salt problems of greatest importance in agriculture arise when previously productive soil becomes salinized as a result of irrigation or removal of natural vegetation and certain dryland agricultural practices (so-called secondary salination). The activities of humans have increased salt-affected areas considerably, either by adding more water by irrigation or by using less, as when dryland agriculture replaces native vegetation. In either case water infiltrated into the soil in excess of that used by the agricultural crops passes beyond the root zone, picking up salts from the soils and substrata and often creating waterlogged sections in low areas. When this occurs, soluble salts stored in the ground are mobilized to accumulate at the surface in the seepage areas, salinizing the soils where the rising water tables approach ground level and increasing solute concentrations in associated groundwaters and streams.

The role of irrigated agriculture in salinizing soils and water systems has been well recognized for hundreds of years. However, it has only relatively recently been recognized that the clearing of lands for dryland agriculture has created analogous problems. The latter problem occurs even in areas such as Australia, where the level of soil salinity under natural conditions is typically very low. Also it is of relatively recent recognition that salination of water resources from agricultural activities is a major and widespread phenomenon of likely even greater concern

122

than that of the salination of soils. Only in the past few years has it become apparent that trace toxic constituents, such as selenium, in agricultural drainage waters can cause serious pollution problems.

## Occurrence and extent of salinity problems

The major naturally saline regions of the world are found in poorly drained low-lying lands under semiarid and arid conditions where large quantities of salts leached from higher regions have accumulated in the slowly flowing groundwater and basin sinks, where the water table is at or close to the soil surface, and where the salts have ascended into the soil because of the high evapotranspiration rate. A close relationship between the depth and salinity of the water table and the extent of salt accumulation in soils is established in naturally semiarid regions for the reasons given above.

The impact of humans on the circulation of salts has been profound. As a consequence of irrigation more water and salt have been applied to soils, more salt has been stored in the soil, deeper soil strata have been affected as more leaching and deep percolation have occurred, and the groundwater table has risen in many places. Large areas of irrigated lands have, therefore, become waterlogged and salinized, and associated surface waters have become increasingly salinized because of a reduction in their volume and because of their reception of salt-laden drainage waters.

It is estimated that nearly 10% of the total land area of the world has been sufficiently affected by salt that its utilization for crop production is limited. These areas of salt-affected soils are widely distributed throughout the world. No continent is free from salt-affected soils. Serious salt-related problems occur within the boundaries of the following countries:
*Europe*—Austria, Bulgaria, Cyprus, Czechoslovakia, France, Greece, Hungary, Italy, Portugal, Romania, the Soviet Union, Spain, Yugoslavia
*North and Central America*—Canada, Cuba, Mexico, the United States
*South America*—Argentina, Bolivia, Brazil, Chile, Colombia, Ecuador, Peru, Uruguay, Venezuela
*Middle East and South Asia*—Afghanistan, Bangladesh, Burma, India, Iran, Iraq, Israel, Jordan, Lebanon, Kuwait, Oman, Pakistan, Qatar, Saudi Arabia, Sri Lanka, Syria, Turkey, the United Arab Emirates, Yemen (Aden), Yemen (San'a')
*North and East Asia*—China, Mongolia, the Soviet Union
*Southeast Asia*—Indonesia, Kampuchea, Malaysia, Thailand, and Vietnam
*Africa*—Algeria, Angola, Botswana, Cameroon, Chad, Djibouti, Egypt, Ethiopia, The Gambia, Guinea, Guinea-Bissau, Kenya, Liberia, Libya, Mali, Mauritania, Morocco, Niger, Senegal, Sierra Leone, Somalia, South West Africa/Namibia, The Sudan, Tanzania, Tunisia, Zaire, Zambia
*Australasia*—Australia and the Solomon Islands

Thus, salt-affected soils occur under widely varying conditions of climate, geology, agriculture, and, of course, social and cultural systems. The economic and social repercussions of soil salination are felt most acutely by the populations of arid zones and mainly by less developed

123

*An irrigation canal is under construction near Manzanillo, Mexico (above), and irrigated fields extend toward the horizon near the Aswan High Dam in Egypt (above right). Irrigation is used to help grow crops in arid and semiarid regions throughout the world.*

nations that depend primarily upon irrigated agriculture for their food production.

The increasing population of the world requires that the viability of the Earth's soil and water resources be maintained in order for the increasing demand for food to be met. The projected increase in croplands for the final quarter of the century is only 10%, yet the world demand for food is expected approximately to double, according to the UN World Food Conference Report of 1974. In addition, it has been predicted that agricultural lands will increasingly be diverted from agricultural production to other uses and increasingly be degraded through various means, a major one being salination. Associated with the latter is the increasing pollution of water resources with various chemicals and salts. Irrigated agriculture is heavily involved in these matters.

While irrigated agriculture makes up only about 15% of the world's agricultural land base, it supplies about 35–40% of the food and fiber because of its higher yields per unit of cropland. The amount of irrigated land increased from about 8 million hectares in the year 1800 to 48 million hectares by 1900. It then approximately doubled in the following 50 years and again doubled during the last 30 years. In some arid countries, such as Egypt, nearly 100% of the agricultural land is irrigated, while in others, such as Pakistan, it is about 50%. In less arid nations irrigated land occupies a much lower proportion of the total cropland, but even there it is continuing to increase and is reaching significant levels; for example, in Thailand the percentage is 26, in France 13, in Spain 10, and in Greece 15. In the U.S. the area under irrigation doubled between 1949 and 1973 to 21 million hectares and by 1987 had more than doubled again. In the Soviet Union about one million hectares of new irrigated land are developed each year. In Hungary the irrigated area has increased tenfold since World War II.

It is estimated that the world's total irrigated area will be about 400 million hectares by the year 2000. This increase has resulted not only in an increased world production in agriculture but also in increased water

124

consumption, in increased waterlogging of irrigated lands, and in increased salt buildup in water supplies and irrigated lands. Unfortunately, no one has predicted how much of this irrigated area will succumb to salt problems, but past experience indicates that the problem of salt in irrigated lands will likely increase at an even faster rate than that of the expansion of irrigation itself.

It is well known that large areas of the world (for example, old Mesopotamia, large parts of the Indus River Valley, and vast territories in South America and China) that previously supplied abundant crops by means of irrigation have since succumbed to salination and waterlogging problems. For example, it is estimated that at one time Mesopotamia fed a population of between 17 million and 25 million people and was a food exporter. At present this area has a population only about one-half of the previous total, and it imports a large quantity of food. People were forced to abandon the affected lands and to develop new areas. As long as new territories were available, the shifting of irrigated agriculture temporarily solved the problem. Today, however, with the growing density of population, increased degradation of land and water resources, and shrinkage of a suitable land base for agriculture, this practice of land abandonment is no longer generally acceptable.

In spite of the general awareness of these problems and past sad experiences, salination and waterlogging of irrigated lands continues to increase. According to the estimates of the UN Food and Agriculture Organization and Unesco, as much as half of the area of all existing irrigation systems of the world is seriously affected by salinity, waterlogging, or both; the area potentially subject to secondary salination is estimated to be equal to or greater than the area presently affected; and ten million hectares of irrigated land are abandoned yearly as a consequence of the adverse effects of salination and waterlogging. This phenomenon is common not only in old irrigation projects but also in areas where irrigation has only recently been introduced.

In some countries the salt problem threatens the national economy. Those countries most seriously affected include Argentina, Egypt, India, Iran, Iraq, Pakistan, and Syria. Roughly half the irrigated land in Syria's Euphrates River Valley has become so saline that crop losses there now total an estimated $300 million annually. Between one-quarter and one-half of all irrigated land in South America is affected by salination, and the problem there appears to be increasing. In India 35% of all irrigated land is seriously saline. In Pakistan, where 80% of all cropland is irrigated, one-third of it (approximately six million hectares) is experiencing severe salt problems, and another 16% is threatened with salination by high water tables.

The future development of planned large irrigation projects, which involve diversions of rivers, construction of large reservoirs, and the irrigation of large land areas, has the potential to cause large changes in the water and salt balances and to affect the salinities of entire groundwater and river systems. The impact will certainly extend beyond that of the immediate irrigated area and can even affect neighboring nations.

125

## Control of soil and water salinity

There are three principal aspects of the salt problem and its control in irrigated agriculture. One is the improvement (reclamation) of soils that are salt-affected under natural conditions or have become so because of mismanagement. A second aspect is the management of productive or only slightly salt-affected soils so as to prevent an increase in their salinity and reduction in crop yields. A third aspect is management to minimize the pollution of groundwater and surface-water supplies with salts and chemicals as a consequence of irrigated agriculture.

Saline soils are reclaimed by improving drainage and by leaching with irrigation water to remove excess salts. The improvement of sodic soils involves (besides drainage and leaching) the replacement of excessive adsorbed sodium by calcium or magnesium and practices that develop better soil structure and permeability. Adequate drainage is essential for the permanent improvement of salt-affected soils. In order to prevent waterlogging, drainage must remove the precipitation and irrigation water infiltrated into the soil that is in excess of crop demand and also any other water that seeps into the area. In order to avoid soil salination, drainage also must provide an outlet for the removal of salts that accumulate in the root zone, and it must keep the water table sufficiently deep to prevent the flow of salt-laden groundwater up into the root zone by capillary forces.

Drainage systems are essentially engineering structures that remove water according to the principles of soil physics and hydraulics. New materials, new methods of installation, and the use of larger and more powerful machinery have revolutionized this industry in recent years, so that drainage facilities can now be constructed much more easily, quickly, and precisely than ever before. Typically, plastic drain tubes enveloped by synthetic "filter-socks" are "plowed-in" at the desired depth and grade. This "plow" is precisely and automatically controlled by a laser-guidance system that is an integral part of a relatively fast-moving,

*An irrigation canal in the Imperial Valley of California is lined with concrete to prevent seepage of the water into the adjacent soil. Such seepage increases the salt content of the soil.*

Soil Conservation Service; photo, Tim McCabe

self-propelled drain-installation tractor unit. Computer models that can simulate water-table levels and salt removal under alternative conditions of cropping and water management are available to better assess and design the drainage needs of the area. Various tillage equipment can even invert whole soil profiles or break up substrata as deep as 2.5 meters (8.2 feet) that impede deep percolation, so that many adverse physical soil conditions causing or associated with salt-affected soils can be modified.

Once drainage has been provided, saline soils are reclaimed by applying water to the soil surface and allowing it to pass downward through the root zone. Leaching efficiency has been greatly increased through improvements in the accuracy and precision of land-leveling techniques and by the ability to apply water uniformly across an area. New theories and guidelines have been developed to predict the amounts of water needed to reduce the soluble salts for various conditions of soil properties and methods of water application. A better understanding of the chemistry of soil permeability has been achieved, and quicker and more cost-effective procedures have been developed for reclaiming sodic soils.

Much more is now known from experience and research about how to manage agricultural lands so as to prevent the excessive accumulation of soluble salts and adsorbed sodium. Management practices include selection of crops and varieties that are appropriately tolerant of salts; use of land-preparation and tillage methods and irrigation techniques that maximize the availability of water (both soil and irrigation water) to the plant and that also minimize deep percolation losses and excess waterlogging while preventing excessive salination within the root zone; the use of special planting procedures and seedbed configurations that minimize salt accumulation in the vicinity of the seed; and construction, maintenance, and operation of water conveyance, delivery, and drainage systems that avoid or control seepage losses and provide water to the fields as needed and in the amount required.

The relative tolerances to salinity of most agricultural crops have been established in controlled studies, and better varieties have been developed through selection processes. Certain practices can also reduce the effects of salinity on crops. Planting on sloping beds or in furrows, transplanting established seedlings, and employing special irrigation techniques can be used to establish a good stand. Closer plant spacings and optimization of irrigation to maintain a high content of soil water can also be used to offset many of the harmful effects of salinity on small and slow-growing plants.

Substantial progress has been made in recent years in controlling soil salinity through improvements in irrigation management. The key to salinity control is close water control that maintains a net downward movement of soil water in the root zone over time while minimizing excess deep percolation. A new theory has been developed, and field experiments have been carried out that show that the optimum salinity control scheme is to provide water to the plants in a way that continuously maintains the soil-water content in the root zone within a narrow range at a relatively high level while at the same time avoiding sur-

*Guided by laser light, an earthmover levels a field (top). When cropland is level, farmers are able to apply the exact amount of water needed—evenly and quickly. This improves crop yields and reduces the salt-producing runoff that results from the need to apply extra water to sloping fields. Above is a lettuce field in Arizona that has been leveled by a laser-controlled earthmover.*

face ponding and minimizing deep percolation. New methods of high-frequency irrigation have been developed that substantially resolve the ponding and percolation problems.

The new methods of irrigation and salinity management improve water-use efficiency by transferring control of the rate of water distribution and infiltration from the soil to an engineering apparatus. In any gravity irrigation system (basin or furrow) the irrigator attempts to provide equal time for water intake across the field. But because soils are typically not homogeneous, even a uniform intake opportunity time does not guarantee uniform intake. If the water ponds on the soil, its rate of infiltration is controlled by the soil's intake rate, which is usually quite variable from place to place within the field and which changes markedly with time. Therefore, typically, excess water is applied to the field to meet the needs of the area of lowest intake rate. This results in excessive deep percolation and salt discharge and also in waterlogging and salt pollution in the areas receiving the drainage. In a closed-conduit system of irrigation (such as sprinkler, bubbler, or trickler) the uniformity of application is more subject to equipment control, and the actual intake may be made as uniform as the application if the rate is less than the soil's intake rate. Thus, closed-conduit systems are being increasingly adopted for irrigation and salinity control.

New developments in gravity irrigation systems improve irrigation efficiency and salinity control, even though surface ponding still does occur. Automated gravity irrigation systems, called cablegation, have been developed for fields irrigated by furrows; these systems progressively "cut back" flow to the furrows in order to reduce losses of tailwater (surface water that drains from a field) and to increase intake uniformity along the row. So-called surge irrigation systems have been developed to reduce runoff losses and increase intake uniformity by pulsing water onto the fields in successive increments. Multiset systems use shallow, buried ditches laid across the furrows at intervals down the field in order

128

to reduce the length of row that is irrigated and thereby increase uniformity and reduce runoff. Systems have also been developed to reduce water losses and increase the efficiency of water use by recirculating and reusing surface runoff from irrigated fields.

Improvements in efficiencies and salinity control are also being obtained in flood irrigation systems by the use of level basins (no grade in any direction) combined with large-flow systems of water delivery. The commercial development of effective, practical, and inexpensive laser-controlled grading equipment provided the impetus for implementation of this method. These relatively small (2–15 hectares) basins, when used with either multiple outlets or single large-flow turnouts, permit a field to be irrigated with less water than used by conventional methods, with higher application efficiencies, with increases in water infiltration uniformity, and with less deep percolation. Consequently, they minimize soil salinity, waterlogging, and salt-loading problems.

Improved irrigation efficiency and salinity control have been enhanced through the implementation of irrigation scheduling techniques. These determine the need for irrigation and the amount required based on calculated evapotranspiration amounts, measured depletion of soil water, or both.

In addition to effective methods of irrigation scheduling and application, effective irrigation and salinity management also require an effective delivery system. As irrigation methods become more efficient, the demands on the distribution system are increased. The operations of delivery systems (usually designed and operated by civil engineers) and of on-farm irrigation systems (usually designed by agricultural engineers and operated by farmers) have typically been in conflict. Delivery systems have generally been designed to provide water on a regular schedule. Efficient irrigation systems require more flexible deliveries that can provide water on demand as each crop and particular field need it. Salinity problems created from poorly designed and operated delivery systems are prevalent throughout the world. Substantial losses

Agricultural Research Service, USDA

*Wastewater laden with salt drains from irrigated land in California's Imperial Valley into the Salton Sea. J. D. Rhoades estimates that as much as 70% of such water can be intercepted and reused to irrigate such salt-tolerant crops as sugar beets and cotton. As well as providing irrigation this would prevent the water from draining into such lakes as the Salton Sea and increasing their salinity.*

*Salt seeps into the Colorado River (top) as a result of irrigation drainage. Bottom, a close-up of a small area in the top photograph reveals a heavy accumulation of salt on the shale that lines the banks of the river.*

from seepage from unlined canals, from spills, and from excessive or unneeded water deliveries have contributed substantially, often primarily, to the excessive waterlogging and salination of irrigation projects. These systems can be improved by lining the canals, by containing the water within closed conduits, and by implementing techniques that increase the flexibility of delivery.

Irrigated agriculture is a major contributor to the salinity of many rivers and groundwaters. The agricultural community has a responsibility to protect the quality of these waters while at the same time maintaining a viable irrigated agriculture. Irrigated agriculture can not be sustained without adequate leaching and drainage to prevent excessive salination of the soil, as discussed above. Yet these processes are the very ones that contribute to the salt loading of rivers and groundwaters. In recent years pollution of water resources has become the major problem involving irrigated agriculture and salinity control in the United States, South Africa, and Australia. Significant increases in understanding not only how salts affect plants and soils but also how cropping and irrigation affect soil and water salinity have been made in recent years; correspondingly new strategies to minimize the pollution generated by irrigated agriculture have been developed and implemented. A brief synopsis of these developments is given below.

The concentration of soluble salts is known to increase in soils as the applied water, but not the salts, is removed by evaporation and transpiration. Evapotranspiration can cause an appreciable upward flow of water and salt from lower soil depths into the plant root zone. By means of this process many soils with shallow, saline water tables become salinized. Soluble salts eventually accumulate in irrigated soils to such an extent that crop yields suffer unless preventive steps are taken. To prevent the excessive accumulation of salts in the root zone, irrigation water (or rainfall) must be infiltrated in excess of that needed for evapotranspiration and must pass through the root zone to leach out the accumulating salts. This is referred to as the leaching requirement. Once the soil solution has reached a salinity level compatible with the cropping system, then subsequent irrigations must remove at least as much salt from the root zone as they bring in, a process called maintaining salt balance. In fields irrigated to steady-state conditions with conventional irrigation management, the salt concentration of the soil water is essentially uniform near the soil surface regardless of the leaching fraction (the fraction of infiltrated water that passes through the root zone), but it increases with depth as the leaching fraction decreases. If the leaching fraction is decreased too much, average root zone salinity increases, and the crop yield will decline. Improved methods to calculate the leaching requirement and salt balance have recently been developed and tested; they show that much less leaching is required for salinity control than was previously advocated.

Irrigation water may contain from 0.05 to 3.5 tons of salt per 1,000 cubic meters (one cubic meter equals 35.3 cubic feet). Therefore, with crops requiring annual irrigations of 6,000 to 9,500 cubic meters of water

130

per hectare, from 0.3 to 33 tons of salt per hectare are added to irrigated soils annually. Reducing the volume of water applied reduces the amount of salt added and the amount needed to be removed by leaching. Additionally, minimizing the leaching fraction by the use of frequent, light, and uniform applications of water minimizes the "pick-up" of weathered and dissolved salts from the soil. The salt load discharged from the root zone can be reduced about 2–12 tons per hectare per year by reducing the leaching fraction from 0.3 to 0.1. The volume of deeply percolating water is reduced in proportion to the reduction in the leaching fraction. Reducing deep percolation generally lessens the salt load that is returned to rivers or groundwater.

The interception of saline drainage water before it is mixed with water of better quality is advocated. Intercepted saline drainage water can be desalted and reused, disposed of by pond evaporation or by injection into some suitably isolated deep aquifer, or used as a water supply in a situation where brackish water is appropriate.

A strategy for salinity control of water systems has been recently developed and successfully tested. In this system salt-sensitive crops (lettuce, alfalfa) are irrigated with "low salinity" water, and salt-tolerant crops (cotton, sugar beets, wheat) are irrigated with drainage water. For the tolerant crops the switch to drainage water is usually made after seedlings are established. The feasibility of this strategy is supported by the following conditions: (1) the maximum possible soil salinity in the root zone resulting from continuous use of drainage water does not occur when the water is used for only a fraction of the time; (2) substantial alleviation of salt buildup resulting from irrigation of salt-tolerant crops with drainage water occurs during the time salt-sensitive crops are irrigated with normal, low-salinity water; (3) proper preplant irrigation and careful irrigation management during germination and seedling establishment leaches excessive salts out of the seed area and from shallow soil depths, permitting good stand establishment; and (4) data obtained in modeling studies and in field experiments support the credibility of this reuse strategy. This strategy conserves water, sustains crop production, and minimizes the salt discharge from irrigated lands and the salt loading of receiving waters. It also reduces the need for diversion of water and for the development of new water supplies for irrigation.

Desalination of agricultural drainage waters is not now economically feasible, but improved techniques for doing this exist and some are being implemented. However, more needs to be done in this regard.

### Research needs and opportunities

A number of ways in which salinity control is being improved were identified in the preceding sections. Yet other control possibilities exist, some of which await advancements in knowledge and technology. For example, additional research is needed to improve the salt tolerance of crop varieties. Research on the genetics of salt tolerance has not been adequately supported, and differences in salt tolerance within species should be exploited. A plant-breeding program for the development of

*Scientists check melons grown on land that had previously been irrigated with salty wastewater for the production of wheat and sugar beets. The yield of melon seeds per acre equaled that from fields that had been irrigated only with water of good quality.*

Agricultural Research Service, USDA

131

salt-tolerant species should be undertaken that would include identifying varieties with superior salt tolerance and crossing them with high-yielding adapted varieties, screening segregated generations for increased tolerance under controlled stress conditions, and testing advanced generations in the field.

An alternative approach to improving the salt tolerance of current crops would be to introduce new crops that grow well under saline conditions. These include atriplex, salicornia, and spartina, among others. If economic uses for them could be found, such as for fuel production, such plants could be developed as crops and grown in salt-affected soils. Unfortunately, though they thrive in adverse environments, such plants tend to grow much more slowly than conventional crops. It may be that those genetic mechanisms that protect them against stress are, at the same time, the ones that restrict their growth rate.

As in the case of breeding, the development of new crops is an area deserving increased attention, but it also is subject to false claims and hopes. The fact that a plant is native to, and survives in, saline environments does not mean that it can be cultivated successfully as a crop because biomass production tends to be proportional to transpiration; plants in saline environments have a low rate of transpiration.

The ability to improve salinity control in crop production should also improve if a better understanding is gained as to how to relate current crop-tolerance information to field conditions. Though an extensive literature exists on the salt tolerances of crops, it mostly deals with information collected in growth chambers or small-plot environments. Knowledge about crop water use as affected by salinity and stage of plant growth is also insufficient, though recently new research has been undertaken in this regard. The salt tolerances of various crops under a variety of water-management practices need more investigation. The

*In a search for salt-tolerant crops a scientist examines a stunted batch of Egyptian wheat that has been grown in a tub of saline water. Behind him is Egyptian wheat that is flourishing in fresh water.*

*Researchers use an electromagnetic monitor to measure soil salinity in the Imperial Valley of California. The device produces a flow of electric current in the soil that increases proportionally to the salinity.*

studies should include evaluations of short-term effects of high salinity at various stages of growth, especially the seedling establishment and flowering stages.

Although increased efforts in genetics and breeding for greater salt tolerance are needed, it must be recognized as a false premise that management research is outdated and no longer needed. The increasing need for conserving soil and water resources dictates that breakthroughs are needed in this regard if a permanent viable irrigated agriculture is to be sustained and, especially, if irrigated agriculture is to be practiced under even higher levels of salinity. The protection of water resources against excessive salination, while sustaining agricultural production through irrigation, will require the implementation of comprehensive land- and water-use policies that incorporate an understanding of the natural processes involved in the soil-plant-water and associated geohydrological systems. For this purpose the long-term effects of alternative irrigation and agronomic practices for salinity control need to be more thoroughly evaluated. Rather than using only crop yield as a measure of the success of salinity-management practices, scientists and engineers should also consider the effectiveness of such practices in the protection of the quantity and quality of water resources. Since crop salt tolerance, soil salt balance, and salt discharge from irrigated fields are interrelated, better techniques for determining optimum leaching requirements are needed, especially for dynamic situations.

Prediction techniques that will describe the quantity and quality of subsurface return flow from different irrigation and management are also needed. To evaluate fully the changes in chemical quality of the flow, the research models should be capable of handling salt precipitation, mineral weathering, adsorption, and the ion-exchange reactions that take place as water moves through the soil and deeper substrata. Present limitations to the use of such models include insufficient knowledge about the pathway(s) of subsurface return flows and about the chemical and physical

133

properties of the substrata in the pathway(s) for the large hydrogeologic systems (such as irrigated valleys or large basins) that are involved. Because of the lack of such models and techniques for acquiring the required information, the problems resulting from the development of new irrigation projects, particularly those involving lands not previously irrigated, will usually be confronted only after the fact.

A need exists to identify and quantify the damages that occur as a result of salination of soils and waters and the benefits of alternative control practices. Such economic studies should also consider effects on water resources, including the local, regional, and national benefits that would accrue from the implementation, in either an irrigated valley or a river basin, of a salinity-control program. For example, a control measure implemented in a particular valley has direct benefits not only to the local area, including the nonagricultural sectors, but to downstream water users as well. Benefits resulting from increased crop yields, saved fertilizer, reduced drainage, reduced pollution, and reduced water costs accrue to both upstream and downstream users.

Improved methods are needed for making areawide investigations to define the need for and potential benefit of salinity-control measures. These studies should pinpoint the sources and causes of salinity and provide the information required for selecting the most appropriate control measures. Once the sources of salts have been defined, more detailed studies should be undertaken to specify how those sources may best be controlled. Demonstration projects and extensive educational programs will be needed to evaluate and demonstrate feasibility and accomplish the implementation of selected programs.

The proper operation of a permanent irrigated agriculture that uses water efficiently requires periodic information on the status of soil salinity. Only with this information can the need for management change and effectiveness of irrigation project operations be assessed with respect to salt balance and water-use efficiency. Suitable inventories of soil salinity either do not now exist or are inadequate; nor are there effective programs to monitor the salinity status of soils and to assess the adequacy of irrigation and drainage systems on a projectwide basis. Presently used methods are primarily based on "salt balance" concepts and models that are inadequate.

The need for monitoring will increase because less water will be available for leaching as the competition increases for water now used in irrigation. In addition, in order to protect water resources, more restrictions will likely be placed on the discharge of salt from irrigation projects. With less leaching there will be a corresponding increase in soil salinity. New instruments for remotely measuring soil electrical conductivity, coupled with computer mapping and satellite-based positioning techniques, have the potential for meeting salinity-monitoring and mapping needs. These methods will have to be integrated into a geographic information system for inventorying salinity. A network of representative soil-salinity-monitoring stations should be established in irrigation projects, especially those projects undergoing changes in operation.

*Symbolizing the destruction that could take place unless effective control measures are carried out, an iodine bush killed by salt in the soil stands at the edge of the Kesterson Reservoir in California (opposite page).*

Ed Kashi © Discover Magazine, Time Inc.

134

The present approach to salinity research, where studies are carried out in artificial, small, controlled, and relatively simple systems that exclude much of the "real world" of irrigated agriculture and the larger hydrogeologic system, leaves much to be desired. This should be corrected with research being undertaken that encompasses the variability and complexity of the real world. In spite of this limitation, much more is known about salinity and its control than is currently being used. Known principles should be adapted, and innovative management systems appropriate to existing field circumstances and crop-production and conservation needs must be developed.

Finally, a proper balance between basic and applied research must be maintained. Accomplishments in basic biotechnology and genetic engineering research should not be expected to supplant the need for research and improvements in management and engineering. Nor should the real goal for research be forgotten: to feed mankind while conserving dwindling soil and water resources.

FOR ADDITIONAL READING

H. Frenkel and A. Meiri (eds.), *Soil Salinity: Two Decades of Research in Irrigated Agriculture* (Van Nostrand Reinhold Co., 1985).

Taylor O. Miller, Gary D. Weatherford, and John E. Thorson, *The Salty Colorado* (The Conservation Foundation, 1986).

S. L. Rawlins and P. A. C. Raats, "Prospects for High-Frequency Irrigation," *Science* (May 9, 1975, pp. 604–610).

I. Shainberg and J. Shalhevet (eds.), *Soil Salinity Under Irrigation* (Springer-Verlag, 1984).

# TUNNELING

## TOWARD THE FUTURE

### by David V. Martin

**Advanced technology is allowing tunnelers to bore faster and more safely through ground once thought impossible to work. A mammoth underwater tunnel in Japan is nearly done, while the long-envisioned Channel link between England and France is just beginning.**

Tunneling, the most unpredictable, expensive, and dangerous field of civil engineering, is also probably the most exciting. Its achievements catch the public imagination, and its failures make the greatest headlines. Without it our lives would be considerably different.

Civilization demands clean drinking water on tap, much of which is now being transported in tunnels. Modern sewerage and wastewater-disposal systems depend to an increasing extent on large interceptor sewers and even underground sewage-treatment plants. Hydroelectric power, currently being expanded in third world countries to save the high and rising costs of fossil fuel stations, often relies on long water-transport tunnels high up in mountain ranges. Increasingly, power plants themselves are being built underground, not only to avoid spoiling the environment but also to make them safer and more secure from terrorists and saboteurs.

In the field of transportation, mountainous countries such as Norway, Switzerland, Italy, and Austria have been busy in the years following World War II driving road tunnels to keep up with the expanding population of private automobiles. Although few new railway tunnels have been built in Great Britain or the United States in the 20th century, France and West Germany have been laying new high-speed rail links, which have demanded extensive tunneling. Confidence in modern tunneling methods has encouraged two of the most ambitious undersea tunneling ventures ever undertaken: the 54-kilometer Seikan twin-track railway tunnel linking the Japanese islands of Hokkaido and Honshu, which will be opened to trains in 1988 after 21 years' work, and the proposed Eurotunnel cross-Channel link between Britain and France, work on which was due to start in July 1987. (One kilometer is about 0.62 mile.)

In congested cities whose central, or downtown, sections have no space to spare for surface transport systems, underground railways—commonly called metros or subways—are being built. London was first in 1863, followed by

*Varied applications of tunnels and underground excavations include a rock-walled subway station in Atlanta, Georgia (right), a water purification plant (opposite page, top left), and a gymnasium beneath a mountain (opposite page, top right), the latter two in Europe.*

Budapest, Hungary, in 1896. By 1950, 17 cities, including Paris (1900), Berlin (1902), New York City (1904), Buenos Aires, Argentina (1913), Tokyo (1927), and Moscow (1935), had metros. By the mid-1980s more than 80 such metros were operating or under construction.

One of the oldest uses of caves and tunnels, for protecting valuable materials, has become fashionable again. The use of underground space for storage, particularly of oil and gas, is common in Scandinavia and in other places where good, hard tunneling rock exists. In some places large food stores are maintained below ground under naturally stable conditions of temperature and humidity. When costs for land purchase, heating and cooling, building maintenance, and security are considered, below-ground facilities are often cheaper than surface facilities.

The pursuit of pleasure and health has not been overlooked in the uses put to tunneling. Large multipurpose sports complexes have been built deep in the rock; in time of war they can be used as secure air-raid shelters. At Holmlia, Norway, ten kilometers outside Oslo, for example, a cavern has been blasted more than 30 meters (one meter is about 3.3 feet) below the surface to provide an area of 6,500 square meters (1.6 acres) for ball games and a swimming pool. Some 53,000 cubic meters (1.9 million cubic feet) of granite were excavated. The facility includes changing rooms, a sauna, showers, a cafe, and an emergency ventilation plant that will support 7,000 people if the complex is used as a bomb shelter. Shelters that double as car parks also have been built.

Deep tunnels throughout the world house factories, breweries, telephone exchanges, sewage-treatment plants, civil defense headquarters and stores, and even offices and housing. Military and defense authorities value underground space for command and control centers, ammunition and ordnance depots, and protected sites for missiles, ships, and aircraft. Today the demand for tunnels and underground excavation of all types seems limitless and has spurred the search for quicker, cheaper, and safer methods of meeting that demand.

**DAVID V. MARTIN** is Editor of Tunnels & Tunnelling *magazine, London.*

*Hard-rock tunnel-boring machine (overleaf) nears completion of a road tunnel in Bergen, Norway. The steel disk cutters on the 7.6-meter (25-foot)-diameter cutterhead produced the concentric scoring on the tunnel face. Photograph, The Robbins Company*

## Hard-rock tunnel-boring machines

Tunneling divides in practice into two entirely different techniques: hard-rock tunneling and soft-ground excavation. Rock tunnels are normally driven either by drilling and blasting or, more recently, by giant full-face tunnel-boring machines (TBMs), or moles. The digging end of a TBM consists of a hydraulically driven cutterhead having a diameter that spans the full face of the tunnel to be bored. As the cutterhead turns against the rock, dozens of hard-steel disk cutters or picks mounted on its surface chip away at the rock surface. The chips drop to the bottom of the tunnel, where they are scooped up by the cutterhead and carried on conveyor belts to the rear of the machine. The first successful hard-rock TBM was built by the Robbins Co. of Seattle, Washington, in 1957.

The Robbins Company

*Newly designed hard-rock TBM from Robbins, destined for a hydroelectric project in California, features a 5.5-meter (18-foot)-diameter cutterhead equipped with 43-centimeter (17-inch) disk cutters, the largest in the industry as of late 1986.*

Three meters in diameter and more robust than earlier types, it could bore for several days before the disk cutters on the head needed to be replaced. Improvements have been continuous since then.

Half a dozen companies now produce successful hard-rock TBMs, but Robbins has made more than any rival. Perhaps the newest design comes from the Swedish company Atlas Copco, which recently began making continuously boring TBMs under the name FORO. In a conventional TBM hydraulic grippers push out against the sides of the tunnel to fix the machine in place while the cutterhead is thrust a certain distance into the rock. Then the cutterhead is retracted and the grippers moved forward for the next advance. By contrast, the FORO machine carries a double set of grippers, which alternately grab and release as the cutterhead continues advancing. The FORO also offers an increase in load per cutter from 20 to 25 metric tons, giving a greatly increased rate of penetration in hard rock. The design allows good access directly behind the cutterhead for immediate support of the tunnel with rock bolts or steel arches.

## Drill-and-blast methods

Drill and blast is still the most widely used tunneling method in granite, limestone, hard sandstone, and rocks with a high compressive strength. A pattern of perhaps 100 holes, each some 5 to 8 meters deep and 45 millimeters (1.8 inches) in diameter, is drilled in the rock face. All except two or three larger holes in the center are filled with explosive, and the face is "blown." When the shattered rock is cleared, the tunnel has advanced by almost the depth of the drilled holes.

Many technical advances both with drilling equipment and with explosives have been made, particularly in the past few years. Early hand-held pneumatic (compressed-air) drills, heavy and cumbersome, were soon mounted on jack legs. Later several units were mounted on chassis

*Atlas Copco's FORO tunnel-boring machine (below and in the diagram at bottom) carries two sets of grippers that alternately grab and release the tunnel walls, enabling the machine to advance continuously. The design allows good access behind the cutterhead for supporting the tunnel with rock bolts or steel arches. As with other TBMs, rocks chipped from the tunnel face are scooped up by the cutterhead and carried to the rear by conveyor belt. In 1987 Swedish tunnelers were using a FORO machine for the Solna water project, a water tunnel passing under central Stockholm.*

(Below) Atlas Copco; (below right) adapted from information obtained from Atlas Copco

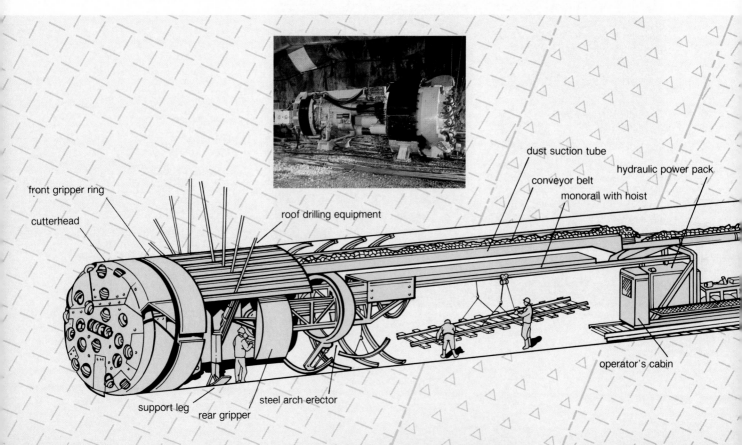

front gripper ring

cutterhead

roof drilling equipment

dust suction tube

conveyor belt

hydraulic power pack

monorail with hoist

operator's cabin

support leg

rear gripper

steel arch erector

to form "jumbos" so that as many as six drills could work on the same rock face at once. Invention of tungsten-carbide-tipped drills having special bit designs dramatically increased the effectiveness of drilling, while introduction of the modern rotary percussive hydraulic rock drill in the mid-1970s by the French firm Montabert further revolutionized drilling technique. Today's hydraulic drills penetrate rock twice as fast as pneumatic drills, consume only one-third the energy, and extend the life of the drill steel. They also improve comfort and safety in the tunnel environment by cutting noise and eliminating the long compressed-air hoses and the airborne oil mist that accompanied use of pneumatic drills.

The very latest advances in drill-and-blast methods announced by Atlas Copco at the 1986 American Mining Show in Las Vegas, Nevada, include the Rocket Boomer, a jumbo boasting a performance twice that

*Large drilling jumbo from Tamrock (above left) is equipped with hydraulic drills mounted on three separate booms and a front platform that can be raised or lowered to accommodate various sizes of tunnel faces. Empty control cab of Atlas Copco's Robot Boomer (above) testifies to the automated capabilities of the machine. Once the operator sets up and starts the rig, a full work cycle can be carried out without continuous supervision.*

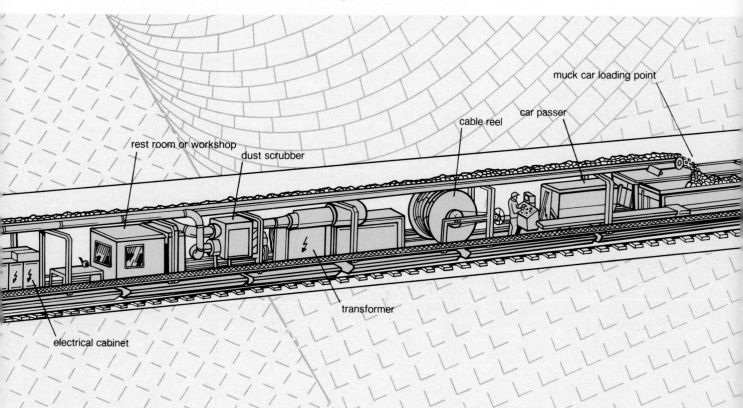

muck car loading point

car passer

cable reel

rest room or workshop

dust scrubber

transformer

electrical cabinet

*Workers load explosives into holes drilled into a tunnel face. Drill and blast is still the most widely used tunneling method in granite, limestone, hard sandstone, and rocks with a high compressive strength.*

of the best previous model, and the Robot Boomer, claimed to be the world's first truly automatic drilling rig. The human operator has been replaced to the extent that complete work cycles can be carried out without continuous supervision. Microprocessor-controlled, the system is intelligent enough to detect and correct its own functional errors. The skilled human operator is not completely replaced; he must set up and start the rig and manually drill the few holes that the rig has rejected.

Although dynamite is still widely used in tunneling, for economy explosives are frequently mixed at the face of the tunnel and fed into the holes through a hose. The most common explosive is ANFO, a mixture of ammonium nitrate and fuel oil. Since the mid-1980s Norwegian tunnelers have started mixing light, cheap, hollow polyethylene granules called Isopor with ANFO to make an even cheaper explosive called Isanol. Only 20–30% ANFO need be used to make the mixture work satisfactorily. Although this technique had been known previously, it became practical only after Dyno Industries A/S of Norway invented a mixer that could homogeneously blend the very light polyethylene granules with heavier ANFO. A half stick of dynamite, however, is still used to initiate the explosion in the top of each hole.

Other developments have been in technique. The Swedes are famous for their "smooth blasting" method around the circumference of a rock face. It gives a less jagged edge to the tunnel wall, saves overbreak (breaking away more rock than necessary) and hence concreting costs, and produces less spoil. Smooth blasting is done by putting less powerful explosives in the outer holes and by careful drilling of the periphery.

One of the most important advances in technique has been nonelectrical detonation of explosive. Electric detonators are commonly used, but they carry some danger of premature explosion and can be set off in thunderstorms. Nonel, as the new method is known, works by percussion and is much safer.

142

## NATM

After a cavity has been bored or blasted out of the rock, it may need temporary support or a permanent lining. A widely used, and sometimes controversial, method is known as the New Austrian Tunneling Method (NATM). Developed between 1957 and 1965, it is not so much a way of excavating and supporting as an entire concept with a set of principles. Thus it has been widely misunderstood by many who think that anyone spraying concrete to line a tunnel is using NATM. Its principal feature is its use of the rock mass surrounding the tunnel, rather than massive steel arches, as the main load-bearing component. Once exposed, the rock is supported as soon and as near to the working face as possible with a thin layer of shotcrete (a sprayable concrete mixture) and with bolts and other primary supports as needed. Meanwhile the rock walls slowly settle, eventually supporting themselves much like a natural cave.

A second distinctive feature of NATM is the use of instruments to monitor the deformations of the excavation and the buildup of load in the support or reinforcing elements. These on-site observations are vital not only for checking on performance and safety but also for guiding the addition of secondary and tertiary support. Early practitioners of NATM were probably the first to make systematic use of instrumentation as an integral part of underground construction.

A third feature of NATM is its potential for fostering a greater sharing of responsibility and risk among owner, engineer, and contractor than conventional contractual arrangements, which often produce adversarial, rather than cooperative, relationships. For example, cost of supporting elements may be based on a classification of rock type on which the contractor and engineer agree after each drill-and-blast round.

A fourth feature of NATM is its versatility and adaptability, which is consistent with its being an approach or philosophy rather than just another method. NATM has succeeded under a wide range of tunneling conditions because of its basic soundness and because of the adaptability of shotcrete as a primary and secondary support material, particularly when used with supplementary support elements.

NATM was originally developed by Austrian engineers for tunneling through Alpine rocks already under high stress. Support was provided

*Following the NATM concept, a tunneler (below) applies a shotcrete layer over newly exposed rock and steel mesh to create a reinforced concrete lining. NATM's principal feature is its use of the rock mass surrounding the tunnel as the main load-bearing component; primary support is added only as needed. One of the first applications of NATM in the U.S was on parts of the Washington (D.C.) metro (below left), which included 53 kilometers (33 miles) of subway construction in bedrock and soft ground.*

(Left) De Leuw, Cather & Company; (right) courtesy, Hochtief

in two distinct parts: an outer ring of reinforced rock with a thin aux-
iliary shotcrete lining (primary support) and an inner ring or lining of
shotcrete (secondary support). By the mid-1980s NATM was in wide use,
especially in South America and the Far East, although it was still new
to the U.S. One of the first U.S. applications was on parts of a subway
tunnel in Washington, D.C., under contract to Austrian builders.

NATM has been tried only relatively recently for near-surface tunneling in soft ground (soils), but spectacular achievements have been
claimed in metro construction in a number of West German cities including Bochum, Frankfurt, Munich, Nuremburg, and Stuttgart. In Bochum,
for example, overlying ground was as thin as 3.5 meters, and tunnel
diameters varied from 8 to 13 meters. Tunneling was variously in marl,
clay, silt, and gravel, and the proximity of existing buildings and surface
transportation imposed stringent limits on how much the surface could
be allowed to settle.

Currently one of the largest and most interesting tunneling jobs in the
world is the construction of no less than 62 double-track railway tunnels
on the new 327-kilometer high-speed railway line between Hannover
and Würzburg, West Germany. Because the trains will travel as fast as
250 kilometers per hour, the lines must be well spaced, fairly straight,
and as level as possible. NATM is being used on all these tunnels to cope
with excavated faces as large as 145 square meters (1,570 square feet)
and widths of about 14.5 meters. It is impressive that modern tunneling
methods have enabled such large excavations to be so speedily and efficiently carried out and such wide arched roofs to be supported safely
with so little material.

The element of controversy surrounding NATM arises from tunnelers
in other countries, notably England and Norway, who regard it more as a
successful marketing exercise for what is just common sense. Norwegians
say that they have been applying these principles, albeit without a formal
definition, for years. Leading English tunnelers point out that quickly
establishing a load-bearing ring and leaving no section of the excavated
tunnel surface unsupported, even temporarily, has long been practiced

*The rectangular shield designed by Sir Marc Brunel for boring the Thames Tunnel (shown in profile) comprised 12 cast-iron frames standing side by side, each pivoting on its own foot. Workers on the frames were protected from the mud, sand, and clay of the tunnel face by a large number of heavy horizontal timbers held in place with small screw jacks. Each timber could be removed independently, the spoil directly ahead of it excavated, and the timber replaced and forced forward with the small jacks. When all the timbers in front of an entire frame had been so advanced, the frame itself was pushed forward with master jacks between frame and brickwork at the roof and floor. The tunnel's brick and masonry lining antedates the invention of Portland cement.*

in all types of soft-ground tunneling. Certainly the shield-based method originally used by Sir Marc Brunel and his son Isambard for constructing the famous Thames Tunnel in London (1825–42) used this principle. English tunneling methods in the 19th century had special merit in that the brick and masonry linings had of necessity to be maintained close to the tunnel face.

Nevertheless, NATM uses a flexible system of providing support, makes systematic use of instrumentation, and encourages everyone associated with tunneling to develop a sound understanding of the method and a cooperative attitude. Encouragement of a thoughtful approach that emphasizes the principles of mechanics and the engineering behavior of geologic strata is NATM's greatest value.

## Tunneling in soft ground

Soft ground, consisting of unconsolidated sediments such as clays, silts, sands, gravels, and alluvial deposits, is usually not self-supporting. It is found typically in plains and valleys—the usual sites of cities—and therefore is the medium for much urban tunneling. When a cavity must be made in soft ground, excavation, immediate support, and management of water interact so closely that they cannot be isolated. Consequently, although soft-ground tunneling and hard-ground tunneling share many features, they differ in practice.

Soft-ground tunneling is normally done inside a shelter, or shield, the development of which was prompted by the intense demand for improved transportation in the densely populated London area of the early 1800s. The elder Brunel devised the shield after watching the boring activities of the shipworm, a mollusk that uses ridged shell plates at its anterior end to tunnel through submerged timber. In 1818 he took out a patent for a circular iron tunneling shield that would hold the ground safely in place during excavation and that could be jacked forward as the tunnel advanced, allowing lining to be installed behind. Thus Brunel invented the shield-driven tunnel, and he established the principle of lining the tunnel at once as the shield advanced. His patent covers every subsequent development in the construction and working of tunnel shields.

Water causes more failures and unforeseen circumstances in soft-ground tunneling than anything else. To control it tunnelers employ a number of techniques. The water table can be lowered by sinking wells and pumping, provided that the source of the water is not unlimited and ground permeability is low. The ground can be grouted or injected with chemicals to fill the pores. Another method, ground freezing, is effective but expensive. Or more traditionally the tunnel can be dug under compressed air.

A necessity with compressed-air tunneling is to seal off the working space from the outside air. This is done with a wall—either an air deck across a vertical shaft or a bulkhead in a horizontal tunnel—fitted with air locks to allow workers and materials to pass through. The health problems associated with compressed-air work—the bends and bone necrosis—are now well known. The risk is thought to result not from

*Decompression chambers, necessary for compressed-air tunneling, prevent such health problems as the bends and bone necrosis by allowing workers a gradual transition between the high-pressure working environment and the outside air.*

Courtesy, Parsons Brinckerhoff Quade & Douglas, Inc.

145

*Hydroshield machine (bottom left) designed by Wayss & Freytag for soft-ground tunneling achieves breakthrough at a metro station site in Antwerp, Belgium. Its specialized cutterhead scoops excavated spoil into a chamber behind the head while a pressurized slurry—maintained at a constant pressure by a cushion of compressed air—supports the soft tunnel face and keeps back groundwater. A Wayss & Freytag Hydrojet Shield (bottom right) built for sewer construction in West Germany uses three oscillating high-pressure water jets to cut through soil.*

working in compressed air but from incorrect decompression procedures. The most recent procedure used in Great Britain and widely elsewhere is known as the Blackpool Tables and dates from 1966. Many authorities believe that the time has come to introduce new and updated regulations.

## Soft-ground machines

Although compressed air is still widely used for tunneling, particularly in Japan and most recently in Hong Kong and Singapore on metro construction, it has been superseded in some countries by the bentonite, or slurry, shield. In its initial configuration the machine resembles a full-face TBM but isolates a specialized soil-scooping cutterhead in a chamber filled with bentonite slurry kept at a pressure sufficient to support the face and keep back groundwater. The slurry from the chamber, carrying the excavated spoil, is pumped to a separation plant, where the spoil is carried away for disposal and the slurry reconditioned for reuse. The first tunnel built by this method was completed in 1973 at New Cross in southeast London.

Meanwhile, in continental Europe and especially in Japan, where a huge public-works program was mounted in the 1970s, the slurry-shield method evolved on a large scale and in many forms. In 1979, of more than 100 tunneling machines at work in Japan, no fewer than 35 were reported to be using the slurry-shield principle. Important effects were reduction in the settlement of overlying ground and buildings and safer working conditions. The beauty of using a slurry rather than compressed air to support the working face is that pressure in the slurry varies naturally from the top of the chamber to the bottom just as does groundwater pressure in the tunnel face; the imbalance of air pressure on a vertical face is thus eliminated, as is the need to apply extra pressure at the top of the face.

When a slurry shield is working well, there are great advantages. Fewer workers are needed, and the spoil is handled automatically by pumping. Conditions in the tunnel are cleaner and safer owing to the

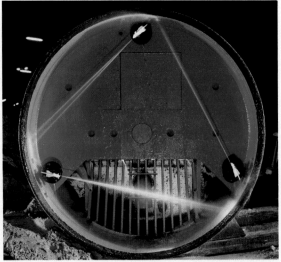

Photos, Wayss & Freytag

absence of noise, dirt, and dust. But if things go wrong, it is difficult to get at the working face, even to replace cutting tools. Although bentonite-shield tunneling is still a specialized and expensive business, it can offer substantial savings of time and money and safety advantages.

One of the most widely used and successful new machines is the Hydroshield, designed by Wayss & Freytag AG and manufactured by Bade & Theelen of West Germany. It differs from its British and Japanese competitors in that the slurry pressure in the digging chamber is held constant by a bubble of compressed air stored behind a partial diaphragm ahead of the main bulkhead and behind the cutterhead. It has been successfully used for metro construction in Antwerp, Belgium; Rome; and Lyon, France. Two U.K.-built Hydroshields are currently employed on the Greater Cairo Wastewater Project in Egypt.

Variations of the German design are intended to cope with mixed ground and boulders. The Mixshield carries away spoil by screw conveyor and can remove or crush boulders. The Hydrojet Shield uses three or more oscillating, high-pressure water jets to cut the soil, with the slurry acting as a stabilizing, excavating, and transporting medium.

The earth pressure balance shield (EPBS), invented in Japan by the Sato Kogyo Co., can tunnel through soft and running ground below the water table. It resembles a slurry shield externally in that the cutterhead consists of a rotating disk fitted with drag teeth positioned along both edges of a number of radially arranged arms. Openings on either side of each cutter arm allow material excavated from the face to enter a drumlike chamber behind the cutterhead. Compressed in the chamber, the material forms a plug that supports the face and keeps out groundwater. A screw conveyor moves material from the drum upward through the bulkhead and through a hydraulically operated sliding gate. When the gate is closed, the tunnel face and drum are completely sealed from the rear of the shield and the tunnel. To maintain a constant pressure at the face, the rotating cutter frame and screw conveyor are kept constantly filled with earth. Thus the soil discharged from the soil chamber is

*Earth pressure balance shield built by Mitsubishi Heavy Industries can bore through soft or watery ground below the water table. Slots on the front face admit excavated material into a chamber behind the cutterhead. Compressed in the chamber, the material forms a plug that supports the ground and keeps out water. Soil leaves the chamber by screw conveyor at exactly the rate that it enters through the cutterhead so that a constant pressure is maintained at the face. The machine is particulary suited to silt and clay soils that form a watertight barrier when compressed.*

Mitsubishi Heavy Industries Ltd.

Photos, American Thrustboring Corporation

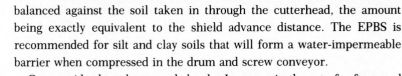

*Pipe-jacking rig drives an Unclemole forward into the ground (above right) as an operator on the surface guides its progress via remote control (above). The Unclemole, a miniature slurry shield machine from Iseki Poly-Tech, can bore underground pipelines having diameters as small as 250 millimeters (10 inches). The pair of hoses visible in the right-hand photo carry slurry to the cutterhead and remove excavated material.*

balanced against the soil taken in through the cutterhead, the amount being exactly equivalent to the shield advance distance. The EPBS is recommended for silt and clay soils that will form a water-impermeable barrier when compressed in the drum and screw conveyor.

Great strides have been made by the Japanese in the art of soft-ground microtunneling; that is, forming underground pipelines having a diameter of about 900 millimeters (35 inches) or less, where it is not possible for a person to enter or work. Microtunneling depends on various types of miniature TBMs operated from the surface by remote control. The Telemole from the firm Iseki Poly-Tech, Inc., is a remotely controlled earth pressure balanced slurry shield for tunnels 600–900 millimeters (24–35 inches) in diameter. A variation is the Crunchingmole, which incorporates rock-crushing equipment in the slurry chamber and disposes of material by the pumped-slurry method. Other similar machines are the Telemouse, for 350–500-millimeter (14–20-inch) tunnels, and the Unclemole, for boring 250-millimeter (10-inch) tunnels that are then lined with pipe jacked forward in sections.

*Tunnel linings of cast concrete reinforced with steel fiber (right) or of bolted precast concrete segments (far right) find wide application in tunneling projects today. One recent advance has been in the use of continuously cast, steel-reinforced linings that are emplaced using formwork carried in the tail of the tunneling shield.*

(Left) Wayss & Freytag; (right) Charcon Tunnels Limited

## Tunnel linings

Permanent linings are always required in soft-ground tunnels and frequently in rock tunnels. They serve two purposes: structurally they contain and support the exposed ground, and operationally they provide an internal surface appropriate to the function of the tunnel. Traditionally linings were made of brickwork and masonry; more recently poured concrete, sprayed concrete, precast concrete segments, and iron and steel linings have been used.

Tunneling researchers in West Germany and the U.S. have been experimenting with continuously cast concrete linings reinforced with steel fibers. The West German company Hochtief has been the most successful using this technique on a number of major tunnels including the Frankfurt and Lyon metros. A casting mold, or formwork, for concrete is accommodated in the tail of the tunneling shield, and as the machine moves forward the concrete is poured in a continuous ring 20 centimeters (7.9 inches) thick. When set, the concrete forms a single-piece, waterproof, reinforced-concrete lining.

Shotcrete linings reinforced with steel fiber, usually applied as part of NATM, are also common, particularly in rock tunnels. The method is constantly being improved, and its use has spread from Europe to the U.S. One variation employs waterproof plastic liners sandwiched between layers of shotcrete lining. In Norway, which has many kilometers of unlined rock tunnels but limited public funds, engineers have developed inexpensive forms of plastic and metal water barriers and insulation that prevent ice from forming in and blocking tunnels in winter.

One of the best and most secure linings for a tunnel is factory-made pipe. In a technique called pipe jacking, pipe sections are pushed from a jacking pit into the excavated tunnel. Although pipe jacking is normally reserved for narrow-diameter tunnels (up to 1.8 meters), larger tunnels can also be jacked. A variety of excavation methods including full-face TBMs can be used at the head of the pipe.

## Other innovations

Some of the most recent advances in tunneling have come out of the search for better ways to direct the lengthening tunnel accurately along its desired direction. Today most TBMs are guided by a system in which a carefully aligned beam of laser light from behind passes through crosshairs mounted on the rear of the machine and hits a target in front of the operator. The operator steers the machine so as to keep the beam trained on a mark on the target—a task made more difficult by the dusty tunnel atmosphere and vibrating machinery. A new improvement from the British firm ZED Instruments allows more accurate steering by replacing the optical target with an array of light-sensitive diodes that, together with information from inclinometers, informs a microprocessor of the machine's alignment to within two millimeters. The microprocessor then determines the amount of correction needed and displays the information to the operator, who may then take the necessary corrective action.

Photos, ZED Instruments Ltd, Hersham, England

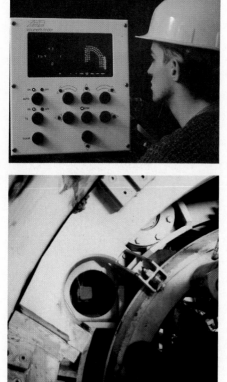

*Laser guidance system from ZED Instruments for tunnel-boring machines replaces the optical target for the laser beam with an array of light-sensitive diodes (above, visible through a hole in the TBM as a small rectangular patch). Rather than observing the beam's position on the target, the operator views a console (top) that displays alignment information gathered from the array and from inclinometers and then analyzed by a microprocessor.*

149

Mucking out and transporting the spoil from the tunnel offers limited opportunity for innovation. Traditionally wheeled dumper trucks or railbound cars have been used. Recently Japanese manufacturers have developed vertical tray lift systems to carry spoil up shafts, and North American firms have produced similar systems using belts. A system known as the Beltavator, borrowed from a technique for loading cargo into ships, sandwiches spoil between two fast-moving rubber belts, which transport it up vertical shafts to the surface. The high-capacity system, designed to keep pace with the increasingly rapid rate of advance of TBMs, was first used on a tunneling application in Montreal in 1985.

Another method, developed in West Germany by the concrete pumping firm Putzmeister but so far applied mainly in Japan, turns the spoil into a slurry (if necessary) by adding water and then pumps it to the surface in a steel pipeline. It has proved particularly useful with wet chalk and is currently in use on construction of the Lille metro in France.

### Underwater tunneling: two ambitious projects

Ever since Brunel drove his tunnel under the River Thames, this type of construction has remained attractive. Most early underwater tunnels were relatively short and took road vehicles, utilities, or railways under rivers or estuaries. The tunnels were either well lined or used the Danish and Dutch technology of immersed tubes. These are large, hollow concrete boxes that can be made at a dock, floated out to the site and lined up end to end, sunk in a trench, and joined to make a tunnel.

After World War II the Japanese perceived the idea of joining two of their islands, Hokkaido and Honshu, with a 54-kilometer undersea railway tunnel designed to take the high-speed Shinkansen, or Bullet Train, then being planned. The first excavations of the Seikan Tunnel took place in 1964, and work continued in spite of many difficulties until "hole through" on the pilot tunnel was achieved in 1983. The undersea section, below the Tsugaru Strait, is 23 kilometers long, but the need to go deep and to keep the grade shallow enough for trains added another 31 kilometers. In addition to the 9-meter-wide, twin-track main tunnel are two subsidiary tunnels: a deep-level drainage tunnel 3.6 meters in diameter, initially driven as a pilot tunnel and serving during construction for access, drainage, and ventilation; and a 4-meter-diameter service tunnel used for maintenance, ventilation, and emergencies. The two subsidiaries merge in the mid-tunnel section; neither are needed under the land sections.

The geology of the seabed under the Tsugaru Strait includes volcanic rocks that are highly fissured and water bearing, sedimentary rocks and mudstones that are stable but have faults, and Tertiary sandy mudstones at the center, the youngest rocks along the route. The method of excavation was drill and blast after early attempts with fullface machines were not entirely successful.

There have been many accidents, fatalities, difficulties, and delays during construction. The worst was when the service tunnel struck a fault 4.6 kilometers out from the Hokkaido shore and water flowed in

*Construction train hauls excavated material from Japan's interisland Seikan Tunnel, which was nearing completion in 1987 after more than two decades of work.*

Kaku Kurita

150

at a rate reaching 70 cubic meters (18,500 gallons) a minute, exceeding the pumping capacity and flooding 3 kilometers of the tunnel. Eventually the tunnel was saved and the fault bypassed, but the operation took eight months. Nevertheless, completion of the Seikan Tunnel must mark one of mankind's most successful tunneling achievements, ranking with the opening of the first big Alpine tunnels in Europe.

More modest but technically interesting undersea tunnels have been built by the Norwegians. At Vardø, north of the Arctic Circle, they drove a 2.6-kilometer-long road tunnel under the sea to an offshore island and left the tunnel mostly unlined. Pumps were installed to remove any water seepage. Other such tunnels have been used to carry North Sea oil and gas pipelines ashore and under deep fjords. Norwegian engineers have even proposed building road tunnels in flexible concrete tubes suspended in the water below shipping depths but well above the deep fjord bottoms.

The biggest, most exciting undersea tunnel under way at present is Eurotunnel, the 50-kilometer-long project for connecting Britain and France under the English Channel with three separate interlinked tubes. One, the pilot and service tunnel, will have a diameter of 4.5 meters; the other two 7.3-meter-diameter tubes will each carry a single high-speed railway track. Work is to start in 1987 and will take about five years, with the first train service expected in 1993. Although Eurotunnel is slightly shorter than the Seikan Tunnel overall, it will have 37.5 kilometers under the sea.

Eurotunnel's construction is expected to take much less time than the 21 years that Seikan demanded. Its geology is much easier to tackle, consisting of easy-to-cut chalk. Six full-face TBMs are to be used on the British side alone, three heading out under the sea and three driving the shoreside tunnels, and another five on the French side. Progress on the British side is expected to average 25 meters per 24-hour working day, but the machines have been designed to cut the chalk as fast as 50 meters per day under the best conditions.

As work progresses, the tunnels will be lined with precast reinforced-concrete segments, or cast-iron segments if the ground demands. Con-

*Profile of the 54-kilometer Seikan Tunnel connecting the Japanese islands of Honshu and Hokkaido shows its 23-kilometer (14-mile) section beneath the Tsugaru Strait. The need to go deep (100 meters [328 feet] below the deepest point of the strait) and to keep the grade shallow enough for trains added another 31 kilometers (19 miles) under the islands. In addition to the 9-meter (30-foot)-wide main tunnel are subsidiary pilot and service tunnels along the undersea portion.*

Adapted from information obtained from Japan Railway Construction Corporation

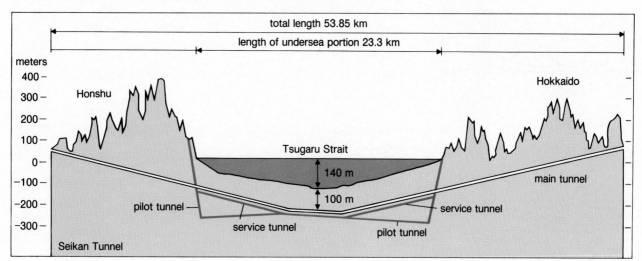

ditions for the 50 or more workers inside the tunnel will be very good. They will make the journey of a half hour or more to the face in fast, clean electric trains and will work in dry conditions at a temperature of about 22° C (72° F). The working environment should remain safe since the pilot tunnel and probing-ahead techniques will reveal any faults or water in front of the main working faces.

When the tunnels open, electric trains traveling at speeds as high as 160 kilometers per hour within the tunnel and 280 kilometers per hour on open ground will convey passengers from London and other British cities directly to Paris, Amsterdam, Brussels, and Frankfurt, with occasional trains going as far as Istanbul or even Moscow. Other travelers will drive their own cars to large loading terminals and then onto two-deck railcar "shuttles" that will convey them in less than an hour to the other side. The British, with their love of French wine and cheeses, will be able to make easy shopping trips across the Channel, and the sophisticated French will be able to call in at English pubs for a pint during an evening outing. The tunneling industry, in its greatest international achievement, will have conquered a barrier that has defied everyone since the Norman invasion of England in 1066. Once long underwater tunnels have been proved technically feasible, financially viable, and popular with their customers, there will be reason for building more.

**The future**

What does the future hold for tunneling? That the use of underground space will increase is undoubted. Already there is talk of connecting Denmark and Sweden, Spain and North Africa, Sicily and Italy, and Japan and South Korea with underwater tunnels. Mechanization during the postwar years has greatly reduced the physical labor involved and cut down the numbers of workers needed to drive tunnels. It is not unreasonable to suppose that a completely unmanned automatic tunneling machine could be built. Such a device might be the product of an international effort—based on the power and mechanization of the American Robbins TBM, guided by the computer-controlled laser system of the

*Eurotunnel will connect England and France by way of twin rail tunnels and a pilot/service tunnel bored 40 meters (130 feet) beneath the Channel bed. Almost four-fifths of its 50-kilometer (31-mile) length will be under the sea.*

Adapted from information obtained from Eurotunnel

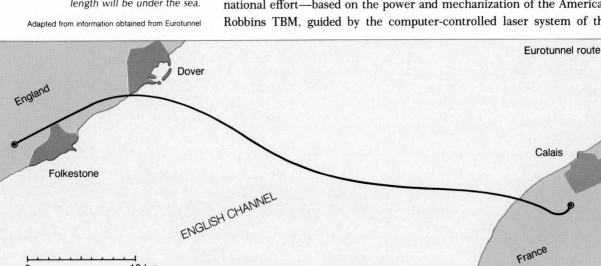

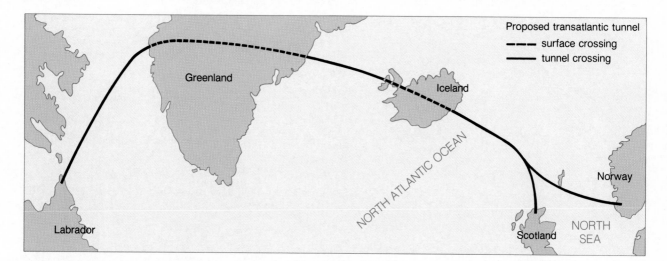

Proposed transatlantic tunnel
‑ ‑ ‑ surface crossing
—— tunnel crossing

Greenland

Iceland

Norway

NORTH ATLANTIC OCEAN

Labrador

Scotland

NORTH SEA

British ZED Instruments, capable of making the continuously extruded lining of the West German Hochtief system, and remotely controlled from the surface using Japan's microtunneling experience. But tunneling is still an art, and however automatic the machines, successful tunnel driving will probably still need the personal touch of master tunneling engineers who will be happy on the job only down at the face.

Frank P. Davidson of the Massachusetts Institute of Technology, in a recently published book on macroengineering titled *Macro: Big Is Beautiful*, calls for an evacuated transatlantic tube sunk in the seabed to carry passengers or commodities at speeds of 3,200 kilometers per hour, making London and New York City only an hour apart. A similar tube could be laid across the length of the U.S., Australia, or Canada. Today such ideas may seem farfetched, but who at the end of the 1950s believed that humans would walk on the Moon within ten years? The dreams of today become the realities of tomorrow, and tomorrow seems ever upon us. Tunneling is as exciting and challenging for engineers as space travel—and will probably be needed when the Moon is colonized.

*Proposal for a transatlantic transport system linking Europe and North America envisions vehicles moving at speeds of 3,200 kilometers (1,990 miles) per hour in an evacuated tunnel or sunken tube in the seabed. A practical route for the system, mapped above, takes advantage of land crossings at Iceland and Greenland. The proposal, devised by a submarine engineer, was inspired by a short story by Jules Verne.*

Adapted from a centerspread drawing of a route selected by J. Vincent Harrington and reproduced in *Macro: Big is Beautiful* by Frank P. Davidson, Anthony Blond, London, September 1986

FOR ADDITIONAL READING

Frank Davidson (ed.), *Tunneling and Underground Transport* (Elsevier Science Publishing Co., 1987).

Frank P. Davidson with John Stuart Cox, *Macro: Big Is Beautiful* (William Morrow, 1983; Muller, Blond & White, 1986).

Sir Harold Harding, *Tunnelling History and My Own Involvement* (Golder Associates, 1981).

E. Hoek and E. T. Brown, *Underground Excavations in Rock* (U.K. Institution of Mining & Metallurgy, 1980).

T. M. Megaw and J. V. Bartlett, *Tunnels: Planning, Design, Construction*, 2 vol. (Ellis Horwood Ltd., 1981–82).

Barbara Stack, *Handbook of Mining and Tunnelling Machinery* (John Wiley & Sons, 1982).

*Tunnels & Tunnelling*, an international monthly subscription journal (Morgan-Grampian Ltd., London).

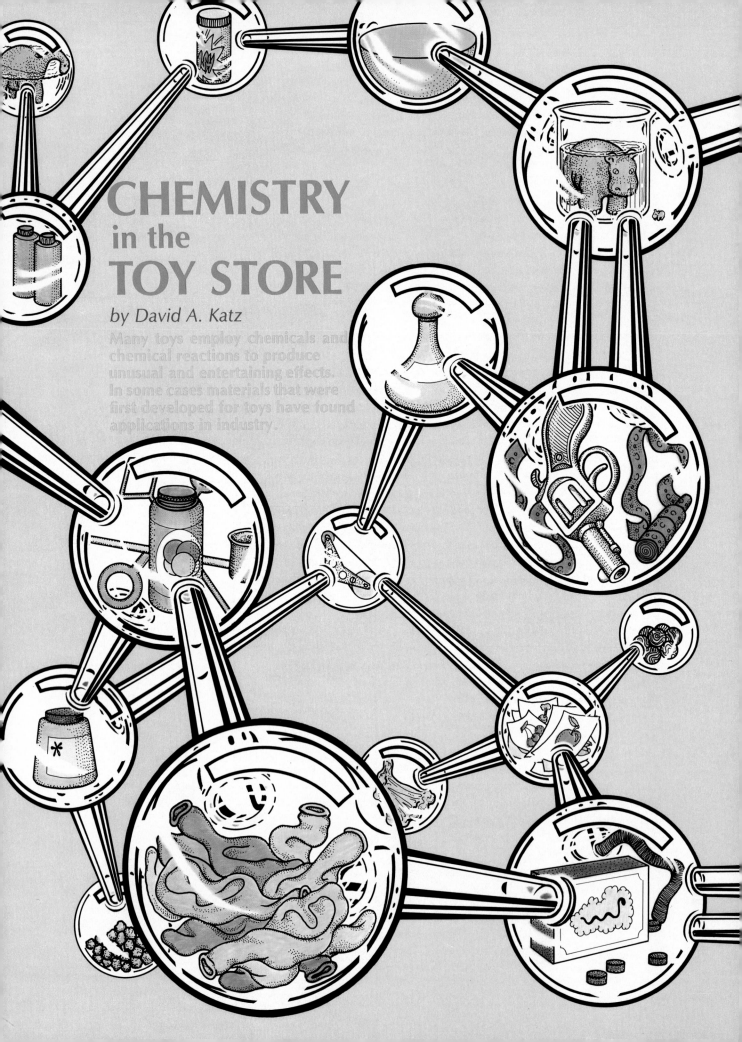

# CHEMISTRY
## in the
# TOY STORE

*by David A. Katz*

Many toys employ chemicals and chemical reactions to produce unusual and entertaining effects. In some cases materials that were first developed for toys have found applications in industry.

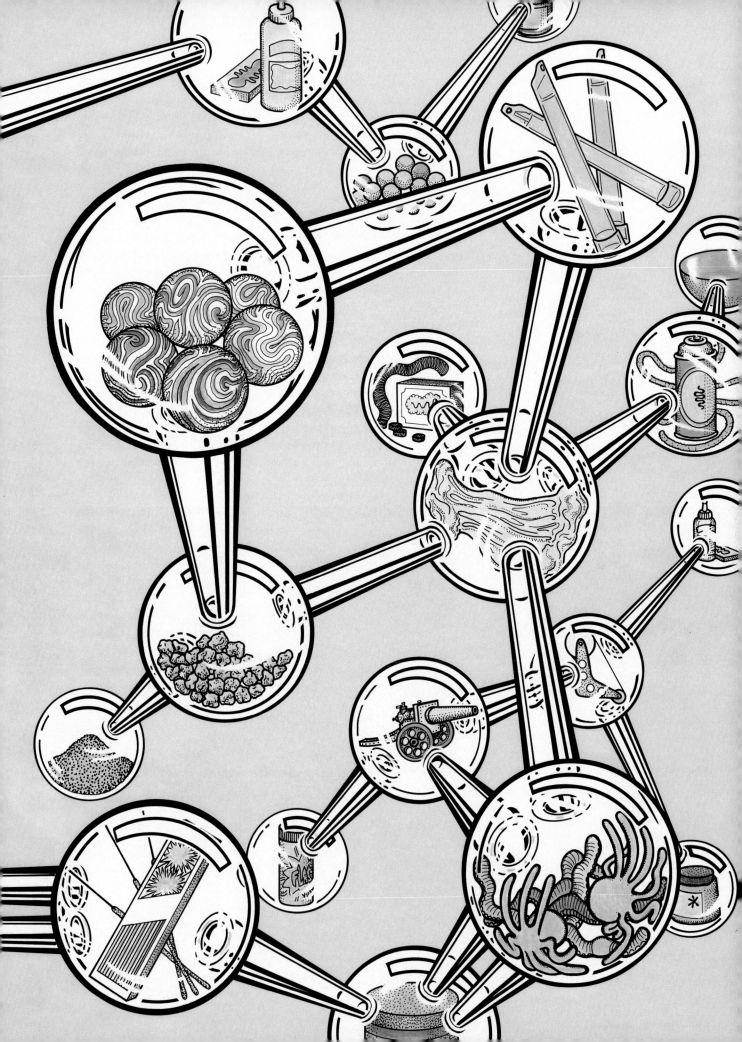

**DAVID A. KATZ** *is an Associate Professor of Chemistry at the Community College of Philadelphia in Philadelphia, Pennsylvania.*

*Illustrations by John Draves*

The chemistry of everyday materials affects our lives in the form of consumer items that are used in the kitchen, laundry, bedroom, workshop, garden, and place of work. One place that is often overlooked is the toy store. Many toys involve chemicals, chemical reactions, and the unique properties of a particular material. Whether the item is a chemistry set, a silicone putty, a polymer with unusual properties, a material to make or mold another plaything, or the batteries used to power mechanical or electronic items, the toy store is a unique place for chemical products.

Chemical toys come from several sources. Some items such as sparklers and flash powders originated in ancient technologies, and some, such as disappearing ink or Magic Rocks, are refinements of experiments that are part of any chemistry course. But most chemical toys are an application of a product used for other purposes or developed through research. Silly Putty is the result of an unsuccessful attempt by General Electric Co. to produce a synthetic rubber in 1941; Slime is an application of a common food ingredient used for thickening or for producing quick-forming gels; Magic Sand® was originally developed for cleaning up oil spills; and Magic Eggs were a result of superabsorbents developed for agricultural applications by the United States Department of Agriculture. In each case someone involved with the material decided that it would make an interesting toy and marketed it. Occasionally the process works in reverse, and a toy provides a way of bringing attention to a new material; this was the case of nitinol, a metal with a memory, used in a Thermobile.

*Soap bubbles have long been a popular item in toy stores. Pipes are among the many devices used to produce the bubbles.*

Charles Cegielski

*Large bubble loop with a smaller one inside (left) produces a small bubble within a large one. A simple loop can be constructed from string and soda straws (below).*

## Soap bubbles

Among the most common items found in toy stores are soap bubbles. The container is usually accompanied by a small plastic wand, consisting of a rod with a loop at one or both ends, or occasionally a bubble pipe or more complicated type of apparatus. Several companies have been producing large bubble loops approximately 19 centimeters (7.5 inches) in diameter; some of these have many smaller loops inside for producing multiple bubbles or concentric loops for making small bubbles in a large one. A large bubble loop can easily be made from plastic soda straws and string. The bubble solutions that accompany these special loops generally are dilute soap or detergent solutions that are not particularly effective for producing strong soap films or large bubbles.

There are many recipes for preparing soap solutions. A simple solution for making soap bubbles or films can easily be prepared by mixing a soap such as Ivory® flakes or a detergent such as Tide® in some distilled or deionized water. A better solution can be made with liquid detergent:

> 10% liquid dishwashing detergent such as Dawn® or Joy®, by
>     volume
> 85% water (distilled or deionized)
>   5% glycerin

The soap mixture should always be stirred, not shaken; otherwise excessive amounts of suds may be produced. A low-suds or "controlled-suds" detergent should not be used.

The glycerin is used to strengthen the soap film. Sugar can also be added, but it is best to use it in the form of a sugar syrup because solid sugar does not dissolve readily. White Karo® syrup also works well. For producing large, long-lasting soap bubbles, one should use:

> 20% liquid dishwashing detergent
> 10% glycerin
> 70% water (distilled or deionized)

A recipe for "super bubbles" calls for:

> 4 parts glycerin
> 2 parts liquid Joy®
> 1 part white Karo® syrup

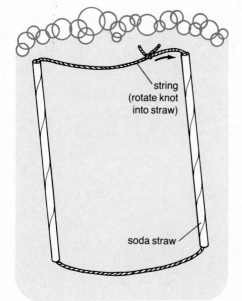

string
(rotate knot
into straw)

soda straw

Distilled water is essential for the prevention of interference from dissolved metal ions, although detergents will not be affected as much as a soap such as Ivory®. (Metal ions in the water are responsible for producing the soap "scum" that forms a ring around the bathtub.). If the solution does not seem to work well, it should be allowed to sit for a few days to a week. Aging improves the characteristics of soap solutions. Super bubbles may even bounce on a clean, smooth floor. A note of caution: super bubbles break with a fair amount of force and so should be kept away from the face. Also, the solutions will make the floor slippery.

As well as blowing bubbles, one can examine the properties of soap films that form on the wire frames that have been dipped into the soap solutions. Simple frames can be made by bending pipe cleaners into various shapes. For more permanent frames heavy-gauge copper wire can be soldered together. Some shapes that can be used are a loop, cube, prism, tetrahedron, and spiral.

A soap or detergent molecule consists of a long, slender nonpolar hydrocarbon chain (a line of consecutively bonded carbon atoms that are bonded to surrounding hydrogen atoms) with a highly polar oxygen-rich group attached to one end. When such molecules are added to

*Molecule of sodium stearate, a typical soap, comprises a long nonpolar chain of hydrocarbons with a highly polar oxygen-rich group attached at one end. Adding such molecules to water, a polar substance, causes them to migrate to the surface and orient themselves so that their nonpolar ends stick out. The diagram below shows the relationship between the soap and water molecules in a soap and water solution.*

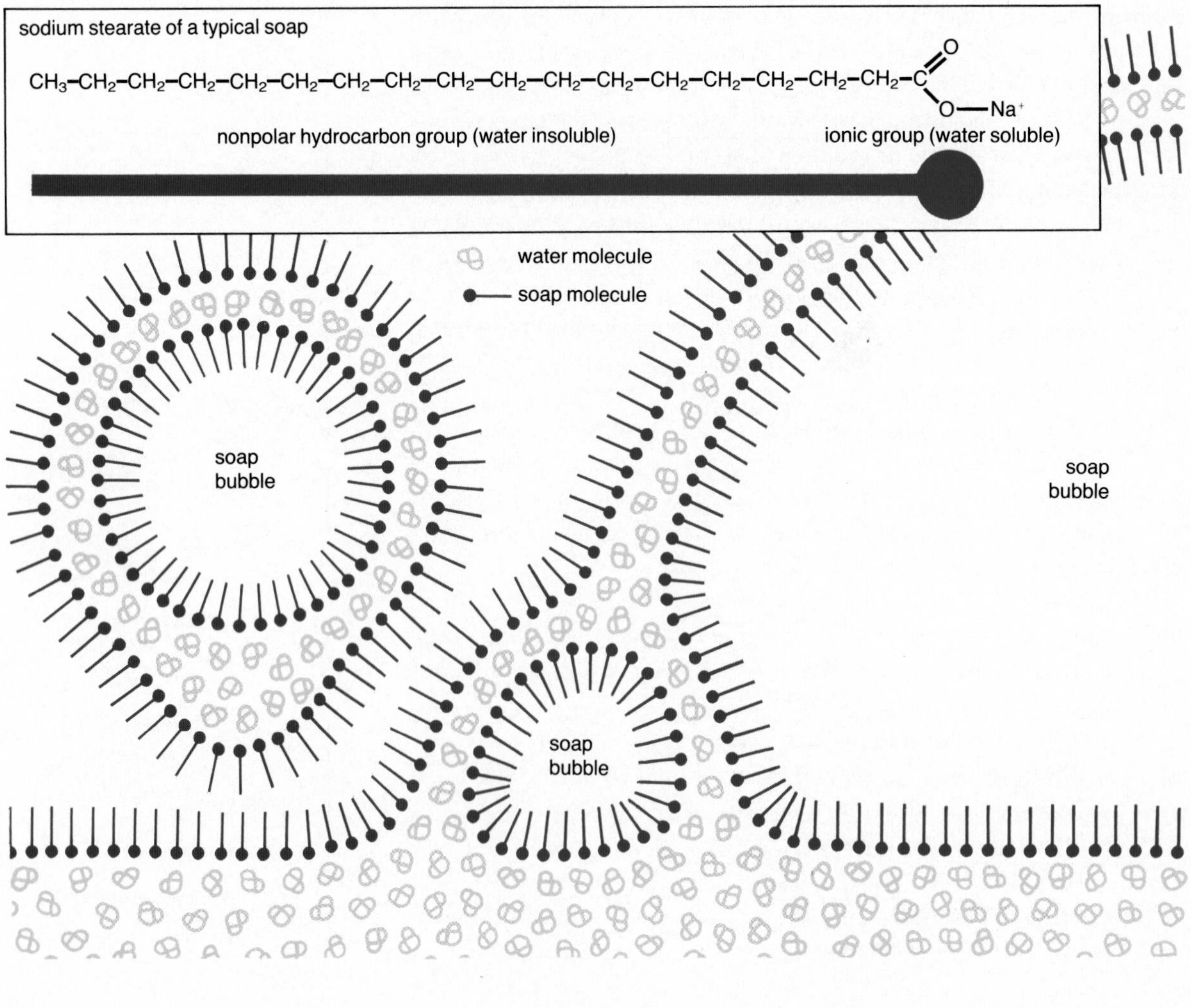

sodium stearate of a typical soap

$CH_3-CH_2-CH_2-CH_2-CH_2-CH_2-CH_2-CH_2-CH_2-CH_2-CH_2-CH_2-CH_2-CH_2-CH_2-CH_2-CH_2-C$

nonpolar hydrocarbon group (water insoluble)　　　　　　　ionic group (water soluble)

water molecule
soap molecule

soap bubble

soap bubble

soap bubble

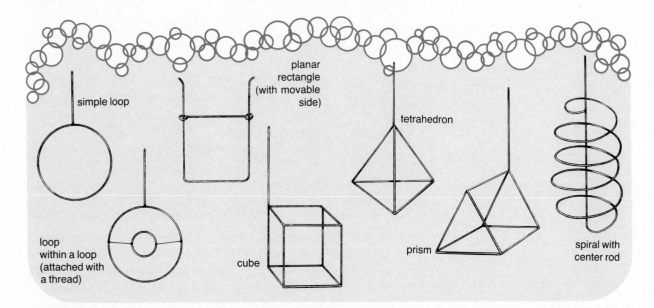

simple loop

planar rectangle (with movable side)

tetrahedron

loop within a loop (attached with a thread)

cube

prism

spiral with center rod

water, a polar substance, they tend to migrate to the surface and orient themselves so that their nonpolar ends are sticking out. The surface of the water is, therefore, covered with a nonpolar layer that drastically reduces the surface tension (the beading-up effect of water on a smooth surface) and adds stabilizing elastic properties to the liquid along with an increase in surface area. When a wire (or plastic) frame is placed in the solution and then withdrawn, the water tends to drain from the inside of the raised surface, making the surface begin to collapse on itself and form a multilayered film. The soap limits the minimum thickness of the film to the length of two soap molecules stacked end to end. Films such as these are self-healing with respect to small punctures.

In the case of a bubble the water drains to the bottom of the bubble, producing a small bump there. One can observe water dripping from the bottom of a large bubble. When the top of the bubble becomes too thin to support the total mass of the bubble, it breaks. The addition of glycerin or other viscous material adds strength to a bubble because this material does not drain out of the soap film readily. The swirling colors observed in the bubble are a result of interference effects of light reflected at opposite sides of the soap film (thin film interference) and the changing thickness of the film due to the draining liquid.

If bubble frames are used, the soap film does not coat the frame but collapses on itself to produce a minimum surface area. This results in the formation of several soap film planes that usually meet at the center of the geometric solid described by the frame. Soap films can meet only at two angles, 120° and 109° 28′. The angle depends on whether there are three or four soap film planes meeting on a line. Other angles are distortions due to physical constraints imposed by the surroundings. For example, if a tetrahedral bubble frame containing the collapsed soap films is dipped halfway into the soap solution, a tetrahedral bubble will form in the center of the soap-film planes. Similar results can be obtained

*Wires are made into frames of different shapes for experimenting with soap films. Heavy-gauge copper wire is used to construct frames intended for long use. When the frames are dipped into a soap solution, films form between the wires.*

159

with a cubic frame, forming a cubic bubble. The shape of these bubbles is a result of the forces exerted by the collapsed films that surround them.

The elasticity of soap films is most easily demonstrated by simply blowing a bubble. To obtain more quantitative data one can measure the elasticity by using a bubble frame with a movable side. If the side is moved up and down, the soap film can be repeatedly stretched and compressed.

When using a large bubble loop, one can easily place a finger, a hand, or even an arm through the film without breaking it by first spreading the soap solution over the skin surface. With a big enough loop and enough soap solution, one could walk through a soap film and stand inside a large bubble.

## Balloons

Among the most common items in toy stores are balloons. They are usually composed of rubber and come in a multitude of colors, shapes, and sizes. Natural rubber is a polymer of isoprene (2-methyl-1, 3-butadiene) in the form of polymeric chains that are joined in a network structure (cross-linked) and have a high degree of flexibility. Upon application of a stress to the balloon material, such as inflating it, the polymer chain, which is randomly oriented, undergoes bond rotations that allow it to be extended or elongated. The fact that the chains are joined in a network allows them to recover their original shapes since the cross-linked chains cannot irreversibly slide over one another. Also, the polymeric material that makes up the balloon is porous, as is evidenced by the deflation of the balloon over a period of time.

An interesting demonstration of some of the properties of the rubber material that composes the balloon is the needle-through-the-balloon trick. For this, one needs a large needle about 35–50 centimeters (14–20 inches) long and balloons of good quality. (Needles about 45 centimeters [18 inches] long are available from magicians' supply stores, as are good rubber latex balloons.) The balloon should be inflated to its maximum size and a small amount of air released from it to allow the molecules some recovery; the end should be tied in a knot. The needle then should be wiped with a cloth containing a small amount of oil, thereby allowing the needle to slide through the rubber more easily. At the end of the

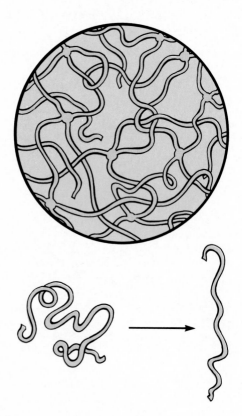

160

balloon, where the rubber is thicker and under less stress, the needle should be slowly pushed into the balloon with a twisting motion. If the needle does not slide easily, more lubrication is needed. If the needle is sufficiently sharp and smooth, it will not tear the rubber but will slide between the polymer chains; this allows the chains to stretch around the needle. The needle should then be pushed through the balloon until it comes through the other side near the knotted end. It can then be either withdrawn or pushed completely through the balloon, leaving two small holes where it passed through. (The rubber does not make a perfect seal in those spots.) After it has been shown that the balloon is intact, the balloon is tossed into the air and popped with the needle to hide the small holes from the audience. With latex balloons of good quality, the needle can also be passed through the balloon from side to side.

## Craft Cast

Craft Cast® is a two-part liquid material that, when mixed in equal amounts, produces a rigid polyurethane foam that can be used for insulating and soundproofing and to make castings of objects. Part A consists of a polymer containing either two or three hydroxyl groups, a blowing agent, a silicone surfactant, and a catalyst. Part B contains a polyisocyanate.

When the two parts are mixed, a polymerization reaction occurs that results in the formation of a large molecule that is rigidly held into a three-dimensional structure. At the same time, the small amount of water present causes a decomposition of some of the isocyanate and the evolution of carbon dioxide that results in foaming. The carbon dioxide bubbles create pores in the viscous mixture as the foam sets into a rigid mass. The cell size and structure of the foam are controlled by the silicone surfactant. A generalized reaction scheme is:

$$R-N=C=O \longrightarrow R-N-C=O \xrightarrow{\text{polymerizes}} \text{polyurethane}$$

$$+ \qquad\qquad | \quad |$$

$$H-O-R \qquad H \quad OR$$

Isocyanate + alcohol      Urethane

*A magician demonstrates the needle-through-the-balloon trick. At the far left he inserts, slowly and with a twisting motion, a large needle into a balloon of good-quality rubber. The balloon should be inflated to its maximum extent and a small amount of air released from it; the end should be tied into a knot. The needle, pointed toward the knotted end, should be wiped with a cloth containing a small amount of oil. If the needle is sufficiently sharp and smooth, it will not tear the rubber but will slide between the rubber's polymer chains and emerge at the opposite side (middle). With the proper equipment even a string attached to the needle can go through the balloon (above).*

Magic effect by Ralph Beck; photos, Bill Arsenault

161

The reaction forming the carbon dioxide is:

$$R-N=C=O \ + \ H-O-H \ \longrightarrow \ R-\underset{\underset{\displaystyle O}{\|}}{\overset{\overset{\displaystyle H}{|}}{N}}-C-OH \ \longrightarrow \ R-\overset{\overset{\displaystyle H}{|}}{N}-H + CO_2$$

Part B may contain toluene diisocyanate (toluene-2, 4-diisocyanate), a substance that is toxic as well as an irritant to the skin and eyes. It may also cause an allergic response. This material should be used only with good ventilation.

A variation of the polyurethane foam is a product called String Confetti. Manufactured in France, it is an aerosol spray producing instant streamers of colored foam that become hardened when they are exposed to air.

### Silly Putty and Slime

*Silly Putty, under low stress as when being slowly pulled apart (below), flows and forms thin strands. When under high stress, such as a sharp pull, it breaks (below right). Transfer of pictures from a newspaper to Silly Putty (bottom right) is accomplished by a reaction between the silicone oil in the putty and the newspaper ink.*

Silly Putty® is a silicone polymer that is marketed by Binney & Smith Inc. and sold under other names by other companies. It is packaged in small egg-shaped containers and is usually pink in color. Some forms of Silly Putty contain phosphorescent material that will allow it to glow in the dark.

Silly Putty tends to dilate (or expand) when sheared, resulting in an increased viscosity under stress. For this reason it has some unique properties: (1) under low stress, such as being slowly pulled apart, the

Reproduced by permission of Binney & Smith, Inc.; photos, Cameramann International, Ltd.

Silly Putty flows, forming thin strands; (2) under high stress, such as a sharp pull, the putty breaks; (3) if rolled into a ball and dropped, the putty will bounce; (4) if a ball of putty is placed on a tabletop and hit with the hand, the ball will hardly be deformed; if hit with a hammer, it will shatter; yet if it is squeezed gently, the ball will flatten; (5) if the putty is stuffed through a tube, it will swell as it emerges from the open end; this is known as die swell. (This works best with freshly prepared putty because the putty tends to harden with age.)

When Silly Putty is prepared in the laboratory, it is initially clear and either colorless or slightly yellow. It will cure within one week to an opaque white solid with properties closer to the commerical Silly Putty, which contains fillers to make it stiff. As it is used, it will pick up foreign matter and become gray in color and slowly improve its properties so that they become similar to those of the commercial product.

One of the interesting properties of Silly Putty is that it picks up pictures from newspapers or the comic sections. This is a function of the ink that is used in newspapers. The ink is composed of mineral oil and carbon black or colored pigments. These inks do not dry readily, as is demonstrated when a finger is rubbed over them. When Silly Putty is placed on the newsprint, the pigment is transferred to the excess silicone oil in the putty.

Slime® is a cross-linked gel made from natural gum. Like Silly Putty, Slime is a fluid that is dilatant. Its properties are also similar: (1) if Slime is pulled slowly, it will flow and stretch; if one is careful, a thin film will form; (2) if Slime is pulled sharply, it breaks; (3) if Slime is poured from

*Slime is poured out of a container and oozes through a child's hand (above left). If Slime is pulled sharply, however, it breaks. In the popular toy Slime Pit (above), Slime is poured into the head of the monster after which it flows from the monster's mouth onto the figure below.*

163

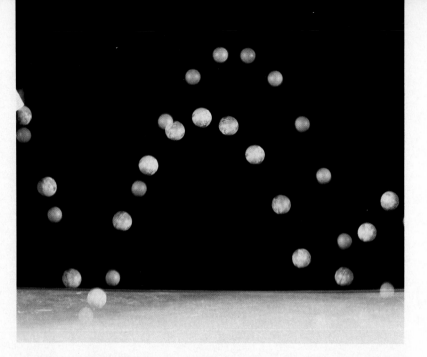

The Super Ball, colored orange, bounces higher than its ordinary counterpart. Consisting of about 100 parts polybutadiene, 0.5 to 15 parts sulfur vulcanizing agent, and 5 to 15 parts of a filler such as hydrated silica or carbon black, a Super Ball has a very high resilience factor and a high coefficient of friction. The relatively large amount of sulfur vulcanizing agent produces the high resiliency.

Wham-O a Kransco Group Company; photo, Cameramann International, Ltd.

its container and the container is then tipped upward slightly, the gel will self-siphon; (4) if a small piece of Slime is placed on a tabletop and hit with the hand, there is no splashing or spattering; if a small piece is thrown onto a hard surface, it will bounce slightly; (5) if Slime is stuffed through a tube, die swell occurs as it emerges.

The natural gum in Slime has a molecular weight of about 220,000. It is used for a wide variety of purposes, including a protective colloid, stabilizer, thickening, and film-forming agent for cheese, salad dressing, ice cream, and soups; as a binding and disintegrating agent in tablet formulations; and in lotions, creams, and toothpastes.

## Super Ball

A Super Ball® is a highly resilient ball that was originally made by the Wham-O Manufacturing Co. Similar products are marketed under other names by other manufacturers; *e.g.*, Bounce Ball. A Super Ball is a ball or sphere having an extremely high resilience factor—in excess of 90%—and a high coefficient of friction. These two qualities cause the ball to react in an extraordinary and unpredictable manner when bounced or struck. Thus, any spin applied to the ball will be accentuated when the ball rebounds from a hard surface.

The Super Ball is composed of about 100 parts polybutadiene, 0.5 to 15 parts sulfur vulcanizing agent, and 5 to 15 parts of filler such as hydrated silica, carbon black, or lithium oxide. There is a higher percentage of sulfur vulcanizing agent in a Super Ball than in products such as automobile tires in order to produce cross-linking between polybutadiene chains; this cross-linking produces the ball's high resiliency. The ball is molded at a pressure of between 500 and 3,000 pounds per square inch for 10 to 30 minutes at a temperature of 140–171° C (285–340° F). Besides the properties described above, a Super Ball exhibits an ability to conserve energy. That is, when bounced, the ball dissipates in the form of heat very little of the energy imparted to it.

164

## A Bad Case of Worms and other wall walkers

A Bad Case of Worms®, once made by Mattel, Inc., is a small plastic case, resembling a suitcase, containing two yellow plastic "worms." The Worms are made of a soft, limp, tackified plastic that is tough enough that a child cannot easily bite off a piece. The plastic, an isoprene polymer, is also washable so that the surface can be restored without losing the tackifier.

To use a Worm, one throws it against a smooth, clean surface, such as a wall, to which it will stick. After a while the Worm will slowly release from the wall and "crawl" down its surface. The rate of motion will depend on the cleanliness of both the wall and the Worm's surface. When the Worm no longer adheres to a surface, it is washed with soap and water to restore its tackiness.

Similar to A Bad Case of Worms are toys in the shape of an octopus, a spider, an insect, a bat, and a skeleton. As one example, the Magic Octopus is made of a soft, limp plastic, probably a styrene or vinyl-

butadiene block copolymer (long segments of polybutadiene separated by segments of styrene or vinyl polymers) that has been tackified so that it sticks to a smooth surface on contact and then slowly releases and "crawls" down the surface. The octopus is stickier than the Worms, and it has better adhesion to surfaces. It does contain excess plasticizer, however, and thus leaves an "oily" residue on the surface that may be difficult to remove. When the octopus ceases to adhere to a surface, its stickiness can be restored by washing it with soap and water.

Variations of the Magic Octopus are the Frog and the Snapper Hand. These are highly tackified and stretchy soft rubber bands shaped as a frog's tongue attached to a frog-shaped handle and a band with a hand-shaped end. They are cast out like a fishing line toward a small object, which will stick to the tacky band and be retrieved when the band snaps back.

## Magic Eggs

Magic Eggs, also called Water Wonder Creatures and Grow Creatures, are named for egg-shaped plastic containers each of which contains a small plastic creature that swells up to 200 times its original size when placed in water. These creatures are composed of a polymer of hy-

*Magic Eggs are egg-shaped plastic containers which hold small plastic creatures. When the creatures are placed in water, they swell to more than 200 times their original size. This is a result of the material from which the creatures are made, a polymer of hydrolyzed starch-polyacrylonitrile mixed with glycerine or ethylene glycol. On drying, the creatures resume their original size.*

165

drolyzed starch-polyacrylonitrile (polyacrylonitrile is commonly known as Acrilan, Orlon, or Creslan) mixed with glycerine or ethylene glycol. This material is commonly called "Super Slurper," and it is capable of absorbing up to 2,000 times its weight of distilled water. The process is reversible, and the Magic Egg creature will shrink almost to its original size on drying.

A recent application of "Super Slurper" is in Pampers disposable diapers. The polymer gel in such diapers can absorb 80 times its weight in liquid.

### Lightsticks

A lightstick is a device that produces a "cool light" by means of a chemical reaction. The reaction is similar to the one that produces light in a firefly, but the chemicals involved are different.

A lightstick is a two-component system consisting of dilute hydrogen peroxide in a phthalic ester solvent contained in a thin glass ampule that is surrounded by a solution containing a phenyl oxalate ester and the fluorescent dye 9,10-bis(phenylethynyl)anthracene. When the glass ampule is broken by bending the lightstick, the hydrogen peroxide and the phenyl oxalate ester react. During the reaction energy is transferred to the dye molecules, and light is produced.

Lightsticks are used as emergency lights, earrings, necklaces, and bracelets. They are also used to light up balls for nighttime playing.

### Thingmaker II

Thingmaker II®, a former product of Mattel, was a molding set that utilized colored material called Goop for making rings, necklaces, pencil holders, flowers for small arrangements, and other articles. Another version was used to make assorted insects.

To be made usable the Goop compound should be placed in the Thingmaker II, where it is heated by a 25-watt light bulb for about one hour

*Goop is poured into Thingmaker II to make flowers and other ornamental objects. The mixture is heated by a 25-watt light bulb for about one hour before it is poured into the molds.*

until it is softened, and then poured into molds. The Goop is described as a lightly cross-linked gelatin with color and bacteriostats (agents that inhibit the growth of bacteria without destroying them) that uses glycerin as a plasticizer. It takes about 15 minutes for the Goop to cool and set before it can be removed from the mold and used for its intended purpose. If exposed to the atmosphere, the molded Goop tends to shrink owing to loss of water.

Goop can be made in a kitchen or a laboratory by dissolving four envelopes of gelatin, such as Knox-brand unflavored gelatin, in 225 milliliters of warm water with 25 milliliters of glycerin. If the resulting gel is too hard or too soft, the quantity of gelatin should be reduced or increased until the proper consistency has been obtained. Food color can be added to produce various colors. The resulting gel should be stored in an airtight container to prevent drying out or growth of mold. When the homemade Goop is going to be used, the container should be set in hot water until the gel becomes liquid. Removal of the Goop from the molds can be facilitated by lubrication of the mold with a thin layer of vegetable oil (a spray-type vegetable oil works well).

## Magic Sand

Magic Sand®, originally produced by Wham-O Manufacturing Co., is sand (silicon dioxide) that has been treated with a colored dye and coated with finely divided hydrophobic silicon. This coating allows Magic Sand to be placed in water to form underwater towers or columns and designs and then to be removed and found to be completely dry. Because of

*Magic Sand, silicon dioxide that has been treated with a colored dye and coated with finely divided hydrophobic silicon, is poured into a jar of water (far left). Its water repellency allows the particles to stay together as a separate phase and to form intricate patterns in water (center). When removed from the water (above), it is completely dry. A similar material has found many industrial applications.*

Wham-O a Kransco Group Company; photos, Cameramann International, Ltd.

this water repellency the particles of Magic Sand will stay together as a separate phase in the water, similar to the phase separation of a polar and a nonpolar liquid such as vinegar and oil.

The Magic Sand is an application of an invention from Cabot Corp., Boston, that originally was used for the removal of oily contaminants from water systems. A similar material is a fumed silicon dioxide, called Cab-O-Sil®, marketed by Cabot Corp., which is used for many applications such as thickening, suspension of solids, and optical clarity in products such as coatings, adhesives, cosmetics, inks, plastics, and rubbers. It is also used to promote the free flow of dry powders.

Magic Sand is prepared by treating an inland sand (which has grains with rounded edges for better flow characteristics) with an organohalosilane such as dimethyldichlorosilane, $(CH_3)_2SiCl_2$. In the reaction the surface of the sand becomes coated with a thin monolayer film of $(CH_3)_2(OH)Si-O-$, which repels water. Materials such as paper, wood, glass, silk, and porcelain can also be coated with a water-repellent film by simply exposing them to the vapor of organohalosilanes.

## Magic Rocks

Magic Rocks, also known as a "chemical garden," consist of small "rocks" colored white, blue, green, red, purple, and orange or yellow. When placed in the "growing solution," the rocks grow and form colored columns. After growth is complete, the solution can be replaced by water so that the garden can be maintained for decoration.

*A "chemical garden" has been grown from Magic Rocks. These are small chunks of differently colored chemical salts such as calcium chloride (white), copper(II) sulfate (blue), cobalt(II) chloride (red), iron(III) chloride (yellow or orange), and nickel(II) nitrate (green). When the salts are placed in a solution of sodium silicate in water, the chunks grow to form colored towers. After the growth is complete, the solution can be poured off and replaced by water.*

Craft House, Toledo, Ohio; photo, Cameramann International, Ltd.

Magic Rocks consist of a sodium silicate solution in water, $Na_2SiO_3$ (the growing solution), and small chunks of various chemical salts. Some commonly used salts and their colors are: calcium chloride (white), lead(II) nitrate (white), copper(II) sulfate (blue), cobalt(II) chloride (red), iron(III) chloride (yellow or orange), nickel(II) nitrate (green), and manganese(II) chloride (pink or purple). The salts are kept stable by being dispersed in an alum or aluminum hydroxide. Attempting to dissolve the colored "rocks" in water or dilute acid results in a gelatinous precipitate.

To make a chemical garden one should mix 100 milliliters of sodium silicate solution (available from chemical supply companies and some hobby shops) with 400 milliliters of water in a 600-milliliter beaker or glass. Enough sand should be added to form a thin layer on the bottom of the container. Then crystals or chunks of any of the above salts should be placed in the solution, though not so many at once that cloudy solutions and heavy precipitates result. After the garden is grown, it can be saved by siphoning off the sodium silicate solution and replacing it with water.

## Smelly Patches and scratch-and-sniff stickers

Smelly Patches are cloth patches backed with a heat-activated adhesive that can be applied to clothing or other objects. They are also marketed in the form of scratch-and-sniff stickers.

Smelly Patches contain a picture of a fruit such as apples, grapes, or strawberries and also smell like the fruit that is pictured. The smell is a result of natural fragrances or esters that are microencapsulated onto the surface of the Smelly Patch. Microencapsulation is a process in which substances such as inks or dyes, adhesives, cosmetics, pharmaceuticals, or fragrances are contained in microscopic capsules, 20 to 150 microns in diameter, that can be broken mechanically, electrically, or chemically to release the contents. The microcapsules consist of different materials, depending on the substance packaged and the method by which it is to be released. Gelatin is widely used as an encapsulating agent. The advantage of microencapsulation is that the capsules remain stable and inert until broken down.

Flavors and fragrances may utilize a single ester or a mixture of esters and other substances. Some esters that smell like common materials are listed below. Esters are made by mixing an alcohol with an organic acid in the presence of concentrated sulfuric acid, which catalyzes the reaction.

| Common esters used for flavors and fragrances | | |
|---|---|---|
| ester | smells like | prepared from |
| isoamyl acetate | bananas | isoamyl alcohol and acetic acid |
| ethyl butyrate | pineapples | ethanol and butanoic acid |
| benzyl acetate | peaches | benzyl alcohol and acetic acid |
| n-propyl acetate | pears | n-propyl alcohol and acetic acid |
| benzyl butyrate | flowers | benzyl alcohol and butanoic acid |
| methyl butyrate | apples | methanol and butanoic acid |
| isobutyl propionate | rum | isobutyl alcohol and propionic acid |
| octyl acetate | oranges | octanol and acetic acid |
| methyl anthranilate | grapes | methanol and 2-aminobenzoic acid |

## Disappearing ink

Disappearing ink is a bright blue water-based solution that, when squirted on various materials, will disappear within minutes, leaving only a colorless "water spot" that will evaporate slowly. When the spot is dry, a small amount of white residue remains.

The ink solution is a moderate to strong base. When an acid, such as hydrochloric acid, HCl, is added to it, the solution becomes colorless and forms a white precipitate. The addition of a base, such as sodium hydroxide, NaOH, dissolves the precipitate and restores the blue color. If the "ink" is squirted on cloth, the colorless water spot that remains after the color fades is slightly acidic. Adding a base to the water spot causes the blue color to return. The blue color is also obtained if a base is placed on the dried "ink" spot.

The material used to make the disappearing ink is an acid-base indicator called thymolphthalein, $C_{28}H_{30}O_4$. The disappearing ink is produced by dissolving a small amount of thymolphthalein in ethyl alcohol and then diluting it with water. The blue color is obtained by the addition of a sodium hydroxide solution.

The change that causes the color to fade is a result of the reaction

*Disappearing ink, a bright blue water-based solution, fades and disappears within minutes after being squirted on various materials. The ink is made from thymolphthalein that is dissolved in ethyl alcohol and then diluted with water. Adding a sodium hydroxide solution produces the blue color. When the sodium hydroxide is exposed to carbon dioxide in the air, the blue color fades.*

of the sodium hydroxide, NaOH, with carbon dioxide, $CO_2$, in the air to form sodium carbonate, $Na_2CO_3$, according to the following reaction:

$$2\ NaOH + CO_2 \longrightarrow Na_2CO_3 + H_2O$$

Once the sodium hydroxide has been neutralized, the acidity of the alcohol changes the "ink" to colorless.

## Thermobile

The Thermobile® is a device consisting of a wire loop around two pulleys, one brass and one plastic, that generates power without a motor or batteries. When the bottom edge of the brass pulley is immersed in hot water (between 50° and 75° C [122° and 167° F]), the Thermobile will within a few seconds begin to spin; it continues to do so as long as the bottom is at a temperature above 50° C.

Left, the Thermobile, a device consisting of a wire loop around one brass and one plastic pulley, begins to spin when the bottom edge of the brass pulley is immersed in water between 50° and 75° C (122° and 167° F). The wire loop consists of a nickel-titanium alloy called nitinol. At low temperatures this wire is soft and can easily be bent, but at high temperatures it becomes stiff (below). Thus in the hot water the wire tries to straighten itself out and in so doing causes the pulley to spin.

The principle underlying the Thermobile is the conversion of thermal energy into mechanical energy by means of a wire loop that is made of a nickel-titanium alloy called nitinol. Nitinol wire is soft at a low temperature and thus can easily be bent into simple shapes. At high temperatures the nitinol wire becomes stiff, reverting to its original shape in what is known as a "memory effect." Thus, the wire, bent around the metal pulley, will attempt to straighten itself out and, in the process, will cause the wheel to spin.

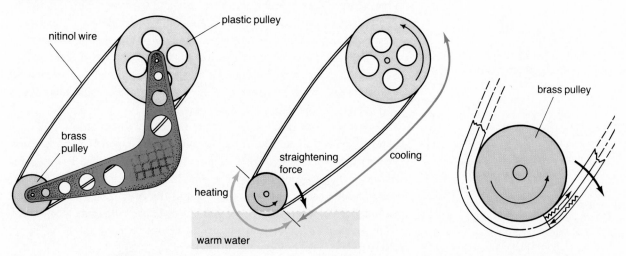

(Top) courtesy, Innovative Technology International, Inc.; photo Charles Cegielski; (bottom) adapted from information obtained from Innovative Technology International, Inc.

*A magician demonstrates Dragon's Breath, which produces a large puff of flame when sprayed into a fire. Dragon's Breath is a fine yellowish powder consisting of club-moss spores and called lycopodium. This powder does not burn in bulk, but the fine particles produced by spraying it into a fire burn because of a high air (oxygen)-to-powder ratio.*

## Flashes and fires

Photographic flash powder, used for special effects by magicians and in the theater, has two components. The metallic component is a mixture of powdered magnesium and powdered aluminum. The second component is an oxidizer, potassium perchlorate, $KClO_4$. After the two components have been mixed, the powder can be ignited by a spark to produce a brilliant flash similar to that of a modern flash bulb. This material is highly unstable and can explode if contained.

Dragon's Breath, also available from magicians' supply stores, produces a large billow of flame when sprayed into a fire. Dragon's breath is a fine yellowish powder composed of club-moss spores and called lycopodium. Although the lycopodium does not burn in bulk, the process of spraying it into a fire results in a dust explosion as the fine particles burn owing to a high air (oxygen)-to-powder ratio. A magician will spray lycopodium from a small rubber bulb into a fire to produce a large billow of flame for special effects during a performance.

172

Sparklers in gold, red, green, and blue colors are manufactured in Taiwan and in Hunan, China, and are often used to decorate birthday cakes or similar items for parties or for celebrating holidays. A sparkler consists of a metal wire about three-fourths covered with a silver or colored hard material. The combustible material most commonly consists of sodium and/or potassium nitrates (chlorates may be used) combined with sulfur and carbon. The sparks are provided by powdered metals such as iron, aluminum, or magnesium. The metal powder is coated with paraffin wax to prevent oxidation during storage and to allow the metal to fall off the sparkler as it burns, producing the characteristic sparks. Colors are produced by adding salts of strontium (red), barium (green), and copper (blue); when these salts have been added, however, it is more difficult to light the sparkler. A lighted sparkler should be kept away from the face and body as well as away from any flammable material. At the completion of combustion, the wire will be hot.

Magic Snakes are small pellets that, when ignited, "grow" into long, curving columns of ash resembling a snake. Originally they were com-

*Sparklers (left) are often used to celebrate holidays. A sparkler consists of a metal wire, three-fourths of which is covered with a hard combustible material. This usually is composed of sodium and/or potassium nitrates combined with sulfur and carbon. The sparks are provided by powdered metals such as iron and aluminum. The metal powder is coated with paraffin wax to prevent oxidation during storage and to allow the metal to fall off the sparkler as it burns. Magic Snakes (below) are small pellets (left) that "grow" into long, curving columns of ash when ignited (right). The pellets are made of a naphthol pitch that has been mixed with linseed oil, treated with nitric acid, washed and air dried, and then broken up and treated with picric acid.*

posed of mercury(II) thiocyanate, $Hg(CNS)_2$, which was bound into a pellet by using dextrin or a gum. However, because of the toxic nature of the mercury(II) thiocyanate and of the combustion product, mercury vapors, the mercury compound has been replaced. The black, nonmercury snakes now available are composed of a naphthol pitch that has been mixed with linseed oil, treated with nitric acid, washed and air dried, and then broken up and further treated with picric acid. The product is then mixed with gum arabic, pelleted, and dried.

## Cap guns

Cap guns and caps have long been popular items in toy stores. Caps used in cap guns usually contain 0.2 grains or less of a pyrotechnical material composed of potassium chlorate, $KClO_3$; red phosphorus, $P_4$; manganese dioxide, $MnO_2$; magnesium oxide, $MgO$, or calcium carbonate, $CaCO_3$; and sand, $SiO_2$; glue is also present to bind the material together. The manganese dioxide catalyzes the decomposition of potassium chlorate to

173

form oxygen and potassium chloride. The magnesium oxide or calcium carbonate acts as an antacid to prevent deterioration due to moisture in storage. The sand helps to produce friction. The mixture of potassium chlorate and phosphorus is explosive and extremely unpredictable in any quantity.

The caps can be individual circles, rings, strips, or rolls that are loaded into cap guns and that will explode with a loud bang on impact. Scraping a cap with a rough object can cause the cap to flare or may produce a small explosion.

### Big-Bang cannons

A Big-Bang® cannon is fueled by a substance called Bangsite, which consists of powdered calcium carbide. The Bangsite is placed in a breech block on the cannon, and a small amount is emptied into the firing chamber, which contains a small amount of water. The reaction of the Bangsite with water produces acetylene:

$$CaC_2 \ + \ H_2O \longrightarrow CaO \ + \ C_2H_2$$

calcium      water                calcium      acetylene
carbide                            oxide

The acetylene mixes with the oxygen that is in the air within the firing chamber. When a spark is produced by the firing mechanism, the acetylene burns rapidly to produce carbon dioxide and water vapor:

$$2\,C_2H_2 + 5\,O_2 \longrightarrow 4\,CO_2 + 2\,H_2O$$

This rapid burning produces heat and results in the almost instantaneous expansion of the gases. This expansion forces the gases out of the muzzle of the cannon. The combustion of the remaining gases is completed outside the cannon, leaving a partial vacuum outside the muzzle

*Diagram below shows the action of a Big-Bang cannon. Powdered calcium carbide, called Bangsite, is placed in a breech block on the cannon (top left), and a small amount of it is then emptied into the firing chamber, which contains a small quantity of water (top right). The Bangsite reacts with the water to produce acetylene, which then mixes with the oxygen that is in the air in the firing chamber. A spark produced by the cannon's firing mechanism begins the process that leads to the explosion (bottom).*

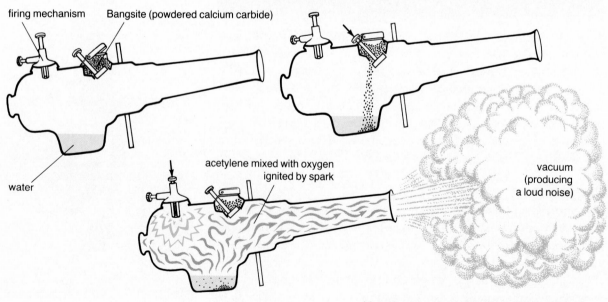

firing mechanism    Bangsite (powdered calcium carbide)

water

acetylene mixed with oxygen ignited by spark

vacuum (producing a loud noise)

Adapted from information obtained from The Conestoga Company, Inc.

and within the cannon. The resulting "inrush" of the atmosphere to fill the void produces a loud noise. Repeating the procedure without allowing fresh air to enter the cannon will result in a muffled bang—because of the lack of oxygen for complete rapid combustion—along with a yellow flash and black smoke at the mouth of the cannon.

*The fuel Bangsite is loaded into a Big-Bang cannon.*

FOR ADDITIONAL READING

Frederick J. Almgren, Jr., and Jean E. Taylor, "The Geometry of Soap Films and Soap Bubbles," *Scientific American* (July 1976, pp. 82–93).

Charles V. Boys, *Soap Bubbles: Their Colors and the Forces Which Mold Them* (Dover, 1959).

Peter S. Stevens, *Patterns in Nature* (Boston, Little, Brown, 1974).

Jearl Walker, "Serious Fun with Polyox, Silly Putty, Slime and Other Non-Newtonian Fluids," *Scientific American* (November 1978, pp. 186–196).

Jearl Walker, "When Different Powders Are Shaken, They Seem to Have Lives of Their Own," *Scientific American* (September 1982, pp. 206–216).

# the Business of
# BABEL
## Cryptology in the '80s

*by David Kahn*

The secret art of cryptology, once
a jealously guarded weapon of national
governments, has become a daily necessity
in the corporate world and an active
field of mathematical research.

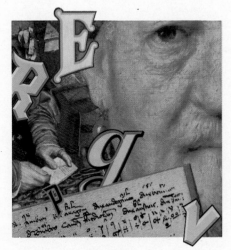

In the fall of 1978 a radio ham in suburban Connecticut overheard some conversations coming from a car radiotelephone in the area. They concerned an impending business deal, and the person in the car seemed to be named Pierre. The eavesdropper called the *Wall Street Journal*, which tentatively identified one of the firms in the deal as AMAX, Inc., a large mining company, and the speaker in the car as its chairman, Pierre Gousseland. The newspaper printed a story that said so. The company denied it. But the deal, which had been rumored for days, never went through—and AMAX stopped using its mobile phone.

On Long Island more recently, another radio ham listened to a woman talking from her car phone to her friend. "I'll talk fast," she said. "Murray's in the florist's. Did you take a lesson from the club's new tennis pro yet?" She said "lesson" with special emphasis, and when her friend asked her what she meant, she described a non-serve-and-volley-type lesson the pro gave. "He's fantastic," she concluded. The radio ham wondered what her husband would have thought had he, too, overheard it.

An oil firm engaged in highly competitive bidding for leases in Alaska put a computer terminal near possible oil lands, from where it presumably transmitted and received information on financial strategies based on the geologic potential. The terminal was linked to a computer in one of the lower 48 states. The firm began to notice that it was being repeatedly outbid by only small amounts. One day it discovered the reason: an identical terminal in a shack a few miles down the road was tapped into the line connecting the company's terminal with the computer. It could only have belonged to a competitor.

The gain in power that accrues to one person from the surreptitious acquisition of information about another was, from the Renaissance until today, almost exclusively a function of government. In curtained, candle-lit chambers, ruffed divines and mathematicians broke codes to further the grand designs of their absolute monarchs. And governments sought, usually successfully, to keep their ability in this area secret. "It is not consistent with the public safety," ruled Britain's House of Lords in 1723, "to ask the Decypherers any questions, which may tend to discover the Art or Mystery of Decyphering." Two centuries later the fact that the British had solved hundreds of thousands of German enciphered messages, or cryptograms, enabling the Allies to sink submarines and win battle after battle on land, was the greatest secret of World War II after the atom bomb.

But what for centuries had been a secret only of state has become a factor of importance to executives and individuals concerned with their privacy. Two technological developments have destroyed governments' monopoly in secret communications: radio and computers. Radio has made it easier than telegraphy or the mail did for a third party secretly to obtain verbal and data messages, which are nowadays increasingly transmitted between microwave towers, between car telephones, and by satellite. Computers have made it relatively easy—easier than penetrating locked safes and filing cabinets—to gain surreptitious access to information. As a consequence cryptology has gone public.

*DAVID KAHN, an editor with* Newsday, *the Long Island daily, is author of* The Codebreakers *and* Kahn on Codes: New Secrets of Cryptology.

*Illustrations by John Craig*

178

## Spreading concern for security

For years the public and business have resisted cryptology. It costs money. It adds people. It invites errors. Normal precautions—for example, discretion on the telephone or keeping confidential data out of the computer and in locked files—generally suffice. Moreover, most computer capers are inside jobs, which cryptology cannot prevent. And many executives believe, probably rightly, that rivals do not eavesdrop on them because the effort is too great and too dangerous for the expected return.

It may take a case in data exposure as sensational as the Chernobyl disaster was in nuclear energy to bring home to most executives the need for cryptology. That such an event has not yet occurred has been the major obstacle to success for salesmen of cryptographic devices. But a number of less dramatic episodes have helped to raise public and business consciousness about security in communications and computers.

Youthful computer enthusiasts have "hacked" into the electronic files of distant hospitals and businesses in recent years, sometimes just to read the files out of curiosity, sometimes to change them out of mischief, sometimes to alter them to get money, goods, or services. Government officials and defectors have disclosed that the Soviet Union intercepts defense-related U.S. telephone conversations from posts near Washington, in San Francisco, and on Long Island, and has bugged the U.S. embassy in Moscow. In 1985 U.S. Pres. Ronald Reagan spoke in the clear with Secretary of Defense Caspar Weinberger about the terrorist seizing of the Italian ship *Achille Lauro*—and was overheard by a radio amateur—because the electronic voice encoder-decoders, or scramblers, in their respective airplanes were not compatible. Subscription television broadcasters have begun to scramble their satellite-transmitted programs, making them unavailable to the thousands of Americans who had bought satellite dishes but refused to pay for decoders.

British intelligence official F. W. Winterbotham's bestseller, *The Ultra Secret*, published in 1974, revealed that the Allies had solved the German Enigma cipher machine and that their solutions had greatly accelerated their victory in World War II. Later a nationwide television news show broadcast a segment on this, and new details have kept the story alive. In the 1970s university scientists claimed that the National Security Agency (NSA), the U.S. government's code-breaking and code-making center (*see* sidebar, page 180), had deliberately weakened a cipher system proposed for communication with government computers not involved in national security. The system was said to be strong enough to keep businesses from cracking it but weak enough to let the NSA solve it.

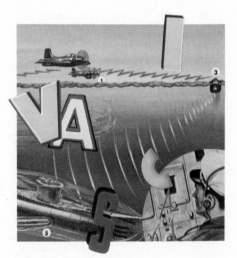

The growing sophistication of the media—and, therefore, presumably of the public—about cryptology is evidenced by the obituary on U.S. network television of a naval codebreaker. He was presented as an unsung hero whose solutions had saved uncounted lives in World War II. That the network thought the public would be interested testifies to its belief in a wider awareness of codes than existed a decade earlier.

At the same time, growing government concern about the potential for the Communist bloc to glean information by monitoring even private

179

## America's big ear

National Security Agency headquarters,
Fort Meade, Maryland.
U.S. Department of Defense

The National Security Agency is the chief code-making and code-breaking organization of the U.S. Within the Department of Defense, it was founded Nov. 4, 1952, by a secret directive of Pres. Harry S. Truman. It is headquartered in a heavily protected complex of modernistic buildings at Fort Meade, Maryland.

Pres. Ronald Reagan's Executive Order No. 12333 of Dec. 4, 1981, assigns it, among other duties, the "collection of signals intelligence information for national foreign intelligence purposes in accordance with guidance from the Director of Central Intelligence" and "executing the responsibilities of the Secretary of Defense as executive agent for the communications security of the United States Government."

The NSA's raw intelligence material consists largely of signals transmitted by foreign radars and radios—messages between people, between computers, from satellites, or from missiles. These are intercepted by U.S. "ferret" satellites and by thousands of radio intercept operators in planes, on ships, and at ground posts around the world. The NSA attempts to crack the cryptosystems in which messages are encased and evaluates the content of solved and plain-language messages to determine foreign nations' strength and intentions. It passes this information to the Central Intelligence Agency for ultimate use by the president and other policymakers.

In 1972, for example, the NSA reported on the Soviet negotiating position during the Strategic Arms Limitation Talks (SALT I). U.S. diplomats maneuvered with it so effectively that they came home with the agreement not to build an antiballistic missile defense system. Walter Mondale, while on the Senate Intelligence Committee, said that he considered the NSA's "work to be possibly the single most important source of intelligence for this nation." But for many years the NSA also improperly eavesdropped on the telephone calls of U.S. citizens.

The NSA's signal security side, less glamorous but more important than its intelligence-gathering operation, devises cryptosystems and procedures to keep the U.S.'s secrets secret as they pass between Washington and generals, admirals, and ambassadors. The delicately balanced strength of the Data Encryption Standard's 56-bit key resulted from a compromise between the two halves of the NSA, one wanting U.S. messages to be truly secure and the other wanting to read foreign DES messages.

communications has led to a presidential directive to help the private sector secure its messages. National Security Decision Directive 145, issued in 1984, is also seen as the NSA's attempt to recapture the cryptologic genie that has escaped from its bottle, to regain control of all cryptology—including private—in the U.S. The directive sets up an elaborate hierarchy, starting with a Cabinet-level committee, to supervise communications security (comsec) throughout the government, extends government communications security control to "unclassified but sensitive information," and mandates the NSA to offer communications security advice to firms that do not even have defense contracts. But opposition has arisen to this sweeping control. Bills have been introduced in Congress to divide defense communications from civil and to put the latter under the jurisdiction of the Commerce Department.

The systems that the NSA is proposing for government and business to protect their messages are not the thick codebooks or the ponderous electromechanical cipher machines made familiar by spy novels or nonfiction best-sellers. Most ciphers today are embodied in the integrated circuits of computer chips. These chips make possible much more complicated and, therefore, potentially stronger systems that also run faster and introduce fewer errors than older cryptosystems.

### Basic strategies

Cryptologists now often divide cipher systems into two types. Block ciphers break the plaintext (the original message) into segments, or blocks, and encrypt one block after another. Stream ciphers encrypt the individual plaintext symbols in succession. Stream ciphers have been more common throughout history. An example is the simplest form of substitution cipher, in which each plaintext letter is replaced by a ciphertext letter, number, or symbol. An instance from the Renaissance is reproduced below.

Such messages are as easily solved as those appearing as puzzles in many daily newspapers. Running words together obliterates many clues, but it does not invalidate the basic method of cryptanalysis: frequency

236

analysis. This technique depends upon the fact that the relative commonness of the letters in English (or in any language) is fairly constant. The stability reflects both a language's phonetic patterns and people's need to refer often to such relationships as those represented by "the," "of," and "her." As a consequence, in most English texts of 200 letters or more, whether Shakespeare or a sports story, "e" will be the most common letter, having a frequency of about 13%. This means that, if a cryptanalyst finds "x" to be the most common letter in a cryptogram whose plaintext is thought to be in English, he can try "x" as "e" to break into the cipher. Other frequency characteristics can help. Three high-frequency letters that do not appear together very often are "a," "i," and "o"; a high-frequency letter that follows vowels in four-fifths of its appearances is "n"; the most common letter pair is "th." With the aid of these characteristics and with guessing, the cryptanalyst can reconstruct the plaintext.

While frequency analysis is a powerful weapon of codebreaking, it can be blunted by not always using the same substitute for a given letter. One way of doing this, called polyalphabetic substitution, is to apply to each letter a key that will determine which substitute the original letter will receive. Different keys will produce different ciphertexts. Today, because of the application of computers, plaintext letters are often represented by groups of zeros and ones—binary digits, or bits. Keys exist in the same form. To encipher a letter, the key bits are added to the plaintext bits. This is done modulo 2, or according to the following rules for adding binary digits: $0 + 0 = 0$, $1 + 1 = 0$, $1 + 0 = 1$, $0 + 1 = 1$. One common binary representation of "a" is the Baudot teletypewriter code 11000. If the key bits are 10011, they will, when added to 11000, produce the ciphertext 01011. If, however, the key bits are 01001, the ciphertext will be 10001.

How, then, can the key bits be generated? The sequence should be long and should be hard for a cryptanalyst to extend forward or backward were he somehow to recover part of it. Such a key is often produced these days by shift registers.

A shift register is an electronic device that consists of a line of connected memory elements. These elements are filled initially with zeros and ones, which the device moves down the line from one element to the next. Cryptographic shift registers contain feedback circuits: the contents of some of the elements are copied by taps and electronically added to or multiplied by one another; the result is fed back into the register's first element, pushing the other digits down one space and outputting the last zero or one. The process then repeats many times, generating a complex sequence of binary digits that can serve as a key. Of course, the electronic circuitry of the register and its initial fill must be known to the intended recipient of the cryptogram but be kept secret from everyone else. Shift registers produce stream ciphers.

If the register has relatively few elements, and if the feedbacks are only added together, a cryptanalyst who obtains or guesses the plaintext for a portion of the cryptogram twice as long as the register length will

182

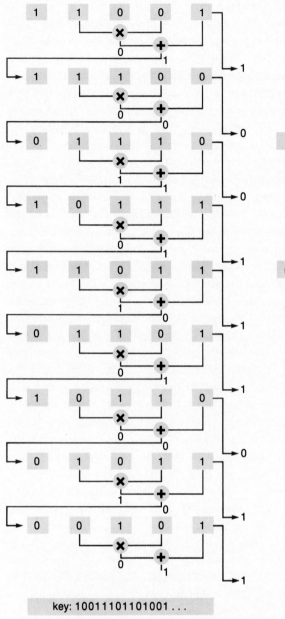

addition modulo 2

$0 + 0 = 0$

$1 + 1 = 0$

$1 + 0 = 1$

$0 + 1 = 1$

multiplication modulo 2

$0 \times 0 = 0$

$0 \times 1 = 0$

$1 \times 0 = 0$

$1 \times 1 = 1$

key: 10011101101001...

be able to reconstruct the shift register and its initial state. He then will be able to read other cryptograms. To help avoid these weaknesses, shift registers must be nonlinear. This requires that the taps be not just added together but multiplied together before the result is fed back into the register. In multiplication modulo 2, $0 \times 0 = 0$, $0 \times 1 = 0$, $1 \times 0 = 0$, $1 \times 1 = 1$. Because three of the four multiplications yield zero as a product, the operation introduces a discontinuity, or nonlinearity, that makes it much harder to trace the feedback circuits and initial state. A simple but effective way of generating nonlinear sequences is to multiply together the output of two linear registers. Properly done, this procedure can produce an extremely long and hard-to-reconstruct sequence.

183

## The Data Encryption Standard

Although shift registers serve widely in many cipher devices today, there exists another commonly used, but totally different, cipher: the Data Encryption Standard (DES). Horst Feistel, an IBM scientist who foresaw some broadened horizons for cryptography, devised the DES system in the late 1960s. IBM offered it in 1974, with modifications, to the U.S. National Bureau of Standards in response to the bureau's advertisement for a standard cipher that could be used by government agencies and those who wished to communicate with them to protect messages and files that were confidential but not related to national security.

But a year later, when the bureau proposed the IBM system as its Data Encryption Standard, protests exploded. One problem was that IBM refused to make public the design criteria for a set of substitution tables used in the DES. Critics feared that this secrecy was hiding a weakness in the system and that someone knowing the design criteria could open a "trapdoor" in the maze of the cipher and reach a solution relatively quickly. IBM replied that in developing substitution tables for the cipher that were stronger than randomly produced ones, it had hit upon principles that the National Security Agency used in its classified systems and wanted kept secret. Moreover, the NSA had tested the future DES for IBM and pronounced it secure.

Instead of calming fears, however, this exacerbated them. Many potential users thought that IBM had, in fact, left a trapdoor in the DES about which the NSA knew and that it could exploit. Another problem stemmed from the fact that the system's strength depends critically on the length of the binary key, which the NSA wanted set at 56 bits. If the key were, to take an absurd example, only one bit long, a cryptanalyst would have only two keys to try. Feistel's original cipher had used 128 bits, and some cryptologists argued for as many as 728, claiming that this would make messages insoluble forever, no matter how fast or how cheap computers got. They claimed that the NSA was advocating a 56-bit key because 48 bits or fewer would allow too many people to solve messages in the cipher while 64 bits or more would make solution too costly even for the NSA should it want to decode any messages. They saw as significant that the NSA would not allow the proposed system to be used for really important, national-security messages.

Articles about the controversy appeared in the technical and general press; workshops were held by the National Bureau of Standards to quiet the fears. Eventually city hall won out. The IBM system became the Data Encryption Standard for the U.S. in July 1977. It rapidly gained broad acceptance. Today dozens of firms manufacture chips for it and cryptosystems using it. Ironically, its very success has doomed it for future government use. Because its wide employment may have made it a lucrative target for foreign cryptanalysts, cipher devices provided under National Security Decision Directive 145 will not use it. But the private sector still employs it extensively, for example, in communicating between automatic teller machines and the bank's central computer, and it remains probably the most widely used cryptosystem in history.

The DES, a block cipher, is so complicated that it was made practical—fast and accurate enough—only by the computer. The system cannot be said to be elegant or to have interesting mathematical properties. Rather it gains its strength from its twistings and foldings, rather like an exceedingly convoluted knot. (*See* sidebar, pages 186–187.)

The cipher's great complexity, paradoxically, has brought it under fire. It is so complicated that its users have never been able to analyze it thoroughly and are unable to predict all its qualities. As a consequence, researchers often find potential weaknesses, such as weak keys. Nevertheless, the DES—provided it is hiding no trapdoors—is an excellent cipher. No method of solution has been proposed in the open literature outside of trying all possible keys. Of course, as was mentioned above, the key length is critical. If it is too short, solution is not hard. If it is very long—several hundred bits—then, even when a cryptanalyst has been given the plaintext for a given cryptogram, testing to discover the proper key will take centuries, even with the most advanced computers.

## Public-key cryptography

The DES and the shift-register cryptosystems require that both encrypter and decrypter have the same key, though one may apply it forward and the other in reverse. This key must be got to the two parties from a central point by a secure means; for example, a courier carrying it in a locked briefcase or in an electronic "gun" that can automatically load the key into the machine. This necessity requires a prearrangement about keys as well as a secure channel for transporting them, which is usually separate from, and slower than, telecommunications channels.

In 1976 an idea surfaced that eliminated these disadvantages. It permitted secret communication without either prearrangement or a separate secure channel. It was the most original idea in cryptology since the

*Mechanical German Enigma cipher machine from World War II (bottom) is compared with one of the smallest cipher devices available today—a set of encryption/decryption chips intended for applications ranging from computers and telephones to wireless pagers and remote control devices.*

(Left) courtesy, Motorola, Inc.

## How the DES works

Like all ciphers, the Data Encryption Standard uses a key. The active part consists of 56 binary digits. Eight others are added as checks of parity (the state of being odd or even) to ensure that the first 56 have not been changed, either by accident or on purpose. The 56 bits that actually control the encryption undergo a complex process before they are applied to the plaintext. They are first shuffled, or permuted, according to a known pattern and then divided in half. This prepares them for use as subkeys in the encryption's 16 iterations, or rounds.

For the first iteration the 28 bits of each half are shifted one space to the left, with each half's first bit moving to last place. Copies of these halves are stored for the next iteration. Then the two halves are put back together; the bits in eight certain positions—the 9th, 18th, 22nd, 25th, 35th, 38th, 43rd, and 54th—are discarded, and the 48 remaining bits are shuffled in accordance with a particular design. They serve as the subkey in the first round. For the second round, each of the copied halves is shifted one place to the left. Again, copies of the new sequences are made and stored for the next iteration, while the sequences themselves drop the eight bits and are mixed for use as key in that second iteration. Subsequent rounds follow the same routine, except that some of the shifts move the bits of the halves two places to the left instead of just one. In the 16 iterations the shifts to the left total to 28 places, the number of bits in each half.

The encryption itself, which these shifting subkeys govern, is done in blocks of 64 binary digits. Consequently, all plaintexts to be enciphered must be in binary form and divided into 64-bit blocks. The encryption consists of 16 repetitions of the following process:

The block of 64 plaintext bits is shuffled in a fixed way—the 58th bit of the block becomes the first bit, the 50th becomes the second, and so on. Because this permutation is known, it offers no additional security but it does destroy patterns such as those of formatting or of stereotyped beginnings and thus presents a somewhat randomized sequence to the rest of the operation. The 64 jumbled bits are divided into a right and a left half. A copy of the right half is made and put aside; in the next round this copy will be moved to become the left half. The original right half is expanded from 32 bits to 48 by repeating some of the bits. For example, the 4th, 5th, 8th, 9th, and others appear twice.

The 48 bits are now added modulo 2 to the 48 bits of the subkey for that round. This sum is divided into eight groups of six bits each. Within each group the first and last bits are cut from the group and put together, leaving the four central bits as another subgroup. Thus 100001 would become 11 and 0000. The tetrad indicates the column and the pair the row in which a substitute for the original six-bit group will be found in a table made up of four rows and 16 columns. Eight such substitution tables exist, one for each group. The table for the first six-bit group is shown below.

|    | 0000 | 0001 | 0010 | 0011 | 0100 | 0101 | 0110 | 0111 | 1000 | 1001 | 1010 | 1011 | 1100 | 1101 | 1110 | 1111 |
|----|------|------|------|------|------|------|------|------|------|------|------|------|------|------|------|------|
| 00 | 1110 | 0100 | 1101 | 0001 | 0010 | 1111 | 1011 | 1000 | 0011 | 1010 | 0110 | 1100 | 0101 | 1001 | 0000 | 0111 |
| 01 | 0000 | 1111 | 0111 | 0100 | 1110 | 0010 | 1101 | 0001 | 1010 | 0110 | 1100 | 1011 | 1001 | 0101 | 0011 | 1000 |
| 10 | 0100 | 0001 | 1110 | 1000 | 1101 | 0110 | 0010 | 1011 | 1111 | 1100 | 1001 | 0111 | 0011 | 1010 | 0101 | 0000 |
| 11 | 1111 | 1100 | 1000 | 0010 | 0100 | 1001 | 0001 | 0111 | 0101 | 1011 | 0011 | 1110 | 1010 | 0000 | 0110 | 1101 |

In this table the substitute for the original 100001 would be found at the intersection of row 11 and column 0000. This is 1111. In the next table the substitute for 100001 is 1101. All eight groups undergo this substitution. The substitution shrinks each group from six to four, undoing the earlier expansion and reducing the half block to its original size of 32 bits. These bits are then permuted according to a fixed formula that moves the 16th bit to the first position, the 7th to the second, and so on. The 32 bits in their new order are then added modulo 2 to the 32 bits of the left half of the original block. The sum becomes the right half of the block for the next round of encryption; the saved right-half copy becomes the left half. Then the next iteration repeats the entire procedure. After the 16th round the two halves are butted together, and the 64 bits undergo a reversal of the initial permutation. The output becomes the cipher block that is transmitted.

DES messages are decrypted by acting on the bits in each round as if they were being encrypted but by running the rounds from 16 to 1. The procedure is made possible by the inverse permutation at the end and by the "autokey" feature—the adding together within each round of the two halves.

The cipher's strength derives from several characteristics that have been realized in extremely clever ways. One characteristic is nonlinearity. The cipher's output is not related either directly or inversely to its input. The disjunction occurs in the substitution tables. That 100001 is replaced by 1111 in the first table is purely arbitrary. The lack of functional or logical connection is shown by the fact that in the next table 100001 gets 1101 as its substitute. The tables themselves are made practicable by what amounts to an ingenious shift in number base from binary (i.e., base 2) to hexadecimal (base 16). It is not possible to construct a table that would substitute all possible groups of six bits into all other possible groups of six bits, for this would require internal connections totaling $2^6!$ or 64! (read "64 factorial"; that is, $64 \times 63 \times 62 \times \ldots \times 1$) or $1.2689 \times 10^{89}$ internal connections. The DES avoids this by expanding the right half from 32 to 48 bits, in effect representing each group of four

plaintext bits by six and permitting the construction of a table with $4 \times 16$ or 64 connections. This makes the arbitrary substitution feasible.

A second characteristic is singularity. This means that a transformation is not invertible. The singular transformations in the DES consist of the replacement, through the table, of six bits by four. Different six-bit groups can produce identical four-bit groups. For example, in the first table 011100, 000001, 111110, and 111011 all yield 0000. A cryptanalyst who might want to trace his way backward through the DES is faced here with four choices as the possible input for 0000. This multiplies his difficulties. Normally, the reduction of six elements to four would cost information, but this is prevented by the earlier reduplication of bits, which adds redundancy.

A third characteristic is strong intersymbol dependence. In the DES each cipher bit results from the interplay of all the plaintext and all the key bits. This interdependence stems from (1) the shift of the key bits, which puts all of them to work at all positions; (2) the repeated permutations, which thoroughly mix the plaintext bits; and (3) the adding of the two halves of the plaintext block, which makes them influence one another. This produces an avalanche effect in which the change of a single bit in a plaintext block yields a totally different ciphertext block. For example, a 64-bit plaintext block entirely of zeros becomes, under a certain key, 11000100 11010111 00101100 10011101 11101110 11011110 01011110 10001011. By comparison, a plaintext block consisting of a 1 followed by 63 zeros becomes, under the same key, 00101100 10010111 01100000 01110110 10100111 00000101 10001101 01000100. The one-bit change has spread throughout the ciphertext. The disadvantage of such interdependence is that an error in a single ciphertext bit will render the entire 64-bit block unintelligible. But the error is at least confined to the block.

development of polyalphabetic substitution ciphers in the Renaissance. It appeared in "New Directions in Cryptography," an article in the November 1976 *IEEE Transactions on Information Theory* by Martin Hellman, a professor of electrical engineering at Stanford University, and Whitfield Diffie, his student. Though this was the first unclassified discussion of the concept, various items of evidence indicate that U.S. or British cryptologists had invented it earlier; the NSA declines to confirm this.

Diffie and Hellman proposed using one key for encryption and another, different key for decryption. A communicator's encryption key could be made public, so that anyone could send him a secret message. But he would keep his decryption key to himself, so that only he could read the encrypted message. The keys would have to be related in such a way that, though one would unlock the other, knowledge of the encryption key would not permit reconstruction of the decryption key.

Diffie and Hellman offered the idea, which they called public-key cryptography, and some suggestions, but no usable systems. But the seeming impossibility of the trick stimulated many people to come up with an answer.

Three mathematicians and computer scientists at the Massachusetts Institute of Technology, Ronald Rivest, Len Adleman, and Adi Shamir, devised an elegant solution. It depends on two characteristics of large numbers that are the product of two large primes. (Primes are numbers divisible only by 1 and themselves.) One of the characteristics is that it is easy to tell whether a large number is a prime or not. The other is that it is hard—at least at present—to determine the factors of a large number once the number is found to be nonprime. On the difference in difficulty between these two problems rests the difference between the encrypting and decrypting keys in the system they proposed.

The RSA (Rivest-Shamir-Adleman) system, as it is called, employs five numbers. Two of them, $n$ and $e$, are public and serve for the encryption; they are derived from three other numbers, $d$, $p$, and $q$, that are kept secret and serve for the decryption. To be encrypted, a message must be converted to numerical form; for instance, "a" = 01, "b" = 02, etc. A long message can be divided into segments of, say, ten digits. Each segment is then multiplied by itself $e$ times, the product is divided by $n$, and the remainder is taken as the ciphertext. In mathematical terms, the plaintext is raised to the $e$th power modulo $n$ to produce the ciphertext.

To be decrypted, the ciphertext is multiplied by itself $d$ times, the product is divided by $n$, and the remainder is the numerical plaintext. In other words, the ciphertext is raised to the $d$th power modulo $n$.

How are $d$, $n$, and $e$ found? Their derivation begins with the random selection of $p$ and $q$. These must be two large prime numbers, each perhaps about 100 digits long. (Such are not hard to find. Primes occur about every 100 numbers or so in the 100-digit range.) Multiplying them together yields $n$. Then, $d$ is another large number chosen at random except for one condition: it must be relatively prime to the product $(p-1)(q-1)$; that is, 1 must be the only number that can be divided into both $d$ and $(p-1)(q-1)$. This relationship is easy to check: a method devised by

188

Euclid finds the greatest common denominator of two numbers; if this denominator is 1, they are prime to one another, though they may not be primes themselves. Finally, $e$ is computed from $p$, $q$, and $d$: $p - 1$ is multiplied by $q - 1$ and the product divided by $d$; the remainder is $e$. This is the multiplicative inverse of $d$ and guarantees that encryption and decryption are inverse operations. The use of modular arithmetic—the raising to powers in the encryption and decryption is done modulo $n$—"closes" the operation, permitting recovery of the plaintext, which would not be possible in ordinary "open-ended" arithmetic.

The system's secrecy resides in the fact that making $n$ public does not disclose its prime factors $p$ and $q$ because of the difficulty of finding the multiplier and multiplicand of a large number. The problem is an old one, and mathematicians of the caliber of Pierre de Fermat and Adrien-Marie Legendre have worked on it, but all the factoring methods known are slow. Factoring a 200-digit number with one of the faster methods known today, doing a million operations a second, would require almost four billion years. The danger in the system is that someone may come along at any moment with an easy way to factor large numbers, for no one has proved that breaking a large number down into its factors is necessarily hard. Furthermore, factoring numbers is currently an intensely active field of research, and mathematicians are bringing ever more powerful computers and computing techniques to bear on the problem. When the RSA system was proposed, 80-digit numbers were considered unfactorable. Today cryptologic researchers are suggesting 200-digit numbers for safety.

## The appeal of public-key systems

Public-key cryptography, or asymmetric or one-way encryption, as it is sometimes called, can help solve two of the most vexing problems in secret communications. One is to eliminate the burden of distributing keys secretly to correspondents. In a telephone or telex network, for example, one person often calls another whom he does not know. To give each subscriber the keys to all the others is, in a large net, administratively impossible. Public keys eliminate this need; each caller just uses the called party's public encryption key. Each subscriber's public key can be printed in a book like a telephone directory and distributed throughout the network. And although public keys often run too slowly for direct use by computers or in speech, they can serve instead to encrypt the keys of faster systems; these keys are then transmitted in this secret form to the recipient.

The other problem that public-key cryptography can help resolve is that of authenticating messages, of making sure that they come from the person they purport to come from. Pen-and-ink signatures testify to the writer, but electronic signatures do not; the latter can easily be forged by either sender or receiver. If, however, they are represented by numbers, public-key cryptography enables them to be put into a form that excludes tampering and thus validates them to both parties. Suppose two suspicious lovers want to make sure that the electronic valentines they

189

receive really come from one another. The ingenious system invented by the three at MIT works like this: He uses his private decryption key (not his public encryption key) to encrypt his love letter (which is, perhaps less than romantically, in numerical form). The result is his signature. He encrypts this with her public key and transmits it to her. She decrypts it with her private key. She now has his signature. She then applies his public encryption key to this, reversing his first encryption and extracting his love letter. He cannot deny the missive, for nobody else knows the private decryption key with which he began. By the same token, she knows that only he could have written the message. Finally, she cannot alter his letter, for it depends upon his private key. The message is thus authenticated.

Press reports touted public-key cryptography as more secure than the older, symmetric systems. This is a misconception. It is certainly more secure than some of the simpler symmetric systems, and it is true that so far nobody has broken the RSA. Nevertheless, at least one other group of asymmetric systems based on a different type of hard mathematical problem, the knapsack problem, has been broken, and the RSA system depends for its security upon the hope that no one will find a fast method of factoring large numbers. By contrast, some of the better symmetric systems, such as the DES with a long enough key, can be demonstrated to be secure even in the face of advances in mathematics and computer speed.

Public-key cryptography can serve in electronic funds transfers by authenticating a transaction. And it will be used to exchange encrypted keys between communicators in the vast, U.S.-government-backed program under National Security Decision Directive 145 to secure the nation's data and voice communciations.

## Cryptosecurity for everyman

This program requires that computers and telecommunications handling classified national-security information be "secured," that such systems handling unclassified but sensitive government information "the loss of which could adversely affect the national security interest" be "protected," and that the government help the private sector to identify possible leaks and to take measures to stop them "in proportion to the threat of exploitation and the associated potential damage." The NSA hopes to have distributed half a million secure telephones throughout the government and to defense contractors by 1991 and to have thousands of encryption devices embedded in office microcomputers.

The NSA will use two levers in doing this job. One is to make security cheap. NSA officials believe that, if security adds no more than 5% to the cost of a device, firms will pay for the extra protection. In large measure the costs can be kept down by designing a security module into the telephone or the personal computer. Such incorporation eliminates both the expense of stand-alone encryption boxes and much of the time and nuisance that they entail. Already some three dozen major manufacturers, with NSA's help, are designing encryption options

190

for their telecommunications devices or computers. The 500,000 secure telephones will scramble talk at the mere turning of a metal key in a lock in the instrument. The economies of scale will help keep prices down. Government-quality scrambler telephones now cost some $27,000; if the three contract manufacturers manage to bring the price down to $2,000, NSA officials feel that business will buy and use scramblers widely. One official foresees 2½ million in use and so a potential market of $5 billion. In fact, however, prices have not sunk nor sales risen to these levels. By early 1987 only 60,000 scramblers had been sold, mainly to government agencies, at prices ranging from $2,600 to $4,000.

The second lever that the NSA will use to achieve its goal of wide cryptosecurity is to ensure that the security is good. For this it is designing its own algorithm, or encryption procedure, which will have to be used by government and contractors; any other firm in the private sector will be able to use either the NSA's system or its own. They will not be able to be made compatible, since the government's system will be kept secret. This system will, moreover, not be the Data Encryption Standard. Said one official, "If I were the Soviet guy, I'm not sure I'd invest the several billion it would take [to read DES messages]. But if DES continues to spread, I might." To prevent the NSA's new system from itself becoming too attractive, the NSA plans to replace it eventually with another, and that in turn with a new one, and so on, each one "backward compatible" with its predecessors.

While this effort, focusing mainly on data in transit, is beginning, another, focusing mainly on data in storage or in processing, is also gathering momentum. The NSA's Computer Security Center directs government computer users and helps private computer users to gain adequate security against such threats as "playful" or malicious intrusion into the computers to read or change data, eavesdroppers tapping computer lines to reproduce what is on a terminal's screen, or destructive programs (called "logic bombs," "Trojan horses," or "viruses") inserted among a computer's programs by disgruntled or dishonest employees.

Can the NSA succeed in this vast task? It is unprecedented in scope, in cost, and in exposure of a traditionally covert agency. It faces many problems. As insurance salesmen must, the program has to persuade people to face an unpleasant possibility and then to spend money for what many perceive as merely a contingency. Business may object that government is getting too close to its sensitive operations. Congressmen have asked whether the NSA is carrying out a national information policy made by executive fiat, which usurps the rights of the legislature. They have introduced bills to block the extension of government control to unclassified data and the NSA's monopoly of communications security by assigning civil comsec to the National Bureau of Standards. Scientists and mathematicians whose work has cryptologic implications fear for unhindered research and the unhampered flow of information; civil libertarians, for personal privacy. But perhaps the greatest problem of all is whether the NSA can stuff back into the bottle the genie that technology has let out—modern cryptology.

# Attending to

# HIDDEN MELODIES

## by W. Jay Dowling

A melody that forms part of a complex pattern of sounds can be detected more easily if a listener is familiar with it and has some idea of where it occurs within the composition.

**W. JAY DOWLING** is an Associate Professor in the Program in Human Development and Communication Sciences at the University of Texas at Dallas, Richardson.

(Overleaf) © Brian Seed—CLICK/Chicago

Picking out a well-known melody when it is embedded in an elaborate pattern of sound is difficult, yet people can do it. It seems as though they can aim their attention at the target melody they wish to hear and then hear it clearly. Hearing the target melody clearly in the midst of complex surroundings is like an auditory version of the visual "hidden figures" test—the task of "find six lions hidden in the jungle" found in children's game books. If one looks at such a drawing without being told to try to find lions, the chances are that none will be seen. But if lions are searched for actively, they eventually will be detected. In fact, after one is noticed, it seems to pop out from the background even if an effort is made to ignore it. It is the same with a previously hidden melody— once it has been noticed, it draws attention and is difficult to ignore.

Finding the lions in the drawing requires knowledge of what lions look like (or at least what simplified drawings of lions look like). It also depends on the knowledge that it is lions that should be sought, and not rabbits or umbrellas. Expecting to find lions leads a person, after searching actively, to find them if they are there. With hidden melodies also, familiarity with the target melody and the expectation of finding it help a listener to hear it clearly.

Young children visiting the "Small World" attraction at Disneyland Park in California encounter animated figures wearing the characteristic dress of various regions of the world, all singing the same song over and over again. This song consists of a set of verses (beginning "It's a world of laughter, a world of tears") and a chorus (beginning "It's a small world, after all"). There are two different tunes—one for the verse and one for the chorus—and the two tunes are repeated alternately over and over. Then at the end, as more and more voices join in singing, the two tunes are presented simultaneously by different groups of singers, along with the harmonizing accompaniment. This creates a much more elaborate and potentially confusing pattern than at the start of the song. The children listening can focus their attention on either the melodic line of the verse or that of the chorus and pick it out of the complex texture. The melody they select stands out perceptually, and the other melody recedes into the background. Having just heard each melody several times by itself, the children are able to select one of them on which to focus, and they can hear that one quite clearly in spite of the fact that it is only a small part of the total mass of sound.

The selective attention exercised by the children in listening to one melody in a complex song is an example of the kind of attention people are often called upon to exert in other situations in life—hearing a friend's voice in a noisy restaurant, detecting a child's cry through wind and rain, listening for a flight to be announced in a bustling airport concourse. Psychologists are interested in how such selective attention works. Psychologically, several processes converge in making the feat of selective attention possible. These processes draw on the listener's knowledge of the particular song, the listener's expectation that that song will be present, and the listener's implicit knowledge of the pattern of pitch relationships in melodies used in the culture.

194

Illustration by Constantino Mitchell

In the "Small World" example the child's knowledge of the particular song makes it easier to pick it out in the complex sound pattern than it would be to focus on an unfamiliar tune. Also important is the child's expectation that this particular melody is likely to be heard again, having just occurred several times earlier. The child is prepared to hear a recurrence of this melody and not, for example, "Happy Birthday" or "Jingle Bells." Familiarity with the tune, along with the expectation of hearing it, can in turn produce even more specific expectancies—expectancies that lead the child's auditory system to be ready to process each note of the melody as it occurs—to literally "follow" the melodic line note for note.

*Picking out a melody that is embedded in a complex pattern of sound is analogous to finding the six lions hidden in the jungle in this visual game; the lions are revealed on the following page.*

### Implicit knowledge and expectancies

The note-for-note expectancies that listeners have are not generally conscious. There is not time in the midst of a piece of music to stop and think, "Now, what note comes next?" But subconsciously the auditory system is actively following the progress of the tune, aiming its focus of attention at specific times when critical events—new notes—are likely to occur and also at regions of pitch (the "up" and "down" dimension of tones) where those notes should be. Thus, the auditory system enhances the clarity of reception of a target melody, picking it out of an elaborate background.

There is yet another sort of tacit, subconscious knowledge that is im-

195

*To perceive melodies it is important to be familiar with the tonal scale system on which the tunes are based. In Western culture this consists of a set of seven pitches in each octave, represented by seven successive white keys on a piano.*

portant in the perception of melodies, namely, implicit knowledge of the tonal scale system that serves as the basis for most melodies in Western culture. European folk melodies do not use all of the infinite variety of pitches that are possible to the human voice (as in imitating a fire siren) but rather use a restricted set of seven pitches in each octave, named *do - re - mi - fa - sol - la - ti* (or, for the key of C, C — D — E — F — G — A — B). These pitches are represented by the white keys on a piano, and their pattern recycles through the seven or so octaves covered by the length of the piano keyboard. Increasingly, through the age range of six to eight years, a child's implicit knowledge of this tonal system becomes more and more sophisticated. Thus, six-year-olds sing more "in tune" (by adult standards) than do four-year-olds, and eight-year-olds perform better than six-year-olds. As can be seen below, this implicit knowledge of the standard set of pitches to be expected in a melody leads the listener to convert unexpected, deviant pitches automatically into expected

196

pitches. All of this knowledge leads to enhanced efficiency in the perceptual processing of auditory events that match expectancies and helps people distinguish them when they are hidden in an elaborate pattern.

The two melodies in the "Small World" song are somewhat difficult to discern in the background unless one has heard them before and expects to hear them in the sound pattern. Nevertheless, they are set off from the background by means of a number of distinguishing characteristics: the sound qualities of the voices singing them, the stream of words being sung, the direction from which they come, their loudness. Though picking them out from the background is easier with knowledge and expectancy, an attentive adult listener could probably hear them clearly even without those aids.

Because they have distinguishing features apparent to the listener, the melodies combined in a pattern like "It's a Small World" differ from the lions in the jungle. The lions are not distinguished from their surround-

*The first page of Johann Sebastian Bach's* Partita No. 3 for Violin Solo, *written in Bach's own hand, reveals the composer's use of rapid alternation between separate regions of pitch to create an impression of two melodic lines arising out of a single succession of notes.*

197

ings by the thickness of the lines or by their color or shading but only by their lion shapes. Knowledge and expectancy are essential in lion detection because there are no obvious perceptual features by which they can be picked out. To demonstrate the analogous importance of knowledge and expectancy in the perception of melodies, then, one needs melodies that are hidden in a corresponding way in their surroundings, without any obvious distinguishing features except for their melodic shapes.

### A hidden-melodies test

To find out how listeners succeed in focusing their attention on one melody in a complex texture, one can give them a "hidden melodies" test analogous to the "hidden figures" test. In such a test the target melody is thoroughly embedded in its background and is not distinguished from it by obvious features of pitch, loudness, or sound quality. To arrive at a pattern with a melody hidden in it in that way, one might start with a pattern in which the melody is distinguished only by pitch. Composers have often used a rapid alternation between separate pitch regions to

*The first page of Johann Sebastian Bach's Cantata No. 29, in Bach's hand, suggests the difficulty of picking out a melody from the complex sound pattern of a piece written for full orchestra.*

create the impression of two melodic lines arising out of a single succession of notes. J. S. Bach in the 1720s wrote sets of pieces for violin alone, as well as for cello alone and flute alone, in which the instrument very quickly skips back and forth between two melodic lines. Figure 1 shows such a pattern with the melody "Mary Had a Little Lamb" on top and "Frère Jacques" below. The listener receives the impression of two simultaneous melodic patterns because the auditory system is unable to follow rapid changes in pitch over such a wide range. The notes making up the two melodic lines are alike in every respect except for the pitch ranges into which they fall. The listener can focus attention on one of the pitch ranges, selecting one of the melodies for perceptual emphasis and ignoring the other.

Now suppose that the difference in pitch between the two melodies in Figure 1 is eliminated. Then all the notes from both melodies will occur in the same pitch range, as shown in Figure 2. Focusing attention on one pitch range will no longer serve to distinguish either melody. When heard with no particular expectation as to what melodies it contains, a pattern like that in Figure 2 sounds like a meaningless jumble of notes. However, if the listener is told that one of the melodies is "Mary Had a Little Lamb," that melody will pop out of the complex texture and be clearly heard, much as the lion pops out of the hidden-figures drawing.

Actively listening for a specific well-known melody leads one to discern that melody in a confusing context, provided it is actually there. This selection of the target melody succeeds despite the fact that the notes of the melody are not distinguished from the irrelevant notes interleaved among them by any obvious features such as pitch or loudness or tone quality. The notes of the target are picked out of the context because they belong to the sought-for melody and thus occur at pitch levels and at times when they are expected.

## Expectancy windows

The ways in which the auditory system accomplishes the task of focusing on a target melody when it is hidden in an homogeneous background are revealed by varying the type of test given the listener. The evidence suggests that the auditory system aims a series of "expectancy windows" at regions of pitch and points in time in which notes are likely to occur (as shown in Figure 3). A person succeeds in selecting the chosen melody because attention can be organized rhythmically. The human auditory system can anticipate the occurrence of an expected event and can prepare itself to be especially sensitive and efficient at just the moment when that event is expected.

That attention can be aimed rhythmically at particular points in time is shown in the following task. The listener hears patterns like those in Figure 2, in which the notes of a familiar melody such as "Mary Had a Little Lamb" are interleaved with distractor notes in the same pitch range. The notes of the combined pattern proceed at a uniform rate. The listener is told what melody to listen for and must say whether that melody is present in the complex pattern. Half the time the tar-

Figure 1 (top) shows the melodies of "Mary Had a Little Lamb" and "Frère Jacques" interleaved in time but played in separate pitch regions. When this pattern is presented at eight or ten notes per second, a listener receives the impression of two melodies at once. But when the same tunes are presented in the same pitch range (Figure 2, bottom), they are almost impossible to distinguish from one another unless the listener is already familiar with them.

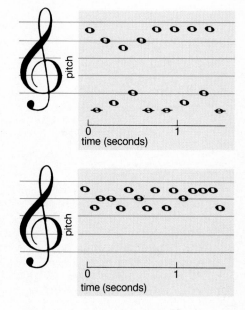

199

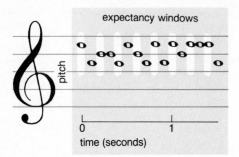

*Figure 3. "Expectancy windows" are drawn around notes of "Mary Had a Little Lamb." Notes within a window's region of pitch and time are processed more efficiently and heard more clearly than are those outside of it.*

get melody is actually present, and half the time another melody is substituted. Listeners perform this task at well above chance accuracy, achieving the correct answer about 85–90% of the time. But they do that well only in cases where the notes of the target occur *on* the beat; that is, where they are the "odd-numbered" notes (1, 3, 5, 7, etc.) in the pattern (*see* Figure 4).

If the target is shifted so as to consist of the even-numbered notes (*off* the beat), the target melody becomes much more difficult to discern, and performance falls to about 70% correct. This happens because it is more difficult to aim expectancies at off-beat time slots in the pattern. The listener has a memory record of the target melody—for example, the memory record for "Mary Had a Little Lamb." To solve the task the listener's auditory system has to match that remembered pattern against the incoming sequence of notes. This is not simple because, among all the notes entering the ears, those that are critical for the comparison do not occur all together in a row. Distractor notes fall in between each pair of target notes. The target notes must be picked out and then compared with memory. That selection is easier if the target notes are on the beat and more difficult if they are off of it.

The relative ease of handling on-beat notes in comparison with off-beat notes can be demonstrated by young musicians in their efforts to learn to play the "oom-pah-oom-pah" rhythmic pattern of marches. In a marching band the "oom" (on-beat) part of the pattern is usually played by the tubas, and they generally have little difficulty producing those notes more or less on time. The "pah" (off-beat) part of the pattern, played by the mid-range French horns, is much more difficult. Young horn players have a tendency to let their "pah" notes drift onto the beat, so that the "oom" and "pah" occur together rather than in alternation. It takes considerable practice before the French horn players learn to hear and produce the pattern accurately.

Listeners find it easier to attend selectively to on-beat notes because it is easier to align their set of expectancies to those notes. But the question then arises as to what happens if listeners are required to direct their expectancies off the beat. This can be done by constructing a pattern in which the target has a syncopated "rhumba" type of rhythm, shown in Figure 5. ("Syncopated" refers to cases in which a strongly accented, emphasized note occurs off the beat.) In this task the beginning and end-

*Figure 4. The notes of "Mary Had a Little Lamb" are shown on the beat, that is, where they are the odd-numbered notes (1, 3, 5, 7, etc.) in the pattern at right and off the beat in the pattern at far right. The melody is much easier to hear when it is on the beat.*

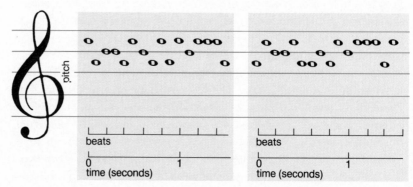

ing of the target pattern remain constant; only the middle note moves. The middle note could move up or down in pitch, and forward or backward in time, to the positions indicated on the grid. The listener's task is to focus on hearing the middle note and tell where it moved. Listeners marked their answers on a grid like the one shown in the figure.

In this task there are two ways of looking at listeners' performances that are especially informative. First, it is important to know whether the occurrence of the target note at the expected time helps a listener judge its pitch correctly. This was the case. When the target note occurred at its expected (though off-beat) time, listeners judged its pitch correctly about 40% of the time; this compared with about 30% correct for target notes occurring at unexpected (on-beat) times. Thus, knowing when to expect something helps people judge what it is when it happens.

Second, one should ask whether hearing the target note at the expected pitch helps a listener tell when the note occurred. That turned out not to be the case. Indeed, listeners were slightly better at telling when unexpected pitches occurred than they were with expected pitches. In this task knowing what to expect did not help in the judgment of when it had occurred.

The results from the tasks described above reveal that time can serve as a framework for the orienting of attention. Attention can be aimed rhythmically with reference to a structure of temporal beats, like the beats in music. It can be aimed both at regular events that occur on the beats and at occasional irregular events that, though they occur off the beat, are expected.

It was suggested above that listeners can discern a hidden melody if they aim their expectancies at a series of "windows" in the pitch/time framework. The tasks just described demonstrate the limitations of those windows in time, but the question remains as to the importance of pitch. The following task demonstrates that the region at which listeners aim attention is limited in pitch as well as in time. As before, one note in a target melody moves—in this case the next-to-last note. The target was presented interleaved with distractor notes, and the next-to-last note either stayed where it was expected in pitch or it moved up or down. As before, the listener had to follow its movement. After the interleaved pattern containing the hidden melody had been played, the listener heard a single note—a "probe" tone. This tone was either the same as the actual pitch of the moving target note or else was slightly higher or lower. If the listeners had been able to follow the critical note in the target to its new pitch, then they should have been accurate in judging the pitch of the probe as higher, lower, or the same. If, on the other hand, they had lost track of the moving note, their performance would have declined.

What happened is suggested by the attentional windows shown in Figure 6. When the pitch of the moving note occurred within the window, above or below its expected position, it was heard clearly and judged accurately. But when it fell outside the window (in this case two or three semitones outside the rest of the notes of the target melody), it was simply lost to the listener, and performance fell to about that of chance. In

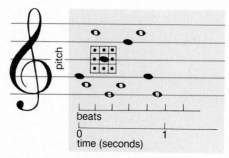

Figure 5. A target melody (solid notes) is interleaved among distractor notes. The second note of the melody can move in pitch and time to the positions indicated on the grid. When the note occurred at its expected time, listeners judged its pitch correctly about 40% of the time as compared with about 30% correct when the note occurred at unexpected times. However, hearing the note at the expected pitch did not help listeners determine when the note occurred.

Figure 6. In the interleaved target melody the next-to-last note can occur at different pitches, either within or outside of the expectancy window. The listener must judge the pitch of the following probe tone in comparison with that of the wandering target note. Listeners were far more accurate in doing this when the target note remained within the expectancy window.

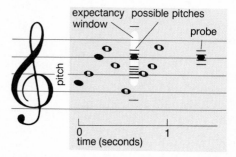

201

fact, when asked (in a separate session), the listeners could not even tell whether the errant notes had gone higher or lower in their wandering.

Performance in this task, in which the target melody was embedded in the interleaved distractor notes, stands in sharp contrast to performance in a task in which the distractor notes were removed. In that case it is easy to judge the pitches of the moving notes, especially when they move into much higher or lower positions. But when certain notes must be picked out of a rapidly moving, distracting context, listeners limit their attention in both time and pitch. They heighten their sensitivities at particular points in time and at the same time restrict them to certain limited regions of the pitch scale.

## Implicit knowledge of the musical scale

So far the tasks described show that knowledge of a familiar melody helps listeners discern it in a confusing context. Earlier in this discussion a reference was made to a more general type of knowledge that plays a role in the perception and recognition of melodies—namely, knowledge of the musical scale framework according to which pitch material in melodies is organized. That knowledge also contributes to efficient processing of expected events.

By the age of eight, children have generally internalized the major scale pattern. They have formed a mental representation of the pitch pattern, a representation that guides their production of pitches when they sing and provides for the interpretation of heard pitches when they listen. This is true of everyone—those who study music as well as those who do not. To test this assertion, one can consider the casual listeners who tune in to "top-40" (popular hits) radio stations but who have had no music lessons in their lives. If the station suddenly started playing songs that did not use the familiar scale pattern—that is, if it started playing "atonal" songs—irate listeners would call the station, demanding that it stop playing "weird" music and return to the type of music they know and love. These listeners might not know exactly what it was that made the music sound strange, but they would certainly notice deviations from their own internalized patterns and object to such changes.

Listeners' pitch judgments in the task illustrated in Figure 6 show the degree to which the mental representation of the standard pitch categories of music guides the interpretation of single pitches as they are heard in a rapid, confusing context. In that task the target note moved to a new pitch, and the listener tried to hear where it had moved. Then the listener compared its new pitch with that of the following probe tone. The pitches to which the target note could move included notes of the major scale (white notes on the piano) and half-step (semitone) intervals outside the major scale (black notes on the piano), but they also included pitches in between those standard ones. The target note could move to "quarter steps," which involved different pitch intervals from any encountered by the listeners in the music they heard every day.

In this task the scale steps and the semitones between them—the notes on the piano—were judged accurately. When the wandering note moved to one of those standard pitches, the probe was judged "equal" most often when it really was equal in pitch. But when the wandering note landed on a quarter step, outside the standard set, the probe tended to be judged "equal" more often when it was actually different from the target note and on a neighboring scale step. That is, it seems that target notes that moved to quarter steps were interpreted by the listener's auditory system as actually having been their scale-step neighbors. In the terms of the Swiss psychologist Jean Piaget, the quarter steps were "assimilated" to their more standard neighbors.

The auditory system took slightly variant pitches that occurred in a rapid-fire context of pitches that all conformed to the cultural standard and interpreted them as instances of the expected pitches. This is similar to experiences that occur when one listens to speech; when a speaker uses a slightly variant pronunciation, it is heard as though the standard pronunciation had been used. In both cases the sounds are interpreted as conforming to cultural categories stored in the brain, even though they actually did not.

Not only did listeners hear the quarter steps as though they were standard scale steps but, perhaps even more remarkable, the absolute pitch level of the melodies was not important to them. That is, when the whole set of patterns was shifted in pitch by a quarter step, so that what had been semitones on the piano became quarter steps and vice versa, exactly the same results were obtained. Thus, what is stored in the brain appears to be a flexible scheme of expected pitch relationships and not a rigid set of fixed pitches that might not match those of the music being heard.

There is a general point to be made concerning the perception of complex works of art, whether by hearing or seeing. Knowing what to expect and being familiar with the materials presented lead listeners and viewers to perceive things differently from the way they would if they were totally naive. This knowledge operates at several levels. In the tasks described, both familiarity with the melody to be heard and expectancies of where it might be hidden aided the efficiency of auditory processing, just as familiarity and expectancy aid vision. And for listening to musical patterns the listener's implicit knowledge of the musical scale system was also important. Most music, symphonies as well as songs as simple as "It's a Small World," is sufficiently complex so that these types of knowledge play an important role in understanding it. In art, as in life, knowledge of what is likely to be seen or heard is a critical component in effective perception.

FOR ADDITIONAL READING

Diana Deutsch (ed.), *The Psychology of Music* (Academic Press, 1982).

W. J. Dowling and D. L. Harwood, *Music Cognition* (Academic Press, 1986).

W. J. Dowling, K. M.—T. Lung, and S. Herrbold, "Aiming Attention in Pitch and Time in the Perception of Interleaved Melodies," *Perception and Psychophysics*, vol. 41 (June 1987).

# NEW LIGHT ON THE
# MAYA

*by George E. Stuart*

Knowledge of the Classic civilization of the Maya has increased greatly in recent years, revealing it to have been a complex and literate society that was less intellectual and more warlike than had been previously believed.

In the centuries between about AD 250 and 900—which archaeologists term the Classic Period—Mayan civilization flourished in the lowlands of the Yucatán Peninsula, a territory now embraced by extreme southeastern Mexico, Guatemala, Belize, and the western parts of Honduras and El Salvador. Our knowledge of the Classic Maya has increased dramatically in the recent past owing to the intensive efforts of a number of scholars in many disciplines. This change not only has added immensely to our understanding of the people themselves but also has transformed the very way in which the subject is approached.

In brief—and in anticipation of what follows below in specific examples—the Maya are now emerging into the light of knowledge in far more detail than has previously been available. They have now been revealed as a complex society featuring a literate elite who recorded the names, places, and events of their own history. This they accomplished by means of the most sophisticated writing system ever developed in ancient America and, often, through the illustrations that accompany their texts. This literacy gives the Maya a unique place in the history of pre-Columbian America, for it allows them to be studied with the aid of their own writings, much as the ancient Greeks and Romans are investigated.

Recent scholarship has also confirmed the close cultural relationship between the Maya and their Mesoamerican neighbors, not only in the practices of warfare and sacrifice but also in the frequency with which those two traits appear. (Mesoamerica in this context extends from central Mexico to Nicaragua.) In short, recent knowledge has served to "humanize" the Maya by transforming our perception of them. Once thought of as an isolated society of peaceful, stargazing intellectuals, they now appear to have been more akin to other civilizations, Mesoamerican and otherwise, that have marked the long story of our collective past.

**Early concepts**

In order to appraise the nature of this change in view and to see it for what it is—more of an accelerated evolution than a revolution—it is appropriate to summarize briefly the history of the knowledge and notions regarding the Maya over the past century and a half. In the early decades of the 19th century, knowledge of the ancient Maya stood, for

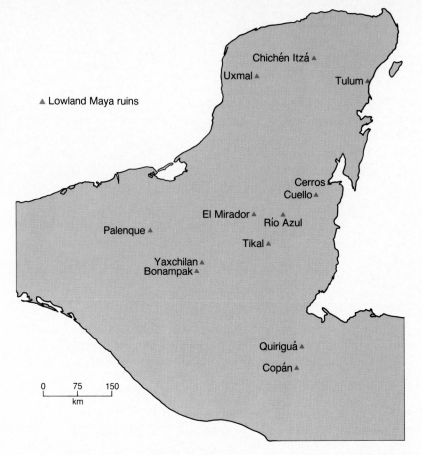

▲ Lowland Maya ruins

Chichén Itzá ▲
Uxmal ▲
Tulum ▲

Cerros ◄
Cuello ▲

El Mirador ▲
Río Azul ▲
Palenque ▲
Tikal ▲

Yaxchilan ▲
Bonampak ▲

Quiriguá ▲
Copán ▲

0    75    150
km

*Maya civilization flourished during the Classic Period (between about AD 250 and 900) in the lowlands of the Yucatán Peninsula.*

**GEORGE E. STUART** *is Staff Archaeologist at the National Geographic Society, Washington, D.C.*

*(Overleaf) Sarcophagus lid discovered at Palenque in 1952 was one of the major discoveries that led to a revised view of Maya culture. Photograph, © Merle Greene Robertson*

all practical purposes, at zero. There were, to be sure, a few available published histories compiled by those who had witnessed—or at least had access to the records of—the Spanish conquest of the Maya area between 1524 and 1697, but these contained observations on the Maya of that period and were, at best, sketchy.

It remained for London publisher Henry Berthoud to issue in 1822 an illustrated report on the ruins of Palenque, the result of explorations made 35 years earlier by Antonio del Río and the artist Ignacio Armendáriz. This landmark publication stands as the first full-fledged, and illustrated, report on a Maya archaeological site.

In a series of short articles between 1827 and 1833, the eccentric naturalist Constantine S. Rafinesque published the first scholarly efforts related to the ancient Maya. He recognized that both the ruins of Palenque and a mysterious hieroglyphic manuscript in the Dresden Royal Library not only were products of the same people but also were quite distinct from "Mexican" (Aztec) material. Although his attempts at deciphering the Maya hieroglyphs were in vain, he did correctly recognize their bar-and-dot numbers as combinations of "ones" and "fives." Most important of all, Rafinesque perceived that the key to decipherment lay in knowledge of the various Maya languages, particularly those spoken in the area of Palenque. The precocious contributions of Rafinesque appeared in the rapidly increasing number of works on ancient America that were published during the time, most notably the admirable summary of prehistoric America by J. H. McCulloh (1829), the much-read *American*

206

*Antiquities* by Josiah Priest (1833), and articles in the popular periodicals of New York City and Philadelphia.

The work of Rafinesque and his colleagues was almost completely overshadowed by the events of the next period of Maya research, which began with the explorations of John Lloyd Stephens and artist Frederick Catherwood between 1839 and 1842. Together they visited numerous ruins of note. Stephens's published narratives (1841 and 1843), accompanied by Catherwood's superb illustrations, proved immensely popular. Moreover, Stephens concluded that the wondrous ruins he had visited were not the work of ancient colonists from Egypt or mythical Atlantis (as most writers of the period speculated) but instead were that of the direct ancestors of the living Maya. Stephens also guessed that the monuments in the ruins commemorated ancient kings—and that the unreadable texts spoke of their exploits.

In the four decades that followed Stephens's remarkable work French explorer Claude-Joseph-Désiré Charnay pioneered the photographic documentation of the ruins, while his countryman, the cleric Charles-Étienne Brasseur de Bourbourg, searched for manuscripts in libraries and archives in Europe and Central America. In 1861 Brasseur published the *Popol Vuh,* the rich 16th-century narrative of myth and cosmic history pertaining to the highland Quiché Maya. Next he discovered an abstract of Bishop Diego de Landa's 16th-century manuscript, *Relación de las cosas de Yucatán,* and published it in 1864. That narrative provided for the first time a highly detailed picture of 16th-century Yucatán and of local Maya customs as the Spanish found them. Landa dealt with virtually all aspects of culture, including social and political organization, religion and ceremonies, native writing, and the calendar. The publication of this priceless document is acknowledged by scholars as one of the most consequential episodes in the entire history of Maya studies.

Also in 1864 a second Maya hieroglyphic book, this one in the Bibliotheque Imperiale of Paris, was reproduced for the use of scholars.

*Drawing of the main tablet of the Temple of the Cross at Palenque is a copy of an original by the Spanish artist Ignacio Armendáriz, who accompanied Antonio del Río on his explorations in 1787. His drawings served as an important reference for scholars of the Maya in the 1820s and 1830s.*

The publication of a third pre-Columbian Maya manuscript, the Madrid Codex, the two fragments of which were published by Brasseur (1869–70) and his colleague León de Rosny (1883), completed this period of noteworthy finds. Thus, by the early 1880s much of the raw material was at hand for the first major advance in the interpretation of ancient Maya culture. That leap was made by a small international group of scholars—and it was accomplished in the span of a single remarkable generation.

## A breakthrough in scholarship

The principal figures in Maya scholarship between 1880 and 1905 were Ernst Förstemann, Paul Schellhas, and Eduard Seler of Germany; León de Rosny of France; and Cyrus Thomas, Daniel G. Brinton, Joseph Goodman, and Charles P. Bowditch of the U.S. The raw material for their collective endeavor continued to accumulate, particularly through the monumental publications of Maya ruins, sculptures, and inscriptions by Alfred P. Maudslay of the U.K. and the series of expeditions by the German explorer-photographer Teobert Maler.

Förstemann, royal librarian at Dresden, worked mainly with the Dresden Codex. From it and the two other manuscripts, from data in the Landa narrative, and from other sources, he single-handedly elicited the complex mechanics of the Maya calendar system and the nature of the "long count," by which the Maya, utilizing the concept of zero in a system of positional notation, recorded the passage of time. Paul Schellhas codified the gods depicted in the Post-Classic codices and, most importantly, recognized their name hieroglyphs. Seler, a brilliant generalist, made profitable comparisons between the cosmological concepts underlying the Maya material and those known from the highlands of central Mexico and thus underscored the fundamental unity of Mesoamerican culture.

*A photograph taken in 1891 reveals vegetation growing over the ruins of the palace at Palenque. The palace was notable for the fragile stucco reliefs on the stone piers.*

Meanwhile, the so-called alphabet in Landa's *Relación* was causing many problems. At first hailed as a sort of "Rosetta Stone" for Maya hieroglyphic writing, it soon became the bone of contention in a debate over whether the Maya system was phonetic. Seler and his German colleagues failed to see any evidence of phoneticism that worked; Cyrus Thomas, on the other side of the Atlantic, sought to make it work but in vain, and by 1904 the problem lay dormant—and unresolved. Brinton, meanwhile, published some of the important *Maya Chronicles* (1882). Goodman's work, which drew upon much of Förstemann's findings on the calendar, culminated in 1905 with his proposal of a correlation between the Maya and the Christian calendar systems—a formula still used by Mayanists to recover absolute dates from the inscriptions.

In 1901 Bowditch suggested that certain stelae (inscribed stone slabs or upright stone monuments) from Piedras Negras, which Maler had photographed, recorded specific data on the births, initiations, accessions, and deaths of rulers. Others, including the archaeologist Sylvanus G. Morley, believed this possibility as well but apparently for only a brief period; in his *Introduction to the Study of the Maya Hieroglyphs* (1915), Morley mentioned the potential historical content of the Maya texts, but he never again addressed the problem. Thus, despite Bowditch's bold yet logical contention, the view of the Maya texts as history receded into limbo for the next half century.

Although important archaeological investigations had taken place in the 1890s—notably the work of George B. Gordon at Copán and Edward H. Thompson in northern Yucatán—it was not until shortly after World War I that intensive excavation was initiated in the Maya area. Under the auspices of the Carnegie Institution of Washington, D.C., long-term programs of excavation were conducted at Chichén Itzá, Uaxactún, and other sites. Under the direction of Morley and Alfred V. Kidder, Carnegie's approach to Maya research was multidisciplinary. Among the various activities, Morley himself worked on dates in the inscriptions; Robert Redfield and Alfonso Villa Rojas devoted themselves to Maya ethnology; Ralph Roys and Alfredo Barrera Vásquez codified the Maya chronicles;

*Among the ruins at Chichén Itzá is a building that the Maya may have used as an observatory. Windows opening out of the dome from an interior spiral staircase probably were used for astronomical sightings.*

*Temples and palaces flank the Great Plaza (above) at Tikal, the largest Maya city in the southern lowlands during the Classic Period. Mural at Bonampak (below), painted about AD 800, depicts a battle scene and reveals that the Maya were not as peaceable as was once believed.*

and, of greatest importance, J. Eric S. Thompson began a half century of work on the Maya hieroglyphs. The University of Pennsylvania conducted a decade of exploration at Piedras Negras, and Frans Blom, Hermann Beyer, and others published important data and analyses under the aegis of the Middle American Research Institute at Tulane University, New Orleans, Louisiana. In Mexico the National Museum—later the Institute of Anthropology and History (Mexico City)—initiated its own programs at Chichén Itzá, Tulum, and Palenque.

### The "establishment" view

This "golden age" of Maya archaeology flourished until 1958, when the Carnegie Institution abruptly abolished its Maya program. But during

that half century or so, scientists and scholars produced a flood of data related to the Maya. And it was the interpretations of these data, largely dominated by Morley and J. Eric S. Thompson, that produced the comprehensive "establishment" view of Maya civilization that so dominated the generation immediately preceding our own—and that has persisted into our very recent past. That view is best expressed in two major works, Morley's *The Ancient Maya* (1946) and J. Eric S. Thompson's *Rise and Fall of Maya Civilization* (1954), and it embraced every aspect of Maya culture and achievement. It may be summarized as follows:

Maya society was largely based on a peasant-priest relationship. The former—farmers of corn, beans, and squash—practiced swidden, or slash-and-burn, agriculture in an unending battle with the ever-encroaching hostile jungle. At the other end of the social scale were the astronomer-priests, the intellectual nobility who continually observed the movements of the Sun, Moon, planets, and stars. Time was not a Maya pastime; it was an obsession, and often the priests of different centers—also the regulators and keepers of the calendar—met, conferred, and agreed on modifications and standardizations of the various day counts and intervals in their system. As a consequence the sculptured stelae depicted priests and, at times, gods—both vague and anonymous beings whose accompanying hieroglyphic texts dealt exclusively with astronomical and/or calendrical matters.

These Maya arranged themselves over the countryside in "centers" marked by the presence of imposing ceremonial architecture. Only the priests occupied such places as Palenque, Tikal, and Copán on a permanent basis. And only on days of ritual would the peasantry gather in these holy places for ceremonials and, perhaps, markets.

The great Maya centers of the southern lowlands (Copán, Tikal, Palenque) were seen by Morley as part of an "Old Empire," which thrived in isolation from the rest of Mesoamerica and the demise of which yielded to a "New Empire" in northern Yucatán; there the Maya,

*In 1952 Alberto Ruz Lhuillier found a five-ton limestone sarcophagus lid (below) in a burial chamber beneath the Temple of the Inscriptions at Palenque (below left). The bas-relief depicts the moment of death–the fleshless jaws of an underworld monster reaching toward a half-reclining man, probably the dying ruler Pacal.*

(Left) D. Donne Bryant; (right) David Alan Harvey—Woodfin Camp Inc.

hybridized by militaristic invaders from the west, continued to flourish until the coming of the Spaniards. Indeed, Morley likened the "Old Empire" Maya to the Greeks of Classical antiquity. By comparison, the Mexicans became the Romans of the Mesoamerican epic.

### New discoveries

This picture of a conservative, peace-loving society of intellectuals, farmers, and artisans appears (with the perfect vision of hindsight) to be excessively idealized, a portrait of a people unique in Earth's past, and so it was. A series of events that began at the very peak of the public and academic acceptance of the Morley-Thompson view described above began to plant the seeds of change.

The first was the fortuitous discovery of murals at Bonampak, deep in the Lacandon Forest of Chiapas. One of the three rooms of incredibly preserved paintings depicted a full-fledged battle. Not only did it include distinct individuals but these same people appeared in scenes of ceremony, dance, and sacrifice that accompanied the great battle mural.

The second major event was the discovery by Alberto Ruz Lhuillier of a remarkable tomb in a crypt beneath the Temple of the Inscriptions at Palenque in 1952. The sarcophagus lid bore a scene and a lengthy hieroglyphic text and provided an indisputable link between actual human remains and the inscriptions.

The third discovery took place simultaneously with the second. While Ruz and his crew recorded the richness of the Palenque crypt, Yury V. Knorozov, a young Soviet scholar, announced the beginning steps of his phonetic decipherment of Maya hieroglyphic writing, based on—of all things—the infamous Landa "alphabet." Knorozov maintained that the Maya signs could function as phonetic syllables and could thus serve to "spell" words.

Considered separately, the first two events appeared at the time to be little more than fascinating discoveries. Thompson interpreted the Bonampak battle scene as a minor raid. George Brainerd, in his revision of Morley's popular book for its third edition (1956), added several photographs of the Ruz tomb and its contents but modified Morley's original

212

text into an even more unrealistic picture of the Maya. And Knorozov's conclusions met with vehement hostility from Thompson and the rest of the Western academic establishment. Considered together from today's perspective, the three events were momentous for they began to lay the foundations for the total revision of the accepted view of the ancient Maya.

The first step in the revision took place in 1958, when Heinrich Berlin recognized a certain class of hieroglyphs, which he termed "emblem glyphs." These appeared to stand for places or family names or both. Only two years later, in the pages of *American Antiquity*, Tatiana Proskouriakoff published what most Mayanists recognize as the key turning point in the path of Maya studies. Her meticulous and unimpeachable analysis of a series of texts from Piedras Negras, Guatemala, demonstrated beyond doubt that the Maya inscriptions, whatever else they might contain, dealt in the main with real people and with history.

In 1962 David H. Kelley tested the historical hypothesis on the inscriptions at Quiriguá and found that they too were concerned with real people and events. That same year Kelley issued the first objective critique of Knorozov's phonetic readings of the hieroglyphs, pointing out that, while there were some shortcomings, the basic approach appeared to be valid. Virtually alone among Western scholars, Kelley applied the Knorozov method and read a name—"Kakupacal"—in the inscriptions of Chichén Itzá, noting that the very same name also appeared in one of the Maya chronicles and in relation to the same place.

The decade between 1963 and 1973 began with a major summary monograph by Knorozov. This was followed by several notable milestones. In 1966 linguists, epigraphers (students of inscriptions), and archaeologists—among them Kelley, Michael D. Coe, Floyd G. Lounsbury, and Norman McQuown—presented papers in Mexico City at a meeting that represented the first productive modern effort to integrate their disciplines. In 1970 one of the largest archaeological endeavors of recent

*A shallow tripod plate from the Late Classic Period (AD 600–800) reveals in allegorical images the Mayan view of the interactions among the underworld, the middleworld, and the heavens.*

© Justin Kerr 1981

*Wall panel from the Late Classic Period, found at Piedras Negras in Guatemala, shows Maya elite at attention in military uniforms.*

Drawing by David Stuart

times, the 14-year program of intensive excavation by the University of Pennsylvania at Tikal (William R. Coe, director), ended. Soon afterward archaeologists attacking the crucial problems of Maya agriculture and subsistence began noting the strange markings on the surface of the land that appeared on remote-sensing images obtained by artificial orbiting satellites. These apparent systems of fields and canals were soon verified on the ground during explorations by Ray Matheny at Edzná and by Dennis E. Puleston, Alfred H. Siemans, and others working in the southern Maya lowlands.

The momentum of the decade continued at a 1971 symposium, Mesoamerican Writing Systems, in Washington, D.C. There George Kubler demonstrated the patterning inherent in whole texts; Kelley reemphasized the astronomical properties of certain Maya date spans; and Lounsbury brought the integration of linguistics and epigraphy to new heights with a brilliant analysis of a hieroglyph representing "lord." This important period of multidisciplinary investigation ended with the publication of Michael D. Coe's *The Maya Scribe and His World* (1973), a work that introduced another whole category of raw material crucial to the understanding of the Classic Maya.

Coe's book began simply as a catalog to accompany an exhibit (by the Grolier Club of New York City) of Maya pottery, sculpture, and a newly found codex; the origins of none of them had been established. In the treatment of the pieces, Coe unveiled a major set of hypotheses. Among them he proposed that scenes painted on Late Classic Maya funerary ceramics bore a direct relationship to the episodes that appear in the *Popol Vuh,* the famed compendium of highland Maya mythology. Second, Coe noted that the hieroglyphs accompanying the scenes and those painted around the vessel rims appeared to be arranged in systematic patterns; thus, he recognized them as bearing significant messages rather than functioning as meaningless ornaments, as Thompson had

214

thought. And third, Coe argued persuasively for the authenticity of the new "Grolier Codex."

At about the same time as the appearance of Coe's provocative work, a small group of Mayanists met at Palenque at the invitation of Merle Greene Robertson, then engaged in documenting the art of the famed site. This first "Mesa Redonda," or Round Table—devoted to art, iconography, and dynastic history at Palenque—proved to be another milestone in Maya research. Among the papers produced by the session, several stood out: Peter Mathews and Linda Schele, working through the enormous body of Palenque hieroglyphic texts, produced the first dynastic list for the site; Lounsbury, building on Berlin's earlier recognition of names on the sarcophagus in the Ruz Tomb, elicited the birth and death dates of Pacal, the occupant of the crypt, along with the roll call of ancestors recorded on the great stone sarcophagus lid; and David Joralemon demonstrated that ritual bloodletting played a key part in the lives of the Maya elite. This point, in particular, led eventually to one of the fundamental revisions of the perceptions of the Classic Maya, namely, the significant role of ritual bloodletting among the elite.

That the theme of blood pervaded the iconography to an astonishing extent was demonstrated by David Stuart in 1982 at a conference held at Princeton University. Drawing upon a wide sampling of Maya art and architecture, Stuart concluded that blood motifs reflected deep Maya concerns with lineage and ancestry and thus referred to the cosmic context of the civilization—the very basis for the legitimacy of dynastic rule by the Classic Maya elite.

Other investigators, meanwhile, had begun to emphasize the warlike aspect of Classic Maya society. In the light of Proskouriakoff's earlier decipherment of the hieroglyph for "capture," the work of Berthold Riese on "war" events in the texts, and contributions by other scholars, the Classic Maya became less and less peaceful—and the famed scene at Bonampak began to make sense. Schele's investigation of human sacrifice among the Classic Maya only reinforced the point.

These analyses of Mayan sculptured and painted images were matched by advances in archaeology, ethnohistory, linguistics, and ethnology. Nor-

*Radar image of the rain forest in the central lowlands of Guatemala reveals gridlike patterns that were discovered to be the remnants of irrigation canals dug by the Maya between 250 BC and AD 900.*

NASA

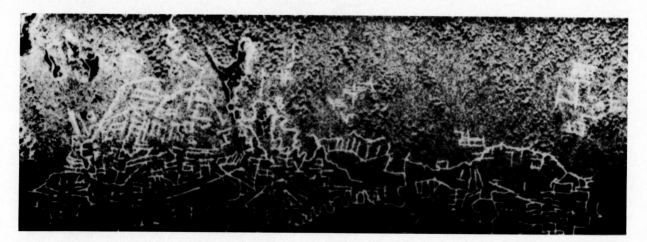

man Hammond's work at Cuello pushed Maya beginnings back through the 2nd millennium BC; David Freidel's excavation of Cerros documented the existence of political iconography in the centuries preceding the traditional beginning of the Classic Period, as reflected in great painted masks on the facade of the principal pyramid there. These masks were marked with hieroglyphic signs—probably the earliest known examples of the complex programs of iconography with which Maya rulers advertised their right to lead. Meanwhile, continuing investigations at Río Azul in Guatemala by Richard E. W. Adams were clarifying the role of Mexican influences in the Classic Maya world. And while these and other efforts proceeded, the Corpus of Maya Hieroglyphic Inscriptions, an important project under the direction of Ian Graham, continued to produce more texts for present and future Mayanists.

## Conclusions and future prospects

Our present state of knowledge of the Maya and their mentality is admirably surveyed in *The Blood of Kings* by Schele and Miller (1986). From it emerges a picture quite different from the Morley-Thompson view of a mere generation ago.

Mayanists now see the subjects of their studies as much more complex than they had previously believed, and much more humanized as well. While the Maya elite were, to be sure, more than routinely interested in time and its passage, they used it for earthly rather than esoteric purposes—as a tool for reaching into eternity in order to link themselves with real and mythical ancestors. Such lineages provided the foundations for legitimate rulership and became manifest in the royal blood motifs and symbols that pervade their art, which, by virtue of this concept,

*Lintel removed from a door at Yaxchilan in Chiapas, Mexico, shows a bloodletting rite that took place on October 28, AD 709. The king holds a huge torch, while his kneeling wife pulls a thorn-lined rope through her mutilated tongue. The king's hairstyle and rope necklace indicate that he will draw blood from himself as the ritual continues.*

Present-day Maya number about two million. They are a primarily agricultural people who occupy the same general region in Mexico and Central America as did their ancestors.

David Alan Harvey—Woodfin Camp Inc.

became political art. Ritual bloodletting and sacrifice thus became for the Maya the continuing reminders that helped perpetuate the dynasties.

In their Classic Period polities—more akin to city-states and thus never an "empire"—the Maya elite waged war, captured neighboring rulers, and sacrificed them. The frequent changing of state boundaries during the period, as demonstrated by Joyce Marcus, Mathews, and others, may have been the final and intolerable source of pressure that fostered the collapse of the cities of the southern lowlands, for war and capture seem to monopolize the texts of those places on the eve of their cultural demise.

The Classic Maya cities were just that—cities. Gone for good is the notion of empty ceremonial centers. The mapping of each ruin, no matter how small it appears at first, reveals more than is at first apparent; and the recent discovery that many of the remains of domestic occupation at Maya sites are buried and thus unable to be seen is resulting in increased population estimates.

Inside each large city dwelt not only the nobility but also many levels of specialists—scribes (often members of the elite or even of the royal family), master architects, painters, merchants, traders, and farmers. The latter, as recent research has shown, were not mere slashers and burners of their forest homeland. Instead, the farmers created sophisticated systems of canals and raised fields, practiced irrigation, and, in short, used whatever worked to sustain themselves and their society. Without such talent the Classic Maya civilization would never have existed.

It would be an act of supreme arrogance to entertain the belief that we now know all there is to know about the ancient Maya—or that all we think we know is correct in every detail. Some of the newest conclusions will doubtless undergo revisions of one degree or another. Even as this is being written, the newest generation of Mayanists is looking at the problems that remain, and the resulting knowledge will only continue its evolution toward an approximation of the truth.

217

GREEN SYMPHONIES AND YELLOW VOICES:
# The Joined Senses of Synesthesia

by Richard E. Cytowic

*When some people hear the phrase
"I see what you're saying,"
they experience it as literally true.*

Most people link their senses only by way of metaphoric speech (saying, for example, that red is a "warm" color; a certain cheese tastes "sharp"; that so-and-so is a "sweet" person). But there are a few who experience the phrase "I see what you're saying" as literally true. For example:

"What first strikes me is the *color* of someone's voice. [Name] has a crumbly, yellow voice, like a flame with protruding fibers. Sometimes I get so interested in the voice, I can't understand what's being said."

The term used to describe such an experience is synesthesia.

The word synesthesia comes from the Greek *syn* ("union") and *aisthesis* ("sensation"), literally a joining of the senses. Synesthesia is an involuntary joining in which the real information of one sense is accompanied by a perception in another. In addition to being involuntary, this additional perception is regarded by the synesthete as real instead of as imagined in the mind's eye, and it also has other interesting features that clearly separate it from artistic fancy or purple prose. Its reality and vividness are what make synesthesia so interesting in its violation of conventional perception. Synesthesia is also fascinating because it logically should not exist in the human brain, where the evolutionary trend has been for increasing anatomical separation of function.

Synesthesia is accepted as a real phenomenon by the medical community, if only because it has been independently noted by many investigators for more than 200 years. Throughout those years, however, attempts to explain the phenomenon have failed, and by the 1920s synesthesia was left with a reputation as a psychological quirk without a basis understandable in terms of current neurophysiology. Despite this, it aroused inquiry in a wide range of disciplines, both traditional and unorthodox. These included neurology, psychology, linguistics, comparative anatomy, artistic creativity, and philosophy.

Only recently have scientists been able to study regional metabolism and, therefore, function, in a living human brain while it is engaged in a specific cognitive behavior. Such research proves that this rare condition is brain-based (perceptual) and not a mind-based condition (such as

imagery). On the evidence of evolutionary and other lines of data, it can be proposed, somewhat romantically, that synesthetes can be regarded as cognitive fossils in that their perception is a fundamentally mammalian (phylum typical) attribute, compared with language, which is uniquely human (species typical).

## Synesthetes speak for themselves

"I remember most accurately scents. At age 2 my father was on a ladder painting the wall. The paint smelled blue, although he was painting it white. I remember to this day thinking why the paint was white, when it smelled blue."

"Colors are very important to me because I have a gift—it's not my fault, it's just how I am—whenever I hear music, or even if I read music, I see colors."

"When I taste something with an intense flavor, the feeling sweeps down my arm to my fingertips, and I perceive that object [weight, shape, texture and temperature] as if I'm actually grasping it."

"When I listen to music, I see the shapes on an externalized area about 12 inches in front of my face onto which the music is visually projected. Sounds are most easily likened to oscilloscope configurations—lines moving in color, often metallic with height, width, and, most importantly, depth. My favorite music has lines that extend beyond the 'screen' area."

Something strange is going on here. The speakers above are all intelligent, responsible people. They are not being artistic, are not on drugs, and are not insane. Yet the incongruous adjectives and nouns come tumbling out with conviction and reflect typical synesthetic sentiments. The speakers have never met, yet their stories are remarkably similar. All apologize frequently. "I know this sounds crazy, but. . . ." They also learned to stop talking about their green symphonies, salty visions, and tastes that feel like glass columns long ago in childhood when they realized that they were different and that no one else understood.

"My parents thought I was very strange. They thought I was making it up to get attention. Everyone was always jumping in with psychological explanations: I had an overactive imagination, I was spoiled and wanted attention, a whole slew of things," says a national coordinator for social worker training. "My mother was the only person that believed me," laments a gerontologist, "and I'm sure she was not truly convinced that what I experience is real."

Other parents may be more sympathetic. When Soviet writer Vladimir Nabokov, as a toddler, complained to his mother that the colors on his wooden alphabet blocks were "all wrong," she understood him to mean that the colors painted on the blocks did not correspond with his own letter-color associations. His mother understood this because she was synesthetic herself.

The appearance of the trait in families is strong evidence that synesthesia is a brain-based condition and not a psychological one. The occurrence of synesthesia in contiguous generations, its transmission from parent to child in any sex combination, and its occurrence in siblings all suggest that it is inherited by means of dominant autosomes (nonsex chromosomes). More familial cases need to be found, however, before

*RICHARD E. CYTOWIC is President of Capitol Neurology and Chief of the Section of Neurology at Capitol Hill Hospital in Washington, D.C.*

*Illustrations by Leon Bishop*

220

the genetic basis of synesthesia is clear. Penetrance (the relative ability of a gene to produce its specific effect in any degree in the organism of which it is a part) may explain, for example, why there is a spectrum of synesthetic performance—from restricted forms in which the stimulus is highly specific to the indiscriminate activation of all five senses by a wide variety of stimuli. In a restricted form the subject may see colored shapes in response to spoken words only, whereas in a polymodal synesthete sounds, sights, and smells might all be seen, felt, and tasted. For example:

"I heard the bell ringing . . . a small round object rolled before my eyes . . . my fingers sensed something rough like a rope . . . I experienced a taste of salt water . . . and something white."

The examples above illustrate two points. First, while any combination or multiple combination of the senses is possible, the most common yoking is sound with sight, called colored hearing or chromesthesia. The second is that color figures quite prominently in the various synesthetic combinations (colored hearing; colored olfaction; word, number and name color associations; colored taste; colored music). Why this should be so is not clear.

### Features of synesthesia

When individual synesthetes compare associations, they find that agreement is coincidental at best. The expectation for homogeneity among synesthetic perception is a presumption that stems from the consensus people have about the perception of everyday objects. We all agree that roses are red and violets are blue, that a square looks like a square, and that a banana tastes like a banana each time we eat one. We can recognize a piano by its sound and not mistake it for a trumpet or a baby's cry. A look at illusions so common in everyday experience that we take them for granted will, however, illustrate that consistency of perception is not absolute.

One such illusion is the perception of a constant color of objects in the varying illumination of daylight. Because there is a marked difference in both the brightness and spectrum of daylight from sunrise to sunset, an object viewed in the morning reflects more blue light than the same object seen toward evening, when it should appear redder. Yet the color of an object is perceived as constant, despite changes in both intensity and incident wavelength. Thus, the color attributed to an object is different from what it "really is." It is different from what the physical properties of the incident light lead one to predict and perceive. The question, then, should be not "Why don't all synesthetes agree?" but rather "Why do the rest of us agree so well? Why do we have common illusions?"

The failure to find such universal correspondences among synesthetes led to the cessation of research by the 1920s. Theories that tried to explain the phenomenon by means of physical processes failed; even Sir Isaac Newton had tried to devise mathematical formulas to "relate" the frequency of sound to an appropriate wavelength of light. It will be seen below, however, that there are generic similarities in the way synesthetes

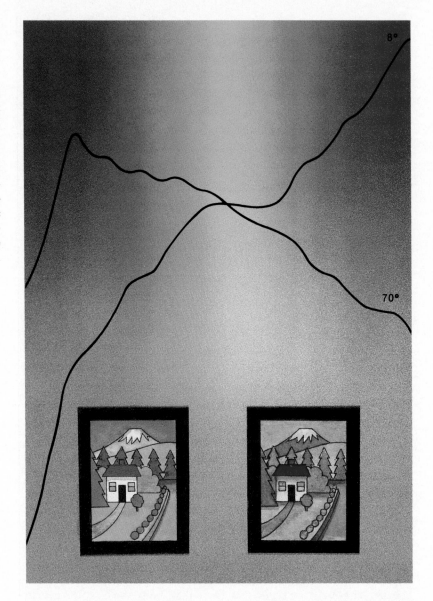

*Daylight from sunrise to sunset varies considerably in both brightness and spectrum. Consequently, objects viewed at midday (lower left) reflect more blue light than those seen in the evening, when they should appear redder (lower right). The curve from lower left to upper right measures the spectrum of the Sun's light at ground level just before sunset when the Sun is 8° above the horizon. The other curve reveals the spectrum when the Sun is high in the sky, near noon. Though the colors of the illuminated objects vary at different times of the day, most people perceive them as the same at all times. This common illusion is called color constancy.*

perceive, even though the end result—the actual perception—is unique for a given individual.

The oldest criticism against synesthesia is that it is subjective; that is, it is a psychophysical phenomenon knowable only through the experiential reports of the subjects themselves. This criticism is an empty one. Many established medical conditions are entirely subjective, such as headache and temporal lobe epilepsy (TLE). TLE is the better example of the two, because while those suffering from this ailment rarely have convulsions, they do have all sorts of peculiar subjective experiences such as disordered time sense, a feeling of leaving one's body, perceptual distortions, and, occasionally, synesthesia.

Because TLE is a relatively common (1/9,600) and well-known entity, a physician can diagnose it by eliciting a patient's history, can confirm the diagnosis by prescribing anticonvulsants and causing the symptoms

222

to go away, and, finally, can prove the diagnosis by demonstrating characteristic waveforms on the electroencephalogram. The word diagnosis means "through knowledge," and the diagnosis of synesthesia is made in the same way as any other diagnosis. While synesthesia is rare (1 in 500,000 by very rough estimate), the stories of synesthetes are so similar that the condition can be diagnosed by the history extracted from the patient, confirmed by meeting five clinical criteria, and proved by objective tests that separate synesthetes from the rest of the population.

The defining criteria of synesthesia are as follows: (1) Synesthesia is involuntary but elicited. It is unsuppressable but cannot be conjured up at will. There must be an objective stimulus. (2) Synesthesia is projected. The elicited sense is perceived as external and not imagined "in the mind's eye." (3) Synesthetic percepts are durable and discrete. The associations for an individual synesthete are constant over his or her lifetime. If a sound is blue, it will always be blue; the context of the stimulus does not have a strong influence. This has been affirmed repeatedly by testing individuals without warning as long as 20 years apart with the same stimuli. The synesthetic percepts are also restricted in their nature. Given choices on a matching task, synesthetes pick only a few, whereas nonsynesthetic subjects show a bell-shaped distribution over the available choices. The generic nature of these percepts is demonstrated by the fact that synesthetes never see complex scenes. The percepts are unelaborated: blobs, lines, spirals, and latticed shapes; smooth or rough textures; agreeable or disagreeable tastes such as salty, sweet, or metallic. Replication, with radial or axial symmetry, is also common. Synesthetic percepts never go beyond an elementary level. A particular stimulus also has a distinctive "signature" for synesthetes. As one synesthete explains, "The shapes are not distinct from hearing—they are part of what hearing *is*. The vibraphone makes a round shape. Each note is like a little gold ball falling. That's what the sound *is*; it couldn't possibly be anything else."

(4) Synesthesia is memorable. Synesthetic percepts are easily and vividly remembered, often in preference to the original stimulus. "She had a green name—I forget, it was either Ethel or Vivian." In this example the actual names are confused because both are green, but the synesthetic greenness is recalled. There is a strong link between synesthesia and eidetic (photographic) memory, and many synesthetes use their condition as a mnemonic aid. The relationship between synesthesia and memory is best depicted in A. R. Luria's *The Mind of a Mnemonicist*. His subject's memory, which was limitless and without distortion, was largely so because of the synesthesiae that accompanied every sensation.

(5) Synesthesia is emotional. There is an unshakable conviction by synesthetes that what they perceive is real. There is often a "Eureka" sensation, such as occurs when people have a sudden insight. The presence of such strong feelings of validity demands investigation of the contribution to synesthesia by the limbic system of the brain. The limbic system deals with emotion and memory and provides the sense of conviction that people attach to their ideas and ideals. Moreover, in this

primitive part of the brain, which reflects the human's inheritance from early mammals (therapsids), there is the opportunity for the blending of information from the various senses.

## Theories of synesthesia

All theories of synesthesia assume that there is a "link" between a sensory stimulus and the synesthetic percept. To the extent that one believes that all psychological phenomena have direct physiological correlates, then some type of physiological theory must be correct. Two centuries of theories fall into three categories.

The first category comprises undifferentiated theories. Popular in the 19th century, they suggested that the condition was caused by an immature nervous system and likened synesthesia to the normal synkinesis ("joined movements") that are seen in all infants. An infant reaching for a toy, for example, will experience involuntary overflow movements of the trunk and extremities. Only when the corticospinal and cerebellar pathways have matured and acquired their myelin insulation is a human capable of finely isolated dexterous movements. Undifferentiated theories fail because they predict an impairment of intellect and an indiscriminate perceptual response to a stimulus—characteristics that are quite unlike the actual specificity of synesthesia and contrary to the usual high intelligence of synesthetes.

Linkage theories are based on the assumption that something is "wrong" with the circuitry of the brain. The assumption of crossed wires or short circuits is the most common intuitive explanation for synesthesia among laymen, but the logical consequences of such an assumption are again contrary to the facts. Linkage theories would especially support agreement of perceptions among synesthetes, which cannot be found.

Linguistic theories suggest that synesthesia is simply a more intense form of the metaphoric speech that everyone uses. The following discussion explains why linguistic theories cannot be correct.

In *De Sensu* Aristotle points out that the senses are never deceived: "Color is an object peculiar to sight, sound to hearing, flavor to taste. . . . Each sense judges the objects peculiar to it and is never deceived as to the existence of the color or sound that it perceives." He also spoke about the discrimination of generic differences:

"Thus sight discriminates between white and black, taste between sweet and bitter, and so on. But we can also discriminate between white and sweet, and in fact between any two sensible qualities. By what means do we perceive generic difference? . . . As white and sweet are recognized as distinct, there must be a single faculty to assess the distinction and hence a single faculty which thinks and perceives them both."

To pursue Aristotle's argument, the same faculty that discriminates white from sweet may fail to discriminate or may perceive the two characteristics as synonymous based on shared qualities, hence, synesthesia. Research during the past century, therefore, focused on shared meanings in language as the link and suggested that synesthesia occurred at the highest levels of abstract processing in the central nervous system.

224

On reflection, however, an Aristotelian "common sensible" is not like a synesthetic percept at all. An Aristotelian common sensible (such as roundedness) cannot be learned by touch alone; it is a concept common to several senses. It is not an association or addition but a filtering out of abstract residues, a subtractive attribute. By contrast, synesthesia adds elementary percepts (sound and color, for example) to form complex ones but without losing the identities of the elementary constituents.

Based on theory alone, therefore, language should have little to do with synesthesia. This conclusion has been supported experimentally by tests called semantic differentials that have revealed no common meanings of words that describe either the stimuli or synesthetic responses. Thus, it appears that the place to go fishing in the brain for explanations of synesthesia is not at the top (in the cortex, where sensory impressions are interpreted in symbolic language) but closer to the bottom.

## Location in the brain

Curiously, no direct comparisons of characteristic perceptual processing between synesthetes and nonsynesthetes were made until 1980. A number of experimental issues are involved in making such comparisons. In a sound-color stimulus-response mapping experiment, for example, one can ask if the highest stimulus of one group of stimuli (such as the highest pitch in a range of notes) causes the same response if it is the lowest stimulus of another group; one also needs to ask how synesthetes perform compared with nonsynesthetic controls. A low-level linkage between two senses should show no context effects; that is, a given stimulus should always evoke the same percept, just as the knee-jerk reflex always produces the same twitch. This is called an absolute effect. If synesthesia were abstractly mediated, however, then the precipitating stimulus should engender a cluster of percepts that share the same meaning, and the range of synesthetic associations should be broad. This is a relative effect.

The results of such mapping experiments show the presence of both absolute and relative effects but are closest to the low level of linkage. Synesthesia seems to occupy an intermediate position in the range from concrete to abstract and from simple to complex brain mechanisms. Physically, this means that synesthesia occurs in the brain below the level of the cortex.

Specific regions of the central nervous system are reserved for specific functions, and for that reason neuroscience has traditionally emphasized the identification of specific regions that are related to specific functions. In all tissues there is more energy metabolism in tissue doing work than in those tissues that are not working. (Energy metabolism comprises the chemical changes in living cells by which energy is provided for the vital processes and activities.) Skeletal muscle does physical work by lifting weight against gravity; the heart does work by pumping blood against a pressure head; and the kidney does chemical osmotic work in concentrating substances against a gradient. While it is not always clear what kind of physical work is taking place in nervous tissue, the measurement

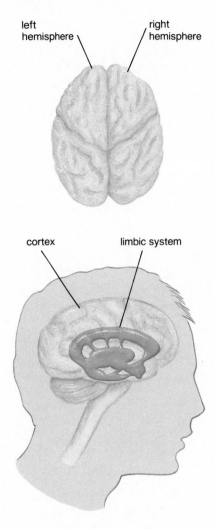

left hemisphere    right hemisphere

cortex    limbic system

*Experiments in which cortical blood flow is measured in synesthetes reveal that synesthesia occurs in the left hemisphere of the brain (top). The blood flow is considerably decreased, indicating that synesthesia takes place below the highest levels of abstract reasoning. Researchers now believe that synesthesia involves a functional disconnection of the language and association regions of the cortex from parts of the brain's limbic system (bottom).*

225

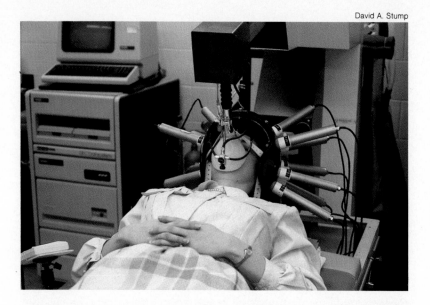

*A synesthetic subject is measured for blood flow in the brain. She inhales radioactive xenon-133, which is inert and saturates body tissues. Scintillation detectors mounted in the helmet she is wearing can then measure the clearance of radioactivity in brain regions while the patient is experiencing synesthesia. Blood flow measurements in regions of the brain can subsequently be derived.*

of energy metabolism can serve as a marker of how much work a given part of the nervous system is doing in any functional state. It is important to localize the measurement to specific regions of the nervous system by a method that can look at all regions simultaneously but independently. The measurement of regional cerebral blood flow (rCBF) fulfills this function because rCBF and metabolism correlate well. It also provides the strongest evidence for reduced cortical brain activity during synesthesia.

After a test subject, a synesthete with geometric taste, inhaled xenon-133, which is inert and saturates body tissues, scintillation detectors mounted in a helmet worn by the subject measured the clearance of radioactivity in the same regions on the right and left sides of the brain while the subject was stimulated and experiencing synesthesia. Blood flow measurements for the gray matter (cortex) and underlying white matter could then be derived. Behavioral states such as reading, remembering, or solving problems normally result in an increase in rCBF over baseline by at least 5%. In the test subject, however, not only was the baseline blood flow low in the left temporal lobe but there also was a dramatic decrease in flow of 18% in the left hemisphere. It is difficult, if not impossible, to produce such a reduction in cortical blood flow with a drug or in other behavioral states. In several areas of the left hemisphere the flow approached the lower limits of the technique to detect flow at all, levels usually seen during a stroke, where the brain tissue is simply dead. Yet no dead tissue was present in this subject. His neurologic examination was completely normal.

This tremendous decrease in cortical blood flow, which reflects decreased metabolism, was dramatic proof that synesthesia occurs below the highest levels of abstract processing. Later evidence for this conclusion also came from drug experiments. Drugs known to stimulate the cortex weakened the synesthetic percept or blocked it altogether, while cortical suppressants intensified the condition. Amphetamine and alcohol are examples of a cortical stimulant and suppressant, respectively.

Surprisingly, synesthesia seems to occur in the left hemisphere, where language resides in almost everyone. The right hemisphere, while also experiencing a reduced blood flow, seems to be responding passively to the forces involved in blood circulation. Thus, synesthesia appears to involve a functional disconnection of the language and association regions of the cortex from parts of the limbic brain in the left hemisphere.

Patients who have had their hemispheres surgically transected have demonstrated that the speech area's ability to describe is no guarantee that it will give an accurate description of perceptions going on in another, disconnected, part of the brain. The patient who speaks is not the patient who perceives; they are separate but usually unified. The proposed disconnection in synesthetes would cause the neural signals to be inadequate to convey all the information about a "true" stimulus to the level of conscious perception, which is then available to language. For this reason a sound may be described as something seen, and the relative enhancement of limbic-emotional brain structures may explain the certainty in a synesthete's mind that what he or she perceives is real and valid. Determining the causes of repetitive and reversible disconnections will require more research on greater numbers of synesthetes.

## Conclusions and future prospects

Human perception is the outcome of an elaborate interaction between stimuli and the apparatus of the brain. Consequently, a visual experience is not a perfect replica of the image received at the retina of the eye. Immense complications of interactions start in the retina and continue through stages of cortex, building in complexity such that certain cells in the temporal lobe respond only to certain geometric shapes or other highly specific attributes of a stimulus.

We are bewildered by such concepts as the shape of a name, blue smells, or symphonies with rising green pyramids because they are not common. But brains are not homogeneous, and uncommon things need to be explained. The neuron, after all, is a storyteller that accentuates some sensory details, ignores others, and is our fragile link to the physical world.

FOR ADDITIONAL READING

R. E. Cytowic and F. B. Wood, "Synesthesia I: A Review of Major Theories and Their Brain Basis," *Brain and Cognition*, vol.1 (1982, pp. 23–35).

R. E. Cytowic and F. B. Wood, "Synesthesia II; Psychophysical Relationships in the Synesthesia of Geometrically Shaped Taste and Colored Hearing," *Brain and Cognition*, vol.1 (1982, pp. 36–49).

R. E. Cytowic, *Synesthesia: A Union of the Senses* (Springer Verlag, 1987).

R. N. Haber, "Eidetic Images," *Scientific American* (April 1969, pp. 36–44).

Vladimir Nabokov, "Portrait of My Mother," *The New Yorker* (April 9, 1949, pp. 33–37).

R. K. Siegel and L. J. West (eds.), *Hallucinations: Behavior, Experience and Theory* (Wiley & Sons, 1975).

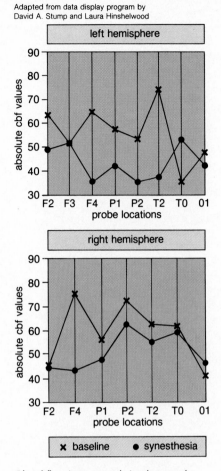

Adapted from data display program by David A. Stump and Laura Hinshelwood

*Blood flow is measured simultaneously at various sites in the left and right hemispheres of the brain of a synesthete. During the baseline state, when the person is not experiencing synesthesia, the mean flow levels in the left hemisphere are low. During synesthesia the left hemisphere flow drops an additional 18%, lending support to the hypothesis that synesthesia is a physically based phenomenon that takes place in the left hemisphere.*

# The SCIENCE and ART of
# PSYCHOTHERAPY

## by Hans H. Strupp

The practice of psychotherapy can be regarded as an art, but because of recent research on its methods and outcomes, it is becoming a scientific discipline as well.

The birth of modern psychotherapy is commonly traced to Josef Breuer's famous patient, Anna O., who, about a hundred years ago, gained relief from her hysterical difficulties by means of the "talking cure." Sigmund Freud, Breuer's young colleague, built on Breuer's early insights, and his subsequent discoveries of psychological dynamics ushered in a revolution that continues to have profound effects on contemporary clinical thinking and practice.

Despite marked advances modern psychotherapy continues to be in a state of turmoil. It is avidly sought by thousands of troubled people who desire relief from such diverse problems as anxiety, depression, personality disorders, alienation, and loneliness. Many forms of psychotherapy are being practiced by an expanding cadre of professionals, including, among others, psychiatrists, clinical psychologists, social workers, nurses, and pastoral counselors. In general, psychotherapy is seen as a major weapon against personal and interpersonal difficulties that are besetting people's lives. On the one hand, it has become a billion-dollar "industry," a recognized "psychosocial treatment" compensable by the government and private health insurance companies; on the other, it is attacked by scores of critics who alternately deny that there is such a thing as psychotherapy, question its effectiveness (more recently, in comparison with psychotropic drugs), or advocate interventions claimed to be superior to "traditional" ones. Coupled with these doubts are the public's growing mistrust of the health professions because of their alleged preoccupation with economic and political power and their lack of concern for the consumer.

Whatever psychotherapy purports to be, certain things are clear today: (1) It is not—and will probably never be—a "miracle drug" or a panacea. (2) Although a substantial percentage of people who have experienced some form of psychotherapy report marked benefits, it is equally true that others in states of crisis overcome their difficulties through their

**HANS H. STRUPP** is a Distinguished Professor in the Department of Psychology at Vanderbilt University, Nashville, Tennessee.

Illustrations by John Zielinski

own adaptive capacities or with the help of family, friends, or members of the clergy who may provide counsel. (3) Individuals who have learned to cope more effectively with adult responsibility and who possess greater personality resources derive more substantial benefits from psychotherapy than persons who lack those strengths or who suffer from emotional disorders of long standing. (4) No form of psychotherapy has emerged as uniquely effective except in some narrowly circumscribed conditions. (5) A number of psychopathological conditions are not helped significantly by available forms of psychotherapy (or any known treatment). (6) The extent to which intensive or prolonged psychotherapy produces radical reorganization of a patient's personality and, therefore, lasting change remains controversial. (7) The quality of the interpersonal relationship between a patient and a therapist plays an important part in determining the course and outcome of the therapy. (8) Once a patient has met certain criteria of suitability, a therapist's personal qualities appear to be more potent factors than any specific set of techniques he or she may use. (9) Finally, in view of the foregoing considerations, the quest for specific psychotherapeutic techniques for specific disorders (analogous to a drug) may turn out to be futile.

Why, in the light of this seemingly pessimistic picture, does the practice of psychotherapy flourish? Why do large numbers of therapists continue to be trained? Why do people continue to enlist the services of psychotherapists? This article will outline major issues confronting psychotherapy research and its relationship to practice and training. It will become apparent that one cannot speak of psychotherapy as an impersonal treatment procedure that exists apart from a particular patient and a particular therapist; instead, the personal qualities of the participants inevitably become intertwined in any therapeutic encounter. At the same time, it is possible for a therapist to employ his or her clinical acumen in understanding complex cognitive (thought), symbolic, and emotional processes that lead to the formation of "symptoms" or other "problems in living" and to help patients resolve or ameliorate these problems. Thus psychotherapy is both a personal and a technical enterprise, and many of the persistent misunderstandings derive from an inadequate appreciation of this fact.

## Definitions

In broad terms psychotherapy is a psychological treatment designed to achieve beneficial personality and behavior change. Patients who seek help for a psychological problem desire such change—they want to feel or act differently, and the psychotherapist agrees to assist the patient in achieving that goal. Major questions in the study of psychotherapy relate to what is to be changed and how change can be brought about. The first part of the question entails definitions of the problem for which the patient is seeking help (for example, depression, marital difficulties, shyness, nail biting, sexual dysfunctions); the second refers to the process and techniques by means of which change is achieved (support, ventilation of feelings, insight through interpretations, systematic desensitization, assertiveness training, etc.). Distinctions are also made with respect to "schools," or theoretical orientations, of therapists and to such variations as individual, group, couples, or family therapy.

Ideally, one would like to state that, given Problem X, the optimal approach is Technique Y. In practice, things are rarely so simple or straightforward; on the contrary, since human problems are often extraordinarily complex, so are the issues facing the therapist who attempts to deal with them. For the same reason, it is unlikely that there can be a single optimal approach to the solution of a psychological problem. Thus it is not surprising that the distinctions between the various forms of psychotherapy pale in significance. This is not to deny that there may be fundamental differences between the philosophies and practices of different therapists, but no therapist, in fact, practices a "pure" technique. In the end, the commonalities in all forms of therapy may turn out to be more crucial than the differences.

Part of the confusion besetting the field relates to the conception of psychotherapy as a "treatment modality," analogous to medical treatment in which a physician ministers to a relatively passive patient. This problem is partly due to the fact that modern psychotherapy has deep roots in the medical tradition. Such terms as "patient," "therapist," and "diagnosis" continue to be used, although in essential respects psychotherapy bears only a superficial resemblance to medical treatment. However, the medical analogy persists because psychotherapy attempts to alleviate human suffering and is therefore regarded as one of the "healing professions." Furthermore, some conditions (such as depression) appear to yield to a combination of psychotherapy and medication, the latter being traditionally the province of physicians. Therefore, it may be asserted that psychotherapy appears to improve a person's "mental health," a rather imprecise term whose utility has frequently been questioned. Yet psychotherapy is typically regarded as a "health care technology" and as such qualifies for reimbursement by insurance companies. Although a growing number of psychotherapists have had their training in such disciplines as clinical psychology and social work rather than in medicine, psychotherapy's allegiance to the medical profession is likely to endure.

Conversely, it is important to note that psychotherapy bears a closer relationship to an educational model than to a medical one. As early as 1905 Freud asserted that psychoanalytic therapy is a form of "reeducation" or "aftereducation," a position he maintained throughout his life. It was clear to him, as it has been to most therapists since, that psychotherapy above all else is a form of psychological influence, a collaborative endeavor in which the patient, from the beginning, is expected to play an active part. From this point of view the majority of neurotic and personality disorders—the prime conditions for which psychotherapy is used—are the products of maladaptive learning dating from early childhood and resulting in low self-esteem, excessive dependency, social inhibitions, and other forms of maladjustment. To overcome these impediments, the patient is typically helped to become more autonomous, self-directing, and responsible. In order to feel better about themselves, their relation-

231

ships with others, and their behavior in general, patients must learn to make changes within themselves and in their environment. The process of therapy is not designed to impose change on the patient but to create conditions that allow internal changes to occur.

Therefore, psychotherapy is essentially a learning process, and the role of the therapist is somewhat analogous to that of a teacher or mentor. If troublesome feelings, ideas, attitudes, and patterns of behavior have been learned, it is possible, within limits, to effect unlearning or relearning. When learning is impossible (for example, in conditions primarily attributable to genetic or biochemical factors), psychotherapy has relatively little to offer. Similarly, if the disturbance is solely due to factors in the person's social milieu (poverty, oppression, imprisonment) or if patients themselves do not desire change but change is mandated by a court of law, school system, etc., psychotherapists encounter great difficulties. Thus psychotherapy works best if patients wish to overcome their problems, are motivated to work toward change, live in an environment that tolerates change, and do not have insurmountable inner obstacles to learning (defenses and rigidities of character). Since all individuals show a tendency to resist personality or behavior change, psychotherapeutic learning is usually beset with difficulties.

## Theoretical orientations

Many models of psychotherapy ("schools") have been proposed. Several of the most important ones are described below.

Psychodynamic forms of psychotherapy derive from the "classical" model of psychoanalysis developed by Sigmund Freud and his followers. The practice of psychoanalysis (the most intensive and ambitious form of psychotherapy) has sharply declined in recent years and has given way to various forms of psychoanalytically informed therapies, including many designed for a shorter period of treatment. In general, the psychodynamic therapies define therapeutic problems in terms of repressed strivings and impulses that underlie the patient's feelings, thinking, and behavior. Unconscious conflicts and the manner in which the patient defends against their emergence in consciousness are implicated as major "causes" of maladaptations that call for therapeutic help. The relationship between patient and therapist (commonly called the therapeutic alliance or working alliance) is viewed as central to therapeutic change. To achieve such change, psychodynamic therapists believe, patients need to gain insight into their unconscious motives. Major attention is paid to understanding the dynamics of the patient-therapist relationship (transference and countertransference) in which the patient unwittingly attempts to recreate with the therapist the interpersonal problems he or she experienced with significant figures of childhood.

Behavioral therapies have achieved prominence during the past several decades. In contrast to those based on the psychodynamic model, these therapies are rooted in principles of learning as originally studied in psychological laboratories. Unlike psychodynamic therapists, behavior therapists attempt to influence directly behavioral processes or processes

*From the wide variety of psychotherapies that are available it is important that a patient receives the one that will be most beneficial. Included among these treatments are client-centered therapy, the behavioral therapies, psychoanalysis, and existential therapy. Some therapists recently have found that by combining one or more of these they can serve their patients more effectively.*

232

close to overt behavior. They achieve their goals through the extinction of anxieties and other maladaptive behaviors by counterconditioning and other specialized techniques. In the more recent past, increasing emphasis has been placed on the role played by cognitive factors in creating and maintaining such symptoms as phobias and depressions. In their attempts to seek specific treatments for specific problems and their insistence on empirical data to document outcomes, behavior therapists have markedly influenced advances in psychotherapy research.

Applications of various behavioral techniques, including biofeedback, have given rise to a new field called "behavioral medicine." Specialized techniques have been developed for the treatment of conditions such as migraine, tension headaches, insomnia, alcoholism, eating disorders, and gastrointestinal disorders. For example, insomnia can be alleviated by training patients in muscle relaxation, and teaching a patient to lower his or her body temperature may be beneficial in treating migraine headaches. As is true of the psychodynamic therapies, behavioral theories and techniques cover a wide spectrum.

Client-centered therapy, founded by the U.S. psychologist Carl Rogers (*see* OBITUARIES), is based on the principle that individuals and groups in conflict possess great resources for self-understanding and personality growth. Rogers stated that the human organism "has one basic tendency and striving—to actualize, maintain, and enhance the experiencing organism." Central to client-centered therapy is the process of "experiencing," which is set in motion and maintained by a set of "facilitating conditions" for the patient, including, among others, empathy and unconditional positive regard. Avoiding "techniques," client-centered therapists attempt to create a therapeutic relationship in which the client can experience increased freedom and personality growth.

Client-centered therapists were among the first to initiate systematic research on the therapeutic process and its relationship to outcomes. Although its popularity appears to have declined, client-centered therapy's influence on research has been considerable.

Existential therapy is a diverse collection of techniques developed by a group of philosophers and psychologists who are united in the belief that the understanding of human behavior is best achieved by focusing on a person's subjective experience. They believe that human beings create meaning and that it is this personal meaning that must be understood in therapy. Two leading proponents, Suzanne Kobasa and Salvatore Maddi, state: "The emphasis in existential psychology is on the importance of developing high levels of awareness concerning life as a series of decisions, the future as opposed to the past, what is possibility and what facticity [givens], and the nature of one's fundamental project."

Maturity, for existential psychologists, is called "authentic being." Its contrast, "existential sickness," is the primary concern of existential therapists. For psychotherapeutic interaction to be successful it must represent an act of love between patient and therapist. While recognizing the powerful influence of one's past, one must seek to transcend it by accepting responsibility for one's actions.

Many critics have expressed increasing dissatisfaction with the inordinate length and cost of psychotherapy, particularly of psychoanalysis. Although Freud was aware of this problem, it failed to receive systematic attention until fairly recently. Major reasons for the renewed focus on this issue have been the greater availability of psychotherapy, the rising cost of health care, and the lack of convincing demonstrations that there is a close relationship between length or intensity of a therapy and its effects. Research is being undertaken to explore the potential of shorter forms of psychotherapy with particular individuals and for particular clinical problems. For example, Hans Strupp and colleagues at the Center for Psychotherapy Research at Vanderbilt University, Nashville, Tennessee, are studying the effects of providing therapists with specialized training in time-limited techniques with adult neurotic patients. It is becoming increasingly clear that in some cases long-term, intensive therapy will remain the treatment of choice, but in many others it will be essential to limit therapeutic efforts and to strive for circumscribed goals. As part of the trend toward greater precision, there has been a notable interest in the development of "treatment manuals." These volumes aid in standardizing training, and they help researchers provide more specific descriptions of therapy.

As the dominance of the major therapeutic "schools" has gradually diminished, an "eclectic" trend has emerged. Concomitant with the decreased competition between major competing schools, both practitioners and researchers have adopted a more pragmatic stance that allows the crossing of theoretical and technique boundaries that were previously considered impenetrable. This trend may have been hastened by the lack of convincing demonstrations that one theoretical framework or set of techniques is uniquely superior; it may also be a function of the search for common factors in all forms of psychotherapy.

The position in favor of common factors has been argued by Jerome D. Frank, a major psychotherapy researcher. He asserts that psychotherapeutic change is prominently a function of a patient-therapist relationship that stems the patient's demoralization and hopelessness. Nonspecific factors involved in such a change include, among others, the therapist's empathy, understanding, respect, interest, encouragement, and acceptance. These common elements may be seen to have beneficial effects in any benign human relationship, including that of psychotherapy. Thus, while the therapeutic schemes and procedures may differ in content, they have common morale-building functions.

Some implications of this formulation for research, training, and practice should be noted. For example, if the effectiveness of different forms of psychotherapy is largely attributable to common factors, the search for "specific" (technique) factors espoused by a particular therapeutic approach may be futile. As research has progressed and carefully controlled studies have become more common, the preponderance of the evidence has tended to support the common factors position. However, it may also be true that the conceptualization of "specific" and "nonspecific" factors is faulty. For example, the quality rather than the form of

235

particular therapist communications may be crucial in effecting change. By this reasoning, the therapist's skill is not exerted by particular "technical" interventions but rather by the quality of the therapist-patient relationship. If this is so, such attributes as empathy and understanding are perhaps quite "specific," and their impact must be assessed by appropriate methods.

## The problem of outcome

The question of psychotherapy's effectiveness is of central interest, but it is clear that, unless terms are properly defined, the question is largely meaningless. By the same token, one cannot answer the question "Is surgery (or internal medicine) effective?" without specifying the pertinent variables.

The problem of psychotherapeutic outcome touches on many facets of human life, and conceptions of mental health and illness cannot be considered apart from philosophy, ethics, religion, and public policy. Inescapably one deals with questions relating to the meaning of human existence and the issue of cultural values. To illustrate: Therapeutic change cannot be measured like changes in temperature; instead, someone must make a judgment that, say, a person's compliance with requests from others is adaptive (that is, "healthy") or, conversely, is an indicator of pathology. Self-assertion may be "good" or "bad," "healthy" or "unhealthy." The question also arises as to who is the final arbiter of change. In some cases one may accept a patient's judgment that he or she feels "better" (as shown by self-reports on psychological tests or rating scales), whereas in others the patient's ability to render an "objective" judgment may be questioned. These decisions are clearly related to the values society assigns to a person's feelings, attitudes, and actions; they are also inherent in conceptions of mental health and illness.

Still, there can be commonsense agreement as to what constitutes a mentally healthy or nonneurotic person. Three major categories of patient behavior have been proposed for judging therapeutic change: (1) disappearance of presenting symptoms; (2) real improvement in mental functioning; and (3) improved reality adjustment. Most therapists and researchers, though they might disagree on criteria and methods for assessing change, would concur that therapeutic success should be demonstrable in the person's (1) feeling state (well-being), (2) social functioning (performance), and (3) personality organization (structure). The first is concerned with the patient's own perspective; the second is that of society, reflecting prevailing standards of conduct and "normality"; the third is the perspective of mental health professionals whose technical concepts (ego strength, impulse control, etc.) partake of information and standards that are derived from the preceding sources but are ostensibly scientific, objective, and value-free. Therapists have continued to assess treatment outcomes with reference to more or less refined clinical impressions, whereas researchers have tended to prefer quantitative indexes that have been derived from standardized tests and rating scales.

236

There are other reasons for qualifying the traditional question of psychotherapy's effectiveness. As already suggested, no form of psychotherapy that is currently practiced is a unitary process nor is psychotherapy applied to unitary problems. Furthermore, therapists cannot be regarded as interchangeable units that deliver a standard treatment in uniform quantity or quality. Patients, depending on differences in their personality, education, and intelligence, the nature of their emotional difficulties, their motivation, and other characteristics, differ in their receptiveness to therapeutic influences. Finally, technique variables, since they are thoroughly intertwined with the person of the therapist, cannot be dealt with in isolation.

There are, by now, clear indications that these strictures are being taken more seriously by researchers although perhaps less so by practicing therapists. There is a long-standing tradition among psychotherapists of viewing their particular approach as the answer to all problems presented by patients, with scant recognition of the possibility that another technique might be more appropriate in a given case. Freud's consistent refusal to view psychoanalysis as a panacea and his insistence upon carefully circumscribing its range of applicability stand as notable exceptions. Researchers have materially contributed to a new climate of opinion characterized by greater tolerance for diverse theoretical viewpoints and techniques, and there recently has been some rapprochement between competing "schools."

Research efforts to study therapy outcomes have been voluminous and sustained. In 1952 the British psychologist H. J. Eysenck charged that psychotherapy produces no greater changes in emotionally disturbed individuals than do naturally occurring life events. Since that time researchers have been spurred to answer this challenge. Analyzing and synthesizing the data from 25 years of research on the efficacy of psychotherapy, Lester Luborsky, Barton Singer, and Lise Luborsky concluded that most forms of psychotherapy produce changes in a substantial proportion of patients—changes that are often, but not always, greater than those achieved by control patients who did not receive therapy. Other reviewers reached similar conclusions. Mary Lee Smith and Gene Glass used specialized statistical techniques to demonstrate that on standardized measures across all types of therapy, patients, therapists, and outcome criteria, the average patient improved and, moreover, did so to a greater extent than did 75% of comparable control patients. In short, the preponderance of the evidence does not support Eysenck's pessimistic conclusion, but neither does it identify particular therapies as impressively superior.

## Patient variables and problems of diagnosis

Therapy outcomes obviously depend to a significant extent on patient characteristics. From the moment the patient meets the therapist, the latter seeks to define the nature of the problem in need of treatment or amelioration. The therapist becomes a diagnostician who attempts to identify a malfunction or a "problem" in order to institute appropriate

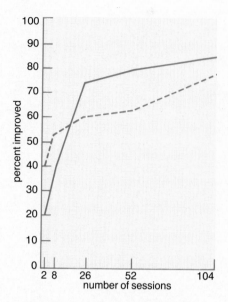

*Statistical techniques have demonstrated that for all varieties of psychotherapy patients improved and did so to a greater extent than did 75% of comparable patients who did not receive any therapy. The solid line indicates ratings of the patients by their therapists at the time that treatment was terminated; the broken line reveals ratings by the patients themselves during therapy.*

"The Dose-Effect Relationship in Psychotherapy," H. I. Howard, S. M. Kopta, M. S. Krause, and D. E. Orlinsky, *American Psychologist*, copyright 1986 by the American Psychological Association. Adapted by permission of the authors.

237

therapeutic action. This requires clinical understanding and appreciation of the vast array of individual differences between patients.

Thus therapists and researchers have come to realize that a phobia, depression, anxiety state, etc., in one patient is not identical to a similar problem in another. Taxonomies of mental disorders such as the *Diagnostic and Statistical Manual of Mental Disorders* of the American Psychiatric Association (DSM-III) are useful, but they may not adequately recognize individual differences. Furthermore, diagnostic categories cannot be directly linked to particular forms of psychotherapy, although efforts along these lines are proceeding.

A major stumbling block is that a patient's "personality organization" often forms an integral part of the therapeutic problem. Phobias, for example, are often found in patients who are generally shy, dependent, and anxious in social situations. In addition, genetic, social, and environmental factors of various kinds influence a patient's current disturbance. Finally, the patient's life history, particularly interpersonal relationships in early childhood, may be crucially important for understanding and treating the current problem. The foregoing variables are typically intertwined in complex ways, thus giving rise to unique constellations that often defy categorization.

## The therapist

As already suggested, the therapist is of crucial importance to the outcome of psychotherapy. Relevant variables in this regard may include the therapist's theoretical orientation, techniques, training, and length of experience. While no single variable has been shown to have a decisive influence on therapeutic outcome, one should not conclude that aspects of the therapist's personality, training, and experience are inconsequential.

There appears to be some agreement that thorough formal training, supervised experience, and, perhaps, personal therapy are essential qualifications for a therapist, but considerable controversy persists. The observation that some persons without formal training can function effectively in the therapeutic role may underscore the importance of such qualities as empathy, respect, understanding, commitment, and caring, but it does not negate the need for systematic clinical training and experience. It should also be remembered that therapists are not solely "change agents"; rather, they are often called upon to make difficult and subtle diagnostic decisions. Furthermore, as professionals they adhere to a code of ethics that assures the client or patient of competent and responsible care.

Training of psychotherapists is being conducted in academic departments of universities and in a growing number of professional schools. Owing to the relative newness of the field, training standards of different institutions are variable, and the selection of trainees may be insufficiently rigorous. However, licensing laws regulating the practice of psychotherapy are having a salutary effect on training and, therefore, on the quality of therapeutic practice, as is society's demand for accountability and cost-effectiveness. Finally, research has called atten-

*Four major types of psychotherapy are among a patient's choices for treatment. From the left they are psychoanalysis, the behavioral therapies, client-centered therapy, and existential therapy. Each approaches the treatment process from a different point of view and uses different methods to try to help patients.*

238

*The patients of Sigmund Freud lay on his couch, photographed in his London home after Freud was forced by the Nazis to leave Vienna in 1938. Freud, the founder of psychoanalysis, sat in the armchair at the end of the couch so that he would not face his patient, an arrangement that he believed would encourage the patient to talk uninhibitedly.*

tion to the occurrence of "negative effects" in psychotherapy, most of which are ultimately attributable to deficiencies in the therapist. Taken together, these developments will continue to strengthen the quality of therapeutic practice.

## Process research

Although the study of therapy outcomes has tended to occupy the limelight, there remain basic scientific questions of how particular outcomes are achieved. To this end it is essential to focus on the transactions between patient and therapist. Of particular relevance is the intensive study of both verbal and nonverbal communications between the participants. While voluminous studies of the therapeutic process have been carried out, progress has been slow. To cite some positive findings, it has been shown that patients who from the beginning of their therapy become actively involved in the treatment process have better therapeutic results; conversely, patients who are negativistic, hostile, and resistant at the beginning of therapy tend to evoke reciprocal attitudes in their therapists. Thus achievements on this front have been relatively modest, but the emergence of new techniques for analyzing content and process (aided by audio and video recordings of therapy hours) has raised hopes for significant advances in knowledge. In this regard research on the therapeutic relationship (alliance) holds particular promise.

## Conclusions

From modest beginnings in the late 1800s, psychotherapy, particularly in the United States, has become a sprawling enterprise. Its increasing availability and popularity, despite diminished support from the govern-

240

ment and insurance companies, is undoubtedly attributable to the fact that it meets important personal and social needs. Once defined as a treatment for a narrow range of "nervous and mental disorders," it has become greatly expanded in scope, as has the cadre of mental health professionals who are called upon to assist a wide band of the population in solving a melange of "problems in living." The recipients of psychotherapy range from children to the elderly, and a large number of theories and techniques have been developed.

Psychotherapy as a field of research is of even more recent vintage; however, during the last several decades a sizable body of literature has focused with increasing precision and rigor on such basic issues as outcomes, patient and therapist variables, and the transactions between patient and therapist. The research tools of modern behavioral science have increasingly been brought to bear on the study of psychotherapy. Although these efforts have not resulted in breakthroughs, psychotherapy research has become increasingly sophisticated and productive. It is playing an increasingly important role in transforming a clinical art into a scientific discipline.

FOR ADDITIONAL READING

Hans J. Eysenck, "The Effects of Psychotherapy: An Evaluation," *Journal of Consulting Psychology* (August 1952, pp. 319–324).

Jerome D. Frank, *Persuasion and Healing,* 2nd ed. (Johns Hopkins University Press, 1973).

Sol L. Garfield and Allen E. Bergin (eds.), *Handbook of Psychotherapy and Behavior Change,* 3rd ed. (John Wiley and Sons, 1986).

Michael J. Lambert, David A. Shapiro, and Allen E. Bergin, "The Effectiveness of Psychotherapy," in Sol L. Garfield and Allen E. Bergin (eds.), *Handbook of Psychotherapy and Behavior Change,* 3rd ed. (John Wiley and Sons, 1986).

Steven J. Lynn and John P. Garske (eds.), *Contemporary Psychotherapies: Models and Methods* (Charles E. Merrill Publishing Co., 1985).

Mary Lee Smith and Gene V. Glass, "Meta-analysis of Psychotherapy Outcome Studies," *American Psychologist* (September 1977, pp. 752–760).

Hans H. Strupp and Jeffrey L. Binder, *Psychotherapy in a New Key: A Guide to Time-Limited Dynamic Psychotherapy* (Basic Books, 1984).

# The San Diego Zoo
## AN ARK IN THE PARK

by Jeffrey L. Jouett

During the years since it was founded in 1916,
the San Diego Zoo has become one of the largest and
most acclaimed in the world. It is now also playing a major role
in the effort to preserve endangered species of animals.

The plaintive bellowing of a leftover lion, heard a half-mile distant by a sympathetic surgeon, evoked an extraordinary response:

"I turned to my brother, Paul, who was riding with me, and half jokingly, half wishfully, said, 'Wouldn't it be splendid if San Diego had a zoo! You know . . . I think I'll start one,' " the late Harry M. Wegeforth recalls in his memoirs. "Taking me at my word, he replied that he would be glad to help, but added dubiously that he did not see how such a project could be put over."

The two were sharing a mid-September 1916 drive through the small seaport city's rambling city park. Quartered there at scattered locations were big cats, wolves, bison, bears, elk, and deer that had been abandoned after the closing of a two-year international exposition celebrating completion of the Panama Canal. Harry Wegeforth turned the car around and parked it in front of the *San Diego Union* newspaper office. The next morning a front-page article relayed the brothers' call for founding members of a zoological society to take charge of Balboa Park's menagerie of misfits and operate a zoo.

Wistful roars still rumble across the same San Diego canyons. Plentiful in 1916, the sonorous Asian lions are today endangered, with fewer than 200 members of the subspecies alive in the wild. In the 70 years since the lion's grumbling inspired him, Harry Wegeforth and his successors have filled the canyons and mesas with nature's most exotic and enchanting wild creatures.

The San Diego Zoo, begun so lightheartedly, has evolved into one of the world's foremost zoological gardens and has prepared for a very serious new challenge. It has become a focal point for a multidisciplinary, modern scientific effort to hedge against the seemingly unalterable progression of wildlife extinctions. Today, and in the future, the San Diego Zoo and other of the world's zoological gardens may prove the last, best hope for survival of the Asian lions and scores more endangered species that find refuge there.

*JEFFREY L. JOUETT is Publicist for the Zoological Society of San Diego in San Diego, California.*

*Photograph of the San Diego Wild Animal Park by Gus Schonefeld—Berg & Associates*

## Postage stamps to Noah's Ark

Providing sanctuary for and sustaining endangered wildlife was not a priority for Zoological Society of San Diego founder Wegeforth, though conservation was endorsed alongside education and recreation in the objectives and bylaws adopted at the society's first meeting on Oct. 2, 1916. To best bring the wonders of nature to the city dweller, Wegeforth set out to fill the San Diego Zoo with popular species such as elephants, apes, giraffes, and zebras, as well as a number of firsts and onlys. "It was never the Zoo's purpose to have a large number of any one species of animals," he later recalled. "A fair collection of the outstanding animals was to be kept, and as the Zoo became more financially robust, we were to replace the most common animals with more select rare specimens."

So in 1925 San Diegans welcomed Cuddles and Snuggles, the first and only koalas exhibited outside of Australia, and in 1931 were quite taken with Mbongo and Ngagi, the first and only mountain gorillas in captivity. To earn the bragging rights of "world's largest animal collection," Wegeforth traded for or had captured as many species of mammals, birds, and reptiles as he could. The majority of the young zoo's animal species were represented by one or two specimens, a "postage stamp collection" of animals, but in regard to variety San Diego's menagerie was considered among the finest in the United States as early as 1925. Modern zoos emphasize larger groups of fewer different species in order to maximize captive reproduction. But until recent years breeding in zoos was not looked upon as a way to replenish casualties in the collection. Replacement animals were, for the most part, available from the wild, and Wegeforth went about attaining them with relish.

A canny and resourceful trader and fund-raiser, Wegeforth bartered common southern California animals such as sea lions, pelicans, rattlesnakes, and king snakes for rare and exotic animals from zoos around the world. He took advantage of the area's mild climate and built outdoor, barless enclosures patterned after those in the Hagenbeck Zoo in Hamburg, Germany (now West Germany). And he enlisted such adventurers as Frank ("Bring 'Em Back Alive") Buck and wildlife photographers Martin and Osa Johnson, among many others, to gather animals for San Diego on their wilderness expeditions. A 1926 expedition to nearby Guadalupe Island netted the San Diego Zoo the first elephant seals seen in captivity and provided Wegeforth with surplus animals and valuable bargaining power. Alarmed at the high prices being charged by dealers in exotic animals, Wegeforth formed an alliance of zoo directors that evolved into the American Association of Zoological Parks and Aquariums.

Quantity, variety, and rarity were the zoo collection values set by Wegeforth and his successor, Belle Benchley, through 1952, when the high cost of attaining animals from the wild and increasing restrictions on the export of wildlife from many countries began to stir the conservation consciousness of the zoo world. Executive director Charles Schroeder determined in 1953 to run the San Diego Zoo as a good business, which meant, among other things, viewing captive breeding both as cost-effective and as a way to dampen the growing criticism of zoos

244

for draining animals from the wild. The San Diego Zoo soon won awards for first births or hatchings of Galapagos tortoises, koalas, Gila monsters, proboscis monkeys, thick-billed parrots, and ruffed lemurs.

By 1966 the crisis of human encroachment on wildlife habitats was all too clear to San Diego Zoo leaders. Not only did the future of zoos depend on the future of wild animals but, more important, the future of an increasing number of wild animals would depend on what zoos could do to help. In October of that year the Zoological Society of San Diego invited zoos from around the world to a landmark conference on "The Role of Zoos in the International Conservation of Wild Animals." From this meeting issued a new cooperative spirit among zoos and a commitment to extend zoo resources toward wildlife conservation education and to buffer dwindling species against extinction.

At Schroeder's urging, San Diegans added a spacious second campus to the San Diego Zoo, beginning in 1969 to construct the San Diego Wild Animal Park on 720 rural hectares (1,800 acres) some 50 kilometers (30 miles) north of the downtown zoo. Called "the zoo of the future" when it opened in 1972, the Wild Animal Park mixes large herds and groups of several species in vast, geographically similar enclosures, some more than 40 hectares (100 acres) in area. More natural interactions and group behaviors result as the animals roam freely while the Wild Animal Park visitors are enclosed aboard a guided monorail tour around the perimeter. The result has been a reproduction rate unparalleled in the zoo world. The abundance of births at the Wild Animal Park has helped bring the southern white rhinoceros off the endangered species list, provided replacement animals for zoos throughout the world, established a genetic reservoir against impending extinction in the wild for many endangered species, and provided animals to return to the wild in projects to reestablish in their natural habitats the Arabian oryx, the tule wapiti, and, soon, the Mongolian wild horse and the California condor.

## Cooperation for conservation

Today the San Diego Zoo's living collection includes 3,300 animals of more than 760 species. The Wild Animal Park adds another 2,500 animals of 280 species to the total tally of the Zoological Society of San Diego. Some 110 of this total are endangered species, and many more are threatened, vulnerable, or rare in the wild. The two campuses are also accredited botanical gardens, where 6,000 species of plants, including nearly 700 kinds of orchids, flourish under the care of horticulturists.

In a 1985 refocusing of goals and philosophies, Zoological Society leaders strengthened the organization's emphasis on the preservation of nature, adopting a mission of "increasing understanding and appreciation of the inherent worth of all life forms by exhibiting animals and plants in natural settings and applying our efforts and influence to the conservation of the earth's wildlife." The new statement of purpose gave voice to a new direction already embarked upon by the San Diego Zoo and the San Diego Wild Animal Park. To accomplish these wildlife conservation goals, the two facilities had begun setting up large areas for

245

The San Diego Zoo contains 3,300 animals of more than 760 species. On the opposite page are (top left) koalas, (top right) aoudads, (center) Malay tapirs, (bottom left) an emerald tree boa, and (bottom right) alligators. At the left are orangutans; above is a lemur; below is a Mandarin duck; and below left is the "Heart of the Zoo Rain Forest Aviary."

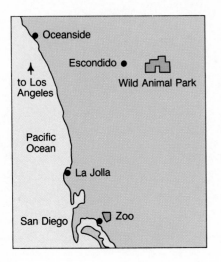

animal breeding compounds out of public view, cooperating with other zoos and government agencies on a far greater scale and establishing a unique research center to concentrate on the reproductive problems of endangered species.

Off-exhibit breeding facilities allow the zoo and the Wild Animal Park to keep more animals of important species and to establish self-sustaining, genetically sound captive populations. Without daily interaction with thousands of zoo visitors, animals in these behind-the-scenes breeding areas are under less stress and are more inclined to natural behaviors, including mating. On a hillside below the San Diego Zoo hospital are a series of breeding groups of lemurs, lion-tailed macaques, douc langurs, tamarins, and other primates. In the same off-exhibit area is the Avian Propagation Center, where thousands of birds' eggs from more than 100 exotic species ranging from Darwin's rheas to tinamous have been artificially incubated and hatched since the complex opened in 1980. The San Diego Wild Animal Park devotes several hundred hectares to off-exhibit breeding groups of antelope species, zebras, and Mongolian wild horses, as well as cheetahs, hornbills, and California condors.

The importance of sharing animals and information among zoos was underlined at a 1979 world conference on breeding endangered species in captivity, at which the Zoological Society of San Diego acted as host. Thomas Lovejoy, director of the World Wildlife Fund USA, told the 300 zoo professionals from 26 nations, "Probably most critical at this time is the willingness of zoos to enter into a new era of collaboration—of which there are encouraging signs—where survival of species takes precedence

over institutional jealousy. Ultimately, the extent of zoo cooperation will determine how full tomorrow's ark will be.''

Breeding loans between zoos are one form of cooperative action that benefits endangered species. Under these relatively new agreements, an animal from one zoo is shipped to another zoo to be matched with an unattached mate. The two zoos share any offspring that result from the prearranged pairing. These exchanges help expand the genetic mixture of a species' captive population and encourage the maximum contribution from each animal toward the next generation of its kind. By 1987 the San Diego Zoo and the Wild Animal Park were participating in more

*Map (opposite page, top) reveals the locations of the San Diego Zoo and the San Diego Wild Animal Park, which are separated from one another by about 50 kilometers (30 miles). An aerial view of the Wild Animal Park (opposite page, bottom) looks toward the southwest with the Asian Waterhole in the foreground. Above, a herd of Indian axis deer, or chital, grazes on the Asian Plains of the Wild Animal Park in view of passengers on the park's monorail line. Nairobi Village (left), the entry complex at the Wild Animal Park, contains three amphitheaters for shows that feature trained animals.*

Attractions at the Wild Animal Park include (top to bottom) Przewalski's horses in the Mongolian Steppe area; some of the 15 different species that coexist peacefully in the Eastern Africa enclosure; and wisent, wild boars, saddleback tapirs, and water buffalo at the Asian Waterhole.

than 300 breeding loans with a score of zoos outside the United States and nearly 100 zoos and private animal collections within the country.

For lemurs, Asian lions, gorillas, black rhinoceroses, and some 40 other extremely endangered animals, a special captive breeding strategy was established by the American Association of Zoological Parks and Aquariums. Called a Species Survival Plan (SSP), this long-range project enlists the cooperation of each zoo that holds a particular species in organizing matings and sharing information on diets and behavior. The SSP programs make the best use of zoological parks' resources by avoiding duplication of effort and making sure that all participating zoos share the best interests of the animals. The International Species Inventory System (ISIS) keeps computerized records of the locations, breeding histories, and mortality factors of zoo animals. The Zoological Society of San Diego is involved with more than 30 of the SSP programs and contributes information on all of the animals in its care to the ISIS system.

## Center for Reproduction of Endangered Species

Since 1975 the Zoological Society of San Diego has spent more than $1 million a year to fund its research program dedicated to applying modern science and medical technology to preserving vanishing wild species. With a staff of 30 scientists and technicians, the Center for Reproduction of Endangered Species (CRES) brings into focus a range of scientific specialties, including genetics, endocrinology, microbiology, behavior, reproductive physiology, and pathology. CRES's work is accomplished with the cooperation of the University of California and other academic institutions, government agencies, and conservation organizations. The pioneering research done by CRES scientists headquartered at the San Diego Zoo has a worldwide impact on wildlife management.

The multidisciplinary approach to endangered species research was proposed and put together by Kurt Benirschke, a professor at the University of California School of Medicine and one of the world's leading

*Plants as well as animals are an important feature of the Wild Animal Park. At the top is the Conifer Arboretum, a display of hundreds of conifers from throughout the world. Visitors to the California Native Plants Trail (left) can view representative species from ten of the state's major botanical communities, ranging from the desert to the high mountains.*

*The southern white rhinoceros (left) and the Arabian oryx (above) have been removed from the endangered species list because of breeding success at the Wild Animal Park.*

authorities on human reproduction. Eager to apply his knowledge and research skills to studying the reproduction of animal species nearing extinction, Benirschke won support for the CRES concept and signed on as its first director and principal scientist. He brought with him from the university a wealth of scientific equipment, a core staff, and an idea that would become a priceless resource for biologists internationally while sparking the imaginations of scientists and laymen alike. Benirschke would start the "Frozen Zoo."

Also dubbed the "20th Century Ark," San Diego's Frozen Zoo is an approximately one-meter-square metal tank chilled by liquid nitrogen to −230° C (−385° F) and filled with semen samples, ova, and fibroblasts from jaguars, pygmy chimps, komodo dragons, gorillas, and roughly 350 endangered or threatened animal species. The cells are stored in a state of suspended animation and can be thawed as needed for studies of chromosomes, aging, evolution, blood cells, or muscle fibers, for example; thus, scientists do not have to seek samples from uncooperative and often unavailable wild animals. Other zoos and outside scientists make continual use of the Frozen Zoo as a genetic library. Reproductive physiologists on the CRES staff draw upon the Frozen Zoo's semen and ova collections for artificial insemination and embryo-transfer procedures with rare tragopan pheasants, komodo dragons, lion-tailed macaques, and other species.

In the CRES endocrine lab, researchers hunt for hormones and try to understand the part they play in wild animal reproduction. While estrogen cycles for human females and many commercially profitable domestic animals are well documented, relatively little is known of the reproductive hormones of thousands of wild species. Monitoring estrogens and other sex hormones is critical to the management of captive breeding populations, particularly for individuals that are reluctant to reproduce. Hormone levels can indicate whether an animal is pregnant, whether it is capable of becoming pregnant, the precise time that mating should occur to achieve pregnancy, whether the fetus is progressing normally, and the time of the impending birth. Such knowledge will enhance the success of artificial insemination of zoo animals.

Human estrogen studies are done with blood samples, but captive wild animals, birds in particular, are traumatized to the point of injury and even death by attempts to catch them in order to draw blood. To subject rare species to such great risks for regular blood samples would be self-defeating. CRES endocrinologists solved this problem by developing methods of measuring minute quantities of hormones in urine and fecal samples that are collected from the wild species without stress to the animals. Reproductive cycles of armadillos, elephants, okapis, rhinoceroses, gorillas, lemurs, bongos, and many other endangered species have been described for the first time through use of this technique.

A basic requirement for successful reproduction is to get the males together with the females. This may be easy enough with mammals, but nearly one-third of all bird species are monomorphic, *i.e.*, males and females look alike to human observers. By charting the ratio of male sex hormones to female hormones, CRES endocrinologists are able to determine a bird's sex by its droppings. Word of this new, noninvasive method

*California condor hand puppet (above) is used to feed and groom a condor chick. Eggs of these birds, which are almost extinct in the wild, are taken for hatching at the zoo so that they will not be lost to predators. Below, food is prepared and an incubator is attended to at the Avian Propagation Center, where thousands of bird eggs from many rare species have been hatched since its opening in 1980.*

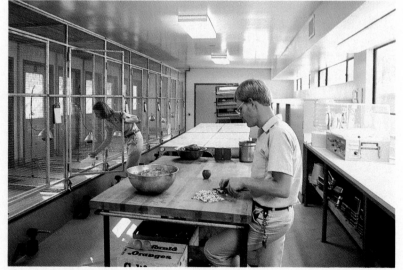

*At the zoo a geneticist works with the International Species Inventory System, which maintains computerized records of the locations, breeding histories, and mortality factors of zoo animals in the United States.*

of distinguishing female from male birds spread quickly, and the San Diego Zoo soon began receiving packets of bird feces from zoos throughout the world. The result has been an increase in the number of couples among the captive kiwis and condors and other monomorphic species. The breeding record of the rare Puerto Rican parrot has improved greatly since the San Diego Zoo helped the U.S. Fish and Wildlife Service biologists discover that they had been pairing birds of the same sex.

Small populations of wild species are susceptible to changes in appearance and behavior as well as to shortened life expectancy owing to the characteristics of limited genetic potential. In zoo collections with inadequate gene pools, unwanted genetic traits can quickly become common when mating of related animals gives disproportionate prominence to recessive genes and chromosome abnormalities. Geneticists at CRES strive to maintain the highest degree of genetic variety among zoo animals by recommending the mating of least-related individuals. For such species as the Mongolian wild horse, extinct in the wild and found only in zoos and preserves, a CRES computer program tracks the pedigree of every individual. All 400 surviving members of this species are descended from only a dozen "founder" animals, and so some inbreeding is unavoidable. But it has been lowered significantly since the genetic-based pairings have been instituted with the cooperation of zoos worldwide. Similar computer-planned matings are improving the genetic foundations of captive koalas, condors, and lemurs, to name a few species. For example, black-and-white ruffed lemur matings are programmmed to avoid a funnel chest deformity that had developed in the rare species' small captive population. CRES genetic evaluations have proved helpful to numerous zoos and species-survival programs internationally. One example is the differentiation by chromosome study of the Bornean and Sumatran species of orangutan. Though long known to be two separate species that do not interbreed in the wild because they inhabit separate islands in Indonesia, some individuals of these species look so much alike that

254

some zoos were pairing them and creating a hybrid orangutan not found in nature. By examining chromosomes found in skin or blood samples, CRES geneticists are able to identify hybrids, Borneans, and Sumatrans and urge appropriate reproductive strategies.

The artificial constraints of captivity impose behavioral changes on wild animal groups, and often the captive environment and its associated behaviors can deter reproduction. For many endangered species in zoos there is a problem both in discovering how captivity may be altering normal behavior patterns and in determining just what normal behavior is, since the majority of species have not been adequately studied in the wild. Social animals, particularly primates, may engage in dominance struggles and intergroup rivalries that interfere with breeding behavior. Behaviorists at CRES observe and record individual animal actions and group interactions in order to recommend changes in captive housing, nutrition, care procedures, or the composition of an animal group that will maximize the breeding potential of each species. An example of behavioral science applied to endangered species reproduction involves the cheetahs at the San Diego Wild Animal Park. Notoriously poor breeders in captivity, the cheetahs were housed together year round. A behaviorist studying the lack of reproduction suggested that the males and females be separated for most of the year and brought together only for the few days that the female was in estrus, thus more closely approximating the cheetah's largely solitary lifestyle in the wild. This recommendation was put into effect, and the result was litters of captive-born cheetah cubs the very next year.

To better sustain wild species in zoos, attention must be paid to the death rate as well as to the birthrate. CRES studies in virology and bacteriology are making important contributions to increasing the life spans and years of fertility of valuable animals. A hepatitis-like virus that causes liver damage in snow leopards; a viral disease called malignant catarrhal fever that affects wildebeest, Pere David's deer, Indian gaurs, and other endangered hoofed species; and neonatal diarrhea, which is a leading cause of death for newborn animals, are among areas of intense investigation by CRES microbiologists.

Artificial insemination and embryo transfer are two complex procedures that are now commonly practiced on domestic animals and that hold great potential as reproductive techniques to bolster dwindling zoo populations. Gazelles and gorillas are among animals that have been successfully artificially inseminated at other zoos, using freshly collected semen. The goal of the San Diego Zoo's CRES, however, is to refine the methodology of insemination so as to make it as consistently successful for a wide range of exotic species as it is already for cattle and other domestic animals. CRES reproductive physiologists also are intent on making routine use of frozen semen and in vitro fertilization. Research progresses on correct freezing and thawing procedures for semen and ova of a broad spectrum of exotic species, while studies of the ovulatory cycles of endangered species will provide insight on the crucial timing of inseminations and embryo transplants.

*The frozen Zoo is a metal tank about one meter (3.3 feet) square that is chilled by liquid nitrogen to −230°C (−385°F) and filled with semen samples, ova, and fibroblasts of approximately 350 endangered or threatened animal species. Stored in a state of suspended animation, the cells can be thawed and used for studies of, for example, chromosomes, aging, blood cells, and muscle fibers.*

© Zoological Society of San Diego, photo, Ron Garrison

The goal of maintaining genetic diversity will be made much simpler once these insemination logistics have been perfected. Currently, a genetic balance of zoo animals is attained by shipping, for example, a male from one zoo to another zoo to breed with an unrelated female. This involves considerable transportation expense; it subjects valuable animals to substantial trauma, risking injury and death; and it holds no guarantee that the new pair will accept each other and produce babies. How much safer, simpler, and cheaper it will be to deliver one small metal thermos containing enough chilled sperm cells to impregnate, through artificial insemination, 100 of the most obstinate gorillas. And semen from the largest elephant weighs the same as and costs no more to ship than semen from the tiniest elephant shrew.

Once perfected, embryo transfer techniques will allow researchers to "mass produce" babies of endangered species, accomplishing population gains in a few years that would take generations to reach by normal reproductive methods. The objective of embryo transfer is to produce up to ten times more babies than normal from each female of an endangered species, using surrogate mothers of similar (though not endangered) species to carry the developing embryos until birth. A female Arabian oryx, for instance, could be injected with a hormone to induce "superovulation." Instead of releasing the normal one egg cell at ovulation, the oryx will release many—perhaps a dozen or more. The ova are then fertilized by Arabian oryx sperm that has been stored in the Frozen Zoo cryogenic bank. When the oryx embryos are just eight cells in size, each will be transferred to the womb of a similar, more common species, such as the relatively plentiful fringe-eared oryx. Following the normal gestation period, these fringe-eared oryx surrogate mothers will give birth to Arabian oryx babies. At CRES work on embryo transfer techniques is being done using rats, hamsters, Barbados sheep, and two endangered species, the Cretan goat and Mongolian wild horse.

*Healthy lamb (above) is the result of an embryo transplant from one Barbados sheep to another. At the right an embryo transplant operation takes place on a scimitar-horned oryx. By means of such transplants, zoo officials hope that many more babies than normal will be produced from females of endangered species, using surrogate mothers of similar (though not endangered) species to carry the developing embryos until birth.*

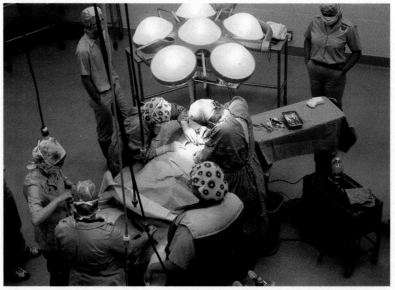

*Among the threatened species represented at the zoo is the Turkomen markhor. It has been depleted in its native habitats of the Soviet Union and Afghanistan because its impressive horns have made it the target of hunters.*

## A wildlife legacy

The prospects facing animals in their wild habitats are grim ones, and the zoos of the world can do only so much on their behalf. The clearing of tropical forests and the devasting impact of human population growth upon wild animals and plants are driven by economic and social forces that show no signs of abating. Hundreds of animal and plant species are destined for extinction in the next 25 years for every one species that zoos can keep alive. Robert Wagner, executive director of the American Association of Zoological Parks and Aquariums, told an international conservation conference in 1979, "Zoological parks and aquariums cannot be considered the last alternative for the survival of all species. But we must be recognized as a waystation, holding some species in trust until the onslaught of habitat destruction can be somehow checked."

The San Diego Zoo and the San Diego Wild Animal Park have joined other zoos in using their animal husbandry expertise and their potential for educating the public to become strong forces for the preservation of nature. Working in concert, zoos of the world are facing an unfortunate future with the hope of holding onto as much of the planet's wildlife legacy as possible.

"At the very least," stated New York Zoo director William Conway at San Diego's conference on breeding endangered species in captivity, "the preservation of a small number of species, even if only for a generation or two, is the preservation of options. All zoos and all people need a new commitment to our vanishing biota in order to make the next few generations of human beings inheritors and not just survivors."

257

# The Lincoln Park Zoo
## AN URBAN OASIS

### by Lester E. Fisher

Confined to a small area less than three miles from Chicago's expanding downtown, the Lincoln Park Zoo for more than a century has sought to entertain and instruct city dwellers.

It began as a drainage ditch for the small community of early Chicago residents. Next the land served as a cemetery. But as the city grew, the cemetery was considered a health hazard, and the bodies were exhumed so that the land could be turned over to open park space. Lagoons were dredged, and two swans were presented by New York City's Central Park as a gift to the area newly designated as Lincoln Park.

The year was 1868, and the swans were soon joined by a bear cub, two peafowl, a kangaroo, a condor, and a goat purchased from the Barnum & Bailey Circus. The small menagerie was called Lincoln Park Zoo, and it was located along Lake Michigan just north of downtown Chicago.

Today, almost a century and a quarter later, Lincoln Park Zoo is known throughout the world as a leader in conservation, recreation, and education. Among its collection of 2,200 animals, it boasts the finest and largest collection of captive lowland gorillas anywhere in the world. Its area has remained at 14 hectares (35 acres) for much of its existence, but within these original boundaries extraordinary change has taken place. This change has been dictated not only by the growth that Chicago has experienced but also by changes realized through advances in medicine and by the decline in populations of the world's wildlife and the resultant new attitudes about the role that captive animals play in zoos of the 20th century.

This is the story of Lincoln Park Zoo, a small zoo located in the heart of the Midwest's largest city. It is also the story of zoos—and their role in conservation today—as well as a story of a living community that coexists with humans and has many of the same problems, dynamics, and aspects of change as any other community in the United States.

### Early years

As Lincoln Park Zoo emerged in the final quarter of the last century, Chicago quickly grew up around it. By 1874 the collection included a variety of birds, mammals, and reptiles, and the nearby conservatory was completed in that same year. Originally 11.8 hectares (29 acres) were

*LESTER E. FISHER, a doctor of veterinary medicine, is Director of the Lincoln Park Zoo.*

*(Opposite page) Photograph © Bill Frantz—CLICK/Chicago*

designated for use by the zoo, but in 1962 a Farm-in-the-Zoo was built
on adjacent land, bringing the zoo's total area to its current 14 hectares.

The early zoo architecture—some of it dates back more than 90
years—was classical in design and typical of the period. It provided great
halls and public spaces for visitors but minimal accommodations for the
captive residents. Animals were to be seen and enjoyed, and great care
was taken to provide optimum viewing for the public and easy cleaning
of cages for the caretakers. Little thought was given to the physical
comfort and psychological needs of the animals. Few animals ultimately
bred under these conditions, but it hardly mattered. New animals could
be taken from the wild at any time. The cost of doing this was minimal,
and availability of animals was not a problem. And so the zoo grew.

An early historic precedent of free admission to the zoo was set by the
first park commissioners, and this policy remains to this day. As a result,
the zoo became not only a neighborhood zoo but one for the whole city,
providing recreation for all Chicagoans. It became a particularly popular
family place, especially for many new immigrants who had enjoyed their
zoos in Europe and could stroll through the park and zoo when they
could afford little else on a Sunday afternoon.

It was in those early years that certain animals gained particular renown
and became citywide favorites. Judy, an Indian elephant, allegedly walked
one night to Lincoln Park through the city from Brookfield Zoo, located
42 kilometers (26 miles) away in a Chicago suburb. Because she refused
to board her truck to be transferred to Lincoln Park Zoo, there was no
other way to get her to her new home. At Lincoln Park she wintered in
the old Small Mammal House for over 40 years and spent her summers
delighting visitors as she performed antics in her outside quarters. Living
to the age of 68, she had set a longevity record for elephants in North
America when she died in 1971.

Another favorite was Mike, a giant polar bear who had been presented as a cub to the zoo by the local Elks club chapter. For years he was "king" of the old line of bear cages that housed more than nine species representing six continents. During his years at the zoo Mike consumed massive quantities of marshmallows offered by visitors. Although this did not contribute to his demise at 30 years of age, it did not help his teeth, and in his later years he was treated on several occasions for extensive cavities.

But perhaps the most popular zoo personality was a lowland gorilla, Bushman, who came to Lincoln Park Zoo from Cameroon, West Africa, in 1931 and died 20 years later on Jan. 1, 1951. At the time of his death he was considered the finest captive specimen of his kind in the world, and after the public heard of his death, they filed for days past his empty cage to pay their respects to an animal that had given so much pleasure to so many Chicagoans for two decades.

But Bushman was far more than just a celebrity animal at Lincoln Park Zoo; he helped establish the interest in lowland gorillas that launched the zoo into its place as the world leader in breeding captive great apes. Bushman had come to the zoo at just one year of age and, although he never bred, he survived at a time when most gorillas were dying in captivity. He had shown that there was hope for the future, and with his death a new era began to emerge in the care and husbandry of all captive animals.

Celebrity status for Lincoln Park Zoo was not, however, restricted to its animals or locally to Chicago. Through an early television show broadcast live across the United States, Marlin Perkins, then zoo director, brought the magic of Lincoln Park and the zoo world to millions of Americans who had no access to or knowledge of exotic animals or a zoo. His popular program, *Zoo Parade*, was broadcast weekly from the zoo every Sunday afternoon for more than 12 years. It was this show that also helped to change many people's attitudes about zoos and the role they would later play in conservation of wildlife.

The concept of housing captive animals originated several thousand years ago in the Imperial Gardens of China. In the 18th century a zoo was constructed at the royal palace in Vienna, and other European monarchs were also soon constructing houses to exhibit their growing menageries. But these zoos were only for the nobility. It was not until relatively recent years that captive animals were exhibited for all the people to enjoy. As mentioned earlier, however, these zoos were designed for pure recreation and public enjoyment, and adequate housing and husbandry for the animals were given little, if any, consideration.

During the last 25 years these outdated concepts have virtually disappeared. Today science plays an ever increasing role in zoo management, and new technologies provide the basis for animal management decisions that help to run zoos in a sensitive but businesslike manner. The zoo today is administered as though it were a community of valuable individuals rather than a collection of replaceable things gathered together purely for public recreation.

*Bushman (top), a lowland gorilla, lived at the zoo from 1931 to 1951 and was perhaps its most popular inhabitant. Below, Marlin Perkins, zoo director from 1944 to 1962, holds a monkey during the filming of Perkins's television show, Zoo Parade.*

*The Lion House (above right), completed in 1912, features a large central hall with cages on each side and a vaulted roof. Indian lions (above) have moved out of the house and into one of the connected outdoor enclosures, which have been designed to simulate the lions' natural habitat as closely as possible.*

## Rebuilding program

At Lincoln Park Zoo this community consists of approximately 2,200 animals, made up of more than 430 species and subspecies of birds, reptiles, amphibians, and mammals. The collection is a dynamic one, ever changing, with births, deaths, illnesses, trades with other zoos, and purchases. Animals must be fed and cared for every day. Because space is limited, optimum use must be made of physical areas, new and old, so that the best environment possible can be provided for each captive animal. Some animals must be kept in groups, while others do better in pairs. Some need height, while others require small hiding places in order to feel secure. Most need a varied diet, but some need a highly specialized and unusual combination of foods. Many animals will eat killed food, while some require the challenge of killing their own meal. Early housing, originally presumed adequate, must now be adapted or changed completely to meet the animals' biologic and psychological needs.

Lincoln Park Zoo's Reptile House was designed as Chicago's first aquarium and, when completed in May 1923 was the largest freshwater fish aquarium in the United States. With the completion of the Shedd Aquarium in 1929, the aquarium at the zoo was closed and converted to the present Reptile House. Then in the 1930s modifications were made to many of the larger tanks by the federal Works Progress Administration (WPA), and today some of the finest examples of WPA art in the Chicago area can still be seen in this historic building.

The Lion House, truly a classic, was completed in 1912. Its huge hall and vaulted tile roof have made it a Chicago landmark. Similarly, the Small Animal House, now called the Primate House, was built in 1927 with classic features and huge open public spaces. The Small Mammal House was built in 1889 and the Bird House in 1904, and although they have since been modified, they remain operational as the zoo's oldest buildings.

*The Primate House (left), originally named the Small Animal House, was built in 1927. It now accommodates a large collection of Old and New World monkeys and several great apes. One of the newest zoo buildings (below left) is the Great Ape House. Completed in 1976, the building lies under a man-made hill. Six large interior habitats provide considerable space for the gorillas, orangutans, and chimpanzees that occupy the house; one inhabitant is the female chimpanzee below.*

With the exception of the Children's Zoo and the Farm-in-the-Zoo, both completed in the early 1960s, Lincoln Park Zoo remained the same in architecture and attitude for most of its first 110 years. Then, in 1976, renewed interest in the zoo provided for a zoo hospital and commissary and a major new building for animals, the Great Ape House.

Remembering the zoo's commitment to Bushman, Lincoln Park Zoo's staff persisted in their goal to achieve good housing for three of the human's closest living relatives: gorillas, chimpanzees, and orangutans. They believed that to achieve good health and viable breeding these animals must be allowed to live in appropriate family groups and must be provided with adequate physical space and psychological aids. As the status of these animals moved from threatened to endangered in only ten years, the urgency of providing for them helped marshal the necessary forces for the zoo to bring about a new and innovative zoo building.

Respecting the limited park space available to the zoo, the architects provided a man-made hill and put the building under it, creating a space 10 meters (33 feet) high with a diameter of 90 meters (300 feet). Six habitats, each three stories high, house the three species of great apes in family groups. Visitors are separated from the animals by special triple-laminated glass that is 4 centimeters (1.6 inches) thick. Interaction between human and ape occurs daily, providing both visitors and animals with constant stimulation and enjoyment.

*The polar bear habitat (above) is part of the Large Mammal Area, completed in 1982. One of the largest exhibits of polar bears in the world, it includes a million-liter (about 266,000-gallon) pool with windows for viewing the bears as they swim underwater. Below, rockhopper penguins occupy an Antarctic habitat that includes ice formations and a pool in the Penguin and Seabird House, which opened in 1981.*

As the master plan to rebuild the zoo continued, the old fenced yards and early bear line were replaced in the late 1970s and early 1980s with a new Large Mammal House, Penguin and Seabird House, and Hoofed Animal Area. The latter was designed to house many varieties of ungulates, from antelope to zebra.

## Daily operations

In keeping with the concern for its community, Lincoln Park Zoo must provide for the ongoing safety of its inhabitants as well as its employees and all zoo visitors. Safety encompasses many concerns, among them health, well-being, and security. The professional staff includes veterinarians and trained biologists, while animal keepers provide day-to-day care for the collection and skilled tradesmen assist administrative managers with the operations aspect of the zoo.

From a physical operations standpoint, ironworkers, carpenters, painters, plumbers, sheet-metal workers, glaziers, masons, heating engineers, and electricians are needed to keep the zoo fully functional every day of the year. Special problems must be considered and remembered when exotic animals are being worked with, including the use of nontoxic play materials and of vermin-control materials; the latter must be effective at controlling such pests but also must be nontoxic to zoo residents.

Food preparation and distribution is a challenging daily chore. Natural food is given to all animals if it is available, but often substitute diets are developed. Freshwater and saltwater fish of varying sizes are offered along with vitamin-mineral supplements. Fresh fruits, vegetables, and massive amounts of hay are used for herbivores and omnivores, while carnivores rely primarily, but not exclusively, on meat and meat by-products. The zoo grows some of its own food, including hydroponic grains grown from wheat, rye, and oat seeds, as well as mealworms, crickets, and mice, which are needed as food for many birds and reptiles. All food

*Grevy's zebras (below left) and Addra gazelles (below) are among the endangered species that occupy the zoo's Antelope & Zebra Area. Completed in 1982, the 1.6-hectare (4-acre) area provides 11 outdoor habitats and a two-story building for camels, zebras, oryx, gazelles, and bison. The endangered species have been assembled in breeding groups as part of the zoo's commitment to wildlife conservation.*

(Left) The Lincoln Park Zoological Society; photo, Susan Reich; (right) James P. Rowan

*The climate-controlled Flamingo Dome (right) allows zoo visitors throughout the year to watch flamingos at their nesting sites. The Zoo Rookery (below) is home to a wide variety of ducks and other waterfowl. During the spring and fall migratory seasons, it is a favorite place for bird-watchers.*

used at the zoo must be of the highest quality and must be handled in a sanitary and timely manner.

Health of the animals also depends on preventive medicine. Handling of animals is avoided whenever possible, as stress in handling can often kill or weaken an exotic animal. When needed, restraint drugs and mechanical darting systems provide safe access to sick animals. This

allows many medical procedures to be completed, including radiology and surgery, which can be done on site or at the zoo hospital.

Ongoing health concerns, such as animal parasites, are monitored and controlled at all times for all species. Immunization is effective for some animals and for some diseases and is practiced whenever possible. An advisory team of human physicians, including pathologists, pediatricians, orthopedists, neurologists, ophthalmologists, surgeons, and dental surgeons also assist the zoo veterinarians when needed and serve in an advisory capacity for the zoo staff. This is particularly important for special cases or when an animal dies, as these physicians often help in autopsying an animal and determining the cause of death.

Within each major section of the zoo—birds, reptiles, and mammals—a curator is in charge, and reporting to him or her are the animal keepers. The keepers serve as the day-to-day contacts with the animals and can help in determining any changes in an animal's health, behavior, and reproductive acitivity. They also are trained to handle any emergency situations that might arise, particularly relating to animal escapes or injuries to employees or zoo visitors.

One area of operation at Lincoln Park Zoo, and at any zoo that exhibits venomous snakes, requires some special safety measures. There are times when venomous reptiles must be handled, and there is always a danger of being bitten or of the animal escaping. As some of these venoms are highly toxic and can kill a person in minutes, special antivenins must be kept on site, available and current, at all times. The zoo also serves as a resource for nearby hospitals when antivenins are needed.

Other areas of the zoo community that are sometimes less visible but are important to the overall operation are the zoo library, housing books and journals on zoology and related topics; a graphics department, responsible for all signs and other print communication at the zoo; and

*The two-hectare (five-acre) Farm-in-the-Zoo allows city dwellers to view the activities that take place on a typical Illinois farm. Cattle, hogs, sheep, horses, goats, and chickens are housed in the Main Barn and in a number of smaller buildings.*

267

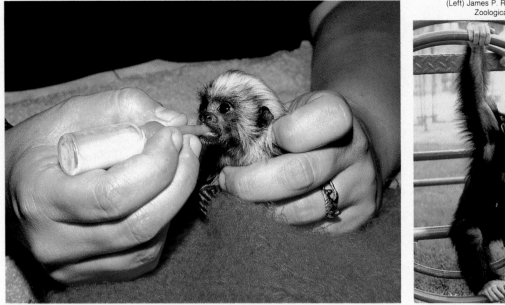

(Left) James P. Rowan; (right) The Lincoln Park Zoological Society; photo, Susan Reich

*In the zoo nursery a cotton-top tamarin is fed (above) and a baby chimpanzee plays (above right). The nursery, a glass-enclosed portion of the Children's Zoo, is an isolation area in which the zoo's staff and volunteers provide food and care for baby animals whose parents cannot or will not do so.*

the education department, which helps fulfill a vital and relatively new role at the zoo. With the advent of conservation issues and concern for vanishing wildlife, education has moved to a top priority at Lincoln Park Zoo and many other zoos throughout the world today. At Lincoln Park Zoo a staff of professional teachers is on site to conduct tours and classes for school groups and other visitors. Volunteers, both on and off the zoo grounds, help to explain about the zoo and animals to all people, young and old, while in-service training to teachers helps them tell the story about zoos and conservation both now and for the future.

While the primary focus of a zoo is on animals, an increasingly important emphasis is being placed on plants and landscaping. Today at Lincoln Park and many other zoos, a professional landscape and floral staff provides indoor and outdoor plantings to enhance the enjoyment and learning of the zoo visitor. When it is possible, similar plant and animal species are shown near or with each other, but considerations of climate and an animal's behavior often limits what can be accomplished. Many zoos experience severe cold or extreme hot weather during the year, and many species of plants must therefore be discarded as unsuitable for use. Also, many animals will either eat or pull out plants that have been added to their habitat. This problem applies equally to small and large animals and to birds, reptiles, and mammals.

## Challenge of a small area

Operating a major collection in a limited space perhaps provides the greatest challenge of all for Lincoln Park and many other zoos. For the zoo and its animals there are as many limitations as there are for the zoo visitor. Decisions about what species of animals will be exhibited in the available space must be made. Some animals require a great deal of space and must be accommodated in large groups, while others require

*Zoo worker tends the "grass machine," which each week produces several hundred kilograms of hydroponic "grass" grown from oat and barley seeds. This grass provides the necessary green food that many of the zoo's animals require for a balanced diet.*

significantly less room and prefer to live as a pair or in a solitary situation. Then there is a question of appropriateness to the zoo's climate, outside space needs and availability, and even availability of certain types of food that may be readily obtainable in some parts of the world but not where the zoo is located.

In earlier days zoos tried to exhibit as many species of animals as possible, given the number of available cages. Often these animals were exhibited alone, in which case there was no chance to promote breeding,

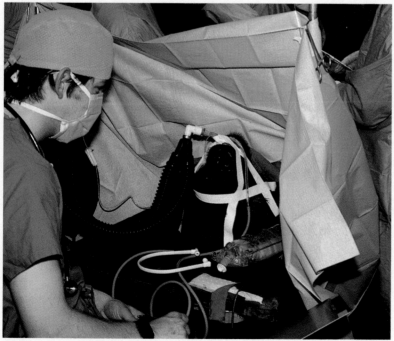

*A gorilla undergoes surgery in the zoo hospital. A full-time veterinarian, an animal health technician, a keeper, and a team of consulting veterinarians and physicians are responsible for medical care of the zoo's animals. Whenever possible, animals are treated in their own habitats.*

*The recently completed Crown-Field Center houses the zoo's Education Department and the offices of the zoo's administrators and of the Zoo Society. The Education Department includes a 200-seat auditorium, two classrooms, a film library, and audiovisual equipment.*

or in pairs that would have promoted breeding except for the total inadequacy of the space that was provided. Little if any thought was given to staff expertise in caring for certain types of animals, the fact that certain animals would not do well in particular climates, or other considerations that are now discussed prior to obtaining an animal for exhibition.

Today animals are chosen for collections on the basis of their potential contribution to long-term breeding programs, their longevity, and their relationship to the particular situation and needs of the zoo. Restrictions on space, such as at Lincoln Park Zoo, play a significant role in determining, for example, how many and what types of hoofed animals will be exhibited. As a city zoo serving a large metropolitan constituency, Lincoln Park Zoo should show a representative group of hoofed stock, but any major breeding programs would have to be accomplished by obtaining access to additional land that would provide for a breeding farm where larger numbers of animals could be housed outside the city. In conjunction with this, back at the zoo, appropriate graphics displays help visitors understand which species are exhibited, why they are exhibited, and which other animals are related to those on and off the exhibit.

Although four million visitors each year must share Lincoln Park Zoo's restricted space with its many animal residents in a highly concentrated area, this often can be an advantage. Families with small children can easily see the entire zoo in a short time without tiring or can return at their leisure to see a specific section in depth. The high concentration of people does, however, present some problems, especially in regard to visitor services. When crowds are large during the peak summer months from Memorial Day through Labor Day, there frequently are not enough

270

places to sit and rest; food operations are pressed to capacity; and the overall cleanup of the grounds, conducted early each morning, is often a major challenge.

School visits each spring and day camp visits each summer, while highly popular, also pose problems with traffic congestion. School buses must be scheduled and routed properly; classes must be quickly conducted and dispersed to allow zoo teachers to cope with the numbers of teachers and students asking for instruction; and zoo volunteers are called upon to answer thousands of questions from children who are often experiencing the zoo—and maybe even touching a rabbit—for the first time. Special consideration is given to visitors who are visually impaired, have other physical handicaps, or need assistance, but there never seem to be enough available strollers or wheelchairs to accommodate all the requests on a busy day at Lincoln Park Zoo.

## Animal conservation

Through its years Lincoln Park Zoo has been, and continues to be, a place for all people to come, enjoy, smile, laugh, and have fun. But these days people also come to learn, especially about animals that are in danger of becoming extinct.

© Peter Pearson—CLICK/Chicago

*An aerial view reveals the close proximity of the Lincoln Park Zoo (in foreground) to downtown Chicago. Having a total area of only 14 hectares (35 acres), the zoo must deal with the challenge of operating effectively within a limited space.*

*Zoos have long provided recreation and information for their visitors. They will continue to do so primarily in order that the relationship that humans have always had with animals can be preserved for the future.*

Conservation has become an important mission of zoos today. It affects their animal management philosophy and operations, and it involves every other aspect of the zoo, from education to graphics and even visitor services. From the animal management side the conservation ideal for zoos is to operate reproductive programs for endangered species of animals so that some of these animals might be released back into the wild should the opportunity present itself. In this way a zoo would complement the work of preserving habitats for animals remaining in the wild.

But returning animals to the wild is not yet a feasible option, and so zoos may play an even more important role in regard to endangered species. They may in the future serve as the last sanctuaries for many of these animals. They may, in fact, be the only places left on Earth where certain species of animals can be seen alive. For additional information on animal conservation, *see* Feature Article: THE SAN DIEGO ZOO: AN ARK IN THE PARK.

## Future prospects

Research and cooperative programs are essential for zoos today if they are to move successfully into the future. Government regulations regarding importation of animals and quarantine regulations have limited the traffic of endangered animals from the wild. This has forced many zoos to make necessary changes from their historic methods of obtaining animals. No longer are wild animals available in abundance; no longer are they easy to obtain even if they are available; and no longer do zoos have the luxury of simply pleasing the public with disregard to the animal.

Behavioral studies between wild and captive populations of animals are beginning. In addition, comparative studies of zoo animals are being undertaken in the areas of nutrition, disease, reproductive biology, anatomy, and even zoonotic diseases—diseases shared by humans and animals. All of this data collection and analysis should help researchers gain a better understanding of captive and wild animals and also help to preserve both the habitats of the animals and the species themselves.

Zoos are, more than ever before, dynamic institutions. They no longer are places for passive enjoyment with occasional interaction but rather are interactive experiences for people of all ages and all walks of life. The zoos of the future will be staffed by highly trained professionals, using the latest technology. They will be better managed and better understood, by both the casual zoo visitor and the professional. And they will no longer be small community recreation areas but rather parts of cooperative networks working across national and international boundaries throughout the world.

Zoos have played and continue to play an important role in the recreational and cultural lives of our citizens. They will do so in the future. But no longer will they do so at the expense of the animals—or at the convenience of humans. Rather they will do so because of the animals, out of consideration for the animals, and for the animals so that the relationship that humans have had with animals for thousands of years can endure—and survive—for thousands of years to come.

# Encyclopædia

# Britannica

# Science Update

# Major Revisions from the 1987 *Macropædia*

The purpose of this section is to introduce to continuing *Yearbook of Science and the Future* subscribers selected *Macropædia* articles or portions of them that have been completely revised or written anew. It is intended to update the *Macropædia* in ways that cannot be accomplished fully by reviewing the year's events or by revising statistics annually, because the *Macropædia* texts themselves—written from a longer perspective than any yearly revision—supply authoritative interpretation and analysis as well as narrative and description.

Three articles have been chosen from the 1987 printing: AUTOMATION, PLATE TECTONICS, and PSYCHOLOGICAL TESTS AND MEASUREMENT. Each is the work of distinguished scholars, and each represents the continuing dedication of the *Encyclopædia Britannica* to bringing such works to the general reader. New bibliographies accompany the articles for readers who wish to pursue certain topics.

# Automation

The term automation was coined around 1946 by the automobile industry to describe the increased use of automatic devices and controls in mechanized production lines. Today, it is widely used in a manufacturing context but is also applied outside of manufacturing in connection with a variety of systems in which there is a significant substitution of mechanical, electrical, or computerized action for human effort and intelligence. An operation is commonly described as automated if it is substantially more automatic than its predecessor.

In its most general usage, automation can be defined as a technology concerned with carrying out a process by means of programmed commands combined with the automatic feedback of data relating to the execution of those commands. The resulting system is capable of operating without human intervention. The development of this technology has become increasingly dependent on the use of computers and computer-related technologies. As a consequence, automated systems have become sophisticated and complex. Advanced systems of this sort now represent a level of capability and performance that surpass in many ways the abilities of humans to accomplish the same activities.

Automation technology has matured to a point where a number of other technologies have developed from it and have achieved a recognition and status of their own. Robotics is one such technology. It is a specialized branch of automation in which the automated machine possesses certain anthropomorphic, or humanlike, characteristics. The most typical humanlike characteristic of a modern industrial robot is its powered mechanical arm. The robot's arm can be programmed to do a sequence of motions to perform useful tasks, such as loading and unloading parts at a production machine or making a sequence of spot-welds on the body of an automobile. The robot will repeat the motion pattern until it is reprogrammed to perform some alternative task. As these examples of robot applications suggest, an industrial robot is typically used to replace a human worker in a factory operation.

This article covers the fundamentals of automation and robotics, including the basic components of an automated (or robotic) system, the technical and economic advantages and drawbacks of such systems, and their key applications. The article also reviews the historical development of automation and considers its impact on society.

This article is divided into the following sections:

The development of automation
The development of robotics
Principles and theory of automation
   Power source
   Feedback controls
   Machine programming
   Decision making
Technology of robotics
Manufacturing applications of automation and robotics
   Machining
   Chemical processing
   Basic metals industries
   Assembly
   Electronics manufacturing

Computer-aided design/computer-aided manufacturing
   (CAD/CAM)
   Robots in manufacturing
Nonmanufacturing applications of automation
   Communications
   Transportation
   Military applications
   Service industries
   Consumer products
Automation and society
   Impact on the individual
   Impact on society
   Advantages and disadvantages of automation
Bibliography

## THE DEVELOPMENT OF AUTOMATION

The technology of automation has evolved from mechanization, which had its beginnings in the Industrial Revolution. (The term mechanization is used to refer to the replacement of human [or animal] power with mechanical power of some form.) Mechanization, in turn, developed out of the human propensity to create tools and mechanical devices.

The first tools made of stone represented prehistoric man's attempts to direct his own physical strength under the control of human intelligence. Thousands of years were undoubtedly required for the development of simple mechanical devices and machines such as the wheel, the lever, and the pulley, by which the power of human muscle could be magnified. The next extension was the development of powered machines that did not require human strength to operate. Examples of these powered machines include waterwheels, windmills, and simple steam-driven devices. More than 2,000 years ago, the Chinese developed trip-hammers powered by flowing water and waterwheels. The early Greeks experimented with simple reaction motors powered by steam. Windmills, with mechanisms for automatically turning the sails, were developed during the Middle Ages in Europe and the Middle East. The steam engine represented a major step forward in the development of these powered machines and marked the beginning of the Industrial Revolution. Since the appearance of the Watt steam engine (developed in 1765 by the Scottish inventor James Watt), powered engines and machines have been devised that obtain their energy from steam, electricity, and chemical, mechanical, and nuclear sources.

**Need for control devices**

Each new development in the history of powered machines has brought with it an increased requirement for control devices to harness the power of the machine. The earliest steam engines required a person to open and close the valves, first to admit steam into the piston chamber and then to exhaust it. Later, the development of a slide valve mechanism that was coupled to the piston shaft made it possible to accomplish these functions automatically. The only need of the human operator was then to regulate the amount of steam that controlled the engine's speed and power. Finally, the requirement for human attention in the operation of the steam engine was eliminated by James Watt's flyball governor introduced during the late 1780s. This device consisted of a weighted ball on a hinged arm, which was mechanically coupled to the output shaft of the engine. As the rotational speed of the shaft increased, centrifugal force caused the weighted ball to be moved outward. This motion controlled a valve that reduced the steam being fed to the engine, thus slowing the engine. The flyball governor remains an elegant early example of a negative feedback control system, in which the increasing output of the system is used to decrease (*i.e.,* add a negative value to) the activity of the system.

Negative feedback is a widely applied means of automatic control used to achieve a constant operating level for a system. A common example of a modern negative feedback control system is the home thermostat. In this device a rise in room temperature causes a bimetallic strip to flex, opening an electrical switch that turns off the furnace. As the room cools down, the bimetallic strip flexes in the opposite direction, closing the switch and turning on the furnace. The switch can be set to start up the furnace at a particular set point (*e.g.,* 70° F).

Another important development in the history of automation was the Jacquard loom, which demonstrated the concept of a programmable machine. This automatic loom, introduced by the French inventor Joseph-Marie Jacquard in 1805, was capable of producing complex patterns in textiles by controlling the motions of many shuttles of different coloured threads. The selection of the different patterns was determined by a program contained in steel cards in which holes were punched. These cards were the ancestors of the paper cards and tapes that control various modern automatic machines. The concept of machine programming was further developed later in the 19th century when Charles Babbage, an English mathematician, proposed a complex, mechanical device that could perform arithmetic operations, data processing, and limited decision making. Although Babbage was never able to complete his so-called Analytical Engine, it is generally considered the precursor of the modern programmable digital computer.

**Building blocks of automation**

The historical developments described above provided the four basic building blocks of automation: (1) a source of power to perform some action, (2) feedback controls, (3) machine programming, and (4) decision making. Over the years these fundamental elements have been refined and enhanced, so that modern automated systems can operate virtually without human intervention.

Some of the most significant refinements and enhancements of the four building blocks of automation have occurred during the 20th century and include developments in electronics leading to the electronic digital computer, improvements in program storage technology, development of new software used to write the programs, advances in sensor technology, and the derivation of a mathematical theory of control systems.

**Impact of computer and related technologies**

The development of the electronic digital computer (the ENIAC [Electronic Numerical Integrator and Calculator] in 1946 and UNIVAC I [Universal Automatic Computer] in 1951) has permitted the control function in automation to become much more sophisticated and the associated calculations to be executed much faster than previously possible. The trend in computer technology has led to machines that are markedly smaller and less expensive than their predecessors yet capable of operating at much greater speeds. This trend is represented today by the microprocessor (and corresponding microcomputer), miniature multicircuited devices capable of performing all of the logic and arithmetic functions of large digital computers.

Along with the advances in computer technology that have occurred since the mid-1940s, there have been parallel improvements in program storage technology for holding programming commands. Modern storage mediums include magnetic tapes and disks; magnetic bubble memories; optical data storage read by lasers; videodisks; and electron beam-addressable memory systems. In association with such developments in computer and storage technology, improvements have been made in the methods by which computers (and other programmable machines) are programmed.

Advances in sensor technology have provided a vast array of measuring devices that can be used as components in automatic feedback control systems. These devices include highly sensitive electromechanical probes, scanning laser beams, systems involving the use of electrical field techniques, and machine vision. Some devices and systems of this type require computer technology for their implementation. Machine vision, for example, requires the processing of enormous amounts of data, and this can only be accomplished by high-speed digital computers. This particular technology is proving to be a versatile sensory capability for accomplishing various sophisticated industrial tasks (*e.g.,* part identification and product inspection), as well as providing the basis for robot guidance systems.

Finally, there has evolved since World War II a highly advanced mathematical and logical theory of control systems. The theory includes traditional negative feedback control, optimal control, adaptive control, and artificial intelligence. Traditional feedback control theory makes use of linear ordinary differential equations to analyze problems such as that of Watt's flyball governor. This theory is basic in modern mechanical, electrical, and chemical engineering curricula. Both optimal control theory and adaptive control theory are concerned with the problem of defining an appropriate index of performance for the process of interest and then operating the process in such a manner as to optimize its performance. The difference between optimal and adaptive control is that the latter must be implemented under conditions of a continuously changing and unpredictable environment. Artificial intelligence is an advanced field of computer science in which the computer is programmed to exhibit characteristics that are commonly associated with human intelligence. These characteristics include the capacity for learning, understanding language, reasoning, solving problems, and rendering expert diagnoses of a condition or situation. Developments in artificial intelligence are expected to provide robots and other "intelligent" machines with the ability to communicate with humans and to accept very high-level instructions rather than the detailed step-by-step programming statements typically required by present-day programmable machines. In the future, a robot endowed with artificial intelligence may, for example, be capable of accepting and executing the terse command "Assemble radio." By contrast, existing industrial robots would have to be provided with a detailed set of instructions that would specify the locations of the radio components, the particular components to assemble first, and so forth.

*Artificial intelligence and robotics*

The various developments described here have made possible a wide range of automated systems both in industrial and nonindustrial applications. Examples of automated systems in industry are numerically controlled machine tools, industrial robots, automated guided-vehicle systems, and automated storage and retrieval systems. Automated systems commonly encountered in everyday life include programmable household appliances, microprocessor-controlled automobile engines, and automatic bank teller machines.

(MIKELL P. GROOVER/ MORRIS TANENBAUM)

### THE DEVELOPMENT OF ROBOTICS

*Importance of numerical control and telecherics*

The field of robotics has its roots in the development of automation technology. Numerical control (NC) and telecherics are two important areas of technology that constitute the foundations of robotics technology.

Numerical control is a method of controlling machine tool axes by means of numbers and other symbols that have been coded on a medium such as punched paper tape. It was developed during the late 1940s and early 1950s. The first NC machine tool was demonstrated in 1952 at the Massachusetts Institute of Technology, Cambridge. Subsequent research there led to the development of the APT (Automatically Programmed Tools) language for programming machine tools.

Telecherics is concerned with the use of remote manipulators controlled by humans. A remote manipulator is a mechanical arm and hand that translates the motions of a human being at one location into motions at a remote location. Such a device is sometimes called a teleoperator. Initial work on the design of teleoperators can be traced to the development of methods for handling radioactive materials in the early 1940s.

Industrial robotics might be regarded as a combination of numerical control and telecherics. Numerical control provided the concept of a programmable industrial machine, while telecherics contributed the notion of a mechanical arm that could be utilized to perform useful work. The first industrial robot was installed in 1961 to unload parts from a die-casting operation. Its development was due largely to the efforts of two Americans—George C. Devol, an inventor, and Joseph F. Engelberger, a businessman. Devol originated the design for a programmable manipulator, the patent for which he titled "Programmed Article Transfer." The U.S. patent for the device was issued in 1961. Engelberger teamed with Devol to promote the use of robots in industry and, together, the two founded the first corporation in robotics, Unimation, Inc., Danbury, Conn.

### PRINCIPLES AND THEORY OF AUTOMATION

As noted earlier, the four basic building blocks of an automated system are (1) a source of power to perform some action, (2) feedback controls, (3) machine programming, and (4) decision making. Any automated system must exhibit at least the first three of these elements. Modern automated systems often possess the fourth element as well.

**Power source.** An automated system is designed to accomplish some useful action, and that action invariably requires power. There are many sources of power available, but the most commonly used form of energy in present-day automated systems is electricity. Electrical energy is the most versatile because it can be generated readily from many sources (*e.g.,* fossil fuel, hydroelectric, solar, and nuclear) and to perform useful work can be converted readily into several types of power (*e.g.,* mechanical, hydraulic, and pneumatic). In addition, electrical energy can be stored in high-performance, long-lived batteries.

*Types of actions performed by automated systems*

The actions performed by automated systems are generally of two types: (1) processing, and (2) transfer and positioning. In the first case, energy is applied to accomplish some processing operation on some entity. The process may involve shaping metal, molding plastic, switching electrical signals in a communication system, or processing data in a computerized information system. All of these actions entail the use of energy to transform the entity (*e.g.,* metal, plastic, electrical signals, or data) from one state or condition into another more valuable state or condition. The second type of action performed by automated systems, transfer and positioning, is most readily conceptualized in automated manufacturing systems designed to perform work on a product. In such cases, the product must generally be moved (transferred) from one location to another during the series of processing steps. At each processing location, positioning of the product is often required. The transfer and positioning actions are called materials handling in automated production systems. In automated communications and information systems, the terms transfer and positioning refer to the movement of data (or electrical signals) among various processing units and the delivery of information to output terminals (printers, video display units, etc.) for interpretation and use by humans.

**Feedback controls.** Feedback controls are widely used in modern automated systems. A feedback control system consists of five basic components: (1) input, (2) process being controlled, (3) output, (4) sensing elements, and (5) controller and actuating devices. These five components are illustrated in the diagram of Figure 1. The term closed-loop feedback control is often used to describe this kind of system.

*Basic components of a feedback control system*

The input to the system is the reference value, or set point, for the system output. This represents the desired operating value of the output. With the previous example of the home heating system as an illustration, the input is the desired temperature setting for the room. The process being controlled is the furnace that provides heat to the room. In other feedback systems, the process might be a manufacturing operation, the rocket engines of the U.S. space shuttle orbiter, the automobile engine in a so-called cruise control system, or any of a variety of other operating mechanisms to which the action power is applied. The output is the variable of the process that is being measured and compared to the input. In the example, room temperature is the variable of interest.

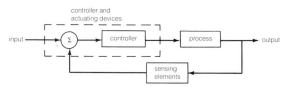

Figure 1: The five components of a feedback control system.

The sensing elements are the measuring devices used in the feedback loop to monitor the value of the output variable. In the home heating system example, a bimetallic strip in the thermostat performs the sensing function. The two different metals in the bimetallic strip possess different coefficients of thermal expansion; accordingly, the flex (deflection) of the strip is directly related to temperature. As such, the strip is capable of measuring temperature.

Many different kinds of sensors are used in feedback control systems for automation.

The purpose of the controller and actuating devices in the feedback system is to compare the measured output value with the reference input value and to reduce the difference between them. In general, the controller and actuator of the system are the mechanisms by which changes in the process are accomplished to influence the output variable. These mechanisms are usually designed specifically for the system and consist of devices such as motors, valves, solenoid switches, piston cylinders, gears, power screws, pulley systems, chain drives, and other mechanical and electrical components. The switch connected to the bimetallic strip of the thermostat is the controller and actuating device for the home heating system. When the output (room temperature) is below the set point, the switch turns on the furnace. When the temperature reaches or slightly exceeds the set point, the furnace is turned off.

**Machine programming.** The programmed commands determine the actions that are to be accomplished automatically by the system. These commands specify what the automated system should do and how the various components of the system must function to accomplish the desired result. The content of the program varies considerably from one automated system to the next. In relatively simple systems, the program specifies a limited number of well-defined actions that are performed continuously and repeatedly in the proper sequence with no deviation from one cycle to the next. In more complex systems, the number of commands could be large and the level of detail in each command could be significantly greater. In relatively sophisticated systems, it is also possible to readily change the program to alter the sequence of actions to be performed by the system.

Programming commands are related to feedback control in an automated system in the sense that the program establishes the sequence of values for the inputs (set points) of the various feedback control loops that make up the system. A given programming command may specify the set point for the feedback loop, which in turn controls some action that the system is to accomplish. In effect, the purpose of the feedback loop is to verify that the programmed step has been carried out. In a robot controller, for example, the program might indicate that the arm is to move to a specified position. The feedback control system in this case would be used to verify that the move has been correctly made. The relationship of program control and feedback control in an automated system is illustrated in Figure 2.

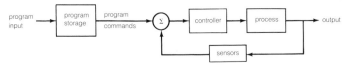

Figure 2: Relationship of program control and feedback control in an automated system.

Some of the programmed commands may be executed in an open-loop fashion—*i.e.,* without the need for a feedback loop to verify that the command has been properly carried out. For instance, a command to flip an electrical switch may not require feedback. An example of the need for feedback control in an automated system exists in a situation where there are variations in the raw materials being fed into a production process, and the system must take these variations into consideration by making adjustments in its controlled actions. Without feedback, the system would not be able to exercise a sufficient level of control over the quality of the process output.

The programmed commands may be contained on mechanical devices (*e.g.,* mechanical cams and linkages), punched paper tape, magnetic tape, magnetic disk, computer memory, or any of a variety of other mediums that have been developed over the years for particular applications. It is common today for automated equipment to use computer storage technology as the means for storing the programmed commands and converting them into controlled actions. One of the advantages of using computer storage technology is that that program can be easily changed or improved. Altering a program contained on a set of mechanical cams involves considerably more work.

**Decision making.** Most highly sophisticated automated systems are capable of making decisions during operation. The decision-making capacity is generally contained in the control program in the form of logical instructions that govern the operation of such a system under varying circumstances. Under one set of circumstances, the system responds one way; and under a different set of circumstances, it responds in another. There are several reasons for providing an automated system with decision-making capability. These reasons include (1) error detection and recovery, (2) safety protection, (3) interaction with humans, and (4) process optimization.

Error detection and recovery is concerned with decisions that must be made by the system in response to undesirable operating conditions. In the operation of any automated system, some form of corrective action must be taken to restore the system when malfunctions and errors occur during the normal cycle of operations. The typical response to a system malfunction has been to call for human assistance. There is a growing trend in automation and robotics to enable the system itself to sense these malfunctions and to correct them in some manner without human intervention. This sensing and correction (referred to as error detection and recovery) can be realized by programming a decision-making capability into the system.

Safety protection is a special case of error detection and recovery in which the malfunction involves a safety hazard. Decisions are required when the automated system detects, through its sensors, that there has developed a safety condition that is hazardous to either the equipment or humans in the vicinity of the equipment. The terms safety monitoring system and hazard monitoring system are typically used to refer to that portion of the automated system that includes the safety sensors and decision-making apparatus. The purpose of the safety monitoring system is to detect the hazardous condition and to take the most appropriate action to remove or reduce it. This may involve stopping the operation and alerting the maintenance personnel of the condition, or it may involve a more complex set of actions to eliminate the hazard.

Some automated systems are required to interact with humans in some way. An automatic bank teller machine, for example, must receive instructions from customers and make decisions according to these instructions. In some automated systems, a variety of different instructions from humans is possible, and the decision-making capability of the system must be sophisticated to deal with the array of possibilities.

A fourth reason to endow an automated system with decision-making capacity is to optimize the process being controlled. This need for optimization occurs most commonly in production situations in which there is an economic performance criterion for the process and it is desirable to optimize this criterion. For example, minimizing cost is usually a key objective in manufacturing. An automated system would make use of optimal control or adaptive control principles in its program to receive appropriate sensor signals and other inputs and make decisions to drive the process toward the optimal state.

### TECHNOLOGY OF ROBOTICS

The most widely accepted definition of an industrial robot is one developed by the Robotic Industries Association:

> An industrial robot is a reprogrammable, multifunctional manipulator designed to move materials, parts, tools, or specialized devices through variable programmed motions for the performance of a variety of tasks.

The technology of robotics is concerned with the design of the mechanical manipulator and the computer systems used to control it. The technology is also concerned with

*Feedback loop*

*Sensing and correcting malfunctions without human intervention*

*Process optimization*

the industrial applications of robots. These will be dealt with below in the section *Manufacturing applications of automation and robotics.*

The mechanical manipulator of an industrial robot is made up of a sequence of link and joint combinations. The links are rigid members connecting the joints. The joints, also called axes, are the movable components of the robot that cause relative motion between adjacent links. Four principal types of mechanical joints are used to construct the manipulator—namely, a linear joint and three types of rotational joints. Figure 3 illustrates the four types. One way to define a robot is by the number of joints used in its construction. Typically three joints are used for a robot's arm and body and two or three joints for its wrist. This

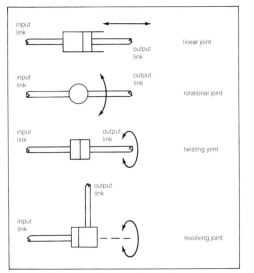

Figure 3: Four types of robot manipulator joints.

permits the robot to position and orient parts and tools in the work space. One possible configuration for a six-axis robot is pictured in Figure 4.

The computer system that controls the manipulator must be programmed to teach the robot the particular motion

By courtesy of Cincinnati Milacron, Inc.

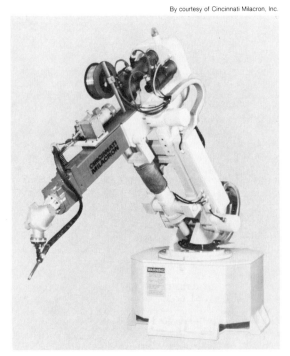

Figure 4: A six-axis, computer-controlled robot equipped for arc welding.

sequence and other actions it must perform to accomplish its task. There are several ways that industrial robots are programmed. One method, called lead-through programming, requires that the manipulator be driven through the various motions needed to perform a given task and that those motions be recorded into the robot's computer memory. This can be done either by physically moving the manipulator through the motion sequence or by power driving the manipulator through the sequence using a control box called a teach pendant.

A second method of programming involves the use of a textual programming language very much like a computer programming language. However, in addition to many of the capabilities of a computer programming language (*i.e.,* data processing, communicating with other computer devices, and decision making), the robot language also includes statements specifically designed for robot control. The latter involves motion control and input/output commands. Motion control commands direct the robot to move its manipulator to some defined position in space. The statement "Move P1," for example, might be used to direct the robot to a point in space called P1. Input/output commands are employed to control the receipt of signals from sensors and other devices in the work cell, as well as to initiate control signals to other pieces of equipment in the cell. For instance, the statement "Signal 3, On" might be used to turn on a motor in the cell by means of output line number 3 in the robot's controller.

Robots of the future are likely to receive instructions (programming commands) by voice input/output. They would therefore have to have artificial intelligence, which would make possible the proper interpretation and execution of the commands. The commands would be expressed in a very high-level language. Unlike today's programming languages in which detailed instructions must be provided in precise syntax, those of the future would be less demanding in terms of format, and the commands would be more task-oriented. That is to say, the programmer would give a command such as "Assemble radio," and the robot would need to develop its own step-by-step procedure for doing the task. The robot would have to possess a high level of intelligence for it to be programmed in this manner. Robots of the future also will necessarily make greater use of sensors for determining positions of objects in the work cell, for safety monitoring, and for error detection and recovery. Machine vision is expected to be an important sensor technology for coming generations of robots.

*Programming industrial robots*

### MANUFACTURING APPLICATIONS OF AUTOMATION AND ROBOTICS

One of the most important application areas for automation technology is manufacturing. To many people, automation means manufacturing automation. Three different types of automation in production can be distinguished: (1) fixed automation, (2) programmable automation, and (3) flexible automation.

The term fixed automation refers to an automated production facility in which the sequence of processing operations is fixed by the equipment configuration. This is sometimes called "hard automation." The programmed commands are, in effect, contained in the machines in the form of cams, gears, wiring, and other hardware that is not easily changed over from one type of product to another. This form of automation is characterized by high initial investment and high production rates. It is therefore suitable for products that are made in large volumes. Examples of fixed automation include machining transfer lines found in the automotive industry, automatic assembly machines, and certain chemical processes.

*Fixed automation*

Programmable automation is a form of automation used in the production of batches (or quantities) of products. The products are made in batches ranging from several dozen to several thousand units at a time. For each different batch of product, the production equipment must be reprogrammed and converted to accommodate the new product configuration. This reprogramming and

*Programmable automation*

changeover (called the setup in many industries) take time to accomplish, and there is thus a nonproductive period followed by a production run for each new batch. Production rates in programmable automation are generally lower than in fixed automation because the equipment is designed to facilitate product changeover rather than for product specialization. A numerical control machine tool is a good example of programmable automation. The program is coded on punched paper tape for each different product style, and the machine tool actions are controlled by the punched tape. Industrial robots are another example of programmable automation.

Flexible automation is an extension of programmable automation. The difficulty with programmable automation is the time required to reprogram and change over the production equipment for each new batch of product. This process takes time, and time is expensive. In flexible automation, the variety of products is sufficiently limited that the changeover of the physical setup of the equipment can be done quickly and automatically. The reprogramming of the equipment in flexible automation is done offline (*i.e.*, the programming can be accomplished without using the production equipment itself). Accordingly, there is no need to group identical products into batches; instead, a mixture of different products can be produced one right after the other. Flexible automation is a relatively new concept in automation. Consequently, there are not many examples of this form of automation compared to the other two types. The economics of flexible automation, however, are advantageous enough that it is expected to become an important method of production in future automated factories.

Applications of automation can be found in nearly all types of production. Many of the important examples are reviewed here.

**Machining.**  The shaping of metal by means of cutting tools was one of the first manufacturing processes to be mechanized and then automated. There are three examples of automation in the machining process that relate to the previous descriptions of the three types of production automation.

The first of these is the transfer line, which is used for machining metal parts in large volumes at high production rates. This is an example of fixed automation, because transfer lines are typically set up for long production runs, perhaps for making millions of parts and running for several years between changeovers. A transfer line is divided into a series of workstations, with each station designed to perform some specific machining operation on a part. The workstations are connected by a parts handling system that moves the parts from one operation to the next. The raw work part enters at one end of the transfer line, proceeds through each workstation, and emerges at the other end as a completed part. In the normal operation of the line, there is a work part being processed at each station, so that many parts are processed simultaneously and a finished part is produced with each cycle of the line. The origins of present-day transfer lines date back to the 1940s and earlier.

The second example of automation in machining is numerical control. The first NC machine tool was invented during the early 1950s. Numerical control is a form of programmable automation in which the machine is controlled by means of numbers (and other symbols) that have been coded on punched paper tape or some alternative storage medium. The program represents the set of machining instructions for a particular part; it is therefore called the NC part program. The coded numbers in the program (specifying $x$-$y$-$z$ coordinates in a Cartesian axis system) indicate to the machine tool the various positions of the cutting tool relative to the work part. By means of a sequencing of these positions in the program, the machine tool is directed to accomplish the machining of the part. A position feedback control system is used in most machines to determine that the coded instructions have been correctly performed. Since the early 1980s, a

microcomputer has typically been used as the controller in an NC machine tool, and the program is actuated from computer memory rather than from punched paper tape. Initial entry of the program into the computer memory is still accomplished by means of punched tape in many cases. This form of numerical control is called computer numerical control (CNC). Another variation in the implementation of numerical control involves the capability of sending the part program over telecommunications lines from a central computer to individual machine tools in a factory, thereby eliminating the use of punched tape altogether. This form of numerical control is known as direct numerical control (DNC).

The third example of automation in machining is the flexible manufacturing system (FMS). The FMS is a form of flexible automation in which several machine tools are linked together by a materials handling system, and all aspects of the system are controlled by a central computer. The materials handling system is capable of delivering parts to any machine in the FMS. Each machine is controlled by CNC, and a central computer sends programs to each controller according to a preplanned schedule. The FMS represents a high level of technological sophistication and a highly integrated form of production automation.

**Chemical processing.**  Some of the most highly automated production facilities are found in the chemical-processing industries. These industries include petroleum refining, food processing, and other operations in which the products are processed in gas, liquid, or powdered form. Such forms facilitate the movement of products through the various steps in the production process. In addition, these products are usually made in large quantities. Because of the ease of handling the products and the large volumes involved, a high level of automation has been accomplished in these industries.

The typical modern process plant is computer-controlled. In one advanced petrochemical system that produces more than 20 different products, the facility is divided into three areas each with several chemical-processing units. Each of the three areas has its own process-control computer to perform scanning, control, and alarm functions. The three computers are connected to a central computer in a hierarchical configuration as illustrated in Figure 5. The central computer calculates how to obtain maximum yield from each process and generates management reports on process performance.

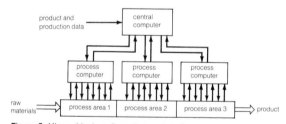

Figure 5: Hierarchical configuration typical of computer process control in a modern plant.

Each process computer monitors up to 2,000 process parameters, such as temperature, pressure, flow rate, liquid levels, chemical concentrations, and other variables required to control the process. These measurements are taken on a sampling basis; the time between samples varies between 2 and 120 seconds, depending on the relative need for the data. Each computer controls approximately 400 feedback control loops. Under normal operation, the control computers maintain operation of the process at or near optimum performance levels. If process parameters exceed the specified normal or safe ranges, the control computer actuates a signal light and alarm horn and prints a message for the technician indicating the nature of the problem.

The central computer receives data from the process computers and performs calculations to optimize the performance of each chemical-processing unit. The results of

*Flexible automation* (margin label)

*Transfer line* (margin label)

*Numerical control* (margin label)

these calculations are then passed to the individual process computers in the form of commands to change the set points for the various control loops.

Substantial economic advantages are obtained from this type of computer control in the process industries. The computer hierarchy is capable of integrating all of the data from the many individual control loops far better than humans can, thus permitting a higher level of performance. Advanced control algorithms can be applied by the computer for optimal process control. In addition, much more quickly than humans, the computer is capable of sensing process conditions that indicate unsafe or abnormal operation. All of these improvements increase productivity, efficiency, and safety during process operation.

**Basic metals industries.** Like the chemical-processing industries, the basic metals industries (aluminum, iron and steel, etc.) have adopted automation for many of their processes. Similar to the chemical industries, the metals industries deal in large volumes of products, and so there is a substantial economic incentive to invest in automation. Metals, however, are typically produced in batches rather than continuously, and handling metals in bulk form is generally more difficult than handling chemicals that flow. Consequently, automation in the basic metals industries has not achieved as high a level as that in the chemical-processing industries.

One example of process automation in the metals industry is the rolling of hot metal ingots into their final shapes (*e.g.,* coils and strips). This was first done in the steel industry; similar processing is also accomplished in aluminum and other metals. In a modern steel plant, hot-rolling is accomplished with the aid of computer control. The rolling process involves the forming of a large, hot metal billet by passing it through a rolling mill consisting of one or more sets of large cylindrical rolls that squeeze the metal and reduce its cross section. In most cases, several passes are required to gradually reduce the ingot to the desired shape. Sensors and automatic instruments measure the dimensions and temperature of the ingot after each pass through the rolls, and the control computer calculates and regulates the roll settings for the next pass.

Control programs have been developed to schedule the sequence and rate at which the hot metal ingots are fed through the rolling mills. In a large plant several different orders for rolled products with different specifications may be in process at any given time. The production control task of scheduling and keeping track of the different customer orders in the mill requires rapid massive data gathering and analysis. In the most modern plants this production control task has been effectively integrated with the computer control of the rolling mill operations to achieve a highly automated production system.

**Assembly.** Assembly operations have traditionally been performed manually, either at single assembly workstations or on assembly lines with multiple workstations. Because of the high labour content and the high cost of manual labour, greater attention has been given in recent years to the use of automation and robotics for assembly work.

For high production work, automated assembly machines have been developed that operate in a manner similar to machining transfer lines. Instead of performing machining operations at the workstations, assembly operations are performed. A typical assembly machine consists of several stations, each equipped with a supply of components and a mechanism for delivering the components into position for assembly. A workhead at each station performs the actual adding and fastening of a component. Typical workheads include automatic screwdrivers, staking or riveting machines, welding heads, and other joining devices. A new component is added to the partially completed product at each workstation, thus building up the product gradually as it proceeds through the line. Assembly machines of this general type are considered to be examples of fixed automation because they are usually configured for a particular product that is made in large quantities.

Since the late 1970s, there has been a growing effort to use robots in assembly operations. Because robots are programmable, the objective in using them for assembly work is to produce parts in medium quantities and to produce a mixture of different models on the same production line. An important research and development project in this general area was the Adaptable Programmable Assembly System (APAS) Project, conducted from 1980 to 1983 in the United States by the Westinghouse Electric Corporation under sponsorship of the National Science Foundation. The assembly of small electric motors was selected as the basis for the APAS development study. The assembly system for the project consisted of six workstations, four of which used robots to perform the assembly operations. A conveyor system was utilized to move partially assembled motors between the stations. Control of the system was accomplished by means of a master supervisory computer, which communicated with local control computers at each workstation. The master computer scheduled and coordinated production and informed the local workstation computers of the tasks that had to be performed.

One of the significant lessons learned from the APAS Project was the importance of designing products for ease of automated assembly. The assembly methods that are satisfactory for humans are not necessarily the most suitable methods for automated workheads. For example, using a screw and nut as a fastening method is suitable for manual assembly but not for automated assembly. Designing the components to be added from the same direction through the use of snap fits and other one-step fastening procedures are much more easily accomplished by automated and robotic assembly methods.

**Electronics manufacturing.** A basic feature of the electronics industry is the need to achieve a high level of coordination in the design, fabrication, and testing of a product. A good example of the need for coordination is in large-scale integration (LSI) and very large-scale integration (VLSI), both of which involve the fabrication of electrical and electronic circuits on small semiconductor chips. LSI and VLSI products are extremely miniaturized and very complex. Computers must be used to perform much of the design analysis and synthesis and then to transfer the design specifications directly to the equipment that produces the chips. Also, electronic components such as LSI and VLSI chips are often produced in relatively low yields, meaning that the proportion of good units to total units made is significantly less than 100 percent. To separate the good units from those that are defective, testing of each unit must be done as part of the production sequence. This need for integration has motivated the introduction of automation into the electronics industry.

Two examples of automation in electronics manufacturing are part insertion machines and wire wrap machines. Part insertion machines are used to position electronic components (LSI chip modules and other devices) relative to a printed circuit board. It is basically an $x = y$ positioning table that moves the printed circuit board relative to the part insertion head, which places the individual components into position on the board. Wire wrap machines are used to make wired connections between terminals on the back of an electrical panel automatically. The wiring head is positioned at the desired terminal pin, after which it wraps the wire around the pin, leads the unconnected end of the wire through a prescribed path to the second terminal pin, and cuts and wraps the wire around the second pin. An electrical test is then made to ensure that the proper terminals have been connected. Faulty connections are identified on a computer-generated report.

Part insertion and wire wrap machines both are production machines that utilize numerical control principles in which programmed commands are communicated to the machine from the design data base for the product. In the part insertion machine, the positioning of the table and the determination of the component to be inserted are contained in the numerical control program. In the wire wrap machine, such a program defines the connections that are to be made. Both the part insertion machine and the wire wrap machine are examples of programmable automation because they can be reprogrammed to accommodate different product configurations.

New inspection and testing equipment is being designed to perform a variety of checks automatically on electronic parts and products. Machine-vision systems are being developed to check the circuits and other quality features of microelectronic chips. These vision systems scan the chips to detect any irregularities from a given standard. Other automated test equipment is designed to perform electrical testing of the circuits more accurately than humans and in a fraction of the time that humans would require to make the tests.

**Computer-aided design/computer-aided manufacturing (CAD/CAM).** Since about 1970, there has been a growing trend in manufacturing firms toward the use of computers to perform many of the functions related to design and production. This trend is popularly known as CAD/CAM. The technology of CAD/CAM is based largely on the capability of a computer system to process, store, and display large amounts of data representing part and product specifications. For mechanical products, the data represent graphic models of the components; for electrical products, they represent circuit information; and so forth. CAD/CAM technology has been applied in many industries, including those involved in machined components, electronics products, and equipment design and fabrication for chemical processing. It reflects not only the automation of the manufacturing operations but the automation of elements in the entire design-and-manufacturing procedure as well.

Computer-aided design entails the use of computer systems to assist in the creation, modification, analysis, and optimization of a design. The designer, working with the CAD system rather than with the traditional drafting board, creates the lines and surfaces that form the designed object (product, part, structure, etc.) and stores this model in the computer data base. By invoking the appropriate CAD software, the designer can perform various analyses on the object, such as stress-strain analysis and heat-transfer calculations. By making adjustments in the design on the basis of these analyses, he develops the final design of the object. Once the design procedure has been completed, the computer-aided design system can be used to prepare the detailed drawings required to make the object.

Computer-aided manufacturing is defined as the use of computer systems to assist in the planning, control, and management of production operations. This can be accomplished by either a direct or an indirect connection between the computer system and the production operations. In the case of the direct connection, the computer is used to monitor or control the process in the factory. Computer process monitoring involves the use of the computer system to observe the manufacturing process, collect data on process performance, and report the performance to plant management. In this way, the plant can be operated more efficiently. Computer process control involves the use of the computer system to execute control actions to operate the plant automatically without significant human intervention. In most cases, process control includes observing the process (*i.e.,* taking feedback measurements) as part of the control function. Several applications of computer process control have been described above, as, for example, in the discussions of the chemical-processing and basic metals industries.

The indirect connections between the computer system and the process are those applications in which the computer is used to support the production operations without actually monitoring or controlling the operations. These applications typically involve planning and management functions that can be performed by the computer (or by humans working with the computer) more efficiently than by humans alone. Examples of these functions include planning of the step-by-step processes for the product, part

programming in numerical control, and scheduling the production operations in the factory.

**Robots in manufacturing.** Today, robotics technology is limited almost exclusively to industrial applications, usually as direct contributors to the production operation. Industrial robot applications can be divided into three categories: (1) material transfer and machine loading/unloading, (2) processing operations, and (3) assembly and inspection.

Material transfer consists of applications in which robots are used to move materials or work parts from one location to another. Many of these tasks are relatively simple, requiring robots to pick parts from one conveyor and place them on another conveyor. Other transfer operations are more complex materials handling tasks, such as placing parts onto pallets in an arrangement that the robot must calculate. In machine-loading and machine-unloading operations, a robot tends a production machine in place of a human worker. Depending on the production operation, the robot either loads parts into the machine or unloads them from it. To perform the task, the robot has to be equipped with a special hand, called a gripper, to grasp a part. In most cases, the gripper must be designed for the particular geometrical shape of the part. An example of a robot load/unload application is an automated machining cell, in which the robot works with a numerically controlled machine tool. The robot loads raw work parts into the machine tool and unloads finished parts from it, and the machine performs the production operation under automatic cycle.  *(margin note: Material transfer and machine loading/ unloading operations)*

By contrast, processing operations require the robot to manipulate some tool to perform a process on the work part. Examples of these applications include spot welding, continuous arc welding, and spray painting. As of the mid-1980s, spot welding of automobile bodies was the most common application of industrial robots in the United States. In this operation, a robot is used to position a spot-welding apparatus against automobile panels and frames to complete the assembly of the basic car body. Arc welding is a continuous process in which the robot must move the welding rod along the seam to be welded. Spray painting involves the manipulation of a spray-painting gun over the surface of the object to be painted. Other processing operations that utilize robots include grinding, polishing, and routing processes in which a rotating spindle serves as the robot's tool.  *(margin note: Robot processing operations)*

Robot assembly applications were discussed above with particular attention to APAS. The use of robots in assembly operations is expected to increase because of the high cost of manual labour in this area. Inspection is another area of factory operations in which the use of robots is growing. In a typical inspection application, the robot positions a sensor with respect to the work part and determines whether the part is consistent with the quality specifications.  *(margin note: Assembly and inspection applications)*

In nearly all of these applications, the robot performs a repetitive operation as a substitute for human labour. Another characteristic of industrial robot applications is that the tasks are hazardous or unpleasant for human workers, as in the case of spray painting, spot welding, arc welding, and certain machine-loading/unloading tasks. Other situations where robots prove attractive as alternatives to humans are those in which the work part or tool is heavy and awkward to handle and in which robots can be used on two or three shifts.  (MIKELL P. GROOVER)

NONMANUFACTURING APPLICATIONS OF AUTOMATION

In addition to the manufacturing applications of automation technology, there have been significant achievements in such areas as communications, transportation, the military, and the service industries. Some of the more significant are described in this section.

**Communications.** One of the earliest practical applications of automation was in telephone switching. The first switching machines, invented near the end of the 19th century, were simple mechanical switches that were remotely  *(margin note: Telephone switching)* controlled by the user pushing buttons or turning a dial on the telephone. The next generation of automatic switching equipment consisted of electromechanical control systems that were developed for public use around the 1920s and 1930s. They were made up of electromechanical relays and switches that performed functions such as monitoring thousands of telephone lines, determining which were demanding service, providing the dial tone, remembering the digits of each telephone number as it was being dialed, setting up the required connections, sending electrical signals to ring the receiver's unit, monitoring the call during its progress, and disconnecting the telephone when the call was completed. These systems also were used to time and bill toll calls and to transmit billing information and other data relative to the business operations of the telephone company. The introduction of these electromechanical systems into the nation's telephone system required many years to complete, but they gradually assumed nearly all of the functions of the human telephone operator.

Modern electronic telephone switching machines are based on highly sophisticated digital computers that perform all of the functions of their electromechanical predecessors with much greater speed, reliability, functionality, and economy. In addition to the functions mentioned above, the newest electronic systems automatically transfer calls to alternate numbers, call the user back when a busy line becomes free, and perform other customer services in response to dialed codes. These systems also perform function tests on their own operations, diagnose problems when they arise, and print out detailed instructions for maintenance personnel.

Other applications of automation in communications systems include local area networks, communications satellites, and automated mail-sorting machines. A local area network (LAN) operates like an automated telephone company within a single building or group of buildings. Such networks are generally capable of carrying not only voice messages but also large quantities of digital data between terminals in the system. Communications satellites have become essential for relaying telephone or video signals across great distances. These satellite communications would not be possible without the automated guidance systems that place and maintain the satellites in a predetermined orbit around the Earth. Finally, automatic mail-sorting machines are being used or installed in post offices throughout the United States to read ZIP codes on envelopes and sort mail according to destination.

**Transportation.** Automation has been applied in various ways in the transportation industries. Major applications include airline reservation systems, automatic pilots in aircraft and locomotives, and automated transit systems.

Airlines utilize automated reservation systems to continuously monitor the status of flights. With these systems, ticket agents at widely separated locations can obtain information about the availability of seats on any flight in a matter of seconds. The reservation systems compare requests for space with the status of each flight, grant space when available, and automatically update the reservation status files. With contemporary systems passengers can secure their seat assignments well in advance of flight time.

Automatic pilots

Nearly all commercial aircraft used by the airlines are equipped with instrument systems called automatic pilots. Under normal flying conditions, these systems can guide an airplane over a predetermined route by detecting changes in the aircraft's orientation and heading from gyroscopes and similar instruments and by providing appropriate control signals to the craft's steering mechanism. Automatic navigation systems and instrument landing systems operate by using radio signals from ground beacons that provide the aircraft with course directions for guidance. When an airplane is within the traffic pattern for ground control, its human pilot normally assumes control.

The BART system

The Bay Area Rapid Transit (BART) system in the San Francisco–Oakland area of California represents an ambitious undertaking in automated rail transportation. It has been a model for rapid transit railways in Washington, D.C., Atlanta, Ga., and various other U.S. cities. The BART system consists of more than 75 miles (120 kilometres) of track, with about 100 trains operating at peak hours between roughly 30 stations. The trains sometimes attain speeds of 80 miles (128 kilometres) per hour with intervals between trains as short as 90 seconds. Each train carries one operator whose role is that of an observer and communicator capable of overriding the automatic system in case of an emergency. The automatic system protects the trains by assuring a safe distance between them and by controlling their speed. Another function of the system is to control train routings and make adjustments in the operation of each train to keep the entire system operating on schedule.

As a BART train enters the station, it automatically transmits its identification and destination, which are flashed on a display board for passengers. Such information is also transmitted to the control centres, from which signals are automatically returned to the train to regulate its time in the station and its running time to the next station. At the beginning of the day an ideal schedule is determined. As the day progresses the performance of each train is compared with the schedule, and adjustments are made to each train's performance as required. If an unexpected situation such as a train breakdown arises, the system can automatically adjust itself to minimize the effect. The entire system is controlled by two identical computers so that if one malfunctions the other assumes control. In the event of a complete failure of the computer control system, the aboard train operators resort to manual control.

**Military applications.** The possibility of using robotics and other advanced automation technologies in military operations has much appeal. As yet, few actual applications have been developed. Many of the routine and sometimes dangerous tasks conducted during land and naval operations and the logistical support of these operations, however, could be performed by sophisticated robots of the future. Some examples include driving trucks in a convoy following a lead vehicle operated by a human, refueling tanks and other vehicles on the battlefield, loading artillery, and working in the engine room on board ship. The possibility of sending soldier robots on a suicide mission deep inside enemy territory is surely a prospect that would interest any military strategist.

**Service industries.** Automation of the service industries encompasses an assortment of applications as diverse as the services themselves. The services include health care, banking and other financial services, government, and retail trade.

In health care the use of computer systems is increasing dramatically and is helping to improve services and relieve the burden on medical staffs. In hospitals computer terminals on each nursing care floor are used to record data on patient status, medications administered, and other relevant information. Besides providing an official record of the nursing care given to individual patients, the computer system facilitates the nurse's task of updating reports at the time of shift changes. Moreover, the system is connected to the hospital's business office so that proper charges can be made to each patient's account for services rendered and medicines provided.

Banks and other financial institutions have embraced automation in their operations because of the large volume of documents and data that have to be processed in their daily business. The sorting of checks and verification of account balances have been computerized by virtually all banks and savings and loans. An increasing number of institutions have gone a step further by establishing systems of electronic banking, including the use of the automatic teller machine (ATM). Located in shopping centres, business buildings, and other convenient places, ATM's permit customers to carry out basic transactions without the assistance of bank personnel.

Electronic banking

Credit card transactions also have become highly automated. Many restaurants and retailers employ systems that automatically check the validity of a credit card and the credit standing of the cardholder as the latter waits for the transaction to be finalized. It is anticipated that future credit card transactions may involve an immediate transfer of funds from the cardholder's account into the merchant's account via high-speed communications lines linking computerized point-of-sale terminals and banks.

Increased reliance on computers and computerized data bases have highly automated the operations of government services. The Internal Revenue Service (IRS) of the U.S. government must review and approve the tax returns of millions of taxpayers each year. The detailed checking of returns—a process known as auditing—is a task that has traditionally been done on a sampled basis by large staffs of professional auditors. In 1985 the IRS began using a computerized system to automate the auditing procedure for the 1984 returns. This system is programmed to perform complex tax calculations on each return being audited. As tax laws change, it can be reprogrammed so as to audit new returns in accordance with the revisions. The IRS expects that the computer-automated auditing system will substantially increase the work capacity of its auditing department without a corresponding increase in manpower.

The retail trade has seen a number of changes in its operations as a result of automation. Selling merchandise has typically been a labour intensive activity, in which salesclerks need to assist customers with their selections and then finalize transactions at the cash register. Each transaction depletes the inventory of the store, and so the item purchased must be identified for reorder. Computer-automated systems have been installed in most large department stores and supermarkets to speed up sales transactions and to provide efficient inventory control. Such a system features a laser light pen or similar sensing device designed to read an identification symbol consisting of a series of bars printed on or affixed to each product. By scanning the symbol with the optical reading unit at the register or checkout counter, the salesclerk quickly identifies the item being sold, records its price into the total of the sale, and enters the transaction into the inventory files of the store. The store's central computer automatically updates these records, subtracting the item sold from the total number of items of the same kind and brand still in stock.

*Automated checkout and inventory control*

**Consumer products.** A wide variety of consumer products have been automated to enhance performance and user convenience. Microwave ovens, washing machines, dryers, compact disc players, videocassette recorders, and a number of other modern home appliances are equipped with a microprocessor that serves as the computer controller for the machine. By simply pressing a series of buttons in proper sequence, the user can program the operation of the appliance. Many videocassette recorders, for instance, can be programmed to automatically tape several television programs transmitted on different channels at different times during the course of a week or longer.

The automobile is another example of a highly automated consumer product. Most recent model cars come equipped with several microprocessors that regulate the operation of the engine (fuel-air ratio and other functions) and of the clock, radio, and automatic speed control (popularly known as cruise control). Special options on some models include the capability to monitor sensors in the car to alert the driver to specific problems (*e.g.,* low fuel, door ajar, and engine temperature) and the ability to compute such information as average gasoline mileage and driving range on remaining fuel supply. One automotive manufacturer has pioneered the use of an electronic voice system, in which the car communicates problems to the driver by means of simple verbal messages delivered through its radio speakers.

(MIKELL P. GROOVER/ MORRIS TANENBAUM)

Over the years, the social merits of automation have been argued by labour leaders, government officials, business executives, and college professors. No doubt the biggest controversy has focused on the employment issue: What is the effect of automation on employment? There are other important aspects of the automation issue as well, including its effect on productivity, economic competition, education, and quality of life. These social issues will be explored here.

**Impact on the individual.** Nearly all industrial installations of automation, robotics in particular, involve a replacement of human labour by an automated system. Therefore, one of the direct effects of automation in factory operations is the dislocation of human labour from the workplace. The long-term effects of automation on employment and unemployment rates are debatable. Most studies in this area have been controversial and inconclusive. Workers have indeed been lost by automation, but population increases and consumer demand for the products of automation have compensated for these losses. Labour unions have argued, and many companies have adopted the policy, that workers who are displaced by automation should be retrained for other positions, perhaps increasing their skill levels in the process. This argument succeeds so long as the company and the economy in general are growing at a fast enough rate to create new jobs as the jobs replaced by automation are lost.

Of particular concern for many labour specialists is the impact of industrial robots on the work force, since robot installations involve a direct substitution of machines for humans at a ratio of from two to three humans per robot. During the first half of the 1980s, however, the effect of robotics on labour was relatively minor in the United States at least, because the number of robots in the nation's factories was small compared to the number of human workers. By the end of 1984, only about 10,000 robots had been installed, while the total work force stood at more than 100,000,000 persons, approximately 19,000,000 of whom worked in factories. This would indicate that the impact of robots on unemployment has been relatively modest to date.

Automation affects not only the number of workers in factories but also the type of work that is done. An automated factory is oriented toward the use of computer systems and sophisticated programmable machines rather than manual labour. Greater emphasis is placed on knowledge-based work and technical skill than on physical work. The types of jobs that must be done in modern factories include more machine maintenance, improved scheduling and process optimization, systems analysis, and computer programming and operation. Thus workers in automated facilities must be technologically proficient to perform such jobs. Professional and semiprofessional positions, as well as traditional labour jobs, are affected by this shift in emphasis toward factory automation.

**Impact on society.** Besides affecting the individual worker, automation has an impact on society in general. Productivity is a fundamental social and economic issue that is influenced by automation. The productivity of a process is traditionally defined as the ratio of output units to the units of labour input. A properly justified automation installation will provide an increase in productivity due to increases in production rate and reductions in labour content. Over the years productivity gains have led to reduced prices for products and increased prosperity for society.

*Increased productivity*

A number of issues related to education and training have been raised by the increased use of automation, robotics, computer systems, and related technologies. As automation has increased, there has developed a shortage of technically trained personnel to implement these technologies competently. This shortage has had a direct influence on the rate at which automated systems can be introduced. The shortage of skilled staffing in automation technologies increases the need for vocational and technical training to develop the required work force skills.

Unfortunately the educational system is also in need of technically qualified instructors to teach these subjects. The laboratory equipment available in schools, moreover, all too often does not represent the state-of-the-art technology typically used in industry.

**Advantages and disadvantages of automation.** The advantages commonly attributed to automation include increased production rates, more efficient use of materials, better product quality, improved safety, shorter workweeks for labour, and reduction of factory lead times.

Automated machines are usually designed to operate at higher production rates than humans are capable of achieving. This increased productivity has been one of the biggest reasons for justifying the adoption of automated systems. Notwithstanding the claims of high quality from good workmanship by humans, automated systems are generally capable of carrying out the manufacturing processs with less variability than humans, thus yielding greater control and consistency of product quality. In addition, the increased process control makes possible more efficient use of materials, resulting in less waste.

Benefits for the factory worker

Automated manufacturing systems often remove workers from the workplace, thus safeguarding them against hazards in the work environment. In the United States, the Occupational Safety and Health Act of 1970 (OSHA) was enacted with the objective of making work safer and protecting the physical well-being of the worker on a national scale. OSHA has had the effect of promoting the use of automation and robotics in the factory.

Another of the benefits of automation noted above is the reduction in the number of hours worked on average per week by factory workers. Around the turn of the century, the average workweek was about 70 hours. This has gradually been reduced, so that today the standard workweek in the United States is about 40 hours. Mechanization and automation have played a significant role in this reduction. Finally, the time required to process a typical job through the factory is generally reduced with automation. Referred to as the manufacturing lead time, this is the amount of time between the beginning of a project or process and the appearance of its results.

Among the major disadvantages associated with automation is worker dislocation. This problem was touched upon earlier. Whatever the ultimate social benefits that might result from retraining displaced workers for other (perhaps more skilled) jobs, in almost all cases the worker whose job is taken over by a machine suffers considerable personal stress. In addition to displacement from work, the worker may be displaced geographically. To find other work, an individual may have to relocate, which is itself another source of emotional stress.

Another significant disadvantage associated with automation is high capital expenditure. Automated systems can cost millions of dollars to design, fabricate, and put into operation. Still other problems characteristic of automated equipment include a higher level of maintenance than is required by manually operated hardware and an inherent lack of flexibility in terms of the variety of products that can be produced.

Also, automation is not without its potential dangers. As often suggested in works of science fiction, the technology associated with automation might ultimately subjugate rather than serve humankind. There is a possibility that workers will become slaves to automated machines, that the privacy of humans will be invaded by vast computer data banks, that human error in the management of technology will somehow endanger the health of civilization, and that society will become completely dependent on automation for its economic well-being.

These dangers notwithstanding, there are substantial opportunities that may arise from the wise and effective use of automation technology. There is an opportunity to relieve humans from boring, repetitive, hazardous, and unpleasant labour in all forms. Then, too, there is an opportunity for future automation technologies to provide a growing social and economic environment in which humans can enjoy a higher standard of living and a better way of life.

**BIBLIOGRAPHY.** Works on the technology of automation and its applications include MIKELL P. GROOVER, *Automation, Production Systems, and Computer-Aided Manufacturing* (1980), an informative survey; N. CAPTOR *et al.*, *Adaptable-Programmable Assembly Research Technology Transfer to Industry: Phase 2* (1982), a final report on technological innovations in manufacturing processes; MIKELL P. GROOVER and EMORY W. ZIMMERS, JR., *CAD/CAM: Computer-Aided Design and Manufacturing* (1984), a comprehensive reference source; and "Automation U.S.A.," *High Technology* 5(5):24–47 (May 1985), a series of articles on factory automation.

Robotics technology and its applications receive focal attention in the following: MARVIN MINSKY (ed.), *Robotics* (1985); V. DANIEL HUNT, *Smart Robots: A Handbook of Intelligent Robotic Systems* (1985); and MIKELL P. GROOVER, M. WEISS, R.N. NAGEL, and N.G. ODREY, *Industrial Robotics: Technology, Programming, and Applications* (1986). A general introduction to robotics applications can be found in ROBERT U. AYERS and STEVEN M. MILLER, *Robotics, Applications and Social Implications* (1983). For more technical material, see JOSEPH F. ENGELBERGER, *Robotics in Practice: Management and Applications of Industrial Robots* (1980). Precise descriptions of robotics applications and a glossary of robotics terminology can be found in DAVID F. TVER and ROGER W. BOLZ, *Robotics Sourcebook and Dictionary* (1983). JOHN HARTLEY, *Flexible Automation in Japan* (1984), is a collection of articles describing Japanese applications of robotics and flexible manufacturing systems. ALAN PUGH (ed.), *Robot Vision* (1983), brings together research papers on this aspect of manufacturing technology.

The impact of automation and robotics technology on the individual and society are discussed in MIKELL P. GROOVER, JOHN E. HUGHES, JR., and NICHOLAS G. ODREY, "The Societal Impact of Factory Automation," *Industrial Engineering* 16(4):50–59 (April 1984); HARLEY SHAIKEN, *Work Transformed: Automation and Labor in the Computer Age* (1985); and ROBERT J. MILLER (ed.), *Robotics: Future Factories, Future Workers* (1983), which also includes the impact on public policy. See also *Exploratory Workshop on the Social Impacts of Robotics: Summary and Issues, a Background Paper* (1982), and *Computerized Manufacturing Automation: Employment, Education, and the Workplace* (1984), with *Working Papers,* 2 vol., published by the Office of Technology Assessment.

(MIKELL P. GROOVER)

# Plate Tectonics

Plate tectonics is a theory dealing with the dynamics of the Earth's outer shell, the lithosphere. Resting on a broad synthesis of geological and geophysical data, it dominates current thinking in the Earth sciences. According to the theory, the lithosphere consists of about a dozen large plates and several small ones. These plates move relative to each other and interact at their boundaries, where they diverge, converge, or slip relatively harmlessly past one another. Such interactions are thought to be responsible for most of the seismic and volcanic activity of the Earth, although earthquakes and volcanoes are not wholly absent in plate interiors. While moving about, the plates cause mountains to rise where they push together and continents to fracture and oceans to form where they pull apart. The continents, sitting passively on the backs of plates, drift with them and thereby bring about continual changes in the Earth's geography.

The theory of plate tectonics, formulated during the late 1960s, is now almost universally accepted and has had a major impact on the development of the Earth sciences. Its adoption represents a true scientific revolution, analogous in its consequences to the Rutherford and Bohr atomic models in physics or the discovery of the genetic code in biology. Incorporating the much older idea of continental drift, the theory of plate tectonics has made the study of the Earth more difficult by doing away with the notion of fixed continents, but it has at the same time provided the means of reconstructing the past geography of continents and oceans. While its impact has, to a considerable degree, run its course in marine geology and shows signs of reaching the limits of usefulness in the study of mountain-building processes, its influence on the scientific understanding of the Earth's history, of ancient oceans and climates, and of the evolution of life is only beginning to be felt.

This article is divided into the following sections:

## PRINCIPLES OF PLATE TECTONICS

The plate tectonics theory has a long and tortuous history. Yet, the theory itself is elegantly simple.

The surface layer of the Earth, from 50 to 100 kilometres (31 to 62 miles) thick, is assumed to be composed of a set of large and small plates, which together constitute the rigid lithosphere. The lithosphere rests on and slides over an underlying, weaker layer of partially molten rock known as the asthenosphere. The constituent lithospheric plates move across the Earth's surface, driven by forces as yet not fully agreed upon, and interact along their boundaries, diverging, converging, or slipping past each other. While the interiors of the plates are presumed to remain essentially undeformed, their boundaries are the sites of many of the principal processes that shape the terrestrial surface, including earthquakes, volcanism, and orogeny.

The most conspicuous feature of the Earth's surface is its division into continents and ocean basins, a division that owes its existence to differences in thickness and composition between the continental and the oceanic crust. The continents have a crust of granitic composition and hence are somewhat lighter than the basaltic ocean floor. Also, they are 30–40 kilometres thick as compared to the oceanic crust, which measures only six to seven kilometres in thickness. Their greater buoyancy causes them to float much higher in the mantle than does the oceanic crust, thus accounting for the difference between the two principal levels of the Earth's surface. The boundary between the continental or oceanic crust and the underlying mantle, the Mohorovičić Discontinuity, has been clearly defined by seismic studies.

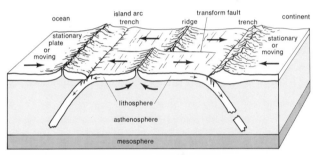

Figure 1: Three-dimensional diagram showing crustal generation and destruction according to the theory of plate tectonics; included are the three kinds of plate boundaries—divergent, convergent (or collision), and strike-slip (or transform).

As conceived by plate tectonics, the lithospheric plates are much thicker than the oceanic or the continental crust; their boundaries do not usually coincide with those between oceans and continents; and their behaviour is only partly influenced by whether they carry oceans, continents, or both. The Pacific plate, for example, is purely oceanic, but most of the others contain continents.

At a divergent plate boundary, magma wells up from below as the release of pressure produces partial melting of the underlying mantle and generates new crust. Because the partial melt is basaltic in composition, the new crust is oceanic. Consequently, diverging plate boundaries, even if they originate within continents, eventually come to lie in ocean basins of their own making. In fact, most divergent plate boundaries seem to have formed within continents rather than in oceans, probably because a hot, weak layer, sandwiched at a depth of about 15 kilometres between two stronger ones, renders the continental crust more vulnerable to fragmentation than its oceanic counterpart. The creation of the new crust is accompanied by much volcanic activity and by many shallow tension earthquakes as the crust repeatedly rifts, heals, and rifts again. *Divergent plate boundaries*

The continuous formation of new crust produces an excess that must be disposed of elsewhere. This is accomplished at convergent plate boundaries where one plate descends—*i.e.*, is subducted—beneath the other. At depths between 300 and 700 kilometres, the subducted plate melts and is recycled into the mantle. Because the plates form an integrated system that completely covers the surface of the Earth, it is not necessary that new crust formed at any given divergent boundary be completely compensated at *Convergent plate boundaries* the nearest subduction zone, as long as the total amount of crust generated equals that destroyed.

It is in subduction zones that the difference between plates carrying oceanic and continental crust can be most clearly seen. If both plates have oceanic edges, either one may dive beneath the other; but, if one carries a continent, the greater buoyancy prevents this edge from sinking. Thus, it is invariably the oceanic plate that is subducted. Continents are permanently preserved in this manner, while the ocean floor continuously renews itself. If both plates possess a continental edge, neither can be subducted and a complex sequence of events from crumpling to under- and overthrusting raises lofty mountain ranges. Much later, after these ranges have been largely leveled by erosion, their remains continue as a reminder that this is the "suture" where continents were once fused.

The subduction process, which involves the descent into the mantle of a slab of cold rock about 100 kilometres thick, is marked by numerous earthquakes along a plane inclined 30°–60° into the mantle—the Benioff zone. Most earthquakes in this planar dipping zone result from compression, and the seismic activity extends 300–700 kilometres below the surface. At a depth of 100 kilometres or more the subducted oceanic sediments, together with part of the upper basaltic crust, melt to an andesitic magma, which rises to the surface and gives birth to a line of volcanoes a few hundred kilometres behind the subducting boundary. This boundary is usually marked by an oceanic deep, or trench, where the overriding plate scrapes off the upper crust of the lower plate to create a zone of highly deformed, largely sedimentary rock. If both plates are oceanic, the deformed sediments and volcanoes form two island arcs parallel to the trench. If one plate is continental, the sediments are usually accreted against the continental margin and the volcanoes form inland, as they do in Mexico or western South America.

Strike-<br>slip plate<br>boundaries Along the third type of plate boundary, two plates move laterally and pass each other without creating or destroying crust. Large earthquakes are common along such strike-slip, or transform, boundaries. Also known as fracture zones, these plate boundaries are perhaps best exemplified by the San Andreas fault in California and the North Anatolian fault system in Turkey.

Most of the seismic and volcanic activity on Earth is therefore concentrated along plate boundaries where mid-ocean ridges, trenches with island arcs, and mountain ranges are generated. Some seismic and volcanic activity also occurs within plates. Interesting examples of this interplate activity are linear volcanic chains in ocean basins, such as the Hawaiian Islands and their westward continuation as a string of reefs and submerged seamounts. An active volcano usually exists at one end of an island chain of this type, with progressively older extinct volcanoes occurring along the rest of the chain. Such topographic features have been explained by J. Tuzo Wilson of Canada and W. Jason Morgan of the United States as the product of "hot spots," magma-generating centres of controversial origin located deep in the mantle far below the lithosphere. A volcano builds at the surface of a plate positioned above a hot spot. As the plate moves on, the volcano dies, is eroded, and eventually sinks below the surface of the sea, while a new one forms above the hot spot. Hot spot volcanism is not restricted to the ocean basins; other manifestations occur within continents, as in the case of Yellowstone National Park in western North America.

The movement of a plate across the surface of the Earth can be described as a rotation around a pole, and it may be rigorously described with the theorem of spherical geometry formulated by the Swiss mathematician Leonhard Euler during the 18th century. Similarly, the motions of two plates with respect to each other may be described as rotations around a common pole, provided that the plates retain their shape. The requirement that plates are not internally deformed has become one of the postulates of plate tectonics. It is not totally supported by evidence,

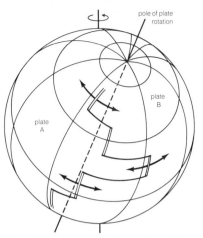

Figure 2: Movement on a sphere of two plates, A and B, can be described as a rotation around a common pole. Circles around that pole correspond to transform faults (single lines connecting divergent plate boundary marked by double line). Note that the pole of rotation of the two plates is not the same as the pole of rotation (spin axis) of the sphere.

but it appears to be a reasonable approximation of what actually happens in most cases. It is needed to permit the mathematical reconstruction of past plate configurations.

The joint pole of rotation of two plates can be determined from their transform boundaries, which are by definition parallel to the direction of motion and so form small circles around the pole. The rate of motion can be computed from the increase in age of the crust away from the divergent plate boundary usually by means of magnetic anomalies (see below *Seafloor spreading*). Because all plates form a closed system, all movements can be defined by dealing with them two at a time.

It is, of course, conceivable that the entire lithosphere might slide around over the asthenosphere like a loose skin, altering the positions of all plates with respect to the spin axis of the Earth and the Equator. To determine the true geographic positions of the plates in the past, which is so important in paleoclimatology and paleoceanography, investigators have to define their motions, relative not to each other, but rather to this independent frame of reference. The hot spot island chains serve this purpose, their trends providing the direction of motion of a plate; the speed of the plate can be inferred from the increase in age of the volcanoes along the chain. It is assumed, of course, that the hot spots themselves remain fixed with respect to the Earth, an assumption that appears to be reasonably accurate for at least some hot spots. Hot spot<br>island<br>chains<br>as a<br>frame of<br>reference

Quite another method of determining absolute plate movements relies on the fact that the equatorial waters of the ocean are, and always have been, very fertile. The high biological productivity yields an enormous quantity of calcareous microfossils, which, like a gigantic natural chalk line, marks a narrow equatorial zone. The displacement of the equatorial deposits over time, traced by means of deep-sea drill cores, enables investigators to determine the direction and rate of plate movement.

Because the plates all interlock, any change in motion anywhere must reverberate throughout the entire system. If two continents collide, their edges will crumple and shorten, but eventually all motion must stop at this boundary and large parts of the system elsewhere will have to adjust. Earth scientists are thus able to reconstruct the positions and movements of plates in the past so long as they have the ancient oceanic crust to provide them with plate speeds and directions. Since old oceanic crust is continuously consumed to make room for new crust, this kind of evidence is eventually exhausted. Little oceanic crust of Lower Cretaceous age (about 100,000,000 to 136,000,000 years old) remains, and none is older than the Jurassic—

the geologic period that began approximately 190,000,000 years ago. Consequently, this method fails for the history of drifting continents during earlier geologic periods (*i.e.,* the Paleozoic and Precambrian eras), making it necessary for investigators to turn to another, less effective technique (see below *Paleomagnetism, polar wandering, and continental drift*).

HISTORICAL OVERVIEW

**Precursors.** Any major new idea in science appears to lead instantly to a search of the past for those who might once have proposed similar concepts and with whom the current proponents should therefore share the credit. In the case of plate tectonics, the primary candidate is obvious: Alfred Wegener of Germany, who explicitly presented the concept of continental drift for the first time at the outset of the 20th century. Though plate tectonics is by no means synonymous with continental drift, it encompasses this idea and derives much of its impact from it.

There might have been predecessors even to Wegener. The outlines of the continents bordering the Atlantic Ocean are so similar that many probably noticed the correspondence, and some might have drawn the conclusion that the lands on both sides were once joined together. The earliest reference to this peculiar geographic feature was made by the English philosopher Francis Bacon. In his *Novum Organum* (1620), Bacon pointed out the correspondence but did not go beyond that. Such was also the extent of the contribution of the great French naturalist Georges-Louis Leclerc, comte du Buffon, a century later. Neither can François Paget qualify as a forerunner of continental drift theorists: even though he stated in 1666 that an undivided continent existed before Noah's flood, he explained the creation of the Atlantic Ocean by having part of that continent sink into the sea.

The first credible proponent of continental drift was Antonio Snider-Pellegrini, a belated advocate of catastrophism (the view that geological history consists of a sequence of numerous violent catastrophic events), who in 1858 ascribed the biblical flood to the former existence of a single continent that was torn apart to restore the balance of a lopsided Earth. More recent and much more sophisticated was the work of the American geologist Frank B. Taylor, who, disdaining the then-prevailing contraction model of mountain building, postulated in 1908 that the arcuate mountain belts of Asia and Europe resulted from the equatorward creep of the continents. His analysis of tectonic features foreshadowed in many ways modern thought regarding plate collisions, and he anticipated Wegener's publications by only a few years. Curiously, however, his work instantly sank into oblivion.

**Alfred Wegener and the concept of continental drift.** Wegener was by training and profession a meteorologist (he was highly respected for his work in climatology and paleoclimatology), but he is best remembered for the foray into geology that led to his formulation of the concept of continental drift. In 1910, again because of the geography of the Atlantic coastlines, Wegener came to consider the existence of a single supercontinent during the late Paleozoic Era (about 350,000,000 to 225,000,000 years ago) and named it Pangaea. He searched the geological and paleontological literature for evidence attesting to the continuity of geological features across the Indian and Atlantic oceans, which he assumed had formed during the Mesozoic Era (about 225,000,000 to 65,000,000 years ago). His efforts proved rewarding, and he presented the idea of continental drift and some of the supporting evidence in a lecture in 1912. This was followed in 1915 by his major work, *Die Entstehung der Kontinente und Ozeane* (*The Origin of Continents and Oceans*).

The idea of large ancient continents composed of several of the present-day smaller ones had been put forth in the late 19th century by the Austrian geologist Eduard Suess. Suess, however, was not thinking of continental drift. In the spirit of his day, he assumed that portions of a single enormous southern continent—designated Gondwana, or

Gondwanaland—foundered to become the Atlantic and Indian oceans. Such sunken lands, along with vanished land bridges, were frequently invoked in the late 1800s to explain sediment sources apparently present in the ocean and to account for floral and faunal connections between continents. They remained popular until the 1950s, stimulated believers in ancient Atlantis, and even made their way into literary works.

Yet, it was already known that the concept of isostasy rendered large sunken continental blocks geophysically impossible, and Wegener characteristically introduced his continental drift proposal by pointing this out. Only then did he proceed to conclude that, if the continents had been once joined together, drift of their fragments rather than their foundering would have been the consequence. The assumption of a former single continent could be tested geologically, and Wegener next displayed a large array of data. Even today his evidence, ranging from the continuity of fold belts across oceans and similarities of sequences of strata on their opposite sides to paleobiogeographic and paleoclimatological arguments, would be judged worthy of serious consideration. He further argued that, if continents could move up and down in the mantle as a result of buoyancy changes produced by, say, erosion or deposition, they should be able to move horizontally as well. The driving forces he considered, however, were unconvincing: both pole fleeing and the westward tidal force appeared to most to be entirely inadequate.

Wegener's proposition was attentively received by many European geologists, and in England Arthur Holmes pointed out that the lack of a driving force was hardly sufficient grounds to scuttle the entire concept. As early as 1929, Holmes proposed an alternative mechanism—namely, convection of the mantle, which remains today a serious candidate for the force driving the plates. Wegener's ideas also were appreciated by geologists in the Southern Hemisphere. One of them, the South African Alexander Du Toit, remained a lifelong believer. After Wegener's death, Du Toit continued to amass further evidence in support of continental drift.

*Evidence supporting the hypothesis.* Much was thus to be said for the idea that the continents were joined together in the Paleozoic, and supporting evidence has continued to accumulate to this day. The opposing Atlantic shores match well, especially at the 1,000-metre (3,300-foot) depth contour, which is a better approximation of the edge of the continental block than the present shoreline, as Sir Edward Bullard demonstrated in 1964 with the aid of computer analysis. Similarly, the structures and stratigraphic sequences of Paleozoic mountain ranges in eastern North America and northwestern Europe can be matched in detail. This fact was already known to Wegener and has been strengthened in subsequent years.

Often cited as evidence have been the strikingly similar Paleozoic sequences on all southern continents and also in India. This Gondwana sequence—so called after one of Suess's large continents—consists of glacial tillites, followed by sandstones and finally coal measures. Placed on a reconstruction of Gondwana, the tillites mark two ice ages that occurred during the long march of this continent across the South Pole from its initial position north of Libya about 500,000,000 years ago until its final departure from southern Australia 250,000,000 years later. The first of these ice ages left its glacial deposits in the southern Sahara during the Silurian Period (which extended from about 430,000,000 to 395,000,000 years ago), and the second did the same in southern South America, South Africa, India, and Australia from 380,000,000 to 250,000,000 years ago. At each location the tillites were subsequently covered by desert sands of the subtropics, and these in turn by coal measures, indicating that the region had arrived near the Equator.

During the 1950s and 1960s, patient work in isotopic dating showed that the massifs of Precambrian time (from about 4,600,000,000 to 570,000,000 years ago) found on

*Marginal notes:*

The super-continent Pangaea

Gondwana sequence

opposite sides of the South Atlantic did indeed closely correspond in age and composition, as Wegener had surmised. It is now evident that they originated as a single assemblage of Precambrian continental nuclei later torn apart by the breakdown of Pangaea.

*Disbelief and opposition.* More common than interest or approval, however, was a disbelief so strong that it often bordered on indignation. One of the strongest opponents was the British geophysicist Sir Harold Jeffreys, who spent years attempting to demonstrate that continental drift is impossible because the strength of the mantle should be far greater than any conceivable driving force. He refused to abandon this viewpoint in spite of the massive evidence in favour of plate tectonics. It was in North America, however, that opposition to Wegener's ideas was vigorous to the point of excess and very nearly unanimous. Wegener was attacked from virtually every possible vantage point, his paleontological evidence attributed to land bridges, the similarity of strata on both sides of the Atlantic called into question, the fit of Atlantic shores declared inaccurate, and his very competence doubted. It also did not escape attention that he did not possess proper credentials as a geologist.

What might have been the cause of this overwhelmingly negative response in the light of such a substantial amount of supporting evidence? The unsatisfactory quality of Wegener's driving mechanism has commonly been cited as the reason, but that seems too simple, especially since the absence of a mechanism did not delay the acceptance of plate tectonics. The roots of the resistance most certainly reached far deeper. It would be unusual for the practitioners of any science to flock to a new concept—particularly a revolutionary one of such profound consequences—before the need for a thorough overhaul of the existing conceptual edifice had become compelling and obvious to most, its supporting evidence daily crumbling, and its explanatory power reduced below any acceptable level.

From T.H. van Andel, *New Views on an Old Planet* (1985); Cambridge University Press

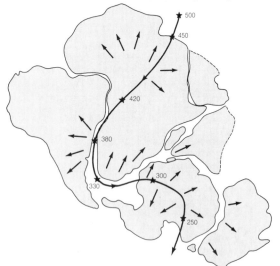

Figure 3: The trail of the South Pole across Gondwanaland during the Paleozoic Era. The numbers indicate its progress by giving the dates of pole positions in millions of years. The arrows show the flow directions of ice caps appearing twice during the long march as ice ages overtook the Earth.

Whatever the cause, continental drift, having been rejected by the vast majority of geologists the world over, retreated into obscurity and remained there for roughly three decades. Ironically, though, Du Toit so successfully kept the fires burning in the Southern Hemisphere that it remained quite respectable there to profess oneself an adherent of continental drift during the very years that such a confession north of the Equator would have exposed one to ridicule and disbelief.

**Renewed interest in continental drift.** *Paleomagnetism, polar wandering, and continental drift.* The fact that some rocks are strongly magnetized has been known for centuries, and geologists recognized more than 100 years ago that many rocks preserve the imprint of the Earth's magnetic field as it was at the time of their formation. Volcanic rocks such as basalt are especially good recorders of paleomagnetism, but some sediments also align their magnetic particles with the Earth's field at the time of deposition. Investigators therefore have at their disposal fossil compasses that indicate, like any magnet suspended in the Earth's field, the direction to the magnetic pole and that yield the latitude of their origin.

During the 1950s paleomagnetic studies, notably those of Stanley K. Runcorn and his coworkers in England, showed that in the late Paleozoic the north magnetic pole—as seen from Europe—seems to have wandered from a Precambrian position near Hawaii to its present location by way of Japan. This, of course, might mean that the magnetic pole itself had migrated or that Europe had moved relative to a fixed pole. Either continental drift or polar wandering was therefore a reasonable explanation. Paleomagnetic data from other continents, however, soon yielded apparent polar wandering paths different from the European one. Separate wanderings of many magnetic poles are not acceptable, but the paths could be brought to coincide by joining the continents in the manner and at the time suggested by Wegener.

Impressed by this result, Runcorn became the first of a new generation of geologists and geophysicists to accept continental drift as a serious proposition worthy of careful testing. Yet, the band of the converted remained small, and most geologists found sufficient reason to doubt the paleomagnetic results, which were often conflicting due to the primitive nature of the early techniques. Since then, more sophisticated methods capable of removing the overprint of later magnetizations have made paleomagnetic data strong supporting evidence for continental drift and a major tool for reconstructing the geography of the past. In the meantime, however, much progress had been made on an entirely different and quite independent front. It was from evidence extracted from the oceanic crust that plate tectonics would be born.

*Gestation and birth of plate tectonics.* When Wegener developed his ideas, and for many years thereafter, relatively little was known regarding the nature of the ocean floor. After World War II, however, rapid advances were made in the study of the relief, geology, and geophysics of the ocean basins. Due in large part to the efforts of Bruce C. Heezen and Henry W. Menard of the United States, these features, which constitute more than two-thirds of the Earth's surface, became well enough known to permit serious geological analysis.

Several major topographic and tectonic features distinguish the ocean basins from the continents. The first of these is the mid-ocean ridge system. Mid-ocean ridges are broad, elongated elevations of the ocean floor rising to about 2.5 or three kilometres below sea level, with widths ranging from a few hundred to more than 1,000 kilometres. Their crests tend to be rugged and are often endowed with a longitudinal rift valley where fresh lava flows, high heat flow, and shallow earthquakes of the extensional type are found. Mid-ocean ridges nearly girdle the globe.

Trenches constitute another type of seafloor feature. In contrast to mid-ocean ridges, they are long, narrow depressions containing the greatest depths of the ocean basins. Trenches virtually ring the Pacific; a few also occur in the northeastern part of the Indian, and some small ones are found in the Atlantic. Trenches have low heat flow, are often filled with thick sediments, and lie at the upper edge of the Benioff zone of compressive earthquakes. Trenches border continents, as in the case of western Central and South America; but they also may occur in mid-ocean, as, for example, in the southwestern Pacific.

Mid-ocean ridges and, more rarely, trenches are offset by fracture zones—transverse features consisting of linear

*The paleo-magnetic studies of Runcorn*

*Significance of ocean basin studies*

ridges and troughs approximately perpendicular to the ridge crest that they offset by a few to several hundred kilometres. Fracture zones often extend over long distances in the ocean basins but generally end abruptly against continental margins. They are not volcanic, and their seismic activity is restricted to the area between offset ridge crests where earthquakes indicating horizontal slip are common.

The existence of these three types of striking, large seafloor features, which had gradually become evident during the late 1940s and 1950s, clearly demanded a global rather than local tectonic explanation. The first comprehensive attempt at such an explanation was made by Harry H. Hess of the United States in a widely circulated manuscript that he had written in 1960 but not formally published for several years. In this paper Hess, drawing on Holmes's model of convective flow in the mantle, suggested that the mid-ocean ridges were the surface expressions of rising and diverging convective flow while trenches and Benioff zones with their associated island arcs marked descending limbs. At the ridge crests new oceanic crust would be generated and then carried away laterally to cool, subside, and finally be destroyed in the nearest trenches. Consequently, the age of the oceanic crust should increase with distance away from the ridge crests, and, because recycling was its ultimate fate, very old oceanic crust would not be preserved anywhere. This, incidentally, took care of an old and troubling paradox: only rocks younger than Mesozoic had ever been encountered in the oceans, whereas the continents bear ample evidence of the presence of oceans for more than 3,000,000,000 years.

Hess's model, later dubbed seafloor spreading by the American oceanographer Robert S. Dietz, appeared to account for most observations and was received with interest by many marine geologists. Confirmation of the production of oceanic crust at ridge crests and its subsequent lateral transfer was not long in coming. Fracture zones had thus far been widely regarded as transcurrent faults that gradually displaced one crestal block to the right or left relative to the other. Given this interpretation, the abrupt termination of many fracture zones against continental margins raised intractable problems. The aforementioned Canadian geologist J. Tuzo Wilson solved these problems in 1965 with a single ingenious stroke. Suppose, he argued, that the offset between two ridge crest segments is present at the outset. Each segment generates new crust, which moves laterally away. Along that part of the fracture zone

*Hess's seafloor spreading model*

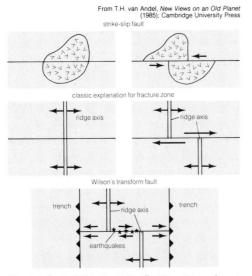

From T.H. van Andel, *New Views on an Old Planet* (1985); Cambridge University Press

strike-slip fault

classic explanation for fracture zone

ridge axis

Wilson's transform fault

trench    trench

ridge axis

earthquakes

Figure 4: Faults that horizontally offset two pieces of crust are called strike-slip faults (top). Fracture zones were initially regarded as classic strike-slip faults until J. Tuzo Wilson demonstrated that they result from the generation of new crust at already offset mid-ocean ridges. The concentration of earthquakes is in the axial part only, and the directions of motion confirm the hypothesis.

lying between crests, the crustal slabs move in opposite directions, even though the axes or rift valleys themselves remain stationary. Beyond the crests, adjacent portions of crust move in parallel and are eventually absorbed in a trench. Wilson called this a transform fault and noted that on such a fault the seismicity should be confined to the part between ridge crests, as is indeed the case. Shortly afterward Lynn R. Sykes, an American seismologist, showed that the motions deduced from earthquakes on transform faults conform to the directions of motion postulated by Wilson and are opposite those observed on a transform fault.

The seafloor spreading model also required that the oceanic crust should increase in age with distance from the ridge axis, and Wilson had already pointed out that volcanic islands in the Atlantic indeed show this pattern. Such islands are few, however, and it is in the nature of these piles of lava and ash that the moment of their birth is difficult to ascertain. Additional evidence was needed, and it soon came from magnetic surveys of the oceanic crust.

A magnetic survey of the eastern Pacific floor off the coast of Oregon and California had been published in 1961 by two geophysicists, Arthur D. Raff and Ronald G. Mason. The results were puzzling and gave rise to many farfetched interpretations. Unlike on the continents, where magnetic anomaly patterns tend to be confused and seemingly random except on a fine scale, the seafloor possesses a remarkably regular set of magnetic bands alternately higher and lower than the average Earth field. These positive and negative anomalies are strikingly linear and parallel with the mid-ocean ridge axis, show distinct offsets along fracture zones, and, when displayed in black and white, generally resemble the pattern of a zebra skin. The axial anomaly tends to be higher and wider than the adjacent ones, and in most cases the sequence on one side is the approximate mirror image of that on the other.

*Magnetic anomalies*

In his convection/seafloor-spreading model, Hess had attributed the formation of the oceanic crust mainly to the hydration of a peridotitic mantle, a process not judged likely to produce such regular magnetic anomalies. Alternatively, it seemed possible that partial melting of the mantle might yield a basaltic magma, which, after congealing, would be a much better medium for retaining a strong imprint of the Earth's magnetic field. This second hypothesis has since been amply confirmed by deep-sea dredging and drilling.

It had further been known since early in the century that the polarity of the Earth's magnetic field reverses from time to time. Studies of the remanent magnetism of stacks of basalt lavas extruded in rapid succession on land had, since the late 1950s, begun to establish a sequence of reversals dated by isotopic methods.

Assuming that the oceanic crust is indeed made of basalt intruded in an episodically reversing geomagnetic field, Drummond H. Matthews of Cambridge University and a research student, Frederick J. Vine, postulated in 1963 that the new crust would assume a magnetization aligned with the field at the time of its formation. If the field were normal, as it is today, the magnetization of the crust would be added to that of the Earth and produce a positive anomaly. If intrusion had taken place during a period of reverse magnetic polarity, it would subtract from the present field and appear as a negative anomaly. Subsequent to intrusion, each new block would split and the halves, in moving aside, would generate the observed bilateral magnetic symmetry. Given a constant rate of crustal generation, the widths of individual anomalies should correspond to the intervals between magnetic reversals. Correlation of magnetic traverses from different mid-ocean ridges demonstrated in 1966 an excellent correspondence with the magnetic polarity reversal time scale just then published by the American geologists Allan Cox, Richard Doell, and Brent Dalrymple in a series of timely papers. This reversal time scale went back some 3,000,000 years, but since then further extrapolation based on marine magnetic anomalies (confirmed by deep-sea drilling)

*The Vine–Matthews hypothesis*

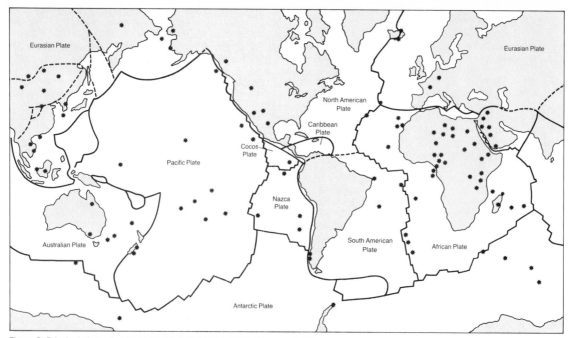

Figure 5: Principal plates that make up the Earth's lithosphere. Very small plates ("microplates") have been omitted. The stars indicate intraplate volcanoes, many of which are thought to be hot spots.

has extended the magnetic anomaly time scale far into the Cretaceous Period, which spanned from about 136,000,-000 to 65,000,000 years ago.

As an aside, it is of interest to note that in Canada Laurence W. Morley, simultaneously with Vine and Matthews but entirely independently, had come to the same explanation for the marine magnetic anomalies, but publication of his paper, delayed by unsympathetic referees and technical problems, occurred long after Vine's and Matthews' work had already firmly taken root.

These confirmations persuaded a large number of marine geologists that seafloor spreading was a reality. Continental drift, however, was not much in their minds, as they focused mainly on the explanations that the concept provided for a host of oceanic features. Land geologists were disinterested, viewing the affair as primarily an issue for their marine colleagues.

Two concerns, however, remained. The spreading seafloor was generally seen as a thin skin most likely having its base at the Mohorovičić Discontinuity—*i.e.,* boundary between the crust and mantle considered of such major importance in the early 1960s that plans were undertaken to sample it by deep drilling in the oceans. If only oceanic crust were involved, as seemed to be the case in the Pacific Ocean, the thinness of the slab was not disturbing, even though the ever-increasing number of known fracture zones with their close spacing implied oddly narrow, long convection cells. More troubling was the fact that the Atlantic Ocean, though it had a well-developed mid-ocean ridge, lacked trenches adequate to dispose of the excess oceanic crust. There, the adjacent continents needed to travel with the spreading seafloor, a process that, given the thin but clearly undeformed slab, strained credulity.

Working independently but along very similar lines, Dan P. McKenzie and Robert L. Parker of Britain and W. Jason Morgan of the United States resolved these issues. McKenzie and Parker showed with a geometric analysis that, if the moving slabs of crust were thick enough to be regarded as rigid and thus to remain undeformed, their motions on a sphere would lead precisely to those divergent, convergent, and transform boundaries that are indeed observed. Morgan demonstrated that the directions and rates of movement had been faithfully recorded by magnetic anomaly patterns and transform faults. He also

proposed that the plates extended approximately 100 kilometres to the base of a rigid lithosphere, which had long been known to be underlain by a weaker asthenosphere marked by strong attenuation of earthquake waves. In 1968 the French geophysicist Xavier Le Pichon refined these propositions with a computer analysis of all plate data and proved that they did indeed form an integrated system where the sum of all crust generated at mid-ocean ridges is balanced by the cumulative amount destroyed in all subduction zones. That same year, the American geophysicists Bryan Isacks, Jack Oliver, and Lynn R. Sykes showed that the theory, which they enthusiastically labeled the "new global tectonics," was capable of accounting for the larger part of the Earth's seismic activity. Almost immediately others began to consider seriously the ability of the theory to explain mountain building and sea-level changes.

Only a few years later, details of the processes of plate movement and of boundary interactions, along with much of the plate history of the Cenozoic Era (the past 65,000,-000 years), had been worked out. Yet, the driving forces—notwithstanding a brief flurry of discussion around 1970—remained mysterious and continue as such. The vast accumulation of data bearing on plate history and plate processes has yielded surprisingly little information about what happens beneath them. Pull by the subducting slab, push at the spreading ridge, convection in the asthenosphere, and even tidal forces have been considered, but in every case the evidence has to be admitted as inconclusive. Many favour convection, but, if this indeed is the driving force, the flow pattern at depth is clearly not reflected in the surface movements of the plates, constrained as they are by each other.

### PLATE TECTONICS AS AN EXPLANATION FOR EARTH PROCESSES

Since its inception in 1967–68, plate tectonics has had a pervasive impact on the Earth sciences. If it has not fully lived up to the proud name "new global tectonics," it has nevertheless exerted enormous influence by clarifying areas of obscurity, reconciling seemingly conflicting evidence, unifying to a remarkable degree events occurring in distant parts of the globe, establishing new pathways toward knowledge, and opening the door to new subjects

The "new global tectonics"

of investigation, all the while raising a myriad of new and important issues. A few examples may suffice to illustrate the dimensions of the revolution it has wrought.

**Pangaea and its breakup.** Magnetic anomalies, transform faults, and hot spot trails permit rigorous geometric reconstructions of past plate shapes, configurations, and movements. As previously noted, reasonable agreement on such reconstructions can be achieved as far back as the late Cretaceous, but beyond that time little oceanic crust remains. Much effort in reconstructing the geography of the past 100,000,000 years or so has shown that, though some reconstructions are straightforward, others imply that the strict application of the assumption that plates are not internally deformed is not justified. Such is the case, for example, for the Pacific basin as opposed to the simple history of the Atlantic.

When dealing with geological time beyond the Cretaceous, other means have to be applied in reconstructing ancient geography. Geological data, for instance, can be used in the time-honoured manner to determine the proper fit of continents to make Pangaea. Only minor controversy continues here, such as in the vexing case of the position of Madagascar or of the many fragments that now constitute the Mediterranean, southeastern Europe, and the Middle East. Old collision boundaries are marked by sutures—*i.e.,* zones of deformation that betray points of contact between formerly separate continents even after much erosion. Good examples include the Urals between the old Central European and Siberian continental blocks, and the Indus suture north of the Himalayas between India and Asia. Some sutures, on the other hand, are well concealed, as, for example, the one in northern Florida and southern Georgia that marks a collision between North America and northwestern Africa during the Paleozoic.

Having reconstructed Pangaea and identified the pieces that came together to form it through largely traditional means, investigators are able to trace continental migrations using paleomagnetic data to obtain their paleolatitudes and orientations for appropriate instants in time. What cannot be determined are their paleolongitudes so that knowledge about the widths of intervening oceans remains limited. Paleolongitudes can be estimated only by relatively crude means such as faunal and floral affinities. Accordingly, Earth scientists will never know as much about the geography of the Precambrian, Paleozoic, or early Mesozoic as they do about the last 100,000,000 years of Earth history. Yet, enough information has become available to permit some undoubtedly flawed but fascinating and useful reconstructions.

A widely used Paleozoic reconstruction by a group of geologists at the University of Chicago shows that throughout the Paleozoic, and probably for some time before then, Gondwana existed, consisting of South America, Africa, and Australia. It was surrounded by an ever-shifting array of landmasses, some large—about the size of North America, China, or Siberia—and others small, though numerous and destined eventually to become parts of Europe and Asia.

**Paleoclimates and ancient oceans.** For Gondwana itself, geological data suffice to recreate in broad outline form not only its coasts, plains, and mountain ranges but also its deserts, polar ice caps, and tropical jungles. These reflect broad climatic zones, which were themselves controlled mainly by insolation, seasonality, and the rotating of the Earth. Large landmasses may sometimes have modified climate to produce monsoons. Given the positions and sizes of continents, paleoclimatic zones may be inferred and then checked against climatic conditions deduced from the fossil record of sedimentary rocks. The results show a satisfactory correspondence between expectations and record, much better than the one obtained by plotting paleoclimatic data on the present-day configuration of continents. They leave little doubt that it is better to accept that the continents have drifted about than to assume that they have remained stationary.

The supercontinent Pangaea was completely surrounded by a world ocean extending from pole to pole and spanning 80 percent of the circumference of the Earth at the Equator. The equatorial current system, driven by the trade winds, resided in warm latitudes much longer than it does today, and its waters were therefore warmer. The gyres that occupy most of the Southern and Northern hemispheres were also warmer, and consequently the temperature gradient from the Equator to the poles was much reduced in comparison to the present.

Early in the Mesozoic, the equatorial current became circumglobal when the Tethys seaway split Gondwana from its northern counterpart, Laurasia. The equatorial surface waters, now able to circumnavigate the world one or more times, became even warmer; but whether the return flows continued to keep the high latitudes warm or diminished in strength and therefore somewhat increased the latitudinal temperature gradients is not certain. Nevertheless, in the middle and later Mesozoic the Arctic and Antarctic surface water temperatures were at or above 10° C (50° F), and the polar regions were warm enough to support forests. As the dispersal of continents following the breakup of Pangaea continued, however, the surface circulation of the oceans became much more complex. During the middle Cenozoic, the northward drift of Australia and South America created a new circumglobal seaway around Antarctica that remained centred on the South Pole. A vigorous circum-Antarctic current developed, isolating the southern continent from the warmer waters to the north. At the same time, the equatorial current system became blocked, first in the Indo-Pacific region, next in the Middle East and eastern Mediterranean, then at Gibraltar, and finally, about 5,000,000 years ago, by the emergence of the Isthmus of Panama. As a result, the equatorial waters were heated less and the mid-latitude ocean gyres were not as effective in keeping the high latitudes warm. Because of this, an ice cap began to form on Antarctica some 20,000,000 years ago and grew to roughly its present size about 5,000,000 years later. This ice cap cooled the waters of the adjacent ocean to such a low temperature that the waters sank and initiated the north-directed abyssal flow that marks the present deep circulation. The Quaternary Ice Age arrived in full when the first ice caps appeared in the Northern Hemisphere about 2,000,000 years ago.

There is no certainty that the changing configuration of continents and oceans can be held solely responsible for the onset of the Quaternary Ice Age, even if such factors as the drift of continents across the latitudes (with the associated changes in vegetation) and reflectivity for solar heat are included. There can be little doubt, however, that it was a major contributing factor and that recognition of its role has profoundly altered all concepts of paleoclimatology.

**Plate tectonics and mountain building.** Subduction and continental collision raise mountain ranges. Consequently, the implications of plate tectonics for the processes of mountain building have attracted much attention. One of the earliest to apply the new theory was the Cambridge geologist John Dewey, who analyzed the Appalachian and Alpine orogenies. Many other researchers have subsequently undertaken similar work in the Mediterranean system and the American Cordilleran ranges, as well as in the Appalachians.

The collisions that gradually joined North America to Pangaea during the Paleozoic exemplify the role of plate convergence in mountain building. Some 500,000,000 years ago, a subduction zone existed along what is now the eastern seaboard of North America. During the course of the next 70,000,000 years—the Ordovician Period—this region underwent a major phase of mountain building. When it was over, the direction of sediment transport had reversed, indicating that a large source area had appeared to the east of the subduction zone. The thick sequence of deposits from this source in eastern North America bears witness to its size, which is incommensurable with the island arcs that normally accompany a subduction zone. Subduction, sedimentation, and volcanism then contin-

Reconstructions of ancient geography

The dispersal of continents and its impact on oceanic current systems

The significance of plate convergence in orogeny

ued until a small continent comprising what is today northwestern Europe collided with the northeastern tip of North America. This collision raised a major chain of folded mountains, the remains of which are now found from New England through eastern Canada and Scotland into Norway. This Caledonian range shed sediments to both sides, forming the Catskill delta in eastern North America and the Old Red Sandstone in northwestern Europe. Subsequently, the southern edge of North America collided with South America, and a little later Africa arrived, producing the southern Appalachians. Miscellaneous fragments, today part of central Europe and the western Mediterranean, filled in the gap and completed this portion of Pangaea.

This account fits the plate model fairly well except for two things: (1) the occurrence of paroxysms of mountain building when no continental collision can be assumed; and (2) the need for sizable landmasses, presumably small continents, floating offshore to provide a necessary sediment source. Both problems appear quite often wherever plate movements are used to explain the details of the formation of major mountain ranges. Yet, the model itself is simple. It allows for three possible cases: ocean–ocean collisions; ocean–continent collisions; and continent–continent collisions. In the first two situations, oceanic crust is subducted either under other oceanic crust or under a continent—a steady process presumably accompanied by an equally steady scraping off and deforming of sediments and basaltic crust at the plate edge and by volcanism farther away. The New Hebrides trench and island arcs in the southwestern Pacific exemplify an ocean–ocean collision, while the Andes Mountain Ranges of South America represent a long-lasting collision of oceanic crust and continental crust at the leading edges of plates.

Even in these cases the process appears to be more complicated than the theory suggests, demanding modifications that, though eminently plausible and often proven, are ad hoc and thus diminish its value as a unifying principle. The South American Andes, for example, have had an episodic history not readily matched to the evidently uneventful spreading of the seafloor in the adjacent Pacific. The volcanism of the segments of the Cascade Range in Oregon and Washington in the northwestern United States is only a few million years old in its present form, whereas subduction along the Pacific coast dates back much farther than that. All along the west coast of North America, mountain building has occurred in distinct major phases, ultimately caused in all probability by changes in the rate and direction of plate movements that complicate the basically simple subduction process.

One of the complicating factors is much in evidence in the coast ranges that extend from California to southern Alaska. Large sections of these mountains fit poorly with the geology of the surrounding terrain and are thought to have originated in the ancient Pacific. Perhaps they once were oceanic plateaus, island arcs, or other thick pieces of oceanic crust that would not subduct but instead lodged against the continental edge, and so disturbed the processes of subduction and mountain building. Some of these "exotic terranes" have been shown by their paleomagnetic properties to have come a long way from their points of origin, perhaps as far as the Southern Hemisphere.

The Indus–Himalayan–Tibetan region in northern India and China represents a continent–continent collision that began 40,000,000 years ago when all of the oceanic crust between northward-drifting India and south central Asia had been consumed and the continent-bearing edges of the two plates met. The suture of this collision, the site of the former subduction zone, lies inconspicuously in the high plateau region north of the Himalayas. This lofty mountain range itself formed long after the collision as India—its momentum not fully spent even today—drove another 2,000 kilometres into the underbelly of Asia. In doing so, Asian lithosphere was displaced laterally along enormous transcurrent faults, which are the sites of the numerous devastating earthquakes in Iran, Afghanistan, and western China. The Himalayas themselves are the product of the northward, low-angle underthrusting of the upper slice of the Indian plate under the Asian plate, making it clear that a continent–continent collision involves a good deal more than the crumpling of opposing front edges.

**Plate tectonics and life.** Inevitably the continuous rearrangement over time of the size and shape of ocean basins and continents, followed by changes in ocean circulation and climate, have had a major impact on the development of life on Earth. Active interest in these aspects of the Earth science revolution has lagged behind that in other areas, even though as early as 1970 the American geologists James W. Valentine and Eldridge M. Moores attempted to show that the diversity of life increased as continents fragmented and dispersed and diminished when they were joined together.

Subsequently, however, the study of plate activity as a force in the evolution of life has leaped forward. A few simple examples of such research must suffice to illustrate the impact of the plate theory. Toward the end of the Paleozoic, during the Permian Period (about 280,000,000 to 225,000,000 years ago), there was a drastic drop in the variety of animal forms inhabiting the shallow seas around Pangaea. Well over half of the total number of known families became extinct. This drop can be attributed in large part simply to the decrease in biogeographic variety that marks a world consisting of a single continent rather than one comprising many widely dispersed landmasses. Other factors, such as a sharp decrease in the area of shallow-water habitats or a change in ocean fertility due to upwelling, have also been invoked. Moreover, the extinction had a complex history. High latitudes were affected first as a result of the waning of the Permian ice age when the South Pole slipped beyond the southern edge of Pangaea. The equatorial and subtropical zones appear to have been affected somewhat later by a global cooling. On the other hand, the extinctions were not felt so strongly on the continent itself. Instead, the vast semiarid and arid lands that emerged on so large a continent, the shortening of its moist coasts, and the many mountain ranges remaining from the collisions that led to the formation of the supercontinent provided strong incentives for evolutionary adaption to dry or high-altitude environments.

The impact of plate movements and interactions on life is perhaps most clearly demonstrated by what happens when continents diverge or collide. When the Atlantic Ocean began to open during the middle Mesozoic, the similarity between the faunas of opposite shores gradually decreased in almost linear fashion—the greater the distance, the smaller the number of families in common. The difference increased more rapidly in the South Atlantic than in the North Atlantic, where a land connection between Europe and North America persisted until well after the middle Cenozoic. The inverse, the effect of a collision between two hitherto separate landmasses, is illustrated by the consequences of the Pliocene emergence of the Isthmus of Panama. In South America a highly specialized fauna had evolved, rich in marsupials but with few predators. After the emergence of the isthmus had made it possible for land animals to cross, numerous herbivores migrated from north to south. They adapted well to the new environment and were more successful than the local fauna in competing for food. The invasion of highly adaptable carnivores from the north contributed to the extinction of no fewer than four orders of South American land mammals. Only a few species, notably the armadillo and the opossum, managed to migrate in the opposite direction. Ironically, many of the invading northerners, such as the llama and tapir, subsequently became extinct in their country of origin and found their last refuge in the south.

**Early plate activity.** Whatever the forces may be that drive the plates, they consume energy. By far the largest part of this energy is derived from the decay of radioactive isotopes within the Earth, and the energy flow has therefore declined through the 4,500,000,000 years of the Earth's history—rapidly at first and then at a slowly diminishing

The effect of plate activity on the evolution of life

though not negligible rate. Accordingly, it is quite likely that the behaviour of the lithospheric plates on the early, more energetic Earth was different from what it is today, and what prevails at present will certainly differ from what will prevail in the future. A thickening lithosphere, a decreasing heat flow, a temperature gradient that decreases with depth within the Earth, and enlarging—though perhaps less vigorous—convection cells in the mantle have all been postulated as unidirectional changes that affected the behaviour of the lithosphere. It is possible, for example, that the initial plates were too small, too hot, and hence too light to be subducted. In this case, the first subduction would mark the coming of age of classical plate tectonics, and, indeed, clear evidence is lacking for subduction until rather late in the Precambrian.

The evidence that bears on the existence, nature, and movements of possible lithospheric plates during the first several billion years of Earth history is very limited. The continental nuclei of the early and middle Precambrian seem to have been small and might be regarded as small plates on a more vigorously convecting mantle. These nuclei are thought to have been embedded in strongly deformed complexes of sediments and basic igneous rocks, the greenstone belts reminiscent of the sutures that mark the closure of ancient oceans. In most cases, however, paleomagnetic data do not leave room for the existence of sizable oceanic areas between such nuclei. Investigators are thus forced to contemplate the possibility that in the Precambrian intensive deformation took place within plates, perhaps commensurate with the postulated thinner lithosphere and higher flow of heat toward the surface. On the other hand, current knowledge of this long but obscure portion of Earth history is so deficient that some geologists have emphatically denied that there might have been a remote past to which classical plate tectonics could not be applied.

### DISSENTING OPINIONS AND UNANSWERED QUESTIONS

**The dissenters.** Scientific revolutions as far-reaching in their consequences as the plate tectonics revolution cannot be expected to be easily, or ever completely, accepted. Nevertheless, once the theory had fully emerged, acceptance was quick and widespread and by the late 1960s its influence in the West was pervasive. Such was, however, not the case in the Soviet Union, a country located largely in the continental interior far from present-day plate boundaries. Soviet scientists viewed as central to any issue of global tectonics the vertical movements of continental interiors, phenomena not satisfactorily dealt with by the plate tectonics theory. A leading spokesman for the Soviet position, the academician Vladimir Vladimirovich Belousov, strongly defended a model of the Earth that postulated stationary continents affected almost exclusively by vertical motions. The model, however, only vaguely defined the forces supposedly responsible for the motions. In recent years, a younger generation of Soviet geologists has very gradually come to regard plate tectonics as an attractive theory and a viable alternative to the concepts of Belousov and his followers.

Opposition to plate tectonics was by no means limited to the Soviet Union. Sir Harold Jeffreys continued his lifelong rejection of continental drift on grounds that his estimates of the properties of the mantle indicated the impossibility of plate movements. He did not, in general, deign to take note of the mounting geophysical and geological arguments that were in favour of a mobile outer shell of the Earth.

Others proffered different explanations of the accumulating evidence, most of which were rather farfetched, as, for instance, the suggestion that new crust was formed at trenches and destroyed on mid-ocean ridges. Still others, notably the American geologists A.A. Meyerhoff and Howard A. Meyerhoff, attempted to assemble data that contradicted the theory and thereby show that the supporting evidence was wrong, insufficient, or simply misconstrued. Demonstrating a remarkable command of often

quite obscure literature, they issued a series of negative commentaries in the early 1970s; but they failed to convince the majority of their colleagues, partly because they did not offer alternative explanations for the evidence.

The only serious alternative had been proposed in 1958 by the Australian geologist S. Warren Carey in the form of a new version of an old idea—namely, the expanding Earth model. Carey accepted the existence and early Mesozoic breakup of Pangaea and the subsequent dispersal of its fragments and formation of new ocean basins, but he attributed it all to the expansion of the Earth, the planet presumably having had a much smaller diameter in the late Paleozoic. In his view, the continents represented the pre-expansion crust, and the enlarged surface was to be entirely accommodated within the oceans. This model accounted for a spreading ocean floor and for the young age of the oceanic crust; however, it failed to deal adequately with the evidence for subduction and compression. Carey's model also did not explain why the process should not have started until some 4,000,000,000 years after the Earth was formed, and it lacked a reasonable mechanism for so large an expansion. Finally, it disregarded the evidence for continental drift before the existence of Pangaea.

**Unanswered questions.** As the philosopher Thomas J. Kuhn has pointed out, science does not always advance in the gradual and stately fashion commonly attributed to it. Major breakthroughs often come from a leap forward that is at least in part intuitive and may fly in the face of conventional wisdom and widely accepted evidence while strict requirements for verification and proof are temporarily relaxed. Revolutions thus often become widely accepted before the verdict from rigorous analysis of evidence is completely in. Such was certainly the case with the geological revolution, which also confirms Kuhn's view that a new paradigm is unlikely to supersede an existing one until there is little choice but to acknowledge that the conventional theory has failed. Thus, while Wegener did not manage to persuade the world, the successor theory was readily embraced 40 years later, even though it remained open to much of the same criticism that had caused the downfall of continental drift. What is the state of the new paradigm? Is it likely to suffer sooner rather than later the same fate that inevitably awaits all scientific theories?

In 1974, almost alone among the doubters who tried to discredit the new theory with contrary evidence, the American geologist John C. Maxwell, in a closely reasoned paper, enumerated all the points on which he believed plate tectonics had failed to offer an explanation. Many of these points have since been resolved, but more than a few remain to suggest that the theory, though in essence valid, may be incomplete.

The greatest successes of plate tectonics have been achieved in the ocean basins where additional decades of effort have confirmed its postulates and enabled investigators to construct a credible history of past plate movements. Inevitably in less rigorous form, the reconstruction of early Mesozoic and Paleozoic continental configurations has provided a powerful tool with which to resolve many important questions. On the other hand, the new paradigm has proved less useful in deciphering mountain-building processes or in offering explanations for the complex history of sea-level fluctuations. The American geologist L.L. Sloss has devoted much effort to demonstrating that continents do indeed rise and fall in unison, but the possible mechanisms for such a process remain elusive.

Where plate boundaries adjoin continents, matters often become very complex and have demanded an ever denser thicket of ad hoc modifications and amendments to the theory and practice of plate tectonics in the form of microplates, obscure plate boundaries, and exotic terranes. A good example is the Mediterranean, where the collisions between Africa and a swarm of microcontinents have produced a tectonic nightmare that is far from resolved. More disturbingly, some of the present plate boundaries, especially in the eastern Mediterranean, appear to be so

*Early opposition to plate tectonics*

*Carey's version of the expanding Earth model*

diffuse and so anomalous that they cannot be compared to the three types of plate boundaries of the basic theory. There is evidence, as held by the American geophysicist Thomas H. Jordan, that the base of the plates extends far deeper into the asthenosphere below the continents than below the oceans. How much of an impediment this might be for the movement of plates and how it might affect their boundary interactions remain open questions. Others have postulated that the lower layer of the lithosphere peels off and sinks late in any collision sequence, producing high heat flow, volcanism, and an upper lithospheric zone vulnerable to contraction by thrusting.

It is understandable that any simple global tectonic model would work better in the oceans, which, being young, retain a record of only a brief and relatively uneventful history. On the continents, almost 4,000,000,000 years of growth and deformation, erosion, sedimentation, and igneous intrusion have produced a complex imprint that, with its intricate zones of varying strength, must directly affect the application of plate forces. Seismic reflection studies of the deep structure of the continents have demonstrated just how complex the events that form the continents and their margins may have been, and their findings sometimes are difficult to reconcile with the accretionary structures one would expect to see as a result of subduction and collision.

Notwithstanding these cautions and the continuing lack of an agreed-upon driving mechanism for the plates, one cannot help but conclude that the plate tectonics revolution has been fruitful and has immensely advanced scientific understanding of the Earth. Like all paradigms in science, it will most likely one day be replaced by a better one; yet there can be little doubt that, whatever the new theory may state, continental drift will be part of it.

**BIBLIOGRAPHY.** J. TUZO WILSON (ed.), *Continents Adrift and Continents Aground* (1976), contains an excellent and readable set of articles on the plate tectonics revolution drawn from *Scientific American,* many written by its protagonists, with fine introductions by the editor. Similarly, ALLAN COX (ed.), *Plate Tectonics and Geomagnetic Reversals* (1973), offers a well-chosen selection of the original classical papers that produced this revolution in the Earth sciences, from Holmes's work in the early 1900s to contributions in the late 1960s. An excellent explanation of the new Earth science is SEIYA UYEDA, *The New View of the Earth: Moving Continents and Moving Oceans* (1978), which discusses plate theory and its application to the study of the Earth's surface structures. Scholarly, but written for a lay audience, is TJEERD H. VAN ANDEL, *New Views on an Old Planet: Continental Drift and the History of Earth* (1985), an application of plate theory to the climatic, oceanographic, and geographic history of the Earth, and the relation of the theory to the history of life. The history of ideas pertaining to continental drift and plate tectonics has been thoughtfully analyzed in ANTHONY HALLAM, *A Revolution in the Earth Sciences: From Continental Drift to Plate Tectonics* (1973). A summary of the revolution, mostly in a critical vein by many of its principal opponents, is CHARLES F. KAHLE (ed.), *Plate Tectonics: Assessments and Reassessments* (1974), a bit dated but a good substantive statement on the subject. More technical, though not forbiddingly so, are three books rich in detail and substance: PETER J. WYLLIE, *The Way the Earth Works: An Introduction to the New Global Geology and Its Revolutionary Development* (1976); ROBERT H. DOTT, JR., and ROGER L. BATTEN, *Evolution of the Earth,* 3rd ed. (1981), for the impact of the plate theory on research in Earth history; and STEPHEN STANLEY, *Earth and Life Through Time* (1985), a newer and more advanced treatment.

(TJEERD H. VAN ANDEL)

# Psychological Tests and Measurement

The Bible records that Gideon was instructed to reduce the number of men who were to accompany him into battle by proclaiming, "Whoever is fearful and trembling, let him return home." This constituted a test, and 22,000 left; but the 10,000 remaining still were too numerous. A further test was ordered: only those who lapped water with their tongues as dogs do, in contrast to those who knelt to drink, were to be retained. They had passed a second test, or hurdle, thus providing an early example of what is known today as the successive-hurdles method of personnel selection.

Again, when Gileadites captured the fords of the Jordan River against the Ephraimites, a simple test was used to detect those who were attempting to masquerade as Gileadites. They were required to say "shibboleth," which Ephraimites could pronounce only as "sibboleth." It is recorded that 42,000 Ephraimites failed this simple, one-item test and were put to death.

The idea of behavioral tests to reveal latent abilities also is found in Plato's *Republic*. Plato states that no two persons are born exactly alike; rather, they differ in natural endowments, making one suitable for one occupation, the other for another. The state, therefore, must select, if possible, "that special order of natural endowments which qualifies its possessor for the guardianship of the state." Plato envisaged tests of military aptitude not unlike those used today.

Not until the end of the 19th century, however, did influences from German experimental psychology, British statistical methods for describing individual differences, and French concern for deviant individuals merge to provide a springboard for modern psychological measurement technique and theory.

The word "test" refers to any means (often formally contrived) used to elicit reponses to which behaviour in other contexts can be related. When intended to predict relatively distant future behaviour (*e.g.,* success in school), such a device is called an aptitude test. When used to evaluate the individual's present academic or vocational skill, it may be called an achievement test. In such settings as guidance offices, mental-health clinics, and psychiatric hospitals, tests of ability and personality may be helpful in the diagnosis and detection of troublesome behaviour. Industry and government alike have been prodigious users of tests for selecting workers. Research workers often rely on tests to translate theoretical concepts (*e.g.,* intelligence) into experimentally useful measures.

This article is divided into the following sections:

## GENERAL PROBLEMS OF MEASUREMENT IN PSYCHOLOGY

Physical things are perceived through their properties or attributes. A mother may directly sense the property called temperature by feeling her infant's forehead. Yet she cannot directly observe colicky feelings nor share the infant's personal experience of hunger. She must infer such unobservable private sensations from hearing her baby cry or gurgle; from seeing him flail his arms, or frown, or smile. In the same way, much of what is called measurement must be made by inference. Thus, a mother suspecting her child is feverish may use a thermometer, in which case she ascertains his temperature by looking at the thermometer, rather than by directly touching his head.

Indeed, measurement by inference is particularly characteristic of psychology. Such abstract properties or attributes as intelligence or introversion never are directly measured but must be inferred from observable behaviour. The inference may be fairly direct or quite indirect. If persons respond intelligently (*e.g.,* by reasoning correctly) on an ability test, it can be safely inferred that they possess intelligence to some degree. In contrast, people's capacity to make associations or connections, especially unusual ones, between things or ideas presented in a test can be used as the basis for inferring creativity, although producing a creative product requires other attributes, including motivation, opportunity, and technical skill.

**Types of measurement scales.** To measure any property or activity is to assign it a unique position along some kind of numerical scale. When numbers are used merely to identify individuals or classes (as on the backs of athletes on a football team), they constitute a nominal scale. When a set of numbers reflects only the relative order of things (*e.g.,* pleasantness–unpleasantness of odours), it constitutes an ordinal scale. An interval scale has equal units and an arbitrarily assigned zero point; one such scale, for example, is the Fahrenheit temperature scale. Ratio scales not only provide equal units but also have absolute zero points; examples include measures of weight, density, and distance.

*Nominal, ordinal, interval, and ratio scales*

Although there have been ingenious attempts to establish psychological scales with absolute zero points, psychologists usually are content with approximations to interval scales; ordinal scales often are used as well.

**Primary characteristics of methods or instruments.** The primary requirement of a test is validity—traditionally defined as the degree to which a test actually measures whatever it purports to measure. A test is reliable to the extent that it measures consistently, but reliability is of no consequence if a test lacks validity. Since the person who draws inferences from a test must determine how well it serves his purposes, the estimation of validity inescapably requires judgment. Depending on the criteria of judgment employed, tests exhibit a number of different kinds of validity.

*Validity*

Empirical validity (also called statistical or predictive validity) describes how closely scores on a test correspond (correlate) with behaviour as measured in other contexts. Students' scores on a test of academic aptitude, for example, may be compared with their school grades (a commonly used criterion). To the degree that the two measures statistically correspond, the test empirically predicts the criterion of performance in school. Predictive validity has its most important application in aptitude testing (*e.g.,* in screening applicants for work, in academic placement, in assigning military personnel to different duties).

Alternatively, a test may simply be inspected to see if its content seems appropriate to its intended purpose. Such content validation is widely employed in measuring academic achievement but with recognition of the inevitable role of judgment. Thus, a geometry test exhibits content (or curricular) validity when experts (*e.g.,* teachers) believe that it adequately samples the school curriculum for that topic. Interpreted broadly, content covers desired skills (such as computational ability) as well as points of information in the case of achievement tests. Face validity (a crude kind of content validity) reflects the acceptability of a test to such people as students, parents, employers, and government officials. A test that looks valid is desirable, but face validity without some more basic validity is nothing more than window dressing.

In personality testing, judgments of test content tend to be especially untrustworthy, and dependable external criteria are rare. One may, for example, assume that a man who perspires excessively feels anxious. Yet his feelings of anxiety, if any, are not directly observable. Any assumed trait (anxiety, for example) that is held to underlie observable behaviour is called a construct. Since the construct itself is not directly measurable, the adequacy of any test as a measure of anxiety can be gauged only indirectly; *e.g.,* through evidence for its construct validity.

A test exhibits construct validity when low scorers and high scorers are found to respond differently to everyday experiences or to experimental procedures. A test presumed to measure anxiety, for example, would give evidence of construct validity if those with high scores ("high anxiety") can be shown to learn less efficiently than do those with somewhat lower scores. The rationale is that there are several propositions associated with the concept of anxiety: anxious people are likely to learn less efficiently, especially if uncertain about their capacity to learn; they are likely to overlook things they should attend to in carrying out a task; they are apt to be under continual strain and hence feel fatigued. (But anxious people may be young or old, intelligent or unintelligent.) If people with high scores on a test of anxiety show such proposed signs of anxiety, that is, if a test of anxiety has the expected relationships with other measurements as given in these propositions, the test is viewed as having construct validity.

**Reliability**   Test reliability is affected by scoring accuracy, adequacy of content sampling, and the stability of the trait being measured. Scorer reliability refers to the consistency with which different people who score the same test agree. For a test with a definite answer key, scorer reliability is of negligible concern. When the subject responds with his own words, handwriting, and organization of subject matter, however, the preconceptions of different raters produce different scores for the same test from one rater to another; that is, the test shows scorer (or rater) unreliability. In the absence of an objective scoring key, a scorer's evaluation may differ from one time to another and from those of equally respected evaluators. Other things being equal, tests that permit objective scoring are preferred.

Reliability also depends on the representativeness with which tests sample the content to be tested. If subjects' scores on some items of a test that sample a particular universe of content designed to be reasonably homogeneous (*e.g.,* vocabulary) correlate highly with those on another set of items selected from the same universe of content, the test has high content reliability. But if the universe of content is highly diverse in that it samples different factors (say, verbal reasoning and facility with numbers), the test may have high content reliability but low internal consistency.

For most purposes, the performance of a subject on the same test from day to day should be consistent. When such scores do tend to remain stable over time, the test exhibits temporal reliability. Fluctuations of scores may arise from instability of a trait; for example, the test taker may be happier one day than the next. Or temporal unreliability may reflect injudicious test construction.

Included among the major methods through which test reliability estimates are made is the comparable-forms technique, in which the scores of a group of people on one form of a test are compared with the scores they earn on another form. Theoretically, the comparable-forms approach may reflect scorer, content, and temporal reliability. This ideally demands that each form of the test be constructed by different but equally competent persons and that the forms be given at different times and evaluated by a second rater (unless an objective key is fixed).

In the test–retest method, scores of the same group of people from two administrations of the same test are correlated. If the time interval between administrations is too short, memory may unduly enhance the correlation. Or some people, for example, may look up words they missed on the first administration of a vocabulary test and thus be able to raise their scores the second time around. Too long an interval can result in different effects for each person of forgetting, practice, or learning. Except for very easy speed tests (*e.g.,* in which a person's score depends on how quickly he is able to do simple addition), this method may give misleading estimates of reliability.

Internal-consistency methods of estimating reliability require only one administration of a single form of a test. One method entails obtaining scores on separate halves of the test, usually the odd-numbered and the even-numbered items. The degree of correspondence (which is expressed numerically as a correlation coefficient) between scores on these half-tests permits estimation of the reliability of the test (at full length) by means of a statistical correction.

This is computed by the use of the Spearman–Brown prophecy formula (for estimating the increased reliability expected to result from increase in test length). More commonly used is a generalization of this stepped-up, split-half reliability estimate, one of the Kuder–Richardson formulas. This formula provides an average of estimates that would result from all possible ways of dividing a test into halves.

**Other characteristics.**   A test that takes too long to administer is useless for most routine applications. What constitutes a reasonable period of testing time, however, depends in part on the decisions to be made from the test. Each test should be accompanied by a practicable and economically feasible scoring scheme, one scorable by machine or by quickly trained personnel being preferred.

A large, controversial literature has developed around response sets; *i.e.,* tendencies of subjects to respond systematically to items regardless of content. Thus, a given test taker may tend to answer questions on a personality test only in socially desirable ways or to select the first alternative of each set of multiple-choice answers or to malinger (*i.e.,* to purposely give wrong answers).

Response sets stem from the ways that subjects perceive and cope with the testing situation. If they are tested unwillingly, they may respond carelessly and hastily to get through the test as quickly as possible. If they have trouble deciding how to answer an item, they may guess or, in a self-descriptive inventory, choose the "yes" alternative or the socially desirable one. They may even mentally reword the question to make it easier for them to answer it. The quality of test scores is impaired when the purposes of the test administrator and the reactions of the subjects to being tested are not in harmony. Modern test construction seeks to reduce the undesired effects of subjects' reactions.

TYPES OF INSTRUMENTS AND METHODS

*Psychophysical scales and psychometric, or psychological, scales.*   The concept of an absolute threshold (the lowest intensity at which a sensory stimulus, such as sound waves, is perceived) is traceable to the German philosopher Johann Friedrich Herbart. The German physiologist Ernst Heinrich Weber later observed that the smallest discernible difference of intensity is proportional to the initial stimulus intensity. Weber found, for example, that, while people could just notice the difference after a slight change in the weight of a 10-gram object, they needed a larger change before they could just detect a difference from a 100-gram weight. This finding, known as Weber's law, is expressed more technically in the statement that the perceived (subjective) intensity varies mathematically as the logarithm of the physical (objective) intensity of the stimulus.

In traditional psychophysical scaling methods, a set of standard stimuli (such as weights) that can be ordered according to some physical property is related to sensory judgments made by experimental subjects. By the method of average error, for example, subjects are given a standard stimulus and then made to adjust a variable stimulus until they believe it is equal to the standard. The mean (average) of a number of judgments is obtained. This method and many variations have been used to study such experiences as visual illusions, tactual intensities, and auditory pitch.

Psychological (psychometric) scaling methods are an outgrowth of the psychophysical tradition just described. Although their purpose is to locate stimuli on a linear (straight-line) scale, no quantitative physical values (e.g., loudness or weight) for stimuli are involved. The linear scale may represent an individual's attitude toward a social institution, his judgment of the quality of an artistic product, the degree to which he exhibits a personality characteristic, or his preference for different foods. Psychological scales thus are used for having a person rate his own characteristics as well as those of other individuals in terms of such attributes, for example, as leadership potential or initiative. In addition to locating individuals on a scale, psychological scaling can also be used to scale objects and various kinds of characteristics: finding where different foods fall on a group's preference scale; or determining the relative positions of various job characteristics in the view of those holding that job. Reported degrees of similarities between pairs of objects are used to identify scales or dimensions on which people perceive the objects.

The American psychologist L.L. Thurstone offered a number of theoretical-statistical contributions that are widely used as rationales for constructing psychometric scales. One scaling technique (comparative judgment) is based empirically on choices made by people between members of any series of paired stimuli. Statistical treatment to provide numerical estimates of the subjective (perceived) distances between members of every pair of stimuli yields a psychometric scale. Whether or not these computed scale values are consistent with the observed comparative judgments is a problem that can be tested empirically.

Another of Thurstone's psychometric scaling techniques (equal-appearing intervals) has been widely used in attitude measurement. In this method judges sort statements reflecting such things as varying degrees of emotional intensity, for example, into what they perceive to be equally spaced categories; the average (median) category assignments are used to define scale values numerically. Subsequent users of such a scale are scored according to the average scale values of the statements to which they subscribe. Another psychologist, Louis Guttman, developed a method that requires no prior group of judges, depends on intensive analysis of scale items, and yields comparable results. Quite commonly used is the type of scale developed by Rensis Likert in which perhaps five choices ranging from strongly in favour to strongly opposed are provided for each statement, the alternatives being scored from one to five. A more general technique (successive intervals) does not depend on the assumption that judges perceive interval size accurately. The widely used graphic rating scale presents an arbitrary continuum with preassigned guides for the rater (e.g., adjectives such as superior, average, and inferior).

*Tests versus inventories.* The term "test" most frequently refers to devices for measuring abilities or qualities for which there are authoritative right and wrong answers.

Such a test may be contrasted with a personality inventory, for which it is often claimed that there are no right or wrong answers. At any rate, in taking what often is called a test, the subjects are instructed to do their best; in completing an inventory, they are instructed to represent their typical reactions. A distinction also has been made that in responding to an inventory the subjects control the appraisal, whereas in a test they do not. If a test is more broadly regarded as a set of stimulus situations that elicit responses from which inferences can be drawn, however, then an inventory is, according to this definition, a variety of test.

*Free-response versus limited-response tests.* Free-response tests entail few restraints on the form or content of response, whereas limited-response tests restrict responses to one of a smaller number presented (e.g., true-false). An essay test tends toward one extreme (free response), while a so-called fully objective test is at the other extreme (limited response).

Response to an essay question is not completely unlimited, however, since the answer should bear on the question. The free-response test does give practice in writing, and, when an evaluator is proficient in judging written expression, his comments on the test may aid the individual to improve his writing style. All too often, however, writing ability unfortunately affects the evaluator's judgment of how well the test taker understands content, and this tends to reduce test reliability. Another source of unreliability for essay tests is found in their limited sampling of content, as contrasted with the broader coverage that is possible with objective tests. Often both the scorer and the content reliability of essay tests can be improved, but such attempts are costly.

The objective test, which minimizes scorer unreliability, is best typified by the multiple-choice form, in which the subject is required to select one from two or (preferably) more responses to a test item. Matching items that have a common set of alternatives for matching are of this form. The true-false test question is a special multiple-choice form that may tend to arouse antagonism because of variable standards of truth or falsity.

The more general multiple-choice item is more acceptable when it is specified only that the best answer be selected; it is flexible, has high scorer reliability, and is not limited to simple factual knowledge. The ingenious test constructor can use multiple-choice items to test such functions as generalization, application of principles, and the ability to educe unfamiliar relationships.

Some personality tests are presented in a forced-choice format. They may, for example, force the person to choose one of two favourable words or phrases (e.g., intelligent–handsome) as more descriptive of himself or one of two unfavourable terms as less descriptive (e.g., stupid–ugly). Marking one choice yields a gain in score on some trait but may also preclude credit on another trait. This technique is intended to eliminate any effects from subjects' attempts to present themselves in a socially desirable light; it is not fully successful, however, because what is highly desirable for one person may be less desirable for another.

The forced-choice technique for self-appraisals is exemplified in a widely used interest inventory. Forced-choice ratings were introduced for evaluation of one military officer by another during World War II. They were an effort to avoid the preponderance of high ratings typically obtained with ordinary rating scales. Raters tend to give those being rated the benefit of any doubt, especially when they are fellow workers. Also, supervisors or teachers may give unduly favourable ratings because they believe good performance of subordinates or students reflects well on themselves.

Falling between free- and limited-response tests is a type that requires a short answer, perhaps a single word or a number, for each item. When the required response is to fit into a blank in a sentence, the test is called a completion test. This type of test is susceptible to scorer unreliability.

Weber's law

Essay and objective tests

Forced-choice items

A personality test to which a subject responds by interpreting a picture or by telling a story it suggests resembles an essay test except that responses ordinarily are oral. A personality inventory that requires the subject to indicate whether or not a descriptive phrase applies to him is of the limited-response type. A sentence-completion personality test that asks the subject to complete statements such as "I worry because . . . " is akin to the short-answer and completion types.

*Verbal versus performance tests.* A verbal (or symbol) test poses questions to which the subject supplies symbolic answers (in words or in other symbols, such as numbers). In performance tests, the subject actually executes some motor activity; for example, he assembles mechanical objects. Either the quality of performance as it takes place or its results may be rated.

The verbal test, permitting group administration, requiring no special equipment, and often being scorable by relatively unskilled evaluators, tends to be more practical than the performance test. Both types of devices also have counterparts in personality measurement, in which verbal tests as well as behaviour ratings are used.

*Written (group) versus oral (individual) tests.* The oral test is administered to one person at a time, but written tests can be given simultaneously to a number of subjects. Oral tests of achievement, being uneconomical and prone to content and scorer unreliability, have been supplanted by written tests; notable exceptions include the testing of illiterates and the anachronistic oral examinations to which candidates for graduate degrees are liable.

Proponents of individually administered intelligence tests (*e.g.,* the Stanford-Binet) state that such face-to-face testing optimizes rapport and motivation, even among literate adult subjects. Oral tests of general aptitude remain popular, though numerous written group tests have been designed for the same purpose.

Interviews viewed as tests

The interview may provide a personality measurement and, especially when it is standardized as to wording and order of questions and with a key for coding answers, may amount to an individual oral test. Used in public opinion surveys, such standardized interviews are carefully designed to avoid the effects of interviewer bias and to be comprehensible to a highly heterogeneous sample of respondents.

*Appraisal by others versus self-appraisal.* In responding to personality inventories and rating scales, a person presumably reveals what he thinks he is like; that is, he appraises himself. Other instruments may reflect what one person thinks of another. Because self-appraisal often lacks objectivity, appraisal by another individual is common in such things as ratings for promotions. Ordinary tests of ability clearly involve evaluation of one person by another, although the subject's self-evaluation may intrude; for example, he may lack confidence to the point where he does not try to do his best.

*Projective tests.* The stimuli (*e.g.,* inkblots) in a projective test are intentionally made ambiguous and open to different interpretations in the expectation that each subject will project his own unique (idiosyncratic) reactions in his answers. Techniques for evaluating such responses range from the intuitive impressions of the rater to complex, coded schemes for scoring and interpretation that require extensive manuals; some projective tests are objectively scorable.

*Speed tests versus power tests.* A pure speed test is homogeneous in content (*e.g.,* a simple clerical checking test), the tasks being so easy that with unlimited time all but the most incompetent of subjects could deal with them successfully. The time allowed for testing is so short, however, that even the ablest subject is not expected to finish. A useful score is the number of correct answers made in a fixed time. In contrast, a power test (*e.g.,* a general vocabulary test) contains items that vary in difficulty to the point that no subject is expected to get all items right even with unlimited time. In practice, a definite but ample time is set for power tests.

Speed tests are suitable for testing visual perception, numerical facility, and other abilities related to vocational success. Tests of psychomotor abilities (*e.g.,* eye–hand coordination) often involve speed. Power tests tend to be more relevant to such purposes as the evaluation of academic achievement, for which the highest level of difficulty at which a person can succeed is of greater interest than his speed on easy tasks.

In general, tests reflect unknown combinations of the effects of speed and power; many consist of items that vary considerably in difficulty, and the time allowed is too limited to allow a large proportion of subjects to attempt all items.

*Teacher-made versus standardized tests.* A distinction between teacher-made tests and standardized tests is often made in relation to tests used to assess academic achievement. Ordinarily, teachers do not attempt to construct tests of general or special aptitude or of personality traits. Teacher-made tests tend instead to be geared to narrow segments of curricular content (*e.g.,* a sixth-grade geography test). Standardized tests with carefully defined procedures for administration and scoring to ensure uniformity can achieve broader goals. General principles of test construction and such considerations as reliability and validity apply to both types of test.

*Special measurement techniques.* Sociodrama and psychodrama were originally developed as psychotherapeutic techniques. In sociodrama, group members participate in unrehearsed drama to illuminate a general problem. Psychodrama centres on one individual in the group whose unique personal problem provides the theme. Related research techniques (*e.g.,* the sociometric test) can offer insight into interpersonal relationships. Individuals may be asked to specify members of a group whom they prefer as leader, playmate, or coworker. The choices made can then be charted in a sociogram, from which cliques or socially isolated individuals may be identified at a glance. Research psychologists have grasped the sociometric approach as a means of measuring group cohesiveness and studying individual reactions to groups. The degree to which any group member chooses or is chosen beyond chance expectation may be calculated, and mathematical techniques may be used to determine the complex links among group members. Sociogram-choice scores have been useful in predicting such criteria as individual productivity in factory work, combat effectiveness, and social leadership.

Sociodrama and psychodrama

## DEVELOPMENT OF STANDARDIZED TESTS

**Test content.** *Item development.* Once the need for a test has been established, a plan to depict its content may be prepared. For achievement tests, the test plan may also indicate thinking skills to be evaluated. Detailed content headings can be immediately suggestive of test items. It is helpful if the plan specifies weights to be allotted to different topics, as well as the desired average score and the spread of item difficulties. Whether or not such an outline is made, the test constructor clearly must understand the purpose of the test, the universe of content to be sampled, and the forms of the items to be used.

Planning the test

*Tryouts and item analysis.* A set of test questions is first administered to a small group of people deemed to be representative of the population for which the final test is intended. The trial run is planned to provide a check on instructions for administering and taking the test and for intended time allowances, and it can also reveal ambiguities in the test content. After adjustments, surviving items are administered to a larger, ostensibly representative group. The resulting data permit computation of a difficulty index for each item (often taken as the percentage of the subjects who respond correctly) and of an item-test or item-subtest discrimination index (*e.g.,* a coefficient of correlation specifying the relationship of each item with total test score or subtest score).

If it is feasible to do so, measures of the relation of each item to independent criteria (*e.g.,* grades earned in school) are obtained to provide item validation. Items that are too easy or too difficult are discarded; those within a desired range of difficulty are identified. If internal consistency is sought, items that are found to be unrelated to either a total score or an appropriate subtest score are ruled out, and items that are related to available external criterion measures are identified. Those items that show the most efficiency in predicting an external criterion (highest validity) usually are preferred over those that contribute only to internal consistency (reliability).

Estimates of reliability for the entire set of items, as well as for those to be retained, commonly are calculated. If the reliability estimate is deemed to be too low, items may be added. Each alternative in multiple-choice items also may be examined statistically. Weak incorrect alternatives can be replaced, and those that are unduly attractive to higher scoring subjects may be modified.

*Cross validation.* Item-selection procedures are subject to chance errors in sampling test subjects, and statistical values obtained in pretesting are usually checked (cross validated) with one or more additional samples of subjects. Typically, it is found that cross-validation values tend to shrink for many of the items that emerged as best in the original data, and further items may be found to warrant discard. Measures of correlation between total test score and scores from other, better known tests are often sought by test users.

*Differential weighting.* Some test items may appear to deserve extra, positive weight; some answers in multiple-choice items, though keyed as wrong, seem better than others in that they attract people who earn high scores generally. The bulk of theoretical logic and empirical evidence, nonetheless, suggests that unit weights for selected items and zero weights for discarded items and dichotomous (right versus wrong) scoring for multiple-choice items serve almost as effectively as more complicated scoring. Painstaking efforts to weight items generally are not worth the trouble.

Negative weight for wrong answers is usually avoided as presenting undue complication. In multiple-choice items, the number of answers a subject knows, in contrast to the number he gets right (which will include some lucky guesses), can be estimated by formula. But such an average correction overpenalizes the unlucky and underpenalizes the lucky. If the instruction is not to guess, it is variously interpreted by persons of different temperament; those who decide to guess despite the ban are often helped by partial knowledge and tend to do better.

A responsible tactic is to try to reduce these differences by directing subjects to respond to every question, even if they must guess. Such instructions, however, are inappropriate for some competitive speed tests, since candidates who mark items very rapidly and with no attention to accuracy excel if speed is the only basis for scoring; that is, if wrong answers are not penalized.

**Test norms.** Test norms consist of data that make it possible to determine the relative standing of an individual who has taken a test. By itself, a subject's raw score (*e.g.,* the number of answers that agree with the scoring key) has little meaning. Almost always, a test score must be interpreted as indicating the subject's position relative to others in some group. Norms provide a basis for comparing the individual with a group.

Numerical values called centiles (or percentiles) serve as the basis for one widely applicable system of norms. From a distribution of a group's raw scores the percentage of subjects falling below any given raw score can be found. Any raw score can then be interpreted relative to the performance of the reference (or normative) group—eighth-graders, five-year-olds, institutional inmates, job applicants. The centile rank corresponding to each raw score, therefore, shows the percentage of subjects who scored below that point. Thus, 25 percent of the normative group earn scores lower than the 25th centile; and an average called the median corresponds to the 50th centile.

Another class of norm system (standard scores) is based on how far each raw score falls above or below an average score, the arithmetic mean. One resulting type of standard score, symbolized as $z$, is positive (*e.g.,* $+1.69$ or $+2.43$) for a raw score above the mean and negative for a raw score below the mean. Negative and fractional values can, however, be avoided in practice by using other types of standard scores obtained by multiplying $z$ scores by an arbitrarily selected constant (say, 10) and by adding another constant (say, 50, which changes the $z$ score mean of zero to a new mean of 50). Such changes of constants do not alter the essential characteristics of the underlying set of $z$ scores.

The French psychologist Alfred Binet, in pioneering the development of tests of intelligence, listed test items along a normative scale on the basis of the chronological age (actual age in years and months) of groups of children that passed them. A mental-age score (*e.g.,* seven) was assigned to each subject, indicating the chronological age (*e.g.,* seven years old) in the reference sample for which his raw score was the mean. But mental age is not a direct index of brightness; a mental age of seven in a 10-year-old is different from the same mental age in a four-year-old.

To correct for this, a later development was a form of IQ (intelligence quotient), computed as the ratio of the subject's mental age to his chronological age, multiplied by 100. (Thus, the IQ made it easy to tell if a child was bright or dull for his age.)

Ratio IQs for younger age groups exhibit means close to 100 and spreads of roughly 45 points above and below 100. The classical ratio IQ has been largely supplanted by the deviation IQ, mainly because the spread around the average has not been uniform due to different ranges of item difficulty at different age levels. The deviation IQ, a type of standard score, has a mean of 100 and a standard deviation of 16 for each age level. Practice with the Stanford-Binet test reflects the finding that average performance on the test does not increase beyond age 18. Therefore, the chronological age of any individual older than 18 is taken as 18 for the purpose of determining IQ.

The Stanford-Binet has been largely supplanted by several tests developed by the American psychologist David Wechsler between the late 1930s and the early 1960s. These tests have subtests for several capacities, some verbal and some operational, each subtest having its own norms. After constructing tests for adults, Wechsler developed tests for older and for younger children.

### ASSESSING TEST STRUCTURE

**Factor analysis.** Factor analysis is a method of assessment frequently used for the systematic analysis of intellectual ability and other test domains, such as personality measures. Just after the turn of the 20th century the British psychologist Charles E. Spearman systematically explored positive intercorrelations between measures of apparently different abilities to provide evidence that much of the variability in scores that children earn on tests of intelligence depends on one general underlying factor, which he called $g$. In addition he believed that each test contained an $s$ factor specific to it alone. In the United States, Thurstone developed a statistical technique called multiple-factor analysis, with which he was able to demonstrate, in a set of tests of intelligence, that there were primary mental abilities, such as verbal comprehension, numerical computation, spatial orientation, and general reasoning. Although later work has supported the differentiation between these abilities, no definitive taxonomy of abilities has become established. One element in the problem is the finding that each such ability can be shown to be composed of narrower factors.

The first computational methods in factor analysis have been supplanted by mathematically more elegant, computer-generated solutions. While earlier techniques were primarily exploratory, the Swedish statistician Karl Gustav Jöreskog and others have developed procedures that permit the researcher to test hypotheses about the structure in a set of data.

Rooted in extensive applications of factor analysis, a structure-of-intellect model developed by the American psychologist Joy Paul Guilford posited a very large number of factors of intelligence. Guilford envisaged three intersecting dimensions corresponding respectively to four kinds of test content, five kinds of intellectual operation, and six kinds of product. Each of the 120 cells in the cube thus generated was hypothesized to represent a separate ability, each constituting a distinct factor of intellect. Educational and vocational counselors usually prefer a substantially smaller number of scores than the 120 implied by this model.

Factor analysis has also been widely used outside the realm of intelligence, especially to seek the structure of personality as reflected in ratings by oneself and by others. Although there is even less consensus here than for intelligence, a number of studies suggest that four prevalent factors can be approximately labeled, namely, conformity, extroversion, anxiety, and dependability.

**Profile analysis.** With the fractionation of tests (*e.g.,* to yield scores measuring separate factors or clusters), new concern has arisen for interpreting differences among scores measuring the underlying variables, however conceived. Scores of an individual on several such measures can be plotted graphically as a profile; for direct comparability, all raw scores may be expressed in terms of standard scores that have equal means and variabilities. The difference between any pair of scores that have less than perfect reliability tends to be less reliable than either, and fluctuations in the graph should be interpreted cautiously. Nevertheless, various features of an individual's profile may be examined, such as scatter (fluctuation from one measure to another) and relative level of performance on different measures. (The particular shape of the graph, it should be noted, partly depends upon the arbitrary order in which measures are listed.) One may also statistically express the degree of similarity between any two profiles. Such statistical measures of pattern similarity permit quantitative comparison of profiles for different persons, of profiles of the same individual's performance at different times, of individual with group profiles, or of one group profile with another. Comparison of an individual's profile with similar graphs representing the means for various occupational groups, for example, is useful for vocational guidance or personnel selection.

**BIBLIOGRAPHY.** DOROTHY C. ADKINS, *Test Construction,* 2nd ed. (1974), a simplified treatment of measurement principles, rules for test construction, and statistical techniques; ANNE ANASTASI, *Psychological Testing,* 5th ed. (1982), an authoritative text and reference book, with emphasis on current psychological tests; LEE J. CRONBACH, *Essentials of Psychological Testing,* 4th ed. (1984), another modern and insightful text and general reference; J.P. GUILFORD, *Psychometric Methods,* 2nd ed. (1954), a widely used book that attempts to integrate psychophysical scaling and psychological measurement methods; HAROLD GULLIKSEN, *Theory of Mental Tests* (1950), a basic theoretical reference; HARRY H. HARMAN, *Modern Factor Analysis,* 3rd rev. ed. (1976), an eclectic treatment of factor-analytic theory and methods; PAUL HORST, *Psychological Measurement and Prediction* (1966), a discussion of practical requirements of psychological measurement as well as of technical problems in prediction; FREDERIC M. LORD and MELVIN R. NOVICK, *Statistical Theories of Mental Test Scores* (1968), a highly technical presentation; GEORG RASCH, *Probabilistic Models for Some Intelligence and Attainment Tests* (1980), with a new model for tests; ROBERT L. THORNDIKE (ed.), *Educational Measurement,* 2nd ed. (1971), with specially prepared chapters by authorities in particular fields of measurement.

(DOROTHY C. ADKINS/ DONALD W. FISKE)

# Science
# Year in
# Review

# Contents

# The Year in Science: An Overview

## by Kendrick Frazier

Two things are certain about science. It does not stand still for long, and it is never boring. Oh, among some poor souls, including even intellectuals in fields of high scholarship, science is frequently misperceived. Many see it as only a body of facts, promulgated from on high in musty, unintelligible textbooks, a collection of unchanging precepts defended with authoritarian vigor. Others view it as nothing but a cold, dry, narrow, plodding, rule-bound process—the scientific method: hidebound, linear, and left brained.

These people are the victims of their own stereotypes. They are destined to view the world of science with a set of blinders. They know nothing of the tumult, cacophony, rambunctiousness, and tendentiousness of the actual scientific process, let alone the creativity, passion, and joy of discovery. And they are likely to know little of the continual procession of new insights and discoveries that every day, in some way, change our view (if not theirs) of the natural world.

The past year was filled with examples of such new developments. I have selected some of them to illustrate seven observations about science and the scientific process. The selections are somewhat personal. The advances are ones I find particularly interesting or significant, or (better!) both. Scores of others could also be mentioned. Furthermore, the categories are somewhat arbitrary, and even the ones selected do not receive equal treatment.

**Science deals with the awesome and bizarre.** This statement is obvious to everyone involved with science, even though scientists usually downplay it in their formal reports. But nonscientists sometimes think that science is conservative or that it deals only with small questions. How wrong they are! In recent years scientists have probed ever further back in time toward the very moment of creation—specifically, to events back to the first $10^{-43}$ second of the universe, when in a fraction of an instant all matter and energy may have been created from virtually nothing. Likewise, physicists and philosophers alike have been grappling with the mind-boggling concepts and seeming paradoxes of quantum theory.

**KENDRICK FRAZIER** is a science writer and editor. He is editor of The Skeptical Inquirer, former editor of Science News, and the author of four books, most recently People of Chaco.

During the past year scientists struggled with promising concepts of superstring theory and cosmic strings (two totally different things). They produced evidence for the large-scale structure of the universe, with its huge and puzzling voids and bubbles. And they gained possible new insights into invisible matter that may make up 90% of the mass of the universe.

Superstring theory emerged out of a longtime quest that has motivated science at the most fundamental level: the attempt to unify the forces and principles of nature. The four forces of nature—the electromagnetic, strong, weak, and gravitational forces—all operate in different domains, on different kinds of matter, at greatly different intensities. Gravity, for instance, reaches across the scale of the universe but has a strength of only one part in $10^{36}$ that of the electromagnetic force; while the strong force, which binds together the heavy particles in the atomic nucleus, has a strength 100 times that of the electromagnetic force but is effective only over scales of the atomic nucleus, $10^{-13}$ centimeters. It is now thought that in the big-bang explosion that created the universe there was for an instant a single kind of force. As the temperature cooled, this force differentiated successively into those that we know today, just as different compounds in a cooling liquid freeze out at different temperatures. All this happened in the first trillionth of a second as the universe "aged" from $10^{-43}$ second to $10^{-12}$ second and cooled from $10^{32}$ degrees to $10^{15}$ degrees C. Thus the search for the underlying unity of nature is an inquiry into the very early evolution of the universe.

Superstring theory is the latest approach to such unification. It improves over earlier unification theories by incorporating their successful predictions while avoiding predictions that either are nonsensical or have been shown false. Moreover, it includes gravity in a natural mathematical way, which the earlier theories could not.

But superstrings involve concepts most bizarre! The theory asks us to think mathematically of the elementary particles of nature not as zero-dimensional points but as one-dimensional strings. The length of these strings, $10^{-33}$ centimeter, is so incredibly short that some $10^{20}$ protons could be strung along them. But this length is enough to make an enormous difference. This string, this proposed fundamental unit of matter, can vibrate. Each vibrational mode of the string corresponds to a different subatomic particle, and the frequency of the mode determines its energy and hence its mass. So, in a sense, the particles we know are the melodies of a submicroscopic violin string, the music of the microcosmos.

There is more. Although the strings themselves may be one dimensional, superstring theories are ten dimensional. They involve nine spacelike dimensions and one timelike dimension. The extra six spacelike dimensions must be curled up tightly into a microscopic ball around each point in space to account for their undetectability. It is as though in the very early universe there were nine spacelike dimensions, but six of them became stuck in an embryonic form, while three developed into the dimensions of length, width, and depth that we know today. Our powers of imagination may be severely challenged by superstring theory, but physicists are rushing to learn and understand the mathematics of this theorized microgeometry of nature.

Cosmic strings are one of the things predicted by superstring theory, but they are nevertheless something entirely different. In this intriguing view of cosmological linearity, cosmic strings are thin threads of energy, $10^{-30}$ centimeter thick, that would be enormously massive, $10^{22}$ grams per centimeter. They would have been produced in abundance in the big bang, whipping throughout the length and breadth of the universe. As these strands and loops passed through the early universe, their gravitational effects would have created sheetlike or circular density fluctuations that helped the primordial matter condense into galaxies and other structures.

Speaking of structures, research during the past year produced intriguing evidence for the three-dimensional structure of the universe. The galaxies were shown to be organized into vast assemblages of matter surrounding even more vast and puzzling voids, like the surfaces of soap bubbles surrounding an interior space of near-nothingness. The universe, in other words, appears to be extraordinarily nonuniform in distribution, with galaxies organized into clusters of galaxies that are in turn organized into clusters of clusters, linked like the beads on a string. One of these superclusters, in the region of the constellations Perseus and Pisces, is a billion light-years long and is the largest known structure in the universe. A wedge-shaped "slice-of-the-universe" map produced during the past year by scientists at the Harvard-Smithsonian Center for Astrophysics, Cambridge, Mass., reveals 1,061 galaxies arranged in striking patterns and shapes and enclosing huge voids 100–150 million light-years in diameter.

Large as these structures are, even more extraordinary are the empty spaces their edges define. These spaces appear to be totally empty—although during the year scientists in New Mexico did discover seven possibly fledgling galaxies inside the Boötes void, the first time anything has been seen inside a void. This apparent emptiness in the face of a need for much more matter than is anywhere visible, in order to account for the gravitational cohesiveness of the universe, leads to the intriguing and increasingly attractive idea that most of the universe consists of "dark matter." This would be some kind of material, perhaps previously unknown elementary particles left over from the big bang, invisible to us but in total having enough mass to make up the 90% deficit

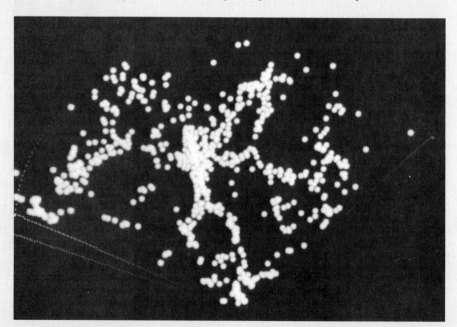

*Chains of galaxies surrounding empty spaces as large as 150 million light-years across is the picture presented by a map of a wedge-shaped slice of deep space. The map, which plots the positions of 1,061 galaxies lying in a region of sky measuring 117° by 6°, suggests a cosmic-foam structure for the universe, with galaxies arrayed on the surfaces of bubble-shaped voids.*

Michael Kurtz and Mathew Schneps, Smithsonian Astrophysical Laboratory

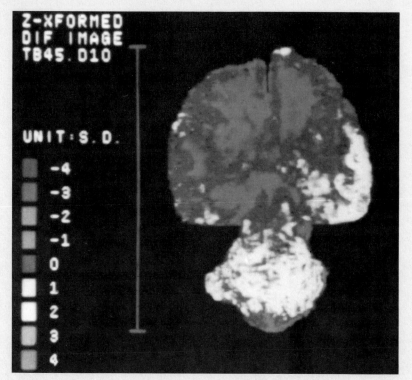

Z-XFORMED
DIF IMAGE
TB45.010

UNIT: S.D.

-4
-3
-2
-1
0
1
2
3
4

*Glucose use as an indicator of metabolic activity in the brain of a cat is tracked using a radioactive tracer and plotted by computer in the form of the metabolic map at left. High levels of activity in the right brain hemisphere, indicated by certain shaded areas, are correlated with the memory of a previously learned cue about the location of food. The left hemisphere, which was experimentally prevented from learning the cue-food association, serves as a control. Researchers found that as much as a tenth of the cat's brain was involved with the memory of the learned cue.*

Courtesy, E. Roy John, New York University; Yong-Nian Tang and A. Bertrand Brill, Brookhaven National Laboratory; Ronald Young, University of West Indies, Jamaica; Kenji Ono, Nagasaki University, Japan

that concerns cosmologists. In this view most of the universe comprises dark matter, while the visible universe represents only the gravitational effects of fluctuations in the distribution of it. It may be then that the voids are areas where both kinds of matter exist but where, for some reason, the familiar kind has not condensed into galaxies.

Lest the physical sciences be thought to have a monopoly on awe-inspiring notions, the results of an experiment reported in 1986 on the physiology of learned memory argue differently. Scientists at New York University, Brookhaven National Laboratory, Upton, N.Y., and elsewhere found a way to reveal how many cells of a cat's brain are involved in the memory of one simple learned response. They had expected that some reasonably small number of brain cells—perhaps 20,000 to 40,000 neurons—in some specific location would handle this chore, which was to remember that food could be found behind a door marked with two concentric circles. Instead, they found the number to be between 5 million and 100 million, or about one-tenth the whole brain. Thus apparently huge numbers of cells throughout the brain contribute to just one single memory, challenging notions that each memory is localized in a specific circuit. Instead, memory seems to be widely distributed and shared among a large proportion of the brain's neurons. The corollary is that each neuron must have roles in handling many memories, for

otherwise there cannot be nearly enough neurons to handle an animal's large catalog of memories.

**Once-ignored hypotheses can gain primacy.** The origin of the Moon has been one of the major unsolved questions of nature. As satellites go, the Moon is very large in relation to the Earth, and the angular momentum of the Earth-Moon system is unexpectedly large. The Moon has a composition much like that of Earth's mantle except for a deficiency of volatile elements. The three leading theories for the Moon's formation—fission, capture, and coaccretion—all have had serious difficulties, and results of the Apollo lunar missions only made them more unsatisfactory.

In the past year a dramatically different theory called the large-impact hypothesis suddenly leapt to the forefront as the best explanation of the many puzzles about the Earth-Moon system. In this view 4.6 billion years ago a Mars-sized object left over from the formation of the solar system struck the young Earth a solid but glancing blow at ten kilometers (six miles) per second. The impact vaporized a considerable section of the Earth's mantle and through some complicated interactions jetted much of it into orbit about the Earth, where it fairly rapidly condensed into the Moon. The Moon was thus born in catastrophe and is composed to a significant degree of Earth material.

The large-impact scenario was first proposed in

the mid-1970s, independently, by scientists at the Planetary Science Institute in Tucson, Ariz., and at the Harvard-Smithsonian Center for Astrophysics. But the time just was not right, and it was mostly ignored. Then, starting with a conference in 1984, planetary scientists at a number of universities and laboratories began looking at the idea from a fresh perspective and suddenly saw that such an impact was not altogether unlikely and that it would explain fairly well many of the enigmas about the Moon. A scientist from the University of Arizona who at first felt the concept was nonsense and set out to lay it to rest did a new series of analyses and found to his great surprise that the evidence strongly supported the large-impact hypothesis. In 1986 many planetary scientists involved in Moon-origin studies were agreeing for the first time that the large-impact idea had become the leading hypothesis. The year also brought strong support for the scenario from numerical simulations on number-crunching supercomputers at two U.S. national laboratories.

Some interesting points can be made here. One is that a previously ignored hypothesis can gain new currency when given a fresh look and when new tools are available to do confirmatory studies not previously possible. Another is that even a highly dramatic theory can at times turn out to be the one that best fits the facts. That is somehow refreshing.

**New forms of matter can still be found.** In 1984 scientists working with an aluminum-manganese alloy discovered an apparently new phase form of solid matter, quasicrystals, never seen before. Since then investigators at many laboratories have been pursuing studies of this curious new material, finding many new ways to make it (including one, solid-state interdiffusion, that does not even require melting the source materials) and producing for the first time quasicrystals large enough to see with the naked eye (at least a half millimeter in diameter) and of a geometry never before seen in crystallography or mineralogy (a triacontahedron, a polyhedron with 30 identical diamond-shaped faces). All this was accomplished with a material that until recently no one had thought possible and that exhibits diffraction patterns in seeming violation of the laws of crystallography.

Quasicrystals are neither crystals nor amorphous materials but something in between. Like crystals they are an ordered structure but of a type not seen before. Whereas crystals are formed from one

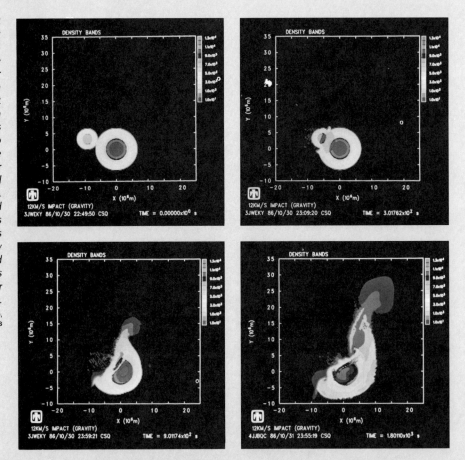

*A Mars-sized protoplanet collides with the young Earth at 12 kilometers (7.4 miles) per second in the sequence of computer simulations at right, which shows the two bodies at the time of impact, then 5, 15, and 30 minutes later (left to right, top to bottom). Much of the ejected material will later condense in orbit around the Earth to form the Moon.*

*The concentric, shaded bands within the two bodies represent different densities of materials. By 1987 many planetary scientists regarded the large-impact model as the leading hypothesis for the Moon's origin.*

Photos, Marlin E. Kipp, Sandia National Laboratories

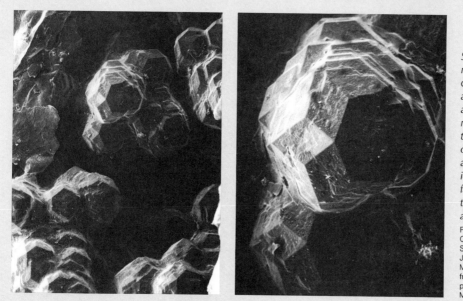

*Scanning electron micrographs of quasicrystals of an aluminum-copper-lithium alloy at two levels of magnification reveal their geometry as that of a triacontahedron, a polyhedron with 30 identical diamond-shaped faces. The large crystal in the right-hand image is about 0.5 millimeter across.*

From "Large AlCuLi Single Quasicrystals with Triacontahedral Solidification Morphology," B. Dubost, J-M. Lang, M. Tanaka, P. Sainfort, and M. Audier; reprinted by permission from *Nature*, vol. 324, no. 6092, pp. 48–50. Copyright © 1986 Macmillan Journals Limited.

basic repeating structure, quasicrystals appear to be formed from two different structures assembled in a nonrepeating array, the three-dimensional equivalent of a tile floor made from two shapes of tile and having an orientational order but no repetition. Thus even a topic so seemingly well settled as the phases of solid matter can yield fundamental revelations from new kinds of inquiries.

At a considerably different size scale was the beginning of the scientific quest at the European Laboratory for Particle Physics (CERN) accelerator in Geneva to create a quark-gluon plasma, a basic form of matter that has not existed in a natural state since shortly after the beginning of the universe. This 18-country scientific effort seeks nothing less than to momentarily create conditions in the accelerator that mimic those a fractional instant after the big bang, when quarks and gluons, now always combined to form the nuclei of all atoms, existed independently. No one yet knows what might be learned from being able to observe free quarks and gluons, but a National Academy of Sciences survey of physics completed in 1986 said such an accomplishment would be of extraordinary importance.

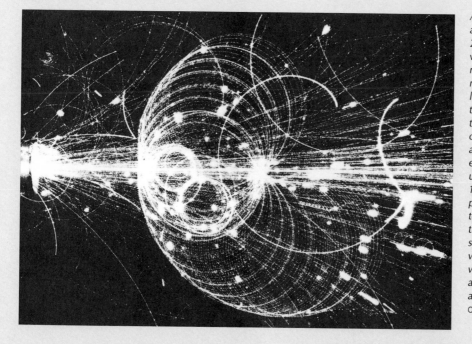

*An oxygen nucleus accelerated to an energy of 200 GeV (billion electron volts) for each of its 16 nucleons (protons and neutrons) slams into a lead target to the left of the image, spewing more than 200 charged-particle collision products into a streamer chamber. In experiments of this kind, under way in 1986 and 1987 at CERN in Geneva, physicists were attempting to recreate conditions that existed a fraction of a second after the big bang, when quarks and gluons were independent of the atomic nuclei in which they are confined today.*
Courtesy, CERN

**Long-accepted theories may still be strengthened.** Even a concept so ingrained in modern science that it has become part of the everyday lexicon—the quantum jump—can resist direct observation for decades. In 1986 the quantum jump was directly observed for the first time. Accomplishing this feat required an ability to perform a demonstration with, literally, a single atom. Only in the past few years, with the development of electromagnetic traps for single atoms, has it become a possibility at all. This and other difficulties were overcome in three separate experiments showing that a single atom does indeed jump from one electronic state to another when it absorbs a photon whose energy corresponds to the difference between those two states. Does this late confirmation mean that scientists had been premature in accepting the reality of the quantum jump? Not at all. Indirect or inferential evidence for the quantum jump had long ago been well established. It is not unusual for a direct demonstration of a fundamental principle to wait until some needed new method of science or technology comes along.

**Insights can come from surprising directions.** It always seems to me extraordinary the way clever scientists can coax so much information about so many diverse aspects of the natural world from the most unlikely sources. The past year produced a fascinating example: subsea structures built by living microbes yielded insights about ancient interrelations of the Earth, Moon, and Sun. The structures are the stromatolites found in various shallow-water pools and tidal flats around the world. They are pillars of rock formed by layers of what were once mats of living microbes, communities of such photosynthetic organisms as cyanobacteria (blue-green algae) that lived and died atop one another. The mats also trapped sediment and other sea debris, all cementing together into an entity of the never alive, the once alive, and the now living. Stromatolites go back about 3.5 billion years to Earth's ancient past, but in western Australia, The Bahamas, and the Persian Gulf they have been found with the top several centimeters still alive, their colonies of microorganisms converting the Sun's light into metabolic energy and matter.

In 1986 scientists from the University of California at Santa Barbara reported the discovery of both fossil and living stromatolites that, unlike most, tilted toward the Sun. What can that tell us? In the course of one year, the pattern of stromatolite growth traces a graceful S-shaped sine wave, which formed as the organisms tracked the Sun from its northernmost to southernmost position in the sky and back again. And since each day's growth produces a new layer, or lamina, the number of such layers within one sine wave gives the number of days in the year. A layer count showed that about 850 million years ago in the late Proterozoic there were 435 days per year, meaning the Earth was rotating faster and by an amount consistent with geophysical expectations and other data. Furthermore, by measuring the maximum angle by which the sine wave deviates from the average direction of the column, the scientists were able to show that the tilt of the Earth's axis may have been about 26.5°, somewhat greater than the 23.5° that it is now. And by similar comparisons to paleomagnetic studies of the rock they were able to show that 850 million years ago the Earth's

White lines added to an aerial photograph of CERN in Geneva trace the location of the Super Proton Synchrotron (SPS), the smaller ring almost completely enclosed within the still uncompleted Large Electron-Positron Collider (LEP). Built for experiments with subatomic particles, the SPS is being "borrowed" by nuclear physicists to collide beams of fairly heavy nuclei like oxygen and sulfur with stationary nuclear targets like lead.
Courtesy, CERN

magnetic axis was close to the axis of rotation. All this from a tiny life form few people know and still fewer appreciate!

**"Fundamental" discoveries may be short lived.** Every year produces examples of potentially important discoveries that turn out not to be true—or at least not to be as certain as had been supposed. Wrong turns and dead ends are encountered in science as in other human activities, and sometimes realization of the mistake dawns too late to avoid the harsh limelight.

One example in 1986 was a well-publicized report of discovery of the most powerful gravitational lens known. A gravitational lens is the result of the presence of some massive object in space nearly along the line of sight of a distant luminous object such as a quasar. The gravitational influence of the object between Earth and the quasar bends its light in such a way that it produces two or more identical images of the quasar. In May an astronomer published a report of an apparent gravitational lens so powerful that it was able to produce multiple images of a quasar 20 times farther apart in the sky than ever seen before. An extremely massive black hole was suggested. By June this particular lens had been shattered. Astronomers at the European Southern Observatory, Santiago, Chile, had taken spectra of the two images and found them to be different. Rather than being images of the same quasar split by the gravitational lens, they were instead images of two different objects, probably quasars that just happen to be fairly close to each other as seen from Earth.

In a slightly different category was a study published in the scientific journal *Physical Review Letters* early in 1986 that suggested the possible existence of a "fifth force." This new evaluation of the so-called Eötvös experiments carried out in the early 1900s found errors in those experiments that could be interpreted as evidence that a small force other than gravity acts on ordinary material objects. Whereas the gravitational attraction between two objects at a given distance depends only on their mass, this speculated new force, a repulsive one, appeared to depend also on the objects' atomic composition. The errors found in the early experiments could be explained if there was a force with a range of about 200 meters (660 feet) that was dependent upon the number of baryons (protons and neutrons) in the interacting substances. Thus the copper, manganese-aluminum alloy, and snakewood Roland Eötvös used in his experiments all appeared to exhibit a slightly different gravitational attraction toward platinum due to the effect of this additional force. This suggestion understandably caused quite a stir. Such a fundamental discovery, if it could be confirmed, would be revolutionary, but the claim would have to pass the most stringent kinds of evaluations. Later in the year two other scientists published a new study proposing a much more mundane explanation for the errors in the Eötvös experiments. They found evidence that the errors could have been due to thermally driven air currents in the laboratory acting on substances of different atomic number and therefore of different bulk. The "fifth force" is not dead yet, but scientists now are not placing too much hope that it will really revive.

Such starts and stops are all part of the vital process of science. Most wrong turns (if that is what they are) tend to get expunged from the record in accounts of scientific discovery. But it is important to realize that for every clear-cut route to discovery many other paths have to be explored as well. And there is no foolproof way to know in advance which is the path to success.

A wrong turn of an entirely different kind blemished the year in an important field of biomedical research. Early in the year several scientists reported in the journal *Science* the discovery of interleukin-4A, a protein molecule that stimulates T lymphocytes, an important type of white blood cell, to leap into action in the process of cell-mediated immunity. In November *Science* published a retraction of the research. One of the scientists who had reported the original discovery, a visiting fellow from Italy, admitted that he had tampered with the research data. His colleagues had to announce to the world scientific community that interleukin-4A does not exist.

Science is a cooperative activity. Although it includes numerous checks and balances, it places a high premium on honesty and integrity in the conduct of experiments and the reporting of research results. But because it is carried out by human beings, human frailties combined with pressures to produce results occasionally come to a regrettable outcome. Nevertheless, most such mistakes are caught and corrected—something else that is refreshing about science in comparison with many other human activities.

**Nature offers never-ending fascination.** Nature always presents new surprises and challenges. Much of the fun of observing science is seeing how these workings of the natural world reveal themselves. Although scientists seldom use the word amazing in their papers, nonscientists do, and that is altogether appropriate.

In the field of animal perception, for instance, investigators reported that the duckbilled platypus uses its bill as an antenna to pick up weak electrical signals. The Australian marsupials were observed swimming under water with their eyes, ears, and nostrils closed, moving their bills back and forth. Experiments showed that they detected direct and

*Duckbilled platypus investigates an active dry-cell battery, having been attracted by its electric field. At a distance of ten centimeters (four inches) the field is similar in strength to that produced by the muscles of live, moving prey.*
G. Langner

alternating electric currents and that they apparently use this ability to sense the electric fields generated by the muscles of moving prey. It is the first time electroreception has been reported in a mammal.

The elephant might seem an unlikely source of further surprises, but scientists during the past year discovered that this largest of land animals produces low-frequency sounds that humans cannot hear but that may well be useful for communicating within herds, particularly over long distances. Also in the realm of animal hearing, praying mantises, which had been thought deaf, were found to have an organ

that detects ultrasonic frequencies and is formed by a thin region of cuticle folded into a groove on the underside of the thorax. This single "ear" (most creatures have pairs of acoustic sensors, the better to triangulate direction) seems to be useful in detecting but not localizing sound. Meanwhile, bees, which have already revealed a rich store of navigational and communicative abilities (they use polarized sunlight to navigate), were shown to have their navigational "maps" embedded in special photoreceptors in their eyes. This array of receptors apparently functions as a template, which the bees use to scan the sky and match its polarization patterns.

Animals of the past produced some surprises, too. Scientists found in Texas the fossil remains of two crow-sized birds that are 75 million years older than the 150 million-year-old *Archaeopteryx*, until now the earliest known bird. Named *Protoavis*, the creature appears to have been capable of true flight, for it has well-developed wing structures and in fact is more birdlike than the famous *Archaeopteryx*. Despite its ancientness, *Protoavis* lends further support to the accepted view that birds originally arose from dinosaurs. It has clawed fingers, a tail, teeth, and other dinosaurian features to go along with its birdlike wishbone.

On the topic of dinosaurs, scientists in New Mexico reported the longest known dinosaur yet, discovered northwest of Albuquerque. An enormous thighbone plus three meters (ten feet) of the tail and eight joined tail vertebrae were removed from the creature's sedimentary graveyard. Paleontologists at the New Mexico Museum of Natural History dubbed it *Seismosaurus*, an appropriate designation for a creature that was 30–37 meters (100–120 feet) long, 5½ meters (18 feet) tall at the shoulder and 4½

*Fossil bones found in western Texas (left) shape the outline of* Protoavis, *a crow-sized bird thought to predate* Archaeopteryx *by 75 million years. An artist's conception (right) fills out the creature.*
(Left) Barbara Laing—© 1986 National Geographic Society; (right) drawing by Michael W. Nickell © 1986

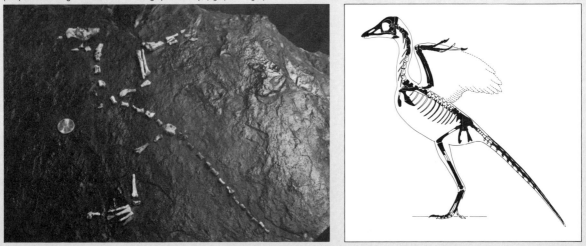

Two enormous, spined tail vertebrae (left) are among the fossil remains of the newly discovered dinosaur Seismosaurus (right, in an artist's conception), so named for its earthshaking physical proportions.
(Left) Courtesy, David D. Gillette, New Mexico Museum of Natural History; (right) illustration by Doug Henderson, Bozeman, Montana

meters (15 feet) tall at the hip, and weighed 80–100 tons. When it walked, it would truly have shaken the ground. Argentine scientists reported discovering the first fossil dinosaur ever found in Antarctica, the only continent on which the prehistoric reptiles had not yet turned up.

Not all discoveries about past animals go back to dinosaurian times. In northern Kenya paleontologist Alan Walker found a 2.5 million-year-old hominid skull that does not fit into any currently accepted schemes for ways in which the human family tree branched back several million years ago. The face has the structure and other characteristics of the previously known genus *Australopithecus* (whose most famous representative is universally known as "Lucy"), but the cranium is by comparison very primitive. It appears that the two-way split of the human family tree has to be replaced by a three-branched model. The discovery is the most important in Africa since "Lucy" and will undoubtedly keep paleoanthropologists busy for some years.

Discovered a few years ago in a Florida peat bog, five well-preserved brains of humans a mere 8,000 years old yielded this past year the oldest known examples of human DNA and cellular structure. Molecular biologists were attempting to clone genes or gene fragments from this ancient DNA in an attempt to compare them with modern genes. It is extraordinary that genetic material from humans just emerging from the last ice age can still be recovered, studied, and perhaps duplicated.

Biochemists and molecular biologists produced a number of important discoveries concerning human genes. Two of them, reported the same week, were the identification of a gene whose disruption leads to a form of cancer (retinoblastoma, a rare eye tumor), and the decoding of part of the gene responsible for Duchenne muscular dystrophy, a serious muscle-wasting disease afflicting thousands of men. The genes involved in red, green, and blue color-vision pigment were also identified, yielding clues to the evolution of color vision. And in 1986 scientists from Purdue University, West Lafayette, Ind., who the previous year had mapped for the first time the structure of a cold virus, pinpointed the site where antiviral agents bind onto a common cold virus and prevent it from spreading infection. This work revealed at the molecular level how two antiviral compounds render the human rhinovirus helpless by preventing it from opening up to release its infectious materials. Yet other scientists put to work in the laboratory a genetically engineered protein known as epidermal growth factor (EGF), which is believed to be what the body uses to spur the growth of skin and similar tissues. Initial experiments on animals showed an extraordinary ability of EGF to speed the healing of wounds. Human trials on eye-injury patients were just beginning.

"Science moves, but slowly, slowly, creeping on from point to point," wrote Alfred, Lord Tennyson. He was obviously writing of an earlier time. Today the only thing anyone can be sure of when looking at a sample of activity on the frontiers of science is that everything changes, quickly, quickly. Science, like nature itself, continually challenges the mind and soul. And that is the way it should be.

# Anthropology

During recent years specialists in human paleontology had generally accepted the idea that human and ape evolution had separated approximately 20 million years ago. A group of fossils called the dryopithecines were viewed as the ancestors of the modern apes, while forms called ramapithecines, which appeared on the order of 13 million to 17 million years ago, were seen as possibly ancestral to humans. David Pilbeam, working with ramapithecine fossils in India, was a leading proponent of this view. However, he recently modified his stance because further analysis indicated that the Asian ramapithecines were already well on the way to becoming orangutans. A ramapithecine from Africa, *Kenyapithecus*, was proposed by some as a possible human ancestor instead.

Work on genetic and biochemical relationships among the hominids, conducted since the mid-1960s, presented quite a different view. This research concluded that the break between the chimpanzee and the human lines occurred as recently as five million to seven million years ago. Indeed, it was shown that humans and chimpanzees share as much as 98% of their genetic makeup, including even the ABO blood system. Pilbeam, when interviewed during the past year, simply stated, "I was wrong."

It has become clear to many researchers that the oldest known hominid, *Australopithecus afarensis*, found in Ethiopia by Donald Johanson and dated to about 3.5 million years ago, is a very early representative of the human line, apparently only about two million years removed from the separation from the chimpanzees. These hominids were well along the way to developing upright posture, a mechanical necessity for the development and enlargement of the brain. *A. afarensis* was only about 1.1 m (3.5 ft) tall and was remarkably human from the neck down. The head, to a nonspecialist, seemed very close to that of a chimpanzee, differing principally in lacking the projecting canine teeth and in the fact that it was balanced atop the spinal column as a result of the upright posture.

The chimpanzees, on the other hand, continued their arboreal adaptation, seen principally in the elongated arms. This development precluded the full development of upright posture and made it mechanically impossible for them to develop the large brain associated with the human line. Such development requires that the skull be balanced atop the spinal column, reducing the need for heavy bone for the attachment of muscles to hold the skull upright.

*A. afarensis* was followed by *A. africanus*, which was very similar but approximately 1.5 m (5 ft) tall. Many physical anthropologists believe that *A. afarensis* split into two lines, one leading via *A. africanus* to *A. robustus* and then to *A. boisei*. These later forms were thought to be an evolutionary line that specialized in eating hard seeds and fruits; hence their designation as "nutcracker man." They are marked by enormous jaws and cheek teeth, the presence of which again precludes the development of the distinctively human brain. The other line led via *Homo habilis* to *H. erectus* and eventually to modern humans.

Other anthropologists believe that the split came slightly later and that *A. africanus* was ancestral to the later *Australopithecus* and *Homo* lines. In either case, the development of the nutcracker jaw was dated to the interval 2.2 million to 1.2 million years ago, with the *A. robustus* form earlier but overlapping *A. boisei* in time.

These views of human evolution, both envisioning a two-way split of the main line, were called into question when Alan Walker of Johns Hopkins University, Baltimore, Md., discovered remains of *A. boisei* at Lake Turkana in Kenya in 1985. The finds were reported in *Nature* in 1986. Walker's new fossils, which have the typical *A. boisei* face and jaw along with a rather primitive skull, date from 2.5 million years ago and thus are far too old to allow *A. robustus* to be ancestral to them.

This new evidence led some anthropologists to conclude that there were three lines of early humans

*Skull that was reconstructed from remains found by Alan Walker at Lake Turkana in Kenya and dated at 2.5 million years old was identified as belonging to the hominid species Australopithecus boisei.*

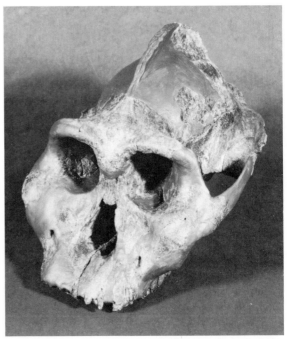

Alan Walker—© 1986 National Geographic Society

Sidney Harris

BRAINS

JAVA MAN   NEANDERTHAL MAN   MODERN MAN

in existence at about the same time. However, as has been pointed out, many of the changes on the way from ape to human took place in all three lines, particularly the flattening of the face from the projecting snout of the ape to the relatively short face of early humans. If there were three separate lines, this would require that all three were evolving in parallel fashion. Parallel evolution occurs when similar species respond to the environment in similar ways and is considered to be rather rare, especially when affecting three forms at once.

Some anthropologists continued to support the two-line approach, pointing out that *A. robustus* has been found only in South Africa and *A. boisei* only in East Africa. This view holds that the two forms are simply geographical races, at most species, of the same animal. In this view there ought to be very old fossils of *A. boisei*.

As has come to be expected in the study of human evolution, every new discovery creates more questions than it answers. Out of the controversy surrounding this new find will eventually come some order, at least until the next discovery.

—Charles W. McNett, Jr.

# Archaeology

Some of the most exciting developments in archaeology during the past year concerned new evidence for the peopling of the Americas and discovery of the oldest and best preserved human brain tissue found anywhere in the world. The year also was notable for the publication of a comprehensive evaluation of the processes by which agriculture was adopted during postglacial times in Europe.

**Colonizing the Americas.** Several important finds relating to the earliest colonization of the New World were reported. One of the most compelling was a well-dated sequence of occupations of a Brazilian

cave that began sometime before 32,000 years ago. These finds were in Boqueirão do Sitio da Pedra Furada in eastern Brazil, as reported by Niéde Guidon of the École des Hautes Études en Sciences Sociales, Paris, and G. Delibrias of the Centre des Faibles Radioactivités, Gif-sur-Yvette, France.

Boqueirão da Pedra Furada is a large rock-shelter with its walls and ceiling covered with prehistoric paintings. It contains a fill deposit more than three meters (ten feet) thick and has evidence of human occupation at all levels. The earliest traces consist of undated scattered charcoal and two stone artifacts near the bottom of the deposit. A continuous sequence of dated hearths, each associated with abundant stone tools, begins in the next highest level; two radiocarbon dates at that level place it at about 32,000 years ago. A series of eight overlying hearths indicate that sporadic occupation occurred between 30,000 and 23,000 years ago, followed by another period of use around 21,000 years ago.

A hearth dated to 17,000 years ago contained painted rocks that had spalled off the walls and ceiling of the rock-shelter, providing the earliest evidence of rock art in the New World. Higher layers without cultural evidence reveal that several thousand years of nonuse occurred between 17,000 and around 11,000 years ago, the date estimated for the next hearth found.

*Prehistoric paintings decorate a rock shelter at Boqueirão da Pedra Furada in eastern Brazil. Radiocarbon dating places its first occupation at about 32,000 years ago, the oldest site of human settlement yet found in the Americas.*

Still higher in the deposits, Guidon and Delibrias found a level of dense occupation between 8,500 and 8,000 years ago, characterized by abundant stone tools, stone-lined hearths, and an apparent emphasis on rock art. Later hearths generally became larger and more variable in form, although they developed an elliptical outline about 6,000 years ago. These younger hearths contained abundant fragments of bone, wood, leaves, and fruit pits. The uppermost sediments were badly disturbed, and no information was obtained on sediments younger than 6,000 years.

Boqueirão da Pedra Furada suggests that human beings entered the Americas prior to 32,000 years ago. While it had not yet been fully analyzed, it added weight to the growing body of data that suggests that colonization of the Americas occurred much earlier than 12,000 years ago, the date currently accepted.

Additional evidence for an early migration was also reported in 1986. Joseph H. Greenberg of Stanford University, Christy G. Turner II of Arizona State University, and Stephen L. Zegura of the University of Arizona argued that, viewed independently, linguistic, dental, and genetic data supported early colonization of the New World.

Greenberg maintained that indigenous American languages could be divided into three major groups: Amerind, Na-Dene, and Aleut-Eskimo. Extensive study of the linguistic relationships between these groups indicates that Amerind contains the greatest number of subclasses and is, therefore, the oldest American language group. Na-Dene languages are somewhat less divergent, and Aleut-Eskimo are the least divergent, indicating that they were more recently introduced. Greenberg argued that these groups were brought into the Americas in three separate migrations across the Bering land bridge from northern Asia: Aleut-Eskimo around 4,000 years ago,

Na-Dene about 9,000 years ago, and Amerind sometime prior to 11,000 years ago.

Studies of dental characteristics also appeared to support the hypothesis that three different groups of peoples entered the New World at different times in the past. Turner argued that the ancestral homeland of all those groups was northern China and that at least 14,000 years had passed since they first diverged from one another. Three distinct stone-working traditions in North America add further support to the three-migration hypothesis.

Zegura's genetic evidence provided the least conclusive support to the linguistic and dental data but did tend to show that at least two—probably three—different periods of genetic diversion from the ancient north Asian base are apparent in the New World. All three authors confused the issue somewhat by equating the postulated migrations with Amerind, Na-Dene, and Aleut-Eskimo language groups, as if dental and genetic variability could be equated with linguistic data. The major thrust of their paper seemed well-founded, however, and they agreed in a separate comment that a departure date of at least 14,000 and possibly as much as 20,000 years ago is reasonable for the earliest split with northern Asia.

Yet another recent study cast light on some of the problems surrounding the first American colonization. D. Earl Nelson *et al.* of Simon Fraser University, Burnaby, B.C., and other Canadian universities reevaluated evidence that they previously had thought supported a date of migration more than 20,000 years ago. Several mammoth limb bones that had apparently been flaked and a flesh-removing tool made from caribou bone were found in 1966 in the Old Crow Basin in northern Canada. At the time of discovery all were radiocarbon dated to around 27,000 years ago, providing what was taken to be strong

*Anatomical sections of two intact brains of human adult males, one of them contemporary (left) and one recovered from an 8,000-year-old burial site in Florida (right), reveal many similarities. The ancient brain section is surrounded by peat and has undergone some fragmentation, but many gross anatomical structures are present. They include: (a) the interhemispheric fissure, (b) corpus callosum, (c) lateral ventricle, (d) insular cortex, (e) putamen, (f) internal capsule, (g) thalamus, and (h) third ventricle.*

contemporary                                                        ancient

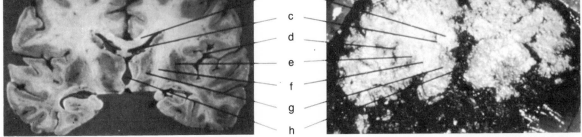

evidence that humans had migrated into northern Canada at least 15,000 years before the date usually accepted. The radiocarbon method used, however, was recently shown to provide incorrect results.

The flesh-removing tool and 35 other bones from the Old Crow vicinity were redated by use of the accelerator mass spectrometry (AMS) method. Twenty-six of those specimens were apparently human-modified mammoth and bison bones; six were from known stratigraphic (buried) locations; and the remaining three were caribou bone and antler tools similar to the flesher. Results showed that the mammoth, bison, and stratigraphic bones ranged in age between 25,000 and 47,000 years old, as their geologic contexts had originally indicated. The caribou bone and antler tools, on the other hand, were shown to be no more than 2,900 years of age, with the flesher dated to only 1,350 years.

The reanalysis thus showed that the tools made from caribou bone and antler are of the Holocene (Recent) Epoch, which began about 10,000 years ago. The more ambiguous flaking patterns on the mammoth and bison bones, however, could still constitute evidence that human beings were in the Americas prior to 25,000 years ago. The problem was to prove that those flaking and stone-working-like breakage patterns on Pleistocene bones were really the work of humans.

**Windover archaeological site.** A project that captured worldwide attention during the past year focused on the Windover site, an 8,000-year-old burial ground in Brevard County, Fla. The remains of more than 40 individuals were recovered from a small swampy pond. One of the most exciting aspects of this excavation was the preservation of recognizable soft tissue, including intact whole brains, in several of the buried individuals. This allowed Glen Doran and David Dickel of Florida State University and researchers at the University of Florida College of Medicine to study anatomical features, remnant cellular structure, and DNA (deoxyribonucleic acid) in the oldest known brain tissue in the world.

Preliminary results showed that this material represents a remarkable anthropological and genetic resource. Scientists at the University of Florida began cloning DNA from some of the brains to compare ancient genes with those of modern humans. These studies could provide the key to understanding and eventually curing such genetic diseases as Down's syndrome and diabetes. Both the brain tissue and skeletal material recovered from the site would allow future studies of protein evolution and genetic mutation. These would greatly improve scientists' ability to determine genetic relationships, especially those between Native American groups and their north Asian ancestors (as discussed above). The University of Florida was also setting up a DNA library

to make genetic material from the 8,000-year-old brains available to brain scientists and geneticists throughout the world.

The Windover site was also providing a pollen record of climatic change beginning about 8,000 years ago. Preliminary indications were that central Florida has become warmer and wetter since that time. In addition, the site yielded a small piece of preserved woven cloth, the oldest yet found in North America. It was made of twined palmetto fibers woven on some sort of loom.

**Postglacial European foragers.** Scientists had long thought that agriculture brought a significant improvement of life to the foraging cultures that adopted it during the Neolithic Period. The ability to grow and store food was thought to be the impetus for such cultural developments as sedentary village life, specialized labor, and the origins of organized religion. While this notion had been shown to be inaccurate in some places, only recently was a model of successful forager-based cultural development proposed for western Europe.

Marek Zvelebil summarized many years of work by himself and others in a survey of postglacial forag-

*Skeletons of a man, woman, and child were found huddled together in the ruins of the Roman city of Kourion on the island of Cyprus, victims of an earthquake that destroyed the city in AD 365.*

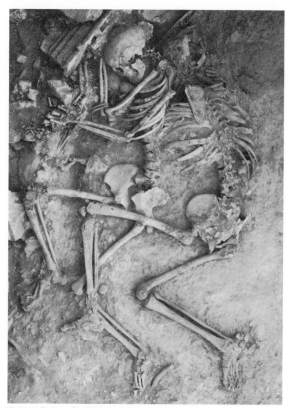

Photos, Honduran Institute of Anthropology and History

*Dark substance inside the shell at the right may be the dried blood of a Maya king, from a ritual bloodletting. In front of the shell are stingray spines, used by Maya men to draw their own blood. The jade figure at the far right was found near the shell, buried beneath an altar in the city of Copan in what is now Honduras. These objects and others were part of a ceremony dedicating a temple-pyramid in AD 756.*

ing in the forests of Europe. He traced the locations and compositions of forests that spread across Europe behind the retreating glaciers and showed that the advent of agriculture had been long delayed in many places because foraging was an equally viable way of life. Foragers in broad regions of Europe developed sedentary village life, ranked societies, and organized religions because of the localized richness of certain resources. These groups apparently delayed adopting full-scale agriculture for as long as 3,000 years, even though they used several species of domesticated plants and animals throughout the period.

Zvelebil argued that specialized exploitation of a few target species, combined with generalized exploitation of opportunistically encountered resources, provided for settled life in the postglacial period. Ungulates (hoofed mammals) were the preferred targets during the early Holocene, but they were gradually replaced by aquatic animals in later times. This shift apparently occurred between 9,000 and 7,000 years ago in the southern Urals, about 7,500 years ago along the Danube River, about 6,000 years ago in Scandinavia, and around 5,000 years ago in the Baltic region.

The Maglemosian culture of northern Europe provides a good example of an effective aquatic adaptation coupled with a generalized forest economy. These people specialized in exploiting seals and other sea mammals between 10,000 and 7,000 years ago. Their material culture consisted of a combination of specialized harpoons for seal hunting and generalized tools called microliths for foraging along the coasts and interior woodlands of Britain, the North Sea basin, Denmark, Poland, and the Baltic region.

In addition to seals, Maglemosian peoples subsisted on aurochs (wild oxen, now extinct), red and roe deer, wild pigs, salmon, pike, migratory birds, rabbits, and beavers. They also utilized hazelnuts, water chestnuts, and water lilies. They lived in set-

tled villages, practiced ritual burial, and apparently had developed notions of wealth and hereditary social status. The question then arises as to why this group would change its subsistence strategy.

Zvelebil argued that Maglemosian subsistence gradually became more specialized, with greater emphasis on seals and other aquatic resources. The later Pitted Ware culture, in Sweden and Finland, was heavily dependent on ring seals between about 5,000 and 4,000 years ago. These people maintained a strong but decreasing inland resource component in their economy throughout this period. However, this arrangement eventually came under pressure as groups in the interior gradually became reliant on domesticated animals and plant horticulture and finally eliminated the generalized forest-based component of their economy. This caused the Pitted Ware people to become even more reliant on seals, with the result that their economy failed because of climate-induced fluctuations in the seal population between 4,000 and 3,800 years ago.

Though he did not directly address the question, Zvelebil implied that agriculture was eventually adopted in northern Europe as the result of increased specialization in foraging, concomitant depletion of target species, population growth, and climatic changes. It appeared that agriculture was an alternative adaptation to reduce risk through intensifying labor and increasing environmental productivity.

A general model such as Zvelebil's can also apply to other regions in the world where agriculture has been developed or adopted. Its value lies partly in its recognition of foraging as a potentially viable way of life rather than as a mean and dreary existence between the times of purported Pleistocene big-game hunting and Holocene agricultural adaptations. Indeed, various foraging economies have probably been the mainstays of human adaptation throughout our tenure on this planet.

—James D. Wilde

# Architecture and civil engineering

**Architecture.** Some architects and prognosticators of architectural trends were pronouncing that "anything goes" in the 1987 world of building design, but in practice this was true only within the context of a particular neighborhood, city, region, or group of buildings. This growing respect for design within the context of the environment was called "contextualism" or "appropriateness." After the furors of modernism and postmodernism, it provided a breathing space. It was an element that architects of different backgrounds and philosophies could agree on (at least until the next fashion appeared) and that most observers could understand.

Architect Antoine Predock's The Beach in Albuquerque, N.M., is a classic example of appropriateness. It is the first building the visitor sees as he approaches the city from the south. A 74-unit medium-to-low-income housing development, the complex is hung like a giant piece of Mexican art against the Sandia Mountains. In The Beach, Predock synthesized the glitter of the old Route 66 strip and the manicured lines of the Albuquerque Country Club, which tenants of the complex can see from their backyards. At the same time he incorporated into his design images of regional history and geography.

The complex steps back from the road in a saw-toothed diagonal line, breaking down the building's long street frontage into half-hidden bays reminiscent of the old motor courts that lined the highway. The sawtooth outline recurs in the exterior stairway parapets and the uneven roofline, which ends in lookouts atop four penthouse towers. The zigzag pattern is reminiscent of a Navajo serape, the terraces of a Zuni pueblo, or the buttes and mesas that dot the New Mexico landscape. The stucco on the highway side of the building complex is painted with big, colorful stripes. The bottom stripe is green, echoing the foliage of the riverside. The middle stripes are warm earth tones, and four pinnacles are sky blue. Despite the vertical towers, the banded walls and the zigzag neon lights that highlight the building at night sustain the horizontal sweep of the entire complex.

Another example of appropriate architecture was built during the year at Seaside near Panama City, in Florida's western panhandle. The 32-ha (80-ac) Seaside development is designed to be a low-rise, high-density community set in a natural landscape of sea grass and scrub oak. Within this context, architects Robert Orr and Melanie Taylor of New Haven, Conn., built the Rosewalk cottages, 14 homes on a 1.2-ha (3-ac) parcel of land. Their work harks back to resort architecture of the past, ranging from the Georgian buildings of The Bahamas to the summer colonies of Nantucket, Mass. The cottages are of

*The Beach, a housing development in Albuquerque, New Mexico, reflects the culture and landscape of the American Southwest. Multicolored horizontal stripes decorate the exterior (left) and zigzag neon lights highlight the building at night (above).*

*Rosewalk cottages at Seaside, near Panama City, Florida, are part of a new low-rise, high-density community set in a landscape of sea grass and scrub oak. Their designs resemble the resort architecture of the past.*

three types: one story with a dormer, one story with an octagonal tower, and two stories. Diversity is achieved through variations in the basic color scheme of creamy roses and yellows and by subtle changes in trim. The houses are clad in cedar or cypress shiplap siding and topped by galvanized steel roofs. Orr and Taylor also designed the project's landscaping, including a fanciful group of outdoor wooden furnishings that revives a tradition of 19th-century garden architecture. Though the cottages have only 75 to 100 sq m (800 to 1,100 sq ft) of living space, a feeling of spaciousness is realized through the use of full-width porches, high ceilings, open-plan layouts, and loft-like balconies.

*The new Lloyd's.* At the opposite end of the appropriateness spectrum is Richard Rogers's spectacular aluminum and concrete headquarters building for Lloyd's of London, a space age giant in the traditional City of London setting. Rogers justified the high-tech design as a contextual effort to capture the dynamic quality of the City's medieval layout of narrow, winding streets.

Roger's standard practice of exposing the structural and mechanical elements suggests a medieval cathedral under construction. Much of this cathedral image stems from the six satellite service towers sheathed in stainless steel. The dramatic focus of the building, however, is the 73-m (240-ft) atrium,

*New headquarters building of Lloyd's of London has exposed structural and mechanical elements (right), suggesting a medieval cathedral under construction. A seven-story-high window (far right) forms one end of the building's most dramatic feature—a 73-meter (240-foot) atrium topped by a glazed barrel vault.*

topped by a glazed barrel vault that looks as though it had been designed in the late 19th century. At the south end of the atrium daylight pours into the interior through a seven-story-high cathedral window. The vault covers Lloyd's famous "Room," where more than 2,000 underwriters trade from computerized workstations. The strength of Lloyd's is not so much in its high technology as in the logical and rigorous adaptation of contemporary engineering technology and building methods. According to Rogers, "There is no high or low technology, just appropriate technology."

**Civil engineering.** For some five years "infrastructure" has been a buzz word in the civil engineering trade press. In the U.S. storm and sewage pipelines have been collapsing at the rate of about 3% per year, and about 75% of the nation's piping systems are performing at 50% capacity. One attempt to remedy the situation was taking place in Chicago, where the mainstream tunnel of the massive Tunnel and Reservoir Project (TARP) opened for service in 1985. Storm water and sewage that would otherwise back up into basements and spill into waterways and Lake Michigan is stored in the tunnel until it can be handled by existing treatment plants. Constructed at a cost of $1.2 billion under the auspices of the Metropolitan Sanitary District of Greater Chicago (MSD), the mainstream tunnel system has eliminated 85% of the sewage pollution problems in the city and 52 nearby suburbs. The 50 km (31 mi) of tunnels were designated Outstanding Engineering Achievement of 1986 by the American Society of Civil Engineers.

The mainstream tunnel is connected to existing sewer systems by 252 collector and 226 drop shafts.

Up to 10.7 m (35 ft) in diameter, the 3.8 billion-liter (1 billion-gal) holding tank-tunnel is 70–90 m (240–300 ft) below ground. The MSD's pumping station, one of the largest ever built underground, has pumps housed in twin chambers 82 m (270 ft) long, 20 m (64 ft) wide, and 27 m (90 ft) high. To construct the pumphouse, about 150,000 cu m (200,000 cu yd) of rock had to be excavated and more than 75,000 cu m (100,000 cu yd) of concrete poured. Phase II of TARP, designed primarily for flood control, would involve adding about 29 km (18 mi) of tunnels to the mainstream system. The quarry at the pumping site would become a reservoir, and another reservoir would be mined.

*The Tenn-Tom.* Another mammoth water diversion project recently completed was the Tennessee-Tombigbee (Tenn-Tom) Waterway in Mississippi and Alabama, connecting the Tennessee River on the north with the Tombigbee River on the south and shortening by hundreds of miles the barge canal route from southern Appalachia to Mobile, Ala. At a cost of almost $2 billion, the 376-km (234-mi) barge canal was the most expensive U.S. Army Corps of Engineers project to date. A major challenge of the Tenn-Tom was moving approximately 230 million cu m (300 million cu yd) of earth, about a third more than was moved to build the Panama Canal. Another was keeping the construction sites dry. To control groundwater, wells were placed at 150-m (500-ft) intervals along both sides of the 460-km (1,500-ft)-wide excavation. The cut floor was kept dry by digging trenches 4.5 to 6 m (15 to 20 ft) deep, parallel to the waterway centerline, at one, two, or three locations across the 230-m (300-ft)-wide canal channel.

*Tunnel-boring machine was one of several used to create 50 kilometers (31 miles) of tunnels for the Tunnel and Reservoir Project in Chicago. The project was designated the Outstanding Engineering Achievement of 1986 by the American Society of Civil Engineers.*

Metropolitan Sanitary District of Greater Chicago; courtesy, Harza Engineering Company

*To build the Tennessee-Tombigbee Waterway in Mississippi and Alabama, approximately 230 million cubic meters (300 million cubic yards) of earth had to be moved. The waterway, connecting the Tennessee River on the north with the Tombigbee River on the south, shortened by hundreds of kilometers the barge canal route from southern Appalachia to Mobile, Alabama.*

Belying its earlier reputation, the Corps of Engineers acted with consistent sensitivity to environmental needs. Thus areas for disposing of the excavation material were located several hundred feet inland, rather than immediately beside the waterway. This removed them from sight and created a strip of earth where the Corps would plant two million tree seedlings. More than 600 consultants, firms, universities, individuals, and organizations assisted the Corps in the planning and design of the project, and some 75 prime contractors and 1,200 subcontractors performed the work.

*Solar generation.* The small town of Daggett, Calif., is the site of another significant engineering feat. In the Mohave Desert, about 110 km (70 mi) east of Los Angeles, more than 120,000 mirrors spread over 160 ha (400 ac) represent three solar power generating systems—Solar I, SEGS I, and SEGS II. The last of the systems, Solar Electric Generating System II (SEGS II), completed in early 1986 with a 30-MW capacity, was the world's largest commercial solar electric plant. Together with Solar I and SEGS I it was capable of producing more than 60 MW of electricity, enough to light about 95,000 homes.

Solar I, a 10-MW generating system, was built by the U.S. Energy Research and Development Administration in 1976 at a cost of $142 million. SEGS I, a 13.8-MW system, built at about half the cost of Solar I, reflected the increasing sophistication of the budding solar power industry. Unlike Solar I, SEGS I has no boiler tower to receive the Sun's reflected rays. Instead, rows of curved collectors concentrate the Sun's rays to heat oil pipes that run parallel to the collectors. Oil flowing through the pipes heats water to produce steam that powers the turbine. A similar system of solar-thermal conversion was used for the $93 million SEGS II.

—John Davis

*See also* Feature Article: TUNNELING TOWARD THE FUTURE.

*Rows of curved mirrors concentrate the Sun's rays to generate electricity at Solar Electric Generating System II in the Mohave Desert of California. When completed in 1986, SEGS II was the world's largest commercial solar electric plant.*

# Astronomy

During the past year the first visits to a comet and the planet Uranus were completed. The birth of a star was observed along with several more bizarre stellar objects. The distance to the center of the Galaxy was refined and its spiral structure confirmed by the study of large molecular clouds. Progress was made in reaching more distant objects in the universe, and the structure of the universe was studied.

**Solar system.** The recent visit of Halley's Comet was not very spectacular for Earth-bound observers, but it became notable in another way when five different spacecraft visited the comet for close-up examination. The Japanese Institute of Space and Astronautical Sciences sent two probes, Suisei and Sakigake; the Space Research Institute of the Soviet Union also sent two vehicles, Vega 1 and Vega 2; and the European Space Agency dispatched one, named Giotto. The spacecraft arrived in quick succession during early March 1986. From relatively large distances the Japanese craft primarily studied the comet's hydrogen cloud and its interactions with the solar wind. The two Vegas came within 8,000 to 9,000 km of the nucleus, and Giotto passed by at a mere 600 km. (One kilometer equals 0.62 mi.)

The Soviet and European measurements of the nucleus showed it to be nonspherical, in the shape of a potato, 7 to 10 km wide and 15 km long. Not only was it larger than expected but it was also much darker than anticipated, reflecting only about 4% of the sunlight falling upon it. The surface of the nucleus was rough, with pits and lumps about 100 m (330 ft) across. The gas in the coma and tail was clearly the result of the evaporation of the ices that make up the bulk of the nucleus. These ices are covered by the dark, nonvolatile crust, which allows the ice to evaporate irregularly from areas estimated to be only 10% of the total surface. Jets of dust and gas feeding the coma and tail were seen coming from localized regions. Of the gases detected in the coma, $H_2O$ was the predominant parent molecule, with the next most abundant being $CO_2$. Other neutral molecules found were $OH$, $C_2$, $CH$, $CN$, and $NH$. The most numerous ionized molecules found were $H^+$, $C^+$, $H_2O^+$, $O^+$, and $He^+$. The $C^+$ was much more abundant than expected and probably came either from dust grains released when the ice vaporized or directly from the dark surface of the nucleus.

Voyager 2 swept within 82,000 km of Uranus in late January 1986. The probe was continuing its outward trip through the solar system and should reach Neptune in August 1989. While it was near Uranus, observations were made of the planet itself, its rings, and its satellites.

The images of the planet, as received from Voyager, were quite featureless. But, by the use of

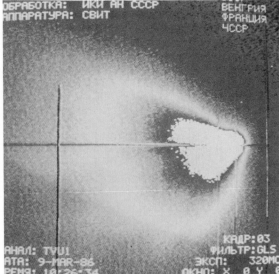

*Nucleus of Halley's Comet was photographed by the Soviet space probe Vega 2 in March 1986 from a distance of about 8,000 kilometers (5,000 miles). Measurements of the nucleus showed it to be nonspherical, in the shape of a potato.*

computer-enhancement techniques, they were made to reveal a banded atmosphere reminiscent of those of Jupiter and Saturn. Bright and dark zones circle Uranus along parallels of latitude. Because the rotational axis of the planet lies nearly in its orbital plane and the planet is now aligned so that the poles point toward the Sun, one side of Uranus has for nearly 42 years been hidden from sunlight. Voyager, however, measured essentially the same temperature for the dark side as the sunlit one; thus, some as-yet-unexplained mechanism must be transferring heat across the predominant wind pattern in the atmosphere. Magnetometers aboard the spacecraft found a somewhat unexpected magnetic field, which, surprisingly, was tilted 55° to the rotational axis of the planet. This tilt is remarkably different from the smaller tilts of other planetary magnetic fields. It was possible that the measurement was made while Uranus was undergoing a reversal of its field, not unlike the reversals in the Earth's field indicated by geologic evidence.

Voyager discovered ten new moons of Uranus, all extremely small, and returned close-up views of the five previously known satellites. All of the moons are quite dark, reflecting only about 4% of the light falling on them. The five larger moons were not expected to show much evidence of recent geologic activity, but they did. Miranda, the innermost of the five, was the biggest surprise. Only 484 km in diameter, it has fault canyons as deep as 20 km and has strongly banded, ridged, and scarped terrain. Its almost bizarre appearance led to the suggestion that

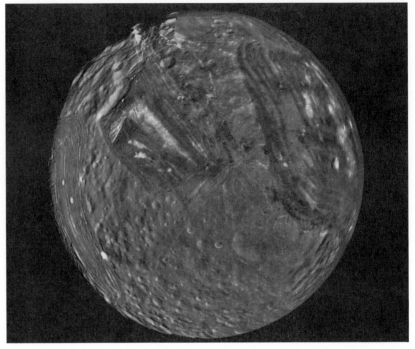

Mosaic of Uranus's moon Miranda, assembled from images obtained by the U.S. space probe Voyager 2, reveals strongly banded, ridged, and scarped terrain. Fault canyons on Miranda are as deep as 20 kilometers (12.5 miles).

it may have suffered total disruption and reassembly one or more times in its history.

The rings of Uranus, already known from stellar occultation observations made from the Earth, were found by Voyager to be extremely dark. The outer and widest ring, called epsilon, is constrained by two tiny shepherd moons, one on either side of it.

**Stars.** A team of observers from the University of Arizona, Christopher K. Walker, Charles J. Lada, Erick T. Young, and Phillip R. Maloney, along with Bruce A. Wilking of the University of Missouri at St. Louis, observed what appeared to be a star actually in the process of formation. They examined IRAS 1629A, a little-studied infrared source in the Rho Ophiuchi molecular cloud, first discovered by the Infrared Astronomical Satellite. The researchers observed at millimeter wavelengths using the 12-m radio telescope that is operated on Kitt Peak in Arizona by the National Radio Astronomy Observatory. By studying the radiation in two emission lines from the carbon monosulfide molecule, they were able to determine the pattern of gas movement around this object. Observing the object directly in visible light was not possible because it is located in a region of great obscuration that can be penetrated only by infrared and radio radiation.

The analysis of the object showed it to be surrounded by a disk of material with jets of gas emerging perpendicular to the disk. The disk itself is about 1,600 astronomical units across (roughly 1.4 billion km). The inner parts of the disk displayed evidence of material collapsing onto a central core, the pro-tostar itself. According to current theories on star formation, the data imply that the collapse started about 30,000 years ago and will continue for another 100,000 years. In the end the protostar will have grown to a mass like that of the Sun. The process now taking place in IRAS 1629A is probably similar to the one that took place when our own solar system formed billions of years ago; it makes this object particularly interesting because it is the first to have shown such clear-cut evidence of being a star actually in the stage of formation.

Until the past year the shortest known period for a binary star was 46 minutes, in a system consisting of two closely spaced white dwarfs. However, William Priedhorsky of Los Alamos National Observatory and Luigi Stella and Nicholas White of the Exosat Observatory at the European Space Operations Centre announced a system with a period of only 685 seconds, less than 12 minutes in duration. While examining data returned in 1984 and 1985 by the European Space Agency's Exosat satellite, they found that the X-ray source 4U 1820–30, located in the core of the globular cluster NGC 6624, showed an extremely regular but gentle variation in its X-ray emission with the very short period noted. This object was already known to be an X-ray burster. Bursters are believed to be binary systems containing a neutron star upon which accreting material gives rise to the bursts in X-ray emission. The first, and obvious, interpretation—that the variation in brightness is associated with a hot spot caused by accreting matter and, therefore, reflects the rotational period

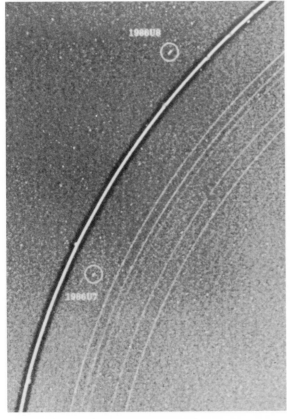

*Two newly discovered satellites on either side of the ninth and outermost ring of Uranus were photographed by Voyager 2. The satellites are called shepherd moons because astronomers believe that their gravitational forces "herd" the rings into narrow shapes.*

of the neutron star—does not work. If that were the case, a small but sure change in the period would be expected as the angular momentum of the star changed owing to the accreting material. But no such period change was detected during the observations, nor was there any noticeable change in archival data from other X-ray satellites dating back to 1976. This leaves the binary period interpretation as the only viable one.

The extremely short period requires a very close system consisting of a pair of objects that, for any reasonable assumed masses, are separated by less than a fraction of the Earth–Moon distance. The best estimate of the components of the system is that they are a helium-rich white dwarf, with a mass $\frac{1}{15}$ that of the Sun, and a neutron star, in mutual orbit about each other. Unfortunately, at the time that the discovery was made there were no functioning X-ray satellites with which to obtain follow-up data.

Astronomers have proposed that black holes occupy the centers of active galactic nuclei and even at our own galactic center, but until recently the only

two binary system candidates known were Cygnus X-1 and an X-ray source in the Large Magellanic Cloud. If the orbital characteristics of a binary system require a component of a few solar masses but such a component cannot be seen, the system probably contains a black hole. Jeffrey McClintock of the Harvard-Smithsonian Center for Astrophysics, Cambridge, Mass., and Ronald Remillard of the Massachusetts Institute of Technology found a third possible black hole. They observed a faint variable star, V616 Monocerotis, which on two known occasions (in 1917 and again in 1975) had become 250 to 1,500 times brighter than its normally obscure appearance. Both outbursts were nova-like in nature, and two satellites determined that the 1975 episode was accompanied by X-ray emissions. For roughly two months in 1975, V616 Monocerotis held the distinction of having the greatest apparent brightness of any known X-ray source in the sky.

McClintock and Remillard followed this variable star photometrically with the 1.3-m McGraw-Hill telescope and also obtained spectroscopic observations of it with the 4-m telescope at Kitt Peak. It was in its quiescent state from 1981 to 1985, the time of their data gathering. The two astronomers found that the object is a binary system with a visible component—an orange, dwarf star with a mass just smaller than that of the Sun—and an invisible component. The orbital period of the system is short, 7.7523 hours, which, when combined with the spectroscopic observations, requires the unseen companion to have a mass of at least 3.2 solar masses. Thus, the dark component is too massive to be a neutron star (beyond the mass limit theoretically permitted for neutron stars), and the only alternative left is that it is a black hole. This possibility fits nicely with the X-ray behavior of the system at outburst. Matter being transferred from the dwarf star to the black hole then would be heated to an extreme temperature by the strong gravitational acceleration of the black hole, resulting in strong increases in both visible and X-ray radiation. The eruptions could be set off when an accretion disk collecting material from the dwarf star becomes unstable and dumps matter into the black hole, or when the dwarf star undergoes an increase in size and the black hole takes gravitational control of some of its outer layers.

**Galactic astronomy.** The precision of very long baseline interferometry (VLBI), whereby radio observations made with radio telescopes separated by distances approaching the diameter of the Earth are combined to give directional accuracy in the submilliarcsecond range, was used to give a new value for the distance of the Galactic center. The previous value for this distance, adopted by the International Astronomical Union, was 8.5 kiloparsecs (a parsec is the distance from which the Earth's orbit would appear to be two seconds of arc in diameter; it is more than 200,000 times the Earth's distance from the Sun, 149.6 million km). This value depended in large measure on photometric distance estimates of the center of the distribution of the RR Lyrae stars lying toward the center of the Galaxy. But interstellar absorption of light and uncertainties in the intrinsic brightness of those stars introduced uncertainties in their distances and that of the center.

Mark Reid of the Harvard-Smithsonian Center for Astrophysics and an international team of astronomers determined the center of the Galaxy to be 7.1(±1.2) kiloparsecs distant from the Earth. They based their conclusion on VLBI data concerning $H_2O$ masers in Sgr B2, a star-forming cloud complex within 300 parsecs of the center. (A maser is an object that utilizes the natural oscillations of atoms or molecules between energy levels for generating radiation in the microwave region of the electromagnetic spectrum.) The analysis required that the observers follow the angular motions of maser clumps in the cloud across the line of sight and also that they measure the clump radial velocities (the line-of-sight velocities) over the course of a year. The radial velocity measurements are used statistically to estimate the space motion of the clumps. This, when combined with the measured angular movements, allows the distance to the cloud to be calculated. The technique is so powerful that it may be applicable to distance determinations for some galaxies that are close to our own. Such determinations are possible only because of the extreme angular accuracy of VLBI data.

Thomas Dame, Bruce Elmegreen, Richard Cohen, and Patrick Thaddeus, who at the time were working at the Goddard Institute for Space Studies, New York City, completed a map of molecular clouds in our Galaxy that lie within an arc of about 120° measured from the Galactic center and are located from the Sagittarius spiral arm inward. The molecular clouds are regions composed mostly of molecular hydrogen and can contain as much as one million solar masses in a volume with a diameter on the order of 300 light-years. They are the regions where many of the young hot stars in the Galaxy formed. They are also the location of the HII, or ionized hydrogen, regions that are associated with hot stars and that mark the spiral arms in our Galaxy. All told, Dame and his colleagues found 17 molecular complexes in the Sagittarius spiral arm. They are located along the arm, more or less like beads on a string, with characteristic distances between them of 3,000 light-years. The roughly equal spacing of the clouds mimics the spacing of HII regions detected in some external galaxies.

The results of Dame and his colleagues are in excellent agreement with the determination of the

Thomas M. Dame and Patrick Thaddeus, Harvard–Smithsonian Center for Astrophysics; Bruce G. Elmegreen, IBM Watson Research Center, and Richard S. Cohen, Columbia University

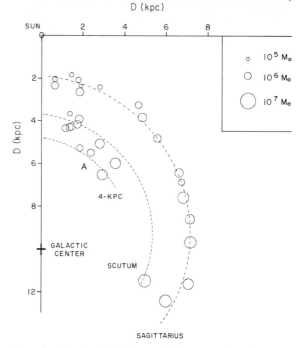

*Map of molecular clouds in our Galaxy comprises those bodies lying within an arc of 120° measured from the Galactic center and located from the Sagittarius spiral arm inward. Such clouds are composed mostly of molecular hydrogen and are the regions where many of the young hot stars in the Galaxy are formed.*

arm made by radio surveys done earlier in the 21-cm line of neutral hydrogen. The scientists also found molecular clouds marking the Scutum arm and the so-called "four kiloparsec" arm, in good agreement with neutral hydrogen maps. The molecular clouds in those inner arms, however, do not reveal the same tendency toward equal spacing. Instead, the arrangement there is indicative of a possible bar-like arrangement in the central region of the Milky Way.

**Extragalactic astronomy.** One of the sources found by the Infrared Astronomical Satellite, labeled IRAS 13348+2438, was shown during the past year to be an infrared quasar by Charles Beichman, B. Thomas Soifer, George Helou, Thomas Chester, and Gerry Neugebauer of the California Institute of Technology; Frederick C. Gillett of the National Optical Astronomy Observatories, Tucson, Ariz.; and Frank Low of the University of Arizona. This object radiates more than 90% of its energy in the infrared, while the roughly 3,500 quasars previously found emit most of their energy in the ultraviolet, visible, or radio wavelengths. The explanation proposed for this object is that it results from the collision of two galaxies, providing large amounts of matter to feed a black hole at the center of one of them. While tremendous amounts of radiant energy would be re-

324

leased by infall into the black hole, it would not be easily visible because of obscuration by interstellar dust released in the collision. The dust, on the other hand, would be heated by this radiation, causing it to emit a great amount of infrared radiation. The radio signal expected from such a vigorous event is squelched by the gas that coexists with the dust, resulting in the very weak radio brightness of this quasar. Its very red color in visible light is caused by the scattering of light by the copious dust surrounding the source. Beichman and his colleagues believe that many more quasars bright in infrared radiation await discovery in the catalog of sources found by IRAS.

The most distant quasar found to date was announced by Stephen Warren and Paul Hewitt of the University of Cambridge. This quasar, in the constellation of Sculptor, is so faint in apparent brightness that it does not have one of the familiar QSO designations. It has a redshift of 4.01, the greatest measured as of 1987. The large redshift implies that the quasar is at a distance of 10 billion to 20 billion light-years from the Sun. The conversion of redshift to distance depends upon the precise curvature of space, which is not yet known. In any case the quasar must have formed within the first 10% of the time since the "Big Bang" (the moment that the universe began from a state of extremely high density and temperature) to have such a huge redshift. The observers employed a search with wide-field photographs, taken in ultraviolet, blue, visual, red, and infrared light, to identify objects that have an energy distribution suggestive of quasars at great redshifts. Candidates, so identified, must then be observed spectroscopically to determine their exact redshift.

Another way of probing deepest space was developed by J. Anthony Tyson of Bell Laboratories and Patrick Seitzer of the National Optical Astronomy Observatories. Using a camera equipped with a charge-coupled device (CCD) at the focus of the four-meter telescope of the Cerro Tololo Inter-American Observatory in Chile, they were able to detect 27th-magnitude galaxies, roughly one billion times fainter than anything that can be seen by the naked eye. (A CCD is a semiconductor device in which charges are introduced when light from a scene is focused on its surface.) Galaxies that faint in apparent brightness must be at distances of the order of ten billion light-years distant from the Earth.

To minimize the number of foreground stars in their measurements, Tyson and Seitzer pointed the telescope toward the South Galactic Pole, thus looking through the thinnest possible part of the disk of our Galaxy. They exposed the CCD for six hours at a time to record the faintest galaxies and took exposures with three different color filters to obtain the colors of the sources that they detected. The colors of the galaxies so found were expected to give a rough indication of relative distance since the redshifts of the galaxies make the more distant ones appear redder. A surprising result of the study, however, was that the faintest and most distant galaxies appeared blue. This means that those galaxies must have an extreme ultraviolet enhancement in order to overcome the reddening that results from the expansion of the universe. Tyson believes that this ultraviolet enhancement results from the production of hot, young stars in the more distant galaxies, which also are the youngest galaxies because at their distances we are seeing them as they were some ten billion years ago.

Combining the counts of galaxies with their colors and current ideas of galaxy evolution, astronomers have concluded that the more distant galaxies might be only a billion or two years into their lifetimes

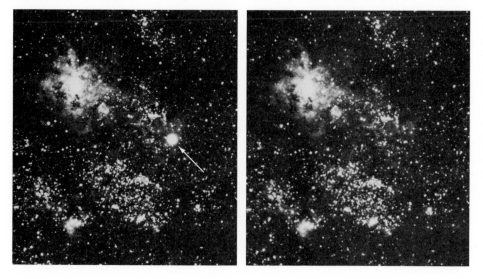

Large Magellanic Cloud as photographed on Feb. 24, 1987 (far left), reveals a supernova (arrow) that was not visible in a photograph taken of the same region on the previous night (left). The exploding star is the brightest supernova since Kepler's star of 1604.

and that galaxy formation started early in the life of the universe. Another surprising result of the measurements was that the images of the faintest galaxies do not decrease in size as one would expect at their greater distances. This implies that we live in a non-Euclidean universe; the curvature of space predicted by Einstein's theory of general relativity actually causes the images to appear larger with increasing distances. These conclusions, although intriguing, still require much refinement before they can be accepted as reliable. Tyson hoped to increase the sensitivity of the CCD camera tenfold during the next few years. If so, galaxies as faint as the 30th magnitude should be reachable, and the necessary data to test the conclusions may become available.

Valérie de Lapparent, Margaret Geller, and John Huchra of the Harvard-Smithsonian Center for Astrophysics released a new map of a three-dimensional slice through the universe based on their observations of the redshifts of galaxies and their directions in space. Because the redshifts can be converted to distances by the redshift law of the expansion of the universe, the three scientists were able to obtain information on the three-dimensional distribution of galaxies in space. Their map included 1,100 galaxies in a thin wedge of the universe, 117° wide with an apex angle of 6° at the Sun and out to a distance of 150 to 300 megaparsecs from the Sun. The galaxies are arranged along what appear to be the walls of huge bubbles in space intercepted by the slice. Voids, lacking in galaxies, were seen with dimensions of 30 to 50 megaparsecs.

The Center for Astrophysics survey employed new techniques for quickly obtaining redshifts and eventually was to be extended to objects as faint as magnitude 15.5 over a large region of the sky. The aim of the program was to determine the large-scale structure of space out to a distance of several hundred megaparsecs. The new sample of space in the map clearly bore out the existence of the voids, reported as early as 1981, and lent credence to the emerging view of the universe as having a sponge-like structure.

On Feb. 24, 1987, Ian Shelton, an astronomer at the University of Toronto who was working at a telescope at Las Campanas Observatory in Chile, discovered on a photographic plate a supernova that had not been visible one night earlier. At approximately 160,000 light-years from the Earth in the Large Magellanic Cloud, the exploding star was by far the brightest supernova since Kepler's star of 1604 and was expected to provide astronomers with information that will help them in deciphering the evolution of the universe.

—W. M. Protheroe

*See also:* Feature Articles: SHIPS TO THE STARS; EXPLORING THE PLANETS; SUPERSTRINGS.

# Chemistry

Among major accomplishments of the past year in chemistry were the syntheses or investigation of numerous biologically active compounds including advanced anticancer metal complexes, antibiotics, unusual molecules from marine organisms, and a natural nighttime inhibitor of photosynthesis in plants. Researchers discovered the identity of the glue that mussels use to bond to underwater objects, generated elemental fluorine chemically for the first time, and devised a way to deposit diamond film on silicon surfaces. Aided by advances in genetic engineering, chemists improved their understanding of the electron-transfer reactions vital to such basic biochemical processes as metabolism and photosynthesis.

## Inorganic chemistry

During the past year inorganic chemists investigated advanced-generation anticancer metal complexes, generated elemental fluorine chemically for the first time, determined the first-ever structure of an electride "salt," and achieved hydration of terminal alkenes (olefins) to primary alcohols by homogeneous catalysis.

**Anticancer metal complexes.** Discovery of the antitumor activity of cisplatin, *cis*-$[Pt(NH_3)_2Cl_2]$ (*see* 1a), in the late 1960s by Barnett Rosenberg and co-workers at Michigan State University initiated an explosive interest in the pharmacology of metal complexes (see *1981 Yearbook of Science and the Future* Year in Review: CHEMISTRY: *Inorganic chemistry*). One continuing effort has involved the syntheses and testing of thousands of metal complexes related to cisplatin. A difficulty with the therapeutic use of cisplatin itself is its toxic side effects. In order to identify a less toxic cisplatin analogue having similar clinical activity, researchers have worked to understand the compound's relative toxicity and

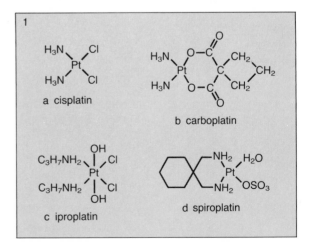

a cisplatin

b carboplatin

c iproplatin

d spiroplatin

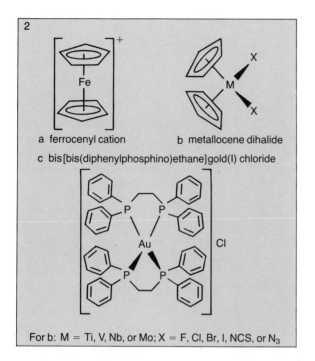

a ferrocenyl cation     b metallocene dihalide

c bis[bis(diphenylphosphino)ethane]gold(I) chloride

For b: M = Ti, V, Nb, or Mo; X = F, Cl, Br, I, NCS, or $N_3$

pharmacology. From their labors has come a second generation of anticancer platinum complexes.

Extensive research in several laboratories including those of Johnson Matthey in England and Bristol-Myers in the U.S. produced the second-generation drugs carboplatin, iproplatin, and spiroplatin (1b–1d). All three have anticancer activity similar to that of cisplatin but appear to have less toxic side effects. For example, Martin Tobe and co-workers at University College, London, demonstrated that for a series of *cis*-[Pt(amine)$_2$Cl$_2$] complexes with alicyclic amines (1d), antitumor potency decreased slightly with increased ring size while whole-body toxicity dropped dramatically. More than 2,000 patients have been treated with carboplatin, and a license was granted in March 1986 for its use in the U.K.

Another generation of antitumor metal complexes was discovered in 1979 by Petra Köpf-Maier and co-workers at the University of Ulm and the Free University of Berlin, both in West Germany (*see* 2). Chemists are justified in calling these compounds third-generation drugs, because from a chemical point of view they are quite different from the cisplatin-type drugs. The compounds most thoroughly tested appear to be the metallocene dihalides, particularly titanocene dichloride. In clinical trials these drugs affected tumors that differed from those against which cisplatin is most effective. Furthermore, the compounds did not impair kidney function, a critical problem with cisplatin, but did cause transient injury to certain liver cells.

Investigators in different laboratories worldwide continued striving to reveal the nature of the chemistry responsible for the antitumor activity of metal complexes. Elegant work by inorganic chemists over several years—much of it coming from the laboratories of Stephen Lippard at Columbia University, New York City, and the Massachusetts Institute of Technology, Cambridge, and of Jan Reedijk at Leiden University in The Netherlands—has been quite successful. Results show that the platinum complex selectively interacts with DNA, specifically at locations termed the guanine N7 sites.

In (3a) a short segment of the sugar-phosphate backbones of the DNA double helix is laid flat in order to view the helix chemically. Of the nucleotide base pairs that form connections across the backbones, each pair comprises one purine base—adenine (A) or guanine (G)—and one pyrimidine base—thymine (T) or cytosine (C). The hydrogen-bonded bases, along with their numbering scheme, are shown in (3b); the N7 site on guanine is identified with an arrow.

In addition to the platinum complex binding at N7 guanine, a second interaction frequently takes place on the same strand of DNA. This one often involves

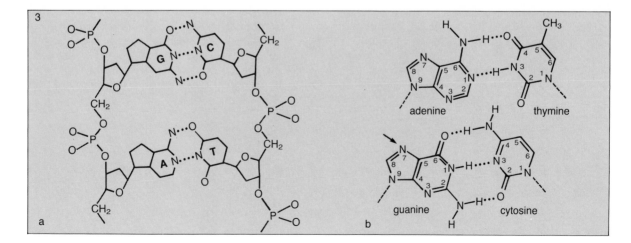

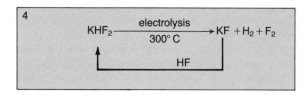

4

$$KHF_2 \xrightarrow[300°\,C]{\text{electrolysis}} KF + H_2 + F_2$$

HF

a next-neighbor guanine and results in a small distortion of the DNA shape. It has been suggested that this distortion is small enough to not be recognized by repair enzymes, at least of certain tumor cells, but large enough to hamper cell replication, thus preventing growth or metastasis of the cancer.

Interestingly, the third-generation anticancer metal compounds, particularly the metallocene dihalides, interact with DNA in a manner different from that of cisplatin-type drugs. Fundamental chemistry studies by Tobin Marks and co-workers at Northwestern University, Evanston, Ill., show that the vanadium form of (2b), $(\eta^5\text{-}C_5H_5)_2VCl_2$, very selectively binds to phosphate groups of the DNA backbone relative to sites on purine or pyrimidine bases. This finding is plausible on the basis of the known chemistry of early transition metals (e.g., the titanium, vanadium, and chromium triads), which have a high affinity to bind to oxygen ligand atoms, whereas platinum(II) chemistry reveals that Pt(II) binds preferentially to ligand atoms of nitrogen over oxygen. In 1986 it was still too early to speculate on the way the differences between these two chemistries translate into differences in anticancer activity of such new drugs as (2a) and (2c). Important, challenging research abounds in this area for capable bioinorganic chemists.

**Elemental fluorine.** In 1886 elemental fluorine was isolated for the first time by French chemist Henri Moissan, who obtained it by the electrolysis of liquid hydrogen fluoride (HF) at low temperature (about −20° C, or −4° F) with added potassium fluoride (KF) to carry the current. His apparatus consisted of a U-tube made of a platinum-iridium alloy and fitted with platinum electrodes. Nothing has changed during the succeeding century in the chemistry involved for the large-scale production of fluorine gas ($F_2$). What has changed is the cell design and the

electrolysis conditions. The modern cell is made of nickel or copper with graphite electrodes, and molten potassium hydrogen fluoride ($KHF_2$) at about 300° C (570° F) is the electrolyte. Although $KHF_2$ melts at 217° C (423° F), the KF product of electrolysis melts at 880° C (1,616° F). Consequently, as electrolysis converts molten $KHF_2$ into solid KF at 300° C, HF must be continuously added in order to maintain the molten $KHF_2$ electrolyte (see 4). Since KF is not consumed during electrolysis, the process amounts to the overall electrolysis of HF to give $H_2$ at the cathode and $F_2$ at the anode.

Chemists have tried for more than 170 years to produce $F_2$ by the chemical means of using a powerful oxidizing reagent to oxidize the fluorine anion $F^-$ to $F_2$. They have failed because fluorine is the most electronegative element; $F^-$ will not give up its electron to become a neutral atom ($\frac{1}{2}F_2$) even to the most powerful of chemical oxidizing reagents. It has long been known, however, that some fluorine compounds react at elevated temperatures to generate $F_2$ (see 5a). Since such compounds as $K_4PbF_6$ require the use of $F_2$ in their synthesis, it follows that their thermal release of $F_2$ is a means of $F_2$ storage but not $F_2$ synthesis.

At long last Karl Christe, a research chemist at the Rocketdyne Division of Rockwell International in Canoga Park, Calif., devised a means of preparing $F_2$ chemically. He reasoned that a Lewis acid such as $SbF_5$ would displace the weaker Lewis acid $MnF_4$ from a salt of the stable complex $MnF_6^{2-}$. Then, since $MnF_4$ is thermodynamically unstable, it would decompose into $MnF_3 + \frac{1}{2}F_2$. His experiments showed this is in fact what happens (see 5b). Christe's method is not just another example of $F_2$ storage but one of chemical $F_2$ synthesis starting with HF. While the discovery is unlikely to supplant the electrochemical production of $F_2$, it does show that research chemists are willing to accept the challenges of old problems for the advancement of basic science.

Elemental $F_2$ and compounds of fluorine have important uses. The classified fluorine research done at Rockwell International, for example, must relate to the use of fluorine in high-energy compounds

5

a (storage and release of $F_2$):

$$K_2PbF_6 \xrightarrow{\text{heat}} K_2PbF_4 + F_2$$

b (chemical synthesis of $F_2$):

$$2KMnO_4 + 2KF + 10HF + 3H_2O_2 \longrightarrow 2K_2MnF_6 + 8H_2O + 3O_2$$

$$SbCl_5 + 5HF \longrightarrow SbF_5 + 5HCl$$

$$K_2MnF_6 + 2SbF_5 \xrightarrow{150°\,C} 2KSbF_6 + MnF_3 + \frac{1}{2}F_2$$

and high-energy reactions of interest to the space program. On the other hand the general public encounters fluorine compounds in such forms as the Teflon coatings that prevent sticking on cooking utensils and snow shovels. Human lives have even been saved by the use of fluorocarbons as a temporary blood substitute.

With regard to the synthesis or manufacture of elements from their natural source on Earth, it should be recalled that while a few elements are found free in nature, most are combined in some compound in which the element has either a positive or a negative oxidation state. Zero is the oxidation state of all free elements. Thus if an element occurs in nature in a positive oxidation state, it must be given negatively charged electrons (be reduced) in order to reach the zero state. The opposite is true for an element that occurs in nature in a negative oxidation state; it must give up electrons (be oxidized) to form the zero valent element. These oxidation-reduction reactions can be either chemical or electrochemical. But, as noted above for the production of $F_2$, with an extremely reactive element it is not easy to find a sufficiently powerful oxidizing or reducing agent to do the job chemically. For this reason $F_2$ is produced electrochemically.

Sodium likewise is manufactured electrochemically—by the electrolysis of molten sodium chloride (NaCl). Sodium is one of the most electropositive elements; $Na^+$ does not accept an electron from even some of the most powerful chemical reducing agents known. Electrochemically it can be forced to accept an electron and form Na, similar to electrochemically forcing $F^-$ to give up an electron to form $\frac{1}{2}F_2$. Perhaps the work of Christe will encourage inorganic chemists to seriously consider ways of chemically generating extremely electropositive elements.

**Sodide and electride salts.** Despite the difficulty chemists face in reducing $Na^+$, it has proved possible to induce Na chemically to accept an electron to form the anion $Na^-$. Discovery of the first salt of an alkali metal anion was reported in 1974 by James L. Dye and co-workers at Michigan State University, and in 1986 they reported the first X-ray crystal structure of an electride salt. Their research was based mostly on the large body of information collected during a period of more than 120 years on solutions of alkali metals in liquid ammonia ($NH_3$). For example, the dissolution of Na in liquid $NH_3$ gives a dark blue solution that is a strong reducing agent and has a very high electrical conductivity. The species present in solution are the ammoniated $Na^+$ and ammoniated electron ($e^-$), which had chemists joking that electrons are blue (*see* 6a). Ammoniated electrons are very good reducing agents and very efficient in carrying an electric current. Dye and co-workers made thermodynamic calculations and esti-

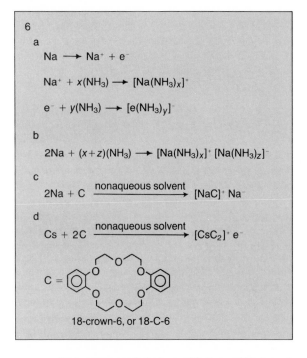

6

a

$$Na \longrightarrow Na^+ + e^-$$

$$Na^+ + x(NH_3) \longrightarrow [Na(NH_3)_x]^+$$

$$e^- + y(NH_3) \longrightarrow [e(NH_3)_y]^-$$

b

$$2Na + (x+z)(NH_3) \longrightarrow [Na(NH_3)_x]^+ [Na(NH_3)_z]^-$$

c

$$2Na + C \xrightarrow{\text{nonaqueous solvent}} [NaC]^+ Na^-$$

d

$$Cs + 2C \xrightarrow{\text{nonaqueous solvent}} [CsC_2]^+ e^-$$

$$C = \text{18-crown-6, or 18-C-6}$$

mates which suggested that equilibrium (6b) is not favorable. The estimates indicated, however, that if $Na^+$ could be stabilized by coordination with a crown ether, then equilibrium (6c) would be favorable. Experiments over the years corroborated their thermodynamic estimates, and several alkali-metal alkalimetalide salts were prepared and studied.

Formation of the anions of the metal depends on the interaction of $e^-$ produced initially from the free metal (6a, first step). With the most electropositive alkali metal, cesium (Cs), the electron initially formed does not react with Cs to form $Cs^-$; instead it pairs with the stabilized Cs cation to form an electride salt (*see* 6d). The X-ray structure of $[Cs(18\text{-}C\text{-}6)_2]^+ \cdot e^-$ turns out to be similar to that of $[Cs(18\text{-}C\text{-}6)_2]^+ \cdot Na^-$, with electrons occupying all of the anionic sites. In 1987 these revolutionary new materials were being thoroughly studied for unique electrical or magnetic properties or both.

**Catalytic hydration of terminal alkenes.** Alcohols in tonnage quantities are manufactured daily by the direct hydration of (addition of water to) alkenes (olefins, $RCH=CH_2$, in which R is a generalized substituent group). Catalysts used in these commercial processes include phosphoric acid, transition-metal oxides, zeolites, or clays. Moderately high temperatures and pressures are required, and primary alcohols ($RCH_2OH$) are not produced. This last limitation is unfortunate because straight-chain primary alcohols are required to produce biodegradable surfactants and detergents. The reason that hydration of terminal alkenes by means of the above-mentioned catalysts do not produce primary alcohols is that

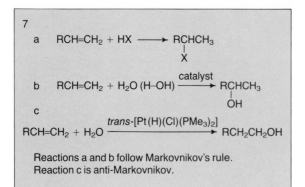

7

a $\quad RCH{=}CH_2 + HX \longrightarrow RCHCH_3$
$\qquad\qquad\qquad\qquad\qquad\quad |$
$\qquad\qquad\qquad\qquad\qquad\quad X$

b $\quad RCH{=}CH_2 + H_2O\,(H{-}OH) \xrightarrow{catalyst} RCHCH_3$
$\qquad\qquad\qquad\qquad\qquad\qquad\qquad\qquad\qquad |$
$\qquad\qquad\qquad\qquad\qquad\qquad\qquad\qquad\quad OH$

c

$RCH{=}CH_2 + H_2O \xrightarrow{trans\text{-}[Pt(H)(Cl)(PMe_3)_2]} RCH_2CH_2OH$

Reactions a and b follow Markovnikov's rule.
Reaction c is anti-Markovnikov.

the addition of water obeys Markovnikov's rule. In 1875 V. V. Markovnikov, a Russian chemist, stated that when a reagent H—X adds to an unsymmetrical olefin ($RCH{=}CH_2$), the positive part of the reagent ($H^+$) will add to the carbon atom of the double bond holding the greater number of hydrogen atoms, and the negative part of the reagent ($X^-$) will add to the carbon atom of the double bond with the lesser number of hydrogen atoms (*see* 7a). When Markovnikov's rule prevails in the addition of water to a terminal alkene, the result is a secondary alcohol (*see* 7b).

One of the earliest uses made of a transition-metal complex as a homogeneous catalyst in a commercial process is in the oxo process. The catalyst is a cobalt carbonyl, and the hydroformylation reaction involves the addition of molecular hydrogen ($H_2$) and carbon monoxide (CO) to an olefin in order to form an aldehyde ($RCH{=}CH_2 + H_2 + CO \to RCH_2CH_2CHO$) that can then be transformed easily to an alcohol. The oxo process produced billions of tons of alcohols over many years, but it suffers from two problems. It requires high temperatures (about 170° C, or 274° F) and high pressures (5,000 psi), and even more troublesome, it produces a mixture, roughly 3:1, of straight-chain and branched-chain aldehydes. Branch-chained alcohols yield detergents and surfactants that are of no value because they are not biodegradable and thus pollute the environment. The problem was largely alleviated a few years ago when Union Carbide started to use rhodium triphenylphosphine complexes as catalysts.

Recently an even more promising solution appeared on the horizon for the production of straight-chain primary alcohols from terminal olefins. It

came as a result of the discovery of William Trogler and co-workers at the University of California at San Diego. They showed that the complex *trans*-$[Pt(H)(Cl)(PMe_3)_2]$, in which $PMe_3$ is $P(CH_3)_3$, is a good homogeneous catalyst for the addition of water to terminal olefins in a way that goes against Markovnikov's rule (*i.e.*, anti-Markovnikov; *see* 7c). The catalytic cycle involves standard organometallic reactions of the types previously described (see *1987 Yearbook of Science and the Future* Year in Review: CHEMISTRY: *Inorganic chemistry*): ligand substitution, ligand migration, reductive elimination, and oxidative addition.

It was too early to speculate on the commercial future of this catalytic hydration reaction. Suffice it to say that it has great potential and that it demonstrates the possibility of one's finding yet undiscovered gems in a well-tilled area of research.

—Fred Basolo

## Organic chemistry

Chemists during the past year made notable progress in developing methods for constructing organic molecules. The reactivity of molecular fragments known as free radicals was exploited in synthesis and was used to explain the action of several clinically important anticancer agents, reagents containing a wide range of less common elements were employed in making or breaking bonds to carbon, and reactions were discovered in which several rings of atoms were created in one step. Marine plants and animals yielded unusual, biologically active compounds with multiple nitrogen and oxygen-containing rings. Investigators reported on the chemical basis for the variation of host-parasite interactions with distance and on a biochemical switch in plants that turns photosynthetic pathways on or off. A variety of molecules were prepared that demonstrated unusual types of bonding.

**Synthetic methods and reaction intermediates.** Free radicals, such as the methyl radical $CH_3 \cdot$ formed by loss of a hydrogen atom from methane ($CH_4$), are short-lived, highly reactive, electrically neutral molecular fragments. Gilbert Stork and co-workers at Columbia University, New York City, found that radicals generated under mild conditions can be made to undergo efficient cyclization (ring

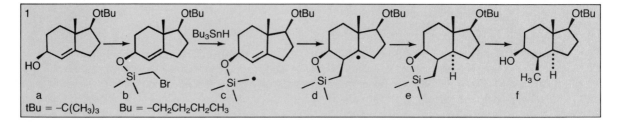

1

a
tBu = –C(CH₃)₃     Bu = –CH₂CH₂CH₂CH₃

b

c

d

e

f

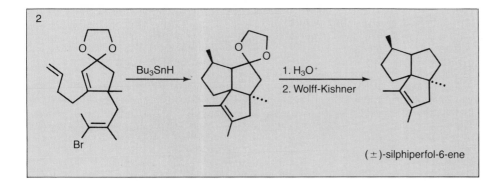

2

1. $H_3O^+$
2. Wolff-Kishner

Bu₃SnH

($\pm$)-silphiperfol-6-ene

formation) in a manner leading to complete control of geometry in the resultant products. With co-worker Michael Sofia, Stork devised a procedure involving generation of a radical (1c) by reaction of a tin hydride with a bromomethyl-silicon substituent (1b), cyclization (1c–1d), and replacement of silicon with hydrogen (1e–1f). In effect the elements of methane are added to a double bond adjacent to a carbon atom bearing an alcohol (OH) function in (1a). The new methyl group is precisely positioned next to the OH. Stork and co-workers Philip Sher and Hai-Lin Chen used a related procedure to synthesize the biologically important molecule prostaglandin $F_{2a}$.

Chemists Dennis P. Curran and Shen-Chun Kuo of the University of Pittsburgh, Penn., combined radical formation promoted by tin hydride with serial cyclization (repetitive ring formation in a single step) in a short synthesis of the tricyclic natural product silphiperfol-6-ene from a precursor with a single all-carbon ring (*see* 2). Chemists Ned A. Porter, David R. Magnin, Bruce T. Wright, Bert Fraser-Reid, and Ray Tsang of Duke University, Durham, N.C., used this procedure to prepare in good yields 10- to 18-membered rings and sugars containing attached multiple-ring systems.

Short-lived organic radicals are also of interest in testing theories of bonding and in understanding the mode of action of drugs. University of Chicago chemists Gerhard L. Closs and O. D. Redwine generated cyclopropen-3-yl (3) by gamma irradiation and studied it at 20–140 K (−423° to −207° F) using electron spin resonance (ESR) spectroscopy. Their work indicated that the free radical (3) is best described as an isoceles triangle with the hydrogen atom at the apex bent substantially out of the ring plane, in good agreement with theoretical calculations. Tetramethyleneethane diradical (4) prepared by Paul Dowd, Yi Hyon Paik, and Wonghil Chang of the University of Pittsburgh is of interest in examining the interaction of two remote radical centers in the same molecule. Employing ESR techniques at 4 K (−452° F; necessary to stabilize this diradical) Dowd found that the spins of the two unpaired

electrons of the diradical are not paired relative to each other but rather are parallel, indicating that the molecule is in a triplet rather than singlet state. This result conflicted with current theoretical predictions. Dowd and Paik also prepared the remarkably strained dimethylenebicyclo[1.1.1]pentanone (5) as a precursor to the dimethylenecyclobutadiene diradical (see *1986 Yearbook of Science and the Future* Year in Re-

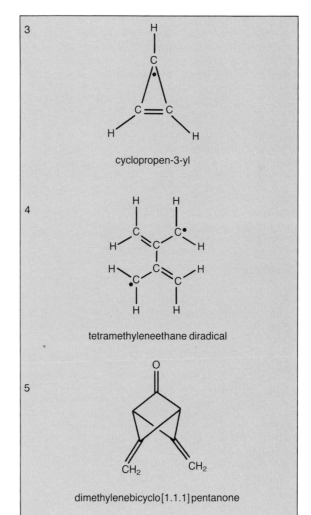

3

cyclopropen-3-yl

4

tetramethyleneethane diradical

5

dimethylenebicyclo[1.1.1]pentanone

view: CHEMISTRY: *Organic chemistry*). Compound (5) decomposes rapidly even at −30° C (−22° F)!

Anticancer drugs known as mitomycins from the microorganism *Streptomyces caespitosus* are themselves inactive and must be metabolically activated prior to reaction with the DNA of tumor cells. Clues about the nature of the activation were provided by Nicholas R. Bachur, Su-shu Pan, and Paul A. Andrews of the University of Maryland Cancer Center, Baltimore; Samuel J. Danishefsky and Melissa Egbertson of Yale University; Maria Thomasz and Roselyn Lippman of Hunter College, New York City; Koji Nakanishi and Gregory Verdine at Columbia University; and Harold Kohn and Nada Zein of the University of Houston, Texas. Biologic transfer of an electron to mitomycin C (6a; one-electron reduction) is thought to give semiquinone radical (6b), which loses methanol giving radical (6c), which in turn is susceptible to attack by the guanine nucleotide bases of DNA. The result is cross-linking of the DNA (6d). These conclusions were drawn following electrochemical studies of mitomycin C by the Baltimore group, chemical reductions of related compounds by the Yale and Houston teams, and studies involving DNA at Hunter and Columbia. Another anticancer antibiotic, fredericamycin A (see *1984 Yearbook of Science and the Future* Year in Review: CHEMISTRY: *Organic chemistry*), was also thought to require conversion to a free radical for biologic activity, according to Bruce D. Hilton and co-workers at the U.S. National Cancer Institute in Maryland.

**Natural product chemistry.** Egg masses of sea slugs (mollusks) seem immune to predation in spite of their brilliant red color and flowerlike shapes. Chemists in Hawaii and Japan isolated from the egg masses remarkable compounds consisting of ni-

trogen- and oxygen-containing rings within larger 28-membered lactone rings. The macrolides were termed ulapualide A and B (in Hawaiian *ula* means "red" and *pua* means "flower") by Jeffrey A. Roesener and Paul J. Scheuer of the University of Hawaii and kabiramide C (after Kabira Bay, Japan, where sample collection took place) by Nobuhiro Fusetani and co-workers of the University of Tokyo. The macrolides show marked antifungal and antitumor activity.

The dinoflagellate *Gymnodinium brevis* often makes up the red tide responsible for massive fish kills and poisoning in humans. Using X-ray crystallography, Yuzuru Shimizu, Hong-Nong Chou, Hideo Bando, Gregory van Duyne, and Jon C. Clardy of the University of Rhode Island and Cornell University, Ithaca, N.Y., characterized brevetoxin A, the most potent algal ichthyotoxin, as a ten-ringed polyether (for the characterization of the related brevetoxin B, see *1983 Yearbook of Science and the Future* Year in Review: CHEMISTRY: *Organic chemistry*).

Marine sponges are a rich source of novel metabolites having antitumor or antiyeast activity. In 1986 manzamine A, containing a complicated array of 5-, 6-, 8-, and 13-membered rings, was isolated from an Okinawan sponge of the genus *Haliclona* by Ryuichi Sakai and Tatsuo Higa of the University of the Ryukyus, Japan, and Charles W. Jefford and Gérald Bernardinelli of the University of Geneva. Calyculin A, a 28-carbon fatty acid linked to two amino acids, was identified in the Japanese sponge *Discodermia calyx* by Nobuhiro Fusetani and co-workers from the University of Tokyo and Yamanouchi Pharmaceutical Co., Japan. Jaspamide, a bromine-containing cyclic modified peptide, was isolated from a Fijian sponge of the genus *Jaspis* by Chris M. Ireland, D.

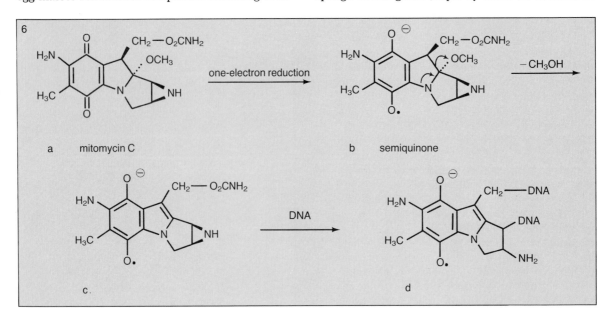

a mitomycin C      b semiquinone      c.      d

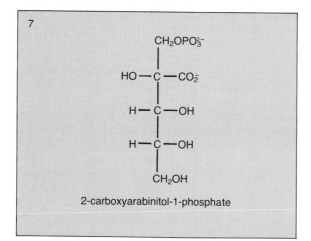

7

$$CH_2OPO_3^{2-}$$

$$HO - C - CO_2^-$$

$$H - C - OH$$

$$H - C - OH$$

$$CH_2OH$$

2-carboxyarabinitol-1-phosphate

John Faulkner, Jon C. Clardy, and co-workers from the University of Utah, the University of California at San Diego, Cornell University, and University Research Park, Salt Lake City.

A curious situation occurs in connection with infestation of *Sorghum* and other grasses by the obligate parasitic plant witchweed (*Striga asiatica*). The seeds of the parasite require a germination stimulant, yet once germinated they survive for less than two weeks in the absence of a host. University of Chicago chemists David G. Lynn and Mayland Chang together with biochemists David H. Netzly and Larry G. Butler of Purdue University, West Lafayette, Ind., identified the molecule hydroquinone from *Sorghum* as an unstable germination stimulant for *Striga*. *Striga* recognizes hydroquinone and commits itself to the host through germination only within the distance through which the labile compound can diffuse before undergoing oxidation to the biologically inactive benzoquinone.

In the absence of sunlight, a plant's photosynthetic pathway shuts down. A team of British and U.S. researchers identified a natural substance, termed a nocturnal inhibitor, that in effect "turns off" a major enzyme in plants with the arrival of darkness. S. Gutteridge, M. A. J. Parry, S. Burton, A. J. Keys, and A. Mudd at Rothamsted Experimental Station, Harpenden, England; J. Feeney at the U.K. National Institute for Medical Research; J. C. Servaites at the University of Dayton, Ohio; and J. Pierce at Du Pont in Wilmington, Del., identified 2-carboxy-D-arabinitol-1-phosphate (7) as the natural substance that inhibits the key carbon-dioxide-fixing enzyme ribulose-1,5-bisphosphate carboxylase in potato plants in the dark. Light decomposes this inhibitor, leaving the enzyme in its activated form primed for action.

The total synthesis of natural products continued to be one of the most active areas of organic chemistry during the year. Notable syntheses completed in 1986 include the 21-membered cyclic lipopeptide antiyeast antibiotic echinocandins by Natsuko Kurokawa and Yasufumi Ohfune of the Suntory Institute, Japan; the antitumor antibiotic cyanocycline by David A. Evans, Carl R. Illig, and John C. Saddler of Harvard University; the potent antihelminthic agent avermectin $B_{1a}$ by Stephen Hanessian and co-workers of the University of Montreal; the biologically active fungal metabolites cytochalasans G and H by Eric J. Thomas and co-workers from Oxford University; the complex monosaccharide hikosamine by Yale chemists Clarence Maring and Samuel J. Danishefsky; and the anticancer antibiotic fredericamycin A by T. Ross Kelly and co-workers of Boston College, Mass.

**Nonnatural product chemistry.** Aromaticity, special stability, and identity of ring carbon–carbon bond lengths in cyclic unsaturated compounds is seen only when the number of pi-electrons corresponds to the Hückel $4n + 2$ rule ($n$ is a small whole number). Manfred Regitz, Richard Mynoff, and Uwe-Josef Vogelbacher of the University of Kaiserslautern and Max Planck Institute in Mulheim, West Germany, succeeded in preparing a stable azacyclobutadiene (8) that with its four pi-electrons violates Hückel's rule and therefore lacks aromaticity. Analysis by nuclear magnetic resonance (NMR) spectroscopy shows that (8) exists as a rapidly interconverting mixture of two rectangular isomers each with distinct long single and short double bonds. The bulky substituents on the ring offer protection against self-coupling. Another non-Hückel fully conjugated ring system was prepared by Klaus Hafner and Volker Kühn of the Technische Hochschule, Darmstadt, West Germany. 9b-Methyl-9b*H*-benzo[*cd*]azulene (9), termed a [12]annulene because it has 12 pi-electrons, is stable only in solution, affording a polymer when concentrated even at −30° C (−22° F).

According to K. Peter C. Vollhardt and Rainer Diercks of the University of California at Berkeley, the instability of four-membered rings with four pi-electrons is responsible for the remarkable bond-fixed central cyclohexatriene ring of tris(benzocyclobutadieno)benzene (10b). This highly strained compound is prepared from the theoretically interesting hexaethynylbenzene (10a) in a cobalt-catalyzed multiple cyclization process. In the central ring of

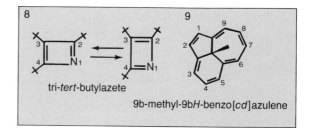

8

9

tri-*tert*-butylazete

9b-methyl-9b*H*-benzo[*cd*]azulene

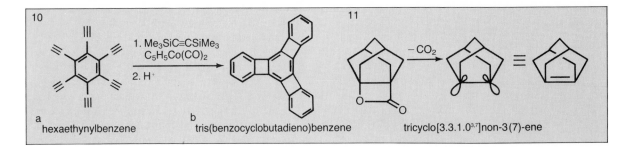

10

11

a hexaethynylbenzene   b tris(benzocyclobutadieno)benzene   tricyclo[3.3.1.0³·⁷]non-3(7)-ene

1. Me₃SiC≡CSiMe₃
   C₅H₅Co(CO)₂
2. H⁺

−CO₂

(10b) the C=C double bonds average 1.33–1.34 Å in length while the C—C single bonds average 1.49–1.50 Å (one angstrom, Å, equals $10^{-8}$ cm). The localized structure avoids cyclobutadiene character in the fused four-membered rings.

The synthesis of reactive small organic molecules continues to challenge chemists. William B. Farnham and Joseph C. Calabrese of Du Pont prepared the crystalline lithium salt of bis(pentafluorophenyl)-iodinanide, $Li^+(C_6F_5)_2I^-$ (a rare organic analogue of $I_3^-$), and an even more unusual fluoride-bridged structure, $C_6F_5I—F—IC_6F_5^-$. The precise nature of the bonding holding the latter ion together was not known. Weston T. Borden and co-workers from the University of Washington presented evidence for the low-temperature trapping of tricyclo[3.3.1.0³·⁷]-non-3(7)-ene (11), in which the C=C bond is pyramidalized (severely distorted from planarity).

Other novel compounds produced in the past year include formaldehyde O-methylide ($^-CH_2OCH_2^+$) by George A. Olah and co-workers from the University of Southern California; thioformaldehyde S-methylide ($^-CH_2SCH_2^+$) by Akira Hosomi, Yumiko Matsuyama, and Hideki Sakurai of Tohoku University, Japan; vinyl phosphine ($CH_2$=$CHPH_2$) by Marie-Claire Lasne, Jean-Louis Ripoll, an André Thuillier of the University of Caen, France; and selenoaldehydes, represented by the general structure $RCH$=$Se$, by Grant A. Krafft and Peter T. Meinke of Syracuse (N.Y.) University and also by Gordon W. Kirby and Andrew N. Trethewey of the University of Glasgow, Scotland. All of these compounds were prepared for the first time in solution. Other novel species, characterized for the first time in the gas phase, include hydroxyacetylene, $HC$≡$COH$, by Helmut Schwarz and co-workers of the Technical University of Berlin and 3-thioxo-1,2-propadien-1-one ($O$=$C$=$C$=$C$=$S$) by Hans Bock, Ralph Dammel, and Dieter Jaculi of the University of Frankfurt, West Germany.

—Eric Block

## Physical chemistry

In 1986 three physical chemists were honored with the Nobel Prize for Chemistry. Their field of study is chemical reaction dynamics, the investigation of the ways in which molecules come together and break apart to form new molecules. It is an exploration of the energies, structures, and reactivities of the reactant and product molecules and an attempt to discover in detail the mechanisms of reactions. Physical chemists also advanced their understanding of electron transfer reactions in proteins, an essential step in energy production and use in living things, and for the first time X-ray crystallographic data were used to predict fundamental physical properties of an atom.

**Chemical reaction dynamics.** Dudley R. Herschbach of Harvard University, Yuan T. Lee of the University of California at Berkeley, and John C. Polanyi of the University of Toronto shared the 1986 Nobel Prize for Chemistry for their work in chemical reaction dynamics. (*See* SCIENTISTS OF THE YEAR.) Herschbach and Lee developed the method of crossed molecular beams, and Polanyi developed the method of infrared chemiluminescence. Both techniques are aimed at helping chemists increase their understanding of reactions.

Chemical reactions take place in the gas state when two molecules, the reactants, collide to form a new molecule or molecules, the products. But not all molecular collisions result in products. The energy can be too high or too low, or the orientation can be wrong. By performing experiments in which reaction conditions are simplified—low concentrations of molecules in gaseous rather than liquid phase—and in which the energies of the reactants and the products are known, chemists can begin to understand the processes of chemical reactions in detail.

In their studies Herschbach and Lee used crossed molecular beams, whereby molecules are carried at high speeds in two jets of gas to a predetermined position where the jets intersect and the molecules collide. The energies, structures, and other variables of the reactant molecules are known in detail, and their concentration is so low that during the experiment the molecules from one beam can only experience one collision each with molecules from the other beam.

The new molecules that are formed and scattered by the collisions are analyzed with regard to their position, energy, and chemical makeup. The technique provides fundamental information applicable to chemical investigations of practical importance; for example, combustion studies directed to the more efficient use of fuel or studies of ozone-destroying reactions that take place in the atmosphere.

Herschbach pioneered the crossed-beam technique, applying it to reactions between alkali metal atoms and other molecules. Crossing beams of potassium atoms and methyl iodide, he found that the product, potassium iodide, formed only if the potassium struck the iodide at just the right angle. The experiment was the first to demonstrate the importance of molecular orientation in reactions. Herschbach also discovered the existence of intermediate reaction complexes, combinations of reacting atoms that survive for a brief, but chemically significant, time before decaying into stable products.

Lee joined Herschbach at Harvard in 1967, and together they set about extending the range of reactions that could be investigated with crossed beams. Lee is credited with making it possible to do experiments involving larger and more complex molecules. He also used lasers to excite molecules and atoms before they collide, a means of precisely controlling their energies. By 1987 his apparatus could detect as few as ten product molecules per cubic centimeter (0.06 cu in) and was being used to study the photodissociation, or break up by light, of polyatomic molecules.

Polanyi developed the technique of infrared chemiluminescence, essentially the measurement of excess energy given off by a molecule subsequent to a chemical reaction. The most striking spinoff of his work has been the development of chemical lasers. First demonstrated in 1965 by J. V. V. Kasper and George Pimentel at Berkeley, chemical lasers have been made that can produce two million watts of power, enough to attract the interest of scientists trying to ignite fusion reactions as well as those involved in new military weaponry.

The feeble infrared radiation given off by product molecules after reaction is measured spectroscopically and analyzed. This information provides researchers with the quantum (energy) states occupied by molecules, giving indirect evidence of the reaction system's potential energy. A description of the potential energies details the chemical behavior of a reaction. Polanyi's method was the first step toward modern laser-based methods for analyzing reactions.

The 1986 Nobel Prize for Physics, also of chemical interest, was given for scanning tunneling microscopy, a method that allows the viewing of atoms and bonds at or near the surface of solids. (*See* Year in Review: PHYSICS: *Condensed-matter physics*; SCIENTISTS OF THE YEAR.)

**Electron transfer.** In 1986 genetic engineering contributed toward understanding a fundamental question in physical chemistry: What are the controlling conditions that modulate the transfer of electrons during oxidation-reduction reactions essential to such biologic phenomena as sugar metabolism and photosynthesis? According to Brian M. Hoffman of Northwestern University, Evanston, Ill., electron transfer between proteins is extremely sensitive to the amino acids, or building blocks of proteins, involved. Along with Nong Liang, Pui Shing Ho, Emanuel Margoliash, and Chae Hee Kang, he investigated the electron transfer from zinc protoporphyrin (ZnP) in a modified enzyme, cytochrome *c* peroxidase, to the ferriheme group [Fe(III)P] of its substrate, cytochrome *c* (a common protein in biologic systems that catalyzes electron transfer).

In this experimental system there is a forward, light-induced electron transfer reaction and a reverse, thermal reaction. The first, by way of a triplet state ($^3$ZnP), reduces the ferriheme in cytochrome *c*:

$$\text{ZnP, Fe(III)P} \rightarrow {}^3\text{ZnP, Fe(III)P} \rightarrow \text{ZnP}^+\text{, Fe(II)P.}$$

The second, a thermal electron transfer step, follows:

$$\text{ZnP}^+\text{, Fe(II)P} \rightarrow \text{ZnP, Fe(III)P.}$$

Hoffman and his colleagues used spectroscopic methods to measure electron transfer reaction rates and found a huge difference between the rate involving yeast enzyme and yeast substrate (triplet, 266/second; thermal, 11,000/second) and that involving yeast enzyme and tuna substrate (triplet, 25/second; thermal, 12/second). Such a remarkably large difference between similar proteins led Hoffman to further investigations. He found that computer studies had suggested that an amino acid, phenylalanine,

*New X-ray microanalyzer developed by researchers at two U.S. national laboratories combines the powers of several existing instruments to detect minute concentrations of elements in material samples.*

in the cytochrome *c* was involved in the electron transfer process. As it happened, biochemists at the University of British Columbia had been engaged in site-directed mutagenesis of cytochrome *c*. A. Grant Mauk, Michael Smith, and Gary J. Pielak produced mutants of the protein in which phenylalanine was replaced with other amino acids: tyrosine, glycine, and serine.

Redoing his experiments with the new proteins, Hoffman found that glycine disrupted the triplet transfer entirely. Triplet rates for serine and tyrosine were similar to those of the native phenylalanine. The big difference appeared in the thermal electron transfer reactions. Tyrosine was similar to native phenylalanine, while serine was on the order of 10,-000 times slower.

Two explanations were offered for the dramatic difference. The different amino acids may dramatically change the enzyme-substrate relationships. Alternatively, since both tyrosine and phenylalanine have aromatic ring components, this region of electron density may have a direct effect on the electron transfer reaction. The electron transfer reaction is exquisitely sensitive to its protein environment. In any case, the ability of genetic engineers to produce subtly different systems for experiments offers physical chemists a tool for observing and understanding important chemical reactions.

Other cytochrome *c* electron transfer studies showed that the reaction is not always reversible. Rolf Bechtold, Stephen S. Isied, and colleagues at Rutgers University, New Brunswick, N.J., found that in experiments with a modified version of the protein containing ruthenium, the rate of transfer in one direction was at least 10,000 times that of the reverse reaction. The difference may be caused by a change in the protein's conformation following transfer.

**X-ray crystallography.** X-rays have long been used to probe the structure of crystals. The rays are passed through a test crystal, and the resultant scatter pattern allows the calculation of relative positions of atoms in the crystal. During the past year, for the first time, X-ray data were used to generate quantum mechanically meaningful wave functions—mathematical descriptions that correspond to allowed energy states—for individual atoms. Scientists calculated wave functions from crystallographic studies of beryllium and used these to calculate such physical properties as electron-nucleus attraction energy, electron kinetic energy, and average electron distance from the nucleus. This achievement involved the efforts of several scientists.

First, Louis J. Massa of Hunter College, New York City, adapted a method of mapping wave functions and mathematical expressions for electron density so they could be applied to X-ray crystallographic data. He put two conditions on the resulting mathematical

Samuel J. La Placa,
IBM Thomas J. Watson Research Center, Yorktown Heights, N.Y.

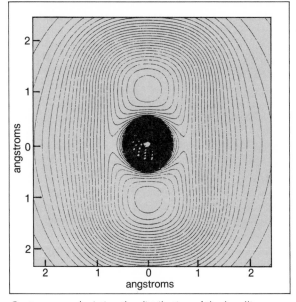

*Contour map depicting the distribution of the beryllium atom's two valance electrons around the nucleus was made from wave functions derived for the first time from X-ray crystallographic data.*

expression—one ensured that the electron density function would map over a permitted wave function, while the other allowed only the right number of electrons.

Samuel J. La Placa of IBM's research center in Yorktown Heights, N.Y., a crystallographer who collaborated with Massa, decided that the best X-ray data would come from beryllium. He needed unusually accurate absolute intensities for scattered X-rays and was able to obtain this data from Finn K. Larsen of Denmark's Århus University and Niels K. Hansen of the Hahn-Meitner Institute for Nuclear Research in West Berlin. La Placa also arranged for scientists at IBM to write the computer programs needed to manage both Massa's equations and the X-ray data.

The final step comprised the calculations, which were done by another of Massa's collaborators, Carol Frishberg of Ramapo College, Mahwah, N.J. Her results from X-ray–derived wave functions agreed well with those from quantum mechanical calculations.

The success of the researchers promises that X-ray crystallographic data for such substances as silicon and gallium arsenide—both important to the electronics industry—may someday be used to predict their physical properties.

—Peter J. Andrews

## Applied chemistry

During the past year research in applied chemistry led to developments in nitrogen fixation, solar energy, a porphin isomer, new cements, mussel glue, organic magnets, glass, and diamond films.

**Nitrogen fixation.** Nitrogen is an important constituent of all plant and animal protein as well as of fertilizers, explosives, and a host of industrial products. Although life literally exists in a sea of this inactive gaseous element, which constitutes about 78% by volume of the Earth's atmosphere, the cells of most living systems cannot assimilate nitrogen from the air for use in synthesizing proteins. Notable exceptions include certain bacteria that live in the root nodules of peas, beans, clover, alfalfa, and other legumes, which have long been cultivated to restore depleted nitrogen to the soil—a technique known as rotation of crops.

The conversion of atmospheric nitrogen into nitrogen compounds that can be used by plants, a process called nitrogen fixation, was first accomplished on an industrial scale in 1909 by the German chemist Fritz Haber. This direct combination of nitrogen ($N_2$) and hydrogen ($H_2$) to form ammonia ($NH_3$), however, requires high temperatures and pressures, and through the years scientists have attempted to fix atmospheric nitrogen under less extreme conditions. In 1939, for example, nitrogen and hydrogen were combined to yield ammonia at room temperature and atmospheric pressure using the known catalytic effects of corona discharge in the research laboratories of Westinghouse Electric Corp. (For more recent examples, see *1979* and *1987 Yearbook of Science and the Future* Year in Review: CHEMISTRY: *Applied chemistry.*)

During the past year Ken-ichi Aika of the Tokyo Institute of Technology, Yokohama, Japan, synthesized ammonia from its elemental constituents nitrogen and hydrogen at room temperature (31° C or 88° F) and atmospheric pressure using a solid heterogeneous catalyst (potassium and ruthenium on active carbon) with a reaction time of two weeks. Although the rate of ammonia generation was very low (0.000187 g per day and per gram of catalyst) compared with, for example, that of ammonia production by the well-studied microbial nitrogenase (enzyme) catalysis (0.00425 g per minute and per gram of protein—10,000 times the rate of the metallic catalyst), the Japanese researcher's discovery represents a key step in the artificial fixation of nitrogen (one gram is about 0.035 oz).

In a related development Robert L. Robson, John R. Postgate, and co-workers at the University of Sussex, England, and the Chemistry and Biology Research Institute, Agriculture Canada, found that the nitrogen-fixing bacterium *Azotobacter chromococcum* contains genes that produce two different forms of its nitrogen-reducing enzyme, nitrogenase. One is the familiar form that contains the metal molybdenum, whereas the second one, which substitutes vanadium

Agricultural Research Service, USDA

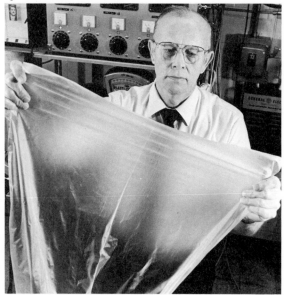

*USDA chemist Felix Otey displays sheets of plastic film synthesized from a blend of corn-derived starch and petrochemicals. Starch-plastic films could find use as biodegradable mulches, food wrap, and biomedical filters.*

for molybdenum, appears when no molybdenum is present in the bacteria's environment. Like the more familiar form of nitrogenase, the vanadium-containing enzyme contains two subunits, the larger of which contains a stoichiometric amount of the metal ion. Since both metals have similar oxidation-reduction properties and since vanadium is more common than molybdenum in some soils, the substitute system is in accord with biochemical concepts.

In an attempt to better understand the nitrogen-fixing *Rhizobium* bacteria in the nodules of leguminous plants, Sharon Long of Stanford University's department of biologic sciences found that the signal from the plant that causes the bacteria to activate the pertinent genes is luteolin, a flavone belonging to the larger family of flavonoids. This discovery marked the first time that a plant flavonoid was shown to be involved in gene regulation. Luteolin, first synthesized in the 1890s, is related to plant dyes used by primitive people. John Frost of Stanford's chemistry department subjected an aqueous organic extract of alfalfa seeds to high-pressure liquid chromatography to isolate the luteolin (identified by mass spectroscopy) from a complex mixture of plant metabolites. What was unusual and different about the chemical analysis was the hooking up of DNA chunks and the creation of a highly sensitive test at the molecular level, which brought together methods of chemistry and biology. According to Frost, "It was a case of biology's providing the essential clue for an otherwise routine chemical procedure." According

337

to Long, "Now that we have begun to understand the process [of nodulation], we can begin to manipulate it." She suggested that microorganisms producing specific chemical compounds could be created with recombinant DNA techniques, using DNA segments such as those characterized by her group. In her words, "Our discovery shows a way to control these microorganisms so they can deliver a desired chemical only to a desired plant. We can thus minimize the need for nitrogen fertilizers and pesticides."

**Solar energy.** Chemists Ruben Maidan and Itamar Willner of the Hebrew University of Jerusalem reduced carbon dioxide ($CO_2$) to methane ($CH_4$) in aqueous solution using visible light, a reaction that may provide a means for storing solar energy in the form of a combustible product. When the system—triethanolamine, as electron donor, in alkaline solution with tris(bipyrazine)ruthenium(II), or $Ru(bpz)_3^{2+}$, as sensitizer, and a ruthenium colloid as catalyst—was illuminated under a gaseous $CO_2$ atmosphere, $CH_4$ was produced with a quantum yield of 0.0025%. The photocatalytic system generates $Ru(bpz)_3^+$, a powerful reducing agent. According to the Israeli researchers, $CH_4$ is produced by electron transfer from this reducing agent to colloid-associated $CO_2$, followed by protonation (addition of hydrogen atoms).

Converting solar energy into usable chemical energy is easy for plants because of their chlorophyll. Chemists Pedatsur Neta of the U.S. National Bureau of Standards, Gaithersburg, Md., and Anthony Harriman of the Royal Institution of Great Britain, London, tried to harness the same mechanism that plants use to split the water molecule into its components and produce hydrogen, a cheap nonpolluting fuel. (For previous attempts to decompose water see *1979, 1982, 1983,* and *1984 Yearbook of Science and the Future* Year in Review: CHEMISTRY: *Applied chemistry.*) The researchers from the U.S. and the U.K. identified new catalysts that allowed them to split water using zinc porphyrin, whose structure is similar to that of chlorophyll. When sunlight is absorbed by zinc porphyrin, a complex chain of reactions begins. The researchers studied the fast reactions (one-millionth of a second) occurring between the time the light is absorbed and the time water is split.

The zinc porphyrin liberates some of the absorbed energy by donating an electron to an accepting molecule, which in turn donates the extra electron to a water molecule to yield hydrogen, a reaction that works best with a platinum catalyst. Meanwhile, because the zinc porphyrin has lost an electron, it has become positively charged. To return to its neutral state, it must absorb an electron from the water molecule, a reaction requiring a ruthenium dioxide ($RuO_2$) catalyst. According to Neta, "The problem is that each molecule of porphyrin can accept one electron, but in order for the water to make oxygen, it has to give up four electrons, so the catalyst serves as a storage place for electrons." The zinc porphyrin reacts with the catalyst, which accumulates and then transfers the charges from the water molecule to make oxygen.

In the future Neta and Harriman intend to add catalysts to the water and porphyrin and leave them outside in a glass container to absorb sunlight. The completed reactions would produce hydrogen fuel on the one hand and oxygen on the other. The two gases could then be recombined in a continuous cycle to form water and liberate energy with little or no pollution. Neta said, "Theoretically, everything we put in just helps the Sun act on the water."

**Porphin isomer.** Emanuel Vogel, director of the Institute of Organic Chemistry, Cologne University, West Germany, and co-workers Matthias Köcher, Johann Lex, and Hans Schmickler refluxed 5,5'-diformyl-2,2'-bipyrrole with a slurry of a low-valent titanium reagent in tetrahydrofuran for four hours to synthesize a novel porphyrinlike compound, which was separated by chromatography on silica gel. An isomer of porphin (the parent compound of the porphyrins), the new air-stable compound, which was christened porphycene (a hybrid between a porphyrin and an acene), has an unusual molecular structure and may be the forerunner of a new series of porphynoid species. Because of the involvement of porphyrins in many essential biologic processes, including photosynthesis and the transport of oxygen in the blood, porphycene should be of interest in various areas of the life sciences. Since it is deeply colored, fluoresces, and has an unusual absorption spectrum, it could open the way to novel dyes and pigments. Such dyes might have application as biologic markers or as sensitizers in the photodynamic treatment of cancer. Although the yield in the synthesis of porphycene was low, 4%, Vogel was confident that it could be improved.

**New cements.** Compared with metals and plastics, cement is inexpensive. Making dry cement requires less energy than making plastics or metals, and it uses inexpensive raw materials—chalk and clay. Set cement is a noncombustible, crush-resistant solid; cement structures made by the Romans still stand after more than 2,000 years. Yet ordinary cement breaks when bent and cracks when something is dropped on it.

Scientists from the United Kingdom developed improved cements that do not possess these disadvantages. J. D. Birchall and co-workers at Imperial Chemical Industries (ICI), Runcorn, England, found that conventional cement contains numerous holes about a millimeter (four-hundredths of an inch) long. These defects are responsible for cement's lack of resilience, the consequence being that cement bridges and beams must be reinforced with steel. Abalone shells, like cement, are made of chalk but are stiffer than aluminum, as tough as Plexiglas, and ten times more resilient than cement because their crystals are orderly and tightly packed. The ICI researchers copied the structure of abalone shell crystals by kneading unhardened cement to remove air bubbles and adding a water-soluble organic polymer that causes the cement particles to slide easily over one another and thus pack more closely. As the polymer dries, it pulls the grains together even more.

Their so-called macro-defect-free (MDF) cement has holes no longer than a hundredth of a millimeter. Because it is 30 times as resilient as ordinary cement, a spring made of it can tolerate 135 kg (300 lb) of tension. It is so tough that a block of it can be turned on a lathe into a tube without breaking. When reinforced with nylon fibers, it can withstand impacts 1,000 times greater than can ordinary cement.

MDF cement may have a multitude of uses. Its strength, stiffness, and good acoustic damping make it ideal for turntables, loudspeaker cabinets, and other high-fidelity audio components. Load-bearing floors, ceilings, and partitions of MDF cement would be strong and soundproof. Pipes and containers would be resistant to acids, alkalis, and solvents and would not be harmed by freezing or thawing. MDF cement, however, fails to hold up well outdoors or in water; either the polymer leaches out, or the solid softens.

In a related development Tom Gardiner and co-workers at Ulster Polytechnic, Belfast, Northern Ireland, reinforced cement with a fabric woven of polypropylene, which impedes the growth of cracks, increases flexibility, and helps to hold the solid together. Asbestos fibers work well, but asbestos is a health hazard; glass fibers also work but rapidly corrode in the alkaline environment of set cement. Polypropylene-reinforced cement (PRC) is free from these disadvantages and is weather resistant.

Gardiner's group coated successive layers of the woven polymer with millimeter-thick layers of cement. In production, fabric is easier to handle than individual fibers; by changing the number of layers or the tightness of the polymer weave, PRC can be tailored to specific applications. Working with several industries, including William Halley & Sons, a textile firm in Dundee, Scotland, the Belfast researchers made PRC flagstones that withstand a three-ton load and are less than half as thick and a third as heavy as natural flagstone. They also built a house entirely of PRC and steel bolts.

**Mussel glue.** Marine mussels secrete a glue that is strong, hardens quickly, and sticks underwater, allowing them to attach themselves to rocks in the surf. No commerical glue works well in wet, saline environments. Until recently mussel glue had to be obtained by a laborious process that yielded one

Courtesy, J. Herbert Waite, University of Delaware, Lewes; photo, Greg Kriss

*Mussels cling tenaciously to underwater objects by means of byssus threads tipped with a strong, waterproof adhesive protein. Synthetic versions of the protein were being developed for medical, dental, and industrial uses.*

gram from 3,000 mussels at a price of $90,000 per gram. Marine biologist J. Herbert Waite, formerly of the University of Connecticut at Farmington and currently of the University of Delaware at Newark, and colleagues devoted more than a decade to gathering the glue in these small amounts from mussels in research supported in part by the U.S. Office of Naval Research and the National Institute of Dental Research. They found the substance to be a polyphenolic protein having a sequence of ten amino acids that repeats 75 times and containing catechol oxidase, which serves as a hardening agent. Genex, a biotechnology firm in Gaithersburg, Md., succeeded in producing an analogue of the precursor to the polyphenolic protein. In 1987 Waite was working on the hydroxylation of the protein produced by Genex, believed to be a critical step in the formation of the glue. Genex executive research scientist David Anderson and colleagues isolated and created a gene of CDNA (copy DNA obtained from RNA isolated from the mussel phenol gland) responsible for producing the predominant decapeptide sequence of the protein glue. Inserted into yeast or bacteria, the gene would then direct the manufacture of the glue in large quantities.

Waite, colleague Christine Benedict, and her husband, an engineer, formed Bio-Polymers, Inc., to make and market substances based on the glue. Because more than three million mussels would be needed to amass about 0.9 kg (two pounds) of the glue, the company planned to make it by solid-phase peptide synthesis for medical and dental applications. Bio-Polymers expected the glue to be available for topical use in dentistry within two years. For the large amounts needed for industrial use, Bio-Polymers would use recombinant DNA techniques.

The mussel glue adheres to almost any kind of surface. In dentistry it could serve as a sealant, for filling cavities, and as an adhesive for bonding teeth. In periodontal surgery it could form a strong bond between gums and teeth. In surgery it could coat sutured tissues to prevent infection and join small broken bones or tendons. The U.S. Navy was interested in the glue for making underwater repairs and coating hulls of ships to prevent corrosion and fouling by marine growth. Bio-Polymers planned to have an ophthalmic glue for cornea and retina repairs ready for FDA testing sometime in 1987.

**Toward an organic magnet.** Creation of a magnet made of organic compounds is a goal that has long eluded chemists. Joel Miller of Du Pont, Wilmington, Del., and William Reiff of Northeastern University, Boston, together with physicist Arthur Epstein of Ohio State University at Columbus took a major step in this direction by preparing for the first time a molecular, organic-like ferromagnetic compound. Ferromagnetism, the ordinary type of magnetism operating in permanent magnets, requires that the individual magnetic moments of a large number of atoms align throughout the solid in parallel, thus creating a large-scale magnetic moment. Ferromagnetism is normally associated with such inorganic solids as iron metal, in part because the atoms of these materials are bonded together very tightly. The new compound, $[Fe(C_5(CH_3)_5)_2]^+[TCNE]^-$, in which the cation (positive ion) is a derivative of ferrocene and the anion (negative ion) is tetracyanoethylene,

is formed of linear chains of alternating cations and anions, with no bonding between the ions. Its solubility and structure make it more like an organic compound than an inorganic solid, and it shows saturation magnetization comparable to that of metallic iron. Miller acknowledged that its practical applications were far in the future, but he stated that it represents brand new chemistry and could lead to the preparation of totally organic ferromagnets.

**Glass.** Kathleen A. Cerqua and Stephen D. Jacobs of the University of Rochester's Laboratory for Laser Energetics developed a method for strengthening the slab of phosphate glass that forms the heart of many lasers so that the instruments can be used at much higher (up to 600%) power or can be fired at faster repetition rates. The process uses ion exchange to put a tough "skin" on phosphate laser glass, making it more resistant to cracking and fracture.

The researchers immersed glass samples for several days in a bath of molten salt rich in sodium and potassium. Lithium atoms normally present in the glass diffused out of the surface and were replaced with the larger sodium and potassium atoms, which had to squeeze into the small "holes" left by the lithium. The exchange builds a compressive stress in a paper-thin outside layer, which strengthens the glass. The process is relatively cheap, and commercial solid-state lasers need not be modified to use the strengthened glass. Such lasers were becoming increasingly popular for industrial robots, surgery, and computer microchip and space applications.

Terry A. Michalske and co-workers at the Ceramics Development Division of Sandia National Laboratories, Albuquerque, N.M., won an award for outstanding scientific accomplishment in metallurgy and ceramics from the U.S. Department of Energy for research that could lead to more reliable glass products. By identifying the chemical reactions in-

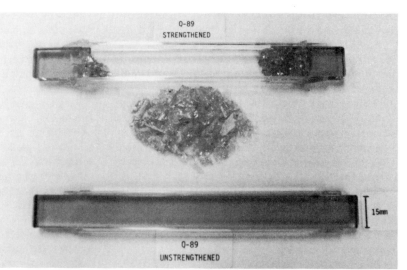

*Slab of phosphate laser glass that was strengthened with a new ion-exchange process developed at the University of Rochester (top) is compared with an unstrengthened slab (bottom) after both samples were subjected to tests in which a flash lamp pumped energy into the slabs. The disintegration of the strengthened glass into fine particles is indicative of the high level of energy it had absorbed before fracturing. By contrast, fracture of the unstrengthened slab, which occurred at a comparatively low pump energy, resulted in a single, nearly invisible crack running the length of the slab.*

Materials Research Laboratory, The Pennsylvania State University, University Park; photos, Teresa Badzian

*Small individual diamond crystals (far left) and continuous polycrystalline diamond film (left), obtained by a microwave plasma chemical-vapor deposition technique at Pennsylvania State University, are revealed in scanning electron micrographs.*

volved in cracking glass, they were discovering ways to predict the occurrence of cracks in glass or ceramics when exposed to various stresses, humidity, and chemicals, ways to treat the cracks, and ways to prevent their growth. Such predictions could help designers improve optical fibers, insulators for high-performance batteries, solar collector covers, underwater windows, and numerous other glass or ceramic products. Better understanding of crack growth should lead to ways to treat glasses with coatings, possibly polymers, that retard or stop crack growth or heal developing cracks.

To understand the silicon-oxygen-silicon bonds that comprise glass the Sandia scientists constructed model compounds made of silicon and oxygen atoms, built distortions into their models, and measured by infrared spectroscopy how these distortions affect surface reactivity. They found that cracks begin to form when water molecules enter the tiny preexisting imperfections present on most glass surfaces. The reaction that occurs between water molecules and the silicon and oxygen atoms ruptures the Si—O—Si bonds. If the moisture level is not reduced sufficiently, these bonds continue to break, and the speed at which breaking proceeds determines how long a material will last. The reaction occurs because of a water molecule's ability to donate both electrons and protons to sites on a neighboring surface, and other molecules with this property, *e.g.*, ammonia, hydrazine, and formamide, attack glass in the same way. Michalske expected that the first application of his work would be in the field of optical fibers.

Chemists at Ensign-Bickford Industries, Simsbury, Conn., who were developing a strong polymer coating for optical fibers found that the coating could be modified to strengthen glass. According to Bolesh Skutnik, research manager of the new product development department, "We can, by design, cre-ate stronger glass material that doesn't corrode in moisture, so there's less chance it will crack. The polymer somehow bonds to the glass, maybe in the same areas that water wants to, making it harder for water to get in."

**Diamond film.** Although synthetic diamonds have been available since the 1950s, creating the hardness, chemical inertness, and thermal conductivity of real diamond in a thin film has eluded scientists until recently. Russell Messier, Rustum Roy, and Karl Spear of Pennsylvania State University claimed to have created a diamond film with a deposition technique in which methane and hydrogen are passed through a plasma-generating zone of microwave radiation that decomposes the gas mixture into atomic carbon and hydrogen. Atomic carbon is then deposited onto a silicon substrate in the diamond's tetrahedral configuration.

The researchers thought that it was probably the atomic hydrogen that made it possible to make true diamond film rather than only a diamondlike one, which had been obtained by previous workers. The atomic hydrogen may alter the film surface such that the carbon never takes on the structure of graphite. The film is completely crystalline, unlike the diamondlike films made by others, which were amorphous or microcrystalline and had components of graphitic bonding. Although a few other scientists remained skeptical, Messier claimed that "electron diffraction has definitely shown that we have diamond. It's beyond any doubt." The diamond film should find electronic and industrial applications, including faster semiconductors and stronger optical fibers. (For additional information on diamond films, *see* Year in Review: MATERIALS SCIENCES: *Ceramics.*)

—George B. Kauffman

*See also* Feature Articles: CHEMISTRY IN THE TOY STORE; FOR FLAVOR, A DASH OF CHEMISTRY.

# Defense research

In the annals of U.S. defense research, 1986 will be remembered as the year in which the nation's aircraft and spacecraft of the 21st century began taking shape. The Department of Defense and the National Aeronautics and Space Administration (NASA) joined forces to develop and build the National Aerospace Plane (NASP), a flying machine of surpassing promise in air and space.

A NASP demonstrator prototype, designated the X-30 and expected to be ready for flight-testing by the mid-1990s, was envisioned as the forerunner of a family of aerospace planes that would be used for a variety of military and civil purposes. The decision to get the program under way, after three years of considering concepts, was based on the judgment that development of its requisite technologies either had finally taken place or was reassuringly near at hand.

This first U.S. step toward a fleet of manned machines for mastering space in the next century caused considerable stir in the aerospace community. For example, Lieut. Gen. William E. Thurman, who in 1986 took charge of the Air Force's Aeronautical Systems Division (ASD) at Wright-Patterson Air Force Base in Ohio, the seat of the NASP program, declared: "We are on the threshold of something marvelous in aviation. The era of the starfighter is upon us—and I'm not talking about technologies of the year 2000; I'm talking about technologies that are with us right now."

Those technologies pervaded the Air Force's Project Forecast II report of 1986. The culmination of an eight-month, Air Force-wide study that generated more than 2,000 "technological possibilities," the Forecast II report identified 70 advanced technologies and systems concepts as having the potential, if given their due, to "revolutionize the way the Air Force carries out its mission in the twenty-first century, guaranteeing continued technological supremacy over any potential adversary."

The aerospace plane received star billing in Forecast II. It was regarded as the eventual repository of a host of the choice technologies, including those of supersonic-combustion ramjets (scramjets), artificial intelligence (AI), microwave millimeter-wave monolithic integrated circuits (MIMIC), optical sensory and computational systems, advanced materials for airframes and engines, and superenergetic fuels for propulsion.

As envisioned the U.S. aerospace plane would be able to take off from and land on ordinary runways. It would be capable of flight in two modes—single-stage into low-Earth orbit and hypersonic (6,500 to 13,000 km/h [4,000 to 8,000 mph]) cruising at altitudes between 30,000 and 105,000 m (100,000 and 350,000 ft). Such capability was also the hallmark of Britain's HOTOL (horizontal takeoff and landing) aerospace plane concept, devised by British Aerospace for possible adoption by the European Space Agency (ESA) for flight beyond the atmosphere in the next century.

West Germany was also in the running to build a combination vehicle for such flight. In 1986 it proposed to the ESA the Messerschmitt-Bölkow-Blohm (MBB) concept for the Sänger space shuttle, which would vault into orbit after having been ferried to an altitude of about 30,000 m atop a much larger aircraft, one to be powered by air-breathing engines and capable of speed about six times that of sound (Mach 6). Both the mother ship and the rocket-powered shuttle craft would land on runways. France, too, had an entry in ESA's spaceflight sweepstakes— Aérospatiale's Hermes space shuttle. With no sig-

*Model of an airplane designed to cruise at hypersonic speeds (6,500 to 13,000 kilometers [4,000 to 8,000 miles] per hour) is tested in a wind tunnel at NASA's Langley Research Center in Virginia. Such a plane also would be able to accelerate into low-Earth orbit.*

Langley Research Center/NASA

*Cray 2 supercomputer, which can perform 250 million computations per second, is part of the Numerical Aerodynamic Simulator. This system will be used to solve complex equations that predict the pattern of airflow around proposed aircraft designs. In the foreground are plexiglass containers that hold the fluorocarbon liquid used for cooling the machine.*

nificant propulsion of its own, the rocket-boosted, delta-winged Hermes would emulate the U.S. space shuttle in gliding to a landing. France was proposing it for launching by ESA's next-generation Ariane 5 rockets in the mid-1990s.

Currently the European concepts had little or no military flavor, whereas the U.S. NASP program most definitely did. Even though NASP held high promise for nonmilitary space and transatmospheric transportation, NASA was committed to providing only about one-fifth of its funding. The lion's share was to be spread among the Defense Advanced Research Projects Agency (DARPA), the Air Force, the Navy, and the Strategic Defense Initiative Organization (SDIO), which was conducting the Department of Defense's research on systems for possible space-oriented defense against ballistic missiles.

DARPA was the leading agency in the NASP program's first phase, which was expected to cost about $600 million and to be completed in mid-1989. During this time, the aerospace plane would be designed, its propulsion modules and key technologies would be developed and tested, and all its technologies would be brought to maturity and marshaled for integration. The second phase, to be led by the Air Force and projected to cost about $3 billion, would bring the X-30 into being as the latest of an illustrious line of X-series experimental aircraft, currently exemplified by the forward-swept-wing X-29 undergoing test flights at Edwards Air Force Base in California.

The X-30, said the Air Force, "will concentrate on the demonstration of technologies for hypersonic cruise and acceleration into low-Earth orbit, and will be sized to accomplish that research at minimum cost." If the test craft performs successfully, the operational aerospace planes will take different forms depending on the particular mission. Large versions could take outsized satellites into space or could even perform the functions of such satellites and become,

for instance, platforms for the directed-energy and kinetic-energy weapons under development in the Strategic Defense Initiative (SDI) program. Smaller variants of aerospace planes could be used for servicing satellites and for ferrying people and supplies to the space station that NASA hoped to have assembled in orbit in the mid-1990s. In 1986 the Department of Defense indicated for the first time that it had some military purposes in mind for that space station.

The Department of Defense had many such purposes in mind for the aerospace plane. In one Air Force scenario the aircraft/spacecraft would climb into a "partial orbit," attack an enemy's space assets (such as reconnaissance satellites and antisatellite spacecraft), reenter the atmosphere to attack a target on land, and then climb back higher in the atmosphere and settle into partial orbit to return home. The aerospace plane "offers strategic force survivability," said Gen. Lawrence A. Skantze, commander of Air Force Systems Command and the leader of Project Forecast II. "A fleet could sit alert like B-52s. . . . We're talking about the speed and response of an ICBM and the flexibility and reliability of a bomber, packaged together in a plane that can scramble, get into orbit, and *change* orbit so [that] the Soviets can't get a reading accurate enough to shoot at it."

The aerospace plane concept was first explored in the early 1960s but was abandoned because some of its key technologies were too immature and its purpose, as perceived at the dawning of the space age, was considered problematic. The concept that now serves as the blueprint for the NASP program was formulated by DARPA, NASA, Air Force Systems Command, and assorted aerospace contractors from 1982 through 1985. In April 1986 NASP competitive airframe design contracts were awarded to Boeing, General Dynamics, Lockheed, McDonnell Douglas, and Rockwell International; propulsion design contracts were given to General Electric and Pratt & Whitney.

NASP program participants concluded that their most difficult task would be to develop the propulsion system and integrate it with the airframe. They referred to the aerospace plane as a "flying engine" because its airframe would be organic to its propulsion. For efficient hypersonic flight, it would have to be configured as a supremely steamlined, totally integrated, aerodynamic-cum-propulsion system that used the airframe to shape airflows into and out of its internally mounted multiple engines, as well as around itself, in an extraordinarily smooth and efficient manner. As James A. Tegnelia, DARPA's deputy director, described the X-30 concept: "The fuselage forebody is an integral part of the engine inlets and the fuselage afterbody is an integral part of the engine nozzles."

The NASP program was justified in great measure by the success of DARPA's experimentation with hydrogen-fueled scramjets—in a project called "Copper Canyon"—and of NASA's work on such engines and on various aerospace plane concepts. NASA had begun looking forward to a space transportation system that would succeed the one now pegged to the space shuttles. The shuttles were expected to have outlived their usefulness in the mid-1990s, and their longevity, utility, and cost-effectiveness were called into question much more critically in the aftermath of the explosion of the space shuttle *Challenger* on Jan. 28, 1986.

The aerospace plane was expected to derive most of its velocity—up to Mach 25 at the point of "orbital insertion"—from hydrogen-fueled scramjets. They could not provide power for rollout and takeoff from a standing start, however, because they needed an intense intake—or ram—of ambient air for oxy-genation and ignition. Thus, the aerospace plane's powerplants were expected to be hybrids, combining scramjets with rockets for takeoff and with subsonic-combustion ramjets for slowest speeds, such as those on approaches and landings. A major challenge for the NASP program was to regulate the supersonic flow of compressed air through the scramjets' combustion chambers in such a way as to prevent shock waves and to keep the engine-ignition process stable and efficient.

Extremely energetic fuels may be in the offing for aerospace-plane propulsion. The Forecast II report noted that "U.S. technology may be able to create stable, high-energy chemical propellants such as tetrahydrogen (to) provide an order-of-magnitude improvement in operational performance of space systems over that provided by conventional fuels." The report also cited the potential of antiproton (antimatter) propulsion, in which negatively charged hydrogen particles called antiprotons and positively charged hydrogen protons would annihilate one another in mixture, thus producing enormous propulsive energy.

In hypersonic flights the aerospace plane would have to withstand temperatures up to 3,300° C (6,000° F) on its airframe, most particularly on leading edges. For that reason, recent breakthroughs in research on lightweight, highly ductile, high-strength materials of great resistance to heat were crucial to the decision to proceed with the NASP program. New processes were devised in rapid-solidification-rate (RSR) powder metallurgy for producing various alloys of probable applicability to the aerospace plane. Superstrong "intermetals," such as titanium aluminide, were also being developed. In store, too, were carbon/carbon materials (those having a carbon matrix that is reinforced with carbon yarn or "fab-

*Trident II intercontinental ballistic missile is launched in January 1987 from the Cape Canaveral Air Force Station in Florida as the U.S. Navy began testing the three-stage offensive weapon. The missile can carry multiple nuclear warheads and has a range greater than the 7,400-kilometer (4,600-mile) range of the Trident I.*

AFP photo

ric'') and ceramic composites that would far surpass the composites and superalloys of 1987 in strength and in resistance to the heat of hypersonic flight. Even the doughtiest of such materials might not be wholly up to the task, however. The aerospace plane was expected to embody a system of fluid coolants and pipes to draw heat away from critical areas. The engine inlets would be among such areas. In keeping with the high degree of streamlining to be required of the airframe, the lips of those inlets would have to be knife-edge thin, and they would heat up fast and furiously.

The NASP program was also made possible by the advent of supercomputers for calculating the aerospace plane's complicated fluid dynamics (the flow of air and of energy around it and into it) and for designing and integrating its airframe and engines accordingly. Data from supercomputers must be validated in flight, however, and NASP officials confessed to grave uncertainty about airflows beyond Mach 8, which in 1987 was the speed limit of existing wind tunnels for testing airframe models and engine modules. It would be up to the X-30 to find out what happens in hypersonic flight beyond Mach 8.

Supercomputers with AI software would almost certainly be central to the aerospace plane's avionics—its electrical and electronic equipment. The Strategic Computing Program that DARPA was conducting in concert with the military services was expected to produce these supercomputers. Called parallel processors, they would be made up of thumbnail-size gallium arsenide (GaAs) semiconductor chips that could process data and perform calculations on many problems all at the same time—in parallel. They would operate at far greater speeds, up to 10,000 times faster, than those of 1987's swiftest mainframe computers, which, while very fast indeed, had to do their calculations in sequence, on only one problem at a time. The parallel processors were designed to be vastly more conducive to the incorporation of increasingly sophisticated AI software and to the storage in their massive memories of data derived from human experience and expertise. This would enable them to make decisions, much as humans do, on the basis of their interpretations of information received from sensors and subsequently cause aircraft to react intelligently.

DARPA and the U.S. Air Force were developing an AI system called ''Pilot's Associate'' to monitor and regulate aircraft engines, hydraulics, and avionics and to assist pilots in planning missions, selecting tactics, taking account of threats, and responding to changing combat situations. Lockheed and McDonnell Douglas were awarded Air Force contracts in 1986 to build such systems. At least some of the elements of the Pilot's Associate were destined for embodiment in the Air Force's Advanced Tacti-

*A screen in front of a pilot flying an F–16 at night displays a daylight-like scene. The view is made possible by LANTIRN (Low Altitude Navigation and Targeting Infrared System for Night).*

cal Fighter (ATF). Two industry teams headed by Lockheed and by Northrop won competitive ATF development contracts in 1986, and General Electric and Pratt & Whitney were developing the fighter's engines. The ATF was scheduled for operational service at about the time that the X-30 was to take to the air.

AI was regarded as the single most pervasive technology in the Air Force's future by Project Forecast II, which described it as ''critical to almost every situation where large quantities of information are managed'' and called for its ''great expansion in our applications across a broad spectrum of uses.'' The aerospace plane's unprecedentedly complex navigational, flight-control, propulsion, and—in its military modes—fire-control demands were expected to make it an especially suitable candidate for AI.

—James W. Canan

# Earth sciences

Major developments of the year in the Earth sciences included research on such diverse subjects as past meteorite collisions with the Earth, the nature and locations of deep-sea hydrothermal vents, the prediction of earthquakes, and the depletion of the ozone layer over Antarctica. Two major earthquakes occurred, and the explosion of the Chernobyl nuclear power plant in the Soviet Union released large amounts of radiation into the atmosphere.

345

# Atmospheric sciences

During the past year research progress continued in the atmospheric sciences. Significant accomplishments occurred in supercomputing and in the development and performance of field experiments to investigate specific weather features. There was increased interest and concern about air pollution and changes in the character of the Earth's surface over vast areas—changes that might be causing irreversible alterations in the Earth's climate.

**Educational and research initiatives.** A U.S. National Science Foundation (NSF) committee recommended that the International Geosphere-Biosphere Program: A Study of Global Change be the major new research endeavor of the world scientific community for the next few decades. Four major initiatives were suggested for priority funding. These included the tropical oceans-global atmospheric program (TOGA), the coupled energetics-dynamics of atmospheric regions study (CEDAR), and studies in the areas of global tropospheric chemisty and mesoscale meteorology (see *Oceanography*, below).

The U.S. Department of Defense in 1986 began to fund a range of basic research programs in the atmospheric sciences. The Army Research Office established a Center of Geoscience at Colorado State University with funding of about $11.5 million over the next five years to study mesoscale meteorology and hydrology. The Office of Naval Research provided substantial funding to Pennsylvania State University and the University of California at Los Angeles (UCLA) to perform auroral ionospheric research; to Dartmouth College and the University of Colorado to conduct atmospheric/ocean/ice numerical model development; and to Penn State to develop a better understanding of mesoscale atmospheric process in the marine environment.

In the fall of 1986 the National Center For Atmospheric Research (NCAR) installed an eight million-word, four-central-processing-unit CRAY X-MP/48 supercomputer so that NCAR and university scientists would have an improved capability for performing computer-intensive simulations of atmospheric flows. Available on the computer were 128 million words on a solid-state storage device. The European Centre for Medium Range Weather Forecasting also installed a CRAY X-MP/48 supercomputer.

**Observational programs.** In 1986 a contract was let to the Sperry Corp. to build 405 MHz wind profilers as part of a National Oceanic and Atmospheric Administration (NOAA) demonstration network in the central U.S. These devices would permit nearly continuous monitoring of the wind within the troposphere (the lowest region of the Earth's atmosphere) and were likely to cause wind measurements from balloon ascent radiosondes to become obsolete within a few years. The first wind profiler was to be installed and tested by NOAA's Wave Propagation Laboratory at Platteville, Colo., in December 1987.

The mechanisms of development of coastal winter storms were the focus of the Genesis of Atlantic Lows Experiment (GALE) and the Canadian Atlantic Storms Program (CASP), which were conducted from January to March 1986. Nine aircraft with more than 1,000 flight hours, two ocean research vessels, eight meteorologic ocean buoys, and a range of other weather-monitoring equipment were utilized during these studies. Such storms, which can develop explosively, often plague the east coast of the United States and Canada with heavy rains and snow and strong coastal winds.

In the Amazon River region, data from a joint U.S.-Brazilian study conducted in July and August 1985, referred to as the Global Tropospheric Experiment/Amazon Boundary Layer Experiment (GTE/ABLE), continued to be analyzed. The large-scale clearing of trees and other vegetation in the Amazon region, the world's largest tropical rain forest, was raising serious concerns regarding possible major effects on global climate. Using ground-based, airborne, and satellite data, the GTE/ABLE program

*The U.S. National Center for Atmospheric Research's Electra research plane was used to study the development of coastal winter storms as part of GALE (Genesis of Atlantic Lows Experiment).*

*Cars entering West Germany from eastern Europe are checked for radioactive contamination following the explosion at the Chernobyl nuclear reactor on April 26, 1986, near Kiev in the Soviet Union.*

confirmed the major influences of tropical forests on the chemical composition of the overlying atmosphere. Large quantities of organic vapors and aerosols are produced by the vegetation and by other biologic activities. These chemicals travel across the Amazon River basin on the prevailing winds, are ingested into the frequent thunderstorms that develop in this humid environment, and are vented into the upper troposphere and the lower stratosphere, where they can be distributed globally. Changes in the biologic activity within the Amazon basin would thus significantly influence the natural global atmospheric chemistry.

Deliberate modification of weather was the focus of the Precipitation Augmentation for Crops Experiment (PACE) in July and August 1986 directed by Stan Changnon of the Illinois State Water Survey. By seeding with silver iodide cumulus congestus clouds that were colder than approximately −5° C (23° F), the experimenters hoped to convert liquid water to ice, thereby releasing latent heat and enhancing the growth of those clouds.

**Air pollution.** A long-term study of air quality in the rural western U.S. was the emphasis of a three-year, $5 million research contract let by the Southern California Edison Co. to the Desert Research Institute, Reno, Nev., in 1986. Referred to as a Program of Excellence in Rural Air Quality Studies (PERAQS), the study focused on atmospheric visibility and on the potential for acid deposition in that region. A study published in *Science* by the Environmental Defense Fund in 1985 had indicated that copper smelters in Arizona and northern Mexico could cause both a serious degradation of visibility and considerably enhanced acid deposition within the National Park Service region of the southwestern United States un-

less stringent control procedures were established at the smelters.

An atmospheric visibility impairment called Arctic haze, which begins in late December and peaks in March and April, was monitored by a NOAA research aircraft during the past year. The aircraft detected a plume 50 km (31 mi) wide with a high soot carbon concentration that moved south from the Arctic Ocean over Alaska. The source of the soot was suggested to be northern Asia and Europe. The soot could significantly alter infrared radiative cooling to space, thereby substantially affecting the Arctic winter climate and, perhaps, weather conditions throughout the Northern Hemisphere.

In the fall of 1986 more than 40 scientists and 60 technical support staff participated in the First International Satellite Cloud Climatology Project Regional Experiment (FIRE) in the upper Midwest of the U.S. The project investigated the impact of cirrus clouds on climate and weather. The direct measurement by aircraft of ice crystal characteristics within the clouds was part of the experiment.

Beginning in the early morning of April 26, 1986, an explosion and subsequent fire at the Chernobyl nuclear reactor near Kiev in the Soviet Union released into the atmosphere vast amounts of radiation that were transported and subsequently monitored at high levels several thousand kilometers from the release point. Excessive ground-level concentrations of radioactive iodine and cesium were found in food materials in parts of Europe. It was possible that areas close to the damaged reactor would be uninhabitable for many years as a result of radioactive contamination.

**Climate change.** Considerable concern regarding the influence of atmospheric inputs of carbon diox-

347

*A dog team pulls a sled and its riders across the snow in front of the Eiffel Tower in Paris in January 1987. Throughout Europe the winter of 1986–87 was one of the coldest in many years.*

ide, methane, chlorofluorocarbons, and oxides of nitrogen continued during the past year. These gases partially absorb long-wave radiation emitted from the Earth and then reradiate it back downward. Higher concentrations of these gases, which were being detected each successive year, could result in warmer surface temperatures over the Earth because of the reduced loss of heat to space. A warmer atmosphere would also increase evaporation and water vapor content in the atmosphere, thereby further increasing the percentage of long-wave radiation from the Earth that is absorbed. Anticipated increases in the concentration of these gases could produce a global mean temperature increase of between 1.5° and 4.5° C (2.7° and 8.1° F) in the first half of the next century.

During the past year, however, it was argued that changes in other aspects of the global atmosphere could negate the temperature increase caused by those gases and could even cause a mean global temperature decrease. In fact, despite a continued increase in the pollutant gases in the atmosphere, Charles R. Bentley, director of the University of Wisconsin-Madison Geophysical and Polar Research Center, indicated that observations over the past ten years suggested that the Antarctic ice sheet was expanding. Using data from conventional weather maps of airflow above the surface, Virginia state climatologist P. J. Michaels found no evidence of any major warming over the last 30 years in the U.S. and southern Canada. Aerosols emitted into the atmosphere by industrial and other human activities and then ejected into the upper troposphere and lower stratosphere could act to cool the climate by

reflecting a greater percentage of incoming solar radiation back into space. In polar latitudes during the winter a low-level pollution layer could cause enhanced cooling since the top of the aerosols would cool radiatively more rapidly than would cold, snow-covered ground in the absence of the aerosols.

Since some types of these aerosols serve as cloud condensation nuclei, which are required for cloud droplets to form in the Earth's atmosphere, a higher concentration of aerosols could slow the natural mechanism of precipitation development and permit clouds to persist longer than they otherwise would. The result would be enhanced outward reflection of incoming solar radiation from the top of the clouds. NASA was conducting a satellite program, called the Earth Radiation Budget Experiment (ERBE), to monitor the Earth's average heat budget with a major emphasis on the magnitude of cloud reflection. On Sept. 18, 1986, the third satellite in the experiment (NOAA-10) was launched into polar orbit, making global coverage complete.

Of major importance during 1986 were the large, systematic changes in the ozone layer over Antarctica. The amount of ozone over Halley Bay in the eastern portion of the Weddell Sea has decreased every spring since 1975, according to the British Antarctic Society. Satellite data revealed that the spring ozone depletion extends over most of Antarctica, creating a hole in the ozone layer about the size of the U.S. The largest rate of depletion has occurred in September, with the total reduction taking place between mid-August and the end of October. Some scientists suggested that increases in pollution gases could be causing the reduction in ozone. The loss of this ozone would eliminate the protection from high-intensity ultraviolet solar radiation as well as change the temperature structure in the stratosphere, with possible catastrophic changes in global climate.

A joint project sponsored by the NSF, NOAA, the National Aeronautics and Space Administration (NASA), and the Chemical Manufacturers Association was performed in the Antarctic spring of 1986 in order to monitor the ozone environment. The University of Wyoming, State University of New York at Stony Brook, the Jet Propulsion Laboratory, and NOAA participated in the project, which was referred to as Winfly and based at McMurdo Station.

Year-to-year changes in hurricane and tropical storm activity in the Atlantic Ocean and Caribbean Sea became the focus of the short-term climate forecast scheme of William Gray of Colorado State University. Based on the wind direction in the upper atmosphere and in the upper troposphere, the presence or nonpresence of an El Niño (unusually warm surface water current) in the eastern Pacific, and the sea-level pressure in the Atlantic, Gray predicted eight and four hurricanes in 1985 and in 1986, re-

*Scientists from the University of Wyoming prepare a balloon for launch in Antarctica as part of an investigation into the annual disappearance of much of the protective ozone layer over the South Pole.*

spectively. The observed occurrence of seven and three hurricanes in 1985 and 1986 demonstrated the accuracy of his forecast technique.

The possibility of a catastrophic change of climate due to even a limited summertime nuclear war in the Northern Hemisphere continued to be debated in 1986. Scientists hypothesized a climate change that would be caused by the injection of tens of millions of tons of elemental carbon smoke into the atmosphere from urban fires generated by even a small number of nuclear weapon detonations. The carbon smoke would shield the Earth's surface from solar heating and thereby cause a rapid cooling, possibly to below freezing, as well as limit or even eliminate photosynthesis for a long period of time. Using more sophisticated numerical models of the Earth's atmosphere, some investigators recently concluded that the cooling might be much less extensive than originally suggested. Nonetheless, most investigators believed that there would be a significant negative impact on the climate and agriculture in the Northern Hemisphere. Possible catastrophic impacts on global climate and ecology even in areas far removed from the thermonuclear impact sites could not be ruled out.

—Roger A. Pielke

## Geologic sciences

Research in the geologic sciences during the past year dealt with such subjects as mass extinctions of species and their possible causes, the evolution of humans, and the prediction of earthquakes. The sharp decline in the price of oil adversely affected academic geology.

**Geology and geochemistry.** The collapse of the price of oil in late 1985 and the consequent dramatic decline in petroleum exploration worldwide was a matter of deep concern in the geologic community during the past year. In his presidential address to the members of the American Association of Petroleum Geologists assembled for the 71st convention of the association, William L. Fisher summarized the recent dramatic events in the petroleum industry. He said, "The cycle we have just experienced was sharp—steep on the upside, with some good, but too much inflation, too much waste, and too many inefficiencies. The cycle was steep on the downside, a collapse of major proportions, and with it a loss of critical production capacity in the U.S. and elsewhere, an inefficient and disastrous reduction of oil and gas activity worldwide, not to mention the massive personal tragedy of professional unemployment and acute underemployment. And perhaps worst of all, the debilitating anxiety of an uncertain future." Despite these conditions the exploration for new petroleum reserves continued, but at a much reduced rate.

The prospect that China might escape dependence upon imported oil appeared to be dimming. In the early 1970s foreign oil companies invested heavily in the expectation that major discoveries of oil and gas reserves would be made in China. After a decade and a half of exploration, the only promising discoveries had been made at a few offshore localities. Melvin A. Conant of Conant and Associates, Ltd., concluded that unless these proved to be important, China could not hope to continue to be an oil exporter. Conant reported that it was generally believed that without the development of new reserves China would not be able to meet its liquid fuel needs from internal sources much beyond the early 1990s.

The collapse of the price of oil during 1985 had a negative impact that reached beyond the petroleum industry to geology in general. Academic geology, for example, had always depended upon the mining and petroleum industry not only as a principal market for its students but also as an important source of funding. By 1987 student enrollment in geology, especially in colleges and universities offering programs in petroleum geology, had already declined dramatically.

A partial solution to the problem of the dramatic impact of the boom and bust cycles of the petroleum

*Oil field workers in Texas shut down a well. Declining consumption of energy coupled with high production levels of petroleum caused oil and gasoline prices to decline and plunged many production areas into recession.*

industry upon colleges and universities might lie in a suggestion made by Hatten S. Yoder of the Geophysical Laboratory of the Carnegie Institution of Washington, D.C. He concluded in the *Journal of Geological Education*, "Universities must resist submission to the current social demands and mission-oriented research funding and preserve their freedom to pursue knowledge that *may* provide solutions to tomorrow's problems."

Although employment opportunities in geology for both sexes generally declined with the increasing economic difficulties in the oil business, educational and employment opportunities for women substantially improved during the past few decades, according to a study undertaken by Mary Sue Coates of the Harza Engineering Co. With its emphasis on field work, geology had been seen as a profession especially unsuited to women. With the removal of this and other barriers, women assumed a much more significant role in all phases of Earth science. Coates's study revealed, however, that women had not yet achieved equality with men in the profession. Although the number of Ph.D. degrees awarded to women had dramatically increased since 1965, the percentage of female full professors in U.S. colleges and universities remained constant at less than 1% during this period. And, reflecting a widespread phenomenon, the salaries of women working in geology were, on the average, substantially lower than those of males in comparable positions.

*Collisions.* The increasing preoccupation with collisions between the Earth and large extraterrestrial bodies such as meteorites and the biologic and physical consequences of such collisions was the most dramatically evident, and perhaps the most significant, feature of geologic research in 1986. Investigators in virtually every subdiscipline of the Earth sciences were turning their attention to this intriguing problem.

In 1980 Luis Alvarez and his colleagues suggested that a collision between the Earth and a large meteorite could have raised a dust cloud sufficient to obscure the Sun, thereby interrupting photosynthesis and leading to a collapse of the food chain. The authors claimed to have evidence that such a catastrophic impact had occurred at the time of the well-documented mass extinction of animals and plants at the boundary between the Cretaceous and Tertiary periods. Since 1980 interest in impacts by large meteors and in catastrophic events of all kinds has dramatically increased. This important development was called by some the "new catastrophism," to distinguish it from the catastrophism that played a significant role in 19th-century geology.

Evidence was growing that a large meteor struck the Earth some 70 million years ago and triggered events that caused widespread animal and plant extinctions. Anomalous concentrations of the element iridium, which Alvarez and his colleagues believed could have been produced only by an impact with an extraterrestrial object, were found at the Tertiary-Cretaceous boundary in more than 50 places in the world. This lent credence to the view that a meteor impact was a causal factor in an episode of extinction.

Attempts to link other episodes of mass extinction known from paleontological evidence to meteor impacts were more problematic. The discovery of an iridium anomaly in late Devonian Period sediments of Australia led some paleontologists to suggest that an impact might have triggered a well-documented episode of mass extinction of marine organisms in Devonian time some 350 million years ago. George R. McGhee of Rutgers, the State University of New Jersey, and his associates reported, however, that signs of meteor impact had not been found in sediments in other parts of the world where paleontological evidence of the Devonian extinction is unmistakable.

Peter M. Sheehan of the Milwaukee (Wis.) Public Museum and Thor A. Hansen of Western Washington University noted that the pattern of extinction at the end of the Cretaceous Period is consistent with the meteor impact hypothesis, which entails a worldwide interruption of photosynthesis. According to their analysis, extinction was indeed concentrated among those animals dependent upon living plants.

It should be noted that there was some resistance to the view that episodes of mass extinction should

A toxic cloud of carbon dioxide and other gases arose from Lake Nyos in Cameroon (left) on Aug. 21, 1986, killing more than 1,700 people living nearby along with thousands of farm animals (right). Scientists believe that carbon dioxide trapped on the bottom of the lake was released into the atmosphere by a subterranean landslide or a small earthquake.

be linked to a catastrophe of extraterrestrial origin. Paul Copper of Laurentian University of Sudbury, Ont., for example, offered quite a different view of the Devonian extinction. He developed a paleogeographic model that considers the extinction, which he believed to be rapid but not cataclysmic, as the result of the elimination of easterly flowing tropical currents caused by the closing of the ocean between the continental masses Laurussia and Gondwana during the course of continental drift.

The work of Copper raised a question that was central to the discussion over theories of catastrophic extinction—just how sudden were the mass extinctions that such events as asteroid collisions had been invoked to explain. If it could be shown that they were not very sudden, then the need for catastrophic events to explain them would plainly be in question. To determine with any degree of precision just how long it took some group of animals or plants to become extinct requires an abundance of paleontological and stratigraphic evidence that is rarely available. The suggestion by R. E. Sloan of the University of Minnesota and his co-workers that the dinosaurs became extinct over a period of millions of years was debated simply because the stratigraphic evidence, while seemingly compelling, had not been accepted by many of those dedicated to asteroid explanations of extinction.

The search for evidence of meteor impact spread beyond that which might be associated with major episodes of extinction. Donald R. Lowe and Gary R. Byerly of Louisiana State University reported evidence of meteorite impact in the form of quenched liquid silicate droplets resembling those found in lunar soils; the droplets were recovered from the greenstone belts of early Archean Age (about 3.5 billion years ago) in South Africa and Western Australia. These rocks are among the oldest relatively unmetamorphosed sediments known.

An attempt to identify a crater with the Tertiary-Cretaceous impact, hypothesized largely on geochemical evidence, was undertaken by a number of geologists during recent months but without much success. At the 17th Lunar and Planetary Science Conference, Jack B. Hartung of the American Geophysical Union and his co-workers reported that while an impact structure near Manson, Iowa, appeared to be the right age, its diameter of 35 km (21.7 mi) was much smaller than the 200-km (124.2-mi) structure that was thought to have resulted from the Tertiary-Cretaceous collision.

The increasing significance attached to meteor impact led to studies, both experimental and theoretical, directed at increasing the understanding of the process of impact. At the 17th Lunar and Planetary Science Conference, John D. O'Keefe and Thomas J. Ahrens of the California Institute of Technology reported on problems relating to scaling relationships for cratering impacts, a crucial consideration for anyone engaged in experimental studies. They determined that, generally speaking, the larger the projectile, the smaller the maximum excavation depth in units of projectile diameter.

*Plate tectonics.* Although the new catastrophism appeared to dominate geologic research in 1986, the theory of plate tectonics was still alive as a source of inspiration for continuing research. Some geologists, for example, began to question the widely accepted

351

*Tracks of dinosaurs in a dry creek bed in Texas were made at the same time as the smaller markings, which some had believed were human footprints. During the past year, however, a scientist determined that most of the "man tracks" were actually scour marks of a kind often found in Texas riverbeds, while others were formed by "flat-footed" dinosaurs.*

view that continental drift and plate tectonics cannot be invoked to explain the generation of very ancient crustal rocks such as those found in Wyoming's Wind River Mountains. According to Richard A. Kerr reporting in *Science*, Gregory Harper of the State University of New York at Albany suggested that these rocks represent a "beached" slice of Archean ocean crust generated in much the same way as later ocean crust has been developed in the course of seafloor spreading. If the work of Harper and a growing number of geologists who agreed with him is verified, it will represent yet another triumph for the "new tectonics."

R. W. Tabor of the U.S. Geological Survey proposed that the development of the theory of plate tectonics has so altered our perception of the structure of the Earth's crust that it might be necessary to reassess the suitability of sites that were only ten years ago considered geologically safe for the loca-

tion of nuclear reactors. The final acceptance of the proposed Satsop site on the Olympic Peninsula in Washington might, for example, be delayed because of the recognition of the potential for the production of major earthquakes by the subducting Juan de Fuca crustal plate.

The use of submersibles to monitor directly the activity along active submarine zones promised to increase scientists' knowledge of the behavior of the Juan de Fuca plate and other plates as well. The U.S. Geological Survey's Juan de Fuca Study Group reported the use of the submersible *Alvin* to study active hydrothermal discharge along the southern Juan de Fuca Ridge.

*Evolution.* The debate between the creationists and the evolutionists continued during the year, and geologists and paleontologists were inevitably drawn into it. The human footprints alleged to be associated with dinosaur trackways, especially in the early

*Jaw fragment of Afrotarsius, a tarsier from the Oligocene Epoch (38 million to 26 million years ago) lies behind that of a contemporary tarsier. The fragment, found in Fayum, Egypt, lends support to the view that Africa was the site of major evolutionary events in the history of primates.*

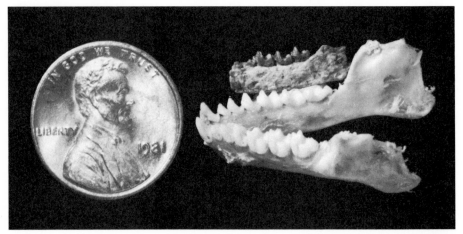

Cretaceous Period sediments of Texas, were cited by creationists as evidence that dinosaurs and humans coexisted in the past, a conclusion dramatically at odds with the view of most geologists. James O. Farlow of Indiana University-Purdue University at Fort Wayne studied nearly all of the relevant sites in Texas and concluded that most of the "man tracks" from the Texas localities are not footprints at all but are solution features or scour marks of a kind frequently found in riverbeds throughout central Texas, while others were formed by bipedal dinosaurs walking in a peculiar "flat-footed" fashion.

Meanwhile, paleontologists continued to assimilate evidence of the evolution within our own order, the primates, which includes monkeys, apes, and humans. Elwyn L. Simons of the Duke University Primate Center, Durham, N.C., reported the discovery of jaw fragment of a tarsier, appropriately named *Afrotarsius*, from the Oligocene Fayum sediments of Egypt. Until this important find, tarsiers, which are primates, had been known only from the living tarsius of southeast Asia. Evidence of the existence of a tarsier at such a remote time in Africa might strengthen the view that Africa was the site of major evolutionary events in the history of the primates.

The expectation, frequently expressed since 1980, that the new catastrophism would substantially alter the direction of geologic research appeared to have been fulfilled by 1987. This "revolution," together with the plate tectonic "revolution" of the 1970s, has had a dramatic impact upon the Earth sciences. There is a tendency to overestimate the importance of our own time in the history of science, a tendency generally to be avoided. It does appear, however, that we have recently witnessed a significant change in the structure of geologic knowledge.

—David B. Kitts

**Geophysics.** The only great (magnitude 8 on the Richter scale or larger) earthquake in 1986 was the magnitude 8.2 shock on Oct. 20, 1986, near Raoul (Sunday) Island, one of the Kermadec Islands northeast of New Zealand. The earthquake was felt in Wellington and Napier, N.Z., and a small tsunami (giant sea wave) that did no damage was generated. Minor damage was reported on Raoul, the only inhabited island in the Kermadecs.

*San Salvador earthquake.* A magnitude 5.4 shock on Oct. 10, 1986, caused severe damage with approximately 1,500 deaths, 10,000 injuries, and 250,-000 left homeless in San Salvador, the capital of El Salvador. The San Salvador quake was typical of the frequent shocks that occur along the Central American volcanic chain. Although the earthquake was only of moderate size, it occurred at shallow depth beneath the thick deposits of volcanic ash that underlie San Salvador.

In contrast to the low-frequency long-duration shaking that devastated Mexico City in 1985, the severe damage in San Salvador was caused by 3–5 seconds of high-frequency (periods of 0.2–0.8 second) shaking with peak accelerations up to 0.72 g. The 1986 San Salvador earthquake is proof that even moderate-size shocks in urban areas present serious hazards, particularly where structures are not constructed to be earthquake resistant.

*Eruption of Augustine Volcano.* Augustine Volcano in Cook Inlet, Alaska, erupted in 1812, 1883, 1935, 1963–64, 1976, and, most recently, during March 27–April 28, 1986. Following the 1976 eruption, the systematic shortening of time between eruptions was noted so that the 1986 event was not unexpected. A swarm of microearthquakes in July 1985 first indicated that Augustine Volcano was reawakening. In February and March 1986 the steady increase of

An earthquake measuring 5.4 on the Richter scale struck San Salvador, the capital of El Salvador, on Oct. 10, 1986. It caused approximately 1,500 deaths, 10,000 injuries, and widespread destruction of property that left 250,000 homeless.

*Augustine Volcano in Cook Inlet, Alaska, shoots massive amounts of smoke and ash high into the air during an eruption on April 1, 1986, disrupting traffic at Anchorage International Airport located 280 kilometers (175 miles) to the northeast.*

seismicity and observations of vapor near the summit of the mountain led to warnings of eruption six to nine days before the start of the 1986 activity.

Because Augustine Island probably has grown by lateral debris avalanche flows, a landslide-induced tsunami is a real danger for every Augustine eruption. A massive landslide during the 1883 eruption extended five kilometers of coastline by two kilometers, generating a tsunami with waves up to 8 m (26 ft) in height in Cook Inlet (one kilometer equals 0.62 mi). Even a small tsunami in a contained estuary like Cook Inlet is cause for serious concern, particularly at high tide. Fortunately, the pyroclastic flow that reached the sea during the March 31 eruption caused no detectable tsunami, though the resulting ash and steam columns reached an estimated height of 11.6–12.2 km.

Eruption of 0.3 cu km of ash during the 1986 eruptions of Augustine Volcano (about $\frac{1}{10}$ the ash erupted by Mt. St. Helens in 1980) did cause serious disruption of Anchorage International Airport, the hub of air traffic in south-central Alaska. Most of the major interstate and international air carriers canceled or diverted flights during the eruption. The last phase of the eruption in April 1986 featured dome-building lava extrusions near the summit of the mountain.

*Very long baseline interferometry.* Very long baseline interferometry (VLBI) uses the simultaneous recording of microwave emissions from extragalactic sources at radio telescope receivers in order to estimate the relative positions and movements of the receiving stations. Since 1980 improved techniques for eliminating errors due to delays in the atmosphere and ionosphere have resulted in typical uncertainties of about 2 cm (0.8 in) in VLBI baseline determinations.

There are few constraints in siting VLBI receivers. In contrast, conventional geodetic techniques are limited to line-of-sight measurements, but they are more accurate than the VLBI method, with uncertainties of about 4 mm (0.16 in) for ten-kilometer-long baselines. Thus, VLBI measurements of baselines of 100 to 1,000 km can provide a valuable complement to conventional geodetic techniques.

For example, VLBI measurements in 1980–84 of three 100- to 300-km-long baselines that cross the San Andreas fault system in southern California indicated substantial crustal movement. Although little motion was indicated between the two receivers located more than 100 km northeast of the San Andreas, the third site, located 35 km southwest of the San Andreas, moved northwest relative to the other two receivers at a rate of 25 ± 4 mm per year. Although this short-term displacement rate is consistent with geologic and conventional geodetic measurements of the slip rate on the southern San Andreas fault, the relative motion between the Pacific and North American plates in California is estimated to be about 6 cm (2.4 in) per year. The usual explanation for the difference in relative plate motion and San Andreas slip rate is that the relative plate motion is accounted for by tectonic processes distributed over a broad region extending from near the California coast to as far east as Nevada and Utah.

While the VLBI baselines did not completely span this region, they did cross the San Andreas fault and other significant active tectonic features, such as the Garlock fault. It is curious that the inferred displacements apparently do not reflect crustal straining along, or movement on, these other active tectonic features. While a completely acceptable explanation of the VLBI results was not available in early 1987, future VLBI and satellite laser-ranging measurements using more sites seemed certain to further the understanding of crustal motions and tectonic processes not only in the western U.S. but throughout the world.

*Extensive damage to an old church in Tumbaco, Ecuador, was caused by an earthquake in early March, 1987. The March 5–8 series of earthquakes killed more than 1,000 people, mainly in the isolated northeastern jungle region of the country.*

*The Parkfield, Calif., earthquake prediction experiment.* Parkfield, located about midway between San Francisco and Los Angeles, is a small farming community that is situated in a sparsely populated area of central California. Since 1857 magnitude-6 earthquakes have occurred on the Parkfield section of the San Andreas fault in 1881, 1901, 1922, 1934, and 1966. Available instrumental recordings and accounts of those shocks are consistent with the hypothesis that essentially the same earthquake ruptures the Parkfield section of the San Andreas every 21–22 years. The anticipated time of the next "characteristic" Parkfield earthquake is January 1988 ±5.2 years (95% confidence interval); therefore, the next shock is now due and is expected to occur sometime before 1993.

The evidence supporting the long-term prediction of the next magnitude-6 Parkfield shock has been recognized as scientifically credible by federal and state of California review panels and has been officially issued as a prediction by the U.S. Geological Survey (USGS), making it the first officially recognized scientific prediction of an earthquake in the U.S. Recent analyses suggest that the strain released by the 1966 shock will most likely be restored between 1984 and 1989, providing independent support for the prediction.

Because the features of the Parkfield earthquakes have been remarkably similar, it is reasonable to assume similar characteristics for the next shock. That is, the detailed observations in 1966 can be used as a template in the design of a focused earthquake prediction experiment near Parkfield. For example, the location of foreshocks in 1934 and 1966 on a two- to three-kilometer-long fault section northwest of and adjacent to the anticipated epicenter is the logical focus of pre-earthquake seismicity studies near Parkfield. Similarly, observations consistent with significant precursory fault creep in 1966 on the 25-km-long rupture zone located southeast of the anticipated epicenter are the bases for the design of observational networks to monitor crustal deformation near Parkfield.

As a prediction experiment the Parkfield study has as its principal goal a detailed description of the final stages of the process by which an earthquake is generated. Observations at Parkfield should aid in the evaluation of the feasibility of intermediate- and short-term earthquake prediction elsewhere. Furthermore, the detailed history of strain accumulation and release over a complete seismic cycle that is being recorded at Parkfield should provide the basis for testing and refining models for earthquake recurrence on other sections of plate boundaries. A secondary goal of the experiment is the issuance of a short-term warning by the USGS to California's Office of Emergency Services (OES), the agency that is responsible for public dissemination of any warning. OES began conducting a Parkfield exercise to determine the best response by state, county, and local governments to a scientifically based earthquake prediction.

*Models of the Earth's mantle.* Knowledge of the structure of the Earth's interior is based on the detailed observations of seismic waves that propagate deep through the Earth. Patterns of seismic-wave arrival times from distant earthquakes were used by seismologists to identify the 10- to 70-km-deep Mo-

*Smoke billows from a new small volcanic island being formed in the Pacific Ocean near Iwo Jima in January 1986. The eruption of an underwater volcano, dormant since 1914, shot lava 300 meters (1,000 feet) into the air.*

horovicic Discontinuity (Moho) between the crust and mantle, the 2,900-km-deep boundary between the mantle and core, and an interface at a depth of 670 km that separates the upper and lower mantle. Geologists' ideas of a mantle composed of concentric layers are founded on the worldwide seismic evidence for boundaries at specific depths.

As part of the theory of plate tectonics, geophysicists explain the occurrence of deep earthquakes in particular regions as the result of a rigid plate thrusting beneath another plate and down into the mantle. In those regions earthquakes occur from the Earth's surface down to a depth of about 650 km and no deeper. That is, earthquakes cease at the depth of the lateral discontinuity that defines the upper- and lower-mantle interface. The inference usually drawn is that the 670-km discontinuity is an effective barrier so that the downthrust plates, like the earthquakes, do not extend into the lower mantle. The implication, that upper- and lower-mantle

*Map reveals the structure of the boundary layer between the Earth's mantle and core based on travel times for seismic waves that traverse the boundary. The peak-to-peak amplitude of 1.2 seconds for the waves appears to be too large to be explained by conventional boundary layer models and may result from the existence of one or more chemical boundary layers.*

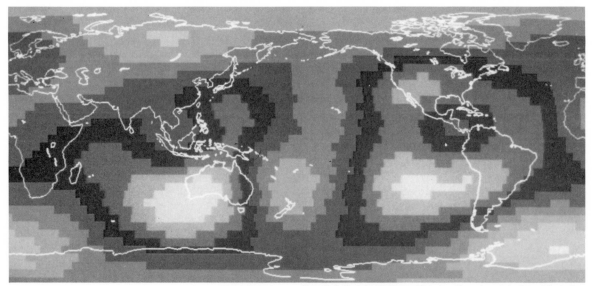

material do not mix, has figured prominently in the development of models of mantle circulation and the possible driving mechanisms for plate motion.

Recent seismological evidence challenged this view of the 670-km discontinuity. The speed of seismic waves in the cold, dense descending plates is 4 to 11% greater than in the surrounding mantle. Recent analyses of seismic waves strongly suggest that these greater seismic velocities extend below the maximum depth of the earthquakes. Thomas Jordan and his colleagues at the Massachusetts Institute of Technology (MIT) presented seismic travel-time evidence for plate penetration to depths of at least 1,000 km at several subduction zones around the western Pacific. Paul Silver and W. Winston Chan of the Department of Terrestrial Magnetism at the Carnegie Institution in Washington, D.C., found that seismic shear waves are bent and split when traversing the mantle just beneath the deepest earthquakes; this finding leads to the conclusion that the subducting plates penetrate at least 300 to 400 km into the lower mantle.

Penetration of subducting plates into the lower mantle has important implications. If the upper and lower mantle do not mix, then the Earth's crust has been derived entirely from the upper mantle. However, mixing of the upper and lower mantle just by plate penetration at subduction zones would result in a volume of matter equal to that of the entire upper mantle being thrust into the lower mantle every billion years. Substantial return flow to the upper mantle by some means seems necessary. The consequences of mantle-wide mixing for the evolution and chemistry of the Earth's crust, oceans, and atmosphere and for the generation of the tectonic processes that shape the world are profound.

*The core-mantle interface.* Although the major elements of the structure of the deep Earth have been known for 50 years, detailed three-dimensional models of the core and the lower mantle depend on adequate models of the crust and upper mantle so that the effects of the more shallow structure can be removed from the seismic data that are sensitive to the details of deep structure. Kenneth Creager and Thomas Jordan of MIT used massive sets of travel times for seismic waves that traverse the core-mantle boundary to map long-wavelength (more than 1,000 km) features with amplitudes on the order of one second in vertical seismic travel time. They explained their observations by the existence on the surface of the core of chemical boundary layers that are perhaps analogous to the continents on the surface of the Earth. The amplitude of the features suggests differences in topography that are greater than those on the Earth's surface.

Topography on the core-mantle boundary might provide keys to understanding important questions.

Topography on the surface of the core may affect convection in the outer core and, therefore, the generation of the Earth's magnetic field since models for the generation of the magnetic field assume convection in the liquid outer core. Since topography suggests stable lateral differences in properties such as temperature in the outer core, it is possible that heat flow and other effects of these lateral differences extend across the interface into the lower mantle, providing a means for coupling of convection patterns in the core and lower mantle. Hot spots on the Earth's surface, such as the Hawaiian Islands volcanic chain, often are associated with vertical plumes that apparently extend deep into the mantle and even to the core-mantle boundary. If the plumes can be associated with the inferred core surface topography, then our understanding of the generation of prominent structural features on the Earth's surface might depend on the details of processes in the Earth's lower mantle and core.

—William H. Bakun

## Hydrologic sciences

New hydrothermal vent systems were discovered on mid-ocean ridges during the past year. Researchers also determined that a single species of fish played a major role in shaping the continental shelf off the east coast of the U.S. The role of computers in hydrologic analysis was a subject of considerable debate.

**Hydrology.** A major theme in hydrologic science in 1986 was a process of review and planning for the future. This included the publication of a special issue of a leading journal, *Water Resources Research,* devoted to trends and directions in hydrology. The editor of this issue, Stephen Burges of the University of Washington, invited an international collection of eminent authors to write on any subject of their choice within the overall title. The results were varied but always stimulating and thought provoking. The collection of papers might prove to serve as a landmark summary of the state of hydrologic science in 1987.

A number of common concerns can be distinguished in these papers. The first is the question of scale. Hydrologists have traditionally been concerned with solving problems in engineering, which has required predictions of hydrologic variables at scales in the range of tens of meters to tens of kilometers. Most hydrologic theory, however, is based on experiments undertaken at much smaller scales. In recent years there has been an increasing recognition that the nonlinear nature of hydrologic systems together with the spatial and temporal variability of vegetation canopies, soil characteristics, and channel form makes it difficult to apply this small-scale theory to large-scale phenomena.

This problem was the subject of a number of the papers. Among them was "The Emergence of Global-Scale Hydrology" by Peter Eagleson of the Massachusetts Institute of Technology, the current president of the American Geophysical Union. He pointed out that there are a range of problems associated with hydrologic circulation at large scales that require dynamic modeling of the coupled ocean-atmosphere-land surface system, in particular defining the spatial linkages that control the impacts of major surface changes or climatic anomalies that are dependent on local persistence in hydrologic variables. Eagleson noted the contributions of remote sensing techniques, modern computing power, and the development of global circulation models in making the analysis of such large-scale assessments of hydrologic systems possible for the first time. Such work is, however, at its very early stages and has often relied on simplifications of the same small-scale theories that have proved difficult to use even at the hillslope scale.

Flood-frequency prediction was the subject of papers by David Pilgrim of the University of New South Wales in Australia, Vit Klemes of Environment Canada, and Ray Linsley of Santa Cruz, Calif. There are elements of unknowability in the assessment of flood risk, for reasons both of the short time scale of most hydrologic records and the impossibility of forecasting major hydrologic events. The adequacy of existing methodologies for predicting such risk and utilizing the predictions in the design of flood-control works was questioned in these papers. The authors were also highly critical of hydrologic training, suggesting that many students who go on to be practicing hydrologic engineers are not provided with the tools for proper application and critical assessment of modern methods of analysis. In this regard both Pilgrim and Klemes pointed to some drawbacks of applying computers to the analysis of problems in hydrology. They suggested that, without proper training in the bases and inadequacies of current hydrologic models, the wide availability of convenient hydrologic modeling packages was likely to lead to predictions and extrapolations that were hydrologically indefensible.

Similar concerns were expressed in a different context. Looking to the future again, a conference was held at Purdue University, West Lafayette, Ind., to discuss the use of supercomputers in hydrology. The conference brought together representatives from the government, industry, and the research community. A review of the meeting written by John Cushman of Purdue highlighted some of the problems inherent in using supercomputers to apply hydrologic theory. Large-scale and more detailed hydrologic predictions will almost certainly require the use of major computer power, and yet the rapid changes in machine architecture and software make it difficult for researchers to combine the roles of an innovative specialist in a particular research area with the changing programming skills required to make efficient use of supercomputers. There is a consequent danger that the attractions of ever increasing computing power may undermine the aim

Flood barrier connecting two man-made islands (top and bottom) was constructed to close off the Eastern Scheldt (Oosterschelde) estuary (left) from the North Sea. The project, completed in October 1986, protects Zeeland Province in The Netherlands from flooding during North Sea storms.

*Spilling over its banks, the Arkansas River invades a community of mobile homes near Tulsa, Oklahoma. Heavy autumn rains in September and October 1986 caused extensive flooding in many parts of the U.S.*

of increasing understanding. It can, in fact, be argued that present knowledge of hydrologic systems is sufficiently limited, and the problems of estimating model parameters are sufficiently great, that the predictions of current models, whether on supercomputers or not, may be totally incorrect. The availability of supercomputers may not, in such a case, be an aid to the advancement of hydrologic science.

These various themes were to be discussed further at an international symposium convened by the International Association of Hydrological Sciences

and the International Association for Hydraulic Research in Rome in 1987 entitled "Water for the Future." These processes of review of past progress and evaluation of current trends in research were perhaps indicative of an underlying concern about the adequacy and applicability of current hydrologic theory and about how the problems posed by the heterogeneity and unknowability of hydrologic systems might be resolved.

It seemed clear that any future advances in hydrologic theory would have to reflect the current

*Boat is stuck in the mud in the Nile River at Cairo, Egypt, in March 1987. A drought that began five years earlier threatened to reduce the flow of the river to its lowest levels in the 20th century.*

Geologist studies a soil density profile chart that has been produced by ground-penetrating radar in the trailer-mounted unit in the background. Such charts help scientists devise methods for keeping chemicals used for agriculture out of groundwater.

lack of knowledge and understanding of hydrologic processes by basing predictions on realistic estimates of uncertainty in the underlying parameters and variables. Such an approach would allow input data, parameter values, and model structures to be considered as sources of uncertainty rather than as physical entities. The value of qualitative knowledge and additional measurements would be assessed in the context of reducing predictive uncertainty. It might be possible to incorporate consideration of processes that are not properly understood, as well as those that are. It would be necessary to develop theory that linked the changing scale of predictions to data requirements and levels of uncertainty.

Some advances toward this end had been made by 1987, particularly in the area of groundwater hydrology, but as a theoretical goal it still seemed a long way off. It might be that, at least initially, it would be necessary to use computer-intensive methods to estimate levels of uncertainty. The power of supercomputers could be then harnessed in a constructive way that would reflect both the knowledge and lack of knowledge about hydrologic systems.

—Keith Beven

**Oceanography.** New discoveries and techniques highlighted a year that was also notable because there was an appearance of a weak El Niño in the tropical Pacific. Formal international approval was given for new interdisciplinary science programs.

*Hydrothermal vents.* Hydrothermal vent systems forming black smoker chimneys with polymetallic sulfide deposits have been found at several places on the mid-ocean ridges since their initial discovery in 1977. During the year scientists found fragments from a "dead" black smoker-type chimney in the Lau Basin near the Tonga Ridge south of Samoa, thus confirming the hypothesis that back arc basins also have vent systems similar to those found on the mid-ocean ridges. Pillows and glass fragments of fresh basalt from the ridge and the relatively unaltered appearance of the chimney fragments suggested that the spreading axis was still alive.

Another newly discovered field of seafloor vents in the eastern Pacific Ocean included every type of venting system already known in the Pacific and Atlantic oceans. The field is on the Juan de Fuca Ridge, about 450 km (280 mi) west of the Washington-Oregon border. The field is accessible, young and growing, and biologically active. It thus appears to be an ideal site for a long-term seafloor observatory for those processes.

*El Niño.* Every few years the climate anomaly known as El Niño changes surface temperatures and currents in the Pacific Ocean, thereby creating global climatic impacts. The 1982–83 El Niño touched off a series of weather events that claimed scores of lives and caused billions of dollars in damage. After that strong event a careful watch was kept on the relevant indexes of an El Niño so that adequate warning could be provided. Late in 1985 the U.S. National Meteorological Center announced that warmings of surface water observed in the equatorial Pacific resembled those associated with El Niño, and a vigil was maintained as the year continued. However, a strong warming trend failed to materialize, and ocean surface temperatures rose no higher than about 1° C (1.8° F) above normal.

It appears that a modest El Niño occurred, but as of early 1987 all the evidence had not yet been gathered. In any case, the observed changes were expected to be useful in further developing the predictive models. Studies continued on the 1982–83 El Niño, which was the best documented and most intensively sampled event of its kind. Using the data from that occurrence along with newly developed numerical modeling techniques, researchers from the National Oceanic and Atmospheric Administration (NOAA) developed a high-resolution computer model that was used to simulate conditions in the Pacific Ocean; the new model produced a remarkably realistic simulation of the 1982–83 event. Later in

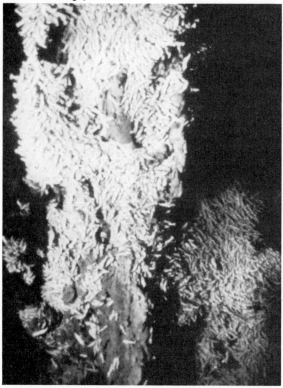

*Previously unknown genus of shrimp was discovered around hydrothermal vents in the Atlantic Ocean by biologists in the submersible* Alvin. *It was not known what food source could sustain so many shrimp in such an area.*

1987 the new model was to be transferred to NOAA's National Meteorological Center for operational use.

Similar events happen in the tropical Atlantic Ocean, but they are not as dramatic. Results presented from a joint U.S.-French field and modeling study in 1983 and 1984 showed a major warming in 1984 on the eastern side of the Atlantic. A weakening of the trade winds appeared to be the cause. The warming event was the strongest one since 1963, when oceanographic and atmospheric conditions were similar. The comparison between El Niño and the Atlantic events helped oceanographers understand the basic physical processes at work. The Tropical Ocean/Global Atmosphere (TOGA) program, sponsored by the World Climate Research Program, was an attempt to look at those processes globally, and in order to do so it established a global monitoring system.

*Biological oceanography.* In one of the major studies based on data from the equatorial Pacific during the 1982–83 El Niño, close agreement was found between the estimates of biological production from shipboard measurements and from satellite measurements of ocean color. This study helped to show that global measurements of ocean color by satellite could disclose some of the secrets of ocean biology. The increased spatial coverage offered by satellites might significantly reduce the errors associated with estimates of primary production. The first of a series of global-scale maps of the distribution of phytoplankton and, thus, of biological productivity in the world's oceans was produced during the year showing the North Atlantic basin in May 1979. The spring "bloom" was seen for the first time as a coherent feature across the entire basin.

In a study of the central North Pacific, oceanographers discovered that they had been underestimating the biological productivity of almost half of the world's oceans. They suspected that sampling of the ocean was not frequent enough to catch the pulses of high productivity that might account for much of the total productivity in open ocean waters.

*Seafloor processes.* Scientists during the year reported observations showing that a single species of tilefish, burrowing and excavating in the ocean floor, has played a central role in shaping the continental shelf off the east coast of the U.S. Apparently, the tilefish protect themselves from sharks by digging shelters, causing grottoes and deep burrows to form along the edge of the continental shelf.

The burrows were observed with the use of a mobile submersible. There were estimated to be more than 1,000 of the burrows per square kilometer (0.386 sq mi), ranging in size up to 3 m long, 1 m high, and 1 m deep (1 m = 3.2 ft). These direct observations disproved long-held notions that the continental shelf is a smooth accumulation of sediment.

*Paleoceanography.* At a conference in Woods Hole, Mass., in September, scientists showed new evidence in support of the Milankovitch theory that the varying distribution of solar radiation over the Earth due to changes in its orbit and orientation is the key to understanding climate changes over the past millennia. A new understanding of paleoclimates was based on the study of ocean sediments. The studies revealed the existence of a measure of atmospheric carbon dioxide in past eras, which can be related to the orbital and climate changes. The fit of the models was improved when atmospheric carbon dioxide concentrations were added to them, but understanding why the 100,000-year cycle of orbital eccentricity plays such a dominant role in changing climate remained a major scientific problem.

In other studies widespread changes in ocean chemistry that can be linked to changes in ocean circulation were revealed. The most extreme events appeared to be associated with changes in North Atlantic deep-water circulation. Other work on detailed oxygen isotope records derived from the study of unicellular microorganisms called foraminifera from deep-sea sediments showed that the temperature of the abyssal ocean has been an actively varying

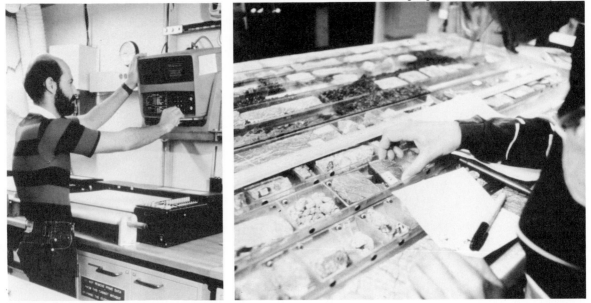

*Deep-sea geophysical conditions are monitored aboard the ocean drilling ship* JOIDES Resolution *(left). Cores obtained by the drilling operations are studied aboard the ship (right). During the past year the* JOIDES Resolution *drilled the deepest hole ever made in the oceanic crust—1,526 meters (5,000 feet) deep—off the west coast of South America.*

component of the climate system. It appears that massive cooling of the already cold abyssal ocean must be considered an important aspect of the ice-age climate.

*Ocean drilling.* The ocean drilling ship *JOIDES* (Joint Oceanographic Institutions for Deep Earth Sampling) *Resolution* continued its operations during the year. A consortium of 12 countries (Belgium, Denmark, Finland, Greece, Iceland, Italy, The Netherlands, Norway, Spain, Sweden, Switzerland, and Turkey) represented by the European Science Foundation joined the U.S., Canada, France, West Germany, Japan, and the United Kingdom, making a total of 18 countries in the program. During the year the ship ranged from the Mediterranean Sea across the tropical Atlantic Ocean through the Panama Canal, down the coast of South America, and then into the Weddell Sea. Topics of study ranged from rifting and basin formation to paleoclimate links between low and high latitudes. Off the Lesser Antilles scientists aboard the ship investigated the geologic processes that formed the islands and the submarine ridge nearby. Drilling results from this cruise allowed scientists for the first time to define the water flow and deformation processes at different stages of plate convergence at the Barbados Ridge.

The deepest hole ever drilled into the oceanic crust lies off the west coast of South America northeast of the Galápagos Islands. The hole was first drilled in 1979 and was deepened during the past year to a total depth of 1,562 m. The hole was of particular interest because its geologic structure was similar to rock formations found on land and because, by examining the chemistry and physical properties of rocks recovered from the hole, scientists can learn how seawater circulates through the basalts and sediments of young ocean crust. Scientists examined the 5.9-million-year-old rocks recovered from the hole to better understand how new rocks form at seafloor spreading centers and how they change in time as they move away from their sources.

In November and December 1986, *JOIDES Resolution* moved to the region that encompasses the Andes Mountains and Pacific Ocean off Peru, where some of the world's most damaging earthquakes and climate changes (for example, El Niños) occur. The ship collected cores of sediment and rock to be examined for clues into the processes associated with active continental margins and the evolution of climate and oceanic circulation in that part of the world.

*New techniques.* Announcements were made during the year of successful new techniques for operating and recovering oceanographic instruments. Of particular interest was the recovery of instruments that had been considered lost on the seafloor. Using an advanced side-scanning sonar device and navigational instruments that included a seafloor acoustic navigation system, oceanographers located and retrieved six separate moorings of oceanogaphic instruments. The moorings were originally lost when flotation devices were damaged or when release mechanisms failed. By recovering the lost hardware, the expedition also retrieved the information con-

362

tained in the instruments' data recorders. The retrieval of the equipment and their data demonstrated that oceanographers now had the capability from surface ships to locate instruments and moorings and recover them from the ocean bottom without the aid of acoustic transponders, a major step toward the establishment of long-term ocean measurements.

In other advances a new version of the GLORIA, a British deep-sea side-scanning sonar device, was built and underwent its first trials during the summer. Mapping with such devices revealed many geologic features, including deep-sea canyons, hundreds of previously unknown submarine volcanoes, faults, metal-rich deposits, and manganese nodule fields. About 2% of the world's ocean floor was mapped with high precision by use of this technique, and the new GLORIA was expected to be used first in the Bering Sea to help map the U.S. Exclusive Economic Zone there.

A new chemical technique that was expected to have important implications for measurements of global-ocean circulation was demonstrated in the Santa Monica Basin off California. In a prototype experiment two tracers, sulfur hexafluoride and perfluorodecalin, both inert and easy to detect, were deliberately injected at mid-depths in the basin and then tracked. Their circulation and diffusion were easily estimated from the data, showing that it would soon be feasible to perform ocean-scale tracer experiments lasting many years. This new technique was to be an important part of the new World Ocean Circulation Experiment (WOCE), also a part of the World Climate Research Program mentioned earlier.

*New programs.* A new international program of research into global environmental change caused by the interactions among the atmosphere, ocean, biosphere, and land, paying particular attention to the impact of the activities of humans on those interactions, was formally agreed to in September by the International Council of Scientific Unions. To be known as the International Geosphere-Biosphere Program of Global Change, it was scheduled to include a series of new oceanography projects that were in the planning stages. Of particular importance were to be studies of the role of ocean biology and chemistry in the cycles of carbon, nitrogen, sulfur, phosphorus, and oxygen, all central to life on Earth.

One such study stemmed from the recent discovery that sulfur compounds produced by biological processes in the ocean can have a major impact on atmospheric composition and, therefore, on global warming. For example, dimethyl sulfide (DMS) produced by planktonic algae escapes into the atmosphere and is oxidized to sulfate aerosol particles in the troposphere (the lower part of the Earth's atmosphere). The amounts correspond to about one-third to one-half of the sulfur that enters the atmosphere from the burning of fossil fuels. But the ocean input is global and, in fact, is dominant in the Southern Hemisphere.

Such research was expected to be just one part of a newly proposed international Joint Global Ocean Flux Study, which would provide the first comprehensive worldwide view of primary productivity in the oceans, carbon flux to the deep ocean, and other variables of critical importance in gaining an understanding of the coupling of marine biogeochemical cycles and the physical climate system. Essential complementary data on the physics of ocean heating, cooling, mixing, and transport processes were to be provided by the TOGA and WOCE programs discussed above. This integration of physics, chemistry, and biology is clearly the direction of the future.

—D. James Baker

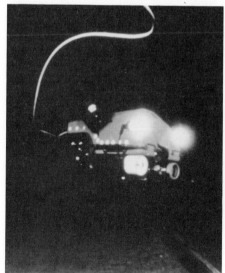 

*A self-propelled robot (far left) is deployed from the submersible* Alvin *to explore inside the sunken ocean liner* Titanic. *Among its discoveries was an electric winch on the* Titanic's *boat deck (left).*

Photos, Woods Hole Oceanographic Institution

# Electronics and information sciences

No phase of modern technological culture is untouched by the products of the electronics industry. By means of computers and associated electronic equipment, people calculate and write, send their voices and receive those of others through the reaches of outer space, drive in greater comfort and safety, increase their chances of physical survival, observe ever faster and smaller phenomena of nature, push back the barrier of the unknown, and increase national security.

## Communications systems

Computers and communications—the two words have been used together for several years, but until recently the two fields remained generally separate. During the past year, however, there was a definite merging and a recognition that although the two exist individually, in combination they increase their effectiveness so that they serve humans around the world in previously unimagined ways.

**ISDN.** For some years the communications industry has been eagerly awaiting the Integrated Services Digital Network (ISDN), a worldwide public telecommunications network that will serve a wide variety of user needs. The concept sounds simple, but the effort required (and being expended) to achieve standards for the various interfaces is enormous. And it must be recognized that, whatever standards are finally accepted, many companies (with their then obsolete equipment) will be unhappy.

Field trials of true ISDN (and ISDN-like) systems were being readied during the past year and in at least one case were under way. Illinois Bell, in conjunction with McDonald's Corp., initiated a full-fledged trial in mid-December 1986. In this experiment some 300 workstations were able to send voice and data simultaneously over simple twisted-pair telephone lines.

**Central office switching equipment.** The recognition by telephone companies throughout the world that computers and communications not only were merging but were also providing significant advantages to those involved expedited the conversion of telephone central offices to "digital switches." Central offices that employ electromechanical switches and relays, and even central offices that employ analog electronic systems, were rapidly being replaced by digital switches.

With digital equipment a voice is sampled many times a second, and the result of each sample is converted to a coded character. This coded character is then transmitted, for a long-distance call, from one central office to another and finally decoded for transmission to the distant telephone.

This sounds simple, but the cost of developing such a system is enormous—on the order of $1 billion. Therefore, it was no surprise that those companies with developed and working digital switching systems were making every effort to sell them. Because the U.S. represented a large part of the worldwide market and because the seven regional operating companies formed as a result of the breakup of the Bell System in 1984 controlled 80% of the U.S. market, a tremendous selling effort was being expended in their direction.

*Conference by videophone takes place using a new system developed by PicTel Corp. in which business users can make video calls over relatively low-cost digital transmission lines. The calls are about twice the price of a conventional long-distance telephone call.*

These Bell operating companies decide for themselves which switching systems they will purchase, but in most cases they have relied on their jointly owned subsidiary firm, Bell Communications Research, to provide guidance. This organization (generally called Bellcore) would, for a fee, evaluate the systems of any manufacturer. As of 1987 two manufacturers—AT&T and Northern Telecom Inc.—had systems that were installed and in operation in Bell operating company territories; in both cases the systems had been installed before the evaluation process was initiated.

**Customer premises equipment.** Most businesses larger than a one- or two-person office utilize small telephone systems called PBXs and key systems. Such systems (often owned by the proprietor and located in a closet or a basement) are connected to the local telephone central office with two or more trunks, thus allowing the employees to access those trunks or simply communicate with one another. During the past decade sophisticated electronics has allowed these systems to be greatly enhanced. For instance, these newer systems are able to display the calling number of internal calls, permit conferencing, indicate that a call is waiting, and facilitate speed calling (call a particular number by depressing one or two buttons). As might be expected, sophisticated accounting features are also included. For instance, a system may be programmed to provide detailed call information (such as the called party and the duration of the call) for particular telephones.

Analysis indicates that the market for key systems will continue at something less than $1 billion per year (at least through the end of the 1980s) and that sales of PBXs will total at least $3 billion annually.

Thus, although some suppliers are bound to become disillusioned and leave the business, the sheer magnitude of demand will lure others into it.

During the year Centrex, another solution to the internal communications problem, experienced a resurgence of popularity. A Centrex system is essentially a PBX, but it is located in the telephone central office rather than with the customer. Responsibility for maintenance passes from the user to the telephone company—but so also does ultimate control of the system. Floor space is saved in the customer's premises, but lines from each individual telephone (rather than just trunks from the system itself) must extend to the central office. Obviously, there are both advantages and disadvantages to such a system. However, telephone companies are uniquely qualified to provide Centrex, and many of them (especially the Bell operating companies) were giving Centrex "flagship" status.

**Fiber optics.** Companies throughout the world continued during the past year to spend millions of dollars on fiber optics and its associated electronics. As many as 8,000 telephone conversations can simultaneously be carried on a single pair of glass fibers and, through the application of a technology called wavelength division multiplexing, that number can be doubled.

US Sprint Communications, a joint venture of GTE and United Telecommunications, planned to have 37,800 km (23,000 mi) of optical fiber in operation by the end of 1987, and construction was proceeding at a rapid rate. The price tag of this undertaking approached $2 billion.

MCI, long dependent on microwaves (indeed, that is what the "M" in the name originally stood for),

Technicians in Atlanta, Georgia, monitor signals in the fiber-optic nerve center of US Sprint Communications, a supplier of long-distance telephone service. Along with many other telephone companies, Sprint was investing heavily in new optical fiber cables.

Roger Allen Grigg—Time Magazine

was rapidly converting to fiber optics, aiming at 11,-300 km (7,000 mi) before the end of 1987. And AT&T Communications, the long-distance arm of AT&T, pegged 16,400 km (10,200 mi) as its near-term goal. Others, including the National Telecommunications Network, a joint venture of seven companies, brought the total to more than 96,500 km (60,000 mi).

The result of this enthusiasm could be an over-abundance of capacity, at least for the foreseeable future. This prospect resulted during recent months in a flattening of the market for fiber, and some nervous users wondered whether there might be previously unrecognized problems with the material. This did not seem to be the case, however, as fiber technology continued to improve. For example, in past years multimode fibers (glass strands about as thick as a human hair) were generally used. But during recent months single-mode fiber (one-tenth the thickness of a human hair) began receiving most of the world's attention. Such fiber allows only one "ray" of light to pass through it, and this in turn permits transmission over much longer distances than is possible with multimode fiber before the signal being transmitted needs to be amplified and regenerated.

Users of single-mode fibers are not limited to a transmission of a single modulated light beam. By multiplexing (mixing) light beams of different frequencies (different colors) on the same strand of glass and then separating those beams at the receiving end, users can greatly expand the capacity of the system.

Until 1987 the long-distance telephone market was responsible for most of the sales of optical fibers, but industry observers expected that the "local loop" market (that segment of the telephone plant that extends from the central office toward the subscriber) would soon take the lead. If that should happen, the total market for fiber would soar once again.

**Customer-owned coin-operated telephones.** A new entrant to the field of high-technology telecommunications was the lowly pay telephone. In past years such a phone depended upon a collection of levers and switches for its operation; in those cases where other than a local call was being placed, a live operator at some distant office was also needed. But coin boxes often filled to overflowing before a coin collector could empty them; just as often a collector arrived only to find that merely a few coins had been deposited. An even more serious problem was the vandalizing of phones—and the inability of the telephone company to do anything about it.

All of this changed during recent months with the introduction of a "smart" payphone called a COCOT (customer-owned coin-operated telephone). The "customer-owned" part of this title refers to the recent decision in the U.S. that coin telephones are similar to other customer-premises equipment and can be owned and provided by anyone. Thus, an owner of a small grocery store could buy his own COCOT, attach it to a telephone line requested of the local telephone company, and be in business. The market, however, was anything but stable. Often the owners of COCOTs (in many cases entrepreneurs seizing on an apparently lucrative opportunity) did not deal fairly with those in whose establishments they placed the phone, nor were they, in turn, fairly treated by the telephone companies. Regulatory commissions stepped in to try to deal with the situation.

*Wavelength division multiplexer, developed by GTE Laboratories, allows two signals to be transmitted within the same optical fiber communications channel, thereby doubling the voice and data capacities of the optical fiber systems used by many telephone companies. Signals enter through optical fiber cables at the right and bottom, are combined in the multiplexer (mixer), and sent out through the cable at the left.*

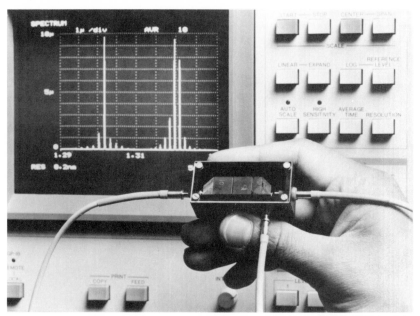

*Copernicus, West Germany's first telecommunications satellite, was scheduled for launch in the fall of 1987.*

Nevertheless, new technology will not be deterred. The "smart" phones include electronic devices that store a table of charges to all parts of the country, taking into account the day of week and time of day. These devices control other devices that generate a synthesized voice, and so a user who places a long-distance call is "told" exactly how much money should be deposited. The COCOTs also measure and store a running total of the money collected and transmit this information to a maintenance center when interrogated. Finally, a number of sensitive points are automatically monitored to protect against vandalism and, if an improper action is noted, a telephone call is automatically placed to the proper authorities.

—Robert E. Stoffels

## Computers and computer science

During the past year advances in technology produced significantly faster microprocessors, some of which emerged in commercially available computers. The year was also marked by the discovery of a new algorithm for testing whether a number is prime. In computer graphics a new way of generating realistic images emerged.

**New and faster microprocessors.** For many years the computer industry has been driven by the availability of new and faster electronic technologies, making it possible to improve computer performance each year without raising prices. The past year followed that trend as several manufacturers announced powerful new computing products.

Motorola, Inc., improved its MC68020 microprocessor "chip" by using a new silicon technology that made it possible to increase the internal clock speed from 16 MHz to 25 MHz (1 MHz is one million Hertz, or one million cycles per second). In addition to increasing the speed of the microprocessor, designers at Motorola were also able to eliminate the need for additional support chips to the processor, which improved its speed still further. As a result, new computer products using the MC68020 executed their tasks much faster than did their predecessors. In addition to improvements in existing processors, Motorola announced plans for another generation of microprocessors that would be named the MC68030.

SUN Microsystems Inc.'s line of computer workstations provided a startling example of how the faster Motorola MC68020 could improve performance. The new SUN computers introduced during the year were rated at 4.1 MIPS (millions of instructions per second, a measure of processor performance). They replaced SUN Microsystems computers introduced less than a year earlier that were rated at less than 2 MIPS. While machines rated at or above 4 MIPS were not unusual, they usually cost in the range of $400,000 to $500,000 and were shared among a small group of users. Because the new SUN Microsystems computer used an MC68020 microprocessor chip to do its computing, the cost was between $50,000 and $100,000, low enough to allow a single user to own one.

In another application of the MC68020, several companies introduced MC68020-based boards that plugged into existing computers and so provided extra processing power. The most interesting MC68020 products plugged into personal computers such as the IBM PC. The PC itself used an older, slower processor, the Intel 8088, which operated at 6 MHz. Thus, the add-on board containing an MC68020 provided more than four times the computing power of the original PC. In addition, the add-on boards usually contained between three and ten times as much memory as the PC and sometimes were equipped with an additional processor chip to increase the speed of addition, subtraction, multiplication, and division operations. To take advantage of the additional speed, software had to be rewritten to perform all processing on the MC68020 and to use the original PC processor only to control input and output devices such as floppy disks and video displays.

Other manufacturers also introduced new microprocessors during the year. Intel Corp. (which made the 8088, 8086, and 80286, all of which became standard in the IBM PC and PC-compatible personal computers) introduced a successor. The new chip, known as the 80386, was faster than its predecessors and differed from them as well. The differences are important because the original 8088 architecture limited memory addressability to regions of 64K bytes (each K is 1,024 bytes, and a byte is 8 bits). The new architecture allowed programs to address the much larger memories that would be available on future personal computers.

Although the IBM PC dominated the personal computer market for several years, Compaq Computer Corp. was the first to introduce a machine that used the new 80386. Its Deskpro 386, announced during the past year, illustrated the power of the next generation of personal computers. The Deskpro's disk storage and processing power are equivalent to those found on engineering workstations and are far greater than the power of other personal computers. At the same time, the Deskpro remains compatible with earlier PCs, allowing it to use software from the vast libraries that have been developed.

Fairchild Camera and Instrument Corp. entered the microprocessor competition by introducing its "Clipper" chip set. The Clipper differs from Motorola or Intel processors because it is a RISC (reduced instruction set computer). RISC technology was pioneered at IBM research centers and at universities such as the University of California at Berkeley. A RISC machine can perform only a few basic operations such as addition and subtraction. By comparison, conventional CISC (complex instruction set computer) machines can perform hundreds of different operations, many of which are seldom or never needed. The motivation for limiting the instruction set is that with fewer instructions the processor can be built to execute tasks much faster. When complex processing is needed, multiple RISC

*The Deskpro 386, developed by the Compaq Computer Corp., was the first personal computer to use the new and powerful 80386 microprocessor. The Deskpro's processing power far exceeded that of other personal computers.*

instructions can be used in place of a single CISC instruction. Fairchild claimed that while CISC chips are limited to between 5 and 10 MIPS, its RISC design would allow later versions of the Clipper to perform at speeds of 25 to 35 MIPS.

**A new prime number test.** Mathematicians say that an integer is prime if it has no factors other than one and itself. That is, a prime integer always produces a remainder when divided by integers other than one and itself. Examples of prime numbers include 2, 3, 5, 7, 11, and 13. The ancient Greeks were the first to ponder prime numbers, and they realized that there are an infinite number of primes but they are not spread out evenly. For example, the next prime after 1,327 is 1,361. The ancient Greeks even devised two methods of determining whether an integer was prime, one that used repeated division and another that enumerated integers in a table and then crossed out multiples.

For hundreds of years primality was a mathematical curiosity but was not of much practical importance. The computer changed all that. Prime numbers now play a key role in the fast Fourier transform algorithms (step-by-step procedures) used for digital signal processing, in generating random numbers used for computer simulation studies of physical phenomena, and in cryptography. These new uses stimulated research into finding methods for generating prime numbers and methods for testing whether a number is prime. The emphasis shifted from methods that are easy to understand to methods that run quickly on a modern digital computer. Some groups even suggested ways to modify computers to make them better at handling prime numbers.

Large prime numbers, those with more than 20 or 30 digits, are of particular importance in computer algorithms, and especially in cryptography. Many modern encryption techniques rely on large prime numbers as the key ingredients in making encoded messages difficult to decipher. Thus, the development of a quick test for primes is important because it would result in a revision of the way that many private and government organizations encrypt data. More important, those organizations want to know whether such a test can be discovered at all. (*See* Feature Article: The Business of Babel: Cryptology in the '80s.)

An advance during the past year came from Shafi Goldwasser and Joseph Kilian, both of the Massachusetts Institute of Technology. Their method tests numbers for primality in "polynomial time," meaning that the amount of time taken by a computer using their method is much shorter than the original enumerative methods. The Goldwasser-Kilian algorithm is not perfect; there is still room for improvement. First, although the method promises to be faster than existing methods when testing very large numbers, it is not competitive when used on the range of numbers tested in most present applications. Indeed, so much effort has been expended on optimizing computer programs for existing methods that it will take time before any newcomer will outperform them. (As of early 1987 a method devised by Leonard Adleman of the University of Southern California and Robert Rumley and Carl Pomerance of the University of Georgia was being used to test numbers with up to 200 digits.) Second, the Goldwasser-Kilian method is probabilistic. It finds the answer quickly with very high probability, but on a few, rare cases it takes longer.

Probabilistic algorithms for primality are not new. Michael Rabin of Harvard University introduced probabilistic algorithms in the mid-1970s. His test is both fast and easy to program on computers, but his algorithm does not always produce the correct answer. If Rabin's method indicates that a number is not a prime, that answer can be trusted absolutely; however, if his algorithm says the number is prime, that answer has only a high probability of being correct. Rabin's algorithm, along with other probabilistic methods that have been developed, is essentially a random search for an answer. The computer is permitted to spend only a limited amount of time ("polynomial in the size of the input" in formal terms) searching for a prime factor. If no prime factor is found in the allotted time, the program declares that the number is prime. By carefully directing the search, Rabin can prove that the probability of missing a prime factor is extremely small. Therefore, the probability of producing an incorrect answer is small.

The small uncertainty in all probabilistic methods bothers mathematicians and computer scientists, who have been seeking an algorithm that is both fast and always accurate. Also in the mid-1970s,

*IBM Personal System/2 Color Display Model 8514, introduced in April 1987, provides high-quality graphics and the capability of choosing up to 256 colors for any given task.*

IBM Corporation

Gary Miller of the University of Southern California discovered a fast primality test that is not probabilistic, but the correctness of Miller's method relies on a mathematical conjecture known as the Riemann hypothesis. Although many mathematicians suspect the Riemann hypothesis is correct, no one has been able to prove it. Thus, a different form of uncertainty plagues Miller's method (*see* MATHEMATICS).

The Goldwasser-Kilian algorithm moves toward the goal of eliminating uncertainty. Like Rabin's method it is fast, but unlike Rabin's method it never gives an incorrect answer. However, the Goldwasser-Kilian method is probabilistic in a different way. It has high probability of running fast, but it may be slow in rare cases. The saving grace is that at its slowest the Goldwasser-Kilian method should perform no worse than the Adleman-Rumley-Pomerance method.

Clearly, the new method takes an important theoretical step forward in the science of computing with prime numbers. It promises to allow computer scientists to test the primality of numbers much larger than current methods can handle. What remains to be seen is how practical the new method will be when used on real computers and how large the primes need to be before it performs better than other methods.

**Computer-generated graphics.** Computer-generated graphics has advanced rapidly in recent years with the discovery of new algorithms and the development of special-purpose graphics hardware. During recent months results of graphics research began to emerge in the form of business graphics packages that produced diagrammatic representations of statistics by the use of pie charts, bar charts, and simple line drawings.

The new business graphics software did not use particularly difficult mathematics, but it did introduce new ways for unsophisticated users to manipulate drawings. It seemed certain to have an immediate impact on nontechnical people who were using personal computers, because it gave them the ability to format and print charts that looked as though they were professionally drawn.

Research on sophisticated computer-generated graphics also advanced during the year, with much attention being focused on making computer graphic drawings more realistic. Good results were obtained by a variety of researchers in the areas of shading and randomness. Early computer graphic drawings were recognizable for their lack of realistic shading. Because the human eye uses shading to help judge shape, texture, and distance, drawings created with simplistic notions of light and shadow look flat and unrealistic. Computing correct shading can be difficult and requires much computing time. However, new algorithms introduced during the year allowed computers to generate drawings with realistic shading even when the picture contained multiple light sources. The algorithms took into account the light sources, their relative intensities, and their effects when combined. As a result, overlapping shadows became darker, and areas reached from multiple light sources became lighter. The research on shading also involved finding ways in which to display realistic shading of colors.

Another interesting idea in computer graphics became popular during the year because it helped solve

*Scientist monitors prototype of West Germany's first supercomputer, SUPRENUM (Supercomputer for Numerical Applications), scheduled to be ready for use in 1988. It was designed to help solve complex scientific and technological problems.*

INP/Authenticated News International

the important problem of randomness. The problem arises when a precise, digital computer is used to generate imprecise, random events. For example, when simulating the effects of air flowing across an airplane wing, the computer needs to introduce some random motion to make the simulation accurate (molecules of air flowing past a real airplane wing do not all follow exactly the same path). To understand why such small randomness is important, one can consider a computer simulation of a football balancing on a razor-sharp edge. Unless some randomness is introduced to account for air moving around the football, the computer will predict that the ball can be balanced without falling. It is well known, however, that such balance would be impossible in practice.

In computer graphics some kind of randomness is essential in making pictures realistic. For example, one might consider a picture of a mountain. Because mountains grow at random, the rocks on a mountain face jut out in random, chaotic ways. If the computer generates a smooth-faced mountain, the kind easily described by mathematical curves, the picture will look artificial.

During the past year computer scientists began using a technique known as fractal geometry to generate impressively realistic drawings of mountains, oceans, and other natural objects. The ideas of fractal growth were first formulated by Benoit Mandelbrot at the IBM Thomas J. Watson Research Center. Mandelbrot observed that many physical objects exhibit a sprawling, somewhat random pattern and also that the pattern remains the same through a large scale of magnification. Using this idea in reverse, a computer can start from a fractal pattern and build up groups of fractals until a large object has been drawn. By constraining growth, the general shape of the object can be controlled. Pixar Corp. began using Mandelbrot's ideas to produce computer-generated graphics for the motion-picture industry. In addition to objects in a landscape, fractals can generate such diverse images as close-up pictures of rusted metal or snowflakes.

Fractal growth has applications in areas outside of computer graphics. For example, scientists use fractals to explain physical phenomena such as crystal growth, movements in fluids, and the shape of polymers. Fractals can also explain what appears to be the disorderly movement of bubbles through liquids. Because of these accomplishments most computer scientists agree that fractals will be increasingly important in computations that deal with physical phenomena; they also may soon be a fundamental part of computer simulation. (See *1981 Yearbook of Science and the Future* Feature Article: FRACTALS AND THE GEOMETRY OF NATURE.)

—Douglas E. Comer

## Electronics

The international market for electronic products and their manufacture became more integrated and expansive during the past year. The government-owned-and-operated West German federal post office entered the fiber-optics field, already under development in both the United States and Japan. Siemens AG, a West German firm, won a $22 million contract to provide China with data-processing equipment; Siemens also bought a site in the U.S. to house its power semiconductors and entered into a joint venture with GTE Corp. for the development and manufacture of telecommunications equipment. The General Instrument Corp. signed with Hyundai to make a new line of silicon chips. The Wang Laboratories Inc., located in Lowell, Mass., established a subsidiary in South Korea.

Even those countries formerly on the edge of the electronic landscape were beginning to enter it. For example, Yugoslavia was attempting to enter the U.S.

*Technician loads circuit boards onto racks for the NCR 9800 computer. Introduced in 1986, the 9800 utilizes 32-bit microprocessor chips.*

market with its ISKRA VME single-board computer. The Israeli electronic industry was manufacturing a version of an IBM machine that was selling at a fraction of the cost of the original.

**Chips.** At the heart of present-day electronic technology is the silicon wafer. Often referred to as a chip, it has many electronic circuits etched in it. Chips of new materials such as lithium niobate ($LiNbO_3$) and gallium arsenide (GaAs) were under development during the year. Also, new manufacturing techniques such as the application of laser technology were used to make chips of increased structural complexity that could handle more information faster with less power required. It was not so long ago that the eight-bit microprocessor capable of representing 256 numbers in one byte (a byte consists of eight bits, each one capable of storing two pieces of information) was the standard in personal computers. By 1987 the 32-bit chip was making its appearance and was beginning to compete for market dominance; a 32-bit word can be made to represent 4,294,967,296 numbers.

As of 1987 three U.S. companies, Intel Corp., Motorola Inc., and National Semiconductor Corp., were making aggressive bids to capture about 70% of the world's chip market, which was $30 million in 1987 and was expected to grow to $215 million by 1990. The personal computer (PC) industry was expected

Computer memory chip developed by IBM can store the equivalent of about 400 pages of double-spaced typewritten text. It can read the data in all of its memory cells in only one-quarter of a second.

IBM Corporation

to provide a major market opportunity for those chip makers. Intel introduced its 32-bit chip, the 80386, which was designed to succeed the 80286 chip installed in IBM PC's and those computers compatible with it. The company hoped that this chip would, because of its ability to run existing software based on the present-day 16-bit chips, secure a major share of the coming 32-bit market.

Together with the efforts by manufacturers to enlarge the data-handling capacity of their chips were their attempts to pack ever more circuits onto a given chip size. This was done to save space and weight, to reduce electrical power requirements, and to increase the rate at which data could be processed. During 1986 the Fairchild Semiconductor Corp. was able to design a chip measuring 2.54 cm (one inch) square that contained about 2.8 million circuit elements. This exceeded the density of many other present-day chips by a ratio of about three to one. Electrical characteristics of the chip were designed to allow for an increased rate of data transmission over that of existing chips.

**Automotive applications.** If the latest electronic-navigational systems from Etak Inc. in the U.S. and the West German firm of VDO Adolf Schindling AG find their way into automobiles, the timely arrival of drivers at their destinations will almost be assured—barring any traffic snarls. Both of these systems use onboard computers with associated video terminals, "smart" magnetic compasses, and the capability to store and compare geographic data against a car's position. For example, the Etak system provides an electronic map of the entire area in California between San Francisco and San Diego, while the Schindling system provides bar-coded city maps against which the position of a car is checked. The Schindling system has been field tested, and its accuracy is claimed to be 97%.

In the opinion of some experts, a revolution in automotive design is under way that will greatly reduce the number of wires found under the dashboards of present-day cars. Despite this reduction, more reliable information is expected to be available to the driver. The 1987 Cadillac Allante was the first production car to incorporate this new technology. Central to the system is an onboard computer that sends signals along a single wire to various subsystems throughout the car. These subsystems contain "smart" power chips, which combine both logic and power functions. For example, the system operates and checks on the status of more than 40 lights in the Allante and also provides data on engine speed, fuel delivery, idle speed, dashboard displays, climatic controls, and the use of fog lights.

Manufacturers of smart power chips saw a vast market potential for this new technology. It was estimated that about 100 of these devices would

*The "Quick Snap" disposable camera, developed by the Fuji Photo Film Co., contains lens, shutter, and film and costs less than $10. After the pictures have been taken, the camera is dropped off for processing the film and is then discarded.*

eventually be installed in every car. The technology was spreading beyond the confines of the U.S. The French automakers Renault and Peugeot joined forces to produce a common system for their cars. In West Germany Robert Bosch GmbH of Stuttgart was working with Intel to produce a high-speed data-transmission system.

**Disaster prevention.** While it was impossible to predict with certainty if a disaster similar to the explosion at the Chernobyl nuclear power plant in the Soviet Union would happen in the U.S., it could be stated that U.S. control systems, partly in response to the lessons learned from the accident at Three Mile Island in 1979 and the fire at the Browns Ferry reactor near Decatur, Ala., in 1975, were more sophisticated than those found in the Soviet Union. Although the shutdown system was working well in 1979 at the Three Mile Island nuclear plant, the plant operators were overwhelmed by the mass of data and consequently made some errors. After that, the computer equipment at the plant was upgraded. Before the accident hundreds of systems provided the operators with an enormous mass of raw data. By 1987 the trend was toward visual displays of systems-analyzed data.

A significant effort was under way at the University of Illinois to prevent future nuclear disasters. Researchers there combined the enormous power of the Cray X-MP/24 supercomputer with the artificial intelligence of an expert system that can simulate and analyze the chain of possible events faster than they can occur in nature. This capability would give operators the needed time for intervention should such be required. Also, by chaining events back in time, the prime causes of a potential disaster could be discerned.

While the accident at the Three Mile Island installation showed the need for analysis of the reams of data generated by the many monitoring systems involved, the fire at the Browns Ferry station indicated the need for increased protection of these systems. Specifically, the fire burned out the station's two monitoring channels, which were contained in the same tunnel. To protect such redundancy systems in the future, the two burned channels were replaced with four, each housed in a separate tunnel.

**Medical applications.** A research effort in nuclear magnetic resonance (NMR) technology at the Max Planck Institute in Göttingen, West Germany, reduced the required exposure time for a usable image of human organs from minutes to seconds. First used as a technique to produce images of human organs in 1976, NMR achieves its results by applying a magnetic field and radiofrequency waves to tissues in the human body. This causes the atomic nuclei contained within the tissue to become excited and emit a signal that is converted by a computer into a visual image. However, it takes about one second for the excited nuclei to resume their magnetic equilibrium; it is only then that a new radiofrequency pulse can be applied, and so considerable time is required to obtain an image.

The new technique uses much weaker radiofrequency pulses that occur much more rapidly. As a result, the time needed for an excited nucleus to return to its magnetic equilibrium position is reduced to 10 to 20 milliseconds. Thus, an image can be completed within seconds. While quantitative studies of blood flow within the human body and dimensions as small as about two millimeters could be measured by the old method, the new technique allows for an extension of NMR to the study of dynamic processes

373

General Electric Research and Development Center, Schenectady, N.Y.

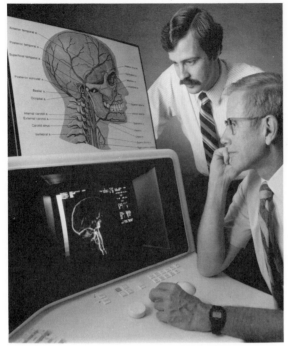

*The velocity of blood flow in a human head and neck is revealed by the use of nuclear magnetic resonance. This noninvasive technique produces its images by applying a magnetic field and radiofrequency waves to body tissues.*

within the human body. For example, the secretion function of the kidneys and the movement of the heart can now be observed. General Electric Co. in the U.S., Philips Industries in The Netherlands, and Siemens AG in West Germany were all incorporating the new technique into their NMR scanners.

**Military applications.** The demands of modern aerial warfare place ever greater reliance upon in-creasingly sophisticated electronic systems for the successful completion of an assigned mission. These systems essentially integrate into a single graphic display the information that had previously been revealed by various gauges and dials. Much of the sensing and the display of the data are based upon infrared sensing and cathode-ray display technology. For example, the U.S. Air Force was placing a system into its fighter planes in which an electronic terrain map stored in its onboard computer is constantly compared to real-time altimeter data. As the airplane nears its target on a low-level approach, an infrared laser/tracker locks onto the target with great precision. The best mode of attack by the plane is automatically calculated by the computer, as is the flight trajectory of any missile that might be released and its release point.

The pilot is automatically warned by audible and visual signals of possible impending disasters. Should he fail to respond to them, the system puts the airplane automatically into level flight and takes over from him.

**Language and speech.** Machines during the past year were becoming more proficient in their ability to understand human language and speech. For instance, computer programs were being developed that translate the romanized pronunciation of Chinese characters into more than 6,000 written ideographs.

Present-day computers have the ability to understand about several hundred words at the most. Patterns of digits that represent individual words are stored in a computer. In operation, the computer compares these patterns with word utterances in real time. Even with their limited vocabulary, the usefulness of such computers in the factory and the laboratory has been proved. The technology is so attractive

*Apple IIgs, introduced in 1986, offers a 16-bit microprocessor with three times the speed that can be achieved by the Apple IIc and IIe. The new model also provides high-resolution graphics (g) and advanced sound capabilities (s).*

AP/Wide World

that the $20 million market of 1986 was expected to increase to more than $1 billion by 1990.

**Other developments.** During the year supercomputers that are able to perform billions of calculations in one-billionth of a second were introduced. A digital tape recorder made its appearance in Japan. X-rays were being used in the production of semiconductor circuits.

An intelligent and high-speed digital oscilloscope, one of the basic measuring tools of the electronic engineer, was introduced during the past year. Other developments included the extended use of computer-assisted design and computer-assisted manufacturing systems.

—Franz J. Monssen

## Information systems and services

During the past year the question of whether the U.S. has an information policy was hotly debated. Andrew Aimes, writing in *Government Computer News,* maintained that information policy was being made by the three branches of government in a piecemeal and relatively unplanned manner. He stated that much of what passed for policy resulted from collisions and frictions between organizations within the government, between the government and groups in the private sector, and between competing countries. He went on to say that the U.S. government had to get its information policy house in order and find practical ways of increasing the level of coordination between and among the principal players.

Some steps in this direction were taken. Circular A-130, released by the U.S. Office of Management and Budget (OMB) on Dec. 12, 1985, provided an initial broad outline of national information policy goals. The circular set basic guidelines for the collection, processing, and dissemination of information by federal agencies and the management of federal information systems. It also revised existing directives on privacy, computer security, and cost-accounting procedures for federal computer and telecommunications facilities. The circular stated that government information is a valuable national resource and that "the free flow of information from the government to its citizens and vice versa is essential to a democratic society." Among the key provisions were that agencies should create, collect, and disseminate information only when necessary for the proper performance of agency functions, and that they should provide public access to government information consistent with the Freedom of Information Act.

A national policy on the transfer of scientific, technical, and engineering information generated as a result of federally funded research was signed by U.S. Pres. Ronald Reagan as National Security Directive 189. The directive, addressed to the heads of executive branch departments and agencies, stated, "It is the policy of this Administration that, to the maximum extent possible, the products of fundamental research remain unrestricted. It is also the policy of this Administration that, where the national security requires control, the mechanism for control of information generated during federally funded fundamental research in science, technology, and engineering at colleges, universities, and laboratories is classification." Each federal government agency was to be responsible for determining the proper classification prior to the awarding of research grants or contracts and for periodically reviewing all such awards for potential classification.

Many professional societies expressed concern about the effects of this policy. The Association of Research Libraries and the Council on Library Resources issued statements reaffirming a commitment to unrestricted access to information and to the principle that the dissemination of ideas is fundamental to a democratic society. These tenets, it was claimed, must take precedence over the principles of national security and economic competition unless a clear and public case can be made for restricting access in a specific instance or to a clearly defined body of information.

U.S. Rep. George Brown, Jr. (Dem., Calif.), speaking at the annual Forum on Information Policies sponsored by the Federal Library and Information Center Committee, voiced his concern that the short-term advantages of the government's attempt to restrict the flow of information and to keep it from commercial and military competitors may do more harm to the U.S.'s own scientific endeavors than it would do to potential competitors. He also made the point that since federal agencies control information relevant to the evaluation of their agency's performance, it is necessary to ensure that this information is not withheld by making it classified in the terms of the OMB Circular A-130.

**U.S. information systems.** U.S. government agencies continued to increase and improve their computerized information services. The U.S. Department of Agriculture (USDA) added the Electronic Food and Nutrition Service to its already extensive electronic information system. Users of this service can access a data base of dietary guidelines, regularly updated press releases, and weekly reports on food costs. In cooperation with the Department of Human Services, the USDA provided the Animal Health Information Service. Users—veterinarians and owners of pets—can retrieve current information on vaccines, regulations, and veterinary research.

The National Library of Medicine's Medlars system produced a cancer data base called PDQ (Physician Data Query). It provides physicians with monthly updated information on advances in treatment of

*Electronic Food and Nutrition Service is provided by the U.S. Department of Agriculture. Users have access to a data base consisting of dietary guidelines, updated press releases, and weekly reports on food costs.*

specific types of cancer. Bioethicsline, another bibliographic data base from the National Library of Medicine, contains information on questions of ethics and public policy in the fields of health care and biomedical research. Included are citations on such topics as codes of professional ethics, patients' rights, organ donations and transplants, euthanasia, and abortion. The approximately 20,000 citations refer to a variety of document types dating from 1973 to the present. Updating is done monthly, with about 2,000 documents added each year.

The Patent and Trademark Office of the U.S. Department of Commerce completed the initial phase of its new automated patent examination process. The Automated Patent System (APS) was designed to handle new patent applications, of which there are more than 120,000 each year. The Patent Office has accumulated more than 27 million patent documents, or about 215 million pages, since 1790, when the first patent was issued. These documents were being converted for storage on optical disks, enabling patent examiners to work at remote stations and have access to a central data base containing U.S. and foreign patent information. The system was expected to reduce the time needed to process patent applications and to improve the quality of patents by allowing examiners more time to study applications.

The National Council on Family Relations produced a Family Resources Data Base consisting of bibliographic information about professionals working in family studies and related fields; information about family life research, education, and training institutions; and information on organizations serving the family. The data base was available on the Human Resources Information Network.

**International information systems.** Worldwide trade in goods, services, and securities has increased the need for international information. Textline, a London-based service, meets those needs by providing English-language abstracts of business-related articles culled from approximately 130 newspapers published in Western Europe, the Middle and Far East, Central and South America, the Soviet bloc, Australia, and Africa. In addition, the service made available abstracts of nearly 500 periodicals covering banking, chemicals, engineering, and insurance. Textline thus became a source of information on international business trends, new products and developments, and political events as they affected the business climate.

ECHO, the European Commission Host Organization, located in Luxembourg, created a data base of information brokers to enable their services and specialties to become more widely known and used throughout the nations of the European Communities. Information brokers, members of one of the new professions to come out of recent technological innovation, are experts in the use of computerized data bases.

The governments of Austria and the Soviet Union signed an agreement to permit mutual access to data bases on the social sciences and economics of both countries. This cooperative effort, launched as an experiment, included access to INION, one of the largest social science and economics data bases in the Soviet Union. The project made Austria the first country outside the Soviet bloc to have access officially to a Soviet data base.

Some lucky Italian farmers had an electronic partner, Agrivideotel, that helped them plan their work and reminded them when something urgent needed to be done. A farmer, using this interactive vidiotex system, reports on the crops that he is currently growing. Agrivideotel might then ask about the local weather and if the land has been irrigated recently, after which it would indicate when the next irrigation is needed. This service was particularly valuable in those parts of Italy where there was a shortage of water.

A vidiotex service in Ireland offered a farm accountancy service and helped farmers calculate whether it would be worthwhile to pursue certain farming risks. Similar systems were being planned for Greece, Spain, and Portugal.

*Optical disc similar to the compact discs used in audio systems can store up to 1.5 million pages of information. A laser records data on the disc, permanently etching the surface while the disc spins. Another laser can retrieve the information by sensing the etching without destroying it.*

**Information science research.** During the year scientists at Case Western Reserve University, Cleveland, Ohio, studied the cognitive processes involved when people seek and retrieve information. The first phase of the study was devoted to methodological problems and to the development of models and measures of information-seeking behavior. During the second phase a series of experiments was conducted to test the previously developed models in relation to the context, structure, and classification of the requests; the search strategies used; and the characteristics and behavior of the searchers.

The Center for Innovation Management Studies was established at Lehigh University, Bethlehem, Pa., to conduct research that would contribute to knowledge about management problems encountered during the technical innovation process and would also identify management practices that may be effective in avoiding or overcoming those problems. Central to the project's research activities was to be the creation of a computer-based bibliography on technical innovation and its management.

The objective of a field study at the Battelle Memorial Institute, Columbus, Ohio, was to investigate the effects of hazard information on the development of risk judgment and action. Data were collected about natural hazards such as mud slides and earthquakes. Interviews with risk-assessment experts, local hazard managers, media representatives, and the general public were used to test and refine a causal model describing the effects of hazard information and a number of background variables on risk judgment and hazard-mitigation behavior. The results of this study were expected to contribute to the understanding of the factors affecting the communication of hazard information from hazard managers to the public and should lead to the development of improved information programs for a wide variety of hazards.

Technological Information Pilot System (TIPS) designated a multinational project that is focused on designing and testing a multinational information network to promote the transfer of technology from industrial nations to less developed countries. The project was funded by the United Nations and supervised by the Office of Projects Execution. The nerve center for the network was located in Rome, and national bureaus were established in each of the participating countries. The main objective of TIPS was to collect and disseminate information on new products and processes, trade investments, and business opportunities.

Dutch-language libraries were participating in a project to create the largest data base of sheet music in The Netherlands. Each library was to use the standards set by the Anglo American Cataloging Rules (AACR2) to process its own holdings. The cooperative activities were expected to process about one million titles of sheet music by 1990.

The Department of Education at Linkoping University in Sweden was studying the conditions affecting the development of information services to small and medium-size industrial companies. The study sought to identify the university information resources available to small companies and the barriers affecting the utilization of information by the individual worker and manager.

—Harold Borko

## Satellite systems

Applications satellites perform three basic functions: communications, Earth observation, and navigation. Designed, constructed, and operated by private industrial concerns, individual countries, and groups of nations, applications satellites proved invaluable throughout 1986.

RCA Satcom K-1 communications satellite is launched from the U.S. shuttle orbiter Columbia in January 1986. The satellite provides television program distribution for hotels, apartment houses, and other multiunit dwellings and institutions.

Progress in expanding networks of applications satellites, however, was severely curtailed during the year. The tragic accident that destroyed the space shuttle *Challenger* and killed its seven crew members in January 1986 canceled a scheduled banner year for U.S. manned space programs. In addition, the failures of unmanned U.S. Delta and Titan boosters, as well as the French-managed Ariane launcher, grounded many planned satellites during the year. While the U.S. and Europe reshaped their competitive satellite-launching industries, Japan, China, and the Soviet Union made significant strides in their national space programs.

**Communications satellites.** The importance of communications satellites for domestic and international purposes was demonstrated throughout the year. In early January 1986 the crew of the U.S. shuttle orbiter *Columbia* deployed an RCA Satcom K-1 communications satellite. The spacecraft was the second of a planned fleet of three operating in the Kµ-band part of the radio spectrum. Each Satcom K-1 was designed to provide coverage of the conterminous 48 states. They would also provide direct satellite-to-Earth television program distribution for hotels, apartment houses, and other multiunit dwellings and institutions.

Competitor to the U.S. space shuttle for payload customers, the French Ariane booster achieved a successful flight in March. From a new launch pad in Kourou, French Guiana, the Ariane placed into orbit a U.S. GTE Spacenet GStar 2 and Brazil's Brasilsat S2 communications satellites. Ariane did, however, suffer a failure in May. Minutes after liftoff the third stage refused to fire. Its Intelsat 5 F14 telecommunications satellite payload was lost in the Atlantic Ocean. As in the case of the U.S. space shuttle, the Ariane booster was then grounded for investigation.

In December a U.S. Atlas-Centaur booster successfully launched the sixth Fleet Satellite Communications spacecraft into geosynchronous orbit. (A satellite in geosynchronous orbit travels above the Equator and at the same speed as the Earth rotates, thus remaining over the same place on the Earth.) From this vantage point the satellite was used by U.S. military services throughout the world, linking ships, aircraft, and land bases.

The failures of the space shuttle, the Ariane, a U.S. Air Force Titan 34D unmanned rocket in April, and a Delta launch vehicle in May led to a virtual loss of U.S. space launch capability. This series of failures prompted China and the Soviet Union to

378

pursue aggressively the marketing of their boosters to the world community.

The China Great Wall Industry Corp. in Beijing (Peking) promoted the Long March 3 rocket, signing up customers from the U.S., Sweden, and Iran. The Soviet Union also offered payload-launch services, including the use of its powerful Proton launcher. A commercial entity, Glavcosmos, was created by the Soviet government to provide a wide range of space services to other nations.

Japan's National Space Development Agency (NASDA) launched a BS-2B in February from its facility at Kyushu. Part of a Broadcasting Satellite Experimental program, these satellites were the world's first to beam signals to individual television sets. Built by Toshiba/General Electric Co., the satellites were used by the Japan Broadcasting Corp. to provide direct color TV transmission to the Japanese mainland and remote islands. In August Japan introduced the H-1 launch vehicle. A product of Japan's NASDA, the H-1 placed in orbit two satellites on its maiden flight: a geodetic laser-reflecting spacecraft and a small Japanese amateur-radio satellite.

China continued to develop a national satellite communications system. A spacecraft designed to relay radio, television, and telegraph signals was launched in February.

Several types of communications satellites were utilized extensively by the Soviet Union. The Ekran, Gorizont, Raduga, and Molniya series of satellites were launched in 1986 to provide reliable, continuous, and economical point-to-point communications.

The Communications Satellite Corp. (Comsat) announced in 1986 the development of a new technique that would permit geosynchronous communications satellites to double their operational lifetimes in space. Designated the "Comsat Maneuver," the life-extension concept would allow communications satellites to drift naturally in orbit without a loss of their locks on Earth-based antennas. The technique would save the fuel that had been used continually to align a satellite's antenna with a ground station.

The 1986 World Cup soccer tournament was the Earth's most watched sporting event, thanks to satellites. During the 52-game series involving teams from 24 nations, the World Cup was viewed by an estimated 12 billion people in more than 100 countries. Mexico's Morelos satellite system and the six satellites of the International Telecommunications Satellite Organization (Intelsat), stationed over the Atlantic, Pacific, and Indian oceans, were utilized.

The largest number of Intelsat satellites ever used for a single event took place in October. Seven Intelsat spacecraft provided worldwide coverage from Reykjavík, Iceland, of the meeting between U.S. Pres. Ronald Reagan and Soviet leader Mikhail Gorbachev.

In 1986 Intelsat continued Project SHARE (Satellites for Health and Rural Education) with a free-of-charge series of continuing medical education pro-

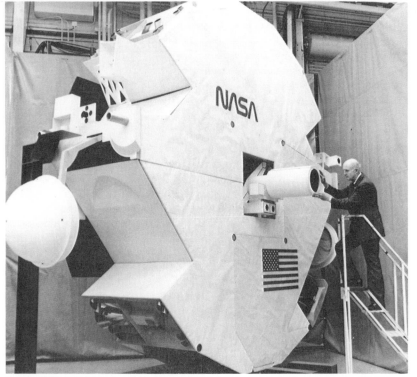

Veteran astronaut Lt. Gen. Thomas Stafford examines the full-scale model of the Orbital Maneuvering Vehicle. Designed by LTV Aerospace and Defense Co. as a companion to the space shuttle, the unmanned vehicle could be launched from the shuttle to repair or retrieve malfunctioning satellites.

AP/Wide World

grams for 5,000 physicians in six Latin-American and Caribbean countries. The project also sponsored video-conference lectures to health-care professionals in five African countries.

Patterned after Intelsat, the International Maritime Satellite Organization (Inmarsat) operated a global system of satellite communications using leased Intelsat, Comsat, and European Space Agency (ESA) satellites. The organization provided high-quality telephone, telex, data, facsimile, and television transmissions to ships, off-shore drilling stations, and coastal Earth stations. Formed in 1982, Inmarsat as of 1987 had 48 member countries and more than 5,000 ship or Earth stations.

Inmarsat during the year led a series of developmental tests of aeronautical satellite communications. Airlines' communications had been confined to conventional radio and thus had been limited as to range, capacity, and reliability. Two types of services were under development, the first relating to airline operational needs and the second to telephone service to airline passengers.

**Earth observation satellites.** This category of applications satellites consists of three major types: weather (meteorologic), Earth resources, and military reconnaissance.

*Weather satellites.* A ninth Geostationary Operational Environmental Satellite (GOES-G) was

*U.S. weather satellite NOAA 10 is launched by an Atlas-E booster from Vandenberg Air Force Base in California in September 1986. Placed in a near-polar orbit, it circled the Earth 14 times each day.*

*Geostationary Operational Environmental Satellite, designed to provide data on precipitation and surface temperatures, is prepared for its launch in May 1986. However, the launch vehicle malfunctioned, and the satellite was destroyed.*

launched on a Delta vehicle from Cape Canaveral, Fla., in May 1986. Destined for stationary orbit above the Equator, it was equipped to relay environmental data on rainfall, river levels, snow depths, and surface temperatures. However, about 71 seconds after lift-off the Delta launcher's main engine shut down, and the rocket and its payload were destroyed.

A U.S. meteorologic satellite, NOAA 10, was launched aboard an Atlas-E booster in September. A third-generation operational weather satellite for the National Oceanic and Atmospheric Administration (NOAA), it was positioned into a near-polar orbit. Circling the Earth 14 times each day, the satellite collected data and transmitted the information directly to users throughout the world to enhance local weather analysis and forecasting.

A Soviet Meteor-2 weather satellite was launched in May as part of the first civil applications-satellite program in the U.S.S.R. Soviet authorities stated that each Meteor satellite gathered more data from one orbit than would 15,000 meteorologic stations on the Earth.

From orbit, weather-satellite sensors were programmed to forecast malaria hazards. NASA scientists began work in 1986 on a pilot project using satellite data to study rainfall and surface water, elements that trigger the breeding of malaria-carrying mosquitoes.

*Earth resources satellites.* Conceived by Centre Nationale d'Etudes Spatiales (CNES), the French national space agency, a SPOT-1 remote-sensing satellite was launched on an Ariane rocket in February 1986. SPOT was the world's first commercial remote-sensing venture, backed financially by the governments of France, Sweden, and Belgium, along with several private shareholders. Orbiting the Earth in a Sun-synchronous orbit, SPOT could image the same area once every 2½ days. Typical applications for SPOT imagery included mineral exploration, crop forecasting, mapping, land-use studies for environmental planning, and management. In certain modes SPOT produced images with a resolution as small as 10 m (33 ft). This was at least three times more detailed than images available from other civilian satellites, such as the U.S. Landsat remote-sensing spacecraft.

Among the commercial users of SPOT's imagery were the news media. Photos "snapped" by SPOT were used by television networks to show the Chernobyl nuclear plant accident in the U.S.S.R., a Soviet nuclear test facility, and preparations for the launching of a Soviet space shuttle.

SPOT's U.S. counterpart, the Earth Observation Satellite Co. (EOSAT), completed a year of commercial operations under a ten-year "government-to-industry" transition contract. EOSAT was developing market strategies for using both previously gathered and newly obtained satellite imagery from the U.S. Landsats 4 and 5.

In late December Chinese and U.S. officials opened a U.S.-supplied satellite station that received

*View of the Atlas Mountains in Algeria is provided by a photograph taken from SPOT-1, the world's first commercial remote-sensing satellite. SPOT-1 was launched from Kourou, French Guiana, on an Ariane rocket in February 1986.*

data daily from the two U.S. Landsat spacecraft. The $10 million facility, the first sold to a Communist nation, was situated in Beijing. Using special receiving and processing equipment, the station could receive satellite images of about 80% of China's territory, as well as areas of the Soviet Union, Japan, and Taiwan.

*A U.S. Air Force Titan 34D rocket lifts off, explodes, and showers debris over Vandenberg Air Force Base in California on April 18, 1986. It carried a KH-11 reconnaissance satellite, reported to be capable of scanning objects only a few meters in size from a 320-kilometer (200-mile)-high orbit.*

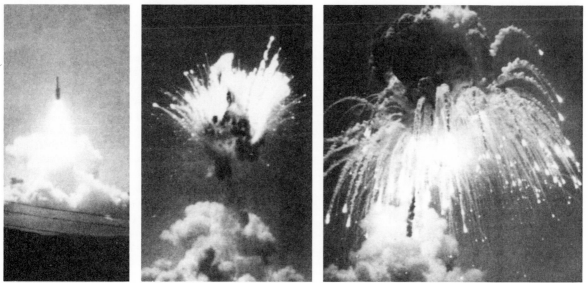

*Military reconnaissance satellites.* The U.S. military space program suffered a severe setback in April when an Air Force Titan 34D exploded less than 350 m (1,000 ft) above its California launch pad. The payload was a KH-11 reconnaissance satellite. An earlier KH-11 satellite, reported to be capable of scanning objects only a few meters in size from a 320-km (200-mi)-high orbit, was still in orbit.

During the past year the Soviet Union launched many photoreconnaissance spacecraft. Designated as Cosmos-class satellites, these spacecraft were designed to obtain images of value to military intelligence. It was widely accepted that such satellites, in use by the U.S. and U.S.S.R. for more than two decades, had had a stabilizing influence on global peace.

In October China's 19th spacecraft was launched from the Jiuquan (Chiu-ch'üan) Launching Center in northwestern China. Apparently a photoreconnaissance satellite, it was recovered a few days later. Chinese officials said that the satellite's mission was land surveillance, mineral prospecting, environmental studies, and "other uses." The satellite utilized improved photographic equipment to transmit better images from space.

**Navigation satellites.** Seven operational satellites of the U.S. Global Positioning System (GPS), also known as NavStar, were in orbit in 1986. Testing of the GPS permitted periodic, three-dimensional navigation positioning, with users of the system increasing in number. Latitude, longitude, and altitude could be provided five to six hours a day anywhere in the world. Applying a similar concept, the Soviet Union broadened the scope of its Glonass navigation satellite program in September, launching three additional spacecraft.

The Search and Rescue Satellite-Aided Tracking (Sarsat) equipment aboard the NOAA 10 satellite was responsible for the rescue of four Canadians in September after their aircraft crashed in a remote area of Ontario. A Sarsat radio beacon in the plane beamed an SOS to the satellite, which relayed the distress call to the search-and-rescue teams. This multinational program was started in 1982 by the U.S., Canada, France, and the Soviet Union. The U.K., Norway, Finland, Denmark, and Bulgaria joined later. Within four years Sarsat was credited with saving more than 700 lives.

—F. C. Durant III

# Energy

Oil prices remained the critical world energy problem during the past year, and the actions of members of the Organization of Petroleum Exporting Countries (OPEC) remained the most important in-

AP/Wide World

*Rilwanu Lukman of Nigeria was elected president of the Organization of Petroleum Exporting Countries (OPEC) in June 1986. OPEC encountered difficulty in maintaining high oil prices during the past year.*

fluence on them. OPEC was finding it increasingly difficult to maintain high oil prices. In 1986 prices dropped sharply and then recovered partially.

**Petroleum.** OPEC finally encountered the dilemma that undermines most price-fixing schemes. For the maintenance of a target price, supplies must be reduced to the amount salable at that price. For such cuts in output to be profitable to the producers involved, the price must rise more than the outputs of those producers fall.

In energy and all other markets the benefits of cutting output and forcing up prices must be shared with the whole industry. Many firms will behave competitively and raise output when prices rise. Consumers will invest in energy-saving technologies. As a result, pressures arise to cut production further. Often the output-cutting process proceeds to the point at which those undertaking it virtually cease production. Thus, their profits also nearly vanish.

This was precisely what happened to Saudi Arabia in the 1980s. It had been undertaking almost all the output cuts of OPEC. By the summer of 1985 its sales had declined close to the vanishing point, and its revenues had dropped sharply. Action to reverse this decline was considered essential.

As usually occurs in such confrontations, Saudi Arabia made its point by increasing its production sharply. Prices then fell sharply. From 1980 to 1985 prices had drifted from their peak of $34 per barrel to about $28. After the 1986 Saudi production increase, prices dropped below $10. Saudi Arabia, nevertheless, gained more from its output rise than it lost from the price decline.

In contrast, those OPEC members already producing at capacity obviously could not raise output enough to offset the loss from the price decrease.

This alerted them to the need to recognize the Saudis' concerns and to assume a greater portion of the output-reduction effort necessary to restore prices.

Saudi Arabia and the rest of OPEC spent most of 1986 in a confrontation over how to secure the desired higher oil prices without eliminating Saudi Arabia's income. Throughout 1986 Saudi Arabia indicated that if others would also cut output, it would cooperate in raising prices—albeit ultimately only to a target of $18 per barrel. An agreement on this price was reached.

As usual in the history of OPEC efforts at price-fixing, the prospects of continued accord remained unclear. It was clear that other countries had to maintain production levels low enough to reconcile $18 oil with Saudi Arabian output objectives. Opinions differed widely as to how well the other OPEC members responded and how long they would remain cooperative. It appeared that OPEC had increased its willingness to cooperate but had not fully resolved the conflicts. Price erosion and possibly even another price break remained likely as disputes over the sharing of production cuts reemerged. An offsetting danger was that U.S. politicians might return to the ill-advised policies of encouraging higher oil prices, maintained from 1945 to 1972.

**Market responses.** Evidence continued to mount on the diversity of useful market responses that have been produced by the gyrations in energy prices since 1971. Among the changes have been the rise of new suppliers, the restructuring of the world energy business, and the development of new arrangements for conducting business.

The available data on energy-consumption trends around the world illustrate the great variation in patterns and their changes since the oil price shocks

that began in 1974. Three main groups of nations are often distinguished—the members of the Organization for Economic Cooperation and Development (OECD, which included the major non-Communist industrialized nations), the rest of the non-Communist world, and the Communist bloc. The three areas differed radically in their overall situations, and further differences prevailed among the regions and countries of each group.

The OECD countries long have accounted for the majority of the aggregate consumption of those energy sources—petroleum, coal, nuclear energy, and hydroelectric power—covered in most energy data reports. The Communist bloc ranked second, and the rest of the world was a distant third. However, the expansion of consumption in the OECD was quite small and involved the combined effect of reduced oil use and increased consumption of other fuels. The Communist bloc and the rest of the world experienced larger consumption increases, which involved rises in oil use.

The share of coal in the rest of the non-Communist world remained similar to that of the OECD. In both areas reliance on coal increased. Conversely, coal comprised a larger share of energy use in Communist countries than in the non-Communist world, but its share of the total was declining.

Many other important differences prevailed. For example, while the rest of the world was sharply increasing gas use, North America was lowering it. The largest coal increases took place in the Communist world and North America. Western European coal use increased only modestly. Nuclear power made big gains that were concentrated in a few countries. The much-discussed U.S. retreat from nuclear power occurred only after a large number of orders had been

**World Energy Consumption by Region and Fuel**
(Million metric tons of oil equivalent)

| Country or region | Total 1973 | Total 1985 | Oil 1973 | Oil 1985 | Gas 1973 | Gas 1985 | Coal 1973 | Coal 1985 | Nuclear 1985 |
|---|---|---|---|---|---|---|---|---|---|
| United States | 1,812.9 | 1,799.4 | 818.0 | 724.1 | 562.5 | 444.5 | 335.0 | 443.4 | 104.6 |
| Canada | 190.9 | 226.6 | 83.7 | 67.7 | 41.8 | 50.4 | 15.6 | 30.6 | 14.0 |
| West Germany | 264.9 | 267.3 | 149.7 | 114.0 | 27.0 | 41.4 | 82.1 | 79.3 | 28.5 |
| United Kingdom | 224.8 | 201.9 | 113.2 | 77.8 | 26.1 | 47.9 | 78.4 | 61.9 | 13.0 |
| France | 186.1 | 189.3 | 127.3 | 83.9 | 15.7 | 23.3 | 29.5 | 24.1 | 45.1 |
| Italy | 137.9 | 140.7 | 103.6 | 85.0 | 14.4 | 27.3 | 9.0 | 15.5 | 1.8 |
| Rest of Western Europe | 391.5 | 436.9 | 242.4 | 206.1 | 44.9 | 52.6 | 43.0 | 74.0 | 34.6 |
| Total Western Europe | 1,205.2 | 1,236.1 | 736.2 | 566.8 | 128.1 | 192.5 | 242.0 | 254.8 | 123.0 |
| Japan | 347.7 | 365.3 | 269.1 | 201.3 | 5.3 | 36.0 | 53.7 | 72.6 | 33.6 |
| Australasia | 64.6 | 91.4 | 32.9 | 30.8 | 3.9 | 15.7 | 22.9 | 36.1 | 0.0 |
| Rest of non-Communist world | 620.0 | 1,104.4 | 378.9 | 559.1 | 75.4 | 171.1 | 117.4 | 238.4 | 14.8 |
| Soviet Union | 874.1 | 1,376.3 | 325.7 | 447.7 | 198.8 | 477.2 | 315.0 | 361.9 | 36.0 |
| China | 362.5 | 634.3 | 53.8 | 87.6 | 6.4 | 11.5 | 292.5 | 509.4 | 0.0 |
| Other centrally planned economies | 431.3 | 580.5 | 99.7 | 124.3 | 43.8 | 92.9 | 273.1 | 330.7 | 11.1 |
| Total centrally planned economies | 1,667.9 | 2,591.1 | 479.2 | 659.6 | 251.2 | 581.6 | 880.6 | 1,202.0 | 47.1 |
| World | 5,909.3 | 7,414.3 | 2,798.0 | 2,809.4 | 1,068.1 | 1,491.8 | 1,667.3 | 2,277.8 | 337.1 |

Note: Hydroelectric is not shown separately but is included in the total.
Source: *BP Statistical Yearbook Review of World Energy* (some 1973 figures supplied by BP).

placed in the late 1960s and early 1970s. Although many of these plans were canceled, many others were implemented. These completed units produced 1985 nuclear generation in the United States that totaled more than twice that of the U.S.'s closest rival, France. Those two countries, along with the Soviet Union, Japan, and West Germany, accounted for almost three-quarters of the world's production of nuclear energy.

Up to the late 1970s coal consumption was increasing in both China and the Soviet Union. While such growth had continued in China, the U.S.S.R. by 1987 was relying almost entirely on natural gas to increase its energy supplies.

The organization of the world's energy industries changed with these market changes. The most striking change concerned the role of the previously pivotal "international major" oil companies. These were the U.S.- and European-based firms that had developed the oil industries of the Middle East. One particularly apt characterization of them was that they were caught in between two forces—squeezed between the diverse pressures exerted by the governments of the producing and consuming countries. Producing countries, as always, wanted more income but were not sure what mix of higher prices, higher outputs, and higher taxes was most desirable for achieving that goal. Consuming countries were seeking to balance consumer demands for cheaper energy with demands by their own energy producers for protection. Given these pressures, the international firms then sought to operate as profitably as possible.

A wide range of views prevails on what occurred in this situation. One group of observers argued that the companies competed as vigorously as political pressures allowed. Another group believed that the companies operated a conspiracy to monopolize the world energy industries. The evidence suggests that the companies were restrained more by the resistance of consuming countries to increased energy imports than by their own ability to limit competition. The oil companies often tried to restrict competition, but the frequency of their efforts and the ultimate necessity for government support to maintain prices suggest that whatever success occurred was fleeting. The companies presided ultimately over a period of declining prices. Concerted action by OPEC then produced massive price increases. As discussed above, however, even these government-supported price rises were difficult to maintain.

With the rise of OPEC many of the arrangements that had been alleged to be indispensable to the oil industry disappeared. At least since the early 20th century, the belief had been widespread that only large experienced companies could succeed in the oil business. Others allegedly could best secure oil under long-term contracts. Good political relations between the governments of consuming and producing countries supposedly were also essential to guaranteeing reliable, cheap supplies.

Among governments these contentions were modified to add nationalistic considerations. Thus, a particular consuming country believed that it could be safe only if a company owned by the nationals of that country developed concessions abroad. These

*Main building of the Qinshan (Ch'in-shan) nuclear power plant rises on the coast of Zhejiang (Chekiang) Province in China. The plant is designed to generate 300,000 kilowatts of electric power.*

*Drawing reveals the essential components of a hot dry rock geothermal power system. A layer of hot dry rock below the Earth's surface is located and cracked open by hydraulic pressure. Water is then pumped through the rock to extract the heat needed to generate power.*

assertions were perversions of the much different proposition that experienced companies were better equipped to initiate oil developments.

Actually, economic and political realities precluded importing countries from benefiting from national oil companies. The need to be profitable encouraged such companies to treat customers on the basis of their willingness to pay rather than their nationality. Also, the establishment by an international firm of operations in many countries forced firms to consider the political pressures in all those nations. For that reason it was difficult for a national company to favor its home country.

All the other beliefs about special arrangements have proved invalid, at least for present conditions. The old order failed to prevent either supply disruptions or price rises. The changes in the world oil industry transferred control of marketing to the OPEC states. Some of the companies retaining vestigial "privileges" to secure oil found themselves committed to paying more than was charged on

open-market sales. Companies thus found it essential to abandon these accords and rely more on open-market purchases.

The transition was a difficult one. Production, refining, marketing, and utilization of crude oil became more distinct. Whenever it was expedient to do so, OPEC countries continued to employ international oil companies or others to assist in the discovery, development, and operation of fields. Such participation, however, was independent of the procurement and use of crude oil.

The market for crude oil became far more open than it had been. Large volumes of oil were sold on a day-to-day basis without the web of contracts that had previously prevailed. Those contracts that had survived were generally agreements to trade at prices set in the open market. Oil thus was no longer considered a good whose economics were so complex that only large experienced companies could efficiently deal in it. It became instead a product as standard, as well understood, and as openly traded and speculated on as wheat.

These developments left the oil industry in considerable disarray. Ventures outside the mineral realm involved several ignominious failures, and a move into nonferrous metals was generally unprofitable. Uranium ventures suffered from strong competition and much slower growth in demand than expected. Several oil companies established significant coal operations. These were probably greater successes than the other efforts but still fell far short of expectations. In short, efforts to develop profitable new businesses fell far short of industry expectations. Thus, it was hardly surprising to see the oil industry move toward concentrating and consolidating its efforts into oil and gas.

*Lightweight fuel cell designed and built by the Argonne National Laboratory near Chicago achieves twice the power and fuel economy of an internal combustion engine of equal weight.*

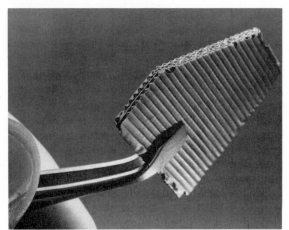

**Natural gas.** Meanwhile, the natural gas side of the business also became altered but in different ways. In the U.S. difficulties were created by the heavy hand of regulation combined with commitments made to purchase gas at prices based on anticipations of continued rises in oil prices from their peak levels. The regulators attempted to achieve a more open market within the limits of their legislative mandates and administrative capabilities.

By contrast, the rise in output of natural gas in the U.S.S.R. made that nation the world's leading natural gas producer. It exported some of that gas to both Eastern and Western Europe. These exports along with those from The Netherlands and Norway allowed Western Europe to increase its consumption of natural gas. Japan also gained its gas from imports, with the majority from Indonesia.

As with coal, natural gas was much less heavily traded internationally than was oil. Gas and coal trade in large part remained governed by contractual arrangements precisely because the trade was so limited that buyers and sellers had few alternatives and needed assurances.

However, the nature of contracting in coal, uranium, and gas was changing, and extensive battles were being fought to alter prior contracts in order to make them more congruent with prevailing economic realities. Means were being sought to adjust the amount bought and the price paid to the market conditions.

**Electricity.** Discussions even began about opening up the most regulation-bound of all energy sectors—

*Vertical-axis wind turbine pumps 130 kilowatts into an electricity grid at Carmarthen Bay in Wales. The two blades are hinged so that they can be angled in high wind speeds and thus control the power output without stalling.*

Courtesy, Sir Robert McAlpine & Sons Ltd.

electricity. Since the early 1970s theorists had suggested that regulation had outlived its usefulness. At the very least, sales among utilities and between utilities and large industrial customers could occur without government regulation.

This argument remained mainly a proposal, accepted by some and criticized by others, including scholars specializing in public utility regulation, utility officials, and a few public organizations. Meanwhile, the industry itself was more concerned with extending existing mechanisms to deal in electric power within the existing regulatory framework. Formal pooling agreements, contracts for power, and increasingly sophisticated networks for trading information and using it to identify and undertake profitable transactions had long been used. Significant efforts were being made to increase the use of those mechanisms. However, regulation received no significant political challenge.

—Richard L. Gordon

# Environment

Environmental concerns during the past year continued to center on three linked issues: the carbon dioxide concentration in the atmosphere, acid rain, and the destruction of tropical rain forests. These issues are linked because the atmospheric carbon dioxide concentration is affected by both combustion of fossil fuels (which causes acid rain) and forest destruction and, in turn, affects climate. Tree mortality rates are affected not only by acid rain but also by climate. The rate at which tropical forests are cut is affected by fuel prices, which regulate the rate of combustion of fossil fuels, and also affects the carbon content of the atmosphere and, hence, climate. The important new development during the year was that the accumulation of additional data caused this linked set of issues to appear more complex than it previously had.

**Carbon dioxide in the atmosphere.** The original carbon dioxide hypothesis consisted of three parts: the rate of worldwide combustion of fossil fuels would increase in compound-interest fashion indefinitely; the carbon dioxide resulting from this combustion would be the principal source of increased carbon dioxide concentration in the atmosphere; and this increased concentration would cause the world to warm. The warming would come about because, as carbon dioxide concentrations increase, air becomes less penetrable by infrared (heat) radiation from the Earth's surface.

During the past year, however, it became clear that serious problems were associated with each of these notions. The worldwide weight of carbon dioxide released into the atmosphere from fuel combustion decreased over 4% from 1979 to 1982; in spite of this the carbon dioxide concentration at the Mauna Loa observatory increased more than 1%. This was not the expected result; it suggested that some factor other than fossil fuel combustion was playing a major, if not dominant, role in the increased concentrations of the gas in the atmosphere.

At least two new publications suggested that in the 19th century the carbon dioxide concentration in the atmosphere was building up at a rate difficult to explain by the small amount of fossil fuel consumed during that period. To illustrate the experimental basis for such a remark, four Australian scientists assessed the concentration of carbon dioxide in air bubbles trapped long ago in Antarctic ice. The ice containing the bubbles was dated by means of oxygen isotope measurements. From such measurements it is possible to obtain the relationship between the age of the Earth and the concentration of carbon dioxide in its atmosphere over four centuries.

These studies revealed that something other than fossil fuel combustion appears to be important in the carbon dioxide issue; that now appears to be mass deforestation. In this view widespread deforestation in North America was important in the carbon dioxide buildup in the 19th century, and the rapid deforestation now taking place in the tropics contributes significantly to the buildup today. The more trees that are cut, the less green tissue there is to use up carbon dioxide and replace it with oxygen.

This discussion suggests that a rethinking of the carbon dioxide issue may be in order. If the global volume of green tissue is healthy and there is an increase in atmospheric carbon dioxide concentrations from fossil fuel combustion, it seems reasonable to assume that the green tissue would simply use up the gas as it would any fertilizer, thus maintaining its concentration in the atmosphere. The fact that this does not happen suggests an alternative hypothesis. The global mass of green tissue does not remove the gas from the atmosphere as quickly as it is introduced into it, because the green tissue either is too unhealthy or is disappearing too fast. Neither of these notions is farfetched. It has been a long time since most high-latitude forest soils have been refreshed by the rock particles that glaciers scoured off the rock surface. Also, the rapid destruction of tropical forests has been widely noted. The volume of forest eliminated each year is in excess of the area of Austria.

The third component of the carbon dioxide hypothesis is perhaps most troubling of all. Instead of there being a warming of the atmosphere, considerable cooling seems to be taking place. One of the factors contributing to the tragic explosion of the U.S. space shuttle *Challenger* on the morning of Jan. 28, 1986, was the coldest temperature ever encountered before a shuttle launch. Indeed, the temperature was outside the range for which the shuttle had been designed. The temperature at Cape Canaveral in Florida was below freezing for ten hours the day of the launch and had dropped to a low of $-4.5°$ C ($24°$ F) at 7 AM. To put this observation into perspective, Cape Canaveral is only about $28°$ north of the Equator, is at sea level, and is on the Gulf Stream, which veers to the northeast to warm all of northwestern Europe. Cairo is $2°$ farther north than Cape Canaveral, and few people would expect freezing temperatures in Cairo. Also, this was not an isolated and completely unpredictable and unexpected accident; the Florida orange producers had been hard hit by four frosts in the last five years.

Other major news stories of the past year supported this picture of a rapidly chilling Northern Hemisphere. Particularly noteworthy were the increases in the levels of Great Salt Lake and the Great Lakes. These levels rose as a result of not one unusual season of weather but many. There was above-average rainfall in the Great Lakes region for five consecutive years. The ability of air to absorb moisture decreases as the air becomes cooler, and the surplus moisture precipitates out as rain or snow.

*Ice forms on equipment used during the launch of the U.S. space shuttle* Challenger *before it exploded in January 1986. NASA officials disregarded warnings to delay the launch because of the icy conditions.*

NASA

*Saltair amusement park is partially submerged by the rising waters of the Great Salt Lake in Utah. In 1986 the lake approached its highest level since 1873, expanding its area by some 2,100 square kilometers (810 square miles).*

Thus, for two widely separated lake systems, high water levels reflect the cumulative effect of years of unusually cold weather. To suggest the severity of the consequences, the U.S. Army Corps of Engineers offered five million sandbags, tons of sand, and miles of plastic sheeting to protect vulnerable shoreline areas along the Great Lakes coasts of Ohio, Pennsylvania, and New York.

These strange weather patterns appear to be associated with a change in wind circulation patterns in the Northern Hemisphere. Instead of moving around the globe, mainly following parallels of latitude, the westerlies have developed a meandering motion, with winds veering southeast to Florida from Alaska.

**Acid rain.** New light was shed on the acid rain phenomenon in an important report from the U.S. National Research Council. It appears as if a widespread climatic cooling is implicated in the increased tree mortality observed at high latitudes and altitudes. The health of red spruce growing at high altitudes in New England began to deteriorate markedly after 1960, as revealed by studies of the thickness of rings in the trunks (a measure of growth each year). This coincided with a marked lowering of winter temperatures in New England that began about 1960 and continued thereafter at an increasing rate.

Other lines of evidence also suggest that mass tree mortality need not be due to pollution. It has been observed in environments relatively free of pollution, such as Hawaii. Also, there were reports of widespread mortality of red spruce in eastern North America between 1871 and 1890. There was little pollution then, but that was a much cooler period than the period from 1940 to 1960, when red spruce flourished in the northeastern United States. To illustrate, the annual mean temperature at New Haven, Conn., from 1871 to 1890 was 8.3° C (47° F) in two years and 8.9° C (48° F) in six years. From 1940 to 1960 it never fell below 9.4° C (49° F) and was 12.2° C (54° F) in two years. From 1780 to 1910 the annual average temperature at New Haven reached as high as 11.7° C (53° F) only once, in 1878. In short, what has been widely perceived as pollution-induced mass mortality of trees may in fact be due to a cooling of the Northern Hemisphere climate to conditions more characteristic of the 19th century than the mid-20th century, which appears to have been atypically warm.

The National Research Council report concluded that the important regional climatic anomalies may have been a factor in the red spruce decline. They were careful to state, however, that there is currently no direct evidence linking acid deposition to elevated tree mortality rates and to decreases in the ring widths of tree trunks. It should be noted that the nature of the acid rain phenomenon is such as to baffle any effort to disentangle the separate effects of pollution and climate change. For example, the effects of each of these factors become more severe with increasing altitude, where trees are growing at the coldest temperatures they could normally withstand; under such conditions any decrease in temperature moves the trees into a lethal climatic range. The moisture in clouds tends to be much more acidic than rainfall, and both the acid rain phenomenon and elevated tree mortality are most serious at altitudes where droplets from clouds are the most important source of moisture.

**Species extinctions.** During the year the potential imminent extinction of perhaps half the world's species of plants and animals, mainly through deforestation, became a major topic of discussion. There were two reasons for this interest: a widely growing perception that tropical rain forests are being destroyed rapidly, and new studies suggesting that enormous numbers of species live in those forests and are vulnerable to extinction before their existence has even been recognized.

There is little disagreement about the fate of tropical forests. Norman Myers estimated that the annual, irrevocable loss of tropical forests is 92,000 sq km (35,500 sq mi), based on remote sensing data of 78% of the relevant land surface. The Food and Agriculture Organization and the UN Environment Program offered somewhat lower estimates, but they projected virtually complete destruction of tropical forests by the year 2135. The World Bank estimated that by that time global human population would be 11 billion.

If, as argued at the beginning of this review, deforestation is much more important than generally recognized in regulating the carbon dioxide concentration of the atmosphere and, therefore, the climate, the prospects are somewhat alarming. One can visualize a population almost three times as dense as at present, confronted with oppressive heat and drought near the tropics and weather too cold to support adequate food production in the countries that are now the world's breadbaskets (the U.S.S.R., Canada, Australia, Argentina, and the U.S.). If the world's forests are eliminated, it has been estimated that about half of all species of plants and animals would become extinct. This would be comparable to the mass extinction of 65 million years ago, when the dinosaurs disappeared along with 60 to 80% of all other animal species.

*Scientist tests chemical that can inexpensively remove more than 70% of the nitrogen-oxide pollutants emitted by coal-burning power plants. Such gases, once in the atmosphere, can contribute to the formation of acid rain.*

Argonne National Laboratory

There are two reasons why the events of the next two centuries would differ from that extinction. First, unlike previous extinctions, large numbers of plant species would be lost. Second, in the past the agent causing extinction ameliorated after some time, allowing a rebound in the diversity of biologic species; this time the cause of the destruction is humans, and they may not become extinct before eliminating large numbers of other species.

During the year a new organization was formed to alert the public to the severity of the mass extinction problem. Called the Club of Earth, it consisted of nine members of the U.S. National Academy of Sciences. This club compensates for its small size with a memorable way of making its arguments. Paul Ehrlich of Stanford University, a club member, pointed out that humans now consume about 40% of the energy trapped by means of photosynthesis by plants throughout the world. If the human population doubled, it would be commandeering 80% of this energy, leaving only 20% for the remaining 5 million to 30 million species.

During the year new data indicated just how much species diversity is found in the tropical forests. Terry Erwin of the Smithsonian Institution's National Museum of Natural History in Washington, D.C., conducted a survey of insects in the canopy of the Peruvian Amazon rain forest. From a single tree he sent ants to Edward O. Wilson of Harvard University, who identified 43 species in 26 genera. That is roughly equal to the number of ant species in the British Isles. In a plot no bigger than one hectare (2½ acres), Erwin discovered 41,000 different species of insects, including 12,000 species of beetles. Peter Ashton of Harvard University found 700 tree species in ten separate one-hectare plots in Borneo, which is equivalent to the tree species diversity for all of North America.

The concern for species extinction has led to considerable recent thought about the possible use of zoos and islands of forests as means of maintaining species diversity. The problem is that as such islands become smaller, the number of species they can maintain indefinitely drops off sharply. When islands are in the size range of one to 25 sq km (0.4 to 10 sq mi), the size of many small parks and nature reserves, the rate of extinction of bird species in the first 100 years is 10 to 50%. Extinction rates rise steeply when the size drops below one square kilometer.

Several other types of habitats contain very large numbers of species and are equally threatened. Coral reefs, coastal wetlands, estuaries, and the large, ancient lakes of Africa all contain large numbers of species that can be lost quickly through pollution, environmental degradation, or invasion of new predators introduced by humans.

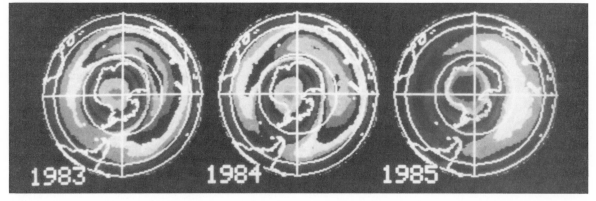

*Computer images derived from data obtained by satellites reveal the progressive thinning of the ozone layer over Antarctica. Variations in the annual concentrations near the center "hole" are shown as ring-shaped zones of differing shades.*

Zoos are inadequate for the amelioration of species extinction. All the zoos of the world contain 540,000 animals in about 4,000 species, a number of individuals equal to about 1% of the number of cats in U.S. households.

Furthermore, if zoos were to be used to ensure the long-term survival of the species they now house, they would have to support larger populations. Consequently, it would be impractical for zoos to sustain more than 900 species for long.

Another means of working to ensure species survival is restoration of natural habitat. This has turned out to be more difficult to accomplish than might be expected. When salt marsh has been restored, for example, the species whose extinction was to be prevented by this measure have not always returned to establish residence there. Animals may have a collective memory as to where they ought to be. Once a habitat has been destroyed, it may be difficult to reteach animals that the place is suitable after it has been restored.

During the year environmentalists became interested in political action to work against species extinction. One strategy was to focus on the World Bank, a major source of development funds for third world countries. Either directly or by lobbying the U.S. Congress, environmentalists sought to influence the bank and other multilateral lending institutions to reduce their funding for such development. Their efforts appear to have had a significant impact. For example, in the U.S. the House-Senate conference on foreign aid funding cut the government's request of $1.4 billion for multilateral banks to $950 million.

The dissatisfaction with bank lending policies to third world country development projects was intensified by information about a number of particularly disturbing projects. Perhaps the most widely publicized was the massive Polonoroeste development scheme in the state of Rondonia in western Brazil. Promoted as a land-reform project, it opened the

tropical region to mass migration and settlement by farmers from impoverished regions elsewhere. In this, as in most similar tropical development schemes, there was concern that the tropical soils would support cultivation for only a few years on new farms, and that the settlers would then be forced to move on to other areas, including those now reserved for the Indians of the region. The World Bank approved nearly a half billion dollars in loans for the project.

The fallacy in this and similar projects is that the luxuriant growth of the tropical forest can be converted to equally luxuriant agricultural productivity. It cannot because the climate and soil are suitable only for supporting the forest. Unlike temperate forest soils, tropical forest soils contain little of the nutrients in the ecosystem, which are mostly bound up in the trees. Furthermore, once the trees have been removed, the iron-rich tropical forest soils develop a bricklike surface and, under the combined influences of great heat and light intensity and torrential rainfall, provide marginal yields. As might have been expected, the Polonoroeste project resulted in soil erosion and river silting on a massive scale.

Another project that attracted criticism was a major livestock scheme in Botswana. This scheme involved the expansion of commercial ranching, which had proved economically and ecologically unsound in previous African ventures. Several studies had shown that livestock imported from other areas do not make as efficient use of some African habitats as native game.

**Species diversity and stability.** Many scientists once believed that very high species diversity occurred in habitats of great stability. More recently, however, the intermediate disturbance hypothesis of Joseph Connell has become popular. This argues that both too much and too little environmental instability are inimical to a high level of species diversity, the latter because it allows for one, or a few, species to gradually become dominant and drive out the rest. Thus, it is at intermediate levels of environmental stability that the greatest levels of species diversity can be found. One notices also that habitats with very high species diversity, such as coral reefs, may be quite violent on occasion.

This issue is linked with that of tropical park management because on occasion one sees a tropical park apparently being destroyed by some disturbance. The question then arises as to whether the appropriate strategy is to attempt to maintain stability or allow the disturbance to run its course. During 1986 the Chobe National Park in northern Botswana confronted park managers and conservation biologists with a particularly thought-provoking example of the stability-diversity problem. The park is a mosaic of grassland and acacia woodland habitat. The acacias, however, are on the verge of destruction. For years no new stands have become established, and many of the existing trees are being destroyed by heavy browsing pressure by various animals and damage by elephants. This situation suggests two interpretations. If the woodlands shrink to mere remnants, then it could be argued that conservation has been a failure. But that is a short-term view. Brian Walker argued during the year that park managers and conservation biologists should welcome change in the habitats that they manage. It is the fluctuating conditions within a habitat that allow for persistence of a large diversity of species over a long time. This interpretation leads to the conclusion that if nature parks and preserves were to achieve equilibrium, the species-rich ecosystems within them would inevitably lose many of their species.

The reasons become clear when one examines the history of the Chobe Park. In the 1890s the Savuti Channel, which had been the major source of surface water, dried up, and the elephant population of the area emigrated to seek water elsewhere. Soon afterward, a rinderpest outbreak wiped out many of the hooved animals. With the relaxation of feeding pressure, acacia seedlings were able to survive to maturity. The population of hooved animals slowly recovered, rinderpest disappeared, water flow resumed in the Savuti Channel, and browsing pressure resumed. Acacias could no longer establish themselves. Thus, a large population of hooved animals and an acacia woodland constitute an unstable, oscillating system. There is a long-term cycle between a thriving acacia population, with few hooved animals, followed by a high population of such animals that prevents establishment of acacia seedlings. Then the channel fills and dries, the population of hooved animals leaves or dies, the acacias become reestablished, and the cycle repeats.

The key to long-term persistence of this ecosystem is periodic decades when elephants and other large hooved animals are kept away from the park so that the acacias can become reestablished. The problem is that tourists like to go to Africa to visit parks so that they can see large numbers of large animals. There is an essential conflict between the goals of always being able to show the tourists what they want and the long-run persistence of the park.

In nature some species are always becoming more abundant and others less abundant in any small habitat. However, the species becoming extinct at one place may be increasing in another area. Humans' overview of nature must become more dynamic to become more realistic: constant migration of species from one small habitat to another and local extinction at each of them occasionally should be considered a normal course of events. If environmentalists are to work effectively against the extinction of large numbers of species, then nature preserves must be arranged geographically in a chainlike fashion so that chance extinction in one park can be compensated for by immigration from surrounding parks. There-

Snap bean plants are grown in controlled environments to test their responses to ozone under various conditions. As the concentration of ozone in the atmosphere increases, crop yields generally decline.

Agricultural Research Service, USDA

fore, to prevent massive species extinction in the tropics, there is a need not only for some fairly large parks but also for parks in appropriate numbers. A token level of support for species diversity, in the form of a small number of widely scattered small parks, will simply lead to the same mass species destruction that would have resulted from complete elimination of the natural habitat.

Recent research indicates that preindustrial societies destroyed their habitats sufficiently to then destroy themselves. The Polynesian society of Easter Island is known from the surviving giant stone statues. From analysis of pollen records it is possible to reconstruct the forest history of the island. When the Polynesians arrived in about AD 400, it was covered with palms, other trees, and shrubs. By 1500 the people had completely destroyed the forest so that when Europeans arrived 200 years later, the island was barren, treeless grassland. In several other cases throughout the world, preindustrial civilizations collapsed because of deforestation, which caused a diversity of problems: no construction timber or fuel, erosion of sloping hillsides, siltation of streams and rivers in the valleys, and gradual destruction of terraces and dams owing to a cycle of flooding after heavy rain and drying up and siltation at other times.
—Kenneth E. F. Watt

# Food and agriculture

Agriculture, along with petroleum, greatly influenced the fortunes of countries in 1986–87 because of the key positions food, fiber, fuel, and forest products have in international trade. The state agricultural experiment station system, which had played a key role in raising the productivity of U.S. agriculture, completed its first century. As its second century began, the major focus of agricultural research would be reducing costs and regaining the competitive edge that the U.S. had lost in the early 1980s. Public interest in diet and health issues continued to increase and was having a marked effect on eating habits in much of the developed world.

## Agriculture

On a worldwide basis, 1986 provided a record harvest. Production of livestock and poultry also rose. Worldwide use of agricultural products, however, was expected to remain below the level of production, causing a further buildup of surpluses in many countries. Declining exports and record imports drove the U.S. agricultural trade balance down to $5.4 billion in fiscal 1986, the lowest since 1972. In late fiscal 1986, lower prices for U.S. rice, wheat, and cotton boosted export volumes of these commodities. Rising volume was expected to help offset lower prices in fiscal 1987.

Sorghum production had been increasing rapidly in the less developed countries since the early 1970s, primarily as a result of the introduction of high-yielding hybrid varieties. The hybrids were widely used in both Asia and Latin America, but in Asia the increased yields had been offset by decreased plantings. In Latin America, Argentina and Mexico had experienced substantial boosts in sorghum output. Even so, Mexico was one of the upper-middle-income countries responsible for shifting the position of the less developed world from net exporter of coarse grains to net importer, as the demand for feed grains surpassed expanding sorghum production.

*Trucks piled high with hay donated by farmers from Clay County in northeastern Florida travel to the Florida panhandle in July 1986 to provide feed for livestock in that drought-stricken area.*

AP/Wide World

*Farmer kneels in a parched potato field in York County, Pennsylvania, in July 1986, displaying the dry earth and tiny potatoes caused by high temperatures and the lack of rain. Under normal conditions one potato should fill his hand by that time of year.*

World meat production increased by 1% in 1986 and was expected to rise again in 1987, with gains in poultry meat, pork, and beef production outside the U.S. accounting for most of the gain. Increased pork production was predicted for China, Japan, and the European Communities (EC). Although beef production would be up worldwide, the rise would be dampened somewhat by a smaller U.S. output. The net result of all these factors could be an outbreak of tariff wars as each country attempted to protect its producers.

**Back to the diversified farm.** There were two million farms in operation in the U.S. in 1986. Of those, nearly 40% were debt free, but 155,000 had a debt-to-asset ratio of 0.41 or more and a negative cash flow, placing them in a very risky position financially. Many farmers were attempting to cope by emphasizing diversification. This trend was not unique to the U.S. but was also apparent in most of the less developed countries. Scientific research in many countries, but particularly in the U.S., was focusing on alternative crops and alternative uses of agricultural products.

For the U.S. agricultural experiment station system, this marked a recommitment to the original goal announced in 1887 with passage of an act sponsored by Rep. William Hatch of Missouri to establish state agricultural experiment stations. When the system was established, most farmers operated widely diversified farms, but in later years, and particularly after World War II, farming became more specialized, In recent years a return to more diversified farming operations has taken place in many parts of the United States. Recent data showed that in virtu-

ally all states except North and South Carolina there had been a major increase in small farms (under 19 ha; 1 ha = 2.47 ac) or farms that could be classified as small-scale.

**The Irish experience.** The parallel between the U.S. and the developed countries of the EC in terms of specialization and consistent production of surpluses demonstates that agricultural science has minimized the crop failures and sweeping losses of livestock to disease that once plagued mankind. Ireland is an excellent example. Ireland is primarily a food-producing country, particularly of meat and dairy products. Irish agriculture has consistently produced food surpluses and thus is export-oriented. Virtually all of the country's 140,000 farms are family operations. Two-thirds are under 20 ha, and one-third are owned and worked by operators over 65 years of age. In recent decades Irish farming and food processing have evolved from a relatively underdeveloped base to a modern high-technology industry.

The An Foras Talúntais (AFT; National Agricultural Research Institute of Ireland) was set up under the post-World War II Marshall Plan. As a result of its work, in conjunction with university research units, Irish farming and agribusiness have been able to realize economic gains from Ireland's membership in the EC. In 1985 gross agricultural output was valued at Irf2,700 million, representing 10% of the gross national product, compared with the EC average of 4%. Cattle, milk, and dairy products accounted for 73% of Irish production. The current challenge of the AFT is to assist Irish farmers with creative approaches to compensate for the quota restrictions imposed by the EC on livestock products.

*David Laurenzo, vice-president of Laurenzo's Italian Gourmet Market in North Miami Beach, Florida, samples a mango that has been treated with cobalt-60 to kill insects and bacteria. The use of irradiation as a method of food preservation continued to be widely debated.*

The AFT is an autonomous body set up to strengthen the use of technology in Irish agriculture, food industries, and related sciences. It comprises several main research centers throughout the country, with headquarters in Dublin. It is required to disseminate research results through a national organization called ACOT and other advisory groups by means of conference, field days, and publications. Among the AFT's accomplishments is the systematic classification of the land of Ireland. Extensive long-term grazing trials have set new benchmarks for animal husbandry, increasing stocking rates from 1.2 to 3.4 head of livestock per hectare. Research work undertaken by the AFT has contributed to the genetic improvement of livestock, taking full advantage of research results from Britain, the United States, and other countries.

Food research is carried out at five centers, with the most attention focused on dairy products. Processing, storage, packaging, transport, and retail

*A peach plant that is resistant to bacterial leaf spot, a major peach disease, was developed by isolating two peach cells from three million cells taken from immature seeds of Sunhigh peaches. Shoots grown from the two cells were used to clone more plants, and thus a disease-resistant plant was produced from cells that came from a disease-susceptible variety.*

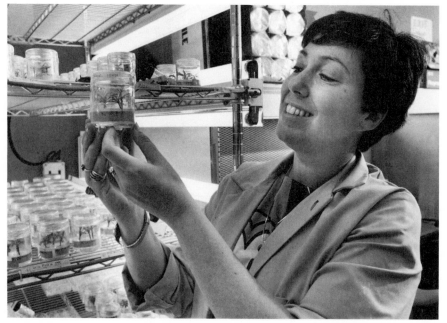

marketing have been target areas. The AFT also has a machinery-testing service to evaluate a wide range of machines coming on the market. It is active in evolving new techniques in fertilizer application, forage harvesting, and grain production and storage. As is true in several developed nations, biotechnology is one of the most promising areas of research in Ireland. The AFT program emphasizes genetic engineering; development of new enzymes and cultures for the food industries, particularly new cheese starters; development of techniques to allow transfer of new genes into cattle in association with embryo transplant work; and plant tissue culture work to develop new virus-free potato varieties and new fruit and forest tree varieties by micropropagation.

**The biotechnology revolution.** "Biotechnology" refers to an array of related sciences that center on the use of new methods to manipulate the fundamental building blocks of genetic information to create life forms that might never emerge naturally. The American Association for the Advancement of Science has termed genetic engineering one of the four major scientific revolutions of the 20th century, on a par with unlocking the atom, escaping the Earth's gravity, and the computer revolution.

Biotechnology makes possible an acceleration of the process of selection and breeding. The basic concept is that every living cell contains the genetic information needed to reproduce its characteristic functions in succeeding generations. The discovery of the structure of genetic material in the 1950s, the unraveling of the genetic code in the 1960s, and the development and refinement of the tools of genetic engineering in the 1970s have led to fundamentally new developments in the biologic sciences. Using enzymes as "genetic sensors," scientists can snip apart the genetic structure of cells and reconstitute it in combinations that are impossible or unlikely in nature. Scientists not only can alter existing genes but can construct synthetic genes that cause the organism to perform desired functions.

The opportunities and applications of biotechnology were summarized by Neville P. Clarke, director of the Texas Agricultural Experiment Station, in the 1986 Yearbook of Agriculture, entitled *Research for Tomorrow*. He points out that one of the early applications of biotechnology has been the use of simple organisms such as bacteria and yeast as "factories" to produce biologically active compounds. For example, through these techniques human insulin is being produced and is replacing insulin from animal sources in the treatment of diabetes. Interferon, an anticancer and antiviral agent previously available only in minute quantities, can be made inexpensively and in large quantities. Diagnostic tests and improved vaccines for both animal and human diseases are also being produced.

In many parts of the world, water is the limiting factor in food production. Biotechnology is being used to enhance the development of plants with a high tolerance to drought. Such plants will maintain yields in environments with little water, and there is promise of developing plants that can use brackish water. Plant growth and development have been investigated for decades but until recently remained poorly understood. Biotechnology makes it possible to isolate, characterize, and manipulate specific genes. Opportunites include altering the chemical composition of plants, improving processing quality, producing plants resistant to stress or herbicides, altering plant size, improving the nutritive value and modifying undesirable properties of plant products, and changing the grain-to-stalk ratio. Genetic engineering also offers an exciting and environmentally sound method of plant pest control through the development of genetic resistance to disease.

Biologic control exploits natural factors in the life cycle of harmful insects. Some possibilities include the use of highly specialized insect pathogens to pro-

*An experimental robot reaches for a plastic orange on an imitation tree while a research engineer watches video monitors. The ability to distinguish colors allows the robot to pick fruit quickly and effectively.*

Agricultural Research Service, USDA

duce insect diseases and utilizing unique viruses to interfere with the insects' immune systems, making them more vulnerable to disease. Such processes are specific to single species and thus are environmentally desirable alternatives to chemical pesticides. The ultimate solution to animal diseases would be to genetically engineer disease-resistant animals. It is now possible to identify the specific genes controlling disease resistance. Identification, mapping, and cloning of these genes, coupled with embryo manipulation, offer dramatic possibilities. In addition, the same technologies can be used to develop diagnostic tests that will determine the presence or absence of specific diseases

While the opportunities for using biotechnology in agriculture seem almost limitless, the new techniques have aroused public concern. There is a need to ensure that biotechnology is used in an environmentally sound manner. To this end, agricultural researchers are enhancing traditional methods of manipulating plant and animal germ plasm as well as following the guidelines for recombinant DNA studies directed toward applications in humans. There is a good track record of safety associated with the research and its products. Recombinant DNA techniques have been employed safely since the mid-1970s. Methods and procedures are being perfected that will assure continued safety in applying recombinant DNA techniques to agriculture and its products.

—John Patrick Jordan

## Nutrition

The public continued to demand information about nutrition for the maintenance of health. Sarah H. Short of Syracuse (N.Y.) University stressed that today's professionals must choose and use the appropriate media and technology to present correct nutrition information effectively to students, clients, patients, and the public.

Increasing numbers of professional organizations were publishing newsletters catering to the interest in nutrition and health. They included, among many others, *Calcium Currents* (National Promotion and Research Board), *Food & Nutrition News* (National Livestock and Meat Board), *Diet and Nutrition Letter* (Tufts University), and *Nutrition and the M.D.* (PM, Inc.). The proliferation of such newsletters raised concern over the validity of the information presented. The potential subscriber needed to assess the intent of the sponsor of the publication, the authors, the research quoted, and the style of writing. Scare tactics usually indicate questionable information or simple "sales pitches."

**Dieting.** Dieting has become a way of life according to *Calorie Control Commentary*, published by the Calorie Control Council, an international association of manufacturers and suppliers of dietary foods and beverages. About 26% of 4,000 households studied had one or more persons on a low-calorie diet. People "on a diet" are avoiding, limiting, or restricting certain specific foods either to lose weight or as part of a general "fitness" program. Many of these people take a "supplement" to keep them going, in the belief that diet supplements can prevent serious illnesses.

Large, repeated doses of nutrient concentrates can amount to "over-the-counter drug abuse." In May 1986 the American Dietetic Association called a panel together to determine specifically when use of a supplement becomes abuse. Most people can consume a supplement containing 100% of the Recommended Dietary Allowance (RDA) of a specific nutrient or group of related nutrients without suffering any ill effects. However, some nutrients have specific, serious side effects if they are taken at higher dosages for an extended period of time. Toxicity is not a problem for water-soluble nutrients that

*Rat is fed a diet rich in selenium in an effort to determine selenium retention in the body. Too little selenium in a child's diet can lead to degeneration of heart muscle, while too much can cause loss of hair and nails.*

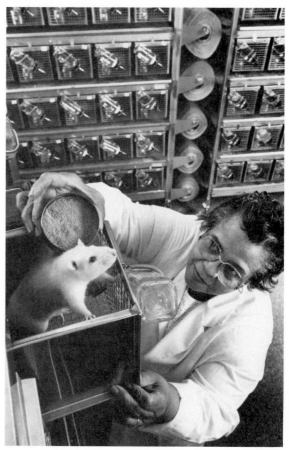

are readily excreted, but this is not the case with fat-soluble or insoluble substances that can be deposited in tissues. Such nutrients can accumulate in certain tissues and may cause serious damage. For example, vitamin A, zinc, and copper become toxic with continued high intakes.

Consumers view concentrated supplements as food and not as drugs, and the U.S. Food and Drug Administration (FDA) does not set upper limits for allowable levels unless a harmful effect has been shown. Physicians are called on to report cases of adverse reactions to vitamin/mineral pills to the FDA just as they do for drugs. It is to be hoped that such physician reports will point the way toward setting limits on how much of a particular nutrient may be put into a given pill.

Additives to foods were first subjected to regulation in the U.S. under the Food and Drugs Act of 1906. The Food, Drug, and Cosmetic Act of 1938 set standards that remained in effect. Additives are classed as direct additives if they are added to a food for a functional purpose (e.g., as sweeteners, coloring agents, or nutritional supplements). A 1958 amendment (Food Additive Amendment) created legal categories of additives: those that require government approval; those approved earlier; and those recognized as safe by qualified scientists (GRAS). Before an additive is approved, it must be proved "safe" under all conditions of use.

**Calcium and osteoporosis.** The widespread publicity given to osteoporosis in recent years caused a 50% increase in the sale of calcium supplements. The disease, which is most common in postmenopausal women, is characterized by loss of bone mass and increased bone fragility. It should be pointed out that bones are not made of calcium alone; the calcium must form a union with other chemical entities to maintain the bone tissue. Since calcium forms many insoluble compounds, formulating a calcium supplement that is soluble after digestion for absorption into the circulatory system is not simple. A study of calcium supplements in stores can be confusing. The compounds include "natural" concentrates of powdered oyster shells (calcium carbonate), calcium lactate, and calcium tartrate.

The RDA for calcium had been raised from 680 mg daily for adults to 800 mg, but members of a Consensus Conference on Osteoporosis of the National Institutes of Health (NIH) recommended a further increase to 1,000–1,500 mg per day. This amount can be supplied by 2¾ cups of milk plus ½ to 1 oz of cheese or other calcium-rich food such as one-half cup of cooked dark-green leaves (collard, turnip, or mustard greens) or nuts such as almonds and filberts. Obviously, the supply of calcium in the diet is heavily dependent on the use of dairy products, mostly milk consumed plain or

used in the preparation of yogurt, custards, puddings, frozen desserts, and other products. The American Society for Bone and Mineral Research asserts that the best way to obtain sufficient calcium is through a balanced diet that includes dairy products in recommended amounts.

**Dietary components.** As life-styles change, concerns about diet and its components change as well. When people worked hard in non-air-conditioned homes and workplaces, salt was needed to offset losses from perspiration. In today's air-conditioned environment, concern about excessive sodium intake dominates the literature. From 1,100 to 3,300 mg of sodium are considered a safe and adequate daily amount, with one level teaspoon of salt supplying about 2,000 mg. A U.S. Department of Agriculture bulletin entitled "Sodium Content of Your Food" states that current estimates of individual intakes of sodium range from 2,300 to 6,900 mg. Foods, drinks, diet supplements, and medications all can be sources of sodium. Excessive sodium intake is believed to contribute to high blood pressure (hypertension).

Salt added during food preparation or at the table is an obvious source of sodium. In addition, the sodium content of many foods is increased by processing methods. This is true of most cheeses (even those classed as "natural"), including cottage, blue, Parmesan, Roquefort, American cheddar, and most processed cheese and cheese spreads. All smoked and cured fish, such as herring and sardines, and canned fish, such as salmon and tuna, are high in salt. So are products in the cured meat group such as ham, bacon, corned beef, and sausages. These foods contain from 400 to over 2,000 mg of sodium per three- to four-ounce serving. A ready-to-eat meal can easily supply more sodium than is needed all day. A higher sodium food should be served with a low-salt food to help control sodium intake. Thus, for example, two ounces of ham and two ounces of chicken can be combined to make a four-ounce entrée. Seasonings made from fruit juices and herbs were being marketed to help make low-salt foods taste better.

The American Heart Association published an "Eating Plan for Healthy Americans" that offers a design for wholesome eating that should prevent obesity, establish blood cholesterol levels below 200 mg, and offer some protection from heart disease. This educational material was also available from the American Dietetic Association and the National Institutes of Health.

Stress was being placed on the need to increase dietary fiber, an indigestible ingredient that passes through the body to be excreted. It dilutes the fats and sugars in foods and has a filling effect that serves to inhibit overeating. Oat bran gained prominence during the year as a fibrous food believed to be beneficial in cancer prevention. Oat bran is the

"Larry never gains an ounce!"

part of the grain left after milling. It contains more than just bran; much of the vitamin, mineral, and protein content of oats is in the bran, making it highly nutritious. Unlike bran from wheat, which is mostly insoluble and, hence, indigestible, oat bran is at least partially soluble in water during cooking. Cooked, it has a creamy/sticky texture. According to H. David Hurt, director of the Quaker Oats Co.'s Nutrition Division, oat bran has been shown to lower blood cholesterol and normalize sugar levels in diabetes, and it may even help to reduce blood pressure. Linda Van-Horn of the community health department, Northwestern Medical School, Chicago, showed that eating two ounces of oatmeal a day has about the same cholesterol-lowering effect as eating two ounces of oat bran. However, "parents in her study who ate oatmeal were happier with their diets than those who ate oat bran."

The national advertising division of the Better Business Bureau (BBB) offered guidelines for the consumer attempting to make decisions on the basis of three types of claims regarding foods as sources of nutrients. (1) Claims for *good sources*, according to the BBB, follow the FDA's rule that "No claim may be made for a food as a significant source of a nutrient unless that nutrient is present in the food at a level equal to or in excess of 10% of the USRDA." (2) Health claims present a problem if fact is not distinguished from truth—literal facts about a food may overstate its real nutritional value. (3) Claims that a food is "natural" are complicated by the fact that the FDA has provided only an inadequate definition of the term, although some 30 decisions involving claims that a product is "natural" have been made. Advertisers look for words with a positive connotation, such as "real" as opposed to "imitation" when applied to a substitute for a natural food; *e.g.*, for pepper or cream.

Laypeople often have great difficulty in assessing the food they eat, and many prefer to rely on a food processor who markets heat-and-eat meals. The fact that these are "warmed-over" and of limited variety seems to make little difference. Research shows that obese people tend to think that they eat less than the actual measurement of the food indicates, while very thin people claim they eat more than is actually the case. Thus, a premeasured meal becomes a help in dieting, provided the diner does not eat additional food.

The amount of physical activity a person undertakes is subject to similar misperceptions. Furthermore, research indicates that the standard tables of resting metabolic rates are 7 to 14% too high. A study of 44 women ranging from 18 to 65 years in age and from lean to obese indicated that less energy is expended (and hence fewer calories used) in normal activities than the tables had predicted. The data help to explain the people who insist that they "eat little and are very active" but who fail to lose—or maintain—weight because they are actually using fewer calories than they had believed. In evaluating diet as related to energy expenditure, only facts will produce reliable results.

—Mina W. Lamb

398

# Life sciences

Several remarkable achievements characterized the past year in the life sciences. A complete set of nerve cells involved in a complex repetitive behavior was described for the first time. Molecular biologists obtained the first high-resolution structure of a crystalline DNA-protein complex. Nitrogen-fixing bacteria that might be useful as biofertilizers for crops in temperate and cold regions were isolated. Other research dealt with such diverse phenomena as endangered species, the recovery of plants from the Mt. St. Helens eruption, and the controversy surrounding the recently discovered skull of a 2.5-million-year-old hominid.

## Botany

The steady progress of discovery and application in botany employed the newest techniques in biology. Typical research findings related to the fossils at the Cretaceous/Tertiary boundary, early $C_4$ photosynthesis, and forest destruction in Africa. Recovery of plants after the Mt. St. Helens eruption, more light on the history of corn (maize), and the molecular biology of plant/parasite relationships were representative of the interests of botanists during the past year.

**Research techniques.** A variety of methods were used during the year to study plant structure, development, and physiology. One interesting application of genetic engineering involved the transfer of luciferase genes from fireflies and bacteria to plants in order to detect the presence of other genes introduced at the same time. One group of researchers, from the University of California at San Diego, was able to splice the firefly luciferase gene into viral

DNA (deoxyribonucleic acid), introduce the modified DNA into the bacterium *Agrobacterium tumefaciens,* and then infect cells of tobacco plants with the bacterium. Because luciferase is an enzyme that promotes luminescence of the pigment luciferin in the presence of ATP (adenosine triphosphate), plants grown from infected cells should glow when their cells receive luciferin just as fireflies do. (ATP is an ester that is found in living cells and plays a fundamental role in most biochemical processes that either produce or require energy.) The researchers were able to produce the glowing effect by watering the infected plants with a luciferin solution that was enhanced by chemicals to promote passage of the luciferin into the plant cells.

Another group of researchers from the Boyce Thompson Institute for Plant Research (Cornell University, Ithaca, N.Y.) and Texas A & M University reported on their success in transferring luciferase genes from a marine bacterium, *Vibrio harveyi,* into the bacteria *Escherichia coli* growing in cultures and *Bradyrhizobium japonicum* growing in soybean root nodules. Such luciferase genes code for enzymes that cause luminescence in the presence of decanal (an aldehyde derived from a liquid paraffin hydrocarbon); this luminescence is readily detected to verify the presence of not only the luciferase genes but any other genes to which they have been spliced.

Paul A. Bottomley and his associates used NMR (nuclear magnetic resonance) to reveal water distribution and transport in root systems. Existing techniques were more difficult to use than were those for aboveground parts of plants because the plant/soil relationship was usually disturbed. The researchers found that NMR techniques helped in studying roots without disturbing the soil. The procedure employs magnetic fields to produce images of water flow;

Illustration by Peter Sawyer; courtesy, National Museum of Natural History

*The Earth as it may have looked 3.5 billion years ago is depicted in a mural at the Smithsonian Institution's National Museum of Natural History, in Washington, D.C. Giant volcanoes rim a shallow sea dotted with stromatolites, moundlike structures of algae and bacteria.*

*A tobacco plant (left) glows in the dark (right) after the gene that codes for luciferase, an enzyme found in fireflies that promotes luminescence, was isolated and inserted into the plant's DNA (deoxyribonucleic acid).*

because soils are largely permeable to these fields, roots can be studied nondestructively in place. Bean plants were germinated and potted in various types of soil. Growth was promoted under controlled conditions of light, temperature, and humidity in greenhouses. One observation showed water moving from the cotyledons (first leaves or one of the first pair or whorl of leaves developed by the embryo of a seed plant) and the associated plant axis when the plant began to wilt. It was suggested that NMR imaging can allow repeated studies of growing plants without harming them. Thus growth, development, and response to environmental factors could be monitored. Plant injury might also be detected.

Paul H. Williams and Curtis B. Hill of the University of Wisconsin developed some plants with a short life history that may be helpful in research and teaching. Early reproductive age and ease of culture are important characteristics in laboratory organisms so that many generations may be produced quickly for observation of experimental results. Flowering plants—unlike microorganisms, simple plants, and some animals—have not been ideal laboratory organisms because they do not reproduce rapidly. Williams and Hill concentrated on selecting individuals in six different species of the genus *Brassica* because of their short reproductive cycles. This genus contains many economically important and scientifically interesting plant groups, such as mustards, cabbages, cauliflower, broccoli, turnips, and rapeseed. The researchers noted that a few plants of each species flowered significantly sooner than the others. Seeds from the fast-flowering plants were germinated, and the resulting plants were raised under controlled conditions. Pollination among plants of the same species produced some plants that were characterized by minimum time from sowing to flowering, rapid seed maturation, absence of seed dormancy, small plant

size, and high female fertility. For the six species of *Brassica*, strains with six to ten reproductive cycles per year were produced.

**Plant history.** Continued study of fossils contributed pieces of the puzzle of plant history. One example of considerable interest related to the now well-known massive extinction of organisms at the end of the Cretaceous Period (65 million years ago), a time often called the Cretaceous/Tertiary boundary. One popular explanation of this devastation is that it was caused by an impact on the Earth by an asteroid. Geologists point to an iridium-rich clay at the boundary as an indication of such an impact because such high concentrations of iridium were most likely produced by an extraterrestrial object. Paleobotanists looked for evidence among plant fossils for such a theory. A report from Tsunemasa Saito and associates from Yamagata University (Japan) supported the idea that vegetation was destroyed by wildfires that could have been caused by a meteoritic impact. Their evidence came from the study of pollen in eastern Hokkaido. They found three distinctive pollen-containing layers in upward sequence: the oldest (Cretaceous) is rich in fern and angiosperm pollen; the next (boundary) has mostly fern pollen and dark charcoal-like woody tissues; and the third (Tertiary Period) has mostly pine pollen. Saito suggested that this is a similar profile to that reported for western North America.

Jack A. Wolfe and Garland R. Upchurch, Jr., of the U.S. Geological Survey believed that the interpretation of pollen findings for the western interior United States was not very clear. They concluded that a study of fossil leaf characteristics showed that extinction was high among gymnosperms, especially evergreens, at the Cretaceous/Tertiary boundary and that survival was high among deciduous plants. Thus, the ability to enter dormancy was a major factor in survival, they reasoned, and an "impact winter" caused by disturbances of a meteoritic collision may have been responsible for the extinctions.

Fossil evidence for the origin of various forms of modified photosynthesis is rare. Since the most common is the so-called $C_3$ (three-carbon acid) form, scientists have believed it to be the original form and that modifications such as $C_4$ (four-carbon acid) are more recent. Three Fort Hayes State University (Kansas) researchers, however, reported finding in northwestern Kansas a leaf fragment that has the appropriate structure for a $C_4$ plant. This is called Kranz anatomy. They dated the leaf at five million to seven million years ago.

Concerning a more recent date but nonetheless interesting was a report from East Africa that forest clearance occurred there at least 4,800 years before the present. Alan Hamilton and David Taylor of the University of Ulster and J. C. Vogel of the Natural Physical Research Laboratory in South Africa ana-

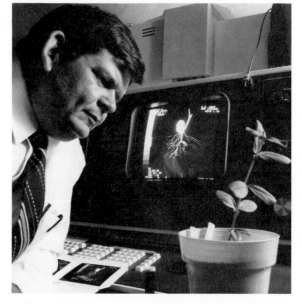

*A plant physiologist views an image of the bean plant at the right on a computer screen. Magnetic resonance imaging allows researchers to see through containers and soil and watch plant roots grow without harming them.*

lyzed a peat core taken from the Ahakagyezi Swamp of southwestern Uganda. They found evidence of agriculture (pollen of plants from agricultural land and human disturbance), soil erosion, and burning down to 10 m (33 ft) below the Earth's surface in their sample core. This level was dated at approximately 4,800 years before the present. The scientists concluded that early phases of forest reduction were associated with soil erosion and burning that were related to agricultural practices. Also they found that there had been periods of forest recovery, but that the last 2,000 years had been marked by forest degradation to supply wood for ironworking practiced by Bantu-speaking people.

**Mt. St. Helens vegetation.** In 1987 it had been seven years since an eruption of Mt. St. Helens devastated 65,000 ha (160,000 ac) of forests, meadows, lakes, and streams in the state of Washington. Trees were uprooted, or at least denuded, and volcanic ash (tephra) and mud were deposited. Whether and how the forest would recover was a subject of interest to scientists, and studies were under way on the 44,500 ha (110,000 ac) of the Mt. St. Helens National Volcanic Monument and other sites. Some researchers concentrated on the recovery of natural vegetation (and animal populations) and others on reforestation techniques.

One example of plant-recovery research was reported by Joseph A. Antos and Donald B. Zobel of Oregon State University. They observed plants belonging to the herb and shrub layer far enough from the eruption that the forest canopy remained intact but close enough that an ash layer covered the ground to a depth of 12 to 18 cm (4.7 to 7 in). They found that numerous species of ground-cover plants possessed enough developmental plasticity to survive and eventually penetrate the ash layer. Some plants did not survive well at all, which, in part, may correspond to the scarcity of some species in that area because of poor recoveries after previous volcanic eruptions. Other species modified their normal structural features to penetrate the ash layer. Most were unable to penetrate with their normal aerial shoots, but some were able to survive up to three years before emerging. Some modifications that were noted included rhizome (underground stem) transformation to long internodes (area between nodes where leaves and shoots are produced); increased vertical rhizome growth as a result of which rhizomes reached the ash-layer surface; unusual vertical shoots; production of growing parts (crowns and bulbs) near the surface; and the very common production of adventitious roots (roots produced along stems where they are not usually found). Antos and Zobel concluded that plants react to being covered with volcanic ash much as they do to being buried by sand and other material.

Research on replanting techniques was being carried out by the Pacific Northwest Forest and Range Experiment Station, the Weyerhaeuser Corp., and a number of other public and private groups. Replanting of seedlings of a number of native tree species was taking place with special attention being paid to such variables as elevation, ability to be planted in original soil (the soil that existed before the ash fall and was not modified by it), fertilizer, shading, and slope. Some preliminary findings indicated that seedlings having roots that could be placed in original soil, even though planted through ash, survived well. If they were fertilized and shaded, they also grew well and might even benefit from the lack of competition for water from other plants. Erosion of the ash proved to be helpful if it uncovered original soil or harmful if it buried the seedlings. It was reported that 25 million trees had been planted on 20,250 ha (50,000 ac) outside the monument boundaries with 80–100% survival rates and approximate growth rates of 30–60 cm (12–24 in) per year (lower elevations) and 10–15 cm (4–6 in) per year (higher elevations).

**New organism.** A group of Dutch researchers reported finding a new organism that contains both chlorophylls *a* and *b*, the photosynthetic pigments found in green algae and higher plants. The most interesting aspect of this new organism is that it is a prokaryote, thereby having characteristics more similar to bacteria than to higher plants. There are bacteria that employ photosynthesis, but they either use a special form of chlorophyll, bacteriochlorophyll, or chlorophyll *a*. Previously, one prokaryotic form was found to contain chlorophylls *a* and *b*. It was placed in a new division called Prochlorophyta but was found to be difficult to study because it could only grow on certain marine organisms. T. Burger-Wiersma and associates were able to isolate another prochlorophyte from some lakes in The Netherlands; this form could be cultured easily and thus was expected to lend itself to the study and understanding of the group. Its utilization of chlorophylls *a* and *b* showed that these pigments were not limited to green algae and higher plants.

**Plants and parasites.** Continuing efforts to understand how fungi attack their hosts revealed the way in which at least one fungus penetrates the cutin barrier that host plants have against such penetration and the means by which another fungus is usually repulsed by an enzyme that the host secretes. (Cutin is an insoluble mixture of waxes, fatty acids, soaps, and resinous material that forms a continuous layer on the outer epidermal wall of a plant.) In the first case it was shown by Charles P. Woloshuk and P. E. Kolattukudy of Washington State University that certain strains of *Fusarium solani* can detect the presence of cutin on the surface of plants and then secrete the enzyme cutinase to break down this surface coat. Spores of *F. solani* landing on a host plant apparently have a small amount of cutinase that can break down a small amount of host cutin into its constituent monomers. These monomers somehow induce the fungus germinating from the spores to produce much more cutinase, which then enables the fungus to penetrate the plant surface and produce infection.

Scientists realized that it also was important to discover the ways in which plants fight back because such information may be used to help plants combat infection when they fail to do so themselves. One recent discovery by four researchers at the University of Basel in Switzerland demonstrated that plants can use enzymes to fight back. Angela Schlumbaum and her associates showed that bean leaves produce chitinase; this breaks down chitin and, therefore, the cell walls of certain fungi and bacteria. Chitinase production is stimulated by ethylene, a normal plant hormone, and also somehow by the presence of the attacking fungus.

**Molecular botany.** Controversy over the origin of corn is long-standing and by 1987 still had not been resolved. One group of investigators was applying molecular methods in an attempt to fit more of the puzzle together. Two main varieties of corn, Southern Dent and Northern Flint, are extremely important crop plants, providing most of the U.S. production, which, in turn, is about 50% of world output. Some corn historians placed the origin of

Northern Flint in the highlands of Guatemala in spite of the great distance between that area and places in the U.S. where it is found. Others placed its origin in the Southwestern and Mexican Indian corns as a way of solving the distance problem. The latter corns, however, differ from Northern Flint in chromosome structure. John F. Doebley of Texas A & M University and Major M. Goodman and Charles W. Stuber of North Carolina State University applied enzyme analysis in an attempt to reveal ancestral relationships. Enzymes occur in somewhat varied forms called isozymes; because enzyme structure is genetically determined, the isozymes can indicate genetic lines and, therefore, ancestry. The analysis of Doebley and colleagues suggests that Northern Flint corn is most closely related to the northwestern Mexican corn, through the southwestern Pueblo Indian corn, and has shown considerable biochemical (isozyme) divergence since then.

A molecular approach to taxonomy was reported by A. R. Hardham, E. Suzaki, and J. L. Perkin of the Australian National University. They used monoclonal antibodies, which react to very specific antigens in organisms, to indicate relationships among fungi. Their techniques could be modified for other plants as well. The monoclonal antibodies are produced by a complex process that begins with the organism being studied and ends with the harvesting of the antibodies from mouse cells.

The value of the procedure is that the antibodies may be selected for specific antigens that indicate a relationship among organisms because the antigens are genetically determined. Thus, by this method, the investigators were even able to determine the difference between strains of the *Phytopthora cinnamomi* species. They also found that some antigens are different among strains of one species, others are the same for all strains of one species but differ among species, and others are the same for all species in a genus.

—Albert J. Smith

## Microbiology

Biotechnology is a discipline that blends together many different areas of science, particularly microbiology, biochemistry, chemistry, engineering, and genetics. It has emerged so quickly, however, that legislation to control it has resulted in considerable confusion. During the past year several federal agencies in the U.S. were involved in forming regulatory guidelines for practical "field" testing of new biotechnological procedures. Many people, however, remained opposed to any type of biotechnological experimentation outside of the laboratory, fearing that genetically engineered organisms would cause unforeseen damage to the environment.

An application for biotechnological testing usually faced lengthy delays in various federal agencies and further delays in states and localities. Even after receiving approval, the test would still be subject to lawsuits. This has led to a paradoxical situation: a bioengineered organism cannot be field tested until it has been proven to be no threat to the environment, but to prove that it will not be hazardous to the environment requires field testing.

A case in point involved genetically altered bacteria designed to prevent the formation of frost on food plants such as strawberry or potato plants. These bacteria, which are normally found on the surfaces of plant leaves, secrete a protein that causes the formation of ice crystals. The organisms were genetically modified by deleting the gene that codes for the ice-nucleating protein. Researchers hoped that the genetically altered organisms, when sprayed on the plants, would replace the normal, unaltered bacteria that secrete the ice-nucleating protein. In this manner the plants would be protected from frost damage. Such genetically modified bacteria were developed independently by scientists from the University of California at Berkeley and from a commercial company in California. Yet, in spite of approval for testing from the Environmental Protection Agency (EPA), local groups were able to block the field testing.

Another company genetically manipulated a common soil bacterium to produce a toxin that is poisonous to cutworms, which attack the roots of corn plants. As of early 1987 field testing of this organism had not yet received approval from federal agencies, which were waiting until more experimental data from the laboratory had been gathered.

A scientist at the Baylor College of Medicine in Houston, Texas, used a genetically altered virus to vaccinate hogs against pseudorabies. Genes were deleted from the pseudorabies virus, thereby making it unable to cause infection in swine. The genetically altered organism, however, was suitable for use as a vaccine for the immunization of animals against the disease. Even though the U.S. Department of Agriculture (USDA) had approved testing, the scientist at Baylor was reprimanded by the National Institutes of Health (NIH), Bethesda, Md., for failure to consult institutional and federal biotechnology safety committees before conducting experiments with this genetically modified organism.

The above situation is curious because the virus used in the study was essentially an attenuated organism. Such an organism has lost the ability to cause disease in at least one host while retaining its ability to be used as a vaccine. Attenuation of a human infectious organism, a procedure that has been used for nearly a century, is achieved by serial transfer of the organism from one experimental animal to

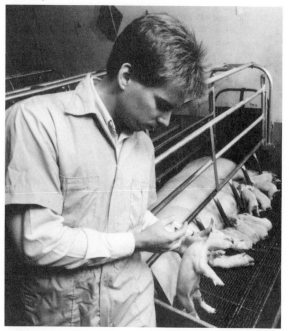

Piglet is injected with a genetically altered virus that provides protection against the disease pseudorabies. The vaccine was later taken off the market because government guidelines for its release had not been followed.

another until the organism is incapable of causing infection in humans but can be used as a vaccine. What happens in attenuation is that the virulence gene(s) has been lost or has undergone mutation. In the case of the pseudorabies virus, the process of attenuation was shortened by the laboratory deletion of the virulence gene.

Biotechnologists in the U.K. had less trouble in field testing genetically modified organisms. British scientists received permission to test a genetically altered virus that infects a pest caterpillar which damages pine trees. They planned to use an altered virus carrying genetic elements that can be identified easily. This would enable the scientists to monitor the virus in the environment. If no evidence of environmental damage is detected, then insect toxin genes will be added to the virus to improve its insecticidal efficiency.

The USDA approved plans of a U.S. company to conduct field experiments with a tobacco plant. Added to the plant was a gene from a bacterium that produces a protein which is poisonous to several caterpillar species that eat plant leaves. Thus the plant itself would produce the insect toxin coded by the added bacterial gene and would be protected from the ravages of caterpillars.

**Applied microbiology.** Other areas employing techniques of biotechnology fared better during the past year than those involving practical testing in the environment. Through the use of DNA (deoxyribonucleic acid) probes, the detection and identification of infectious organisms from patients or in such substances as food, water, or soil appeared to hold much promise. The procedure is based on the genetic principle of reassociation of nucleic acids that are complementary. (Complementarity is the capacity for precise pairing of purine and pyrimidine bases between strands of DNA and sometimes RNA, ribonucleic acid, such that the structure of one strand determines the other.) Thus an organism can be detected and identified when single-strand DNA prepared from a known infectious organism binds to single-strand DNA extracted from tissues of the patient or from other substances. This promises to be a sensitive, accurate, and rapid diagnostic procedure. It can be performed quickly on unlimited numbers of samples.

Tests employing DNA probes can also be based on the binding of DNA to complementary RNA. The U.S. Food and Drug Administration (FDA) recently approved such tests to aid in the clinical diagnosis of two microorganisms that cause atypical pneumonia. The FDA also approved a similar DNA-probe technique to identify the bacterium that causes tuberculosis.

Microbiologists from Laval University in Quebec, Canada, developed DNA probes that detect and identify bacterial resistance to antibiotics. In this assay procedure, regions of DNA from bacteria known to

*"So, until next week—Adios amoebas."*

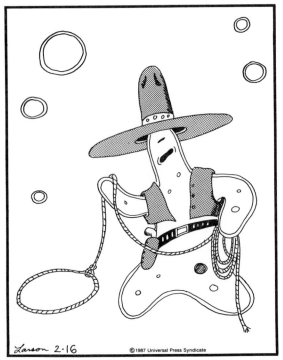

be resistant to antibiotics were tailored by various DNA-cloning procedures and used as probes for the detection of antibiotic resistance genes in bacterial isolates.

Gene probes were also being developed to detect microorganisms that can degrade man-made chemicals which have found their way into the environment as a consequence of industrial and agricultural activities. These chemicals persist in the environment for various periods of time, and they are a concern to society. Scientists from the University of Tennessee developed a DNA probe to detect microorganisms in the environment that degrade certain polychlorinated biphenyls (PCBs). Other workers from the University of Nevada used a similar procedure to detect organisms that degrade a commonly used herbicide, 2,4-D. The results from procedures such as these are expected to be useful in predicting the rate at which xenobiotics may be degraded naturally in the environment. The techniques also should help identify new organisms capable of degrading xenobiotics.

Under laboratory conditions a team of scientists from Oklahoma and Tennessee successfully removed common polluting chemicals from experimentally contaminated groundwater aquifer samples. The researchers used a genetically engineered bacterium with genes added to code for enzymes that degrade the pollutants. They showed that, by using specific DNA probes, it was possible to monitor accurately the genetically engineered bacteria when they were released in the environment. These results suggested that genetically engineered microorganisms can be used to clean up chemically contaminated groundwater and that genetic monitoring would reduce the uncertainties and fears associated with the environmental release of genetically modified microorganisms.

Scientists from the U.K. began using genetic-engineering techniques to produce new antibiotics. One technique involved cloning genes for more than one type of antibiotic into a single organism in order to produce hybrid antibiotics. Such antibiotics were expected to have more than one inhibitory action and to be resistant to inactivation by enzymes from bacteria that are resistant to the usual antibiotics.

A research team in Belgium reported finding in *Azospirillum* a region of DNA that is involved in the interaction of that bacterium with plant roots. Although *Azospirillum* is a common soil organism, it is important because it fixes atmospheric nitrogen. (Nitrogen fixation is the metabolic assimilation of atmospheric nitrogen by soil microorganisms and its release for plant use.) The bacterium is found in association with the roots of many forage grasses and grains. Nitrogen-fixing organisms collectively fall into the category of biofertilizers. Thus the discovery of plant-interactive genetic determinants in *Azospirillum* causes this soil bacterium to become a candidate for genetic engineering to realize its biofertilization potential.

The traditional method for converting coal to a gaseous fuel is catalytic gasification of the coal at high temperatures and pressures. Scientists at the University of Arkansas, however, reported that such gases (carbon monoxide, carbon dioxide, and hydrogen) can under conditions in which free oxygen is absent be biologically converted to methane by certain bacteria.

**Environmental microbiology.** *Azolla* is a common water fern in the leaf cavities of which are found symbiotically associated nitrogen-fixing cyanobacteria. Scientists from the University of Chicago reported that the plant regulates the nitrogen-fixing activities of the cyanobacterium. The plant thus makes a "slave" of the bacterium. When it needs nitrogen, it "tells" the bacterium to produce it. The mechanism by which this takes place remained unclear, but evidence indicated that the plant controls the level of transcription of various genes in the cyanobacterium. (Transcription is the process of communicating the genetic code from DNA to RNA.) The plant, therefore, exerts control over the bacterium at the molecular level.

Canadian scientists isolated nitrogen-fixing bacteria that colonize roots of plants that grow in Canada's Arctic regions. It is possible that these bacteria, which have the combined capabilities of nitrogen fixation and root colonization at low temperatures, may be useful as biofertilizers for crop plants in temperate and cold regions.

Bacteria that swim toward one or the other magnetic pole when placed in a magnetic field are designated magnetotactic. The sensing organelles in the bacteria are termed magnetosomes, and they contain magnetite ($Fe_3O_4$), a mineral in which one group of magnetic ions is polarized in a direction opposite to the other. Magnetosomes orient the bacteria in a magnetic field and determine in which direction they swim. Magnetotactic bacteria from the Earth's Northern Hemisphere are north seeking, and those from the Southern Hemisphere are south seeking. The Earth's magnetic field is inclined downward in northern latitudes and upward in southern latitudes. Thus by swimming along magnetic lines, the magnetotactic bacteria, which require either very little or no free oxygen, swim to the bottom of the sea where oxygen is either absent or exists at a low level.

Residual magnetism in marine sediments has been used extensively for many years to calculate the geological time scale, to study geomagnetic reversals of the Earth, and to measure the rates of seafloor spreading. Magnetite is usually the material studied and measured. Recently scientists from West Ger-

many and from California independently concluded that magnetite in marine sediments having natural residual magnetization is fossil bacterial magnetite. Previously it had been thought that this type of magnetite arose from physical and chemical sources.

Scientists from several laboratories reported that certain deep-sea animals, such as mussels, clams, and tube worms, use methane as an energy and food source in symbiosis with microorganisms. These symbiotic bacteria have the ability to use methane as a carbon and energy source, and they make substances that the animals in turn use for energy and food.

A team of researchers from Maryland and California found that certain Arctic starfish in their larval stage preferentially consume bacteria and not algae. The adult forms consume algal phytoplankton. Thus the food web of the starfish is uncoupled from the phytoplankton web. This means that the starfish can grow in the ocean throughout the year by eating bacteria during those periods when the growth of phytoplankton is limited owing to low light and nutrient levels.

Surprisingly, Canadian workers reported that some common species of lake algae "graze" on bacteria to supplement photosynthesis. In fact, the algae appeared to obtain about half of their total carbon from ingested bacteria.

—Robert G. Eagon

## Molecular biology

A large number of vital cellular processes depend upon the interaction of proteins with DNA. These include the replication of DNA, the transcription of RNA (the process of communicating the genetic code from DNA to RNA), and the regulation of those processes. To study the molecular details of such interactions scientists have used a variety of methods, including analyses of the rates of biochemical reactions and sophisticated chemical probes that determine precisely which nucleotide pairs are involved in binding a particular protein. The ultimate in structural information, however, is provided by X-ray diffraction analysis of crystalline material. During the past year the first high-resolution structure of a crystalline DNA-protein complex was obtained by John Rosenberg and collaborators at the University of Pittsburgh.

The complex contains two components: the protein part is the restriction endonuclease (an enzyme) known as *Eco*RI, and the DNA part is a short double-stranded fragment of 13 nucleotides (the basic building blocks of the DNA molecule), of which the *Eco*RI recognition site GAATTC is a central part. The structure provides both a precise picture of how the enzyme recognizes this particular sequence in a

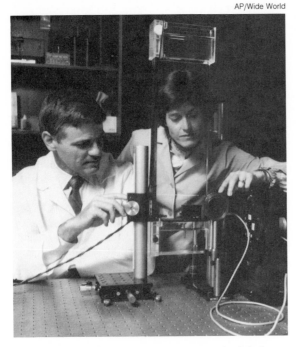

*Scientists work with a sequenator, a computerized device developed during the past year at the California Institute of Technology that can quickly and automatically analyze (or sequence) the structure of DNA.*

long DNA molecule and a likely mechanism for the specific cleavage of DNA between the G and A units.

Restriction endonucleases are enzymes, produced by bacteria, that recognize short sequences of nucleotides in DNA. They bind to DNA at these sequences and, in most cases, hydrolyze (split the bond and add elements of water) one phosphodiester bond in each DNA strand. (DNA consists of two polynucleotide strands, each of which has a backbone consisting of sugars [deoxyribose] linked together by phosphodiester bonds. Each sugar is attached to one of the four bases—adenine [A], cytosine [C], guanine [G], or thymine [T]. Specific hydrogen bonds between A and T and between G and C hold the two strands together in a helical structure.) More than 100 different restriction endonucleases, each from a different bacterial species, are known. The convention for naming these enzymes uses the first letter of the bacterial species and the first two letters of the genus, followed by a Roman numeral to cover cases in which a given bacterium produces more than one enzyme. For example, *Hemophilus influenzae* strain d produces three different restriction endonucleases, known as *Hind*I, *Hind*II, and *Hind*III. Each recognizes and cuts a different sequence in DNA.

The enzyme *Eco*RI is produced by *Escherichia coli* carrying an R plasmid. (A plasmid is an extrachromosomal genetic element that is present in some species of bacteria.) It is the first restriction enzyme

for which the target sequence and site of cutting were determined. It should be noted that the *Eco*RI target sequence is symmetric: the complement of GAATTC is GAATTC, recalling that the two strands of a DNA molecule have opposite polarity. The enzyme is believed to bind to DNA and then to scan along the DNA molecule. When the enzyme encounters the sequence GAATTC, the binding becomes tight and two phosphodiester bonds, between the G and A residues on each strand, are broken. The result is a staggered break in the DNA double helix. Mild heating ruptures the hydrogen bonds holding the A-T pairs together at the nicked ends, allowing the DNA to be separated into fragments. If a very large DNA molecule is incubated with *Eco*RI and then heated gently, the resulting population of DNA fragments will vary in length (determined solely by the distribution of GAATTC sequences in the original molecule), but each fragment will have identical ends, which look like this:

AATTC————————G
G————————CTTAA.

Regardless of its source, each DNA fragment produced by digesting DNA with *Eco*RI will have the end structure described above. A useful consequence is that any DNA fragment produced by *Eco*RI can be annealed with any other. The single-stranded protruding ends are complementary in the sense that they can form specific hydrogen bonds as follows:

An enzyme called DNA ligase is capable of reforming the phosphodiester bond between the G and A residues on each strand, restoring the continuity of each DNA strand. Recognition of these possibilities led Herbert Boyer and Stanley Cohen to propose the insertion of DNA fragments from foreign sources, such as humans, plants, and insects, into plasmids by means of restriction endonucleases. Thus was born recombinant DNA methodology and the billion-dollar biotechnology industry.

Before returning to the structure of the *Eco*RI endonuclease-DNA complex, it is useful to review a few of the facts known about each of the partners in the complex. DNA structural information, of course, began with the historic work of James Watson and Francis Crick and the group of Maurice Wilkins in London. Their results are well known, but it should be recalled that their experimental data were fiber diffraction patterns rather than information derived from single crystals. The fiber diffraction data were interpreted in terms of two models: the so-called B helix, in which the nucleotide pairs are perpendicular to the fiber axis, and another structure, the A helix, observed at very low humidity, in which the base pairs are tipped with respect to the fiber axis.

More recently a series of short DNA fragments was crystallized, and their structures were determined to high resolution by Alexander Rich and his colleagues at the Massachusetts Institute of Technology and by Richard Dickerson and his colleagues, first at the California Institute of Technology and later at the University of California at Los Angeles. These fragments, each having a different nucleotide sequence, display a surprising variety of secondary structure, including the B helix, the A helix, and a left-handed zigzag called Z DNA. Except for the latter, which occurs in some sequences of alternating purines and pyrimidines (such as GCGCGCGC), there is no discernible correlation between nucleotide sequence and the observed crystal structure.

A rather large number of proteins that bind to DNA also were crystallized and their three-dimensional structures determined. Most of these were proteins that regulate the expression of bacterial genes by binding to specific DNA sequences at or near the site where transcription of the gene's messenger RNA begins. In each case the high-resolution structure that was obtained made it possible to build an atomic model of the protein and then to examine, by the use of computer graphics, how the protein *might* bind to its specific DNA target. These modeling studies usually assume that the DNA is in the B-helix configuration, although it is known that frequently the binding of protein to DNA induces kinks, bends, or other deformations of the free DNA structure.

It was, therefore, a substantial advance to have at hand a high-resolution structure of both the DNA fragment and its bound protein in a complex. Before looking at the structure in detail, one further comment about the experimental work is in order. Generally speaking, X-ray diffraction studies require substantial amounts of pure protein in order to grow crystals. Regulatory proteins and many enzymes are normally present in cells only in small amounts. All of the structural work on these proteins was made possible by recombinant DNA technology. When the genes encoding these proteins are cloned in suitable vectors, bacteria can produce 20% or more of their total protein as the cloned gene product. (A vector is a genetically engineered DNA molecule used for propagation and expression of cloned genes.) Thus the formerly rare materials are made available in amounts inconceivable prior to the introduction of recombinant DNA. When one recalls that restriction endonucleases, such as *Eco*RI, made recombinant DNA technology possible, it seems fitting that the crystals of *Eco*RI complexed with DNA were grown from preparations of the enzyme that was itself the product of a cloned gene.

The structural results were breathtaking. The *Eco*RI endonuclease consists of two molecules. These two identical subunits contain involuted clefts that bind segments of the DNA backbone. The overall appearance of the protein is globular, with each subunit containing a single domain, a local region of a protein structure formed by the folding of the polypeptide chain. The DNA lies in a groove formed where the two protein subunits are joined, wrapped in place by short arms protruding from each subunit. Each subunit domain contains a pair of α-helical segments roughly perpendicular to the DNA axis and pointing at the DNA. At the end of one helical segment is an arginine residue (arginine and lysine are the two basic amino acids of the 20 that occur in proteins) that forms a pair of hydrogen bonds with the backside of the G nucleotide in the recognition sequence GAATTC. At the end of the other helical segment are two amino acids, an arginine and a glutamic acid, both of which make a pair of hydrogen bonds to the two A nucleotides. Altogether, three amino acids on the two helical segments make a total of six hydrogen bonds to the sequence GAA. This set of bonds is repeated in a symmetric way: the complementary DNA strand of the recognition sequence is also GAATTC, but it extends in the opposite direction. The second subunit of the endonuclease protein makes exactly the same six hydrogen bonds to the GAA of the other strand. Thus the TTC residues do not participate directly in the bonding of the protein to the DNA recognition sequence.

A consequence of the protein-DNA interaction is distortion of the DNA B-helix. The structure of the DNA is actually deformed in three places. One is in the center of the recognition sequence, between the

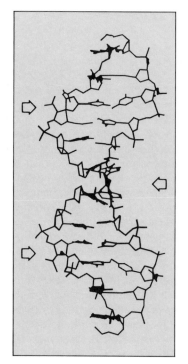

*Diagram of the DNA B-helix reveals three deformations in the structure as indicated by the arrows. Described as neokinks, they were caused by the interaction of the DNA and a protein (see text).*

A and the T, where the helix is unwound by 25°. Two other deformations, symmetrically placed, are centered on the phosphates attached to the G residues. If these deformations occurred in free DNA, they would be called "kinks." Since in this case they are formed as a consequence of the interaction with the protein, the researchers introduced the term "neokink" to describe them. One of the remarkable and unexpected results to flow from the analysis of this structure is the idea that the enzyme *induces* the structural deformation in the recognition sequence that permits the sequence-specific binding manifest in the 12 hydrogen bonds described above.

Other significant discoveries were made. The enzyme requires the $Mg^{++}$ ion in order to cleave DNA. To form stable structures for crystallization, $Mg^{++}$ was omitted from the solutions of DNA and protein from which the crystals were grown. Therefore, the structure obtained was that of a precursor to the enzymically active complex. Indeed, the structure contained a solvent cavity that is likely to be the place where $Mg^{++}$ binds to help catalyze the phosphodiester bond cleavage between the G and A residues. When $Mg^{++}$ was diffused into the crystals, the DNA was cleaved and the structure was changed, without destroying the crystals.

As a result of this work two crystal structures are eagerly anticipated: that of the *Eco*RI endonuclease itself and that of the DNA-enzyme complex after cleavage of the DNA. When these results are combined, they will provide a view of the mechanism of an enzyme's action unprecedented in biochemistry.

—Robert Haselkorn

## Zoology

A major concern of biologic science in recent years has been the accelerating extinction of animal species, especially those living in tropical forests. Several aspects of this crisis were discussed during the past year at a symposium sponsored by the U.S. National Academy of Sciences and the Smithsonian Institution. Discussion centered on the danger to the great diversity of life in tropical forests, most of which had yet to be identified and studied. Approximately 1.7 million species of animals throughout the world had been described by 1987, but recent studies in the tropics indicated that the total number in existence could exceed five million. Of these, half live in the tropical forests. These forests, which cover only 7% of the world's land surface, were rapidly being destroyed by logging and by being cleared for farming and cattle raising. Taking place along with the loss of the forest was the extinction of large numbers of known and unknown animals and plants. David Raup of the University of Chicago made the point that the predicted loss of 50% of all species

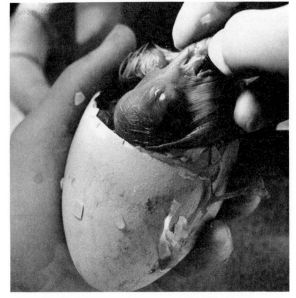

*California condor chick hatches at the San Diego Zoo. The zoo reported in 1987 that its 13 condor chicks were growing well. This represented nearly half the known number of living California condors.*

by the year 2135 would be comparable to the mass extinctions of dinosaurs and other organisms that occurred at the end of the Mesozoic Era. Unlike the controversy concerning the latter, this time there would be no doubt about the causative agent.

On a somewhat more hopeful note, steps were taken to help ensure the survival of three species of animals, the California condor, the black-footed ferret, and the monarch butterfly. By 1987 the California condor was on the brink of extinction. The last known wild female was captured and taken to the San Diego Wild Animal Park to take part in a breeding program that would, it was hoped, continue the existence of the largest bird of the United States. Three males remained to be captured, one of which was the mate of the female. The San Diego program was successful in breeding condors. Bill Toon, associate curator for birds, was pleased to state that in 1987, 13 condor chicks were growing well and represented nearly half of the known number of living California condors. (*See* Feature Article: THE SAN DIEGO ZOO: AN ARK IN THE PARK.)

Another capture and breeding program was instituted for the black-footed ferret. This animal had been living on the edge of extinction for many years. Though they were once thought to be extinct, a thriving colony of these ferrets was found in Wyoming in 1981, living in association with a large prairie dog city. However, like all isolated populations, these ferrets faced the danger that some disaster might suddenly destroy all or most members of them. Two epidemics did sweep through the area. First sylvatic plague devastated the prairie dog colony, thereby killing off most of the ferrets' food supply. Then canine distemper killed half of the remaining ferrets. The last census, in 1986, indicated that only 21 ferrets might still be living, including six in captivity. Because of these low numbers and the distances that separate the individuals, the U.S. Fish and Wildlife Service decided to capture the remaining individuals and add them to a breeding program at the Sybille Research Station near Laramie, Wyo. This, it was hoped, would ensure the future of the black-footed ferret and eventually allow its reintroduction to the wild.

In the mid-1970s, Fred Urquhart, a Canadian entomologist, discovered the wintering site of the eastern monarch butterfly. This is an area of oyamel fir forest in mountains near Mexico City. Since that time small-scale logging operations have gradually been reducing that forest and threatening the existence of the butterflies. Efforts by the Monarca A.C. (a Mexican wildlife organization) and the World Wildlife Fund resulted in an edict by the Mexican government proclaiming the site to be an ecological preserve. Steps were also being taken to provide alternative sources of income for the tenants who lived by logging the firs.

**Primate evolution.** A major development in primate evolution was the description of a skull found in northern Kenya west of Lake Turkana in 1985 by Alan Walker of Johns Hopkins University. This new specimen, designated as KNM-WT 17000 in the National Museums of Kenya, is a hominid australopithecine, but at that point agreement about it ends. The skull is 2.5 million years old, making it the oldest known hominid that is not on the line leading to modern man.

The description of the skull by Walker, Richard Leakey of the National Museums of Kenya, John M. Harris of the Los Angeles County Museum of Natural History, and Frank H. Brown of the University of Utah, indicated it to be very massive, with very large frontal and occipital crests, extremely large teeth, and a small braincase. It presented a puzzling mixture of primitive and specialized features. Its age and characteristics were forcing a considerable revision of the prevalent idea that one ancient primate, *Australopithecus afarensis,* was the ancestor of only two lines of australopithecines. One line led to modern man; the second led to the other australopithecines and ended in extinction. The new find suggested that there might have been three or four lines of hominids and that their common ancestor possibly lies farther back in time than previously thought.

Another of the problems in hominid evolution was the dating of the earliest primate fossils. These fossils were from the Jebel Qatrani Formation in the Fayum depression of Egypt. This area also has provided important fossils of many other mammalian groups. Because the deposits there have undergone considerable disruption through time, the age of the fossils was uncertain, but it was estimated to be about 27 million years. Recently, John G. Fleagle of the State University of New York at Stony Brook, Thomas M. Brown and John D. Obradovich of the United States Geological Survey, and Elwyn L. Simons of Duke University reexamined this problem. Based on geological and faunal evidence, they found that a minimum age for this formation would be 81 million years. This increase in age is important because it provides a more reasonable length of time for the evolutionary changes that are apparent between the Fayum fossils and other fossil remains. It also reveals that there is a gap of 10 million years, between 30 and 20 million years ago, from which there are essentially no primate remains. It was during this period that great evolutionary changes of the monkeys took place.

Another important question about the Jebel Qatrani Formation was answered by Storrs L. Olson of the Smithsonian Institution and D. Tab Rasmussen of Duke University. Because important phases of primate evolution took place there, it is of considerable interest to know what environmental conditions existed there at that time. Olson and Rasmussen noted that a considerable proportion of the fossil birds from the Jebel Qatrani are members of living families. By studying the distribution and habitats of these modern relatives, they found that many of the modern forms shared only one habitat. This region, in Uganda north and west of Lake Victoria, is an area of swampland bordered by grasslands and forest. Interestingly, the next oldest primate forms are mostly from the shores and islands of Lake Victoria, indicating that this kind of aquatic-associated habitat was important in early primate evolution.

**Central nervous system.** While a complete understanding of the central nervous system of even the simplest animals was far from being achieved, a number of advances were made. For the first time a complete set of nerve cells involved in a complex repetitive behavior was described. Peter Brodfuehrer and W. Otto Friesen at the University of Virginia found in the subesophageal ganglia that trigger undulatory swimming in the medicinal leech a pair of nerve cells, designated Tr1. These cells constitute the last in a set of five levels of nerve cells involved in this behavior. Rhythmic activities, such as this swimming pattern, are usually thought to be controlled by (1) a central oscillator, which is a network of nerve cells that generates rhythmic timing cues and that connects to the (2) motor and inhibitory nerve cells going to muscles. The oscillator nerve cells are controlled by (3) gating and (4) trigger nerve cells. Gating nerve cells allow the oscillator network to stimulate the muscles while the oscillator cells are active; by contrast, the trigger nerve cells need only fire briefly to initiate and continue activity of the oscillator network. The two Tr1 cells are trigger cells and produce their effects by stimulating gating cells in the leech's segmental ganglia. A short burst of activity in the trigger cells produces a long-lasting stimulation of the gating cells. In the leech the trigger cells, in turn, are stimulated by endings of various (5) sensory nerve cells that are associated with sense organs in the skin of the leech. Thus, the complete pathway from sensory input, via the skin, to a complex motor response, swimming, is now known.

The mechanisms of memory continued to fascinate and mystify investigators. The most common concept of memory retention by the brain suggests that repetitive stimulation of a series of nerve cells modifies their connections (synapses) in such a way that that pathway becomes easily stimulated and constitutes a "memory." Such a memory would involve quite a few nerve cells but not extremely large numbers of them.

In an elegant series of experiments, E. Roy John of New York University, Tang Yong-Nian and A. Bertrand Brill of Brookhaven (N.Y.) National Laboratory, Ronald Young of the University of the West Indies, and Kenji Ono of Nagasaki University reported that a memory in the cat brain may involve millions of nerve cells. They observed the incorporation of radioactively labeled glucose in the brain as the cat observed new situations and compared it with the incorporation of glucose when the cat was presented with a "memorized" situation. The cats had been trained to know that two concentric green circles on a small door meant that it could be pushed open to obtain food. A red contact lens placed over an eye would prevent the cat from perceiving the green circles. By surgically separating the right and left cerebral hemispheres of the cat's brain after training, the investigators could present the "memory stimulus" to one cerebral hemisphere without presenting it to the other hemisphere. Computer processing allowed the investigators to compare the radioactivity incorporated in the left and right brain cells during the presentation of the stimulus. They found that very large areas of the cerebral hemispheres and other areas of the brain increased their metabolic rates when the stimulus was present.

The controversial interpretations of these experiments is that a given memory may involve the diffuse participation of millions of nerve cells and that a given nerve cell may be involved in the retention of many memories. If true, this will make the memory mechanism even more difficult to unravel.

Information exchange is not restricted to the nerve cells within an individual but frequently occurs between individuals of a single species and, less commonly, between individuals of different species. Two interesting examples involving birds were recently reported. Cliff swallows live in breeding colonies in the western half of the United States. They build clusters of mud nests on the undersides of overhanging cliffs or rocks and in protected areas such as the undersides of highway overpasses. Raising of broods within a colony takes place at approximately the same time so that many adults in the colony will be foraging for food for chicks simultaneously. Cliff swallows feed on temporary aggregations of flying insects. Since these aggregations usually exist only for several minutes before dispersing, the swallows must continuously locate new feeding locales. Charles R. Brown at Princeton University observed colonies of swallows over four consecutive summers and found that unsuccessful foragers frequently would watch those swallows that returned to their nests with food and would then follow a successful bird as it returned to its feeding site. Because success in finding food appeared to vary more or less randomly among

*Cliff swallows use their summer nesting colonies (right) as places to share information about where to find food. At the far right a cliff swallow feeds its young.*

Photos, Mary Bomberger Brown

*Stegosaurus had only one row of bony plates extending from its neck and back (left) rather than two (right) as had been previously believed. This conclusion was reached by a scientist in Los Angeles after a careful reexamination of the most complete stegosaurus skeleton. He found no evidence that any of the plates overlapped or had asymmetric bases.*

the individuals of the colony, this behavior benefited the entire group and might be a major advantage of nesting in a colony.

An interesting example of advantageous information exchange between individuals of different species was reported by Charles A. Munn of Wildlife Conservation International in New York City. Many birds while feeding rely on sentinel birds to warn them of approaching predators, especially flying ones such as hawks and eagles. Munn found this to be true of two populations of birds in the Peruvian forests. Species feeding in the understory of the forest utilized the bluish-slate antshrike as a sentinel, while those occupying the forest canopy used the white-winged shrike-tanager. In both cases only about 50% of the warning cries from the sentinel corresponded to the sighting of a predator. The other 50% were deliberate false alarms. The false alarms were designed to distract momentarily a nearby bird that had just flushed an insect from cover. This momentary hesitation allowed the sentinel bird to fly over quickly and catch the insect for itself. The birds appear to realize that not all alarm calls are genuine, but also know they cannot take the chance of ignoring any of them. While the loss of an occasional insect is not much in return for the protection supplied by the sentinel, it does somewhat call to mind a protection racket.

**Sensory physiology.** A number of interesting observations were made in the area of sensory physiology. For many years scientists speculated on the possible existence of a magnetic sense in animals. Since that time evidence has accumulated that many species of animals are able to sense magnetic fields. During the past year John Phillips at Cornell University found that migratory salamanders can use magnetic cues. Phillips stimulated these animals to leave their pond by raising the temperature of the water, but before they could reach the shore he quickly

removed them and carried them to a laboratory in which the magnetic environment could be manipulated. In the laboratory the salamanders moved in the direction that would have taken them to the shore of the pond. This is an orienting response that these salamanders have in their home ponds. Salamanders not temperature-stimulated to leave their pond would, in the laboratory, move in directions that would take them back to their home ponds. This is a homing response. Both orientation and homing directions were changed by a corresponding angle as the horizontal (polar) component of the magnetic field in the laboratory was rotated. The direction of the vertical component (the Earth's magnetic lines incline down in the Northern Hemisphere) also influenced orientation. If these lines were reversed, that is, made to slope up, the direction of orientation was shifted by 180°. The homing response was not affected by the direction of the vertical component of the magnetic field.

Besides confirming the existence of a magnetic sense in salamanders, these results imply two magnetic sensing systems, one of which is sensitive to the vertical component of magnetic fields and one that is not. The homing response also implies that these salamanders may have a "magnetic map" sense. The ability to home using natural magnetic patterns should require an extraordinary sensitivity to magnetic variations.

Electroreception in many fishes is a well-established sense and is known to occur in amphibians as well. Surprisingly, this ability to detect electric fields has been found in a mammal. Henning Scheich of the Technical University of Darmstadt, West Germany, and Anna Guppy of the Australian National University reported the presence of electroreceptors in the bill of the duck-billed platypus. They suggested that the receptors may be located in the ducts of cutaneous mucus glands. All animals generate electric

411

potentials when muscles contract, and the platypus possibly uses these to locate and catch the small aquatic animals on which it feeds.

Like the large whales, elephants have been found to produce and hear sounds of very low frequency. Katharine Payne, William Langbauer, Jr., and Elizabeth M. Thomas of Cornell University reported vocalizations of 14–24 Hz by African elephants. These sounds, which are normally below the threshold of human hearing, carry for long distances. The extent to which these sounds are used for communication is not known, but they could be the explanation for the puzzling coordinated behavior patterns observed in herds of elephants.

A major step in understanding the mechanism whereby honeybees can use the "waggle" dance to locate food sources was made by Samuel Rossel and Rudiger Wehner of the University of Zurich. A bee's eye is made up of approximately 6,000 units called ommatidia. Each ommatidium has a group of eight receptor cells in which the light-sensitive components are fine tubes that lie parallel to the surface lens and point toward the central axis of the ommatidium. Rossel and Rudiger found that certain of these light receptors were specialized for the reception of polarized ultraviolet light and were arranged in a pattern such that the degree of stimulation of the receptors would vary with the bee's orientation relative to the source of the polarized light. When blue sky is visible, the maximum polarization of sunlight will be at a right angle to the position of the Sun. The dancing bee indicates a food source at a particular distance and at a particular angle relative to the Sun. The observer bee leaves the hive, flies in a circle to determine the maximum direction of light polarization, and then uses that information to determine the proper direction in which to search.

Another insect, the praying mantis, was found to possess a unique auditory apparatus. After observing nerve signals in the central nervous system of the mantis in response to sound stimulation, David Yager and Ronald Hoy of Cornell University found the ear of the mantis to be a single structure located on the underside of the thorax between the bases of the legs. Other insects have sound receptors located in various parts of the body, but in all other cases these organs are paired and have the potential for sound localization as well as detection. Being single, the ear of the mantis should not be able to determine the direction of sound, and preliminary experiments support this. The function of the ear is uncertain, but observations on an Asian species indicate that one possibility is that it detects the ranging sounds of flying bats and triggers evasive maneuvers by the mantis.

**Other developments.** A number of marine invertebrate animals that live in the areas of hydrothermal vents or hydrocarbon seepage are known to utilize sulfur compounds as a food source. These animals do not metabolize those compounds directly but use materials produced by intracellular symbiotic bacteria that employ the sulfur compounds as a primary energy source. During the past year scientists obtained evidence that other animals may use methane gas in a similar fashion. James J. Childress, C. R. Fisher, and A. E. Anderson of the University of California at Santa Barbara, and J. M. Brooks, M. C. Kennicut II, and R. Bidigare of Texas A&M University reported that an as yet unnamed mussel of the family Mytilidae has intracellular symbiotic bacteria that metabolize methane. These mussels were trawled from depths of 600 to 700 m from the Gulf of Mexico off Louisiana in an area of oil seepage. The bacteria are located in the cells of the gills and can utilize methane at high rates. The ratio of different isotopes of carbon found in other tissues of the mussels support the contention that the mussel is deriving its carbon source from compounds produced from methane by the bacteria. The use of symbiotic bacteria as a source of nutrition is apparently a major mode of life among the marine invertebrates.

A growth factor discovered in the 1950s by Stanley Cohen of Vanderbilt University was reported during recent months to have an unexpected function. Osamu Tsutsumi, Hirohisa Kurachi, and Takami Oka of the U.S. National Institutes of Health found that epidermal growth factor (EGF) was produced by the submandibular salivary glands of mice. They also noted that removal of those glands caused the EGF to almost disappear from the blood and reduced the number of sperm produced by the testes to about one-half the normal level. Interestingly, neither the level of the sex hormone testosterone nor behavior was altered. Administration of EGF restored the sperm count to normal. In the female mouse EGF plays a role in the growth of the mammary glands. EGF is the first hormone-like substance having a direct reproductive role that is not produced either by the brain-pituitary complex or by the gonads themselves.

The use of the degree of similarity in the genetic material, DNA (deoxyribonucleic acid), as a measure of ancestral relationships continued to produce controversial family trees. By comparing the DNA compositions of birds, Charles G. Sibley and John E. Ahlquist of Yale University determined that the new-world vultures are more closely related to storks than to old-world vultures; swifts are most closely related to hummingbirds; swallows belong with the songbirds; and starlings are related to mockingbirds rather than to crows. The investigators concluded that many anatomical features which have been used to indicate common ancestry are the results of adaptations to similar environments and life-styles and, consequently, can be misleading indicators of genetic relationships.

It has long been known that sex determination among the hymenoptera (bees, wasps, ants, and their relatives) is based on whether the egg receives one X chromosome or two. A male is the result of development of an egg that has not been fertilized and consequently has one X chromosome contributed by the female producing the egg. A female results if the egg is fertilized and carries an X chromosome from each parent. Some truly fascinating modifications of this pattern occur in the parasitic wasp, *Nasonia vitripennis*. This wasp lays its eggs on fly pupa, on which the wasp larvae feed after hatching. Normally, the female wasp can control the proportion of male and female offspring by regulating the release of sperm from a storage sac as the eggs are laid. Some females carry an inherited "maternal sex ratio factor" that induces closure of the sperm sac, reducing the number of eggs fertilized and thereby increasing the percentage of female young. Some male wasps carry a "paternal sex ratio factor" that causes only males to hatch. This factor is carried in the sperm and, following fertilization, causes the destruction of the male-derived X chromosome. The resulting egg now has only one X chromosome and produces a male wasp, which again carries the paternal sex ratio factor. To complicate matters further, some females are infected by a bacterium that selectively destroys most of the unfertilized eggs before they hatch, resulting in mostly female offspring.

It is theorized that the two sex ratio factors help maximize the numbers of wasps, but the action of the bacterium appears only to benefit the bacterium. But however the system operates, the continued existence of the wasps indicates that it must work.

—J. R. Redmond

# Materials sciences

Progress in converting other forms of carbon to diamond was made during the past year. Researchers also discovered that introducing porosity to some ceramics improves the mechanical properties of those materials. New procedures were developed for producing high-quality, low-cost ceramic powders, and metallurgists used plasma furnaces to recover metals from their ores.

## Ceramics

Advances were made during the past year concerning several new or significantly improved ceramic materials. Significant developments also occurred in the areas of the processes used to shape these materials into useful products, and of their applications.

General Electric Research and Development Center, Schenectady, N.Y.

*Researchers at General Electric Co. have developed a computer sofware package for designing parts made from structural plastic foam. Here they examine an intricately shaped pallet for shipping fragile jet engine components.*

**New materials.** One of the most striking of the new materials was vapor-deposited diamond. Unlike previously reported diamondlike coatings, which contained appreciable amounts of hydrogen and which had only a preponderance of real diamond character in their atomic bonding, the new materials truly appeared to be high-quality diamond. Researchers had long sought to convert into the cubic, very hard diamond structure either carbonaceous gases or the more common forms of carbon, which are stable at room temperature and atmospheric pressure. Until recently, however, the only successful approach to obtaining synthetic diamond was to heat graphite to very high temperatures in specialized equipment that could simultaneously apply very high pressures. Although large, gem-quality diamonds formed in that way would be extremely expensive, the process was used to make industrial-grade diamond powder for use in grinding and cutting.

Research on the deposition of diamond from carbonaceous gases offered the potential for low costs, but early attempts to obtain diamond in that way did not work. The most successful early effort was W. G. Eversole's demonstration in 1958 that thin diamond films could actually be formed by the pyrolysis of methane gas. (Pyrolysis is chemical change brought about by the action of heat.) Unfortunately, Eversole's process produced films that were a mixture of both diamond and graphite. The next major advances

413

were made by Boris Derjaguin and his colleagues at the Institute of Physical Chemistry in Moscow in the late 1970s. They showed that atomic hydrogen in the gas phase prevented the deposition of graphite without affecting the formation of diamond, and they suggested that the atomic hydrogen acted as a selective solvent. Though Derjaguin and his colleagues have since that time grown a number of thin single-crystal and polycrystalline diamond films, their work was largely overlooked or ignored elsewhere.

Japanese researchers were among the first to follow up on Derjaguin's work. Beginning in the early 1980s, a number of them explored various ways of producing high concentrations of atomic hydrogen within the reactant gases to speed the deposition process and improve the quality of the films. By 1987 some of their efforts appeared to be nearing commercial applications. Within the U.S. interest picked up markedly during the past two years, and substantial research was under way.

Much of the current work was focused on plasma-assisted chemical-vapor deposition and other methods aimed at further improvements in the quality and speed of the deposition process. However, there was still a great deal to be learned about how diamond forms from the gas phase. Some of the recent studies, for example, suggested that it is the energy of excited states in the gas phase that is responsible for diamond formation rather than the presence of atomic hydrogen itself.

The interest in diamond films stemmed not from the familiar beauty of gemstone-quality diamonds but rather from the amazing physical and mechanical properties of diamond for a wide variety of potential commercial applications. For example, diamond is the hardest material known, and a coating even a few micrometers thick might provide exceptional cutting ability and wear resistance. At room temperature and above, it conducts heat better than any other material, including copper and silver, yet it can also be a good electrical insulator. This combination of properties may open important applications in the packaging of high-power, high-speed chips for the electronics industry. When a suitable impurity has been added, diamond also has exceptional potential as a semiconductor. The electron velocities achievable in diamond are higher than those in gallium arsenide, the best candidate at present for high-speed semiconductor applications. One research group, the Crystallume Co. in California, was even investigating the fabrication of bulk ceramic forms of diamond for possible structural applications.

In regard to other new materials, researchers at the Naval Research Laboratory, Washington, D.C., showed that carefully introduced porosity can actually improve the mechanical properties of some ceramics. Using photolithographic techniques to control the placement, size, shape, spacing, and orientation of the pores, they showed that they could control crack propagation and reduce stress concentrations near the random flaws normally present in lead zirconate titanate, one of the principal materials used for high-power sonar transducers. The result was a substantial increase in toughness and nearly a doubling of strength.

Researchers at Sandia National Laboratories, Albuquerque, N.M., showed that the strength and toughness of glass-ceramics, materials that are formed in a glassy condition and then treated by heat to convert them to largely crystalline ceramics, can be substantially improved by the incorporation of about 10% zirconium dioxide. While such toughening has been applied extensively to crystalline ceramics, this appears to be its first application to glass-ceramics, and the results may prove useful in the further development of glass-ceramic composites.

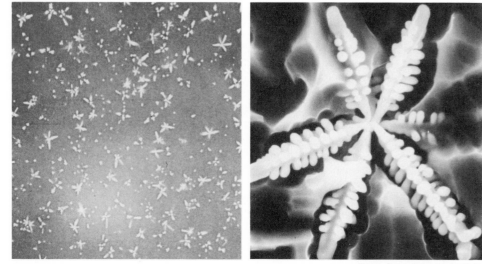

*Zirconium oxide crystals, revealed on the polished surface of a glass-ceramic (right), add toughness and strength. A crack in the glass-ceramic that occurs near such a crystal would essentially be closed because the crystal would spontaneously convert to its larger monoclinic form (far right).*

Photos, Sandia National Laboratories

**Processing.** In the processing area several new low-temperature powder-making approaches having the potential for the production of high-quality, low-cost ceramic powders emerged. One approach used hydrothermal synthesis, in which raw materials are dissolved and desired particle compositions are precipitated out in an aqueous solution under a combination of moderate temperatures and applied pressures. The process appears to produce high-quality, sinterable powders and to have considerable commercial potential. (A sinterable powder is one that will form a coherent mass when heated, without melting.) For example, researchers at Battelle Columbus Laboratory and the Tokyo Institute of Technology used this process to produce fine, uniform, partially stabilized zirconium oxide powders.

Spray processes also showed promise for powder production. In the spray pyrolysis method a solution containing appropriate salts is atomized into droplets in a heated reaction chamber. The solvent is then evaporated, and the resultant solids are decomposed into the desired ceramic compounds in a single step. Pennsylvania State University researchers used this method to produce fine-grained, very reactive powders for a variety of electronic applications. Soviet Academy of Sciences researchers used cryochemical processing to achieve similar objectives; instead of heating the droplets, they froze them and then immersed them in acetone to extract the aqueous solvent.

One of the most novel of the new techniques to produce powder was rapid precipitation from supercritical fluid solutions, under development at Battelle Pacific Northwest Laboratories. A liquid can exist only up to a certain critical temperature. Above that temperature there is just a single, supercritical fluid phase that exists regardless of the applied pressure. These supercritical fluids have many interesting physical and chemical properties, including the ability to dissolve some materials that would not be nearly as soluble in ordinary liquid solvents. Once dissolved, the materials can be precipitated out in the form of very finely divided ceramic powders by rapidly expanding the fluid to produce a sudden decrease in pressure, density, and solute solubility.

**Applications.** There were also several important developments in the applications of ceramics. Piezoelectric ceramics were finding increasing use as actuators and even as small electric motors. (Piezoelectric ceramics are those that exhibit electric polarity due to pressure.) A major factor in this development was their ability to provide precise, controlled linear displacements as small as one micrometer (a millionth of a meter) with accuracies routinely of the order of ten nanometers (ten billionths of a meter). The ability to position and manipulate materials or objects on so fine a scale was taking on increasing importance in many fields, including precise visible and laser optics, deformable mirrors, precision machining and manufacturing, and the construction of new scientific instruments and electron optic devices such as the scanning tunneling microscope.

There were also interesting new applications for ion implantation in improving the electro-optical properties of ceramics. Sandia National Laboratories researchers showed that the photosensitivity of ferroelectric lead lanthanum zirconate titanate can be increased by a factor of 10,000 in the near-ultraviolet part of the spectrum by means of the implantation of a combination of inert ions, such as argon, neon, and helium, or by a combination of inert ions and active ions such as aluminum or chromium. The resultant material is the most sensitive, nonvolatile image-storage medium yet developed and has potential for erasable and reusable applications. The improvement and tailoring of the properties of electro-optical materials by the implantation of inert and electrically active ions was also under investigation at the University of Sussex, Falmer, England, where researchers were focusing on materials such as lithium niobate and lithium tantalate.

—Norman M. Tallan

## Metallurgy

During the past year attention was focused on the interrelated topics of alternative sources of energy, usage of energy for the extraction and refining of metals, and recovery of valuable metals from industrial waste materials. In most conventional extraction processes, the melting temperatures and chemical stabilities of the materials being processed require that the processes be conducted at temperatures in the range of 1,000–1,500° C (1,800–2,700° F). Fossil fuels are normally used in these processes as both the chemical reductants for the oxides being reduced and also as the fuels themselves, the chemical combustion of which increases the temperature of the reactants to a level at which the required reduction reactions occur readily. However, when the required temperatures are in excess of 1,600° C (2,900° F), the use of electrical energy becomes more efficient. In view of the projection that by the year 2000 electricity will be the cheapest and most abundant form of energy, research and development were being concentrated on the use of electrical energy for the extraction, refining, and remelting of metals. Particular attention was being paid to the development of plasma furnaces.

A plasma is a partially ionized, electrically neutral, and electrically conducting high-temperature gas that is produced by the passage of an electric arc through the gas. Two major types of electrode geometry are employed in the generation of a plasma. In one a

*Technician adjusts valves on a new electrogalvanizing production line. Coils of sheet steel are rust-proofed on the line with a thin coating of zinc, enabling automakers to offer ten-year warranties against corrosion damage.*

nozzle is formed by a central cathode and a ring-shaped anode, and the gas, which is ionized by being passed through the nozzle, forms a plasma "torch." In the other the arc is transferred from the cathode to an external anode, which can be the surface of the liquid metal that is being melted or processed.

Relatively large-scale plasma equipment was first constructed by the U.S. National Aeronautics and Space Administration for the purpose of producing a plasma torch capable of generating thermal energy at temperatures similar to those experienced by space vehicles during their reentry to the Earth's atmosphere. This development was followed by an industrial application of plasma technology, using existing equipment, which was more rapid than the development of the fundamental understanding of the principles required for rational and efficient design. Research in 1987 was involved with the study of the physics and electrical characteristics of plasma generators, power supply systems, reactor engineering, and process chemistry.

In addition to the production of temperatures that are much higher than those that can be attained by the combustion of fuels or by resistance heating, the attractions and potential advantages of plasma reactors include the ability to supply a concentrated heat source in a compact system; this permits a high processing rate per unit volume of reactor, control of the gaseous atmosphere in the reactor, and operation in a closed system, which is important for the containment of pollution.

In one experimental design, called an in-flight reactor, the plasma generated from a hollow cathode is transferred vertically downward to a ring-shaped anode and, by electrochemical means, is then made to travel around the ring at rates of 2,000–10,000 rpm. This rapid rotation expands the plasma into a conical form with a base diameter and height each measuring 12.5 cm (five inches). With argon as the plasma gas and operating with a current of 290–400 amp at 140–220 v, a maximum temperature of 7,700° C (13,900° F) is obtained in the plasma. Mixtures of oxide and carbon particles with diameters in the range of 40–200 µm were fed through the cone and allowed to fall into a long vertical chamber in which the reaction products were quenched. (One µm, micrometer, equals one one-millionth of a meter.)

The reduction of ores of chromite ($Cr_2O_3$) and taconite ($Fe_3O_4$) was studied in an in-flight reactor. It was found that the processing of the chromite ore produced a metallic Fe-Cr alloy containing up to 12% by weight of carbon in solution and a large proportion of the carbide ($(FeCr)_7C_3$), whereas processing of the $Fe_3O_4$ produced iron containing between 1 and 3% by weight of carbon. This study showed that, as predicted by thermodynamics, the reduction with carbon of the more stable oxides, such as those of chromium, titanium, and silicon, tended to produce metal carbides rather than metal, whereas reduction with carbon of the less stable oxides, such as those of lead, nickel, and iron, tended to produce the metallic state. The researchers considered this process to be well-suited to the production of high-carbon ferroalloys, which could be decarburized in a subsequent step, and to the bulk production of silicon carbide and tungsten carbide.

A different arrangement was used in the falling film plasma reactor, which has been employed to reduce iron oxide and vanadium oxide. This reactor is equipped with a long, hollow electrode containing a methane-hydrogen plasma. Oxide powder is introduced at the top of the electrode, where it melts and then falls as a liquid film. Since the film is located in the path of the plasma, it is heated by resistance as well as by radiation and convection from the plasma. The relatively long time of residence of the film in the reactor and the intimate contact between the film and the plasma, which, being hydrogen and methane, is also the chemical reducing agent, provides a high degree of chemical reduction; also, the film is sufficiently fluid that slagmaking additions need not be made to the feed material. The specific power consumption decreases with decreasing size of the oxide particles, higher proportions of reactant to the plasma, higher throughput rates, and lower gas enthalpies. (Enthalpy is a measure of the quantity of thermal energy required to raise the temperature of a given amount of substance through

*Stainless steel bars are shaped to form the ribs to which the Statue of Liberty's copper "skin" is attached (left). The original wrought steel ribs had corroded. A special aluminum scaffolding was erected around the statue (center) during its restoration. At the right is the Statue of Liberty after the restoration was completed in 1986.*

a given interval.) In a 1 Mw unit that is making iron, the specific energy consumption of 2.6 kw-hr per kilogram of iron was only 15% greater than the theoretical value and was approximately equivalent to the total energy equivalent input per kilogram of conventional steelmaking.

In Japan research was being conducted on a plasma induction furnace for melting alloys based on copper, manganese, and nickel. In the generation of plasma by induction there is no direct resistive coupling of the plasma with the power source, and electrode contamination problems are therefore eliminated. In this furnace a protective inert argon atmosphere is maintained over the liquid pool.

Plasma technology was being applied in the United Kingdom to the recovery of valuable metals from the fume produced during the making of stainless steel. This fume, which is collected on filters as fine dust, typically contains, by weight, $Fe_2O_3$ (41.8%), $Cr_2O_3$ (15.6%), $SiO_2$ (8.3%), ZnO (7%), CaO (6.8%), MnO (6.5%), MgO (3.5%), NiO (3.5%), MoO (1.8%), $Pb_3O_4$ (1.7%), $Al_2O_3$ (0.5%), and CdO (0.13%) and is produced at a rate of 1.5–2% of the rate of production of the stainless steel. Because Pb, Cd, and $Cr^{6+}$ can be leached by groundwater, their presence in the fume places it in the U.S. category of federal hazardous waste, which requires that it be encapsulated before being discarded or be dumped in a controlled landfill.

The fume and anthracite are fed to a vertical cylindrical furnace in which an argon plasma is transferred from a cathode located in the center of the roof to the surface of the slag, which acts as the anode. In this mode of transfer most of the energy of the plasma is dissipated at the anode by the reassociation of the ionized gas. The furnace, which operates at 380 v and 2,500 amp with an arc length of one-half meter (1.6 ft), is sealed and runs at a slightly positive pressure to prevent the infiltration of air. The slag is formed in the furnace by the mutual fluxing of the CaO, $SiO_2$, MgO, and $Al_2O_3$, which are present in the fume in relative proportions that produce a fluid slag at the operating temperature of 1,500° C (2,700° F). After dissolution in the slag the oxides of iron, chromium, nickel, and molybdenum are reduced to form a carbon-saturated liquid ferroalloy containing typically, by weight, 25.5% chromium, 5.4% nickel, and 1.7% molybdenum, and the volatile metals are vaporized and then recovered as a fume containing typically, by weight, 30.8% ZnO, 5.5% $Pb_3O_4$, 2.7% $K_2O$, and 1.3% CdO. The ferroalloy is recycled to the electric arc furnace where the stainless steel is made; the fume is suitable for sale to zinc producers; and the slag can be safely discarded.

The greatest potential of plasma technology lies in the possibility of its being used to convert waste material generated by one process into a form suitable as the feed material for another process. For example, the more than 700 million tons of coal burned in the U.S. each year produce 70 to 105 million tons of ash, 85% of which is blown out of the stacks of electric power plants as fly ash. One aim of plasma technology research is the development of a means of recovering alumina and ferro-silicon from this fly ash.

—David R. Gaskell

417

# Mathematics

The major event during the past year in the mathematical world was the International Congress of Mathematicians. Held at the University of California at Berkeley, this quadrennial meeting took place in the United States for the first time since 1950. Almost 3,600 mathematicians attended from throughout the world to share discoveries and generate ideas. Unfortunately—as in the past—a number of invited speakers from the Soviet Union were prohibited by their government from attending.

**Fields Medals and Nevanlinna Prize.** A prime feature of the Congress was the announcement at the opening ceremonies of the winners of Fields Medals and the Nevanlinna Prize. Carrying the prestige of Nobel Prizes (but no monetary award), two to four Fields Medals are awarded at each Congress to mathematicians under 40 years of age for outstanding research of a seminal nature.

The 1986 recipients of Fields Medals were Simon Donaldson of the University of Oxford, Michael Freedman of the University of California at San Diego, and Gerd Faltings at Princeton University. Leslie Valiant of Harvard University was awarded the Nevanlinna Prize, which is given to recognize the achievements of a young mathematician working on mathematical aspects of information science.

Donaldson, 29, was cited for work done as a second-year graduate student. His 1982 result, taken together with methods of Freedman's, implies that there exist "exotic" 4-spaces. A standard Euclidean 4-space is like familiar 3-space but possesses a fourth spatial dimension together with the familiar distance measure determined by the Pythagorean theorem. Spaces that are locally Euclidean—around each point there is a small neighborhood of points that is indistinguishable from any other neighborhood in a Euclidean space—are called manifolds. A sphere is an example of a two-dimensional manifold (or 2-manifold); so also is the surface of a doughnut.

It had been thought that any four-dimensional manifold that has the same topological properties as Euclidean 4-space must also share all of its differential structure. Topological properties reflect the basic shape of the manifold without regard to distance, including the number (but not the size) of its holes. (A doughnut is an example of a one-holed manifold.) Differential structure involves how calculus can be done on the manifold.

An "exotic" 4-space is topologically but not differentially equivalent to Euclidean 4-space. Donaldson's discovery of such spaces was especially remarkable because exotic spaces do not exist in any other dimension. Surprisingly, Donaldson used instantons, the solutions in Euclidean space of the Yang-Mills equations of theoretical physics, which are generalizations of James Clerk Maxwell's equations for electromagnetism. Some of Donaldson's results reflect back to physics, in the form of describing properties of magnetic monopoles.

Faltings, 32, was honored for 1983 work proving the 60-year-old Mordell conjecture, which is about the relationship between the number of solutions to an algebraic equation and the geometry of certain surfaces associated with the equation. Faltings's theorem is remarkable both for its simplicity (it takes only two lines to state) and for its applications. His apparently theoretical work was applied in 1986 by computer scientists Leonard Adleman and Ming-Deh Huang of the University of Southern California to devise an efficient probabilistic test (a test that does not provide absolute certainty) for whether an integer is prime, which has applications in cryptography. The outstanding application, however, was major progress in resolving a 340-year-old claim by number-theory genius Pierre de Fermat. Fermat wrote in the margin of one of his books that he

*Richard M. Schoen of the University of California addresses the International Congress of Mathematicians at Berkeley, California, in August 1986. Winners of the Fields Medals and the Nevanlinna Prize were announced at the congress.*

had found a "truly marvelous" proof that there are no nonzero integer solutions to the Pythagorean-like equation $x^n + y^n = z^n$ if $n > 2$. He also wrote that his proof would not fit in the margin.

If $n = 2$, the equation has an infinite number of basic solutions—ones that are not multiples of others—such as the 3–4–5 right triangle known to the ancient Egyptians and Babylonians. Over the centuries mathematicians gradually eliminated some other values of $n$, including $n = 3$, as having no solutions, but they were unable to eliminate all $n > 2$. The vast majority of mathematicians believed that Fermat must have deluded himself about having a valid proof. In 1978 Sam Wagstaff of Purdue University, West Lafayette, Ind., used a computer to help show that Fermat's "last theorem" (as the conjecture is known, because it is the last of Fermat's assertions to elude proof) is true for all $n < 125,000$; the practical consequence is that if there is a solution for some $n$, it will involve too many digits ever to write out.

Faltings's result, however, shows that for each $n > 3$, there are at most finitely many basic solutions to the Fermat equation—as opposed to the cases $n = 1$ and $n = 2$, which have infinitely many basic solutions. The result relies on a curious idea that is quite common in mathematics. Normally a mathematician would graph an equation by drawing a curve or surface corresponding to all real numbers that satisfy the equation. Since the solutions sought involve only integer values, it seems paradoxical indeed to construct the higher-dimensional graph that results from allowing $x$, $y$, and $z$ to be complex numbers. (A complex number is of the form $a + bi$, in which $a$ and $b$ are real numbers and $i$ is the square root of $-1$.)

Even more surprising is the simplicity of the key fact about the complex surface resulting from an algebraic equation: its "genus" (the number of holes that it has) characterizes the number of solutions in rational numbers of the equation. (A rational number, or fraction, is one of the form $a/b$, where $a$ and $b$ ($\neq 0$) are integers; integer solutions of $x^n + y^n = z^n$ correspond to rational solutions of $a^n + b^n = 1$ with $a = x/z$, $b = y/z$.) If the surface has no holes, the equation has either no rational solutions or infinitely many. If the surface has exactly one hole, the equation has at most a finite number of basic solutions. After proving this latter fact in 1922, L. J. Mordell conjectured that the same holds true for surfaces with more than one hole. Faltings proved Mordell's conjecture for a wide class of generalizations of algebraic equations.

The surface for $a^n + b^n = 1$ has $(n - 1)(n - 2)/2$ holes, which is more than 1 if $n > 3$. Consequently, the corresponding equation has at most a finite number of rational solutions, and the original Fermat equation $x^n + y^n = z^n$ can have only a finite number of basic solutions for each $n > 2$. It is still an enormous step to Fermat's last theorem—that for each $n > 2$, this finite number is in fact 0—but Faltings's work raises new hope of resolving the question.

Freedman, 35, proved in 1982 the four-dimensional Poincaré conjecture and provided classification theorems for important classes of 4-manifolds. For an ordinary sphere in three dimensions (known to mathematicians as the 2-sphere because its surface is two-dimensional), a loop drawn on its surface can be shrunk continuously to a point (as if the loop were a loop of string that was slowly pulled tight from both ends). The surface of a doughnut does not have this property, as a loop around the outside edge surrounds the hole and hence cannot be shrunk to a point. This property of shrinkability of loops is called simply-connectedness; the two-dimensional Poincaré conjecture asserts that if a closed and bounded manifold is simply-connected, then it is topologically equivalent to a sphere. The truth of this two-dimensional version was known to Henri Poincaré in 1904, when he suggested that the analogue should be true in higher dimensions. Thus, the three-dimensional Poincaré conjecture claims that objects equivalent to 3-spheres are ones in which the appropriate generalization of simply-connectedness holds: not only can all loops be shrunk but also all "balloons" (so that the solid "surface" can have no cavities).

The higher-dimensional analogues have proved easier to verify. In 1961 Stephen Smale proved the $n$-dimensional Poincaré conjecture for $n > 7$ (and in 1966 received a Fields Medal for his work); the cases $n = 5$ and 6 were proved by Smale, Christopher Zeeman, and John Stallings. Freedman's work, which used the strategy successful in the two-dimensional case (classifying manifolds), left only the case $n = 3$ open.

That remaining case was the subject of intense work and controversy in 1986. Early in the year Colin Rourke of the University of Warwick, England, and Eduardo Rêgo of the University of Oporto, Port., claimed to have proved it. A brief announcement was made in Britain's *Nature* magazine in February. But their announcement, unusual because it leapfrogged the established channels for verification of mathematical scholarship, may have been premature. Presenting the work at a seminar in Berkeley in November, Rourke was forced to admit to a gap at a crucial point—a gap that he expressed confidence he would be able to bridge. At the beginning of 1987 the mathematical jury was still out on what, if confirmed, would be the greatest achievement in the 1980s in the branch of mathematics known as topology.

Finally, Leslie Valiant, 37, was honored with the Nevanlinna Prize for his wide-ranging research in

*Leslie Valiant of Harvard University won the Nevanlinna Prize in 1986 for his work in computer science, which included discovering fast algorithms for parsing sentences in context-free grammars (see text) and investigating the potential of parallel computers.*

computer science, including discovering fast algorithms (step-by-step procedures) for parsing sentences in context-free grammars (ones that allow indefinitely deep nesting of grammatical rules), enlarging the theory of computational complexity, and investigating the potential of parallel computers.

**Zero-knowledge proofs.** Throughout the late 17th and early 18th centuries, Isaac Newton and Gottfried Wilhelm Leibniz and their followers carried on a vicious battle over who deserved credit for the invention of calculus. This debate resulted in part from the fact that Leibniz's independent discoveries took place in the long interval between Newton's discoveries and their publication. At one point, to establish his priority, Newton sent Leibniz an enciphered message containing what Newton regarded as a central idea; the intention was that Leibniz would be unable to decipher the message and that Newton then could subsequently reveal the cipher's key and thereby display knowledge of the idea at the time the message had been sent.

In 1986 computer scientists described a much more elegant interactive protocol for the same purpose—to convince a person beyond a shadow of a doubt that one has a proof of a particular theorem without revealing the slightest clue about the nature of that proof. The idea of such a protocol, called a zero-knowledge proof, was introduced in 1985 by Shafi Goldwasser and Silvio Micali of the Massachusetts Institute of Technology and Charles Rackoff of the University of Toronto. In 1986 Micali, with Oden Goldreich of the Israel Institute of Technology (Technion) and Avi Wigderson of Hebrew University of Jerusalem, showed how to construct a zero-knowledge proof that a problem from a large class of very difficult problems (called NP-complete problems) has a solution. Then at the International Congress Manuel Blum of the University of California at Berkeley demonstrated a protocol that could be applied to any mathematical theorem.

His scheme converts the theorem to an equivalent theorem about the existence of a round-trip tour of all the vertices of a certain graph; the latter question is an NP-complete problem and, therefore, a zero-knowledge proof for it can be constructed.

Zero-knowledge proofs, like the cryptosystems devised by mathematicians in recent years, rely on trapdoor functions—ones that are easy to compute (code) but whose inverses are difficult to compute (decode). The ideas of a zero-knowledge proof can be combined with cryptographic work to provide a practical and secure identification scheme, devised by Adi Shamir and Amos Fiat. In the context of a user signing onto a computer system or a banking machine, the machine would ask not for the password or secret number—whose secrecy could be compromised by its entry being observed—but instead would ask a series of always-different questions about the password or secret number. It would be unlikely for a person to give answers that are all correct without knowing the secret, yet answering some questions correctly would not give away the secret number or help in answering subsequent questions. (*See* Feature Article: THE BUSINESS OF BABEL: CRYPTOLOGY IN THE '80s.)

Like Adleman and Huang's new probabilistic primality test, zero-knowledge proofs continued the trend in mathematics away from absolute certainty. Just as their primality test provides only "almost certainty" that a tested integer is prime, a zero-knowledge proof provides only "almost certainty" that the respondent indeed possesses a proof; there remains a small probability, decreasing as the number of questions answered correctly rises, that the respondent has answered them all right by accident or coincidence.

**Milestones.** In July 1986 the International Mathematical Olympiad took place in Warsaw, Poland. Competing in this 27th annual competition were 210 high-school students from 37 countries. The U.S. team tied with the U.S.S.R. for first place, continuing a tradition of U.S. teams finishing in the top five since U.S. participation began ten years ago. The U.S. team was coached by Cecil Rousseau of Memphis (Tenn.) State University and Gregg Patruno of Columbia University, New York City, and the First Boston investment firm, who also coached the 1985 team to second place (behind Romania). Joseph Keane of Pittsburgh, Pa., was the only one of the 1986 participants to receive a Special Award, for a particularly elegant solution to one of the six challenging problems in the two-day contest.

In June 1986 an 81-digit number was factored, setting a new record for the largest integer factored by a general-purpose factoring method. Surprisingly, the task was accomplished not by a supercomputer but by eight linked Sun microcomputers, each of which required about 150 hours before all the factors of $2^{269} + 1$ were found. That microcomputers could so quickly factor large integers posed a possible threat to the security of secret codes that rely on the difficulty of such factoring.

—Paul J. Campbell

# Medical sciences

The disease AIDS (acquired immune deficiency syndrome) dominated the year in the medical sciences. Progress was made in understanding the virus that triggers the syndrome, but no cure was found or vaccine developed. Research on interferons revealed that these proteins are effective in treating certain cancers and the common cold. Dental scientists continued to make advances in combating tooth decay and gum disease, and the first genetically engineered vaccine to be licensed by the U.S. Department of Agriculture was introduced for swine pseudorabies.

## General medicine

In medical research during the past year major advances occurred in understanding how and in what way interferons work. Results were announced on the use of lasers for vaporizing atherosclerotic deposits and also for obliterating small segments of the heart that disturb its normal beat. The AIDS epidemic continued on its deadly path.

A disease that can have serious long-term consequences—rheumatic fever—might be mysteriously returning. The hepatitis B virus and an occasional coinfectant were beginning to give up their secrets. The problems that exposure to smoke causes nonsmokers continued to be enumerated, and the genes that cause certain diseases were pinpointed.

**Interferon.** The immune-system proteins known as interferons were heralded in the late 1970s as potential treatments for viral infections and cancers, but determining their usefulness has entailed careful clinical trials. While the first interferon was discovered in 1957 by Alick Isaacs and Jean Lindenmann of the National Institute for Medical Research in London, the marketing of members of the interferon family is only a recent development.

A genetically engineered alpha-2 interferon, already marketed in Europe, received U.S. approval in 1986 for use against hairy cell leukemia, a rare blood cancer. The disease has a varying course; a three-to-five-year survival is average, but some people can live longer. It was previously treated either by removal of the spleen or with drugs that had generally unsatisfactory results. In clinical trials with alpha-2 interferon, over 90% of patients with the leukemia improved. Side effects were minimal. All the people in the U.S. trials reported fatigue and symptoms resembling influenza, and some reported mild, transient confusion and drowsiness; half or more had a loss of appetite. This was the first U.S. approval of an interferon. The drug was already available in Canada and the United Kingdom for treating hairy cell leukemia; in Ireland and the Philippines it was marketed for hairy cell leukemia, multiple myeloma, Kaposi's sarcoma, malignant melanoma, and venereal warts. Other countries in South America and Europe had approved it for various purposes.

Investigations of other members of the interferon family continued for use in other cancers and viral diseases. In one, chronic myelogenous leukemia (CML), alpha-A interferon appeared to eliminate the leukemic cells. The disease generally kills its victims in 2½–3 years. In a study of 17 patients with CML, the interferon reduced the number of white blood cells and platelets to normal levels in 13 and near normal levels in one. In six of the patients, the presence of a chromosomal anomaly—a rearrangement—that marks the final and usually fatal stage of the disease disappeared.

Interferons also demonstrated antiviral activity. In studies conducted in Australia and the United States alpha-2 interferon limited the spread of colds. In the Australian study 120 people used interferon nasal sprays whenever a family member had a cold. They had 33% fewer days with cold symptoms and 41% fewer colds than did 109 people who used placebo sprays. In the U.S. study 52 of 222 people using a placebo spray got colds, while only 32 of 226 taking interferon did. In a second U.S. experiment volunteers were exposed to cold viruses and then given either interferon or a placebo. While 12 of the 34 placebo recipients subsequently developed colds, only 2 of the 27 who took interferon did so. In both studies there was some minor nasal bleeding.

As for how interferons work, researchers from the University of Zurich, Switz., found that interferon's protective effect against influenza in mice depends on its ability to prompt the production of a particular protein that acts to stimulate the immune system. When they injected mice with antibodies to interferon, the protein production ceased and mice failed to fight off the infection.

**Lasers in the heart.** Lasers advanced their way into the human heart. Following extensive animal trials, physicians began using lasers carried by optical fibers into leg veins of people with a painful condition called intermittent claudication, in which atherosclerotic plaque in the main artery feeding the leg partially blocks circulation. Lasers were tried in cases where the symptoms did not respond to exercise, drugs, or surgery.

When a heart condition was first treated with lasers, in 1983, the procedure was done during heart bypass surgery. U.S. surgeons traveled to France, where they worked with French surgeons on several patients. These initial procedures were done on arteries being bypassed; during the operation a laser was inserted into the artery and used to vaporize nearby fatty deposits. But after the operation the main blood flow went through the transplanted, wider vessel, and so the other newly opened arteries in many cases were not held open.

At the annual scientific session of the American Heart Association, where scientists announce research advances in cardiovascular disease, a group from Boston University described their experience in using lasers on arteries not being bypassed; the technique does not require open-chest surgery or stopping the heart.

In the procedure a laser transmitted by fiber optics is inserted through a blood vessel into the patient's leg and then threaded through the circulatory system up to nearly closed arteries in the beating heart. The laser's metal tip is heated to 400° C (752° F); this essentially melts the fatty deposits, opening an artery that is 90 to 95% closed into one that is only 20 to 30% closed. The artery is then fully opened by inserting into it a balloon that is then inflated. Researchers involved with this technique said that the laser might someday do all the work on its own, without the balloon backup.

Also at the meeting other researchers described their use of lasers to destroy cardiac cells that were responsible for causing the heart to beat erratically. These areas are usually treated when possible by drugs or surgery. Surgeons from a New Jersey hospital used lasers to vaporize trouble spots on the inner walls of hearts of people who had ventricular tachycardia (rapid heart beat), and North Carolina surgeons used laser power to kill rather than vaporize areas responsible for tachycardia.

A Milwaukee heart surgeon described the use of lasers directly on the muscle tissue itself. The procedure was done on hearts temporarily stopped to allow conventional bypass operations aimed at other areas of the heart. Mahmood Mirhoseini used a laser to blast about 12 paths through the heart muscle into one of the chambers of the heart—the left ventricle. The entry point clotted, leaving a channel from the ventricle into the muscle. The channel allowed fresh blood to circulate through the heart muscle.

**Immunology.** Immunologists during the year were working to define major and minor activities of the components of the immune system. One potentially important component was discovered in 1986—a protein receptor that lies on the surface of T cells, one of the immune system's major cell types. T cells rid the body of foreign organisms and virally infected cells by recognizing signs of foreignness and reacting to them. The cells can directly kill the organisms or

help other immune cells to do so, and they also help to turn off the immune response. The T cell already has two well-characterized receptors that recognize foreign matter. The purpose of the newly discovered protein remained to be determined. The researchers who found it believe that its function might explain properties of the immune system that are not now well understood.

The existence of the protein was heralded by its gene, one that is active early in the development of T cells. Two groups of researchers, at Columbia (New York City), Harvard (Cambridge, Mass.), and Tufts (Medford, Mass.) universities, found the receptor. One group exposed T cells to monoclonal antibodies to remove cells that carried the known receptors and found the new one in the cells that remained. The other group looked for signs of the active gene in juvenile T cells and isolated the product. About 5% of T cells carry only the new receptor.

**AIDS.** The number of new AIDS cases in the U.S. during the past year dropped below the annual doubling that had previously taken place, and a drug was found that appeared to lengthen the lives of certain people with AIDS. The rest of the news in 1986 was not so good.

At a midyear international AIDS research conference held in Paris, a World Health Organization official estimated that as many as 100,000 people in the world had AIDS and that between five million and ten million people had been infected. A physician in Zaire reported that the disease was widespread in Africa, affecting an estimated 6% or more of the population. In Africa the syndrome had struck males and females in equal numbers.

In the United States AIDS began to establish itself among heterosexuals who were not drug abusers. Researchers from several universities found the virus in vaginal and cervical secretions of infected women.

More was learned about the basic biology of the virus and the cells that it infects. University of Alabama researchers found that its mutation rate is up to one million times faster than that of other DNA (deoxyribonucleic acid). Scientists at Harvard University identified a second self-stimulating AIDS gene which produces a protein that promotes viral production of other AIDS proteins. Epidemiologically, further evidence was gathered showing that the virus is not spread by casual contact.

In regard to vaccines researchers at Duke University, Durham, N.C., and the U.S. National Cancer Institute isolated a protein from the outer covering of the AIDS virus that caused several species of animals injected with it to form antibodies; in the test tube these antibodies neutralized the virus. Other researchers identified a segment of a human hormone that is similar to an AIDS protein. This segment, they concluded, might be useful as a vaccine. Antibodies to the hormone protected cultured cells from infection by the AIDS virus.

U.S. National Institutes of Health researchers spliced AIDS genetic material into the virus that is used to vaccinate against smallpox. This hybrid virus produced a protein found in the AIDS virus coat and was being evaluated as a vaccine. Scientists from Genentech Inc. announced at the Paris meeting in June that Chinese hamster cells had produced one of the coat proteins.

Other vaccine candidates included an engineered version of the AIDS virus that was missing two key genes. Without those genes, scientists found, the virus cannot kill its target immune cells. But one of the proteins that surround the virus was found by several laboratories to be capable, on its own, of killing immune system cells. That ability makes at least this protein an inappropriate candidate for a vaccine.

Prospects for the development of a vaccine raised questions about who would use it. Until the virus and its attendant proteins are fully understood, researchers cannot say with certainty that an altered virus or protein might not cause the same problems as the original organism. A vaccination could expose people at low risk to a potentially harmful substance; many people at high risk have already encountered the virus, and those who have not can avoid exposure by safe sex practices.

New members of the virus family were identified. One, first isolated from healthy Senegalese prostitutes by Myron Essex and his co-workers at the Harvard School of Public Health and collaborators in France and Senegal, is apparently harmless and may even protect bearers from infection by the AIDS virus. Researchers led by Luc Montagnier from the Pasteur Institute in Paris identified another virus in several Europeans; although those people had no antibodies against the original AIDS virus, they did have an AIDS-like illness, and on magnification the virus itself looked just like the AIDS virus. And Swedish researchers found yet another virus in several West African AIDS patients living in Sweden.

The group of viruses believed to be responsible for AIDS finally got a name. While its various discoverers have called it lymphadenopathy-associated virus (LAV), human T-lymphotropic virus type III (HTLV-III), and AIDS-associated retrovirus (ARV), an international taxonomy commission settled on human immunodeficiency virus (HIV).

The first evidence that a drug could slow the lethal progress of the virus was found by researchers during the past year. Called azidothymidine (AZT) and manufactured by Burroughs Wellcome Co., the drug was matched against a placebo in a double-blind study in which neither patients nor doctors knew who was receiving which treatment. Over a six-month trial 145 patients with AIDS or AIDS-related

*Crystal of azidothymidine (AZT) is photographed in polarized light. AZT was the first drug to demonstrate that it could slow the deadly progress of the virus that causes AIDS (acquired immune deficiency syndrome).*

complex were given the drug every six hours, while 137 patients with the same condition got a placebo every six hours. One person died while receiving AZT, but 16 of the placebo recipients died, prompting the U.S. government to halt the trial and make the drug available to all the people in the study.

But the drug has some drawbacks. It suppresses bone marrow function in many recipients, leading to anemia. And it was tested only in adults who had had an AIDS-related pneumonia. While those people comprised about 60% of the AIDS population, the remaining 40% were not assured of receiving any benefits from the drug. Meanwhile, other drugs, some of them structurally similar to AZT, were being developed.

**Cancer.** Scientists from Beth Israel Hospital in Boston developed a blood test for cancer. While several blood tests were already available, they were not particularly reliable, accurate, or easy to perform and were generally used to monitor the course of a cancer rather than as a population-wide test to detect it in the first place.

The Beth Israel test relied on the presence of a particular type of fat in the blood. Before it could be widely applied, it had to be backed up by more data and further study.

The blood fats were studied by means of nuclear magnetic resonance spectroscopy. In this technique a strong magnetic field is applied to the sample in question. The magnetic field aligns the spins of certain atoms, in this case hydrogen. Then a burst of radio waves unaligns the spins. As the atoms then realign themselves with the magnetic field, they

423

Merck Sharp & Dohme

emit radio signals; the timing and strength of those signals indicate the composition of the sample.

After analyzing blood from 311 people by nuclear magnetic resonance spectroscopy, researchers found that these fats were different in people with cancer. Among the people in the study were healthy controls, patients with malignant and benign tumors, noncancer patients, and pregnant women. In 81 people with untreated cancer the fats gave off a slightly different signal than they did in other members of the study group, with two exceptions; pregnant women and men with benign enlarged prostates were in the cancer range, though they did not have cancer.

Why the blood fats would be different in people with cancer is a mystery. Researchers involved in the project suggest that the change represents the body's response to a tumor, rather than something that comes from the tumor itself. What remained to be seen was whether these changes occur early enough in the cancer process to be useful in diagnosis.

**Rheumatic fever.** The incidence of rheumatic fever began to increase in the U.S. during recent months. This disease, a constellation of symptoms including heart inflammation, arthritis, spasms, and rash, was a major public health problem in developed countries in the first half of the 20th century and in 1987 was still a major problem in the third world.

While the symptoms usually disappear quickly, the disease often leaves behind a damaged heart. As many as two million adults in the United States have heart damage that resulted from a childhood bout with rheumatic fever. The disease had until recently been so rare in the U.S. that government officials had stopped their surveillance program.

But at a medical meeting in 1986 researchers described outbreaks in Utah; Colorado; Pittsburgh, Pa.; and New Haven, Conn. In Utah there were at least 100 cases in 18 months during 1985 and 1986; in the previous ten years there had been an average of six cases per year in that state.

The disease often follows strep throat and is believed to be caused by antibodies to the streptococcus bacteria mistaking body tissues for bacteria and attacking the tissues. The initial drop in the incidence of rheumatic fever, which began before the modern age of antibiotics, has gone largely unexplained, as has its recent upsurge. The disease is clinically the same as the one that occurred in the early 1900s, though the current outbreak appears mostly to be affecting middle-class rather than underprivileged children. Another difference is that in the majority of cases the disease has not been preceded by a sore throat.

**Hepatitis B.** Great advances were made during the year in the understanding and prevention of hepatitis B infection, a disease for which there was no cure. Hundreds of millions of people in the world

*Technician makes Recombivax HB, the first recombinantly engineered vaccine available for human use. It protects against the hepatitis B virus and is made by using yeast that is saddled with a gene from the virus.*

carry the culprit virus. While many carriers remain asymptomatic, others suffer from liver infection, cirrhosis, and liver cancer. More was also learned about the delta agent, a mysterious "obligate" virus that can infect only those cells already infected with the hepatitis B virus.

In research done during recent months, scientists at a Harvard University laboratory discovered how to grow the hepatitis B virus in a test tube. They infected cells that originally came from a liver cancer, and the hepatitis B survived and reproduced itself. Though this feat had no immediate practical implications, it would allow researchers to learn more about how the virus reproduces itself and might suggest ways to intercede in the process.

Researchers from The Netherlands, California, and Maryland determined the sequence of subunits that the delta agent gene comprises. The agent is a single-stranded circle of RNA—most genes are double-stranded—and looks somewhat like certain plant viruses.

Currently, delta agent infection is diagnosed by the finding of cellular changes in bits of removed liver. The discovery of the genetic sequence was expected to promote the development of a blood test.

Scientists might also get a chance to see how the delta agent and hepatitis B viruses interact.

A new tool in the prevention of hepatitis B infection became available—a vaccine against the virus made by recombinant engineering. It was the first recombinantly engineered vaccine available for human use. While a vaccine of isolated hepatitis B protein collected from infected humans was already in use, the new vaccine was made by yeast saddled with one of the virus's genes. The yeast makes a protein that usually enrobes the viral DNA; when the body sees the protein, it makes antibodies to it. Therefore, when a person becomes infected, he or she has already been "primed" to fight it off.

**Smoking.** The Worldwatch Institute announced in 1986 that tobacco was the leading cause of premature death among adults. More than one billion people throughout the world smoked. In the U.S. in 1985 smoking was claimed to have contributed to about 375,000 deaths from emphysema, lung cancer, and heart disease; worldwide, smoking was estimated to have caused 2 million to 2.5 million deaths.

On the issue of "passive" smoking, the U.S. National Research Council released a report stating that smoke from cigarettes is a definite health hazard to nonsmokers. The council spent a year analyzing numerous studies on the incidence of smoking-related disease among nonsmokers exposed to smoke at home or at the workplace, as well as physiological studies of the constituents of smoke and the way the smoke is absorbed by nonsmokers.

Among their conclusion were:

(1) Children of smoking parents wheeze, cough, and produce more sputum than children not exposed to smoke in the home. Exposed infants have more respiratory infections. Exposed adults have slightly reduced lung function.

(2) The rate of lung cancer is 30% higher among nonsmokers married to smokers than among nonsmokers married to other nonsmokers.

(3) The evidence of an increased development of cardiovascular disease by nonsmokers exposed to smoke is more hazy, and more study is needed in that area.

An analysis of Danish health statistics showed that the birth weights of babies born into households where the mother or father smoked were lower than those of babies born to two nonsmokers—9.2 g (0.32 oz) less per daily cigarette smoked by mothers and 6.1 g (0.21 oz) less per cigarette smoked by the father. The total loss in cases where both parents smoked 20 cigarettes a day was about 300 g (10.7 oz).

A University of California at San Francisco study of more than 7,000 nonsmoking women aged between 30 and 59 found that those who were married to smokers suffered heart attacks at triple the rate of wives of men who had never smoked. But a British study from the Institute for Cancer Research found no discernible effect from passive smoking. That conclusion was based on a study of previous exposure to smoke among 12,000 hospital patients and the incidence of smoking-related disease among them.

**Genetics.** The genes—or at least their approximate chromosomal location—for several genetic disorders were identified during the past year. One such assignment was made for phenylketonuria (PKU), one of the longest known and best understood inborn errors of metabolism. PKU results from the lack of a functioning enzyme that normally breaks down the amino acid phenylalanine; loss of this enzyme causes a phenylalanine buildup and severe mental retardation. Researchers from the College of Medicine at Baylor University, Houston, Texas, pinpointed a long

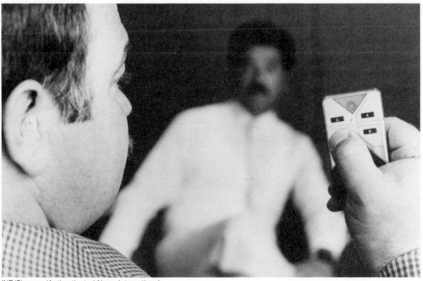

*Small and lightweight hearing aid, developed by the West German firm Siemens, can be controlled by pushing buttons on a tiny box held in the user's hand.*

INP/Siemens/Authenticated News International

gene that can vary greatly from person to person; by following the inheritance pattern of just part of the gene and the association of that part with PKU, they were able to find four forms of the gene in 90% of people with PKU.

Blood screening can be done to determine if an infant has PKU; if the disease is present, a diet low in phenylalanine limits its effects. The new test, claimed one of its founders, will enable prenatal screening.

Defects in a particular gene that result in Duchenne muscular dystrophy were pinpointed to a specific section of the X chromosome by Harvard University researchers, who have characterized 10% of the gene. With further characterization the protein coded for by the gene can be determined, and the process involved in causing the muscle-wasting disease can be further understood. Eventually, it may be possible to supply the correct protein as a treatment.

Researchers from several institutions in Boston found that the absence of a normal gene causes retinoblastoma, a rare eye cancer that if caught in time can be treated by removal of the eye. The scientists found the "address" of the normal gene on chromosome 13. For a person to develop the cancer, the pair of genes—one on each chromosome 13—must be affected in eye cells. If a person with retinoblastoma has an abnormality in one chromosome 13, as shown by blood analysis, the cancer probably resulted from a chance mutation in eye cells in the other, normal chromosome 13. Such a person could pass the bad gene on to offspring, who would develop the cancer if their other chromosome 13 mutated. A person with retinoblastoma and two normal chromosomes can be presumed to have a tumor caused by two spontaneous mutations in the eye and thus would not be likely to pass on the retinoblastoma propensity to offspring.

—Joanne Silberner

## Dentistry

In a new twist on the trend toward the greater use of credit cards to pay health care costs, Bank of America and Blue Cross of California teamed up to offer a new dental plan for individuals. Personal Dental Net, billed as "the alternative for people who don't have employee or group health insurance," became available to MasterCard and VISA cardholders in California's major metropolitan areas. The plan maintained contracts with about 300 dentists to provide care. Cardholders could use their cards to pay the annual premium, which totaled $147 for individuals, $264 for the cardholder and one family member, and $369 for an entire family. They could also pay the premium directly, bypassing the card's

annual 19.8% interest rate. Cardholders were able to save 42% on a filling and 54% on a crown, compared with typical dentists' charges in California. These estimates were based on calculations by Blue Cross of California of customary and reasonable fees in the Los Angeles area.

**Gum disease.** Technology such as computers and lasers was expected to have an impact soon on periodontal (gum) disease, which remained the greatest cause of tooth loss in adults. "We are in a renaissance period. All the research in the past 10 years is finally coming to fruition," declared Michael Newman, a periodontics professor at the University of California at Los Angeles. Some new methods of diagnosis that were beginning to become available to dentists included automated probing and a pressure-sensitive probe that beeped when it reached the proper pressure in the periodontal pockets, which are caused by the disease. Other new diagnostic steps included laser probes to look at blood-vessel flow, infrared photography to determine the level of gum-tissue inflammation, and X-rays coupled with sophisticated computers that could assess jawbone loss.

Bacteriology was making major strides in the diagnosis of juvenile periodontitis (inflammation of the tissues surrounding a tooth) and in other types of disease. "Virulent bacteria groups are responsible for the initiation and progression of periodontal disease," Newman said. Immunofluorescence and latex glutination were newly developed methods that employed antibodies to look for bacteria. "Within a year we should be able to take a plaque sample, put it on a slide, drop a reagent, shake it up, and see if the plaque clumps. If it clumps, bacteria are present. If we know it's there, we know where to go with treatment," Newman concluded.

Additional progress in the fight against periodontal diseases was reported by a researcher from the University of Maryland who said that an individual's internal-defense mechanism, namely, white blood cells, may play a major role in the development of the disease. "Based on recent research from the fields of microbiology and immunology, it appears a defect in the white blood cells probably is the primary cause and plaque is the secondary cause of at least one form of the disease," said Jon B. Suzuki. "This form of disease apparently is not related to the amount and type of toothbrushing and plaque on the teeth," he added.

Always present in gums, white blood cells normally seem to guard against bacteria in the mouth. Abnormal white blood cells, however, permit bacteria to spread and cause infection at an early age. Studying subtle changes in these cells could help distinguish this form of gum disease. Researchers in the last five years discovered a blood test that isolates the white blood cells for clinical observation, but as of 1987 the test was not widely available. Along with X-ray techniques that show changing patterns in bone structure, the test would be used to assist in diagnosing periodontitis. Future periodontal research would look into possible hereditary factors, according to Suzuki. Isolated cases from the last two decades had demonstrated that many young persons had gum problems "that tend to run in families."

**TM disorders.** Using an amplifier, dentists can listen to the sounds produced by abnormal jaw joints to make an accurate diagnosis of a painful condition. Comparing statistics from normal and abnormal temporomandibular (TM) joint sounds, Mark A. Piper of St. Petersburg, Fla., said that the amplifier, called a Doppler auscultator, is "100%" reliable in determining if a problem exists and 95% accurate in identifying the specific trouble. Speaking at the annual session of the American Dental Association (ADA) in Miami, Fla., Piper pointed out that many people suffer from certain types of headaches, tenderness of the jaw muscles, or dull, aching facial pain. These can occur because the chewing muscles and jaw joints do not work together properly.

Use of the Doppler auscultator involves the placement of a pencil-shaped probe on the skin over the jaw joint. The probe, held against the skin with cream, is attached by wire to the amplifier, which records sounds on a paper printout.

Doppler auscultation led to a clearer understanding of the joint when compared with other techniques. "It can pick up irregular sounds associated with conditions such as a displacement of the jaw disk or a perforation or hole in the disk ligament and it helps to characterize various stages of arthritis," Piper said. "Until now we've had some difficulty in defining what exactly we're dealing with by identifying a sound associated with a particular jaw joint problem," he said. Using this technique, a dentist is able to give the patient information about the extent of the problem and expectations on the results of treatment. Treatment can range from soft-food diets, bite splints, biofeedback techniques for stress, and drug therapy to surgery to correct jaw alignment. The technique was also used successfully by physicians to detect blood-vessel and heart problems.

**"False fingernails" for teeth.** Dental "facades" called veneers can make aesthetically unpleasing teeth look as though they have always been perfect and whole, claimed a University of Southern California dental scientist. Veneering is a variation of cosmetic dental bonding, likened to false fingernails, in which tooth-colored plastic, ceramic, or porcelain materials are applied over teeth to repair and mask such dental imperfections as chips, cracks, and stains, said Mark Friedman of Los Angeles. With the direct method, a dentist applies a composite or plastic resin directly to the tooth and then sculpts

it "freehand" into the desired shape. With the indirect method, the veneer is prefabricated in a dental laboratory according to average tooth contours or is custom molded and then is applied to the tooth.

The indirect method has shown some advantages over direct application primarily because it employs better materials, Friedman said. "Indirect veneers can now be made of porcelain; this material does a superior job of covering stains, especially the dark brown stains caused by some tetracycline medications and other drugs," he explained. "These indirect porcelain veneers provide more complete coverage of such stains than traditional bonding materials do. They also produce more natural restorations because they are able to reproduce the translucence of natural teeth," he added.

To apply porcelain veneers, a dentist must first make an impression of the tooth. A veneer is then created from the impression. According to Friedman, "Indirect porcelain veneers are the closest thing currently available to a replacement for natural tooth enamel. Though this technique has been used for only a short time, there is no question that it produces more durable as well as more natural-looking restorations. Indirect porcelain veneers may last at least twice as long as restorations using traditional bonding materials." Although indirect porcelain veneers look more natural and are more durable, they are also more expensive and involve the "buffing" of enamel. This buffing, which removes a minute layer of enamel with a diamond stone, prevents the restored tooth from looking "bulky."

**Adult orthodontic treatment.** Bioprogressive therapy, an orthodontic technique in which only one or a few teeth are moved at a time, offers for adult patients an alternative to traditional orthdontic treatment. Treatment can be accomplished within about two years, the same time required by traditional procedures. "A great deal of skill and judgment are needed to determine which tooth or teeth should be moved first. This sets in motion a sequence of movements or realignments that eventually result in an improved bite and straight teeth," said Robert Ricketts of Pacific Palisades, Calif. "Thus, the orthodontist must establish a hierarchy of teeth—a predetermined sequence in which teeth should be adjusted to achieve the best possible results. The end result is similar to results achieved with standard orthodontic treatment, but the way in which the end is achieved is very different."

Bioprogressive therapy allows the use of orthodontic appliances with lighter, smaller wires that apply less pressure to the teeth than do traditional devices. Each adjustment—each movement of teeth—takes from about four to six weeks, while traditional treatment requires adjustments by the orthodontist about every two weeks. By 1987 approximately 25%

of orthodontists were using bioprogressive therapy, according to one estimate. The procedure could also be used for children.

**Dental implants.** Improvements were made during the year in dental implants, alternatives to dentures for missing teeth. An increasing variety of implant types made it possible "to combine different types to best enhance treatment," according to Burton Balkin of Philadelphia. For example, two different implant types made with the same metal might be used, or metals and nonmetals that are compatible might be appropriate. "Fewer questions arise now as to the effectiveness of this form of treatment (implantology). The same person is not limited to one system as long as the implants are compatible," Balkin explained.

Dental implant devices attach replacement teeth to gums or bones in the mouth. There were several types, including those that were placed into the bone with posts projecting through the gums to which replacement teeth were attached. Another type involved a metal framework made to fit the jaw's shape and surface. This framework had posts that projected through the gums and attached to replacement teeth. The framework was not embedded into the bone but rested on the bone beneath the gums. A third type of implant was used to help retain natural teeth that were loose. It passed through the root of the tooth and into the underlying bone, thus stabilizing the tooth.

**Tooth decay.** Tooth decay had long been considered an irreversible process, one that ended in a cavity that needed to be filled by a dentist. New research demonstrated, however, that the decay process might be halted or reversed, depending on a

*Dental implant device, one of several varieties now in use, consists of posts that are placed in a patient's jawbone and extend upward through the gums. Replacement teeth are then attached to the posts.*

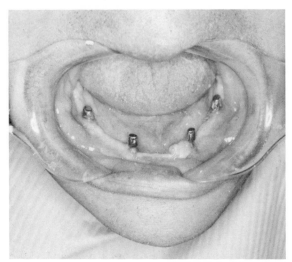

Courtesy, Burton E. Balkin, D.D.S.

number of factors. This reversal is called "remineralization." When it occurs, there is often no need to drill and fill the tooth, said R. W. Valachovic of Boston. At the Veterans Administration outpatient clinic in Boston, his research team studied a group of healthy males and followed their decay rate over a nine-year period. They noted that approximately 3% of the decayed teeth underwent complete reversal of the decay process and remineralized. Decay in an additional 10% had not progressed in three years, while that in 8.5% had not progressed by six years, and decay in 5% had not progressed by nine years. The researchers concluded that a small percentage of decayed teeth seen on X-rays either remineralize or do not become more decayed over a nine-year period.

In recent years researchers repeatedly demonstrated that cavity prevention is nearly 100% effective for children's back teeth that remain completely sealed. A sealant is a clear or shaded plastic resin applied to the chewing surfaces of the back teeth, where decay most often occurs. It acts as a barrier, protecting the decay-prone areas of the back teeth from oral bacteria. While fluoride protects the smooth surfaces of teeth, sealants are most effective in the tiny indentations of the back teeth that are too small for even a single toothbrush bristle to clean.

—Lou Joseph

## Veterinary medicine

The manpower issue continued to be a major concern in veterinary medicine, based on projections of an American Veterinary Medical Association (AVMA) study that predicted a 73% growth in the supply of veterinarians by the year 2000, compared with a growth in demand of 31% for pet-animal veterinary services and of 23% for food-animal veterinary services. However, the veterinary profession sought to address this issue in a positive way. Multistate conferences were held in the Northwest and the Southeast to explore ways to better market veterinary services, and the AVMA established a Committee on Veterinary Manpower. The committee explored nonprivate-practice opportunities that did not require additional training beyond the doctor of veterinary medicine (DVM) degree and programs that would facilitate mid-career changes into nonprivate-practice careers. The *Journal* of the AVMA planned to begin publishing in early 1987 a series of articles on private- and nonprivate-practice opportunities for veterinarians.

A U.S. Department of Agriculture (USDA) report entitled "Employment Opportunities for College Graduates in the Food and Agricultural Sciences" noted a number of agriculture-related fields that could use a veterinarian's education and skills. A surplus of job opportunities in those fields was projected over the next five years. In addition, a report of the U.S. Department of Health and Human Services entitled "Fifth Report to the President and Congress on the Status of Health Personnel in the United States" noted the existence of 623 geographic areas, with a population of nearly 14.6 million persons, that were considered to have shortages of veterinarians. Examples of shortage areas include Banks County in Georgia, Chase County in Kansas, and Teton County in Idaho.

Practice opportunities were expanding in selected areas such as pet-bird medicine, wildlife medicine, and exotic-animal medicine. Membership in the 14 AVMA-recognized veterinary specialties continued to grow, and several were adding subspecialties. For example, the American College of Veterinary Internal Medicine had subspecialties in cardiology, internal medicine, and neurology, while the American College of Veterinary Microbiologists recently added bacteriology/mycology, immunology, and virology subspecialties. Other specialty areas were reflected by the establishment of societies such as the American Veterinary Cancer Society and the British Veterinary Cardiovascular Society.

The British Small Animal Veterinary Association sponsored a presentation on veterinary dentistry by an Idaho veterinarian, Jean Hawkins. Hawkins reminded the veterinary attendees that "every animal that comes into your practice has a mouth." As the life spans of companion animals increased, so did the likelihood that periodontal (gum) disease—the primary reason for the "bad breath" in dogs and cats—would become a major problem. Since cavities were rare in dogs, routine fluoride treatment was not necessary. Home dental care was now being recommended and included brushing the teeth.

The facilities of a number of veterinary programs underwent major renovations and additions during the past year. Included was the addition of a completely new veterinary college, Canada's fourth. Located at the University of Prince Edward Island, the Atlantic Veterinary College accepted its first class of 50 students in 1986. Cost of construction was $42 million and was shared by the Canadian government, New Brunswick, Newfoundland, Nova Scotia, and Prince Edward Island. When the college graduates its first class in 1990, the total number of graduates of Canadian veterinary colleges will increase by 20%.

The Queen Mother Hospital for Animals was officially opened at the Royal Veterinary College in London. This new small-animal referral hospital was designed to be capable of dealing with up to 10,000 animals per year. The new Sefton surgical wing of the equine hospital at the Royal Veterinary College also opened during the year. This new facility provided improved surgical services for horses and enhanced student training in advanced equine surgical techniques.

The Michigan State University School of Veterinary Medicine initiated a $46.8 million project that would expand and remodel the school's Veterinary Clinical Center. The project was expected to require three years for completion and would provide improvements in facilities for the clinical and instructional programs needed for full accreditation of the school by the AVMA. Plans for a Midwestern regional veterinary college in Nebraska were replaced by plans to build a $7 million center for advanced studies in food-animal medicine. In addition to research, the center would provide training for senior veterinary students from Kansas State University's School of Veterinary Medicine, which agreed to accept up to 30 Nebraskan students per year beginning in 1987.

**Historical veterinary medicine.** In May the Nebraska Veterinary Medical Association dedicated the restored Phillipson Veterinary Infirmary in Grand Island at the Stuhr Museum of the Prairie Pioneer. The infirmary was used by pioneer veterinarian Pete Phillipson during his 75 years of practice in Nebraska. Phillipson graduated in 1908 from the former Kansas City Veterinary College and retired from veterinary practice at the age of 100.

After being lost for nearly seven decades, a charcoal portrait of Daniel E. Salmon, one of veterinary medicine's founding fathers in the U.S., was discovered in a storage area of the New York State College of Veterinary Medicine at Cornell University; it was restored and placed in the library of the college, of which he was an 1876 graduate. Salmon was chief of the former Bureau of Animal Industry, a past president of the AVMA, and the first recipient of the DVM degree from a regular academic veterinary program in the U.S.

Myron Essex was the recipient of an Albert Lasker Clinical Medical Research Award in recognition of his research contributions toward the understanding of AIDS (acquired immune deficiency syndrome). Essex was the second veterinarian to receive a Lasker Award since the prize was established in 1944.

**Human-animal relationships.** The Delta Society and the AVMA cosponsored the first Bustad Companion Animal Veterinarian Award. William McCulloch of the College of Veterinary Medicine at Texas A & M University was the recipient. Leo Bustad and McCulloch were involved in founding the Delta Society, a nonprofit resource for information on human-animal interactions and animal-facilitated therapy. McCulloch's brother, the late Michael McCulloch, a psychiatrist, was a pioneer in research on the benefits to humans of relationships with animals. A survey of physicians and psychiatrists revealed that dogs were recommended as companion animals to

*Morris, the "spokescat" for 9–Lives Cat Food, receives a checkup from his veterinarian to help publicize National Cat Health Month in September 1986. The campaign focused on the health needs of pet cats.*

humans by 94% of the prescribing professionals; cats by 71%; birds, fish, gerbils, and other small animals by 15–20%; and horses by 10%.

Massachusetts veterinarian Anita Migday acted as host of a 26-part public television series entitled "Cats and Dogs." It explored the relationship between people and pets and included such topics as the training of dogs as companions for the hearing impaired, the use of pets for therapy for elderly residents of hospitals, and the testing of a dog for its personality type.

The AVMA and the makers of 9-Lives Cat Food collaborated in publicizing the first National Cat Health Month with the aim of improving the level of feline health care and educating cat owners about the health and medical needs of their pets. Morris, the 9 Lives cat, served as Cat Health Month "spokescat" and met the news media in several major cities. He was accompanied by his traveling companion, Laura Pasten, a veterinarian from California.

In the U.S. in 1986 cats outnumbered dogs 50 million to 49 million, and in some areas the difference was much higher. For example, in Spokane, Wash., there were nearly twice as many cats as dogs. The demand for more comprehensive medical care for cats was increasing. With improved health care cats were living longer but consequently were becoming afflicted with ailments of the elderly such as heart disease. The first implantations of cardiac pacemakers in pet cats were done in 1986 by surgeons at the Virginia-Maryland Regional College of Veterinary Medicine and at Cornell University's veterinary college. Many pacemakers had previously been implanted in pet dogs.

**Pet insurance.** A new pet insurance company offered injury and illness coverage for dogs in most of the U.S. The program was endorsed by the American Humane Association and the New York State Veterinary Medical Society. Another firm that had been in operation for five years offered coverage in 26 states. Nine hundred veterinarians were shareholders in that company. More than 30 pet health insurance programs had failed in the U.S. In the U.K. a pet health insurance company, established in 1932, continued to provide coverage in Britain and Europe. An insurance program was recently established in Australia, while in New Zealand a dozen plans had been proposed but none implemented.

The Sacramento Valley Veterinary Medical Association and the School of Veterinary Medicine at the University of California at Davis developed a pet-loss group to help pet owners, including children, deal with their grief over the loss or impending loss of their animals. The group met twice each month with owners who had been referred by their pet's veterinarian. The service was provided without cost to the owner.

A Texas veterinarian initiated a care and companionship program for pets whose owners had died or were otherwise unable to care directly for them. The nonprofit program was operated by the Companion Animal Retirement and Education (CARE) Center and was intended primarily for horses, dogs, and cats, though other animals would be considered.

**Animal disease problems.** New disease problems or diseases occurring with increased incidence during the past year included feline hyperthyroidism, which might reflect exposure to environmental pollutants; deaths in pet birds exposed to toxic fumes produced by overheating nonstick surfaces of cookware; a canine distemper epidemic in south London that was characterized by unusually severe brain damage; and deaths of horses from Potomac fever at certain racetracks. A new five-minute diagnostic test for Potomac fever was developed and was expected to be available soon for clinical use if licensing was approved by the USDA.

An outbreak of African swine fever occurred in The Netherlands. By 1987 this serious swine disease had not yet appeared in the U.S., but it had been diagnosed in swine on several Caribbean islands. The presence of African swine fever on the European continent led to concern by some in the U.K. that it and other diseases could be introduced into Britain via the English Channel Tunnel should that structure be built.

*"You both appear to be in excellent health."*

*Nematodirus battus*, a new parasite of sheep in the Western Hemisphere, was isolated from flocks of sheep in Oregon by veterinary parasitologists from Oregon State University. The parasite had been a problem in the U.K. since 1951 and was considered to be the most pathogenic parasite of lambs. The disease was of considerable concern to the sheep industry as the mortality rate in infected flocks reached nearly 30%.

Equine infectious anemia (EIA) is a serious disease that can be fatal in horses. While the disease does not affect human beings, the retrovirus that causes it is a relative of the human AIDS virus. Researchers at Washington State University's College of Veterinary Medicine were using a molecular approach to develop a vaccine that would not only prevent the clinical disease but also allow diagnostic differentiation of vaccinated and carrier horses. The Chinese developed a successful attenuated live virus vaccine for horses, but the USDA would not approve its use in the U.S. because of the possibility that the modified virus would revert to a virulent form and because response to the vaccine could not be distinguished from the carrier state that provides the reservoir for spread of the disease.

An increase in rabies occurred during the past year in the mid-Atlantic and southeastern states of the U.S., and the disease was moving into the northeast. The increase was attributed to a rise in the raccoon population. Efforts were under way to develop techniques for vaccinating wild populations of raccoons against rabies by the use of new molecular biology and genetic engineering methods. The goal of this research was to develop an oral rabies vaccine that could be applied to bait that would be dropped by airplane in wilderness areas, where it would be eaten by wildlife and thereby provide them with immunity to the disease.

A new swine pseudorabies vaccine was the first genetically engineered vaccine to be licensed by the USDA. Because of this action the department was the subject of much criticism by opponents of genetic engineering. Although the vaccine contained a live virus, a gene was removed that prevented the virus from replicating in nervous tissue and from reverting to its virulent state. A genetically engineered vaccine for infectious bovine rhinotracheitis was undergoing regulatory agency evaluation at the year's end.

Farmers, environmentalists, and animal welfare advocates opposed approval by the U.S. Food and Drug Administration of a genetically engineered bovine growth hormone (BGH). The hormone could increase milk production by up to 40%, which might result in such overproduction of milk that 25 to 30% of U.S. dairy farmers would be forced out of business. The impact of BGH on veterinary management of dairy herd health was unknown at the year's end but was being evaluated. The establishment of the first dairy for camel milk in Saudi Arabia offered veterinarians in that country a new challenge in herd-health management.

—John M. Bowen

# Optical engineering

During the past year the semiconductor laser reached a new level of maturity and eliminated gas lasers from consideration in many applications. The major growth area continued to take place in semiconductor diode lasers. The number of such lasers was reported to have increased by more than 60%, but sales in dollars rose only about 4% because of the drastic drop in the price per unit item. In 1987 a single moderate-power diode laser sold for as little as $18 and for much less when purchased in quantity. It seemed likely that most offices and homes would be the possessors of at least one laser during the next year or two.

The principal consumer product using diode lasers continued to be the audio compact disc player. More than four million such players were sold in the past year. A new threat to the disc player market, however, was high-density digital audio tape, which was competitive with optical discs in the quality of reproduced sound.

A major new market was the application of laser printers to small computer systems. At least 30 different makes of such printers were on the market, with average prices of $2,000 to $3,000. With their excellent print quality—resolutions of more than 300 spots per inch—these printers were a major growth force in the microcomputer industry in 1986.

Other areas of application included that of optical memories. The use of compact disc technology permitted 500 million to one billion words to be stored on an inexpensive, computer-addressable disc that was less than 12.5 cm (5 in) in diameter. Most of the hardware development had been carried out by early 1986, but as of early 1987 the software that would be capable of handling such huge data bases had not yet appeared, inhibiting the growth of the market. Only a few specialized applications had been introduced by early 1987.

The very nature of diode lasers changed. The most common type had a power of about 20 milliwatts and emitted in the near-infrared range of the spectrum. However, diode lasers with up to 500 milliwatts of continuous or 10 watts of pulsed power operation were demonstrated. The linking of several separate diodes to provide higher power was also shown to be feasible.

A red, visible-wavelength diode laser was demonstrated in the laboratory. Diodes with very-narrow-wavelength output, competitive with gas lasers in spectral purity, were produced. Diodes with the ability to be electronically scanned over a reasonable angular range were also available. A solid-state laser pumped by a diode laser was developed for machining and other high power uses, including long-range space communications. The potential applications of such devices in machining very small parts or even in biologic applications appeared to be enormous, and the reliability, economy, and simplicity of devices using such lasers were already noteworthy.

In more traditional optics both Corning and Eastman Kodak in the U.S. and Hoya and Ohara in Japan demonstrated the capability and willingness

*The 35–millimeter camera regained popularity during the past year. Autofocus devices and full-exposure automation were offered on almost all of the new models.*

to produce direct-molded finished glass lenses of up to 2.5 cm (1 in) in diameter. It seemed likely that the traditional fabrication methods of grinding and polishing of small lenses would be reserved for prototype quantities in the future. Because of the high cost of production of the molds the use of these techniques seemed likely to be economical only for quantities of lenses exceeding a few hundred.

Optical fiber communications benefited from technical advances in couplers, switches, and new diode detectors. There was, however, a major decrease in the long-distance communications optical fiber supply business, brought about by the tremendous overcapacity that had already been installed. The next likely growth in this area was expected to be in the development of inexpensive local area networks. A lively debate was under way as to whether less expensive semiconductor diodes could replace laser diodes effectively for fiber applications within a building or neighborhood.

New detectors in the visible and infrared spectral regions were announced. Of special interest was the availability of array detectors for direct imaging of infrared scenes. For visible detectors inexpensive charge-coupled-array video cameras appeared on the market. (In a charge-coupled array, semiconductor devices are arranged so that the electric charge at the output of one provides the input stimulus to the next.) These were used in new formats of 8-mm-wide videotape in a compact form. The cost of such cameras was similar to that of a good-quality photographic camera. A remarkable achievement was the development by Tektronix Inc. of a detector array consisting of 2,048 by 2,048 separate light-sensing elements for technical imaging purposes. The resolution achieved by this quantity of image elements in a detector was becoming competitive with that of good photography.

During the year the standard 35-mm camera format returned as a popular medium. As a result of continued improvements of such cameras, autofocus devices and full-exposure automation were features of almost all of the new models.

Although the electronic still camera was available for purchase, this product as of 1987 had not yet found any large market. The general public still preferred to have photographic prints in hand.

The construction of large astronomical telescopes took a step forward with the beginning of the fabrication of the optics for a telescope with an aperture of 10 m (394 in) for the University of California. Other projects that had been announced earlier for telescopes with apertures of 6 and 8 m (236 and 315 in) failed to gain sufficient construction funding.

Space optics experienced a major downturn in activity following the shuttle *Challenger* disaster in January 1986. Because the decision had been made

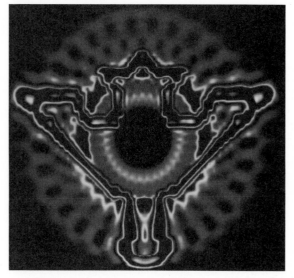

*Computer-enhanced photo resembling a delta-wing aircraft was produced using a new optical pattern recognition system. The "lock-and-tumbler" hologram, developed by scientists at Sandia National Laboratories in New Mexico, allows computers to recognize target objects regardless of angle of view, rotation, brightness, or image scale. Existing systems must match their holographic templates exactly.*

several years ago to use the shuttle as the only vehicle for launching heavy payloads, the grounding of all shuttle orbiters after the *Challenger* accident resulted in the stoppage or stretchout of most major programs and the cancellation of some. A decision to begin building some unmanned launch vehicles in 1987 was expected to have some positive effect, but it was not yet known when active space astronomy would be resumed. Especially hard hit was the Hubble space telescope. It appeared that this instrument would not be launched until the fall of 1988 at the earliest. The costs of maintaining that payload, as well as others, in a ready state adversely affected the availability of funds for all astronomical projects.

The support of the U.S. government for the Strategic Defense Initiative program continued. In the area of optical engineering several demonstrations of satellite tracking and attack were carried out. However, a major decision to abandon the laser-in-space concept, at least for the present time, eliminated many of the advanced programs in large-scale space optics that were previously considered to be likely. Therefore, no major advances in that field were reported.

Because the field of optical engineering continued to expand, the demand for trained people in the discipline remained strong. Several universities and colleges added optical engineering courses to their engineering curricula.

—Robert R. Shannon

433

# Physics

For many physicists the most exciting news of the past year was the discovery of a class of materials that become superconducting, *i.e.*, lose all resistance to the flow of electric current, at temperatures far higher than previously reported. In other research investigators synthesized large, high-quality artificial diamonds, succeeded in trapping individual particles of antimatter in a "bottle" of electric and magnetic fields, intensified the search for evidence of proton decay and the existence of the magnetic monopole, and neared their goal of creating a new form of matter, quark-gluon plasma, in the energetic collisions of heavy nuclei.

## General developments

Century-old attempts to measure gravity, decade-old efforts to make artificial diamonds, and multiyear-old experiments to trap atoms were reexamined or redone in 1986—with interesting new results.

**An "antigravity" force?** Geophysical experiments by Australian scientists, particle experiments by U.S. scientists, and gravity experiments by Hungarian scientists all combined to suggest that there may exist a new type of force between masses. This postulated force is repulsive, 1% as strong as the normal, attractive gravitational force, and larger for materials like iron than materials like wood. If these speculations are correct, then attempting to repeat Galileo's apocryphal experiment at the Leaning Tower of Pisa with iron and wooden balls would result in the wooden ball's hitting the ground first.

For many years Frank Stacey and co-workers at the University of Queensland, Australia, had been measuring the gravity of the Earth in tall towers, on the Earth's surface, and in deep mine shafts. Their gravity meter could easily sense the decrease in gravity as they increased its distance from the center of the Earth. After taking these expected variations out of their data and correcting for the variations in the density of the ground, they found that their calculated value of the gravitational attraction of the surface layers of the Earth remained about 1% higher than expected.

Meanwhile, U.S. theorist Ephraim Fischbach, experimentalist Sam Aronson, and others had been puzzling over a small anomaly in the lifetime of an esoteric subatomic particle called a neutral K meson. Einstein's special theory of relativity predicts that the faster an unstable particle travels, the longer it takes to decay. But the change in the lifetime of the K meson with velocity did not follow Einstein's theory exactly.

Recently Fischbach proposed that both anomalies are caused by a previously unrecognized, fifth force of nature, which he called hyperforce, that is proportional to the hypercharge in a body. The amount of hypercharge in an ordinary body is proportional to the number of nucleons (protons plus neutrons) in the body. The mass of a body is almost, but not quite, proportional to the number of nucleons in the body. The hyperforce between any two bodies would be repulsive, with a strength about 1% of the gravitational attraction between the same two bodies. Unlike the gravitational attraction, which drops off slowly as the square of the distance between the bodies, the hyperforce repulsion would reach out to about 200 m (600 ft), then drop off rapidly beyond that.

Since the hyperforce repulsion would be greater for some materials than others, Fischbach and co-workers turned to a collection of data taken between 1889 and 1908 by Hungarian scientist Roland Eötvös and his Budapest colleagues. They had compared the gravitational and inertial masses of many different kinds of substances. There had been differences, but Eötvös had ascribed them to experimental error. When Fischbach and co-workers reanalyzed the data, ordering the substances by the ratio of the total number of nucleons divided by the mass, they found a significant trend suggesting a slight variation of gravity with the number of nucleons.

The variations seen are close to the experimental limits, and much of the data is old. Everyone involved suggested caution in saying that a new fundamental force had been found. In fact, two other scientists who reexamined Eötvös's results found evidence that the discrepanices might well be due to air currents created by subtle temperature variations in Eötvös's laboratory. Nevertheless, a number of experiments involving gravitational gradiometer instruments, freely falling masses, trapped antiprotons, and modernized versions of the Eötvös and Cavendish types of gravity-measuring instruments were in the planning stages in 1987. Perhaps these efforts would determine whether hypercharge is real or just another will-o'-the-wisp of modern physics.

**Hold that atom.** In 1986 scientists succeeded in trapping and studying individual atomic particles—in one case, an antiparticle. When an atom is ionized (has an excess or deficit of electrons), it carries an electric charge and can thus be trapped easily with electric and magnetic fields. Such ion traps have been successful in the past in holding single barium ions for long periods of time. (See *1986 Yearbook of Science and the Future* Year in Review: PHYSICS: *General developments*.) Shining a laser beam at a barium ion can cause an electron around the ion to jump to a higher energy state. The electron almost immediately jumps down again, emitting a photon. If the laser light is intense enough, these quantum jumps can occur millions of times a second, allowing the ion to be "seen" by its emitted photons.

Using this observation technique scientists during the past year observed single ions taking quantum jumps from one level to another. Independent groups at the University of Washington and the University of Hamburg, West Germany, used barium ions, while a team at the U.S. National Bureau of Standards in Colorado used mercury ions. In each case the teams first "watched" their trapped ion as it jumped from the ground state to a short-lived excited state, then back again. They then sent into the trap a weak laser beam of a color different from the one used to produce the short-lived excited state. Occasionally a photon from that beam would excite the ion into a different, longer-lived excited state. When this quantum jump occurred, the ion could no longer drop repeatedly to the ground state to be excited by the first laser; the ion in effect "turned off" and was no longer visible. After staying in the metastable excited state for a time, it then dropped back to the ground state where it became visible again. Thus, by watching the ion turn on and off, the scientists could time the quantum jumps of single atoms.

A more exotic ion was recently captured for the first time. It was an antiproton, which can be thought of as an ionized atom of antihydrogen. Gerald Gabrielse of the University of Washington led an international team that included scientists from Fermi National Accelerator Laboratory, Batavia, Ill., and the University of Mainz, West Germany, in a visit to the Low Energy Antiproton Ring (LEAR) at the European Laboratory for Particle Physics (CERN) in Switzerland. They set up their ion traps, adjusted the electric and magnetic fields, then signaled the LEAR engineers for a "dump" of a billion antiprotons in less than a millionth of a second. The high-speed antiprotons lost most of their energy traveling through a sheet of beryllium at the entrance to the trap. A few straggled into the trap at an energy low enough for them to be captured when the trap voltages were pulsed on. In a typical run as many as 200 antiprotons were captured. They were usually held for 100 seconds (although once for ten minutes); then the trap voltages were turned off, allowing the antiprotons to annihilate on the trap walls so they could be counted.

Further experiments would be done in late 1987 when the improved LEAR facility resumed operation. Those experiments were to use a precision trap to compare the inertial masses of an antiproton and a proton to one part in a billion or better. Then would come experiments to measure the gravitational masses. Because the hypercharge of the antiproton is −1, while that of the proton is +1, a gravitylike hyperforce that is dependent on the hypercharge should certainly show up in these experiments.

In addition to advances in the trapping of charged ions, a team at AT&T Bell Laboratories, Holmdel,

Adapted from information obtained from AT&T Bell Laboratories

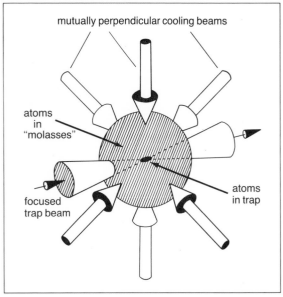

*Laser trap for neutral atoms uses a two-stage approach: three pairs of mutually perpendicular, unfocused beams to create a region of "optical molasses" and an intense trap beam focused to a tiny spot within the molasses.*

N.J., led by Arthur Ashkin reported the first laser beam trap for neutral atoms. When an atom moving toward the laser absorbs a photon of laser light, the recoil from the absorption process gives the atom a push away from the laser. A short time later the atom reemits the photon, which gives the atom another push, but because the emitted photon can go off in any direction, those pushes that the atom receives from a large number of emitted photons average out to zero. The result of thousands of absorption and emission cycles—in which photons are received from one direction but are thrown off in all directions—is an effective slowing of the atom by the laser beam, a technique called laser cooling.

Trapping begins with the formation of a region of "optical molasses" made by using six unfocused laser beams coming from six different directions. The streams of laser photons hinder the escape of the atoms from the region but do not make a perfect trap. They do, however, collect a large cloud of atoms and cool them down, allowing the trap itself to be more effective. The real trap is a tiny region of strongly focused laser light. Atoms are attracted to the focal point, where the laser beam is most intense. The strong light used for trapping soon would heat the atoms enough to escape the trap but for a technique invented by French scientists from École Normale Supérieure, Paris, in which the focused trapping beams and the unfocused cooling beams are switched back and forth, thus alternately trapping and cooling the atoms. The scientists at Bell Labs

435

successfully trapped about 500 sodium atoms in a fluorescent orange cloud at a temperature a fraction of a degree above absolute zero.

**An engineer's best friend.** Technologists have always been fascinated with the innate properties of diamond. It is the hardest material known, is strong in both tension and compression, conducts heat better than copper, transmits light better than any glass, and can withstand temperatures as high as 1,600° C (2,900° F) provided air is kept away so that the diamond does not burn up. Diamond also has the same crystalline structure as silicon and so should be an excellent semiconductor material. Until recently, however, the supply of high-quality diamonds has been limited to small expensive stones found in the ground.

The techniques for making artificial diamonds in the laboratory have been known since the 1950s, but the cost of the machines, slow growth speeds, and the size and quality of the diamonds produced have prevented artificial diamonds from competing with natural diamonds. This changed recently when Sumitomo Electric in Japan started mass-producing high-quality synthetic diamond crystals as heavy as two carats. The Gemological Institute of America examined a number of specimens and found that they are transparent, yellow, single crystals that are gem-quality but easily distinguishable from natural diamonds.

Sumitomo Electric was not planning to enter the jewelry trade but instead was selling its diamonds for dressing tools, ultraprecision cutting tools, and heat sinks for high-power laser diodes (diamond conducts heat five times better than copper yet is an electrical insulator). Their light yellow color comes from the strong ultraviolet absorption of single nitrogen atoms replacing carbon atoms in the crystal. These combine with other defects in the crystal to form "color centers" that fluoresce in visible light under ultraviolet illumination. Steven Rand, a scientist at the Hughes Research Laboratories in California, used the fluorescent light from these color centers to make a diamond laser.

A recent patent by Kazuo Tsuji of Sumitomo Electric describes the company's diamond growing process, which includes a new twist that may have significant implications for the technological use of diamonds. In the high-pressure (60,000-atmosphere), high-temperature (1,600° C) process, carbon in the form of graphite is put at the hot end of a pressure cell, and a seed crystal of diamond is put at the cold end. The space in the pressure cell is filled with a molten metal such as iron, nickel, or cobalt that readily dissolves carbon. The temperature gradient across the pressure cell causes the graphite to dissolve at the hot end and deposit as single-crystal diamond on the seed at the cold end.

The typical pressure cell has a large diameter; such a cell slowly grows a faceted lump of diamond. Tsuji found that if the cell was filled mostly with molten salt and contained just a long, thin column of molten metal in the middle, diamond growth would proceed only along the molten metal column to form a diamond rod. The shape of the initial metal column determined the shape of the final diamond rod. For example, Tsuji grew diamond rods having rectangular, square, and triangular cross sections. It was obvious that more complex shapes, such as hollow tubes and perhaps even single-crystal diamond turbine blades, could someday be fabricated by means of this growth technique, eliminating the difficult problem of cutting, grinding, or otherwise machining diamond parts.

—Robert L. Forward

## High-energy physics

The past year in high-energy physics was characterized more by consolidation and refinement of earlier observations than by new breakthroughs. Some of this comparative quiet was due to the effort expended on the construction of new facilities, which took place in part at the expense of the operation of existing facilities.

The standard model is now quite firmly entrenched in particle physics. In this model the electromagnetic and weak forces, or interactions, between matter particles are unified in the Weinberg-Salam electroweak theory. A crowning achievement in 1983 was the observation at the European Laboratory for Particle Physics (CERN) near Geneva of the $W^+$, $W^-$, and and Z intermediate vector bosons, the field particles of the weak interaction, exactly as predicted by the theory. The other major component of the standard model is the quantum chromodynamics (QCD) theory of strong interactions. This model, which treats all strong interactions in terms of the exchange of particles called gluons, differs from the

**Table I. The Elementary Particles of Physics**

| | Electric charge[1] | Generation I | Generation II | Generation III |
|---|---|---|---|---|
| quarks | $+2/3$ <br> $-1/3$ | $u$ $(0.3)$[2] <br> $d$ $(0.3)$ | $c$ $(1.5)$ <br> $s$ $(0.5)$ | $t$ $(?)$[3] <br> $b$ $(5)$ |
| leptons | $-1$ <br> $0$ | $e$ $(5.1 \times 10^{-4})$ <br> $\nu_e$ $(0?)$ | $\mu$ $(0.106)$ <br> $\nu_\mu$ $(0?)$ | $\tau$ $(1.784)$ <br> $\nu_\tau$ $(0?)$[3] |

[1] Electric charge is in units of the magnitude of the charge of the electron.
[2] Numbers in parentheses are masses in units of GeV/$c^2$ (energy in billions of electron volts divided by the square of the speed of light). Quark masses are approximate.
[3] The $t$ quark and the $\nu_\tau$ (tau neutrino) have not been experimentally observed.

**Table II. The Basic Forces or Interactions of Physics**

| Force | Field particle and rest mass | Strength relative to strong force at $10^{-13}$ cm distance | Particles that experience force |
|---|---|---|---|
| electro-magnetic | $\gamma$ (photon); 0 | $10^{-2}$ | all electrically charged particles; all quarks and all charged leptons |
| weak | $W^{\pm}$; 81.8 GeV/$c^2$ $Z^0$; 92.6 GeV/$c^2$ | $10^{-13}$ | all particles |
| strong | g (gluon); 0 | 1 | quarks and hadrons (particles composed of quarks) |
| gravita-tional | G (graviton)[1]; 0? | $10^{-38}$ | all particles with mass |

[1] The graviton has not yet been observed.

quantum theory of electromagnetism (quantum electrodynamics, or QED) chiefly in that there are three aspects (called colors) of the particles that experience the strong interaction whereas there are only two aspects, or signs, of electric charge (positive and negative). In the standard model of QCD all hadrons, or strongly interacting particles, are made up of combinations of six (or more) kinds of quarks, and it is between these quarks that the gluon-exchange force acts. The six quarks and six leptons of the standard model, with some of their properties, are listed in Table I. The basic interactions of the standard model are summarized in Table II.

**Quark scattering and jets at the CERN collider.** As an example of the parallel between QED and QCD, the elastic scattering of two electrically charged particles and the corresponding scattering of two quarks can be compared. The scattering of two electrons is understood in QED as mediated by the exchange of a virtual photon (the quantum of electromagnetic radiation) between the two particles. The classical inverse-square law of electrostatics leads to a very specific angular distribution for the scattered electron. This process is illustrated schematically in Figure 1a.

The corresponding process in QCD is the scattering of one quark by another, mediated in this case by the exchange of a gluon. Although the QCD force at very small distances (less than $10^{-13}$ cm) also follows an inverse-square law, at large separations quarks are attracted by a force that does not vary with separation, so that the energy required for separation grows continually with distance. The practical consequence is that free quarks are not found and that the elastic scattering of two quarks must there-

fore be studied indirectly. This scattering process is illustrated in Figure 1b, in which a quark in each of two nucleons (a proton and an antiproton) scatter by means of the exchange of a gluon.

As the scattered quarks fly off, the theory predicts that quark-antiquark pairs will be generated from the vacuum, thus avoiding the infinite energy required for unpaired quarks to separate completely. The consequence is that experimentally one observes "jets" of mesons (two-quark particles) produced in the directions of the scattered quarks. Other meson jets are produced along the directions of the incident nucleons.

The classical electrostatic scattering (Coulomb repulsion) of alpha particles (positively charged nuclei of helium) by the positively charged nuclei of gold was a landmark experiment in the early years of the 20th century in establishing the nuclear model of atomic structure. The angular distribution of the alpha particles as predicted by theory [$1/\sin^4(\theta/2)$] was observed, and small deviations from this dependence were correctly ascribed to the fact that the gold nucleus is not a dimensionless point but has a finite size.

From recent experiments at the CERN proton-antiproton collider, physicists have analyzed thousands of events wherein jets are produced from collisions having an energy as high as 600 GeV (billion electron volts) in the proton-antiproton center of

*Figure 1. In a, elastic scattering of two electrons, e⁻, takes place via the exchange of a virtual photon γ. In b, elastic scattering of a u quark and a d̄ quark (a d antiquark) is mediated by the exchange of a virtual gluon g. The u and d̄ quarks are shown as constituents of a colliding proton p and antiproton p̄, respectively.*

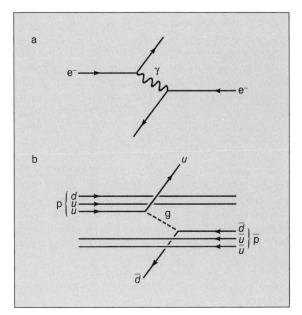

mass. For those events producing energetic jets that fly off at large angles to the original particle direction and that consequently have high transverse momentum, the data can be analyzed in terms of quark-quark elastic scattering, in which the energy, angle, and tranverse momentum of a jet is taken to represent the corresponding parameters for the scattered quark. From this analysis the data fit excellently with the QCD prediction, corresponding to the $1/\sin^4(\theta/2)$ of electrostatic scattering, after account is taken of the internal momentum distribution of quarks in the nucleon. This remarkably simple interpretation of data at so high an energy is strong support for the standard model of strong interactions.

It has been known for some time that the cross section for nucleon-nucleon scattering (the effective area that one nucleon presents to another as a collision target) rises with increasing energy above about 200 GeV (or 20 GeV in the center of mass). From cosmic-ray data reported in 1985 the cross section at 500 million GeV (30 thousand GeV center of mass) has been interpreted to be three times the value at 200 GeV. The CERN jet-production data over the range of 200–900 GeV in the center of mass suggested that most of the rise in cross section can be ascribed to the increasing cross section for the hard (essentially head-on) scattering of nucleon constituents leading to jets. Other data from the CERN collider added to physicists' confidence in the electroweak aspect of the standard model as well. The production of W and Z particles in terms of absolute cross sections and angular distributions and of certain of their decay characteristics were all in accord with predictions.

All of the new results from the CERN collider, however, have not been quite so positive. In 1984 the largest detector at the collider produced a positive signal for the most massive quark of Table I, the $t$ quark. Based on six events the data were interpreted as evidence for a $t$ with a mass of 40–60 GeV. Subsequent running of the experiment including data at higher energies failed to confirm the earlier results, and theorists argued that the earlier reported result appeared to correspond to a greater cross section than their calculations could accommodate. As of early 1987 no one could claim positive evidence for the $t$ quark, but neither was there reason to believe that it does not exist with a mass greater than 30 GeV. It was clear that finding the $t$ among the complex jet signals would be more difficult than was first expected. Similarly, other results from the CERN collider suggesting "new" physics did not hold up following the examination of additional data, detector improvements, and better analysis.

**Nonaccelerator experiments.** A synonym for high-energy physics is elementary particle physics, and many of the interesting frontiers in this field do not require the high energies of large accelerators. A small but increasing fraction of the high-energy community conducts nonaccelerator experiments that relate to elementary particles.

One group of such experiments relates to the search for the spontaneous decay of the free proton. Grand unified theories, which attempt to unite the strong and electroweak interactions, predict that quarks and leptons are not absolutely immutable but may transform one into the other, albeit at an extremely slow rate. An inevitable consequence of this conjecture is that a proton is not stable against spontaneous radioactive decay into a positron (positively charged electron) and a meson. The simplest of these theories predicts a lifetime for the proton of about $10^{30}$ years. Alternatively, if $10^{30}$ protons are observed, one can expect a proton decay rate of one per year.

Based on these predictions, groups in India, Italy, France, Japan, and the U.S. built large detectors designed to find this decay. For the largest detector, located near Cleveland, Ohio, a group from the University of Michigan, the University of California at Irvine, Brookhaven (N.Y.) National Laboratory, and Boston University built a container in a salt mine (to reduce unwanted cosmic-ray backgrounds) containing about 8,000 metric tons of water observed by 2,048 photomultiplier tubes. From their observations this group established a lifetime of at least $3 \times 10^{32}$ years for the predicted most prevalent type of decay. In other words, to the limit of the detector's sensitivity they found no evidence for proton decay. Recently the detector was improved, making backgrounds from cosmic-ray neutrinos less of a problem. Together with results from the European and Asian experiments, the most current data suggested that any successful form of grand unified theories must be more complicated than at first believed. Theorists still expect that the proton is unstable at some level, and experiments in progress should push the lifetime sensitivity beyond $10^{34}$ years.

Other nonaccelerator experiments seek evidence for the magnetic monopole, a predicted particle having a single north or south magnetic pole and a mass about $10^{16}$ times that of the proton. These particles would be too massive to be produced by the most energetic accelerators currently available, but they might remain as relics of the big bang origin of the universe. Searches so far have been negative, but a detector being built in Italy by a U.S.-Italian collaboration would be about 1,000 times more sensitive than previous devices.

Neutrinos may be altogether massless particles, as is the photon. Yet nothing in the standard model or in present experiments precludes a mass on the order of a millionth that of the electron. If neutrinos have mass, even a very small mass, profound consequences for particle physics, astrophysics, and cosmology would follow. Although earlier experiments indicated some evidence for a nonzero mass, more recent data from a variety of sources, in particular studies of reactor-produced neutrinos and of the radioactive decay of tritium, found no evidence for neutrino mass. One new conjecture relates to the possibility that a long-standing anomaly between the expected and observed emission of neutrinos from the Sun is due to effects related to a nonzero neutrino mass. New improved measurements of solar neutrinos being planned in Japan, Italy, and the U.S.S.R. would be sensitive to these effects. In the U.S., physicists were continuing an existing solar neutrino experiment in a South Dakota gold mine.

**Unresolved problems and new theories.** The more scientists understand, the more sophisticated are the questions they can ask of nature. For example, three generations of quarks and of leptons are now clearly established. An obvious question follows. Are there further, undiscovered generations? In fact, the very small mass (be it zero or nonzero) of all known neutrinos provides a possible probe of this question independent of the masses of the charged leptons and quarks. One mode of the decay of the Z intermediate vector boson is into lepton-antilepton pairs, such as an electron and a positron or a neutrino and an antineutrino. The decay rate for each of these lepton-pair possibilities should be equal, including decays to still undiscovered neutrino species. Therefore, a limit on the observed rate of decay to neutrinos, given known and observed decays to pairs of charged leptons, provides a limit to the number of kinds, or generations, of neutrinos. One result from the CERN proton-antiproton collider is that there are almost certainly no more than five generations of neutrinos (*i.e.*, no more than two beyond the three known).

It is not known why there are different generations or, indeed, why different particles—the quarks, for example—have different masses. All evidence suggests that the electron is a geometrical point (*i.e.*, has a physical radius of zero). Having learned that first atoms, then nuclei, and now protons and neutrons have internal structure, physicists naturally ask if quarks are also composite or whether, like the electron, they are fundamental entities without internal structure. As of 1987 there was no evidence for an internal structure for quarks, although the experimental arguments were not nearly as tight as for the electron.

There are, however, very strong theoretical predictions and definitive tests at energies beyond those currently available. At energies below 1 TeV (trillion electron volts) in the quark-quark center-of-mass system, answers to the questions discussed above should be found. It was for this reason that so much effort was being focused on new facilities.

**New accelerator facilities.** During the past year a significant number of accelerators were in various stages of construction around the world. It was a measure of the excitement generated by the search for answers in high-energy physics that effort and resources on this scale were being expended on these machines and their detectors.

At the Fermi National Accelerator Laboratory near Chicago, the world's first superconducting accelerator, the Tevatron, operated at 900 GeV. In November 1986, proton-antiproton collisions at 1,800 GeV (1.8 TeV) were achieved, and the first physics experiments were scheduled to be carried out in early 1987 at the Tevatron using a newly completed Collider Detector Facility.

At the Stanford Linear Accelerator Center in California a novel electron-positron collider was being completed. This Stanford Linear Collider (SLC) would produce 100 GeV in the electron-positron center of mass, sufficient to create a Z particle directly. The SLC was scheduled to be turned on during 1987 for the first time.

In Japan a circular electron-positron storage ring came into operation at the end of 1986. At the KEK Laboratory near Tokyo, this machine, named Tristan, achieved electron-positron collisions of more than 50 GeV at the center of mass and was designed to reach 70 GeV. Should the *t* quark be light enough, this facility could be the first to observe definitive evidence for it.

In 1989 CERN was slated to complete LEP, the largest electron-positron collider currently under construction. In its first years of operation it would function at about 100 GeV (near the mass of the Z particle); later its energy would be approximately doubled, and studies of the production of $W^+W^-$ pairs would be carried out.

In Hamburg, West Germany, a unique facility was being built to collide 800-GeV protons with 30-GeV electrons. Electron-proton collisions have been a rich source of new physics for 20 years, and extending these studies to a new energy domain would address many questions inaccessible to the proton-antiproton or electron-positron colliders.

The Serpukhov laboratory south of Moscow was constructing a 3-TeV superconducting synchrotron named UNK. It was to be used as a conventional accelerator but would also achieve proton-proton collisions utilizing a 600-GeV proton synchrotron in the same tunnel.

Finally, planning in the U.S for the 20-TeV Superconducting Super Collider (SSC) was well advanced. Through collisions between two proton beams of 20 TeV each, an energy of 40 TeV in the center of mass would be achieved, and this with a luminosity, or interaction rate, thousands of times greater than that achieved in proton-proton or proton-antiproton colliders in the past. During 1986 a detailed accelerator design was completed, and prototype magnets were engineered, built, and tested.

The high-energy physics community is confident that this succession of new facilities will resolve many current questions. Yet, if history is any guide, the most interesting results from these machines will take the form of complete surprises and are likely to reveal more new puzzles in the fundamental nature of matter and energy than they will resolve.

—Lawrence W. Jones

## Nuclear physics

The past year for nuclear physics was exciting. As several new experimental facilities became operational, entirely new areas of nuclear science opened to exploration. Among them were the behavior of the nuclear many-body system under very high angular momentum and centrifugal forces, the behavior of nuclei very far from stability, and the behavior of heavy nuclei involved in collisions at very high energies. The development of new detection instrumentation for nuclear gamma radiation resulted in a renaissance in nuclear spectroscopy.

**Nuclei at high angular momentum.** Extensive spectroscopic studies in recent years have demonstrated that the shapes of nuclei change systematically as their angular momentum, or spin, increases. At low spin nuclei having few valence nucleons (protons and neutrons in orbits outside the specially stable, closed core of the nucleus) are essentially spherical. As the number of valence nucleons increases, the spherical systems become increasingly soft and susceptible to quadrupole vibration relative to their equilibrium shape. When the number of valence nucleons is large, the shape is stabilized to that of a prolate spheroid or football. With increasing spin, however, almost all nuclei except those with very large numbers of valence nucleons first transform into oblate spheroids (doorknob shapes). In the case of rare-earth nuclei, for example, the transformation occurs at angular momenta above perhaps 20 units, up to the maximum experimentally accessible—about 40 units. (The usual unit of angular momentum is Planck's constant divided by $2\pi$.) At higher spin, above perhaps 55–60 units, it had been thought that a rather abrupt transition would occur to a so-called superdeformed, very elongated, prolate spheroid as a consequence of the increasing centrifugal forces brought about by rotation; this state, however, had been inaccessible to all experimental studies.

Particular interest attached to the possibility of finding the superdeformed shapes because, many years earlier, the late Sven Gösta Nilsson of Lund University, Sweden, had demonstrated theoretically that when a nucleus becomes superdeformed it may

Adapted from information obtained from D. Allan Bromley

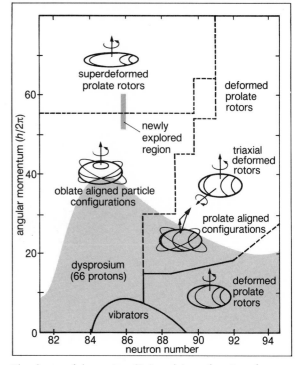

*The shapes of dysprosium (Dy) nuclei as a function of angular momentum and neutron number are diagramed schematically. The shaded region is that studied prior to 1986; the unshaded region is open to some conjecture. Superdeformed shapes of $^{152}$Dy at angular momenta in the 50–60-unit region recently have been detected.*

exhibit a totally new kind of stability and a new type of shell structure having magic numbers of neutrons and protons different from those characteristic of spherical systems. These magic numbers are simply the signature that a gap has developed in the quantum level spectrum at that particular number, effectively creating a closed shell of nucleons. Nilsson showed that an entirely different set of closed shells occurred when the ratio of the major to minor axis of the superdeformed nucleus was 2:1 or 3:1 and that certain very highly deformed nuclei, which corresponded to the closure of these new shells, might be expected to be particularly stable.

During the past year Peter Twin and Paul Nolan of the University of Liverpool, England, and the Daresbury Laboratory, together with their colleagues, brought into operation the TESSA 3 spectrometer system, which for the first time made possible the experimental study of these superdeformed nuclei as they are created from the fusion of target and projectile nuclei. The TESSA 3 device surrounds the bombarded target with some 62 hexagonal, close-packed crystals of bismuth germinate chosen for their high gamma-ray absorption and used to detect the large number of simultaneous gamma rays emitted as the product nucleus undergoes deexcitation, or slows down, from its high-spin states. While the bismuth germinate system determines the multiplicity of gamma rays, a surrounding network of germanium detectors permits detailed study of the deexcitation patterns. In a study of palladium-108 target nuclei bombarded by a calcium-48 beam, Twin and his collaborators were able to see discrete gamma radiation resulting from the deexcitation of quantum states as high as 60 units of angular momentum. This technological tour de force thus increased the angular momentum of states that could be studied with a precision of 50% above that previously accessible. From their data they were able to demonstrate that they had indeed detected the fusion product dysprosium-152 in its superdeformed shape and that it did have a major-to-minor-axis ratio of 2:1.

Whereas this behavior was in accord with expectations, similar measurements on other rare-earth nuclei showed totally different behavior. Cerium-132 was found to stretch slightly under centrifugal forces, while dysprosium-152 stretches dramatically to achieve the 2:1 axis ratio. Erbium-158, with only six nucleons more than dysprosium-152, changes its behavior altogether with increasing angular momentum: its nucleons cease moving collectively as one body and instead adjust their orbits one by one in the nucleus, leading to a noncollective overall shape change from prolate to oblate. Adding only four more nucleons to give erbium-162 results in a remarkably stable, collective nuclear structure that deforms hardly at all under centrifugal forces. Such striking differences in behavior in the new spin

The TESSA 3 spectrometer encloses a target in an array of gamma-ray detectors made of bismuth germinate, which in turn are surrounded by germanium detectors. A beam of accelerated ions strikes the target, creating fast-spinning nuclei that emit telltale gamma rays upon deexcitation.

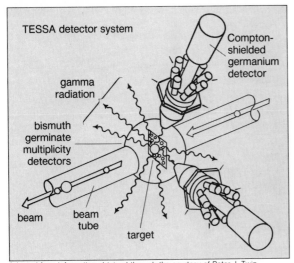

Adapted from information obtained through the courtesy of Peter J. Twin, Nuclear Facility, Daresbury Laboratory

regime that was opening to detailed study provided a clear signature for entirely new physics. Of particular interest was the possibility that, at least in some cases, the change from prolate to oblate shape could occur abruptly as a phase transition in hot, high-spin nuclear matter.

This area would be actively explored in all laboratories that could give access to it. The success obtained at Daresbury depended on the availability not only of the TESSA spectrometer but also of very high-quality projectile beams from the 25-MV (25-million-volt) tandem electrostatic accelerator installed at Daresbury. In 1987 the only comparable facilities elsewhere were the Holifield accelerator at Oak Ridge (Tenn.) National Laboratory and the ESTU-1 accelerator just coming into operation at Yale University. Other accelerator installations, including the tandem-linac (linear accelerator) ATLAS configuration at Argonne National Laboratory in Illinois, the tandem cyclotron system TASCC at Chalk River Nuclear Laboratories in Canada, the double-cyclotron facility GANIL at Caen, France, and the Super-HILAC linear accelerator facility at the University of California at Berkeley would also be used to probe these new phenomena.

**Nuclei on the edge of stability.** Nuclei that are very far from stability and on the edge of spontaneous disruption provide particularly sensitive systems in which to test and refine physicists' understanding of nuclear structure and nuclear forces. In the past attention had been focused primarily on neutron-rich nuclei that are far from stability because these could be made in the fission process. Proton-rich nuclei far from stability, on the other hand, can only be made in nuclear reactions that have been induced by heavy, accelerated nuclear projectiles. Of particular interest among the proton-rich nuclei are those having equal numbers of neutrons and protons, since with increasing mass these nuclei become increasingly unstable.

During the past year C. J. (Kim) Lister of the University of Manchester, England, and his colleagues, using the recoil mass separator system at the Daresbury Laboratory, succeeded in extending the known kinds of such nuclei all the way from zinc-60 to zirconium-80. The latter nucleus was especially interesting because Lister and his collaborators were able to demonstrate that at this very edge of stability zirconium-80 in its ground state, rather than at very high spin, was superdeformed, having an axis ratio of 2:1. Whereas the technology of Twin and his colleagues opened the nuclear stratosphere to precision study, that of Lister and his collaborators opened the distant reaches of the nuclear valley of stability. Both represent new frontiers and should provide vital new information about the behavior of the nuclear, many-body system.

**Heavy-ion collisions at relativistic energies.** A number of years ago T. D. Lee and Gian Carlo Wick of Columbia University, New York City, suggested the possibility that in high-energy collisions of heavy nuclei it might be possible to create entirely new kinds of matter. In contrast to elementary particle physics wherein the goal is that of delivering ever more energy to ever smaller volumes in the hope of materializing some of it in the form of new particles, the goal of heavy-ion collisions is that of delivering ever more energy to relatively large volumes containing large numbers of nucleons, and therefore of their constituent quarks and gluons, so that new kinds of collective behavior, interactions, and matter may result.

At very high energies the expectation is that nuclei become effectively transparent to one another so that an accelerated projectile can pass entirely through a target nucleus, heating both to temperatures sufficiently high to liberate the constituent quarks in the nucleons and thus create a quark-gluon plasma. Only at extraordinarily high energies, however, is the quark-gluon plasma expected to be separable from the superheated projectile and target remnants.

During late 1986 a critically important step toward the goal of studying these ultrahigh-energy collisions was taken both at the Brookhaven (N.Y.) National Laboratory and at CERN in Geneva. At Brookhaven, oxygen ions were accelerated in the Alternating Gradient Synchrotron (AGS) to an energy of 14.6 GeV (billion electron volts) per nucleon, both these and sulfur ions at the same energy were to be used for seven weeks of experimentation in early 1987. At CERN, oxygen ions were accelerated to 200 GeV per nucleon and used in preliminary experiments; sulfur ions of equivalent energy were to be used for a 17-day experiment in September 1987.

Preliminary results from CERN demonstrated that the oxygen beams delivered to the experimental targets are remarkably clean and free from contamination, for example, by alpha particles that might result from fragmentation of the oxygen projectiles during the kilometers-long flight path. Furthermore, earlier fears that the CERN energy of 200 GeV per nucleon would be so high that the oxygen projectiles would pass directly, and largely unaffected, through a lead target were shown to be unwarranted. During the initial few days of running, data were obtained in photographic emulsion experiments, in experiments on the production of muon pairs, and in calorimetric experiments, while several thousand streamer-chamber pictures were taken to provide a preliminary overview of this new domain. The streamer-chamber pictures confirmed that the nuclear stopping power at the energies produced at CERN is still high and led to considerable optimism that these experiments, as

well as future ones at higher energies, would enable investigators to probe the equation of state of nuclear matter, perhaps the most fundamental question in the field, and to study the phase transition between normal matter and quark matter, as represented by the quark-gluon plasma.

Even at an energy of 200 GeV per nucleon, only 20 GeV per nucleon is available in the center-of-mass system for a projectile–fixed-target arrangement, and the center-of-mass energy in such a geometry increases only very slowly with the laboratory beam energy. Recent calculations at least suggested that, in order to bring about the transition to quark matter at low density, a temperature equivalent to approximately 200 MeV would be required; alternately, at low temperature a density somewhere between five and ten times normal would be needed. In order to separate clearly the quark-gluon plasma, when formed, from the target and projectile remnants, simple calculations showed that center-of-mass energies in the range of 50–100 GeV per nucleon would be required, energies simply beyond any reasonable access in a projectile–fixed-target geometry.

Fortunately, at Brookhaven National Laboratory the tunnel, the refrigeration system, and a wide range of facilities and equipment representing more than half the total cost of a relativistic heavy-ion collider system already exist as a consequence of initial construction for the planned but later abandoned Isabelle high-energy physics accelerator. These facilities have now been incorporated into a detailed design for a relativistic heavy-ion collider (RHIC) facility currently at the top of the U.S. nuclear physics community's priority list for new construction. Because of the dimensions of the tunnel, it should be possible to build a cost-effective system that collides 100-GeV-per-nucleon beams, resulting in 200 GeV per nucleon in the center of mass for all ions up to gold. If construction on this facility starts in 1989, then experiments at these energies could be initiated in 1994.

**Relativistic electron studies.** Reflecting the fact that the nuclear physics community had agreed upon a high-energy, high-duty-factor electron accelerator as its highest priority for new construction in the early 1980s, the U.S. Department of Energy recently approved construction of the Continuous Electron Beam Accelerator Facility (CEBAF) at Newport News, Va. When the machine was originally proposed, the existing technology dictated a room-temperature, linear accelerator with a stretcher ring to provide electron beams as high as 4 GeV in energy and at roughly 100% duty factor. During the past year, however, because of the rapid progress made in the technology of superconducting radio-frequency (RF) cavities, the decision was made to change the design, eliminating the stretcher ring, and recirculating the beam four times through two superconducting linacs. Among its many technological advantages are reduced power consumption, smaller facility size, and better beam quality. Although the facility was designed for a maximum energy of 4 GeV, preliminary tests on the RF accelerating cavities suggested that a maximum energy of 6 GeV might be obtained in the original configuration. Furthermore, the design is such that, if and when the research requires it, the maximum energy can be readily extended to 16 GeV. Current schedules called for completion of CEBAF in 1992, and detailed planning for the experimental program was under way.

CEBAF will permit mapping out the detailed transition from nuclei considered as complexes of neutrons and protons to nuclei in which the neutrons and protons are themselves in excited states (the so-called nucleon isobars), to at least the beginning of quark deconfinement, in which the excited nucleons begin to melt into one another and in which the beginning of the transition from ordinary to quark matter takes place. This is a very complex region where quantum chromodynamics, the theory of the strong force holding the nucleus together, cannot be applied in its perturbative limit. Yet the understanding of this transition is of critical importance, and high-energy electrons provide the optimum probe for its study.

Although the research under way at the large electrostatic accelerators, at the heavy-ion accelerators, and at the electron accelerators superficially appears quite different, they are very much related and interdependent. Only with the results of all three will physicists truly begin to understand the richness of the phenomena that the nuclear many-body system makes available.

—D. Allan Bromley

## Condensed-matter physics

The 1986 Nobel Prize for Physics was awarded for two significant inventions which, although separated by approximately 50 years in time, are highly topical today in both basic and applied research. Both inventions provide means for fulfilling the old dream of being able to "see" atoms. Half of the prize was awarded to the West German physicist Ernst Ruska, retired from the Fritz Haber Institute of the Max Planck Society in West Berlin, "for his fundamental work in electron optics and for the design of the first electron microscope" in the early 1930s. The other half of the prize was divided between Gerd Binnig, also a West German physicist, and Swiss researcher Heinrich Rohrer of the IBM Zürich Research Laboratory for their design of the scanning tunneling microscope in 1981. (*See* SCIENTISTS OF THE YEAR.) This instrument is described in the *1984 Yearbook of Science and the Future* Year in Review: PHYSICS: *Solid-state physics.*

Each of the inventions is based on a specific quantum mechanical property of electrons. Only a few years before Ruska's invention of the electron microscope, the wavelike nature of the electron had been predicted by French physicist Louis-Victor de Broglie and experimentally verified by U.S. investigators Clinton Davisson and Lester Germer in an electron diffraction experiment. The electron microscope is built on the same concepts as the light microscope, substituting electrons for light and exploiting their wavelike characteristics in focusing them with magnetic lenses. Modern electron microscopes are sophisticated instruments having electron energies in the million-electron-volt range, computer-controlled magnetic lenses, modern image-detection and image-analysis systems, and resolutions better than two angstroms ($\mathring{A}$) making it feasible to see rows of atoms clearly. (One angstrom is one hundred-millionth of a centimeter.)

In contrast to the transmission electron microscope the tunneling electron microscope is a wonder in its simplicity, yet it boasts atomic-resolution performance. A fine stylus in the form of a sharp metal tip is scanned across the surface to be imaged in a raster pattern and only about 10 $\mathring{A}$ above the surface. Applying a voltage of only a few volts causes a flow of electrons between the tip and the sample, even though they are not in electrical contact in the classical sense. The small distance of 10 $\mathring{A}$ is in the space regime governed by the laws of quantum mechanics, and a "tunneling" current flows through the potential barrier between the tip and the sample. By monitoring the tunneling current as the probe stylus is scanned across the surface, an image of the atomic arrangement of the surface is obtained in which the individual atoms are clearly visible.

The ability of the tunneling microscope to image individual atoms makes it an ideal tool to see atomic-scale surface defects and individual adatoms (adsorbed atoms) on the surface; by contrast, other instruments like the electron microscope require an array of atoms, as in a single crystal. As Figure 1 illustrates, the scanning tunneling microscope can be made small enough to be held in the hand, and it can easily fit into laboratory-scale chambers and other equipment for surface studies, complementing such tools as electron spectrometers and electron-diffraction instruments. It is therefore rapidly becoming an important diagnostic tool for surface scientists. Most modern surface studies must be performed in elaborate ultrahigh-vacuum chambers to avoid contamination of the sample surface with residual gases. The tunneling microscope, however, has proved remarkably capable of imaging samples in a variety of environments, many of them much more realistic

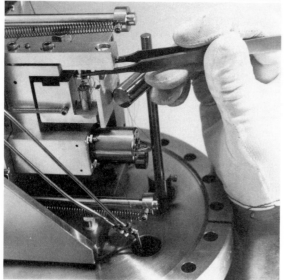

*Figure 1. A small scanning tunneling microscope can fit easily into a conventional vacuum chamber.*

and similar to the environment of technologically important processes. Scientists at the University of California at Santa Barbara, for example, obtained excellent surface images of samples in air and even in water and were able to study the initial phases of corrosion in aqueous solution.

By varying the voltage between tip and specimen one can also conduct tunneling spectroscopy and probe the wave functions of the surface atoms. Because the environment of surface atoms differs from that of bulk atoms, the surface will exhibit specific electronic states, or surface states. These states play a very important role in determining, for example, the electronic behavior of a catalytic surface or the electronic properties of a semiconductor surface. Much of present-day surface-physics research is aimed at studying the correlation between the geometric structure of a surface and its electronic structure. The tunneling microscope for the first time provides the means to analyze both structures with the same instrument on an identical sample area. It should advance scientific understanding of such applications as Schottky barrier formation, a key process in modern electronic devices, and the surface chemistry in such important processes as corrosion and catalysis.

**Superconductivity.** The IBM Zürich laboratory was also the origin of one of the most revolutionary breakthroughs in condensed-matter physics in recent years, a collection of discoveries and observations having technological implications of the same magnitude as the invention of the transistor. The event also is interesting sociologically as an example of the way modern scientific research is practiced and the way its progress is accelerated through international communication. The discovery occurred in the field of research dealing with superconductivity, the absence of electrical resistance in a substance at very low temperatures. In April 1986 J. Georg Bednorz and K. Alexander Müller of the IBM Zürich laboratory submitted a paper to the European physics journal *Zeitschrift für Physik* in which they reported the onset of superconductivity at a temperature as high as 30 K. (Subtracting about 273 from a temperature in kelvins [K] gives its equivalent in degrees Celsius [° C]; *e.g.*, 30 K = −243° C.) The previous record high superconducting temperature had been set in 1973 when the record was increased by a mere two degrees, from 21 K to 23 K. The new discovery was also revolutionary in that it occurred in a new class of superconducting materials, consisting of complex metal oxides. The samples in which it was discovered contained the elements barium (Ba), the rare-earth element lanthanum (La), copper (Cu), and oxygen (O).

When the paper appeared in the fall of 1986 and the results were confirmed at several laboratories in the U.S., Japan, and China, it stimulated feverish activity among physicists and materials scientists all over the world. New finds came quickly and were exceedingly rewarding. Within weeks new materials were synthesized in which the critical temperature for superconductivity approached 100 K. As of early 1987 the frontier of this field was advancing so rapidly that it was difficult to put it into perspective. Most of the signs, however, pointed in the direction of a fundamental discovery that would have vast scientific and technological implications.

The phenomenon of superconductivity was discovered by the Dutch physicist Heike Kamerlingh Onnes in 1911 and was made possible by his success in liquefying helium three years earlier. While measuring the electrical resistivity of mercury as a function of temperature, he found a decrease with decreasing temperature as expected until the resistivity suddenly went to zero at the temperature of liquid helium, 4 K (*see* Figure 2). In subsequent years other metals (presently 21) and metal alloys (presently several thousand) were found to be superconductors when cooled to temperatures in the vicinity of liquid helium. In the superconducting state the material is perfectly "frictionless" for a direct current. Currents set up experimentally in superconducting rings have persisted undiminished for years. It is estimated that the lifetime for such a superconducting current is greater than 100,000 years.

The technological importance of superconductivity was early recognized for electrical applications. A superconducting power line could transmit power without losses, which can reach 3–4% per 160 km (100 mi) in a normal long-distance power line. A

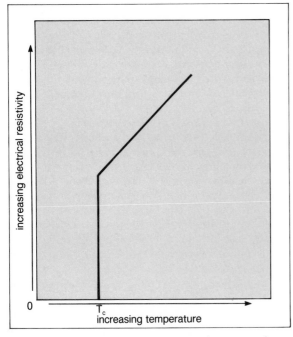

Figure 2. Electrical resistivity in a superconducting metal is plotted as a function of temperature. With decreasing temperature, resistivity falls gradually until it drops abruptly to zero at the superconducting transition temperature $T_c$.

circulating current in a superconducting ring could act as an electrical storage device, similar to a rechargeable battery but without energy loss or deterioration. Electrical energy from utilities could be stored in such a device at night when consumption is low and then tapped during peak daytime demand periods. Superconductors could be used to create large magnetic fields for applications ranging from magnetically levitated trains to high-energy particle accelerators. The major hindrance in realizing these applications has been the awkwardly low temperatures needed to reach the superconducting state, which requires liquid helium as a refrigerant. Much effort, therefore, has been devoted to finding materials with a high transition temperature. Progress has been exceedingly slow. In the beginning the lack of a satisfactory explanation of the phenomenon of superconductivity hindered the pace of research even more. It was not until the 1950s that U.S. researchers John Bardeen, Leon Cooper, and John Schrieffer provided a theoretical framework in a theory coined the BCS theory after the initials of the originators. In 1972 the three men were awarded the Nobel Prize for Physics, the second for Bardeen who had also shared a Nobel for the invention of the transistor.

The Ba-La-Cu-O compound has a so-called layered perovskite structure, a model of which is shown in Figure 3. The copper atoms are arranged in layers with each copper atom surrounded by six oxygen

atoms in an octahedral arrangement. By applying a hydrostatic pressure to the sample, the scientists were able to raise the transition temperature above 50 K. This led to the suggestion that one could obtain the same effect by replacing some of the metal atoms with others of different size. By replacing barium with strontium, which is chemically similar to barium but has a smaller atomic radius, researchers indeed verified the predicted increase in transition temperature. By following the trends in the change of the transition temperature with the substitution of atoms, scientists Maw-Kuen Wu of the University of Alabama at Huntsville and Ching-Wu (Paul) Chu of the University of Houston, Texas, together with several co-workers homed in on a class of superconductors having transition temperatures close to 100 K, well above the 77 K boiling point of liquid nitrogen.

The newer compounds contain the metal yttrium (Y) instead of lanthanum and have an overall composition corresponding to the formula $(Y_{0.6}Ba_{0.4})_2CuO_4$. In order for these materials to be superconductors, however, they must contain less oxygen than the formal composition. They were made in a relatively simple way by heating yttrium and copper oxides with barium carbonate in air at about 1,000° C (1,830° F). As of early 1987 detailed knowledge about these materials was still lacking; much work remained in order to understand their synthesis and to characterize them fully.

Figure 3. The new superconducting materials have layered perovskite structures, with each copper atom surrounded by six oxygen atoms. For their high transition temperatures to appear, however, they must be oxygen deficient.

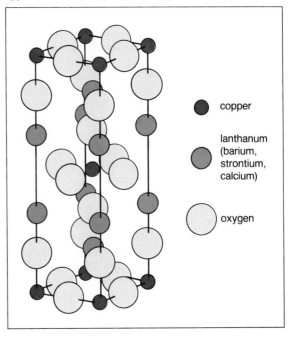

copper

lanthanum (barium, strontium, calcium)

oxygen

The demonstration of a practical superconductor above the temperature of liquid nitrogen should have dramatic technological implications. In contrast to cumbersome and expensive liquid helium, liquid nitrogen is cheap (cheaper than milk) and easy to fabricate. It remained to be seen if the new materials could be made in useful forms, such as sufficiently strong, ductile wires or as layers plated on a substrate that had the necessary mechanical properties. Nevertheless, despite the short time since the discovery of the new superconducting materials, remarkable progress had been made in the art of manufacturing them in suitable forms. At the March 1987 meeting of the American Physical Society, which was dominated by news of the superconductor discoveries, researchers from AT&T Bell Laboratories, Murray Hill, N.J., demonstrated one of the materials in the form of a flexible tape, which could be formed to the desired shape and then converted by heat to a final ceramic form. In another effort scientists from Stanford University proposed using an evaporation deposition technique to make the new materials in thin film form suitable for electronic applications.

Another unknown parameter, which is of extreme importance for many proposed technical applications, is the critical current density that these materials can carry before their superconductive properties are destroyed. In addition to the disappearance of electrical resistivity at the onset of superconductivity, another important effect, the Meissner effect, occurs. At the transition temperature a superconductor expels all magnetic flux from its interior, either fully, for what is called a type I superconductor, or only partially, for a type II superconductor. This effect shows up as a large negative magnetic susceptibility below the transition temperature. In fact, it is the measurement of such large negative susceptibilities that provide the most conclusive evidence of a true superconducting state. When a superconductor is exposed to a sufficiently large magnetic field, it is unable to sustain its superconducting state. For the new superconductors to be useful for large-scale applications, they must be able to remain superconducting at high magnetic fields and carry large electric currents. Whereas the first measurements of the ability of these materials to resist magnetic fields was quite encouraging, their critical current densities were still unknown.

The existing BCS theory can readily explain superconductivity up to about 40 K. It remained to be shown whether the same basic theoretical model could accommodate the new high-temperature superconductors. The salient feature of the BCS theory is the binding of electrons into pairs (Cooper pairs) by means of an attractive force—created by the interaction between the electrons and the vibrations of the material's crystal lattice—that is larger than the electrostatic repulsion between electrons. Above the superconducting transition temperature the thermal energy becomes high enough to break up the Cooper pairs. Theorists still needed to determine if attractive forces stronger than the interaction between electrons and lattice vibrations are necessary to explain superconductivity at such high temperatures as 98 K and above.

A dramatic illustration of the rapid progress that occurred during the past year is provided by Figure 4, which follows the attainment of record-setting superconducting temperatures over time. Will the curve continue upward? Will it reach room temperature? These natural questions may soon be answered as a result of the effort currently under way to explore the new discoveries in superconductivity. Even as soon as late March 1987 researchers were claiming evidence for signs of superconductivity as high as 240 K in a Y-Ba-Cu-O compound. Perhaps in the not-too-distant future on a trip to the hardware store for electrical wire, one may have to choose between "regular" and "superconducting."

—Stig B. Hagstrom

*See also* Feature Article SUPERSTRINGS.

*Figure 4. The new superconductors have raised the record transition temperature dramatically, well above the temperature of liquid nitrogen (77 K).*

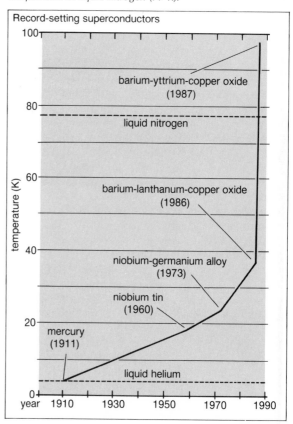

# Psychology

The past year was marked by the appearance of a number of unorthodox ideas, mainly relating to the practice of psychology. In addition, there was the usual continuing advance of psychological research on a wide range of basic topics.

**Cooperation and competition.** One of the most refreshingly provocative new emphases centered on the value of cooperation as an alternative social framework in contrast with competition. The arguments in support of cooperation were comprehensively advanced by Alfie Kohn in his *No Contest: The Case Against Competition* (Houghton-Mifflin). An intensive survey was made by University of Minnesota educators of 122 studies, from 1924 to 1981, comparing educational performance in cooperative and competitive classrooms. A majority (65) of these showed superior performance under cooperation, with only a small number (8) indicating the opposite result; the remainder did not reveal statistically reliable differences. Cooperation was found to produce higher achievement than individual work in 108 of the 156 students.

Three major reasons for the superiority of cooperation were cited by Kohn. First, the anxiety produced by a competitive situation interferes with learning and performance. Second, efficient sharing of diverse resources is difficult under competitive compared with cooperative conditions. Third, learning and performance under competition depend more on extrinsic reinforcers (gold stars, honor rolls, and the like) than on intrinsic motivation, which is more durably related to high achievement.

**Parents as teachers.** Another recent example of capitalizing on intrinsic rather than extrinsic motivation is the "New Parents as Teachers" program arranged by the Missouri State Department of Education. This project was directed by educational psychologists Michael Meyerhoff and Burton White. It was based on the premise that much crucial learning (or failure to learn) occurs during the first three years of a person's life. Thus, the home is the first schoolhouse, and the parents, or other caretakers, are the first teachers.

The Missouri program involved an intensive, carefully planned effort to train parents to be effective teachers of their newborn children. This model parent-education program was run during the calendar years 1982–85. Four districts, with 60 to 100 families in each, were each provided with the services of one full-time and two part-time parent educators. The districts represented a cross section of the state's population: one urban, one suburban, one small town, and one rural. The program, which was privately funded by the Danforth Foundation, was said to have cost approximately $800 per family per year for the three years of its operation.

Toward the end of the third year a randomly selected group of 75 of the children from the program was compared by an independent research organization with 75 closely matched children who had not been enrolled in the program. The children who had been in the project achieved significantly higher scores on intellectual and linguistic tests. Moreover, they were also described as having "outstanding" social development.

One of the most attractive features of this ap-

Parent educator (left) and mother watch 22-month-old boy carry a cup on a plate. As part of the "New Parents as Teachers" program arranged by the Missouri State Department of Education in 1982–85, one full-time and two part-time educators were hired in each of four school districts to train parents to be effective teachers of their young children.

Bob Greenspan

proach to parenting is the fact that it requires little in the way of special devices or treatments. Quite to the contrary, a major focus of the program is that the parents simply open up the home, allowing the children to have as free access to its ordinary living conditions as possible rather than restricting their training to special times or special kinds of educational learning toys. As Meyerhoff and White said in their September 1986 *Psychology Today* article, "Unlike the many 'infant stimulation' or 'superbaby' programs that have sprung up in recent years, the Missouri program focused on a comfortable, constructive style of parenting designed to make the early educational process enjoyable as well as effective rather than intensive and highly structured."

**Intelligence.** The most exciting recent development in the studies of intelligence was the "triarchal theory" of Yale University psychologist Robert Sternberg. The crux of his theory is the recognition of the existence of three different types of intelligence. The orthodox type, which Sternberg called componential, is based on analytic, critical thinking and is the type measured by most intelligence tests to yield the standard IQ. The second type, called experiential because it depends upon the innovative utilization of one's experiences, is concerned with creativity and insightful solutions to problems. The third type, called contextual because it is based on the effective manipulation of the environment, produces "street-smart" adjustments.

The relatively independent way in which these three essentially different types of intelligence develop makes it important that the functioning of the latter two, which are not measured by the orthodox intelligence test, be more generally recognized.

Sternberg's *Beyond IQ: A Triarchic Theory of Human Intelligence* (1985) and his *Intelligence Applied* (1986) provide detailed accounts of the triarchal theory and how it can be applied. A broader spectrum of contemporary perspectives on this topic can be found in some 1986 volumes edited by Sternberg and Douglas Detterman.

**Successful coping.** A number of indications of successful coping by handicapped persons were reported during the past year. For example, Australian psychologist Linda Viney studied more than 500 chronically ill hospital patients and found that their expressions of positive emotions and the accompanying maintenance of "psychological integrity" were highly correlated with satisfactory interpersonal relationships, as reflected by complimentary comments about the nurses. Viney concluded that hospital staff should be more vigorously encouraged to improve their relationships with individual patients.

Adjustment by mentally retarded persons was studied 40 years after initial diagnosis by a research group headed by California psychologist Robert Ross.

These researchers were able to locate 160 men and women who as children in San Francisco had IQ scores between 60 and 80. As adults, these persons still scored low on a standard intelligence test and did, of course, have some significant intellectual deficiencies. Nevertheless, they were found to have made, in the main, surprisingly good social and occupational adjustments. It was concluded that standard intelligence test scores alone provide an insufficient basis for the diagnosis of "retarded" because the demands of, and support from, the environment play so crucial a role in actual adjustments. This conclusion confirmed the interpersonal-relationship emphasis described in the previous paragraph, and the limitations of the standard IQ test are predictable on the basis of Sternberg's triarchal theory, described above.

A more dramatic instance of the overcoming of a disability was afforded by Donald Lyman in his book *Making the Words Stand Still: How to Rescue the Learning Disabled Child.* Lyman was, and still is, handicapped by what is now generally labeled as a Specific Learning Disability. He estimated in his book that between 10 million and 15 million otherwise relatively normal children have similar difficulty in the mastering of written language. His own struggle against this disability—culminating in a Ph.D. degree and a distinguished teaching career—offers much hope to similarly disabled children and their parents.

**Therapy.** One of the interesting developments in clinical psychology has been the resurgence of interest in "hypnotherapy," the use of hypnosis as a therapeutic treatment. This trend is part of a more general renewal of interest in hypnosis, an as yet poorly understood form of relaxation-induced suggestivity in which some dramatic behaviors can occur.

Within clinical psychology German-born psychotherapist Erika Fromm argued strongly for the greater use of hypnoanalysis. She stated that hypnosis offers a "road that goes down to the unconscious more steeply and much faster than psychoanalysis does." She also commented, "Had Freud used permissive hypnosis—which was not yet known in his time—I'm convinced that he'd never have given up hypnosis."

Directed dreaming is one technique that hypnoanalysis uses in common with psychoanalysis. But there are two other useful therapeutic techniques that are unique to hypnoanalysis: age regression and hypermnesia (the recapturing of an especially vivid memory).

The long, slow therapeutic process that is characteristic of most psychotherapies, and especially of orthodox psychoanalysis, has been the cause of growing discontent. Psychologist Kenneth Howard and associates of Northwestern University, Evanston, Ill., analyzed the case records of more than 2,400 clients who had been given various forms of psychotherapy. They found that half of these clients had shown marked improvement within the first eight sessions and that three-quarters of them had done so by the 26th session. Depressed persons were the quickest to improve, with anxiety cases next.

Some implications of this timely and suggestive study were encouraging. First, excessively protracted therapeutic sessions are not necessarily required for positive results. Second, it may be wise to consider changing the type of therapy, or at least the particular therapist, if some progress is not evident within a reasonable number of sessions. (*See* Feature Article: THE SCIENCE—AND ART—OF PSYCHOTHERAPY.)

**Psychophysiology.** Intensively studying 51 brain-damaged children, a West German research team found a relationship between the size of the brain injury and the detrimental effect on IQ; each 1% additional brain damage accounted for a decrease of approximately four points in the IQs of children aged five years or older. The generality of this relationship contrasts with the much more specific effects, depending on the location of the injury, in brain-damaged adults.

For the past decade the Type A personality pattern has been generally regarded as closely associated with a high risk of coronary heart disease. During recent months a team of researchers at Duke University Medical Center, Durham, N.C., found that the best indicator of heart disease is just one feature of the Type A syndrome: hostility. The features of impatience and competitiveness do not seem to be as important. When measured by a relatively simple questionnaire, hostility scores were clearly more highly predictive of actual coronary blockage than were the other standard Type A symptoms.

These results were corroborated by psychologists Ted Dembroski and James MacDougall of Eckerd College in Florida. The only Type A characteristic found to correlate with blockage of the coronary arteries was the potential for hostility. These researchers also found that keeping anger bottled up (''anger-in'' characteristic), not ordinarily a part of the Type A syndrome, predicted coronary blockage. However, letting anger out was also identified as a predictor of coronary blockage by psychologist Aron Siegman and his associates at the University of Maryland. Thus, anger along with hostility (which may be regarded as a more personally directed form of anger and aggression) seems to put people at high risk for heart disorders.

Some interesting and suggestive results on the problem of male competitiveness and dominance were recently reported by British endocrinologist W. N. Jeffcoate. In a small but nonetheless potentially important study, five British physicians were closely confined during a two-week boating holiday. They were (unobtrusively) observed by three women passengers, who assessed their social dominance.

The males with the highest dominance scores, as assessed by the women passengers, also had the highest testosterone levels when tested at the end of the holiday. This result confirmed earlier results from both monkey and human studies. But there was an additional, and quite unexpected, result: the dominant males also had higher prolactin levels. That result was perplexing because prolactin is associated with anxiety and tends to inhibit the sexual dominance that is produced by testosterone.

—Melvin H. Marx

**Developments in Europe.** In an attempt to remove the restrictions preventing psychologists and members of other professions from providing professional services in member nations of the European Communities other than in those in which the professional person trained, the EC Council of Ministers proposed a directive on a general system for the recognition of higher education diplomas awarded on completion of vocational courses of at least three years' duration. The directive would not become law until it was approved by the Council of Ministers.

In general, the intention to seek the mutual recognition of qualifications in psychology throughout the EC was welcomed by psychologists in the member nations. However, severe reservations were expressed about certain components of the proposed directive. Major differences in the ways psychologists are trained and in the content of the training were found to exist within the different countries of Europe. These disparities and the need for psychologists to be fluent in the language of the country in which they are to practice were proving to be major obstacles inhibiting the free movement of professional psychologists from one member nation to another. As discussion continued, it was becoming increasingly apparent that major revisions would be needed if the proposed directive was to provide a viable legislative framework.

Increasingly, psychologists in Europe were appreciating the need for the science of psychology to be applied in practical ways. Within the British Psychological Society special initiatives were started to promote research into the psychology of food consumption, health, and nutrition. A new Health Psychology Section of the society was formed, and a major position statement was being prepared on substance abuse, addressing the issues of drug addiction and related problems. These same topics and others, such as the need for human factors to be taken into account in the design and implementation of information technology systems, were discussed in several conferences in Europe.

—Colin V. Newman

# Space exploration

The accidental destruction of the U.S. space shuttle orbiter *Challenger* on Jan. 28, 1986, resulting in the deaths of all seven crew members, dominated the remainder of the year in space exploration in the United States. Not only were all shuttle missions canceled until at least 1988 but also the many probes and satellites that had been scheduled for launch from the shuttle orbiters were either postponed or eliminated entirely.

On a positive note, several space probes achieved close encounters with Halley's Comet and provided considerable data about its makeup. Voyager 2 flew past Uranus and made new discoveries about that planet. Also, the Soviet Union successfully launched a new space station and sent several spacecraft to dock with it.

## Manned flight

The year 1986 marked a period of transition for the U.S., Soviet, and European manned space flight programs. For the U.S. it was a year of frustration, anger, and sorrow in the wake of the *Challenger* accident. Problems with Titan and Delta rockets, coupled with the *Challenger* tragedy, pointed to a crisis in the U.S. space program. A larger crisis for Western space capabilities in general occurred with the failure of a European Ariane rocket and the subsequent grounding of that fleet in the spring of 1986. Thus, for four months during 1986 the West was completely without a launch capability. For the Soviet Union the transition was one of technological progression from its venerable Salyut series of space stations to the new Mir space station, more complex space operations, and commercial activities once the preserve of the West.

**Space shuttle.** The year began with ambitious plans to launch 15 shuttle flights, to send probes to Jupiter and the Sun, and to deploy the Hubble Space Telescope in orbit. But events of late 1985 carried over into January, and the U.S. National Aeronautics and Space Administration (NASA) found itself beginning the new year with its top official under indictment and its most immediate priority, the flight of Mission 61-C, frustrated again and again by launch delays. In early January NASA administrator James Beggs resigned in the face of charges that he had defrauded the government while an executive of the General Dynamics Corp.

During the same period, Mission 61-C endured seven postponements before finally being launched on January 12. Aboard were crew members Robert L. Gibson, Charles F. Bolden, Jr., George D. Nelson, Steven A. Hawley, Franklin R. Chang-Diaz (the first Hispanic-American to journey into space), pay-

load specialist Robert J. Cenker of RCA, and U.S. Rep. Bill Nelson (Dem., Fla.). Nelson was the second member of the U.S. Congress to fly aboard the shuttle, the first having been Sen. Jake Garn (Rep., Utah) in April 1985. The crew of the 61-C mission successfully deployed a communications satellite for RCA and operated the Materials Science Laboratory, an infrared imaging experiment, and 13 small, self-contained experiments known as Getaway Specials. The flight concluded on January 18, after three landing delays due to weather, with a problem-free touchdown at Edwards Air Force Base in California.

The next mission, 51-L, marked the first use of Pad B at Launch Complex 39 of the Kennedy Space Center. Mission 51-L was intended to carry into orbit the second Tracking and Data Relay Satellite and two experiments associated with the return of Halley's Comet. The mission carried added significance because it was to be the first flight of a private, nontechnical citizen, high-school teacher Sharon Christa McAuliffe of Concord, N.H. Other members of the crew were Francis R. Scobee, Michael J. Smith, Ellison S. Onizuka, Judith A. Resnik, Ronald E. McNair and Gregory B. Jarvis, a payload specialist for Hughes Aircraft Co.

The flight was postponed four times prior to the launch on January 28. When the launch did finally take place, tragedy struck and the U.S. space program was in crisis. Less than one second after the solid rocket boosters (SRBs) ignited, there were ominous indications of trouble, unseen by those on the ground or aboard the orbiter *Challenger*. Photographs and film analyzed after the accident showed prominent puffs of smoke—at first gray but becoming increasingly blacker—coming from the aft field joint on the right-hand SRB. This indicated to investigators that the joint was not sealing properly, and the color of the smoke puffs suggested that grease, joint insulation, and the rubber O-ring seals were being burned and eaten away by the hot gases within the booster. But even before the shuttle cleared the launch tower, residue from the burning propellants within the booster temporarily sealed the breach.

At 58 seconds into the flight, however, the seal was again breached, and a plume of flame began to leak through; it cascaded backward in the slipstream of the shuttle, setting up a blowtorch effect against the side of the large external fuel tank. At 72 seconds the lower strut linking the right-hand SRB and the tank broke loose, and the booster rotated about its upper attachment point, striking the tank and causing structural failure. When the tank came apart, the structural integrity of the entire vehicle was fatally compromised, and it broke into pieces. Fuel from the tank billowed out into a massive cloud and ignited, but the fireball itself was more an effect of *Challenger*'s destruction than its cause.

Severe aerodynamic loads broke the orbiter into several large identifiable pieces that emerged from the fireball; one of these was the crew compartment. After several months of study NASA was unable to say if the seven crew members were conscious as the crew cabin plunged 14,240 m (47,000 ft) into the Atlantic Ocean, although there were indications that such may have been the case for at least some of them.

The accident shocked the nation and threw NASA into the deepest crisis of its history. The event dominated the remainder of the year for the space agency and was listed by both United Press International and the Associated Press in December as the top news story of 1986. In the immediate aftermath of the accident, NASA began the largest air and sea salvage operation in history to recover wreckage in support of the investigation. A presidential commission, headed by former U.S. secretary of state William Rogers, was appointed to investigate the tragedy independently of NASA and in February determined that the agency's decision-making process was "flawed." Rear Adm. Richard H. Truly, a former astronaut, was appointed to head the shuttle program, and James C. Fletcher, administrator of NASA during the development of the shuttle in the early 1970s, was again named to the agency's top post in May. The directors of the three field centers responsible for manned space flight were replaced, and a series of management changes followed throughout the year.

As the Rogers Commission investigation unfolded, NASA's reputation for excellence lost much of its luster. A complicated management structure, bureaucratic handling of problems with the solid rockets, and questions about the design and development of the shuttle from the program's inception raised doubts in the minds of many and overshadowed the

*A presidential commission on the space shuttle* Challenger *accident, headed by former U.S. secretary of state William Rogers (front row, center), included former astronaut Neil Armstrong and astronaut Sally Ride (front, left and right).*

Timothy A. Murphy—U.S. News & World Report/Special Features

affairs of the agency. In June the Rogers Commission released its report and made nine major recommendations in such areas as design, safety, management, launch and landing escape options, independent oversight, and maintenance safeguards. In July NASA submitted a plan to U.S. Pres. Ronald Reagan for the implementation of all nine recommendations. Two task forces were set up to study NASA's management structure, and efforts to define future space flight programs were initiated on an agency-wide level. A new series of tests was begun on the SRBs, and contracts were awarded in September for the study of completely new, alternative booster designs. A space flight safety panel was formed to study new designs for crew escape, and NASA's safety and reliability organization was strengthened with an infusion of additional money and people. Management of the agency also was overhauled, with control of the shuttle and space station programs moved from the field centers back to a central authority at NASA headquarters in Washington, D.C.

While these internal actions were under way, other events of 1986 dramatically altered the nature and outlook of the U.S. manned space flight effort. A week after the *Challenger* accident, President Reagan pledged continued support for manned flight in his state of the union address and called for development of a "National Aerospace Plane." The craft, a combination air and space plane, would employ highly advanced propulsion and materials technology to achieve horizontal takeoff and single-stage flight to orbit, or it could be used within the atmosphere as a hypersonic transport plane. A joint program between NASA and the Department of Defense began with the goal of flight-testing a vehicle in the 1990s and beginning regular operations after the year 2000 (*see* Year in Review: DEFENSE RESEARCH). At the same time, NASA continued its own effort to design a more immediate successor to the space shuttle.

In April a U.S. Air Force Titan rocket exploded shortly after launch from Vandenberg Air Force Base in California. This was the second consecutive Titan failure in five months and prompted the Air Force to ground the Titan fleet. In early May a NASA Delta rocket went out of control shortly after launch and was destroyed. Because the Delta rocket had many similarities to another expendable booster, the Atlas Centaur, both rockets were taken out of service and the U.S. was left without a launch capability.

Congress urged NASA to fix the problems with the unmanned rockets and rely on them more in the future. As a result of this crisis in launch capability, national policy was changed in the U.S. in August. At that time President Reagan announced his intention to fund construction of a replacement orbiter for the *Challenger,* but he also prohibited NASA from engaging in any future commercial launch agreements

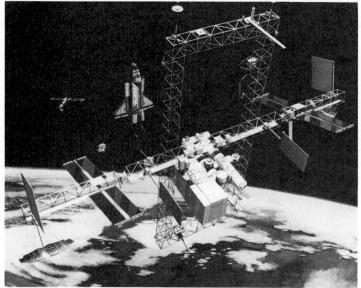

*Proposed United States space station (left) consists of a framework that supports resource modules and visiting spacecraft. Cutaway drawing (above) reveals the possible configuration of a laboratory module on the space station.*

for the shuttle. This implied a greater reliance on expendable rockets for launches of commercial payloads and more emphasis on government research and development payloads on the shuttle.

Also in 1986 a second presidential panel, the National Commission on Space, released a report detailing the possible space-faring efforts of the U.S. over the next 50 years. The commission recommended that the country seek low-cost access to near-Earth space and to the solar system, that the technology base of the U.S. be revitalized to support that effort, and that a large spaceport be built in orbit to establish what the commission called "a bridge between worlds." NASA was expected to release a detailed response to the report in mid-1987. In the meantime, the agency requested increased funding for efforts to spur the nation's technological development.

Work on NASA's other major project, the space station, became highly politicized during the past year as management changes took effect. Congressmen from Texas reacted strongly in July to NASA's plans to move part of the work on the station from the Johnson Space Center in Houston to the Marshall Space Flight Center in Huntsville, Ala. This prompted a review of the entire program and resulted in major redesigns of policy in regard to both hardware and management.

On the international front NASA reached agreements with Japan, Canada, and the European Space Agency (ESA) for their continued participation in the space station program. Japan agreed to study designs for a multipurpose research laboratory module. Canada worked on its designs for a servicing center consisting of manipulator arms that would help assemble and maintain the station. Europe continued its work on the design of an attached laboratory module and a free-flying unmanned platform to be launched into polar orbit. ESA and NASA also agreed to study a free-flying, man-tended platform that would fly in formation with the larger U.S. space station.

**Soviet manned flight.** While the West reeled from the *Challenger,* Titan, Delta, and Ariane failures, the Soviet Union began a new era of expanded space operations with the launch of the Mir ("Peace") space station in February. Mir, the third generation of Soviet space stations, featured six docking ports (compared with two on earlier Soviet stations), expanded living quarters, greater available power, and modernized research equipment. The station had a mass of 21 metric tons (46,295 lb) and was 13.13 m (43.08 ft) long and 4.2 m (13.78 ft) wide at its maximum diameter. The U.S.S.R. said that Mir would become the core of a larger, permanently manned orbital facility that would be augmented by the launch of specialized modules.

On March 13 Leonid Kizim and Vladimir Solovyev, carrying with them mementos in honor of the *Challenger* crew, were sent aloft aboard Soyuz T-15 to rendezvous with the new station and become its first occupants. They spent 53 days at Mir installing and adjusting equipment and bringing the complex to life. During their stay they were visited by two unmanned Progress cargo ships. One of those, Progress 26, delivered two tons of material, one-fourth of which was intended for installation on the Salyut 7 space station.

On May 5 Kizim and Solovyev separated from Mir aboard Soyuz T-15 and made a 3,000-km (1,860-mi) journey to Salyut 7, where they both had spent

*Carrying cosmonauts Vladimir Solovyev and Leonid Kizim, the Soyuz T-15 spacecraft is launched (left) by the Soviet Union in March 1986 to rendezvous with the new space station Mir (top right). Mir had more docking ports, larger living quarters, and greater available power than previous Soviet stations. Bottom right, Solovyev (left) and Kizim return to the Earth on July 16 after making the first trip between two orbiting vessels in history; they visited both Mir and an earlier station, Salyut 7.*

237 days in 1984. Salyut 7, workhorse of the Soviet program since 1982, had not been occupied since November 1985. It was the first journey between two orbiting vessels in space flight history, and analysts of the Soviet efforts predicted that it was a harbinger of things to come, with the Soviets planning "constellation operations" of several space platforms at once.

While the two cosmonauts were at Salyut 7, a new-generation Soyuz vehicle was launched and sent on an unmanned flight to Mir. The new vehicle, Soyuz TM, featured improved rendezvous and tracking equipment, updated propulsion and communications systems, increased cargo capacity, and a redesigned cockpit. The Soviets said that the unmanned tests were successful and that the Soyuz TM series would soon replace the older Soyuz T series. Soyuz TM separated from Mir on May 29 and landed successfully on the Earth on May 30.

On May 28 Kizim and Solovyev made a 3-hour 50-minute space walk outside Salyut 7 to retrieve experiments left there by a previous crew. On May

31 they again ventured outside for a five-hour space walk and erected a truss as part of a large-scale assembly program. The lattice framework was unfolded, erected, and attached to the hull of the space station.

The two cosmonauts left Salyut 7 on June 25 and arrived back at Mir on June 26. On July 7 Kizim became the first person to log a full year (366 days) in space. The cosmonauts left Mir in July and landed on July 16 near Arkalyk in the U.S.S.R.

On Feb. 5, 1987, cosmonauts Yuri Romanenko and Alexander Laveikin were launched to Mir aboard Soyuz TM-2 in the first manned use of the updated Soyuz vehicle. They were expected to stay in orbit for as long as 290 days, which would set a new endurance record.

**European manned flight.** The year was also one of transition for the 14 member nations of ESA. Ten of those countries agreed in 1986 to a formal program for the development of a European manned space flight capability. The agreement grew out of the French Hermes manned orbiter program, which

453

was conceived by the French CNES national space agency for launch aboard the Ariane 5 heavy booster.

Hermes was being designed for a variety of manned missions, including satellite servicing and Earth observation flights. As of 1987 ESA's plans called for the construction of two Hermes orbiters, expected to enter service in the mid-1990s.

During the year France conducted talks with the Soviet Union to discuss a design that would allow Hermes to dock with the Mir space station. The U.S. also indicated interest in 1986 in providing Hermes with the capability of docking with the U.S. station.

—Brian Welch

## Space probes

The loss of the space shuttle *Challenger* in January 1986 left the U.S. planetary exploration program in disarray. Europe, Japan, and the Soviet Union, however, forged ahead with probes to Halley's Comet and plans to sample the solar system.

Although the U.S. had failed to fund and launch a mission to Halley's Comet earlier in the decade, 1986 had promised to be bright for planetary exploration, with planned launches for the Galileo orbiter-and-probe to Jupiter and for the Ulysses International Solar Polar Mission. Also scheduled were two missions that, while not probes, would have aided in the exploration of the solar system: the ASTRO battery of three ultraviolet telescopes was to travel aboard the space shuttle in March as the international armada flew past Halley, and the Hubble Space Telescope, with five instruments to study the planets and stars, was to be launched in the fall.

*Challenger,* destroyed with its seven-person crew on January 28, carried a small retrievable satellite called Spartan Halley that would have looked at the comet shortly before its closest approach to the Sun. The disaster grounded the remaining three shuttles at least until early 1988 while a new booster design was developed. Unrelated accidents with expendable rockets and the increasing reliance on the shuttle as a launcher caused a crisis in the space community (see *Manned flight,* above).

Renewed emphasis on safety in the shuttle program led NASA to cancel the so-called Widebody Centaur, a shuttle-size version of the Centaur upper-stage rocket that had been in use since the 1960s. Problems with an all-solid Inertial Upper Stage rocket earlier in the shuttle program had prompted NASA to redesign Centaur for the shuttle so that it could launch both Galileo and Ulysses from the shuttle. Both spacecraft were to be aimed at Jupiter, a trip requiring a large change in velocity. Problems in building the upper stage and worries about dumping its volatile liquid oxygen and hydrogen propellant in an emergency raised doubts about the Cen-

taur's safety in the wake of the *Challenger* accident. Canceling Centaur effectively grounded both spacecraft—already delayed from early 1980s launches—and forced them into storage until the late 1980s.

Galileo was to be equipped with a sophisticated array of instruments to study Jupiter and its moons for almost two years. About a month before insertion into orbit around Jupiter, the spacecraft would release a probe that would enter the atmosphere to measure conditions down to a depth equivalent to ten times the pressure at sea level on Earth (the same as under 100 m [330 ft] of water).

Ulysses, designed and built by the European Space Agency, was to carry instruments to measure the solar wind and magnetic fields above the poles of the Sun. In order to do so it would use the intense gravitational field of Jupiter to execute a hairpin turn that would place it above the plane of the ecliptic (the plane of the Earth's orbit).

Galileo and Ulysses were scheduled to be launched from the space shuttle during 1989–90 by the solid-propellant Inertial Upper Stage but would detour to Venus to use its gravitational field. The Magellan also was scheduled to be launched in 1990 by a commercial version of the Inertial Upper Stage.

**Halley's Comet.** Five spacecraft from the U.S.S.R., ESA, and Japan's Institute of Space and Astronauti-

*Galileo orbiter-and-probe (envisioned in the drawing below) was designed to be launched from a space shuttle to investigate the atmosphere of Jupiter. After the* Challenger *accident, the probe was temporarily grounded.*

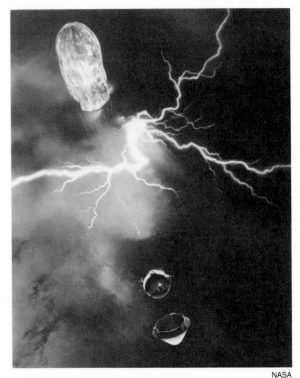

NASA

NASA/JPL

*Color composite of Uranus's moon Titania, taken by Voyager 2 from a distance of 480,000 kilometers (300,000 miles), shows evidence of impact scars and past geologic activity.*

cal Sciences flew past Halley's Comet during March 1986. The Soviet Vega 1 and 2 spacecraft, launched, respectively, on Dec. 15 and Dec. 21, 1984, first flew past Venus to deposit landers and balloon-borne observatories. Japan launched Sakigake (Pioneer) on Jan. 8, 1985, and Suisei (Comet) on Aug. 19, 1985. Europe's Giotto (named for a Florentine painter who depicted Halley's as the Star of Bethlehem) was launched on July 2, 1985. The missions were timed to fly quickly past Halley as it rose through the plane of the ecliptic. Halley's retrograde (clockwise), sharply inclined orbit demands large expenditures of energy for a slow flyby like that of Voyager at Uranus. A ballistic intercept without leaving the plane of the ecliptic was the easiest way to get a close look at the comet.

The first close encounter was achieved by Vega 1 at 8,889 km on March 6, 1986, followed by Vega 2 at 8,030 km on March 9. (A kilometer is about 0.62 mi.) Giotto dived through the tail and behind the nucleus on March 13 within 600 km. The Japanese probes passed at greater distances, Suisei at 151,-000 km on March 8 and Sakigake at 6,990,000 km on March 11.

Detailed reports in *Nature* magazine on May 15 and elsewhere released many of the preliminary findings of the various Halley's science teams. Uppermost in everyone's mind was the shape and size of the nucleus, enshrouded in a ghostly show of illuminated water vapor and gas for centuries. It appeared to have a double-lobed shape, 7.5 × 7.5 × 14 km in size with a rough, cratered terrain and at least one mountain. At least four bright spots, scalloped features resembling craters on the order of 800 m wide and a few hundred meters deep, were associated with gases spewing from inside the comet. The surface, which reflected only 4% of the light that struck it, seemed to be insulated with carbon dust.

Following the unexpected survival of Giotto—contact was lost for half an hour during passage through the comet tail—ESA scientists were considering the possibility of retargeting it for an encounter with a second comet, Grigg-Skjellurup, in July 1992.

**Uranus.** Detailed analysis of Uranus, the outermost planet explored by humans, started soon after Voyager 2 flew by it on Jan. 24, 1986. Uranus was the first of the planets to be discovered by telescope. The inner six were known to the ancients.

One discovery by the space probe was that the planet's methane atmosphere may cover an 8,000-km-deep ocean of superheated water surrounding a rocky core about the size of the Earth. The ocean might have been generated by countless collisions with comets since the planet formed.

Radio signals from the planet were not detected until a few days before the closest encounter because the axis of the planet's magnetic field is skewed 55° from the axis of rotation, itself almost parallel to the orbital plane. One intriguing possibility is that the magnetic pole is reversing, something never observed elsewhere (although geologic evidence shows that it has happened on Earth). Because of this sideways tilt the geographic north pole was in darkness as Voyager approached the sunlit south pole. The winds, at up to 362.5 km/h, blew in the direction of rotation rather than opposite to it.

The number of rings known to circle the planet increased to about 100, most of them as dark as the carbon of which they are believed to consist and many existing only as partial arcs. The lack of fine dust particles indicates that the rings have been cleaned up and may exist only for 100 million years before being destroyed by drag and gravity.

Ten new moons were discovered by Voyager as it flew through the Uranian system. Their sizes ranged down to a diameter of 40 km, in contrast to 1,610 km for Uranus's largest moon, the long-known Titania. Six of the newly discovered satellites orbit at about the same altitude, implying a common origin, perhaps in the breakup of an older moon.

The four major moons, all known long before the Voyager encounter, were found to be quite varied rather than being identical iceballs. Oberon has a 20-km mountain and escarpments, indicating strong volcanic activity. Titania's surface bore similar evidence. Umbriel is rich in ice but uniformly dark, suggesting that it is covered with debris. Ariel has mountains and cliffs but also smooth valley floors that may have been flattened by tidal heating or filled with water-ammonia ice. And a smaller moon, Miranda, with its curious plowed-field features—named Trapezoid, Ridged Ovoid, and Banded Ovoid—may have been resculpted several times by collisions with objects capable of making craters almost the size of a small moon.

A planned 1987 firing of Voyager's onboard thrusters was adjusted to retarget its August 1989 flyby of Neptune from a miss of 1,280 km to 4,800 km to avoid possible ring debris and radiation belts. Voyager would fly over Neptune's north pole and then past its moon Triton, which might have lakes of liquid nitrogen.

**Continuing studies.** Teams analyzing data from two French-built science balloons released into the atmosphere of Venus by the Vega probes reported new findings about the cloud-covered planet. The balloons drifted for 11,000 km at about 7° north and south of the planet's equator from night into day for 46 hours before their batteries faded.

Data indicate that Venus has planet-wide vertical winds that move at 2 to 4 km/h. When one balloon passed 50 km above Aphrodite, a 5-km-high mountain, the winds gusted to 11 km/h, indicating that Venus, like the Earth, has planetary waves in the atmosphere caused by surface features. Temperature differences of 6.5° C (11.7° F) between the two probes suggested that there are large eddies in the atmosphere at the equator. The balloon instruments also saw no breaks in the clouds and detected no lightning. The latter observation supported a 1986 challenge to the 1978 report that lightning-related radio noise had been detected by the Pioneer Venus Orbiter.

A four-year study of Viking Orbiter images of Mars indicated that the planet's surface was shaped by volcanic activity and flowing water, and that enough water remains locked in the crust to flood the planet to a depth of 300 m (990 ft). Evidence of lakes that were once five kilometers deep also was found.

**Future missions.** Even as the data from the Halley's probes were being assessed, plans were being made for several missions ranging from modest to ambitious. A team of principal investigators was selected for the U.S. Mars Observer (earlier called the Mars Geochemical/Climatology Observer). The new Observer series of spacecraft was intended to provide low-cost missions to the planets by adapting existing spacecraft designs and undertaking narrow lines of investigation. In the case of the Mars Observer, an RCA Satcom communications satellite would be used. Instruments selected for the spacecraft included infrared and visible light sensors to scan the surface and atmosphere of the planet. A high-resolution mapping camera had not been planned for the spacecraft but was tentatively selected because of its innovative design. It would use a reflector telescope with a composite structure based on the design of the Hubble Space Telescope. Because imaging instruments demand large quantities of power and transmission bandwidth, the camera, with a resolution of one meter (3.3 ft), would view selected targets rather than map indiscriminately.

The Mars Observer was scheduled to be launched in 1990 and to orbit Mars at an altitude of 361 km. However, NASA delayed the launch until 1992 for budgetary reasons.

NASA also selected investigators for a Comet Ren-dezvous/Asteroid Flyby mission, dubbed CRAF, that would be the first of the new Mariner Mark II series of spacecraft. Several comets and asteroids were selected as targets but then were discarded when the program was not included in new budget plans. NASA had hoped to include CRAF in its 1988 budget plan. That would have allowed a September 1992 launch and flybys of asteroids Malautura and Hestia in 1993 and 1995, respectively, followed by a long-term rendezvous from December 1996 to December 1999 with comet Tempel 2.

The Mars Observer and CRAF originated in a core program recommended in 1982 by NASA's Solar System Exploration Committee (SSEC) in its report, "Planetary Exploration Through Year 2000." In 1986 "An Augmented Program" report was released. At its heart was the collection of samples of material from Mars and from a comet by means of missions that easily would cost $2 billion or more.

"The collection and return of samples from other worlds by automated spacecraft for analysis in terrestrial laboratories is potentially the most powerful technique for extending our understanding of the solid bodies in the solar system: inner planets, asteroids, and comets," the SSEC wrote. The Soviet Union performed such missions, on a limited level, with its Luna spacecraft in the 1970s. Highly sophisticated spacecraft employing advanced automation and other technologies would have to be built for gathering a variety of scientifically valuable samples from Mars and a comet.

For the Mars Surface Sample Return mission the space shuttle would launch a spacecraft weighing about 9,000 kg (20,000 lb). A second shuttle would launch the orbital transfer vehicle that would fire the probe to Mars. For a November 1996 launch (now seen as unlikely) the probe would arrive at Mars in September 1997. The entire spacecraft would enter the atmosphere of Mars, using it as a brake to reduce the weight required for retrorockets, and then skip back out to orbit. After final mapping the lander would be deployed to touch down on the planet's surface in a fashion similar to that of the Viking landers in 1976. A remote-control rover would be deployed to spend the next few months wandering within a 100-m radius of the lander.

Through the distant senses of the rover's instruments and stereo cameras, scientists on Earth would examine soil and rock and select samples, each weighing a few grams. About October 1998 the return capsule would be boosted to orbit, where it would dock with the orbiter and be returned to Earth orbit in September 1999. The 5 kg (11 lb) of samples would be placed in a quarantine laboratory for initial examination. This would reduce the chance of releasing Martian organisms into the Earth's environment. Meanwhile, the rover would be

*Pioneer 9, launched into solar orbit on Nov. 9, 1968, was given up for dead in March 1987, about four years after it was last heard from. The spacecraft had been designed for a lifetime of six months.*

sent on a wider ranging, less cautious exploration of the planet, perhaps to pick up samples for a second probe a few years later.

A Comet Nucleus Sample Return would resemble the Mars mission in many respects but would have its own technical challenges. It would require more energy to start the journey and travel to the comet. Because comets are so small and are made up largely of frozen liquids and gases, the landing would resemble a docking with another spacecraft. At touchdown the lander would have to anchor itself to the surface in some manner. But even the makeup of the surface is unknown and could range from glacial ice to soft snow, the SSEC noted. Samples would be gathered by drilling a core sampler to a depth of one meter. Preserving the sample in its natural state would also be a challenge, since melting would mix whatever layering might be present. The need to provide protection from dust and gas jets emanating from the comet would also complicate the spacecraft designer's job.

The U.S.S.R., meanwhile, revealed many details of its future probes. The mission to Mars and its satellite Phobos would feature a unique pair of instruments that would allow direct sampling of the chemical makeup of the asteroid-like moon. A laser would fire from a distance of 50 m (165 ft) every five to ten seconds during the 15-minute encounter.

Small bits of Phobos would be vaporized by the powerful light (equivalent to one billion watts per sq cm) and analyzed by a Bulgarian mass spectrometer. A French instrument would fire an ion beam at the surface and analyze the secondary ions that are scattered back to the spacecraft. A small "hopper lander" carrying an X-ray fluorescence spectrometer also would touch down on Phobos and gently skip about the surface to study different sites. The Soviets were also studying the possibility of retargeting one of the spacecraft to study the Martian moon Deimos as well.

A tentative accord was struck by the United States and the Soviet Union to renew cooperation in the space sciences. The agreement, born of the Apollo-Soyuz mission in 1976, had been allowed to lapse by the U.S. in 1982 as a sign of displeasure over Soviet pressure on Poland. Renewal was stymied by Soviet insistence that the U.S. stop its Strategic Defensive Initiative program as a condition for any joint venture. Cooperation continued, though, on a low-key basis and was renewed through the Inter-Agency Consultative Group, which coordinated the Halley observations.

The new general agreement between the U.S. and U.S.S.R. called for cooperation in several areas, including the joint selection of landing sites on Mars and the sharing of data from Venus, Mars, and comet missions. A Soviet invitation to participate in a Mars Surface Sample Return mission, planned for a 1996 launch, was declined because the U.S. had no such project approved. However, each nation agreed to add coinvestigators from the other nation to its own Mars probes.

The Earth's closest planetary neighbor was not being ignored. The Soviets reported plans for a Polar Lunar Orbiter mission. To be launched in 1991, it would carry double the payload of a mission the U.S. had tried to start for several years. The spacecraft would be equipped with mapping and spectrometer instruments to study the makeup of the Moon's surface.

ESA was considering a Saturn orbiter/Titan probe mission, called Cassini, which it might undertake with the U.S., and the Comet Atmosphere Earth Sample Return (CAESAR) mission. Perhaps the most ambitious mission yet proposed was called TAU for Thousand Astronomical Units (the distance from Earth to the Sun is one astronomical unit, or 150 million km), suggested by a team at the Jet Propulsion Laboratory. This would be a 50-year deep-space probe to the edge of the solar system, where billions of comets are believed to orbit the Sun in the so-called Oort Cloud.

—Dave Dooling

*See also* Feature Articles: SHIPS TO THE STARS; EUROPE'S GROWING POWER IN SPACE.

# Transportation

Continued sharp competition during the past year for both freight and passenger traffic—in an environment of lessening regulation—had a dual effect on research and development activity. The need for greater productivity stimulated more interest in technological innovation, but lower profit margins were forcing cuts in expenses. Also, the U.S. government's aggressive efforts to reduce the huge annual budget deficits made it difficult to maintain current levels of spending on research and development.

**Intermodal transport.** The trend toward intermodal transport—joint movements by two or more different modes—continued, spurred by railroad movement of double-stacked ship containers (one on top of the other). The railroad industry viewed merchandise intermodal traffic as its major growth market in the immediate future because of steadily declining bulk traffic. In fact, eight of the ten concepts under study for futuristic "integral trains" were intermodal: four to move containers, three to move truck trailers, and one to move interchangeable highway/rail trailers.

The last concept was not new because the Road-Railer had long been under development. The interchangeable units—which can use either rubber-tired trailer wheels for highway travel or train wheels for rail movements—were operated between a number of cities during the past year. Each unit cost about $40,000, needed only one set of interchangeable wheels, and was linked directly with another Road-Railer for integrated rail hauls. The transition from rail to highway, or vice versa, required only four minutes through use of a compressed-air system. A recent change permitted the heavy rail wheel carriage to be detached for more economical highway operations.

The operational tests were made possible by an agreement with rail unions to permit a two-man crew (engineer and conductor), no caboose, and extended running (operation without the distance limits prescribed in union work rules). A spokesman for the Norfolk Southern Corp., which operated RoadRailer trains between Detroit and St. Louis, Mo., noted that their use resulted in lower transportation costs, less cargo damage, greater speeds, and less expensive transfer facilities. More recent operations were with a 28-unit RoadRailer train from Detroit to Kansas City, Mo., hauling General Motors Corp. auto parts over Conrail and Burlington Northern tracks. If the 18-hour one-way time could be maintained, the test could become a regular run, a Burlington Northern spokesman stated.

Growing concern about international terrorism and drug smuggling was having a negative impact on intermodal container movements that must pass through customs. Proper examinations of sealed containers are not possible without highly sophisticated screening equipment; thus, slow, personal inspections could be made of only a selected number of the many thousands of containers moving in foreign trade. Three companies—Bechtel National, Varian Associates, and American Science and Engineering—joined in developing a high-tech device that could rapidly screen fully enclosed and sealed cargo in containers. It was capable of screening cargo to detect hidden contraband such as explosives, drugs, and weapons. Bechtel claimed that the system could screen 85 air cargo containers an hour.

**Air transport.** While the historic flight of the small, lightweight *Voyager* nonstop around the world did not represent any major technological breakthroughs for commercial air transport, it clearly demonstrated the strength and durability of light, all-composite aircraft structures. The graphite-composite aircraft's 40,244-km (1 km = 0.62 mi) flight encountered without mishap a number of extreme weather conditions, including severe turbulence. The flight also illustrated the value of the use of satellite weather data, which enabled the craft to fly around or over the most dangerous conditions, including Typhoon Marge. Such data also enabled *Voyager* to maximize tail winds, which helped save fuel and thus shortened the trip by a full day.

The aviation industry continued to expand its use of automation and computerization in virtually every area: aircraft construction, engines, reservations,

*The lightweight experimental aircraft* Voyager *prepares to land at Edwards Air Force Base in California in December 1986, becoming the first plane to circle the Earth nonstop without refueling.*

458

*Prototype fuel-efficient propfan engine is tested on a Boeing 727 (left) for possible use on Boeing's new-generation B-7J7 airliner. CATIA computer system (right), which uses a three-dimensional model, is being used in the designing of the 7J7.*

airport facilities, and air traffic control. For example, United Air Lines was spending $1 billion to expand and further automate its Apollo computer reservations system. The advanced "Enterprise" system, to be installed by mid-1987, was designed to simplify an agent's task in obtaining ticketing and related data from Apollo. In regard to aircraft design and construction, Boeing Co. was seeking to utilize a system called CATIA (computer-graphics-aided three-dimensional interactive applications) in its automated designing of a new-generation, 150-passenger transport, the B-7J7. The system, developed by Dassault-Breguet of France and marketed in the U.S. by the IBM Corp., allowed computer-aided designing in a three-dimensional mode. Boeing stressed the need to develop an "electronic work statement," a fully computerized document outlining the many functions involved in the aircraft's design and production—a costly process that at present was labor intensive and paper intensive. Another expensive problem was created by the great variation in aircraft configurations demanded by airlines, which the new system could ease by automating the earlier phases of the program.

The 7J7 would also be unique in another way, assuming that Boeing carried out plans to use prop-fan propulsion (ultrahigh-bypass engines driving counter-rotating propellers). This was just one of several programs under way to develop fuel-saving propeller engines. The British Aerospace Advanced Turboprop (ATP) 65-passenger transport, powered by two six-bladed Pratt & Whitney of Canada turboprop engines, began flight tests. Lockheed Corp.

announced plans for in-flight tests in April 1987 of a new, fuel-efficient propfan, which it described as "probably the best new transport technology to come along this decade." Lockheed claimed that the new engines, to be in commercial use by early 1992, would use half as much fuel as a comparable B-727 and 20% less than the most fuel-efficent transports of 1986, such as the B-757.

The propfan project of General Electric Co. appeared to be the farthest along in development, with flight tests already performed as one of three engines on a B-727 test aircraft. This design used an unducted fan engine consisting of two rows of counter-rotating curved blades; during its first tests it performed without cracking or other major problems. Reduction of normally high propeller noise, a major reason for the demise of propeller engines, and of vibration were the biggest challenges facing the new technology. Both the Lockheed and General Electric projects were being financed in part by the U.S. National Aeronautics and Space Administration (NASA).

The roadblock to commercial helicopter service, its high cost, could be overcome if a joint European project proved successful. Aircraft manufacturers from five European nations (France, Great Britain, West Germany, Italy, and Spain) joined, with their governments' approval, in developing a European Future Advanced Rotorcraft (Eurofar) able to carry 25 passengers at speeds in excess of 483 km/h for distances up to 965 km. Utilizing two 9.9-m (32.8-ft)-diameter rotors—one on each end of the aircraft's wing—the vehicle would take off and land

United Technologies/Sikorsky Aircraft

*Artist's drawing shows an aircraft with an X-wing that can operate as a rotor for vertical takeoff and landing (VTOL) and at speeds up to 370 kilometers (230 miles) per hour. At that speed the wing would be stopped from rotating and become fixed for speeds up to 740 kilometers (460 miles) per hour.*

from downtown heliports like a helicopter and then would make the transition to winged flight for high-speed cruising. Following a $45 million study of tilt-rotor technology, the manufacturers planned to build a test aircraft for a first flight in 1991 or 1992. The goal was to cut direct operating cost per hour to about 84% of that for a helicopter, which would then become only 42% because of a doubling of operating speed and, thus, effective payload. Use of light, all-composite airframes and wings to reduce weight, plus active controls and advanced electronics, should help meet the technology problems, but the obstacles could include market acceptance and the availability of in-city heliports.

A long-time air technology goal of achieving very high-speed horizontal flight in vertical takeoff and landing (VTOL) aircraft might be reached by the end of 1987 if a four-phase project of NASA and Sikorsky Aircraft Co. proved successful. The concept called for the use of an innovative X-wing that operates as a rotor for takeoff/landing and speeds up to about 370 km/h, at which time it is stopped in flight for use as fixed wings for speeds up to 740 km/h. The X-wing provides lift by blowing air through slots in the leading and trailing edges of the wide blades, which become fixed at a 45° angle from forward flight.

Two sets of engines were to be used in the initial tests of the VTOL, one for the X-wing and the other for horizontal flight. The flight tests' four phases would include: (1) normal flight with supporting fixed wings and then with the X-wing mounted but not used; (2) full operation of the X-wing blowing systems in fixed position in horizontal flight; (3) ground testing of the X-wing in rotary mode; and (4) flights during which conversions would be made between the rotary and horizontal modes.

**Pipelines.** The petroleum-pipeline industry, al-

ready highly automated and computerized, continued in that direction during the past year—with emphasis on the use of so-called lap-top computers. The major carriers initially had stressed the use of large mainframe computers at company headquarters for overall automated operational control. This was followed by the use of supplemental and smaller "desktop" computers at the district station level as the key to a supervisory control and data acquisition (SCADA) system. The latest step involved the use of very small computers; it was made possible by the sharp increases in the power, speed, and memory capacities of these machines.

*Univeyor conveyor system, shown being assembled at an FMC Corp. plant in Florida, is designed to move objects longitudinally, laterally, and circularly more efficiently than other loaders now in use.*

AP/Wide World

The small, light computers could be transported easily at the field level and could be used to replace many manual procedures. They also replaced the former extensive use of standard U.S. mail and high-cost express transmissions of data from the field to home and district offices. An example was the storing and processing of tank and meter data by field inspectors and their rapid and reliable transmission via any field-located telephone jack. Crude oil inputs from widely dispersed locations were being measured and evaluated by "gaugers," which now were equipped with the tiny lap-top computers that stored and processed the data as well as making checks on their validity—a step formerly done only at the home office. These small computers were also being used to expedite scheduling, monitor pump and compressor station facilities, analyze tank farm operations, and enhance both leak detection and corrosion monitoring.

The Shell Development Co. introduced a system to measure continuously and automatically the full sediment and water (S and W) content of streams of crude oil. Sizable quantities of S and W can be costly if not measured, because they otherwise would be paid for as oil.

Colonial Pipeline Co. developed a new information system to permit rapid and continuous tracking of shipments. The firm transported 50 different classes of refined petroleum products over its 8,470-km system from refineries in Texas, Louisiana, Mississippi, and Alabama to terminals in 13 states and the District of Columbia. At any given time more than 70 shippers were "active" on Colonial's system. The communications network included 250 video terminals and nine dial-in lines for shipper use. Each shipper had three primary telephone numbers to the computer, each of which automatically tried three numbers before giving a busy signal.

The Colonial system provided shippers with detailed information in three general areas: nominations (shipper requests for pipeline space to move a product), which advised where the shipment would be received and delivered as well as all parties involved; schedules, which showed arrival and departure times for shipments; and revenue accounting, which provided shippers with information regarding their inventory on Colonial's system for both pipelines and tank farms.

**Highway transport.** The potential of computerization appeared ready in 1986 to be exploited to the fullest by the U.S. trucking industry. One innovative development was vehicle tracking, which enabled the company's home base to be aware of the location of all its motor vehicles at all times. United Parcel Service (UPS) of Greenwich, Conn., the nation's largest trucking firm, announced plans to buy II Morrow, Inc., of Salem, Ore., for $15.3 million. The major objective was to utilize II Morrow's already proven vehicle-locating-and-tracking system.

The II Morrow system was linked to Loran C satellite transmitting stations maintained by the U.S. Coast Guard. Each truck was fitted with a receiver that picked up Loran C data and then automatically radioed this information back to the home base, where it was transferred to a computer screen. The computer system had separate chips for the display of different maps, each one for a specific geographic area covered by the company's operations. Signals of different colors indicated on the screen whether a vehicle was on its way to a job or returning, whether it was parked, or whether it was facing an emergency (flashing red light); all of these displays were controlled by the driver, who merely pressed the appropriate button on a transmitter in the cab. No voice communication was required.

UPS, which operated about 60,000 trucks throughout the U.S., planned to install the devices on a graduated basis. II Morrow was expected to continue to provide similar tracking systems for the aviation and maritime industries.

The Federal Highway Administration began efforts to improve truck safety by means of a newly developed information-exchange system called Safetynet. To be used by both federal and state governments, the system would feed data developed by the latter, using standardized computer programs, into a national motor carrier safety data base. The data would be collected from roadside inspections, federal safety audits, accident statistics, and, later, safety-management audits. Federal funding was provided to help finance the program.

Noting their use in most European countries, the Insurance Institute for Highway Safety (IIHS) urged the Federal Highway Administration to require on-board automatic records systems (black boxes) on all large trucks. The purpose would be to record, with tachographs, such data as the truck's driving time, vehicle speed, distance traveled, and rest breaks. IIHS claimed that the present system—the use of logbooks written by drivers—was too easy to falsify, especially in regard to whether drivers were complying with the ten-hour-a-day driving limit. IIHS cited a study by the American Automobile Association showing that 41% of all heavy-truck accidents involved overworked truck drivers, with one of every three drivers violating the daily driving limit.

It appeared that the use of front brakes on the steering axles of tractor trailers in the U.S. would soon be mandated, despite opposition from many drivers who said that such brakes tended to lock, thus reducing control and increasing the possibility of jackknifing. While U.S. truck manufacturers had been required to build front brakes into such trucks since 1980, the Bureau of Motor Carrier Safety

(BMCS) had permitted carriers to remove them. The U.S. Congress directed the Federal Highway Administration to close the loophole. Subsequent demonstrations by the BMCS, using combination trucks in a wide range of configurations and on both dry and wet pavements, clearly showed that front-wheel braking helped stop trucks in shorter distances and with better control.

The fear of locking brakes resulted in the development of new antilock technology in the U.K. While drivers of large trucks had been using a load-sensing device, which mechanically proportions braking on the various axles to the load imposed on them, this did not prevent brake locking. One answer was the use of a new system called SkidChek, produced by the British firm Lucas Girling. The system was capable, proponents claimed, of replacing load sensing. SkidChek could electronically sense the speed of the wheel and then, just before the time that brake locking would occur, provide data to the black box, which in turn would instantly reduce the air pressure in the brake chamber. The major drawbacks to SkidChek were the cost—$600 to $1,125 per axle—and the need for sophisticated maintenance.

P.*I.*E. Nationwide, Inc., of Jacksonville, Fla., reported that it had developed the trucking industry's first electronic bill-of-lading transmission system that was capable of being operated with a personal computer. Called the Shipmaster, it performed transactions that previously could be handled only by mainframe computers. P.*I.*E. also used the system to process bills of lading for shippers. Other services included rate quotations, shipment tracing, and actual preparation of bills of lading.

**Railroad transport.** The two major programs that U.S. railroads hoped would achieve great techno-logical leaps forward—integral trains and advanced train control—progressed during the year but did so more slowly than had been expected because of both traffic and financial constraints. The Association of American Railroads began evaluation of some of the ten concepts of high-productivity integral trains proposed by manufacturers, most of whom were trying to gain acceptance for their design by such means as cutting train weight through the use of lightweight materials, improving suspension and braking systems, and distributing locomotive power more evenly. The overall goal was to reduce operating costs by up to 35% for bulk service and 50% for intermodal service.

Greater progress was reported on the Advanced Train Control System (ATCS), which was under development by U.S. and Canadian railroads. ATCS would offer "intelligent trains" capable of being operated at maximum efficiency because of up-to-the-minute data access through use of a combination of transponders (radio or radar sets that receive designated signals and then emit signals of their own for purposes of identification and location of objects) located along the track and interrogators on locomotives to read their coded messages. The data would then be fed into onboard computers that already contained detailed information regarding the physical characteristics of the route, speed restrictions, location of work gangs, etc. Thus, the engineer could be warned of dangers of delays ahead, and the computer, if necessary, would reduce the throttle setting and apply the brakes. The Union Pacific Railroad began an operation test of the ATCS on its North Platte subdivision in Nebraska.

The partially successful efforts of U.S. railroads to eliminate cabooses at the ends of freight trains

*Pres. François Mitterrand of France and British Prime Minister Margaret Thatcher meet in Canterbury, England, on Feb. 12, 1986, to sign the treaty governing the operation of a tunnel railway system across the English Channel between Cheriton, near Folkestone, England, and Fréthun, near Calais, France.*

were given another boost when the Federal Railroad Administration (FRA) formally approved new rules allowing the use of end-of-train telemetry devices as an alternative. The FRA said that the devices, which also contained automated warning lights, should be capable of initiating an emergency brake application and informing the train engineer about the status of the train's air-brake system throughout the trip. The Canadian Transport Commission authorized the Quebec North Shore & Labrador Railway to use the devices in its limited market area but as of early 1987 had not given the Canadian National and CP Rail carriers authority to eliminate their cabooses and substitute the rear-of-train devices.

The Association of American Railroads announced that the railroad industry could now obtain a rail with a service life 2.7 times longer than the standard carbon rail. The head-hardened rail utilized technology developed by the Broken Hill Proprietary Co. of Whyalla, Australia, and was designed for long life in high-wear operations (heavy loads and curves). The head-hardening process was described as virtually automatic, with "the head of the rail heat-treated by a two stage controlled induction heating process, followed by accelerated cooling with air quench that results in the formation of a fine pearlitic microstructure that is superior to others for wear resistance."

Continued availability of low-cost diesel fuel discouraged rail investment in advanced locomotives utilizing other forms of energy. A new U.S. Department of Energy study said that modification of diesel engines to burn coal slurry (a mixture of coal particles and water) appeared to offer the best opportunities for railroads to return to coal for powering trains when oil prices rose.

The Burlington Northern Railroad successfully tested a locomotive powered by natural gas in a 214-km haul of a 29-car general freight train. The test engine employed a single control to burn either diesel fuel for lower speeds or natural gas for higher speeds. The combustion system involved injecting the compressed, but not liquefied, gas (methane) into the cylinder during a portion of the cycle when both the intake and exhaust ports were closed. A small amount of diesel fuel was also injected to ignite the mixture. A one-year service evaluation was planned, subject to approval by the Federal Railroad Administration.

Greater operational and pricing freedom made possible by deregulation might give the TankTrain its long-needed marketing boost. The 15-year-old concept utilized an interlocking hosing system that enabled an integrated train of special GATX Leasing Corp. tank cars to be quickly loaded and unloaded at a single point. Already used to a limited extent on hauls from 160 km to more than 1,600 km in carrying liquids such as crude oil, petroleum products, nitrogen

fertilizer solution, and superphosphoric acid, GATX foresaw its use for just about any liquid commodity, including petroleum chemicals and food products.

The high cost of breaking up old freight cars for reuse of parts and sale of the remainder as scrap was sharply reduced by the use of a machine called EGOR, for Efficiency on the Go for Reclamation. According to Conrail, 38 people previously had been needed to cut up surplus boxcars as well as 70-ton hopper and gondola cars; however, only 8 were needed with EGOR. The machine contained a huge shear to cut up the cars and a grapple to move the parts for either reuse or scrapping. Both were mounted on construction equipment. Previously the cars had been lifted by a gantry crane for removal of parts by blowtorches, a method that often resulted in injury from falling pieces. Savings in labor costs approached $1 million a year.

**Water transport.** Research and development programs relating to ocean transportation were being stretched out or phased out because of the stringent cost-saving measures required as a result of the poor market conditions. On the other hand, such conditions also led to greater reliance on automation and computerization when they could improve efficiency and thus reduce costs.

Det Norske Veritas, the Norwegian ship classification society that certified seaworthiness and technical standards of vessels, claimed that within

*Unmanned motor car is tested near Tokyo. Suspended by 12 semiconductors about ten centimeters (four inches) above its "track," the car can attain a speed of 420 kilometers (260 miles) per hour.*

AFP photo

three years it would be technically possible to man medium-sized bulk carriers ranging from 8,000 to 10,000 tons deadweight with only six men: one master, two mates, two engineers, and one cook/general assistant. This would be a dramatic decline from the average crew of 36 persons in 1950 and 13 in 1987. These reductions were possible mostly because of automated operations, such as an unmanned engine room.

Sea-Land Corp. unveiled what it claimed to be the container shipping industry's first data-communication link that would allow shippers to track their export/import shipments by direct access to the carrier's computer network. Called the Sea-Trac System, it could provide such data from the carrier's worldwide intermodal ship/rail/truck network as vessel schedules, bookings, cargo tracking, documentation, teletype transmission, and immediate hot-line assistance.

Ship icebreaking technology first used in the salt water of the Baltic Sea was successfully tested in the fresh water of the Great Lakes by the Finnish-flag vessel *Kiisla*. The ship utilized two giant air compressors, called bubblers, that were able to emit streams of air against the ice surrounding a ship in sufficient force to either push the ice away or, if this was not possible, "lubricate" the ice sufficiently for a ship to slide through it. The captain of the vessel said the compressors were used only when the ship was in danger of getting stuck. The purpose of the trial was to enable Sun Chemical Co. of Canada to provide year-round water-transport movements of petrochemicals from Sarnia, Ont., to Chicago. In clear waters the trip would take about 36 hours, but another 14 hours were required in winter ice conditions. The established technology was called a gamble in this instance because freshwater ice is more difficult to break through than saltwater ice and also refreezes more quickly.

Two scientists at the U.S. National Oceanic and Atmospheric Administration and Northern Technical Services of Anchorage, Alaska, developed new charts to help ocean vessels determine when icing conditions were becoming hazardous. The charts, called nomograms, were developed following a five-year study of 85 severe icing incidents during that period. The study showed that ice can accumulate up to three times faster than was previously believed, with a buildup of more than three-fourths of an inch per hour in severe conditions. This causes a rapid increase in topside weight that makes a vessel top-heavy and susceptible to overturning in rough seas— as often had happened with small craft. The new charts would provide early warnings, giving a ship's captain advance notice to seek shelter or divert the vessel to a safer route.

—Frank A. Smith

# U.S. science policy

Looking back over the year past, the editors of the British magazine *New Scientist* asked plaintively: "Was there ever a worse year for science and technology than 1986?" They ticked off the evidence. The *Challenger* space shuttle disaster in January marked the "end of innocence" for technology in the U.S. In April the explosion at the Chernobyl nuclear power plant in the Soviet Union demonstrated not only the heavy cost of human error in nuclear technology but also how poorly prepared even the most technologically advanced nations were to deal with radioactive clouds that cross international boundaries. And around the world the steadily mounting toll of AIDS (acquired immune deficiency syndrome) provided a grim reminder of the limits of medical research despite its massive resources.

**Financial support.** U.S. scientists had an additional worry. As 1986 dawned there were indications that academic scientists not primarily engaged in military research would suffer crippling cuts in federal support. Primary among these were gloomy forecasts about the impact of Gramm-Rudman-Hollings, a congressional measure to zero out the federal deficit by the 1991 fiscal year. The dominant view of the scientific leadership was that this legislation would slice 12% off the top of the federal science budget—with the added complication that defense-related research and development might be protected at the expense of research in the civilian sector. Indeed, when fiscal 1986 was almost half over, the National Science Foundation (NSF) warned its academic clientele not only to prepare for cuts of up to 10% in continuing and new programs but also that grant awards already made might be cut retroactively.

Overall federal support for academic research and development was also in retreat. The decade had begun with a decline averaging nearly 4% annually during 1980–82. Beginning in 1982 the administration of Pres. Ronald Reagan did a turnabout and effected an average annual growth rate of 8%, although much of that growth was reflected in support of defense-related research. In 1985–86 growth once again stopped, and in 1987 funding declined an additional 3%. For many academic scientists, a *New York Times* reporter observed, even the growth that began in 1982 "may be scarcely noticeable." David Sanger wrote: "Both Government statistics and interviews with researchers across the country indicate that the Administration has concentrated much of its basic research funding in unusually large projects, such as establishing supercomputer and advanced engineering centers around the country, or in technologies it considers critical to industrial or military competitiveness. As a result, scholars say that funds for individual scientists, especially those not working in the heavily favored areas of advanced computer science, biotechnology, or composite materials, may be scarcer than ever."

Private industry spending for research and development also began to level off. A survey by the NSF predicted that nongovernmental funding would increase by only 5% in 1987, down from an annual growth rate of 13% during the previous decade.

Nor could cheer be found in the U.S. Office of Management and Budget (OMB). Hugh Loweth, a 35-year veteran of the science section of the White House budget office, thus attributed his decision to retire in mid-1986: "It became clear to me that science was entering a period of diminishing returns in Washington. Under Gramm-Rudman-Hollings, the budget would suffer a serious crunch and science would be a victim. It's been my observation that the science community cannot save government funding for scientific research without the help of allies from outside its own borders. It's going to require the pressure of political and industrial interests as well as public opinion to make the situation come out right."

The scientific community began to hear the message. At a colloquium on research and development

*Artist's drawing shows a laser beam generated on the Earth being reflected toward a high-altitude target by a space-based mirror. It is one of the concepts being considered in the U.S. Strategic Defense Initiative program.*

U.S. Department of Defense

sponsored by the American Association for the Advancement of Science in March, the audience was, in the words of the sponsors, "advised to practice up on the martial arts, to climb into the ring and fight for their scientific lives, interests, and projects." As it turned out, a few sectors of the scientific enterprise found a powerful ally in the White House itself. President Reagan ordered that basic research be protected.

The budget for fiscal 1987 proposed to the Congress in early February 1986 justified the early optimism. Total federal obligations for research and development, including new facilities and equipment, reached $63 billion—a generous 16% above the $54 billion in fiscal 1986, even after the impact of Gramm-Rudman-Hollings. The research and development portion of the budget had a familiar look. The Defense Department's portion totaled $41.8 billion, 25% higher than in fiscal 1986. The nuclear weapons program of the Department of Energy (DOE) brought the total for military research and development to $44.4 billion.

The largest single program in military research and development was the Strategic Defense Initiative (SDI), commonly referred to as "Star Wars." It was slated to receive $4.8 billion within the Department of Defense and an additional $603 million in DOE. Virtually every element in the SDI program was to be doubled.

The NSF was earmarked to receive some $1,690,-000,000 in 1987, an increase of $130 million, or 8% above the $1,560,000,000 that had been budgeted for fiscal 1986. Physics obtained the smallest rise (only 6.7% above 1986) and materials science only a trifle more (7%), while mathematics (with 15.7%) and chemistry (12.5%) gained significantly. A substantial increase was proposed for the NSF's Engineering Research Centers. They were slated to receive $12 million more than in the previous year, achieving a total of $35 million in 1987; the increase would enable the NSF to enlarge the number of engineering centers at universities from 6 to 11 by the end of 1987.

In announcing its proposed budget for the NSF in fiscal 1987, the agency's director, Erich Bloch, took pains to note that, coming in a time of financial austerity, this budget clearly signaled the importance that the Reagan administration placed on increasing its investment in civilian basic science and engineering research and education. "Present and future economic competitiveness are built on fundamental science and engineering research and education. They lead to the products and services that improve the well-being of all citizens and help to guarantee our national defense. Investing in these activities is investing in the future of our country."

Few in the director's audience could quarrel with

his observations. On the other hand, similar views had been frequently voiced over the past several years with no visible effect. The recommendations of the President's Commission on Industrial Competitiveness had been politely received by the president and then left to gather dust on Washington bookshelves. What had changed? The most likely answer was that the repeated cries of alarm from U.S. high-technology industries simply became more audible—and credible—as the U.S. trade deficit with Japan became more visible.

In addition, the concept of integrated science and technology centers at major universities had a definite attraction for those of the new scientific leadership who had strong backgrounds in industrial and military technology, such as NSF director Bloch. According to Philip M. Boffey, science policy reporter for the *New York Times*, the chief promoter of the new approach in the Reagan administration was George A. Keyworth II, who had served as White House science adviser until the end of 1985. Keyworth saw the new centers as a way to "change the very fabric of U.S. research universities," principally by gathering researchers from several disciplines to work on critical problems in collaboration with industrial scientists. He described the program as "probably the single most important initiative in the Reagan Administration's science policy. This is not a program—it's an incipient revolution." The idea also struck fire within academia. When the foundation had originally asked for proposals for its modest program of six centers budgeted at $10 million, it had received 142 applications, seeking a total of more than $2 billion. Suddenly international competitiveness seemed to be on everyone's agenda. By the end of 1986 a bipartisan group in Congress had formed the Congressional Caucus on Competitiveness, with the new speaker of the House of Representatives, Jim Wright (Dem., Texas), declaring that "competitiveness may be the dominant economic issue of the remaining years of the 20th century."

At the U.S. Department of the Treasury, a Working Group on Global Competitiveness began to assemble a list of proposals for a plan to deal with the problem. If the message needed reinforcing, President Reagan, in his state of the union message in early 1987, told the Congress that it would "soon receive my comprehensive proposals to enhance our competitiveness, including new science and technology centers and strong new funding for basic research."

The new religion in the Congress came almost too late for the NSF fiscal 1987 budget. After surviving the scrutiny of three authorizing committees, the administration's proposed budget for the foundation was savaged by the House Appropriations Committee in August. The appropriations measure that was passed on to the Senate had been slashed by $146

million and was little more than that of fiscal 1986. The blow sent a severe shock wave through the scientific leadership. Only recently the chairman of the National Science Board had been seriously advocating that the NSF abandon the traditional approach of seeking incremental increases and start asking—in the bullish phrase of one Washington science advocate—"for the kind of money that is required to accomplish its mission."

A panel created by the White House Science Council and headed by David Packard, chairman of the board of Hewlett-Packard Co., and D. Allan Bromley, physics professor at Yale University, had issued a report in January that called for a doubling of university basic research funding over a five-year period. Reagan himself had followed by announcing the five-year doubling rate as administration policy. In point of fact, when the budget for fiscal 1988 was in preparation, friends in the OMB made it known that the NSF budget request for that year would indeed call for a whopping increase of about 20%—but only if the fiscal 1987 request survived the legislative process more or less intact. In March the presidents of 28 scientific, engineering, and mathematics societies, in an unprecedented show of solidarity and initiative, had signed letters to each of the members of the House and Senate budget committees, expressing their concern over the possible consequences of an inadequate investment in research. News of the House action sounded the alarm once again, and once more the heads of the societies cosigned letters to the members of the Senate and House Appropriations Committees, this time urging support for the full amount of the administration's fiscal 1987 budget request for the NSF. For whatever reason, the Senate Appropriations Committee heard what its House counterpart had not. It approved the administration's full request and then added another $10 million for science education. The two conflicting measures then went into conference.

By the end of the year, the NSF budget for research and related activities that had been proposed to climb to a level of $1,479,000,000 had been pared down and reshaped to $1,406,000,000, still representing a 4% increase over fiscal 1986. Overall, Congress had considerably reshaped the proposed research and development budget. According to an analysis by the American Association for the Advancement of Science, Congress cut $6.6 billion from the Department of Defense budget for research and development and added $1.9 billion for civilian research and development, much of it to the National Institutes of Health.

White House support for academic research and development in the face of the general budget slashing drew gratitude from the scientific leadership but did not quiet their concerns. Granting that the proposed budget for the NSF was "excellent," Robert M. Rosenzweig, president of the Association of American Universities, testified before the House Committee on Science and Technology that related efforts to cut deficits, reduce overhead, and reform taxes imposed a "special and largely unintended jeopardy" on major research universities.

Rosenzweig pointed to (1) proposed cuts in student aid, in the budget of the National Institutes of Health, and in Medicare and Medicaid reimbursement coupled with (2) proposed limitations on the ability of universities to recover the indirect costs of research activities and (3) the potential damping effect on private philanthropy of changes in the tax law affecting deductibility of alumni giving. "Several essentially unrelated policy lines seem to be converging," he warned. If they do meet, he continued, "there is the real prospect of very serious damage" to the fundamental research capability of U.S. universities.

Proposed new limitations on reimbursement of indirect research expenses alone could cost research universities $300 million annually, declared Donald Kennedy, president of Stanford University. "In order to pay these unreimbursed costs," he said, "Stanford will have to divert funds . . . which would otherwise have been spent for . . . critical academic endeavors. While this proposal may produce some immediate budget savings, in reality it is a costly undertaking; by undermining the basic research capacity of universities, it will ultimately harm American science and technology."

If university administrators were mystified by the new federal policies, they had good reason. Only a few months earlier the Packard-Bromley panel created by the White House Science Council seemed to share the same worries. Citing obsolete equipment, aging buildings, and shortages of students and faculty in many important fields, the panel had concluded: "Our universities today simply cannot respond to society's expectations for them or discharge their national responsibilities in research and education without substantially increased support."

**Scientific manpower—and womanpower.** In a statement published in *Science* magazine in early 1987, NSF Director Bloch reminded his readers that economic competitiveness was not a problem that could be solved merely by throwing money at it. In a series of essential requirements he listed human resources first. "Too few of our best students study science and engineering," he said, "and of those who do, too few finish the Ph.D. We need to make careers in science and engineering more attractive." He added: "We also need to broaden participation among women and minorities . . . not now participating fully in the educational and research process. We simply cannot afford to waste their talent."

Bloch had support from other scientific organizations. In April 1986 the National Research Council of the National Academy of Sciences reported that only 900 students a year were receiving a doctorate degree in physics, compared with 1,550 per year in 1970. "Such a decline," the report said, "could have serious consequences for national defense and the economy, which rely heavily on the development of new technologies." The report also pointed out that an increasingly smaller proportion of physics graduates were U.S.-born. In 1982, the most recent year for which data were available, nearly 40% of enrollees in graduate physics programs in the U.S. were citizens of other countries.

The Research Council was also concerned about the lack of participation by women and minorities in graduate physics programs. Data reported by the NSF in January provided some reassurance that affirmative action was slowly working in the scientific and engineering communities. Both women and minorities had made substantial gains since the mid-1970s, the government agency reported. Employment of women in those fields had increased by 157%, up from 9% of the work force to 13%. Black employment was increasing twice as fast as was white (140% versus 70%), but as of 1987 blacks still accounted for only slightly more than 2% of all employed scientists and engineers.

The foundation also reported that the number of foreign scientists and engineers in U.S. firms was growing at an unusual rate. Between 1972 and 1982

WHEN SCIENCE CATCHES UP TO SPORTS

I WANT $400,000 A YEAR, A BONUS FOR EACH STEP THAT LEADS TO A NEW PRODUCT AND A FIVE-YEAR CONTRACT. OR TRADE ME TO ANOTHER LAB.

Sidney Harris

the proportion of noncitizens among the U.S. population of scientists and engineers had increased from 10 to 17%. The foundation's most recent data showed that foreigners represented 14% of all newly hired scientists and engineers in electronics firms and 12% in independent research and development laboratories. A third survey reported that non-U.S. citizens had earned 28% of all U.S. science and engineering doctorates awarded in 1985.

As part of a broad effort to increase the human resources available to the scientific enterprise, the foundation announced in January 1987 that grants totaling $6.6 million had been awarded to help upgrade science education in grades kindergarten through six. According to Bill G. Aldridge, executive director of the National Science Teachers Association, more than curriculum development was required. He charged, "About 30 to 40 percent of all science courses in American schools are staffed by teachers who are drastically unqualified." He attributed the problem to the coincidence of a teacher surplus at a time of decreasing enrollments and a new emphasis on increased science requirements. With an eye to minimizing budgetary outlays, he complained, school superintendents were haphazardly assigning surplus teachers to new courses—assigning business teachers, for example, to courses in mathematics.

**Insecurity about military security.** The imposition of military security on scientific communications and its repressive effect on research continued to concern the scientific community. In recent years scientific societies had been protesting the sudden suppression, at scientific meetings, of papers reporting the results of openly conducted research.

Among new concerns were regulations that sought to restrict the participation of non-U.S. students in unclassified research programs. Considering the increasing role of foreign research assistants, many senior investigators began to worry whether they would be able to complete research programs already started. Typical was a curious new clause that began to appear in grant contracts for unclassified research funded by DOE. It stated, "If the grantee believes any information developed or acquired may be classifiable, the grantee shall not provide the potentially classifiable information to anyone except the Director of Classification and shall protect such information as if it were classified until notified by DoE that a determination has been made that it does not require such handling."

A dispute between the NSF and the Department of Defense over access to supercomputers had to be referred to the National Security Council for resolution. Pentagon hardliners insisted on a no-exceptions ban on use by citizens of Warsaw Pact nations, including students who would use the supercomputers as part of their classroom assignments.

Another case of head butting between the scientific community and the Department of Defense was occasioned by a report from the National Academy of Sciences. The academy, a private organization of distinguished scientists whose operation was largely dependent on contractual arrangements with agencies of the federal government, had already shown itself willing to oppose the Department of Defense in defending scientists' right to communicate openly with each other in unclassified areas of research. In January 1987 it again chose to question the correctness of Pentagon policies, this time in an area of concern far larger than the scientific community: competitiveness. Produced by a panel who had impeccable credentials and headed by Lew Allen, Jr., formerly chief of staff of the U.S. Air Force and director of the National Security Agency, the report found that recent regulations designed to impede Soviet acquisition of militarily sensitive commercial technology were, in fact, "overcorrecting" previous weaknesses and were failing "to promote both military security and economic vitality." While export controls did serve to hamper Soviet acquisition of sensitive technologies, the panel said, they also tend to have "an increasingly corrosive effect" on U.S. relations with European allies and make it more difficult for U.S. industry to compete in the international arena.

Meanwhile, quarrels between the administration and members of the scientific community on questions of military weaponry continued to proliferate. The merits of the Strategic Defense Initiative remained on center stage. In March 1986 a nationwide poll taken at the request of the Union of Concerned Scientists reported that, by almost two to one, physicists viewed SDI as a step in the wrong direction for the national security policy of the United States. Among those who claimed a high level of familiarity with SDI, the ratio was still higher. Even among those who derived a majority of their funding from the Department of Defense, only 38% thought it was a step in the right direction.

Such polls did not sit well with Donald Hicks, undersecretary of defense for research and advanced technology. In an interview with *Science* magazine, Hicks said that Defense Department funds might be withheld from scientists who publicly opposed Pentagon programs. The firestorm that followed spread to Capitol Hill, with some members of the Congress calling for Hicks's resignation and others calling for sharp cuts in the SDI budget. Later, the Pentagon explained that Hicks had been speaking hypothetically. "It is not DoD policy to review researchers' opinions prior to awarding them contracts. This is not written or unwritten policy. Awards to researchers are made strictly on a merit basis."

—Howard J. Lewis

# Scientists of the Year

## Honors and awards

The following article discusses recent awards and prizes in science and technology. In the first section the Nobel Prizes for 1986 and the Britannica Awards of 1987 are described in detail. The second section is a selective list of other honors.

### Nobel Prize for Chemistry

The Nobel Prize for Chemistry in 1986 was divided equally among the three principal creators of the scientific specialty called chemical reaction dynamics, the study of time-dependent details of chemical processes. The prizewinners were Dudley R. Herschbach and Yuan T. Lee of the United States and John C. Polanyi of Canada.

The quantitative study of chemical reactions started late in the 18th century, when the French scientist Antoine Lavoisier demonstrated by accurate measurements that mass is neither created nor destroyed in chemical changes. Within the next few decades the English scientist John Dalton put forth his idea that each chemical element consists of indivisible particles of a single kind and that all matter is composed of these particles. As a name for these particles Dalton revived the word "atoms," which had been introduced by the ancient Greek philosopher Democritus. The properties of various substances differ because their particles are composed of different atoms or combinations of atoms. In chemical reactions, according to Dalton, changes take place in the arrangements of atoms, but investigations of the details of these changes had to be postponed for many decades, until after the development of concepts of how atoms are bound together in molecules. Late in the 19th century the Swedish chemist Svante Arrhenius made two major contributions to the solution of the problem. First, he improved Dalton's atomic theory by showing that many dissolved substances must exist in the form of electrically charged particles, or ions. (For this achievement he received the Nobel Prize for Chemistry in 1903.) Second, he explained the effect of temperature on the rates of chemical reactions by proposing that the colliding particles do not react unless their energy exceeds a required minimum. His interpretation became the basis for all later theories about reaction rates.

During the 20th century there arose a chemical specialty—chemical kinetics—focused on how the rates of chemical changes are influenced by numerous conditions that are subject to experimental control, such as temperature, pressure, the concentrations of the reacting substances, and the presence of catalysts. Practitioners of this specialty measured the speeds of chemical reactions and interpreted them as to their consistency with differing mechanisms, that is, schemes involving the collisions of molecules, the breaking of certain chemical bonds, and the formation of others.

Until late in the 20th century practically all research in chemical kinetics and mechanisms depended on the measurement of changes in the concentrations of substances—commonly in the gaseous state or in solution—as reactions proceeded. Although it was clearly understood that even the most complicated reactions were sequences of steps, each involving only one or two atoms or molecules, the available techniques could be applied only to phenomena associated with large numbers of these particles. Under the conditions of the experiments, the reacting species suffer so many collisions with the surrounding particles that their energies and motions are quickly randomized; therefore, only the average behavior of the molecules could be observed. Polanyi offered a lucid analogy, comparing classical chemical kinetics to sociology, "dealing with the behavior of societies," and modern reaction dynamics to psychology, "recognizing only the rules of behavior of individuals."

Herschbach was one of the first scientists to adopt the technique of molecular beams for chemical research purposes. Since the early 20th century physicists had used narrow streams of particles moving at known speeds through a vacuum to study properties of matter that could not be conveniently observed otherwise. A great advantage of beam techniques is

*Dudley Herschbach*

Harvard University News Service;
photo, Jane Reed

that the particles are so far apart that they do not collide or otherwise interact with one another. In 1959 Herschbach built a vacuum apparatus in which two beams, each consisting of particles of a single substance, could be made to intersect. When atoms and molecules of different species collided, they reacted with one another, and the newly formed products would fly away from the site at which the beams crossed. Because small numbers of particles traversed this region, the products formed at a very low rate, and to detect them Herschbach and other scientists adopted a sensitive technique that had been demonstrated in 1955 by Ellison Taylor and Sheldon Datz at the Oak Ridge (Tennessee) National Laboratory. These scientists made use of the fact that measurable electrical signals are produced when atoms or ions of potassium or other alkali metals strike heated filaments of tungsten or platinum. In the early 1960s Herschbach used this method to study the reaction between potassium atoms and methyl iodide molecules. He found that one of the products, potassium iodide, left the point of reaction in the direction opposite to that of the incoming beam of potassium atoms. He concluded that the reaction is most likely when the potassium atom approaches the methyl iodide molecule along the axis of the bond connecting the iodine atom with the methyl group. No earlier technique could have provided such clear evidence of the necessity for a particular orientation of the particles of reacting substances.

In certain reactions the final products were not the immediate result of the collision but were formed indirectly, by the disintegration of intermediate species that persisted for unexpectedly long intervals. Using a variety of particle detectors, Herschbach was able to measure the energy of the reaction products and to determine how this energy was distributed among the different possible forms, such as translation (motion of the molecule as a whole), vibration (internal oscillations of the parts of the molecule), and rotation (tumbling or spinning). In studying the relative amounts of products detected at various angles from the direction of the crossed beams, Herschbach correlated this distribution with the lifetime of the unstable intermediate species. If one of these entities does not remain intact long enough to undergo a single rotation, the fragments formed when it breaks apart will fly off in directions closely related to those of the colliding beams. In contrast, if the intermediate can tumble about before disintegrating, the products will be detected over a wide range of angles.

Herschbach designated Lee "the Mozart of chemical physics" for his experimental skills and ingenuity, which often have meant the difference between success and failure in challenging situations in the laboratory. Though previous investigators had tried

University of California, Berkeley

*Yuan Lee*

to use mass spectrometers for detecting the products of crossed-beam experiments, they had not been able to obtain useful results. Lee identified the source of the problem as insufficiently high vacuum in the reaction chamber. Under these conditions the detector was swamped by meaningless signals resulting from collisions of extraneous particles. He devised a method of reducing the pressure to one ten-thousandth of that formerly achieved. Under these conditions it became possible to take advantage of the ability of the mass spectrometer to distinguish among molecules that are very similar in atomic composition. This capability is essential in studying reactions such as those involved in the combustion of large molecules or in the behavior of pollutants in the Earth's atmosphere.

Herschbach was born in San Jose, Calif., on June 18, 1932. He earned a B.S. in mathematics (1954) and an M.S. in chemistry (1955) at Stanford University and a Ph.D. in chemical physics at Harvard University in 1958. He joined the faculty of the University of California, Berkeley, in 1959, then moved to Harvard as professor of chemistry in 1963. During the period 1961–68, Lee—first as a doctoral candidate, then as a postdoctoral fellow—was one of Herschbach's principal collaborators.

Lee was born at Hsin-chu, Taiwan, on Nov. 29, 1936. He earned a bachelor's degree from the National Taiwan University, Taipei, in 1959 and a master's degree from the National Tsing Hua University, Hsin-chu, in 1961. He then moved to the University of California at Berkeley, where—conducting research under the supervision of Herschbach—he received a Ph.D. in chemistry in 1965. He remained with Herschbach at Berkeley as a postdoctoral fellow until 1968, when he joined the faculty of the University of Chicago. In 1974 Lee returned to the Berkeley campus as professor of chemistry; in the same year, he was naturalized as a citizen of the United States.

Polanyi was cited for his investigations of infrared chemiluminescence, the emission of radiation by molecules as their internal vibrations and rotations slow down. Analysis of this radiation provides information about the distribution of energy within chemical species and the relation of this distribution to the details of the sequences of events occurring during reactions. Polanyi's technique is a valuable complement to the molecular-beam approach developed by Herschbach and Lee.

Earlier chemists had shown that many reactions of simple compounds are quite complicated. For example, the reaction between hydrogen and chlorine, forming hydrogen chloride and releasing considerable energy, occurs at a rate best explained by proposing that a long series of steps, instead of simple two-body collisions, must take place. This account, however, leaves open the question of the precise origin of the liberated energy. Studying one of the proposed steps, Polanyi found that when hydrogen atoms and chlorine molecules collide at 77 K the newly formed hydrogen chloride molecules emit faint infrared radiation in patterns showing that they are vibrating as if their temperature were 3,000 K. That is, much of the energy released in the reaction must first appear in the form of vigorous vibration of the product molecule. For this radiation to occur, it is essential that the molecules not first dissipate their excess vibrational energy in collisions with other particles. Polanyi reduced the number of such collisions by carrying out the experiments in evacuated vessels.

*John Polanyi*

The Nobel Foundation, Stockholm

In extensions of his research, Polanyi obtained evidence that the molecules of newly formed reaction products also rotate much faster than they would if they were in equilibrium with their surroundings. Still later research has provided insights into how reaction rates are affected by selectively exciting different modes of translational, vibrational, and rotational energy of the reacting substances.

Polanyi was born on Jan. 23, 1929, in Berlin. In 1952 he received a Ph.D. in chemistry from the University of Manchester, where his father, the late Michael Polanyi, a noted physical chemist, had been a professor until 1948. He carried out postdoctoral research at the National Research Council of Canada in Ottawa and at Princeton University and then joined the faculty of the University of Toronto in 1956. In 1974 he was named University Professor of Chemistry.

## Nobel Prize for Physics

The Nobel Prize for Physics was divided among three European scientists who devised instruments that produce detailed images of objects far too small to be seen with the aid of optical microscopes. Half of the prize was awarded to Ernst Ruska of West Germany, who constructed the first electron microscope in the early 1930s and continued research on it until his retirement four decades later. During his long career Ruska witnessed the adoption of electron microscopy as one of the primary research techniques of a wide spectrum of scientific disciplines; a noteworthy example is the study of viruses, which are beyond the reach of optical microscopes but are well within the range of electron microscopes.

The other half of the prize was split between two members of the staff of the Zurich Research Laboratory of the International Business Machines Corp. (IBM), Gerd Binnig of West Germany and Heinrich Rohrer of Switzerland, for developing the scanning tunneling microscope. Since its introduction in the early 1980s, this instrument has provided scientists with views of individual atoms and even smaller features of the surfaces of solids.

The choice of the laureates provoked some criticism. This year one of the biggest questions concerned the long delay in recognizing Ruska, particularly in comparison with the prompt citation of Binnig and Rohrer. The Swedish Academy of Sciences, in announcing its selections, admitted that Ruska's share of the prize honored a promise fulfilled, while Binnig and Rohrer's share recognized a promising future. The academy does not publicly justify its decisions, but commentators pointed out that the academy may have been deterred by the difficulty of assigning credit for the electron microscope because of unresolvable claims of priority.

Until the 1930s the examination of very small objects depended on optical microscopes, in which glass lenses form an image by focusing a beam of light that passes through the specimen. In the course of nearly five centuries of development, the various defects of these lenses were analyzed and corrected, and the magnifying power of the microscope was pushed close to the theoretical limit imposed by the wavelengths of visible light. Present-day optical microscopes can produce useful images about 2,000 times larger than the object, in which it is possible to distinguish features that are about eight millionths of an inch apart. To study objects in finer detail than that, another technique is needed.

During the 1930s a prediction made in the preceding decade—that electrons should show some of the properties of waves much shorter than those of light—was confirmed by George Paget Thomson in Britain and Clinton J. Davisson in the United States. For this demonstration they shared the Nobel Prize for Physics in 1937. If electron beams could be focused as sharply as light beams, magnifications 100,000 times greater than those of optical microscopes should be possible. Glass lenses absorb and scatter electrons, so they are useless for this purpose, but in 1931 Ruska took advantage of the facts that electrons are electrically charged and that the paths of moving charged particles can be controlled by electric or magnetic fields. He built the first electron lens, an electromagnet that created a field of the shape and strength required to furnish the short focal length essential for high magnification. By 1933 he had improved the electron microscope so that it gave greater magnification than the best optical microscopes. Electron lenses are subject to all the distortions of light lenses, and it has not been possible to correct them completely. Even so, electron microscopes now produce magnifications about 1,000 times greater than their optical predecessors.

Unable to obtain financial support for his research in electron microscopy, Ruska left that field in 1933, finding employment in television technology. For the next few years he stayed in touch with developments on his invention and continued to seek commercial backing, while other scientists tried to cope with major objections to his idea. One of these objections was the possibility that biologic specimens would be destroyed by the high vacuum needed in the instrument to minimize scattering of the electron beam by air molecules; another was that the beam itself would burn up the specimens. Progress in overcoming these drawbacks persuaded Siemens & Halske, a leading German electronics firm, to underwrite Ruska, who resumed his active research in 1937. Within two years he had built two commercial prototypes capable of magnification 30,000 times and resolution 20 times better than that attainable by

The Nobel Foundation, Stockholm

*Ernst Ruska*

any possible light microscope. Siemens would have undertaken commercial production of these instruments by 1940, but World War II intervened. Ruska continued his research until his laboratory was destroyed late in the war.

Ernst August Friedrich Ruska was born in Heidelberg, Germany, on Dec. 25, 1906, and began his higher education at the Technical University of Munich. He transferred to the Technical University of Berlin, which awarded him a doctor's degree in engineering in 1934. Thereafter he held industrial research positions until 1955, when he became director of the Institute of Electron Microscopy of the Fritz Haber Institute of the Max Planck Society in West Berlin. He was named professor of electron optics and electron microscopy at the institute in 1959 and held that position until he retired in 1972. For many years he combined his research career with teaching positions at the Technical University and the Free University of Berlin.

Binnig and Rohrer's scanning tunneling microscope (STM) depends on a physical principle completely different from that of the electron microscope to produce images of the surfaces of conducting or semiconducting materials. In the electron microscope a beam of energetic electrons must be focused on a thin film of the material to be studied. In the STM two electrodes (the extremely fine tip of a metallic probe and the surface of a conductive material) must be manipulated so that the distance between them can be controlled with unprecedented precision. If this gap can be made small enough, without allowing the electrodes to touch, an electric potential of a few volts will induce enough electrons to cross it to produce a measurable current.

By the end of the 19th century the idea that atoms do indeed exist had been accepted by practically all physicists. Since then strenuous efforts have been made in the search for devices that could generate images of them. By the 1980s the most highly refined versions of Ruska's electron microscope could resolve objects less than 2 angstroms in diameter (an angstrom is one ten-billionth of a meter), very close to the size of a typical atom, but could not be adapted to the study of surfaces because the electron beam passes completely through the specimen.

During the operation of the STM an electric current passes between the surface being studied and a tungsten probe that is caused to move in a path covering a selected area. The strength of this current depends very strongly on the distance of the probe from the surface, and this distance is kept constant by measuring the current and using it to control the position of the probe. To form an image sharp enough to reveal single atoms, the tip of the probe itself must consist of a single atom, and its elevation above the surface must be monitored with a precision of a few hundredths of an angstrom. The probe is steered through its invisible motions by programming minute alterations in the lengths of the legs of a supporting tripod; these legs are made of a ceramic piezoelectric material that changes its dimensions under the influence of an electric field. In the early versions of the STM, an elaborate suspension system was required to protect the apparatus from the disastrous consequences of even the slightest vibrations. More recent models, much smaller than their forerunners, are rigid enough to eliminate this problem. Since the operation of the first STM was demonstrated, it has been found that high vacuum is not necessary; the electron flow occurs even if the probe and surface are exposed to the atmosphere or if they are under water.

The current is a consequence of the quantum mechanical phenomenon called tunneling, in which the wavelike properties of electrons and other minute particles make it possible for them to appear in places where, under the rules of classical physics, they would not be found. A record of the elevation of the moving probe is a topographical map of a surface on which the contour intervals are so small that individual atoms are clearly recognizable.

During the first few years of the STM's application, it was used to study the arrangement of the atoms at the surface of crystals of silicon, a feature of importance in seeking an understanding of the behavior of such crystals in computer chips and other semiconducting devices. Even finer details of the silicon surface were revealed by scanning it at different voltages. The regions of high electron density that define the chemical bonds between the atoms were mapped by this technique. Because the STM has been shown to operate with water between the probe and the surface, it has been possible to begin examinations of biologic specimens under conditions similar to those in which they ordinarily function. Such investigations still lie outside the capabilities of electron microscopes.

Many metals and alloys become superconductors when they are cooled to very low temperatures. In

*Heinrich Rohrer (far left) and Gerd Binnig (left)*

studies that would have been impossible without the STM, the surfaces of several of these materials were examined at temperatures above and below that at which their electrical resistance disappears, and associated structural changes were observed.

Rohrer was born in Switzerland on June 6, 1933, and was educated at the Swiss Federal Institute of Technology in Zurich, receiving a Ph.D. in physics in 1960. He held a two-year postdoctoral fellowship at the State University of Rutgers, New Brunswick, N.J., before returning to his native country and joining the staff of the IBM Zurich Research Laboratory.

Binnig, the youngest of the Nobel prizewinners of 1986, was born on July 20, 1947, in Frankfurt, West Germany. He graduated from the Johann Wolfgang Goethe University in Frankfurt and earned a Ph.D. in physics from the University of Frankfurt in 1978. He then joined the IBM Zurich Research Laboratory, where he and Rohrer immediately initiated the research program that resulted in the first STM. One of the pleasant surprises that they experienced in the project was the rapidity with which they reached their goal.

## Nobel Prize for Physiology or Medicine

The Nobel Prize for Physiology or Medicine in 1986 was divided equally between Rita Levi-Montalcini of the Institute of Cellular Biology in Rome, which is one of about 150 constituent bodies of the National Research Council of Italy, and Stanley Cohen of the Vanderbilt University School of Medicine, Nashville, Tenn. Levi-Montalcini, whose professional activities have encompassed medicine, embryology, and neurobiology, is a citizen of both Italy and the United States; Cohen, a biochemist, is a U.S. citizen. The two scientists also shared the Albert Lasker Award for Basic Medical Research in 1986 for the same achievements that brought them the Nobel Prize, namely, the investigation of natural substances that promote the growth of nerve cells and numerous other tissues and organs.

Levi-Montalcini, who was born in Turin, Italy, on April 23, 1909, graduated from the medical school of the University of Turin in 1936. She remained at the university, carrying out research in embryology, until 1939, when she was dismissed from her position because of the anti-Semitic policies of Benito Mussolini's Fascist government. She found a new post in Brussels, Belgium, but left that country when it was invaded by the Germans in 1940. Returning to Turin, she improvised a laboratory in a bedroom of her parents' home and continued her experimental work, using chick embryos secretly provided by her friends. At the same time she dispensed clandestine medical care to the residents of the poor neighborhoods of Turin. Driven from the city in 1942 by

The Nobel Foundation, Stockholm

*Rita Levi-Montalcini*

heavy air raids, she set up a second makeshift laboratory in a small country house, where the supply of eggs was as unreliable as the electric power service. When the Germans occupied Italy in 1943, Levi-Montalcini went into hiding in Florence and resumed her ministrations to the civilian population after the Allies expelled the Germans.

After the war she recovered her academic appointment at the University of Turin and continued her studies there until 1947, when she accepted a position as a research associate in the zoology department of Washington University in St. Louis, Mo. There she joined a group directed by Viktor Hamburger, who had been favorably impressed by an article written by Levi-Montalcini that had been rejected by the Italian authorities but published in a Belgian scientific journal. Hamburger had already begun an investigation of the process by which cells of the peripheral nervous system in chick embryos establish connections with the organs that they will influence in the mature animal. When the Royal Caroline Institute in Stockholm announced that the Nobel Prize was to be awarded to Levi-Montalcini and Cohen, some experts in developmental biology expressed surprise and disappointment that Hamburger was being denied a share of the honor.

In 1948 another scientist had found that if a fragment of sarcoma 180, a tumor that can affect the connective tissues of mice, was implanted in a three-day-old chick embryo, it was quickly invaded by nerve fibers from the embryo. In 1952 Levi-Montalcini—by then an associate professor—extended this experiment and proved that the nerve growth was caused by a soluble substance released by the tumor and carried to the embryo in the bloodstream. In 1953 she showed that the material produced by sarcoma 180 caused the same vigorous growth in nerve tissue that had been removed from the embryo and kept alive in a culture medium. Levi-Montalcini's use of cultures, rather than intact eggs, formed the basis of a practical bioassay procedure that was thereafter adopted as the standard method in many laboratories for studies of the soluble substance, which has been known as nerve growth factor (NGF) since 1954.

Levi-Montalcini continued to be active in the study of NGF, remaining in St. Louis until 1961 and then returning to Italy to become a senior scientist at the Institute of Cellular Biology. She had become a U.S. citizen in 1956, and as of 1987 she still held the rank of professor (emeritus since 1977) at Washington University.

Cohen was born on Nov. 17, 1922, in Brooklyn, N.Y. After graduating from Brooklyn College in 1943, he continued his education at Oberlin College in Ohio and at the University of Michigan, receiving a Ph.D. from the latter in 1948. He engaged in pediatric research at the University of Colorado until 1952 and then joined Hamburger's research group at Washington University as a postdoctoral fellow. There he and Levi-Montalcini promptly established a close and lasting collaboration, in which Cohen's initial objective was to isolate and purify the nerve growth factor from the cells of sarcoma 180.

After separating the tumor cells into several different fractions, Cohen traced the activity to a component that consisted of proteins and nucleic acids. In an attempt to find which of these two types of material was responsible for the nerve growth, he and Levi-Montalcini treated the mixture with a small amount of a snake venom that would disintegrate the nucleic acid molecules but leave the proteins unaffected. The outcome of this procedure was a

*Stanley Cohen*

striking increase in the activity of the tumor extract. This surprising result was the scientists' first clue that snake venom itself was a more abundant source of NGF than sarcoma 180. Taking advantage of this discovery, Cohen isolated the factor from the venom, purified it, and proved that it is a protein.

The identification of the growth factor in snake venom prompted the investigators to examine a third possible source, the submaxillary salivary gland of rodents, because it was known that this gland bears certain resemblances to the venom gland of snakes. The salivary gland indeed proved to be richer in NGF than either of the earlier sites. The substance could be isolated from these glands in amounts large enough to permit studies of its chemical structure by another group of biochemists at Washington University. By 1971 they had been able to decipher the arrangement of the amino acids present in the protein molecule. They found that the structure is remarkably similar to that of the hormone insulin, although the physiological functions of the two substances are entirely different. It has been suggested, however, that the two proteins may have evolved from a common precursor.

While studying impure preparations of NGF obtained from mouse salivary glands, Cohen injected them into newborn mice and was particularly intrigued by the result; the eyes of the mice opened, and the teeth erupted from their gums several days sooner than those of mice not given the extract. These effects, not related to the development of the nervous system, suggested to Cohen that a second growth factor must be present in the extract. The study of this new factor became Cohen's principal activity when he joined the faculty at the Vanderbilt School of Medicine in 1959. He developed methods of isolating and purifiying the substance, which is designated epidermal growth factor (EGF) although it has been found to influence many tissues in addition to the skin, including the cornea, immune system, liver, blood cells, thyroid, ovaries, and pituitary gland. It was also found to be necessary for the production of sperm cells in mice.

By 1972 Cohen and his small group of collaborators had analyzed the structure of the new protein molecule and turned their attention to the process by which EGF moves from the bloodstream to the interior of the cells on which it exerts its effects. They found this phenomenon to be closely analogous to the mechanism by which cholesterol-carrying particles are transferred into cells. Clarification of that action, called receptor-mediated endocytosis, was one of the achievements for which Michael Brown and Joseph Goldstein won the Nobel Prize for Physiology or Medicine in 1985.

In situations governed by this phenomenon, a molecule penetrates a cell wall only if there is a site on the wall that first recognizes the molecule. Such a specific site, called a receptor, becomes firmly attached to the molecule, apparently through the action of a structural complementarity and not as the result of a chemical reaction that forms a covalent bond. When this binding occurs, a dimple develops on the cell surface and continues to deepen until the molecule becomes enveloped in a sac that eventually is pinched off inside the cell, where the sac opens, presumably under the influence of substances present there. The empty receptor finally returns to the cell wall to await the arrival of the next matching molecule. The external membrane of each of the numerous cells in the body of any organism incorporates the specific receptors appropriate for each kind of molecule needed by that cell.

Gene-splicing techniques, which brought a share of the Nobel Prize for Chemistry to Paul Berg of the United States in 1980, have been applied to the preparation of EGF. Considerable demand for the protein has developed because it has many possible applications in investigations of diseases marked by abnormalities of growth. The Nobel Assembly's citation suggested that continued research on the growth factors appears likely to enlarge the present poor understanding of birth defects, degenerative changes in senile dementia, delayed wound healing, and cancer. EGF has already become established as one of the valuable components of the culture medium in which films of human skin are grown for use as grafts for victims of severe burns.

—John V. Killheffer

## Britannica Awards

Britannica Awards for 1987, honoring exceptional excellence in the dissemination of learning, were presented to five persons. Two them, a British naturalist and television broadcaster and a U.S. physicist and science writer, were scientists.

Although many medals and prizes mark original contributions to the world's sum of knowledge, the Britannica Awards, presented for the first time in 1986, celebrate both exceptional skills in imparting learning to others and a passion for its dissemination. The persons singled out to receive the awards have demonstrated these skills in the media of broadcast and print journalism, lecturing, and books, and in doing so they have made fields of highly specialized knowledge intelligible and accessible to a wide general audience.

The Britannica Awards embrace the whole spectrum of knowledge. Candidates for the award are nominated by members of Britannica's Board of Editors and its Editorial Advisory Committees drawn from the faculties of great universities in the United States, Canada, Japan, Australia, the United Kingdom, and continental Europe. Final selections are made by a committee consisting of the chairman of the corporation's Board of Directors, the chairman of its Board of Editors, its president, and its editor in chief.

The award consists of a gold medal, $15,000 in cash, and an allowance for the expenses of attending the presentation and subsequent lectures. The awards were presented on Feb. 16, 1987, at a celebratory banquet at the United Nations Delegates' Dining Room in New York City.

**Attenborough, Sir David.** David Attenborough was at the top of his profession when he decided to quit the British Broadcasting Corporation (BBC), where he was director of television programming and a member of the Management Board, to become a free-lance filmmaker and author. He had long since harnessed the enormous potential of television for popular education in both natural history and human culture.

He was born David Frederick Attenborough on May 8, 1926, in London and grew up in Leicester, where his father was principal of University College. Many of his forebears were educators, and both his son and daughter became teachers. But the classroom was not David's métier. From childhood he was a passionate inquirer into the ways of nature. He attended Wyggeston Grammar School for Boys and went on to Clare College, Cambridge, where he earned an M.A. in zoology and geology in 1947. He finished two years in the Royal Navy as a lieutenant and in 1949 got a job as an editorial assistant in an educational publishing house.

In 1952, after completing a training program at the BBC, he became a producer and quickly found his niche. One of his early shows featured reptiles brought from the London Zoo by a curator, Jack Lester, with whom he soon dreamed up a series to show animals both in the wild on film and live in the studio. The idea won approval from both the BBC and the zoo and resulted in a joint venture that led to a landmark series called "Zoo Quest" that was a hit for ten years.

Early in the "Zoo Quest" series Jack Lester, who had been the presenter or narrator, became ill and died, and Attenborough, a bit tentative about the idea, went before the cameras in his stead. He proved to be a natural and continued his backstage role as well. He also wrote a series of "Zoo Quest" books telling the story of the globe-girdling expeditions to film the TV programs. Then in 1963 he gave up television to study anthropology in graduate school.

In 1965 the BBC persuaded him to return as controller of its new second television channel, BBC-2. His innovative programming quickly expanded its audience, and he helped launch such dramatic productions as "The Forsyte Saga" and cultural-educa-

*Sir David Attenborough (far left) and Jeremy Bernstein (left)*

tional series such as Jacob Bronowski's "The Ascent of Man" and Kenneth Clark's "Civilisation."

This track record moved the BBC to give Attenborough the programming helm of both of its television networks, but the joys of management soon palled, and in 1972 he quit to free-lance. He was not idle; he resumed writing and producing seminal TV series of the general sort that had made his reputation, including "The Tribal Eye" (1975), "Life on Earth" (1978), and "The Living Planet" (1984). All won large audiences, and he turned all of them into successful books.

Attenborough was knighted in 1985. His brother is Sir Richard Attenborough, the distinguished actor and director.

**Bernstein, Jeremy.** There is little interglobal conversation among other occupants of the three worlds in which Jeremy Bernstein operates. He is a major channel of communication among them: the worlds of the physicist, the mountaineer, and the interpreter of science for the intelligent nonprofessional reader. He has won distinction in all three. In the last, he has been celebrated for two decades for the clarity of his writing about the major issues of modern physics.

Bernstein was born Dec. 31, 1929, in Rochester, N.Y. He was educated at Harvard University, where he earned B.A. (1951) and M.A. (1953) degrees in mathematics and a Ph.D. in physics in 1955. After working as a research associate in physics at Harvard's Cyclotron Laboratory, he was appointed to the Institute of Advanced Studies at Princeton, N.J. In 1960 he went to the Brookhaven National Laboratory in New York and while he was there won (1961) a position on the staff of *The New Yorker*.

Mountain climbing was a major avocational interest for Bernstein, and he was able to arrange his dual career so that he could spend three months every year climbing—usually in Switzerland or France. In 1962 he became associate professor of physics at New York University, and in 1967 he was named professor of physics at Stevens Institute of Technology at Hoboken, N.J. He also became an adjunct professor at Rockefeller University in New York City. At various times he has held a National Science Foundation fellowship and concurrent appointments at the University of Oxford; CERN (Conseil Européen pour la Recherche Nucléaire), near Geneva; the University of Islamabad, Pak.; France's École Polytechnique, Paris; Columbia University, New York City; and, twice, as Ferris professor of journalism, at Princeton University. He writes for his peers as well as for nonscientists and is the author of some 50 technical papers.

In interpreting science to the general public, usually initially through the pages of *The New Yorker* and then through books into which the articles evolved, Bernstein has shed light on topics ranging from cosmology to the origins of the computer. He has published a dozen books addressing such diverse topics, and he also writes a biennial column, "Out of My Mind," for *The American Scholar*. His science writing for the general reader has brought him many honors, including the American Physical Society-U.S. Steel Award (twice) and the American Association for the Advancement of Science-Westinghouse Award. His autobiographical memoir, *The Life It Brings,* was published in 1986.

—Bruce L. Felknor

477

| AWARD | WINNER | AFFILIATION |
|---|---|---|

### ARCHAEOLOGY

| | | |
|---|---|---|
| MacArthur Prize Fellow Award | David N. Keightley | University of California, Berkeley |

### ARCHITECTURE

| | | |
|---|---|---|
| Albert S. Bard Award | Buttrick White Burtis, Architects and Planners | New York, N.Y. |
| Albert S. Bard Award | Davis, Brody & Associates | New York, N.Y. |
| Albert S. Bard Award | Abe H. Feder | New York, N.Y. |
| Albert S. Bard Award | Hardy Holzman Pfeiffer Associates | New York, N.Y. |
| Albert S. Bard Award | Pasanella & Klein, Architects | New York, N.Y. |
| Albert S. Bard Award | Prentice & Chan Ohlhausen, Architects and Planners | New York, N.Y. |
| Albert S. Bard Award | Weintraub and di Domenico | New York, N.Y. |
| International Pritzker Architecture Prize (1986) | Gottfried Böhm | Cologne, West Germany |
| International Pritzker Architecture Prize (1987) | Kenzo Tange | Tokyo, Japan |

### ASTRONOMY

| | | |
|---|---|---|
| Arctowski Medal | John A. Eddy | High Altitude Observatory, Boulder, Colo. |
| Bruno Rossi Prize for High-Energy Astrophysics | M. van der Klis | European Space Agency |
| Crafoord Prize | Gerald Wasserburg | California Institute of Technology, Pasadena |
| Dannie Heineman Prize for Astrophysics | Hyron Spinrad | University of California, Berkeley |
| James Craig Watson Medal | W. Kent Ford, Jr. | Carnegie Institution, Washington, D.C. |
| Maria Goeppert-Meyer Award | Judith S. Young | University of Massachusetts, Amherst |
| Robin Prize | Jacques Lequeux | Observatory of Marseille, France |

### CHEMISTRY

| | | |
|---|---|---|
| Anna Louise Hoffman Award | Bridget A. McCortney | Rice University, Houston, Texas |
| Arthur C. Cope Award | Ronald Breslow | Columbia University, New York, N.Y. |
| Arthur C. Cope Scholar Award | Robert G. Bergman | University of California, Berkeley |
| Arthur C. Cope Scholar Award | Thomas C. Bruice | University of California, Santa Barbara |
| Arthur C. Cope Scholar Award | Emil T. Kaiser | Rockefeller University, New York, N.Y. |
| Arthur C. Cope Scholar Award | Satoru Masamune | Massachusetts Institute of Technology, Cambridge |
| Arthur C. Cope Scholar Award | Albert I. Meyers | Colorado State University, Fort Collins |
| Arthur C. Cope Scholar Award | K. C. Nicolaou | University of Pennsylvania, Philadelphia |
| Arthur C. Cope Scholar Award | Leo A. Paquette | Ohio State University, Columbus |

| AWARD | WINNER | AFFILIATION |
|---|---|---|
| Arthur C. Cope Scholar Award | Nicholas J. Turro | Columbia University, New York, N.Y. |
| Arthur K. Doolittle Award | J. M. J. Frechet | University of Ottawa, Canada |
| Arthur K. Doolittle Award | F. M. Houlihan | AT&T Bell Laboratories |
| Arthur K. Doolittle Award | C. G. Willson | IBM Research Laboratory, San Jose, Calif. |
| Challenges in Chemistry Award | George C. Pimentel | University of California, Berkeley |
| Distinguished Achievement in Fiber Science Award | Edwin L. Thomas | University of Massachusetts, Amherst |
| Ernest O. Lawrence Memorial Award | C. Bradley Moore | University of California, Berkeley; Lawrence Berkeley Laboratory, Calif. |
| H. A. B. Dunning Award | Hoechst-Roussel Pharmaceuticals | Somerville, N.J. |
| Henry Draper Medal | Joseph H. Taylor | Ball Chemical Co., Glenshaw, Pa. |
| Jacob F. Schoellkopf Medal | Herbert A. Hauptman | State University of New York, Buffalo |
| National Academy of Sciences Award in Chemical Sciences | Herbert C. Brown (Emeritus) | Purdue University, West Lafayette, Indiana |
| Pfizer Award in Enzyme Chemistry | Joanne Stubbe | University of Wisconsin, Madison |
| Polanyi Medal | Sidney W. Benson | University of Southern California, Los Angeles |
| Priestley Medal | John D. Roberts | California Institute of Technology, Pasadena |
| Richard C. Tolman Medal | Arnold O. Beckman | Beckman Instruments, Fullerton, Calif. |
| Robert A. Welch Award | George C. Pimentel | University of California, Berkeley |
| Science Award | Andrew Van Hook (Emeritus) | College of the Holy Cross, Worcester, Mass. |
| Superior Civilian Service Award | David L. Venezky | Office of Naval Research, London |
| Wilfred T. Doherty Award | Zoltan A. Schelley | University of Texas, Arlington |
| Willard Gibbs Medal | Jack Halpern | University of Chicago, Ill. |
| Wolf Prize | Elias J. Corey | Stanford University, Calif. |
| Wolf Prize | Albert Eschenmoser | Swiss Federal Institute of Technology, Zürich |

## EARTH SCIENCES

| | | |
|---|---|---|
| Alexander Agassiz Medal | Wallace S. Broecker | Columbia University, New York, N.Y. |
| Arthur L. Day Medal | E-an Zen | U.S. Geological Survey |
| Arthur L. Day Prize and Lectureship | Harmon Craig | University of California, San Diego |
| Award for Outstanding Services to Meteorology | For Spacious Skies Foundation | Boston, Mass. |
| Carl-Gustaf Rossby Research Medal | Michael E. McIntyre | University of Cambridge, England |
| Charles Doolittle Walcott Medal | Andrew H. Knoll | Harvard University, Cambridge, Mass. |
| Charles Doolittle Walcott Medal | Simon C. Morris | University of Cambridge, England |
| Charles L. Mitchell Award | John A. Brown, Jr. | National Oceanic and Atmospheric Administration, Washington, D.C. |
| Charles L. Mitchell Award | Leo C. Clarke | U.S. Navy |

| AWARD | WINNER | AFFILIATION |
| --- | --- | --- |
| Clarence Leroy Meisinger Award | Isaac M. Held | Princeton University, N.J. |
| Cleveland Abbe Award | Alfred K. Blackadar | Pennsylvania State University, University Park |
| Crafoord Prize | Claude Allègre | Institut de Physique du Globe, Paris |
| Francis W. Reichelderfer Award | Robert E. Muller | Raleigh Weather Service Forecast Office, N.C. |
| George P. Merrill Award | Günter W. Lugmair | Scripps Institution of Oceanography, San Diego, Calif. |
| G. K. Warren Prize | Stanley A. Schumm | Colorado State University, Fort Collins |
| J. Lawrence Smith Medal | Gerald J. Wasserburg | California Institute of Technology, Pasadena |
| Jule G. Charney Award | Richard A. Anthes | National Center for Atmospheric Research, Boulder, Colo. |
| MacArthur Prize Fellow Award | John R. Horner | Museum of the Rockies, Montana State University, Bozeman |
| MacArthur Prize Fellow Award | Richard P. Turco | R & D Associates, Marina del Rey, Calif. |
| Mary Clark Thompson Medal | J. William Schopf | University of California, Los Angeles |
| Penrose Medal | Lawrence L. Sloss | Northwestern University, Evanston, Ill. |
| Robert Leviton Award | Gregory Byrne | University of Houston, Texas |
| Special Award of the American Meteorological Society | Leonard W. Snellman | University of Utah, Salt Lake City |
| Sverdrup Gold Medal | James J. O'Brien | Florida State University, Tallahassee |

## ELECTRONICS AND INFORMATION SCIENCES

| | | |
| --- | --- | --- |
| John Tyndall Award | Robert D. Mauer | Corning Glass Works |
| Miles Conrad Memorial Award | H. Edward Kennedy | Biosciences Information Service |
| Navanlinna Prize | Leslie G. Valiant | Harvard University, Cambridge, Mass. |

## ENERGY

| | | |
| --- | --- | --- |
| Esclangon Prize | M. Pigeon | Commissariat à l'Énergie Atomique, Paris |
| Foucault Prize | R. Campargue | Commissariat à l'Énergie Atomique, Paris |

## ENVIRONMENT

| | | |
| --- | --- | --- |
| Barrington Moore Memorial Award | Elbert L. Little, Jr. (Retired) | U.S. Forest Service |
| Charles Porter Award | C. Herb Ward | Rice University, Houston, Texas |
| F. H. Waring Award | Paul E. Flathman | O. H. Materials Co. |
| F. J. Zimmerman Award in Environmental Science | William H. Glaze | University of California, Los Angeles |
| Hugh Hammond Bennett Award | William C. Moldenhauer (Emeritus) | Purdue University, West Lafayette, Ind. |
| John A. Beale Memorial Award | Lloyd P. Blackwell (Emeritus) | Louisiana Tech University, Ruston |

| AWARD | WINNER | AFFILIATION |
| --- | --- | --- |
| John Burroughs Award | Gary Nabhan | Desert Botanical Garden, Phoenix, Ariz. |
| J. Paul Getty Wildlife Conservation Prize | Henry and Jean de Heaulme | Madagascar |
| J. Paul Getty Wildlife Conservation Prize | Sir Peter Scott | Wildfowl Trust, Gloucester, England |
| Kyoto Prize | G. Evelyn Hutchinson | Yale University, New Haven, Conn. |
| MacArthur Prize Fellow Award | Lester R. Brown | Worldwatch Institute, Washington, D.C. |
| Murray F. Buell Award for Excellence in Ecology | Kate Kajtha | Duke University, Durham, N.C. |
| Public Service Award | William C. Ashe | U.S. Fish and Wildlife Service |
| Public Service Award | Thomas Cabot (Emeritus) | Cabot Corp., Weston, Mass. |
| Public Service Award | Larry Henson | U.S. Forest Service |
| Public Service Award | Larry J. Wilson | Conservation Commission, Iowa |
| Sir William Schlich Award | Murlyn B. Dickerman (Retired) | U.S. Forest Service |
| Sol Feinstone Environmental Award | Ray L. Boice | Gering, Neb. |
| Sol Feinstone Environmental Award | Arthur P. Cooley | East Patchogue, N.Y. |
| Sol Feinstone Environmental Award | Ernest M. Dickerman | Swoope, Va. |
| Sol Feinstone Environmental Award | Lloyd C. Hulbert | Manhattan, Kan. |
| Sol Feinstone Environmental Award | Lenore N. McCullagh | Orange Park, Fla. |
| Technology Transfer and Extension Award | Marvin W. Blumenstock | University of Maine, Orono |
| Young Forester Leadership Award | Gary A. Moll | American Forestry Association, Washington, D.C. |

## FOOD AND AGRICULTURE

| | | |
| --- | --- | --- |
| Application of Agricultural and Food Chemistry Award | Tom J. Mabry | University of Texas, Austin |
| Bristol-Myers Award for Distinguished Achievement in Nutrition Research | Clement A. Finch | University of Washington, Seattle |
| Conrad A. Elvehjem Award for Public Service in Nutrition | Alfred E. Harper | University of Wisconsin, Madison |
| Crop Science Research Award | Glenn B. Collins | University of Kentucky, Lexington |
| Cyrus Hall McCormick Jerome Increase Case Gold Medal Award (1986) | Joseph K. Jones | Cotton, Inc. |
| Cyrus Hall McCormick Jerome Increase Case Gold Medal Award (1987) | Francis J. Hassler | Raleigh, N.C. |
| Hancor Soil and Water Engineering Award | R. Wayne Skaggs | North Carolina State University, Raleigh |
| Harvey W. Wiley Award | Jonathan W. White (Retired) | U.S. Department of Agriculture |
| Japan Prize | Henry M. Beachell | International Rice Research Institute, Philippines |

| AWARD | WINNER | AFFILIATION |
|---|---|---|
| Japan Prize | Gurdev S. Khush | International Rice Research Institute, Philippines |
| John Deere Medal | C. Glenn E. Downing (Retired) | North Vancouver, B.C., Canada |
| Kishida International Award | Bill A. Stout | Texas A & M University, College Station |
| Lederle Award in Human Nutrition | Mary Frances Picciano | University of Illinois, Urbana |
| Massey-Ferguson Medal | Gordon L. Nelson | Ohio State University, Columbus |
| Mead Johnson Award for Research in Nutrition | Dale A. Schoeller | University of Chicago, Ill. |
| Osborne and Mendel Award | Aloys L. Tappel | University of California, Davis |
| Wolf Prize | Sir Ralph Riley | Agricultural and Food Research Council, U.K. |
| Wolf Prize | Ernest R. R. Sears | University of Missouri, Columbia |

## LIFE SCIENCES

| | | |
|---|---|---|
| Albert Lasker Basic Medical Research Award | Stanley Cohen | Vanderbilt University, Nashville, Tenn. |
| Albert Lasker Basic Medical Research Award | Rita Levi-Montalcini | Institute of Cell Biology, Rome |
| Applied and Environmental Microbiology Award | Marvin P. Bryant | University of Illinois, Urbana |
| Bio Expo 86 Award | U.S. Office of Technology Assessment | Washington, D.C. |
| Burroughs Wellcome Toxicology Scholar Award | Daniel Acosta, Jr. | University of Texas, Austin |
| Carski Foundation [Distingushed Teaching] Award | Samuel Kaplan | University of Illinois, Urbana |
| Charles Thom Award | Shukuo Kinoshita (Retired) | Kyowa Hakko Kogyo Co., Japan |
| Eli Lilly Award in Biological Chemistry | James E. Rothman | Stanford University, Calif. |
| European Molecular Biology Organization Prize | John Tooze | European Molecular Biology Organization, Heidelberg, West Germany |
| Experimental Animal Nutrition Award | Robert D. Steele | Rutgers University, New Brunswick, N.J. |
| Fankuchen Award | Michael G. Rossmann | Purdue University, West Lafayette, Ind. |
| Gairdner Foundation International Award | James Darnell | Rockefeller University, New York, N.Y. |
| Gairdner Foundation International Award | Phillip A. Sharp | Massachusetts Institute of Technology, Cambridge |
| Gairdner Foundation International Award | Michael Smith | University of British Columbia, Vancouver, Canada |
| Gilbert Morgan Smith Medal | Richard C. Starr | University of Texas, Austin |
| International Prize for Biology | Peter H. Raven | Missouri Botanical Garden, St. Louis, Mo.; Washington University, St. Louis, Mo. |
| John J. Carty Award for the Advancement of Science | Motoo Kimura | National Institute of Genetics, Mishima, Japan |
| J. Roger Porter Award | Barbara J. Bachmann | Yale University, New Haven, Conn. |

| AWARD | WINNER | AFFILIATION |
|---|---|---|
| Kyoto Prize | Nicole M. LeDouarin | Institut d'Embryologie, Nogent-sur-Marne, France |
| Lawrence Memorial Award | Andrew J. Henderson | City University of New York and New York Botanical Garden, N.Y. |
| Louis and Bert Freedman Award for Research in Biochemistry | Arthur Karlin | Columbia University, New York, N.Y. |
| Luigi Provasoli Award | Annette W. Coleman | Brown University, Providence, R.I. |
| Luigi Provasoli Award | Lynda J. Goff | University of California, Santa Cruz |
| MacArthur Prize Fellow Award | David Page | Massachusetts Institute of Technology, Cambridge |
| MacArthur Prize Fellow Award | Robert M. Shapley | Rockefeller University, New York, N.Y. |
| MacArthur Prize Fellow Award | Allan C. Wilson | University of California, Berkeley |
| Meritorious Service Award of the U.S. Department of Interior | Paul Eschmeyer | U.S. Fish and Wildlife Service |
| New York Academy of Sciences Award in Biological and Medical Sciences | Kjell G. Fuxe | Karolinska Institutet, Stockholm, Sweden |
| New York Academy of Sciences Award in Biological and Medical Sciences | Tomas Hokfelt | Karolinska Institutet, Stockholm, Sweden |
| Repligen Award | Gregorio Weber | University of Illinois, Urbana |
| Selman A. Waksman Award in Microbiology | Harland G. Wood (Retired) | Western Reserve University, Cleveland, Ohio |
| U.S. Steel Foundation Award in Molecular Biology | Thomas R. Cech | University of Colorado, Boulder |
| V. D. Mattia Award | Gunter Blobel | Rockefeller University, New York, N.Y. |
| Wolf Prize | David M. Blow | Imperial College, London |
| Wolf Prize | Sir David Phillips | University of Oxford, England |

## MATHEMATICS

| AWARD | WINNER | AFFILIATION |
|---|---|---|
| Cole Prize in Number Theory | Dorian M. Goldfeld | Columbia University, New York, N.Y. |
| Cole Prize in Number Theory | Benedict H. Gross | Harvard University, Cambridge, Mass. |
| Cole Prize in Number Theory | Don B. Zagier | University of Maryland, College Park; Max Planck Institute, West Germany |
| Fields Medal | Simon Donaldson | University of Oxford, England |
| Fields Medal | Gerd Faltings | Princeton University, N.J. |
| Fields Medal | Michael Freedman | University of California, San Diego |
| Leroy P. Steele Prize | Rudolf E. Kalman | University of Florida, Gainesville |
| Leroy P. Steele Prize | Donald E. Knuth | Stanford University, Calif. |
| Leroy P. Steele Prize | Saunders MacLane | University of Chicago, Ill. |
| MacArthur Prize Fellow Award | Benedict H. Gross | Harvard University, Cambridge, Mass. |
| National Academy of Sciences Award in Applied Mathematics and Numerical Analysis | Oscar E. Lanford III | University of California, Berkeley |

| AWARD | WINNER | AFFILIATION |
| --- | --- | --- |
| Third World Academy of Sciences Mathematics Prize | Liao Shan Tao | China |
| Wolf Prize | Samuel Eilenberg | Columbia University, New York, N.Y. |
| Wolf Prize | Alte Selberg | Institute for Advanced Study, Princeton, N.J. |

## MEDICAL SCIENCES

| AWARD | WINNER | AFFILIATION |
| --- | --- | --- |
| A. Cressy Morrison Award in Natural Sciences | Janet D. Rowley | University of Chicago, Ill. |
| Albert Lasker Clinical Medical Research Award | Myron Essex | Harvard University, Cambridge, Mass. |
| Albert Lasker Clinical Medical Research Award | Robert C. Gallo | National Institutes of Health, Bethesda, Md. |
| Albert Lasker Clinical Medical Research Award | Luc Montagnier | Pasteur Institute, Paris |
| Becton-Dickinson Award in Clinical Microbiology | Stanley Falkow | Stanford University, Calif. |
| Behring Diagnostics Award | Thomas F. Smith | Mayo Clinic, Rochester, Minn. |
| Bio Expo 86 Award | Genentech, Inc. | San Francisco, Calif. |
| Burroughs Wellcome Molecular Parasitology Award | John Boothroyd | Stanford University, Calif. |
| Burroughs Wellcome Molecular Parasitology Award | Jeffrey Ravetch | Memorial Sloan-Kettering Cancer Center, New York, N.Y. |
| Borden Award in Nutrition | Barry Wolf | Medical College of Virginia, Richmond |
| Distinguished Service Award of the American Medical Association | G. Valter Brindley, Jr. | Texas A & M University, College Station |
| Distinguished Service Award of the American Medical Association | Kenneth M. Brinkhous (Emeritus) | University of North Carolina, Chapel Hill |
| Dr. William Beaumont Award in Medicine | Bergein F. Overholt | University of Michigan, Ann Arbor |
| Dr. William Beaumont Award in Medicine | F. Douglas Scutchfield | University of California, San Diego |
| Gairdner Foundation International Award | Adolfo J. de Bold | University of Ottawa, Canada |
| Gairdner Foundation International Award | Jean-François Borel | Sandoz Ltd., Basel, Switzerland |
| Gairdner Foundation International Award | Peter C. Doherty | Australian National University, Canberra |
| Gairdner Foundation International Award | T. Geoffrey Flynn | Queen's University, Kingston, Ont. |
| Gairdner Foundation International Award | Harald Sonnenberg | University of Toronto, Ont. |
| Gairdner Foundation International Award | Rolf M. Zinkernagel | University of Zürich, Switzerland |
| Gairdner Foundation Wightman Award | Aser Rothstein | Hospital for Sick Children, Toronto, Ont. |
| Hammer Prize | Tadatsugu Taniguchi | Osaka University, Japan |
| Hammer Prize | Steven A. Rosenberg | National Institutes of Health, Bethesda, Md. |
| Hoechst-Roussel Award | Julian E. Davies | Pasteur Institute, Paris |

| AWARD | WINNER | AFFILIATION |
| --- | --- | --- |
| Inventor of the Year Award | David F. Mark | Cetus Corp., Emeryville, Calif. |
| Inventor of the Year Award | Leo S. Lin | Cetus Corp., Emeryville, Calif. |
| Inventor of the Year Award | Shi-Da Yu Lu | Cetus Corp., Emeryville, Calif. |
| Joseph B. Goldberger Award in Clinical Nutrition | Albert J. Stunkard | University of Pennsylvania, Philadelphia |
| Joseph B. Goldberger Award in Clinical Nutrition | Theodore B. Van Itallie | St. Luke's Hospital Center, New York, N.Y. |
| Louis Jeantet Foundation Prize | Michael Berridge | University of Cambridge, England |
| Louis Jeantet Foundation Prize | Sydney Brenner | Medical Research Council, U.K. |
| Louis Jeantet Foundation Prize | Désiré Collen | Catholic University of Louvain, Belgium |
| Louis Jeantet Foundation Prize | Walter Gehring | University of Basel, Switzerland |
| Louis Jeantet Foundation Prize | Luc Montagnier | Pasteur Institute, France |
| Louis Jeantet Foundation Prize | Dominique Stehelin | Pasteur Institute, France |
| Madison Marshall Award | John Montgomery | Southern Research Institute, Birmingham, Ala. |
| Paul Ehrlich and Ludwig Darmstaedter Prize | Abner L. Notkins | National Institutes of Health, Bethesda, Md. |
| Richard Lounsbery Award | Alfred G. Gilman | University of Texas, Dallas |
| Scientific Achievement Award | George E. Burch (Deceased) | Tulane University, New Orleans, La. |
| Scientific Achievement Award | Solomon H. Snyder | Johns Hopkins University, Baltimore, Md. |
| Wolf Prize | Pedro Cuatrecasas | Duke University, Durham, N.C.; University of North Carolina, Chapel Hill |
| Wolf Prize | Osamu Hayaishi | Osaka Medical College, Japan |

## OPTICAL ENGINEERING

| | | |
| --- | --- | --- |
| C. E. K. Mees Medal | Adolf W. Lohmann | Friedrich Alexander University of Erlangen-Nurnberg, West Germany |
| David Richardson Medal | John W. Evans | National Solar Observatory, Sunspot, N.M. |
| Distinguished Service Award of the Optical Society of America | John N. Howard (Retired) | Air Force Geophysics Laboratory, Hanscom Air Force Base, Mass. |
| Frederic Ives Medal | Anthony E. Siegman | Stanford University, Calif. |
| Joseph Fraunhofer Award | Jerzy A. Dobrowolski | National Research Council, Ottawa |
| R. W. Wood Prize | David E. Aspnes | AT&T Bell Laboratories |

## PHYSICS

| | | |
| --- | --- | --- |
| Aimé Cotton Prize | Jean-Luc Destombes | University of Lille, France |
| Ancel Prize | Daniel Beysens | Center for Nuclear Research, Saclay, France |
| Brelot Prize | Françoise Hippert | University of Paris, Orsay, France |
| Bruno Rossi Prize | Allan S. Jacobson | Jet Propulsion Laboratory, Pasadena, Calif. |
| Charles Hard Townes Award | Hermann A. Haus | Massachusetts Institute of Technology, Cambridge |
| Commonwealth Award in Science | Alain Aspect | Collège de France, Laboratoire de Spectroscopie Hertzienne de l'Ecole Normale Supérieure, Paris |

| AWARD | WINNER | AFFILIATION |
| --- | --- | --- |
| Copley Medal | Sir Rudolf Peierls (Emeritus) | University of Oxford, England |
| Dannie Heineman Prize | Alexander M. Polyakov | Landau Institute for Theoretical Physics, Moscow |
| Davisson-Germer Prize | Daniel Kleppner | Massachusetts Institute of Technology, Cambridge |
| Dirac Medal | Yoichiro Nambu | Enrico Fermi Institute, Chicago, Ill. |
| Dirac Medal | Alexander M. Polyakov | Landau Institute for Theoretical Physics, Moscow |
| Ellis R. Lippincott Award | Wolfgang Kaiser | Technical University of Munich, West Germany |
| Enrico Fermi Award | Ernest D. Courant | Brookhaven National Laboratory, Upton, N.Y. |
| Enrico Fermi Award | M. Stanley Livingston (Deceased) | Massachusetts Institute of Technology, Cambridge; Brookhaven National Laboratory, Upton, N.Y. |
| Ernest Orlando Lawrence Memorial Award | James J. Diederstadt | University of Michigan, Ann Arbor |
| Ernest Orlando Lawrence Memorial Award | Helen T. Edwards | Fermi National Laboratory, Batavia, Ill |
| Ernest Orlando Lawrence Memorial Award | Joseph W. Gray | Lawrence Livermore National Laboratory, Calif. |
| Ernest Orlando Lawrence Memorial Award | James L. Smith | Los Alamos National Laboratory, N.M. |
| Excellence in Plasma Physics Research Award | Alfred Y. F. Wong | University of California, Los Angeles |
| Grand Prize of the Académie Française | Charles Peyrou (Retired) | CERN |
| Grand Prize of the Académie Française | Jacques Prentki (Retired) | CERN |
| Holweck Prize | Denis Jérôme | University of Paris, Orsay, France |
| Hughes Medal | M. M. Woolfson | University of York, Heslington, England |
| James Clerk Maxwell Prize | John H. Malmberg | University of California, San Diego |
| Japan Prize | Theodore H. Maiman (Retired) | Marina Del Rey, Calif. |
| Jean Ricard Prize | Jacques Villain | Jülich, West Germany |
| J. J. Sakurai Prize | David J. Gross | Princeton University, N.J. |
| J. J. Sakurai Prize | H. David Politzer | California Institute of Technology, Pasadena |
| J. J. Sakurai Prize | Frank Wilczek | Institute for Theoretical Physics, Santa Barbara, Calif. |
| Joliot-Curie Prize | Jean-Jacques Aubert | University of Aix-Marseille, France |
| King Carlos I Prize | Luis E. Ibanez | Spain |
| King Olav Gold Medal | Jan Wroldsen | CERN |
| Langevin Prize | Mannque Rho | Center for Nuclear Research, Saclay, France |
| Lenin Prize for Science and Technology | Sergey P. Denisov | Institute of High Energy Physics, Serpukhov, U.S.S.R. |
| Lenin Prize for Science and Technology | Yury D. Prokoshkin | Institute of High Energy Physics, Serpukhov, U.S.S.R. |

| AWARD | WINNER | AFFILIATION |
|---|---|---|
| Leo Szilard Award for Physics in the Public Interest | Arthur H. Rosenfeld | University of California, Berkeley |
| MacArthur Prize Fellow Award | Albert J. Libchaber | University of Chicago, Ill. |
| Maria Goeppert-Mayer Award | Judith S. Young | University of Massachusetts, Amherst |
| Max Born Award | Emil Wolf | University of Rochester, N.Y. |
| National Academy of Sciences Public Welfare Medal | Dale R. Corson (Retired) | Cornell University, Ithaca, N.Y. |
| Nishina Memorial Prize | Toyoichi Tanaka | Massachusetts Institute of Technology, Cambridge |
| Otto Laporte Award | Hans W. Liepmann | California Institute of Technology, Pasadena |
| Ramon y Cajal Award | Alberto Galindo | Spain |
| Ramon y Cajal Award | Pere Pascual | Spain |
| Robertson Memorial Lecture | Yakov Zeldovich | Institute of Chemical Physics, Moscow |
| Rumford Medal | Hans G. Dehmelt | University of Washington, Seattle |
| Rumford Medal | Martin Deutsch | Massachusetts Institute of Technology, Cambridge |
| Rumford Medal | Vernon W. Hughes | Yale University, New Haven, Conn. |
| Rumford Medal | Norman F. Ramsey | Harvard University, Cambridge, Mass. |
| Third World Academy of Sciences Physics Prize | E. C. G. Sudarshan | India |
| Tom W. Bonner Prize in Nuclear Physics | Lowell M. Bollinger | Argonne National Laboratory, Ill. |
| Wigner Medal | Feza Gürsey | Yale University, New Haven, Conn. |
| William F. Meggers Award | Hans R. Griem | University of Maryland, College Park |
| Wolf Prize | Mitchell J. Feigenbaum | Cornell University, Ithaca, N.Y. |
| Wolf Prize | Albert J. Libchaber | University of Chicago, Ill. |

## PSYCHOLOGY

| | | |
|---|---|---|
| MacArthur Prize Fellow Award | Paul R. Adams | State University of New York, Stony Brook |
| National Academy of Sciences Award for Scientific Reviewing | Gardner Lindzey | University of Texas, Austin |
| Troland Research Award | Laurence T. Maloney | University of Michigan, Ann Arbor |
| Troland Research Award | Brian A. Wandell | Stanford University, Calif. |

## SPACE EXPLORATION

| | | |
|---|---|---|
| Arthur S. Fleming Award | Samuel L. Venneri | NASA |

## TRANSPORTATION

| | | |
|---|---|---|
| Arthur S. Fleming Award | Bruce J. Holmes | NASA |
| British Gold Medal | Ronald W. Howard | GEC Avionics, Rochester, Kent, England |
| British Silver Medal | Frank G. Willox | Eurofighter Jagdflugzeug GmbH, West Germany |

| AWARD | WINNER | AFFILIATION |
|---|---|---|
| Bronze Medal of the Royal Aeronautical Society | David C. R. Link | British Aerospace, U.K. |
| Elder Statesman of Aviation Award | J. B. Hartranft, Jr. | Aircraft Owners and Pilots Association of the U.S. |
| Elder Statesman of Aviation Award | Anthony Levier (Retired) | Lockheed Corp., Calif. |
| Elder Statesman of Aviation Award | John P. Riddle | Embry-Riddle Aeronautical University, Daytona Beach, Fla. |
| Elder Statesman of Aviation Award | John Worth | Academy of Model Aeronautics, Reston, Va. |
| Frank G. Brewer Trophy | Charles A. Anderson (Retired) | Tuskegee Institute, Ala. |
| Gold Air Medal of the International Aeronautic Federation | Ralph P. Alex | Ralph P. Alex & Associates, Fairfield, Conn. |
| Gold Medal of the Royal Aeronautical Society | Ralph S. Hooper (Retired) | British Aerospace, U.K. |
| National Academy of Sciences Award in Aeronautical Engineering | Thornton A. Wilson | Boeing Co. |
| Pecora Award | Allen H. Watkins | U.S. Department of the Interior |
| R. P. Alston Medal | Richard J. Poole | British Aerospace, U.K. |
| Silver Medal of the Royal Aeronautical Society | Peter G. Wilby | Royal Aircraft Establishment, Farnborough, England |
| Wakefield Gold Medal | John G. Jones | Royal Aircraft Establishment, Farnborough, England |
| Wright Brothers Memorial Trophy | Joseph F. Sutter | Boeing Co. |

## SCIENCE JOURNALISM

| AWARD | WINNER | AFFILIATION |
|---|---|---|
| American Association for the Advancement of Science-Newcomb Cleveland Prize | Maria Chow | Massachusetts Institute of Technology, Cambridge |
| American Association for the Advancement of Science-Newcomb Cleveland Prize | David J. Filman | Scripps Clinic and Research Foundation, San Diego, Calif. |
| American Association for the Advancement of Science-Newcomb Cleveland Prize | James M. Hoyle | Scripps Clinic and Research Foundation, San Diego, Calif. |
| American Institute of Physics Science-Writing Award | Donald Goldsmith | San Francisco, Calif. |
| MacArthur Prize Fellow Award | Thomas Whiteside | *New Yorker* magazine |

## MISCELLANEOUS

| AWARD | WINNER | AFFILIATION |
|---|---|---|
| Forum Award | Spurgeon M. Keeny, Jr. | Arms Control Association, Washington, D.C. |
| International Hall of Fame World Award of the Inventors Clubs of America | Yoshiro Nakamatsu | Tokyo, Japan |
| Jean Perrin Prize | G. Meurgues | Paris Museum |
| Jean Perrin Prize | J. M. Pelt | University of Metz, France |
| MacArthur Prize Fellow Award | Richard M. A. Benson | Yale University, New Haven, Conn. |

| AWARD | WINNER | AFFILIATION |
| --- | --- | --- |
| Presidential Award of the Inventors Clubs of America | Yoshiro Nakamatsu | Tokyo, Japan |
| Scientific Freedom and Responsibility Award of the American Association for the Advancement of Science | Chilean Medical Association | Santiago, Chile |
| Scientific Freedom and Responsibility Award of the American Association for the Advancement of Science | Victor Paschkis (Emeritus) | Columbia University, New York, N.Y. |
| Washburn Award | Robert D. Ballard | Woods Hole Oceanographic Institute, Mass. |
| Westinghouse Science Talent Search | 1. Louise Chia Chang | University of Chicago Laboratory Schools High School, Illinois |
| | 2. Elizabeth L. Wilmer | Stuyvesant High School, New York, N.Y. |
| | 3. Albert Jun-Wei Wong | Oak Ridge High School, Tenn. |
| | 4. Joseph Chen-yu Wang | Forest High School, Ocala, Fla. |
| | 5. Daniel J. Bernstein | Bellport High School, Brookhaven, N.Y. |
| | 6. Stephen A. Racunas | Valley High School, New Kensington, Pa. |
| | 7. Maxwell V. Meng | Centennial High School, Ellicott City, Md. |
| | 8. Todd A. Waldman | Walt Whitman High School, Bethesda, Md. |
| | 9. Maria J. Silveira | Bronx High School of Science, New York, N.Y. |
| | 10. Michael P. Mossey | Greenhills High School, Cincinnati, Ohio |

# Obituaries

**Bonestell, Chesley Knight, Jr.** (Jan. 1, 1888—June 11, 1986), U.S. architect and artist, earned the reputation of "dean of space artists" because of the realistic conceptualizations of planets in his paintings. Born in San Francisco, he became fascinated with astronomy when he was a child and began painting on the subject at the age of five. His first paintings of Saturn, however, were destroyed in the great San Francisco earthquake (April 18, 1906) and ensuing fire.

At the age of 12 Bonestell began formal instruction in art, and in 1911 he began architectural studies at Columbia University in New York City. Though he never graduated from college, he passed the California state board examination and became a certified architect, working for Willis Polk, who pioneered glass "curtain wall" construction. Bonestell later worked in New York City before he went to London in 1922. He made an extensive tour of Italy (1925–26) before returning to New York in 1927. He moved back to San Francisco in 1931 and launched a career in Hollywood in 1938, working for RKO studios as a special-effects matte artist. His unique talents were used for such motion pictures as *The Hunchback of Notre Dame* (1939) and *Citizen Kane* (1941) and later for such science-fiction films as *Destination Moon* (1950), *When Worlds Collide* (1951), *War of the Worlds* (1953), and *Conquest of Space* (1955).

Bonestell established a career as a space artist in 1944 with a series of paintings of Saturn that he sold to *Life* magazine. His astronomical paintings were lauded because of his mastery in depicting planets as viewed from their satellites. He was a perfectionist

*Chesley Knight Bonestell, Jr.*

Courtesy, Bonestell Space Art; photo, Cedric Braun

in attaining an authentic representation that corresponded with known scientific data. Later, when more up-to-date scientific information was available, it was discovered that Bonestell's finely crafted scale drawings were more accurate than anyone had imagined. Besides providing space illustrations for such magazines as *Collier's*, *The Magazine of Fantasy and Science Fiction*, and *Galaxy Science Fiction*, he collaborated with German rocketeer Wernher von Braun and science writer Willy Ley to produce such illustrated books as *The Conquest of Space*, *Conquest of the Moon*, and *The Exploration of Mars*.

Bonestell continued to paint throughout his life, and during the early 1970s, after years of historical research, he recreated in oil the Spanish California missions as they appeared during the 17th and 18th centuries. In 1986, in recognition of his contributions to the development of the space program, an asteroid was named "Bonestell."

**Busemann, Adolf** (April 20, 1901—Nov. 3, 1986), German aerospace engineer, was dubbed "the father of supersonic flight" for his invention of the swept-back-wing design used in U.S. F-86 and Soviet MiG-15 jet fighters during the Korean War. His invention, which he unveiled at the Volta Congress in Rome in 1935, permitted jet planes to exceed the speed of sound. After earning a Ph.D. in engineering from the Technical University of Brunswick in Germany, he served (1925–31) as a research scientist at the Max Planck Institute in Germany and was a privatdocent (unsalaried lecturer [1931–35]) at the University of Dresden. After immigrating to the U.S. in 1947, Busemann served as a research scientist for the National Aeronautics and Space Administration (NASA). There he designed a rotating space station and recommended that ceramic tiles rather than aluminum be used as heat shields on the space shuttle. From 1963 to 1969 he was professor of aerospace engineering at the University of Colorado and from 1969 he was professor emeritus.

**Cooper, David Graham** (Feb. 11, 1931—July 29, 1986), South African-born psychiatrist, was, with R. D. Laing, a proponent in the 1960s of "antipsychiatry"; later he claimed that the age of "nonpsychiatry" was beginning. A Marxist, he came to regard psychiatry as a tool of capitalism and maintained that "all delusion is political statement," the individual's protest against bourgeois conformism. "Antipsychiatry" (later rejected by Laing) was represented as the struggle against medical manipulation. In the 1970s, convinced that capitalism was already in its death throes, Cooper asserted that with "nonpsychiatry" disturbed behavior would be channeled as a source of social creativity.

Cooper studied medicine at the University of Cape Town before going to England, where he held a series of posts in London hospitals. He became di-

*David Graham Cooper*

rector of Villa 21, an experimental unit for young schizophrenics. He and Laing founded the Philadelphia Association, which established such therapeutic communities as Kingsley Hall in London's East End (1965–70). Cooper became an "antidirector" of the so-called Institute of Phenomenological Studies and in 1967 organized a Congress on the Dialectics of Liberation. From 1974 he lived mainly in Paris, lecturing in psychopathology at the University of Vincennes (University of Paris VIII); by that time he had abandoned all psychiatric practice. He traveled extensively, visiting the U.S., South America, Mexico, Japan, Belgium, and Italy. His books include *Psychiatry and Anti-Psychiatry* (1967), *The Death of the Family* (1971), and *The Language of Madness* (1978).

**Deng Jiaxian** (TENG CHIA-HSIEN) (1924—July 29, 1986), Chinese physicist, was acknowledged shortly before his death as the "father of China's nuclear bomb." He was the architect of the country's first atomic bomb, exploded on Oct. 16, 1964, and the first hydrogen bomb, exploded in June 1967. After Deng graduated (1945) from China's Southwest Associated University, he went to the U.S. (1948), where he earned a Ph.D. in physics from Purdue University. He returned to China in 1950 after the Communist victory there and in 1958 was appointed head of the theoretical department of the Nuclear Weapons Research Institute. Working without the aid of a model, his dedicated team of scientists successfully constructed the design for China's first atomic bomb in 1959. Deng, who directed 15 of China's 32 nuclear tests, was instrumental in developing the country's nuclear weapons arsenal. Besides his scientific contributions, he was a member of the Communist Party Central Committee and at the time of his death held a number of high government posts.

**Doisy, Edward Adelbert** (Nov. 13, 1893—Oct. 23, 1986), U.S. biochemist, won the 1943 Nobel Prize for Physiology or Medicine for the discovery of vitamin K. Doisy shared the prize with Henrik Dam, who independently isolated the vitamin in 1939. After earning A.B. and M.S. degrees from the University of Illinois, Doisy received (1920) his Ph.D. from Harvard University and then joined the faculty of Washington University School of Medicine in St. Louis, Mo. Doisy, working with embryologist Edgar Allen, isolated a variant form of vitamin K, vitamin $K_2$, and such sex hormones as estron (theelin, 1929), the first estrogen to be crystallized; estriol (theelol, 1930); and estradiol (dihydrotheelin, 1935). After helping to establish the biochemistry department at Washington University, Doisy was named chairman of the department in 1924. His accomplishments were recognized in 1955 when the university's department of biochemistry was named for him. Doisy retired in 1965. Some of his scientific writings include *Sex Hormones* (1936) and *Sex and Internal Secretions* (1939), with Allen and Charles H. Danforth.

*Edward Adelbert Doisy*

**Espenschied, Lloyd** (April 27, 1889—June 21, 1986), U.S. electrical engineer, together with Herman A. Affel invented (1929) the coaxial cable, a high-frequency transmission line that made television transmission possible. Espenschied's coaxial cable for wide-band, long-distance transmission significantly improved voice traffic. While attending Manual Training High School in Brooklyn, New York City, Espenschied constructed (1905) one of the first amateur wireless telegraph stations; he left school to become a wireless telegraph operator aboard a ship but recognized that he required more formal education. He entered Pratt Institute, Brooklyn, where he studied engineering and earned a degree in 1909. The following year he joined the engineering department at American Telephone and Telegraph Co. in New York City and five years later played a vital role in the first experiments with radio voice transmission overseas. In 1935 Espenschied's department was incorporated with Bell Telephone Laboratories, Inc., and he was appointed director of the high-frequency transmission department. During his long career he also worked on electric reflection systems and was the inventor of the radio altimeter, which used the reflection of radio waves from the Earth for the determination of altitude. The device was first applied to aerial navigation in 1938. Espenschied, the holder of more than 100 patents, retired in 1954.

**Hanfmann, George M(axim) A(nossov)** (Nov. 20, 1911—March 13, 1986), Russian-born archaeologist, as field director (1958–76) and then director (1976–78) of the Harvard-Cornell archaeological expedition in Sardis, Turkey, unearthed a treasure trove that included evidence of gold refineries, a marble-paved shopping street, and a mammoth synagogue constructed in the 3rd century AD. Hanfmann, who earned (1934) a Ph.D. in classical philology from the University of Berlin, emigrated to the U.S. in 1934 and the following year received a Ph.D. in philosophy from Johns Hopkins University, Baltimore, Md. He joined the faculty at Harvard University in 1935 and for many years served as professor of fine arts. In 1947–48 he participated as a member of an archaeological expedition conducting excavations in Tarsus, Turkey. Besides teaching he also served (1946–74) as curator of ancient art at Harvard's Fogg Art Museum, where he organized such exhibitions as "Ancient Art in American Private Collections," "Master Bronzes of the Ancient World," and "The Beauty of Ancient Art." He was probably best known, however, for his excavations in the ancient city of Sardis, the capital of the kingdom of Lydia and a leading cultural and commercial center of the Mediterranean and Near Eastern world. During his excavations Hanfmann found evidence that Sardis was seized by wandering Greek veterans of the Trojan War in the 12th century BC; he also discovered tons of pottery and jewelry and Bronze Age burial urns dating from 2500 to 2200 BC, a find that indicated that civilization in Sardis was at least 1,000 years older than had been believed. The rich archaeological site of Sardis yielded inscriptions in six languages; gold artifacts predating the reign of Croesus (560–546 BC); the tomb of King Gyges, who ruled Lydia in the 7th century BC; a monument to the Lydian mother-goddess, Cybele; and a Roman bath with a heating system. These discoveries helped archaeologists define the transition from the Bronze Age to the Iron Age in western Asia Minor. Hanfmann chronicled his achievements in nine volumes published by the Harvard University Press and in *Sardis from Prehistoric to Roman Times* (1983), a condensed version of his scholarly work. The author of more than 350 books, articles, and reviews, he

served as senior editor and adviser for the Sardis expedition until his death.

**Hass, Henry Bohn** (Jan. 25, 1902—Feb. 13, 1987), U.S. chemist, discovered gas chromatography, an important technique used in analytical chemistry to separate chemical substances. In this method the material to be separated is carried by a moving gas stream through a tube packed with a finely divided solid that may be coated with a film of a liquid. It is widely used to analyze mixtures and purify chemical compounds. An expert in organic chemistry, Hass earned (1925) a Ph.D. in chemistry from Ohio State University before joining (1928) the faculty of Purdue University, West Lafayette, Ind., where he taught until 1949. He then entered the field of industrial chemistry as manager of research and development for General Aniline and Film Corp. In 1952 he became president of the Sugar Research Foundation and helped discover that sugar could be used in the manufacture of newsprint, cosmetics, phonograph records, insecticides, and explosives. As an inventor he held more than 50 patents for new chemical processes and new products. He was also recognized as an authority on active carbon, which has high absorptive properties and is used in gas masks to absorb poisonous vapors; he developed a process for deinking paper that utilized active carbon. Hass was credited with inventing the heat-and-mix method of thermal chlorination and the vapor-phase nitration of saturated hydrocarbons, a discovery that made explosives and other important products commercially available. During World War II he worked on the development of the atomic bomb in the top-secret Manhattan Project. At the time of his retirement in 1970, he was director of chemical research with M. W. Kellogg. Hass was the recipient of the Perkin Medal of the Society of Chemical Industries and the Gold Medal of the American Institute of Chemists.

**Herbert, Frank Patrick** (Oct. 8, 1920—Feb. 11, 1986), U.S. science fiction writer, was the object of a cultlike following as the best-selling author of the "Dune" series of futuristic novels. He produced carefully researched, highly complex works that explored such themes as ecology, human evolution, the consequences of genetic manipulation, and mystical and psychic possibilities. Herbert's fiction, which reflected present-day political and social realities rather than escapist fantasy, included the epic *Dune* (1965), which was translated into 14 languages and sold more than 12 million copies, and its sequels *Dune Messiah* (1969), *Children of Dune* (1976), *God-Emperor of Dune* (1981), and *Chapterhouse: Dune* (1985). Though Herbert worked for several newspapers, including the *San Francisco Examiner* and the *Seattle* (Wash.) *Post-Intelligencer*, he left journalism in 1972 in order to devote all his time to writing. Included among his more than two dozen novels were

*Frank Patrick Herbert*

the highly acclaimed *Dragon in the Sea, The Green Brain, The God Makers, The Santaroga Barrier, The Heaven Makers, The Dosadi Experiment,* and *The Jesus Incident.* At the time of his death, Herbert was working on the next novel in the "Dune" series.

**Hynek, J(osef) Allen** (May 1, 1910—April 27, 1986), U.S. astrophysicist, was instrumental in obtaining a measure of respectability for the study of unidentified flying objects (UFOs) by neither discounting nor sensationalizing the possibility of their existence. The "Galileo of UFOlogy" earned a Ph.D. (1935) from the University of Chicago and taught astronomy (1935–41 and 1946–56) at Ohio State University. In 1948 he became scientific consultant on UFOs to the U.S. Air Force, and his levelheaded and open-minded approach gained him respect in the scientific community. Though Hynek believed that most "flying saucers" could be explained as meteors, weather balloons, aircraft, hallucinations, or hoaxes, he claimed to have studied more than 10,000 sightings and concluded that at least 500 were unex-

*J. Allen Hynek*

plained. In 1966, when an unusually high number of sightings occurred in Michigan, he was summoned to investigate; he discovered that the strange celestial lights probably were caused by luminous marsh gas.

In 1956 Hynek joined the Smithsonian Astrophysical Observatory as associate director to Fred L. Whipple. In preparation for the 1957–58 International Geophysical Year and the orbiting of artificial satellites to gather data, Hynek was placed in charge of predicting the satellite orbits and supervising optical tracking of the satellites by 12 observatories strategically placed throughout the world. The project became known as Operation Moonwatch.

From 1960 until his retirement in 1978, Hynek was chairman of the department of astronomy at Northwestern University in Evanston, Ill., and director of its Dearborn Observatory. He was the author of *Challenge of the Universe* (1962) and *The UFO Experience* (1972), in which he coined the phrase "close encounters of the third kind" to describe contact with a UFO or an alien being. For many years he published a monthly newsletter, *International UFO Reporter,* and in 1973 he established the Center for UFO Studies in Evanston, which he relocated in Scottsdale, Ariz., when he moved there in 1985.

**Jolly, Hugh Reginald** (May 5, 1918—March 4, 1986), British pediatrician, was physician in charge of the pediatrics department of the Charing Cross Hospital, London (1965–84). He was internationally known for his widely translated *Book of Child Care* (1975) and was largely responsible for the current, more relaxed attitudes toward all aspects of child rearing. He encouraged the presence of fathers at their children's births and promoted breast-feeding on a system he called "ask feeding." Jolly also pioneered in allowing unrestricted parental visits with children in the hospital.

Educated at Marlborough College and at Sidney Sussex College, University of Cambridge, he completed his medical studies at the London Hospital, qualifying in 1942. Following service as a captain in the Royal Army Medical Corps (1944–47), he worked at the Hospital for Sick Children, Great Ormond Street, London, before spending the 1950s as consultant pediatrician at Plymouth. Jolly was also professor of pediatrics at University College, Ibadan, Nigeria (1961–62) and visiting professor of child health at Ghana Medical School (1965–67). Although his contributions to psychoanalysis are not explicit, Jolly believed that the problems of children are often really those of their parents. He stressed the psychological necessity of mourning and encouraged the maternity staff to treat the parents of stillborn babies with greater understanding. Jolly was renowned in Britain as a medical journalist in both broadcast and print media, as well as for such books as *Sexual Precocity* (1955) and *Diseases of Children* (1964).

**Lehninger, Albert Lester** (Feb. 17, 1917—March 4, 1986), U.S. biochemist, was credited with developing bioenergetics, the branch of biology dealing with energy transformations in living organisms. Specifically, Lehninger studied mitochondria, a submicroscopic structure that takes the form of spherical granules, short rods, or long filaments and is found in almost all living cells. In 1948 Lehninger, together with Eugene P. Kennedy, discovered that cell respiration, the process whereby metabolically useful energy is extracted from nutrient raw materials, takes place in the mitochondrion. This find helped advance knowledge of cell structure and function. Lehninger also conducted investigations into biological oxidations and phosphorylations.

After earning a B.S. (1939) from Wesleyan University, Middletown, Conn., Lehninger received an M.A. (1940) and Ph.D. (1942) from the University of Wisconsin, where he served as an instructor from 1942 to 1945. In the latter year he joined the University of Chicago, and in 1952 he went to Johns Hopkins University School of Medicine, Baltimore, Md., as DeLamar Professor of Physiological Chemistry and director of the department. In 1978 Lehninger was appointed university professor of medical science at Johns Hopkins. Some of his most important works included *The Mitochondrion* (1964), *Bioenergetics* (1965; 2nd ed. 1971), and *Biochemistry* (1970; 2nd ed. 1975), one of the most influential textbooks on the subject.

**Lipmann, Fritz Albert** (June 12, 1899—July 24, 1986), German-born U.S. biochemist, was the corecipient (with Sir Hans Krebs) of the 1953 Nobel Prize for Physiology or Medicine for the discovery of coenzyme A, an important substance in cellular metabolism. Lipmann earned his M.D. (1924) and his Ph.D. in chemistry (1927) from the University of Berlin. He conducted research at the Kaiser Wilhelm Institute of Biology, Berlin and Heidelberg (1927–30), and at the Biological Institute of the Carlsberg Foundation, Copenhagen (1932–39), before immigrating to the U.S., where he joined the staff of the Cornell Medical School, New York City (1939–41). He then moved to Massachusetts General Hospital, Boston (1941–57), where he was director of the Biochemistry Research Department, and to Harvard Medical School (1949–57), where he was professor of biological chemistry.

Lipmann first discovered the enzyme in 1945 and identified it as an important factor in providing physical energy for the human body. While conducting research on pigeon liver extracts, he found a catalytically active, heat-stable factor that aids in converting fatty acids, steroids, amino acids, and hemoglobins into energy. He subsequently isolated, named, and then determined the molecular structure of this factor—coenzyme A. In 1957 Lipmann joined the

*Fritz Albert Lipmann*

Rockefeller Institute (now Rockefeller University), New York City, and served as professor until 1970, when he became professor emeritus. He continued to operate a laboratory and to conduct research there until shortly before his death. In addition to his Nobel Prize, Lipmann in 1966 received the National Medal of Science, the highest award for scientific achievement in the U.S. His autobiography, *Wanderings of a Biochemist,* was published in 1971.

**Livingood, John Jacob** (March 7, 1903—July 21, 1986), U.S. physicist, was the first person to produce a radioactive isotope artificially. After graduation from Princeton University in 1929, he became an associate at the radiation laboratory of the University of California at Berkeley. While working there with Ernest O. Lawrence's group in experimental nuclear physics, Livingood helped design and operate

*John Jacob Livingood*

the first cyclotron. In 1936 he used this accelerator for the artificial production of bismuth-210, a naturally occurring radioactive substance. Livingood and Glenn Seaborg later used the cyclotron to produce many other radioactive isotopes, including radioactive iodine. After leaving Berkeley in 1939 Livingood taught at Harvard University, worked in private industry, and, from 1952, was a research physicist and administrator at the Argonne National Laboratory near Chicago.

**Loewy, Raymond Fernand** (Nov. 5, 1893—July 14, 1986), French-born U.S. industrial designer, created streamlined designs for automobiles, railroad cars, buses, airplanes, and even spacecraft. Loewy also changed the appearance of such everyday items as electric shavers, office machines, soft-drink dispensing machines, radios, and refrigerators, thereby establishing industrial design as a profession.

After graduating from the University of Paris in 1910, he studied advanced engineering at the École de Lanneau but interrupted his education to serve in the French Army during World War I. Loewy earned his degree in 1918 and the following year immigrated to the U.S., where he launched a career as a fashion illustrator for such magazines as *Vogue* and *Harper's Bazaar*. In 1929 he started his own design firm; he scored a major success in 1934, when he designed the Coldspot for Sears, Roebuck and Co. This nonrusting, aluminum-shelved refrigerator was a commercial triumph, and it won first prize at the Paris International Exposition of 1937.

Loewy, the first to introduce functional styling to industrial products, formed Raymond Loewy Associates in 1945 with five partners. The firm produced designs for a myriad of products, including lipsticks, electric shavers, automatic pencils, and labels

*Raymond Fernand Loewy*

UPI/Bettmann Newsphotos

and packaging for soaps, toothpastes, and cigarettes. Loewy was responsible for a dramatic increase in sales of Lucky Strike cigarettes during World War II when he eliminated the green from the packaging and declared, "Lucky Strike green has gone to war." Loewy's sleek designs transformed the U.S. landscape and reinforced his artistic credo, "Good design keeps the user happy, the manufacturer in the black, and the aesthete unoffended." He was responsible for designing Studebaker automobiles, locomotives and passenger cars for the Pennsylvania Railroad, buses for Greyhound, and Air Force One for Pres. John F. Kennedy. Loewy later designed the stamp commemorating the assassinated president. From 1967 to 1973 he worked for the U.S. National Aeronautics and Space Administration, producing spacecraft designs for the Apollo and Skylab projects. His writings include *The Locomotive* (1937), *Never Leave Well Enough Alone* (1951), and *Industrial Design* (1979).

**Mair, Lucy Philip** (Jan 28, 1901—April 1, 1986), British anthropologist, served as professor of applied anthropology (1963–68) at the London School of Economics and Political Science (LSE). She conducted her fieldwork in Africa and New Guinea and had a particular interest in the relations between developed and third-world countries. Educated at St. Paul's Girls' School and at Newnham College, University of Cambridge, where she studied classics, she was drawn to anthropology by a connection with Gilbert Murray's work for the League of Nations. She was appointed assistant lecturer in the international relations department of the LSE (1927), lecturer (1932), and reader (1946). Influenced by Bronislaw Malinowski, professor of social anthropology, she went to Uganda (1930–31) and studied the Ganda people. After World War II she was assigned to the Australian Land Headquarters Civil Affairs School (1945–46) to help train those who were to implement the Australian Labor Party government's radical policies for Papua New Guinea. She returned to Papua New Guinea after her retirement (1968) and also held teaching posts at the Universities of Durham and Kent, ceasing active work only at the age of 77. Her first book, based on her 1930 studies, was *An African People in the Twentieth Century* (1934). She also wrote *The New Africa* (1967) and a series of anthropological studies, including *Primitive Government* (1962), *Witchcraft* (1969), *Marriage* (1971), *African Societies* (1974), and *African Kingdoms* (1977).

**Matthews, Sir Bryan Harold Cabot** (June 14, 1906—July 22, 1986), British scientist, was professor of physiology at the University of Cambridge (1952–73) and made an important contribution to the efficiency of the Royal Air Force during World War II with his studies on the effects of high altitude on the human body. He studied the effects of thin air, low temperatures, swift acceleration, and decompression, and he designed and advised on equipment that would counteract them. He was also consulted by the Royal Navy in the interest of submarine crews.

Matthews was educated at Clifton College and at King's College, Cambridge, where he studied physiology, and was elected a fellow of King's College in 1929. He initially studied the relationship between the central nervous system and muscle spindles, and he devised new and more efficient apparatuses for measuring neurological activity. He became interested in the problems of high altitude while taking part in the International High Altitude Expedition in the Andes Mountains in 1935. With war imminent, he was moved to the Royal Aircraft Establishment at Farnborough, Hampshire, and was placed in charge of aviation medicine. After the war he returned to Cambridge. Matthews was knighted in 1952 and was vice president of the Royal Society (1957–58). He was the author of *Electricity in Our Bodies* (1931).

**Matthews, L(eonard) Harrison** (June 12, 1901—Nov. 27, 1986), British zoologist, as scientific director of the Zoological Society of London (1951–66) conducted valuable research, notably on marine mammals, and with his many popular books helped to interest the general public in wildlife and nature conservation. The son of a chemist, he was educated at Bristol Grammar School and at King's College, University of Cambridge, where he took a first class degree in the natural sciences (1922). In 1923 he visited the mangrove swamps of Brazil, and the following year he was a scientific member of the *Discovery* expedition to South Georgia, where he made special studies of whales and seals. This experience was chronicled in his first book, *South Georgia, the Empire's Subantarctic Outpost* (1931). Matthews left the *Discovery* in 1929 to become a special lecturer of the University of Bristol. After serving as a radio officer during World War II, he returned to Bristol as a research fellow (1945–51). His best-known works included *British Mammals* (1952), which formed part of the Collins New Naturalist series, and *Man and Wildlife* (1975).

**Menard, H(enry) William** (Dec. 10, 1920,—Feb. 9, 1986), U.S. geologist, was a pioneer in the study of plate tectonics, the scientific theory that present and past earthquakes and volcanism, with associated mountain building, can be explained by the relative movement and jostling of enormous blocks (plates) of the Earth's crust. Menard, who earned a B.S. from the California Institute of Technology, served in the U.S. Navy as a photograph interpreter and intelligence officer before earning a Ph.D. in geology at Harvard University in 1949. During the 1950s he was one of the first geologists to use the aqualung to study the seafloor and logged more than 1,000 dives.

*H. William Menard*

Menard was particularly interested in the Pacific Ocean, and he led or participated in 25 expeditions there. In 1950 his party discovered the chain of submerged seamounts that continue the Hawaiian chain 3,200 km (2,000 mi) northwest toward Wake Island. En route home from the same voyage, the group found and named the Mendocino Escarpment, a huge submarine cliff extending west 3,200 km from California's Cape Mendocino. In 1955 Menard joined Scripps Institution of Oceanography in La Jolla, Calif., as professor of geology, and from 1978 to 1981 he headed the U.S. Geological Survey. He was also the recipient of the Bowie Medal, the highest honor of the American Geophysical Union.

**Mulliken, Robert Sanderson** (June 7, 1896—Oct. 31, 1986), U.S. chemist and physicist, was awarded the 1966 Nobel Prize for Chemistry for "his fundamental work concerning chemical bonds and the electronic structure of molecules." Mulliken graduated from the Massachusetts Institute of Technology in 1917 and earned a Ph.D. from the University of Chicago in 1921. After conducting research on war gases for the Army during World War I, he began studying (1923) molecular spectra and molecular structure. In 1928 he joined the faculty of the University of Chicago.

Mulliken, who was dubbed "Mr. Molecule" by his colleagues, was the creator of the molecular orbital theory, which postulates that when atoms combine to form a molecule their electrons no longer orbit the original nuclei but form new orbital configurations around groups of nuclei to create bonds that hold the molecule together. His work, which laid the foundation of molecular science, was so original yet so technical that he never attempted to explain it for the layman. It was not until high-powered computers became available that he was able to describe accurately the orbitals for important molecules. During World War II Mulliken worked on the development

*Robert Sanderson Mulliken*

of the atomic bomb. In 1965 he joined the Institute of Molecular Biophysics at Florida State University but also retained his position at the University of Chicago, where he conducted research until 1985.

**Mycielski, Jerzy** (Feb. 23, 1930—Feb. 10, 1986), Polish physicist, gained international recognition for his research on the physics of semiconductors. He wrote widely acclaimed papers on such subjects as hopping conductivity (the "hopping" of a single electron from one molecular complex to another), the absorption of radiation during hopping, and diluted magnetic (semimagnetic) semiconductors. Mycielski also contributed significantly to the growth and effectiveness of the scientific community in Poland by his encouragement of interactions among scientists. His colleagues praised him for his ability to make difficult problems easy to understand without resorting to oversimplification. Mycielski's interest in mathematical economics led to his appointment to serve on the UN Committee on Asian and Far East Economics in 1966. During 1980–81 he was a strong representative in academic circles of Poland's Solidarity movement. Mycielski was graduated from Boleslaw Bierut University of Wroclaw. He taught at Wroclaw University, Wroclaw Technical University, and the University of Warsaw, and from 1973 he served as the head of Poland's Research Center for Solid State Theoretical Physics.

**Perkins, (Richard) Marlin** (March 28, 1905—June 14, 1986), U.S. zoologist and television personality, delighted millions of television viewers as the genial and unflappable narrator of "Zoo Parade" (1949–58) and as the host of "Mutual of Omaha's Wild Kingdom" (1963–85), two programs that extolled the importance of preserving endangered species. While growing up on the family farm, Perkins became fascinated with animals. He studied zoology for two years before joining (1926) the St. Louis Zoo as a laborer. His talents were soon recognized, and

he became reptile curator, a post he held until 1938, when he became director of the Buffalo (N.Y.) Zoo. In 1945 he became director of the Lincoln Park Zoo in Chicago, and in 1949 he launched "Zoo Parade," a behind-the-scenes glimpse at animals in the zoo. The show went on network television the following year. In 1962 Perkins returned to the St. Louis Zoo as director, and the following year he also assumed duties as the host of "Wild Kingdom." The safari-format program, which was lauded for its unique footage, won four Emmy awards and was seen on 200 stations in North America and in more than 40 countries worldwide.

Perkins, who appeared unperturbed after being charged by an irate bull seal, sprayed by a baby elephant, and bitten by a cottonmouth moccasin and a rattlesnake, helped dispel superstitions about feared animals by maintaining his composure on camera. He dedicated his career to the preservation of wildlife and was the author of four books: *Animal Faces, Marlin Perkins' Zoo Parade, I Saw You from Afar,* and his 1982 autobiography, *My Wild Kingdom.*

**Rainwater, (Leo) James** (Dec. 9, 1917—May 31, 1986), U.S. physicist, together with Danish physicists Aage N. Bohr and Ben Roy Mottelson, shared the 1975 Nobel Prize for Physics for "the discovery of the connection between collective motion and particle motion in atomic nuclei and the development of the theory of the structure of the atomic nucleus based on this connection." Work on the theory began in 1949. The shape of the atomic nucleus had been accepted as spherical, but in his research Rainwater theorized that some atomic nuclei assumed different asymmetrical shapes because of the velocity of movement in the particles that shape the inner and outer nucleus. His colleagues in Denmark experimented and proved his theory.

Rainwater earned a physics degree (1939) from the California Institute of Technology and an M.A. (1941) and Ph.D. (1946) from Columbia University in New York City, where he then spent the rest of his professional career teaching physics. He twice served (1951–54 and 1957–61) as director of Columbia's Nevis Cyclotron Laboratories in Irvington, N.Y., and in 1983 he was appointed Michael I. Pupin Professor of Physics at Columbia. He also participated in Atomic Energy Commission (AEC) and naval research projects and was awarded the AEC's Ernest Orlando Lawrence Prize for Physics in 1963.

**Rogers, Carl R(ansom)** (Jan. 8, 1902—Feb. 4, 1987), U.S. psychologist, was a pioneer in the development of humanistic psychology, which broke with the behaviorist and psychoanalytic approaches to psychotherapy and instead focused on the concept of the self and the individual's perception of the world according to his or her own experiences. Rogers stressed that in developing his or her personality a person strives for "self-actualization (to become oneself), self-maintenance (to keep on being oneself), and self-enhancement (to transcend the status quo)." His influential approach emphasized the role of the patient, referred to as the client, who actively participates in therapy by determining the course, speed, and duration of treatment. While completing his Ph.D. studies at Columbia University's Teachers College, Rogers engaged in child study at the Society for the Prevention of Cruelty to Children, Rochester, N.Y. He became director of the agency in 1930 and the following year earned his Ph.D. From 1935 to 1940 he was lecturer at the University of Rochester, and in 1939 he wrote *The Clinical Treatment of the Problem Child*. As professor of psychology at Ohio State University (1940–45), he created a stir with his article, "Newer Concepts of Psychotherapy" (1940), which introduced his client-centered theory. He expanded on his approach in *Counseling and Psychotherapy* (1942) by suggesting that a trusting relationship between a therapist and client can help resolve difficulties and help clients gain the insights necessary to restructure their lives. From 1945 to 1957 he served as a professor at the University of Chicago, where he founded a counseling center and conducted studies to determine the effectiveness of his therapy. In 1957 he became a faculty member of the University of Wisconsin and in 1961 wrote his most popular book, *On Becoming a Person*. In 1963 he left the university to help found the Center for Studies of the Person in La Jolla, Calif., where he spent the remainder of his professional career. Some of his other books included *Freedom to Learn* (1969), *Personal Power* (1977), and *A Way of Being* (1980).

**Woolley, Sir Richard van der Riet** (April 24, 1906—Dec. 24, 1986), British astronomer, served as the U.K.'s astronomer royal from 1956 to 1971. A leading authority on the Sun, he was an eminent figure in British and Commonwealth astronomy although his work may have been underestimated because of his unwillingness to recognize the importance of space travel and radio astronomy. He studied in Cape Town, South Africa, and at Gonville and Caius College, Cambridge, England, after which he spent two years as a Commonwealth fund fellow at Mount Wilson Observatory, Calif. Woolley returned to Cambridge for two years, after which he joined the Royal Observatory, Greenwich, in 1933 and, with Sir Frank Dyson, wrote *Eclipses of the Sun and Moon* (1937). In 1939 he became director of the Commonwealth Solar Observatory in Canberra, Australia, where, until his appointment as astronomer royal, he made a major contribution to the development of astronomy through his work at Mount Stromlo Observatory. He spent the last four years of his career as director of the Astronomical Observatory in South Africa (1972–76). As an administrator he helped

*Sir Richard van der Riet Woolley (left).*

to coordinate research in Britain and abroad and to encourage education in astronomy, while his own work, especially that recorded in *The Outer Layers of a Star* (1953; with D. W. N. Stibbs), advanced knowledge of the Sun and other stars. Woolley was knighted in 1963.

**Zhang Yuzhe** (CHANG YÜ-CHE) (1902—July 1986), Chinese astronomer, as director (1942–84) of the Zijinshan Observatory in Nanjing (Nan-ching), discovered three comets and nearly 1,000 minor planets with his assistants. Zhang, who was regarded as the founder of modern Chinese astronomy, discovered his first minor planet in 1928 while conducting graduate research in the U.S. In 1964 he was elected deputy for Jiangzu (Chiang-tzu) Province, and in 1973 he served as chairman of the Astronomical Society of China. His many accomplishments were recognized in the 1970s when Harvard University named a minor planet that he had discovered after him.

*Zhang Yuzhe (right)*

# Contributors to the Science Year in Review

**Peter J. Andrews** *Chemistry: Physical chemistry.* Science writer, Rockville, Md. Winner in 1984 of the National Award of Excellence of the Society for Technical Communications.

**D. James Baker** *Earth sciences: Oceanography.* President, Joint Oceanographic Institutions Inc., Washington, D.C.

**William H. Bakun** *Earth sciences: Geophysics.* Research Geophysicist, U.S. Geological Survey, Menlo Park, Calif.

**Fred Basolo** *Chemistry: Inorganic chemistry.* Morrison Professor of Chemistry, Northwestern University, Evanston, Ill.

**Keith Beven** *Earth sciences: Hydrology.* Hydrologist, Department of Environmental Science, University of Lancaster, Lancaster, England.

**Eric Block** *Chemistry: Organic chemistry.* Chairman and Professor, Department of Chemistry, State University of New York at Albany.

**Harold Borko** *Electronics and information sciences: Information systems and services.* Professor, Graduate School of Library and Information Science, University of California, Los Angeles.

**John M. Bowen** *Medical sciences: Veterinary medicine.* Associate Dean for Research and Graduate Affairs and Professor of Pharmacology and Toxicology, College of Veterinary Medicine, University of Georgia, Athens.

**D. Allan Bromley** *Physics: Nuclear physics.* Henry Ford II Professor of Physics, Yale University, New Haven, Conn.

**Paul J. Campbell** *Mathematics.* Associate Professor of Mathematics and Computer Science, Beloit College, Beloit, Wis.

**James W. Canan** *Defense research.* Senior Editor, *Air Force Magazine,* Washington, D.C.

**Douglas E. Comer** *Electronics and information sciences: Computers and computer science.* Professor of Computer Science, Purdue University, West Lafayette, Ind.

**John Davis** *Architecture and civil engineering.* Editor, Publications Manager, The Asphalt Institute, College Park, Md.

**Dave Dooling** *Space exploration: Space probes.* Program Developer, U.S. Space Academy, Space & Rocket Center, Huntsville, Ala.

**F. C. Durant III** *Electronics and information sciences: Satellite systems.* Aerospace Historian and Consultant, Chevy Chase, Md.

**Robert G. Eagon** *Life sciences: Microbiology.* Professor of Microbiology, University of Georgia, Athens.

**Bruce L. Felknor** *Scientists of the Year: Britannica Awards.* Editorial Consultant, Encyclopædia Britannica, Inc.

**Robert L. Forward** *Physics: General developments.* Senior Scientist, Hughes Research Laboratories, Malibu, Calif.

**David R. Gaskell** *Materials sciences: Metallurgy.* Professor of Metallurgical Engineering, Purdue University, West Lafayette, Ind.

**Richard L. Gordon** *Energy.* Professor of Mineral Economics, Pennsylvania State University, University Park.

**Stig B. Hagstrom** *Physics: Condensed-matter physics.* Professor and Chairman of the Department of Materials Science and Engineering, Stanford University, Stanford, Calif.

**Robert Haselkorn** *Life sciences: Molecular biology.* F. L. Pritzker Distinguished Service Professor, Department of Molecular Genetics and Cell Biology, University of Chicago, Ill.

**Lawrence W. Jones** *Physics: High-energy physics.* Chairman and Professor, Department of Physics, University of Michigan, Ann Arbor.

**John Patrick Jordan** *Food and agriculture: Agriculture.* Administrator, Cooperative State Research Service, U.S. Department of Agriculture, Washington, D.C.

**Lou Joseph** *Medical sciences: Dentistry.* Senior Science Writer, Hill and Knowlton, Inc., Chicago.

**George B. Kauffman** *Chemistry: Applied chemistry.* Professor of Chemistry, California State University, Fresno.

**John V. Killheffer** *Scientists of the Year: Nobel prizes.* Associate Editor, *Encyclopædia Britannica.*

**David B. Kitts** *Earth sciences: Geology and geochemistry.* Professor of the History of Science, University of Oklahoma, Norman.

**Mina W. Lamb** *Food and agriculture: Nutrition.* Professor Emeritus, Department of Food and Nutrition, Texas Tech University, Lubbock.

**Howard J. Lewis** *U.S. science policy.* Managing Editor, National Association of Science Writers, Bethesda, Md.

**Melvin H. Marx** *Psychology (in part).* Professor Emeritus of Psychology, University of Missouri, Columbia, and Senior Research Scientist, Department of Psychology, Georgia State University, Atlanta.

**Charles W. McNett, Jr.** *Anthropology.* Professor of Anthropology, American University, Washington, D.C.

**Franz J. Monssen** *Electronics and information sciences: Electronics.* Instructor, Department of Electronic and Computer Engineering Technology, Queensborough Community College, New York, N. Y.

**Colin V. Newman** *Psychology (in part).* Scientific and Professional Secretary, British Psychological Society, Leicester, England.

**Roger A. Pielke** *Earth sciences: Atmospheric sciences.* Professor of Atmospheric Science, Colorado State University, Fort Collins.

**W. M. Protheroe** *Astronomy.* Professor of Astronomy, Ohio State University, Columbus.

**J. R. Redmond** *Life sciences: Zoology.* Professor of Zoology, Iowa State University, Ames.

**Robert R. Shannon** *Optical engineering.* Professor and Director, Optical Sciences Center, University of Arizona, Tucson.

**Joanne Silberner** *Medical sciences: General medicine.* Biomedicine Editor, *Science News,* Washington, D. C.

**Albert J. Smith** *Life sciences: Botany.* Professor of Biology, Wheaton College, Wheaton, Ill.

**Frank A. Smith** *Transportation.* Senior Associate, Transportation Policy Associates, Washington, D.C.

**Robert E. Stoffels** *Electronics and information sciences: Communications systems.* Editor, *Telephone Engineer & Management* magazine, Geneva, Ill.

**Norman M. Tallan** *Materials sciences: Ceramics.* Chief, Metals and Ceramics Division, Materials Laboratory, Wright-Patterson Air Force Base, Ohio.

**Kenneth E. F. Watt** *Environment.* Professor of Zoology, University of California, Davis.

**Brian Welch** *Space exploration: Manned flight.* Public Information Specialist, NASA Johnson Space Center, Houston, Texas.

**James D. Wilde** *Archaeology.* Codirector, Office of Public Archaeology, Brigham Young University, Provo, Utah.

## Contributors to the Encyclopædia Britannica Science Update

**Dorothy C. Adkins** (d. 1975) *Psychological Tests and Measurement (in part).* Psychologist and Professor of Education, University of Hawaii, Honolulu.

**Donald W. Fiske** *Psychological Tests and Measurement (in part).* Emeritus Professor of Psychology, University of Chicago, Ill.

**Mikell P. Groover** *Automation (in part).* Professor of Industrial Engineering, Lehigh University, Bethlehem, Pa.

**Morris Tanenbaum** *Automation (in part).* Executive Vice President, American Telephone and Telegraph Co., New York, N.Y.

**Tjeerd H. van Andel** *Plate Tectonics.* Wayne Loel Professor of Earth Sciences, Stanford University, Calif.

# A
# Science
# Classic

On a new method of treating Compound Fracture, Abscess &c.,
with observations on the conditions of Suppuration. By Joseph Lister Esq.
F.R.S., Professor of Surgery in the University of Glasgow.
Part I On Compound Fracture.

The disastrous consequences of in Compound Fractures contrasted with
the complete immunity from danger to life or limb in Simple
Fracture is one of the most striking as well as
melancholy facts in surgical practice.

If we enquire how it is that an external wound communicating
with the seat of fracture leads to such grave results, we
cannot but conclude that it is by access of the atmosphere
the blood which is effused in greater or less amount
around the fragments & among the interstices of the tissues,
& decomposition through the influence of the
losing its natural bland character & assuming the
properties of an acrid irritant, occasions both local & general
disturbance.

We know that blood kept exposed to the air at the temperature
of the body in a vessel of glass or other material chemically inert
soon decomposes, & there is no reason to suppose that the
living tissues surrounding a mass of extravasated blood could
preserve it from being affected in a similar manner by the
atmosphere. On the contrary it may be ascertained as a matter of
observation that in a compound fracture twenty four hours after
the accident the coloured serum which oozes from the wound
is already distinctly tainted with the odour of decomposition,
& during the next two or three days, before suppuration has
set in the smell of the effused fluids becomes more & more
offensive.

This state of things is enough to account for all the bad

# Sir Joseph Lister

# On the Antiseptic Principle in the Practice of Surgery

In this volume of the *Yearbook of Science and the Future* the editors
continue for the second year the Science Classic, a feature that
celebrates past achievements in science and technology. The article
below, honoring Sir Joseph Lister on the 75th anniversary of his
death, sets forth the discoveries that established Lister as the founder
of antiseptic medicine. First read as a paper before the British Medical
Association on Aug. 9, 1867, the article was published in volume ii of
the *British Medical Journal* in 1867.

In the course of an extended investigation into the
nature of inflammation, and the healthy and morbid
conditions of the blood in relation to it, I arrived,
several years ago, at the conclusion that the essential
cause of suppuration in wounds is decomposition,
brought about by the influence of the atmosphere
upon blood or serum retained within them, and, in
the case of contused wounds, upon portions of tissue
destroyed by the violence of the injury.

To prevent the occurrence of suppuration, with
all its attendant risks, was an object manifestly desirable; but till lately apparently unattainable, since
it seemed hopeless to attempt to exclude the oxygen, which was universally regarded as the agent
by which putrefaction was effected. But when it
had been shown by the researches of Pasteur that
the septic property of the atmosphere depended,
not on the oxygen or any gaseous constituent, but
on minute organisms suspended in it, which owed
their energy to their vitality, it occurred to me that
decomposition in the injured part might be avoided
without excluding the air, by applying as a dressing

some material capable of destroying the life of the
floating particles.

Upon this principle I have based a practice of
which I will now attempt to give a short account.

The material which I have employed is carbolic
or phenic acid, a volatile organic compound which
appears to exercise a peculiarly destructive influence upon low forms of life, and hence is the most
powerful antiseptic with which we are at present
acquainted.

The first class of cases to which I applied it was
that of compound fractures, in which the effects of
decomposition in the injured part were especially
striking and pernicious. The results have been such
as to establish conclusively the great principle, that
*all the local inflammatory mischief and general febrile
disturbance which follow severe injuries are due to
the irritating and poisoning influence of decomposing blood or sloughs.* For these evils are entirely
avoided by the antiseptic treatment, so that limbs
which otherwise would be unhesitatingly condemned
to amputation may be retained with confidence of
the best results.

In conducting the treatment, the first object must
be the destruction of any septic germs which may
have been introduced into the wound, either at the

---

*The first page of the first draft of Sir Joseph Lister's articles
describing antiseptic surgery was written by Lister's wife. The
articles were published in 1867.*

moment of the accident or during the time which has since elapsed. This is done by introducing the acid of full strength into all accessible recesses of the wound by means of a piece of rag held in dressing-forceps and dipped in the liquid.[1] This I did not venture to do in the earlier cases; but experience has shown that the compound which carbolic acid forms with the blood, and also any portions of tissue killed by its caustic action, including even parts of the bone, are disposed of by absorption and organization, provided they are afterwards kept from decomposing. We are thus enabled to employ the antiseptic treatment efficiently at a period after the occurrence of the injury at which it would otherwise probably fail. Thus I have now under my care in the Glasgow Infirmary a boy who was admitted with compound fracture of the leg as late as eight and a half hours after the accident, in whom nevertheless, all local and constitutional disturbance was avoided by means of carbolic acid, and the bones were firmly united five weeks after his admission.

The next object to be kept in view is to guard effectually against the spreading of decomposition into the wound along the stream of blood and serum which oozes out during the first few days after the accident, when the acid originally applied has been washed out, or dissipated by absorption and evaporation. This part of the treatment has been greatly improved during the last few weeks. The method which I have hitherto published consisted in the application of a piece of lint dipped in the acid, overlapping the sound skin to some extent and covered with a tin cap, which was daily raised in order to touch the surface of the lint with the antiseptic. This method certainly succeeded well with wounds of moderate size; and, indeed, I may say that in all the many cases of this kind which have been so treated by myself or my house surgeons, not a single failure has occurred. When, however, the wound is very large, the flow of blood and serum is so profuse, especially during the first twenty-four hours, that the antiseptic application cannot prevent the spread of decomposition into the interior unless it overlaps the sound skin for a very considerable distance, and this was inadmissible by the method described above, on account of the extensive sloughing of the surface of the cutis which it would involve. This difficulty has, however, been overcome by employing a paste composed of common whitening (carbonate of lime) mixed with a solution of one part of carbolic acid in four parts of boiled linseed oil, so as to form a firm putty. This application contains the acid in too dilute a form to excoriate the skin, which it may be made to cover to any extent that may be thought desirable, while its substance serves as a reservoir of the antiseptic material. So long as any discharge continues, the paste should be changed daily; and, in order to

*Sir Joseph Lister*
By courtesy of the Wellcome Trustees, London

prevent the chance of mischief occurring during the process, a piece of rag dipped in the solution of carbolic acid in oil is put on next the skin, and maintained there permanently, care being taken to avoid raising it along with the putty. This rag is always kept in an antiseptic condition from contact with the paste above it, and destroys any germs that may fall upon it during the short time that should alone be allowed to pass in the changing of the dressing. The putty should be in a layer about a quarter of an inch thick, and may be advantageously applied rolled out between two pieces of thin calico, which maintain it in the form of a continuous sheet, that may be wrapped in a moment round the whole circumference of a limb, if this be thought desirable, while the putty is prevented by the calico from sticking to the rag which is next the skin.[2] When all discharge has ceased, the use of the paste is discontinued, but the original rag is left adhering to the skin till healing by scabbing is supposed to be complete. I have at present in the hospital a man with severe compound fracture of both bones of the left leg, caused by direct violence, who, after the cessation of the sanious discharge under the use of the paste, without a drop of pus appearing, has been treated for the last two weeks exactly as if the fracture were a simple one. During this time the rag, adhering by means of a crust of inspissated blood collected beneath it, has continued perfectly dry, and it will be left untouched till the usual period for removing the splints in a simple fracture, when we may fairly expect to find a sound cicatrix beneath it.

We cannot, however, always calculate on so perfect a result as this. More or less pus may appear after the lapse of the first week; and the larger the wound the more likely is this to happen. And here I would desire earnestly to enforce the necessity of persevering with the antiseptic application, in spite of the appearance of suppuration, so long as other symptoms are favourable. The surgeon is extremely apt to suppose than any suppuration is an indication that the antiseptic treatment has failed, and that poulticing or water dressing should be resorted to. But such a course would in many cases sacrifice a limb or a life. I cannot, however, expect my professional brethren to follow my advice blindly in such a matter, and therefore I feel it necessary to place before them, as shortly as I can, some pathological principles, intimately connected not only with the point we are immediately considering, but with the whole subject of this paper.

If a perfectly healthy granulating sore be well washed and covered with a plate of clean metal, such as block-tin, fitting its surface pretty accurately, and overlapping the surrounding skin an inch or so in every direction, and retained in position by adhesive plaster and a bandage, it will be found, on removing it after twenty-four or forty-eight hours, that little or nothing that can be called pus is present, merely a little transparent fluid, while at the same time there is an entire absence of the unpleasant odour invariably perceived when water dressing is changed. Here the clean metallic surface presenting no recesses, like those of porous lint, for the septic germs to develop in, the fluid exuding from the surface of the granulations has flowed away undecomposed, and the result is absence of suppuration. This simple experiment illustrates the important fact, that granulations have no inherent tendency to form pus, but do so only when subjected to a preternatural stimulus. Further, it shows that the mere contact of a foreign body does not of itself stimulate granulations to suppurate; whereas the presence of decomposing organic matter does. These truths are even more strikingly exemplified by the fact, which I have elsewhere recorded, that a piece of dead bone, free from decomposition, may not only fail to induce the granulations around it to suppurate, but may actually be absorbed by them; whereas a bit of dead bone soaked with putrid pus infallibly induces suppuration in its vicinity.

Another instructive experiment is to dress a granulating sore with some of the putty above described, overlapping the sound skin extensively, when we find in the course of twenty-four hours that pus has been produced by the sore, although the application has been perfectly antiseptic; and, indeed, the larger the amount of carbolic acid in the paste the greater is the quantity of pus formed, provided we avoid such a proportion as would act as a caustic. The carbolic acid, though it prevents decomposition, induces suppuration—obviously by acting as a chemical stimulus; and we may safely infer that putrescent organic materials (which we know to be chemically acrid) operate in the same way.

In so far, then, carbolic acid and decomposing substances are alike—namely, that they induce suppuration by chemical stimulation, as distinguished from what may be termed simple inflammatory suppuration, such as that in which ordinary abscesses originate, where the pus appears to be formed in consequence of an excited action of the nerves, independently of any other stimulus. There is, however, this enormous difference between the effects of carbolic acid and those of decomposition—viz. that carbolic acid stimulates only the surface to which it is first applied, and every drop of discharge that forms weakens the stimulant by diluting it. But decomposition is a self-propagating and self-aggravating poison; and if it occurs at the surface of a severely injured limb, it will spread into all its recesses so far as any extravasated blood or shreds of dead tissue may extend, and, lying in these recesses, it will become from hour to hour more acrid till it acquires the energy of a caustic, sufficient to destroy the vitality of any tissues naturally weak from inferior vascular supply, or weakened by the injury they sustained in the accident.

Hence it is easy to understand how, when a wound is very large, the crust beneath the rag may prove here and there insufficient to protect the raw surface from the stimulating influence of the carbolic acid in the putty, and the result will be, first, the conversion of the tissues so acted on into granulations, and subsequently the formation of more or less pus. This, however, will be merely superficial, and will not interfere with the absorption and organization of extravasated blood or dead tissues in the interior; but, on the other hand, should decomposition set in before the internal parts have become securely consolidated, the most disastrous results may ensue.

I left behind me in Glasgow a boy, thirteen years of age, who between three and four weeks previously met with a most severe injury to the left arm, which he got entangled in a machine at a fair. There was a wound six inches long and three inches broad, and the skin was very extensively undermined beyond its limits, while the soft parts generally were so much lacerated that a pair of dressing-forceps introduced at the wound, and pushed directly inwards, appeared beneath the skin at the opposite aspect of the limb. From this wound several tags of muscle were hanging, and among them there was one consisting of about three inches of the triceps in almost its entire thickness; while the lower fragment of the bone, which was broken high up, was protruding four and a half inches, stripped of muscle, the skin being tucked in under it. Without the assistance of the antiseptic treatment, I should certainly have thought of nothing else but amputation at the shoulder-joint; but as the radial pulse could be felt, and the fingers had sensation, I did not hesitate to try to save the limb, and adopted the plan of treatment above described, wrapping the arm from the shoulder to below the elbow in the antiseptic application, the whole interior of the wound, together with the protruding bone, having previously been freely treated with strong carbolic acid. About the tenth day the discharge, which up to that time had been only sanious and serous, showed a slight admixture of slimy pus, and this increased till, a few days before I left, it amounted to about three drachms in twenty-four hours. But the boy continued, as he had been after the second day, free from unfavourable symptoms, with pulse, tongue, appetite, and sleep natural, and strength increasing, while the limb remained as it had been from the first, free from swelling, redness, or pain. I therefore persevered with the antiseptic dressing, and before I left, the discharge was already somewhat less, while the bone was becoming firm. I think it likely that in that boy's case I should have found merely a superficial sore had I taken off all the dressings at the end of three weeks, though, considering the extent of the injury, I thought it prudent to let the month expire before disturbing the rag next the skin. But I feel sure that if I had resorted to ordinary dressings when the pus first appeared, the progress of the case would have been exceedingly different.

The next class of cases to which I have applied the antiseptic treatment is that of abscesses. Here, also, the results have been extremely satisfactory and in beautiful harmony with the pathological principles indicated above. The pyogenic membrane, like the granulations of a sore, which it resembles in nature, forms pus, not from any inherent disposition to do so, but only because it is subjected to some preternatural stimulation. In an ordinary abscess, whether acute or chronic, before it is opened, the stimulus which maintains the suppuration is derived from the presence of the pus pent up within the cavity. When a free opening is made in the ordinary way, this stimulus is got rid of, but the atmosphere gaining access to the contents, the potent stimulus of decomposition comes into operation, and pus is generated in greater abundance than before. But when the evacuation is effected on the antiseptic principle, the pyogenic membrane, freed from the influence of the former stimulus without the substitution of a

An atomizer mounted on a tripod and operated by a foot treadle was used by Lister to spray carbolic acid into the air surrounding a patient with an open wound.

new one, ceases to suppurate (like the granulation of a sore under metallic dressing), furnishing merely a trifling amount of clear serum, and, whether the opening be dependent or not, rapidly contracts and coalesces. At the same time any constitutional symptoms previously occasioned by the accumulation of the matter are got rid of without the slightest risk of the irritative fever or hectic hitherto so justly dreaded in dealing with large abscesses.

In order that the treatment may be satisfactory, the abscess must be seen before it has opened. Then, except in vary rare and peculiar cases,[3] there are no septic organisms in the contents, so that it is needless to introduce carbolic acid into the interior. Indeed, such a proceeding would be objectionable, as it would stimulate the pyogenic membrane to unnecessary suppuration. All that is necessary is to guard against the introduction of living atmospheric germs from without, at the same time that free opportunity is afforded for the escape of discharge from within.

I have so lately given elsewhere a detailed account of the method by which this is effected, that it is needless for me to enter into it at present, further than to say that the means employed are the same as those described above for the superficial dressing of compound fractures—namely, a piece of rag dipped in the solution of carbolic acid in oil, to serve as an antiseptic curtain, under cover of which the abscess is evacuated by free incision; and the antiseptic paste, to guard against decomposition occurring in the stream of pus that flows out beneath it: the dressing being changed daily till the sinus has closed.

The most remarkable results of this practice in a pathological point of view have been afforded by cases where the formation of pus depended upon disease of bone. Here the abscesses, instead of forming exceptions to the general class in the obstinacy of the suppuration, have resembled the rest in yielding in a few days only a trifling discharge; and frequently the production of pus has ceased from the moment of the evacuation of the original contents. Hence it appears that caries, when no longer labouring, as heretofore, under the irritation of decomposing matter, ceases to be an opprobrium of surgery, and recovers like other inflammatory affections. In the publication before alluded to I have mentioned the case of a middle-aged man with psoas abscess depending on diseased bone, in whom the sinus finally closed after months of patient perseverance with the antiseptic treatment. Since that article was written I have had another instance of success, equally gratifying, but differing in the circumstance that the disease and the recovery were both more rapid in their course. The patient was a blacksmith who had suffered four and a half months before I saw him from symptoms of ulceration of cartilage in the left elbow. These

had latterly increased in severity, so as to deprive him entirely of his night's rest and of appetite. I found the region of the elbow greatly swollen, and on careful examination discovered a fluctuating point at the outer aspect of the articulation. I opened it on the antiseptic principle, the incision evidently penetrating to the joint, giving exit to a few drachms of pus. The medical gentleman under whose care he was (Dr. Macgregor of Glasgow) supervised the daily dressing with the carbolic-acid paste till the patient went to spend two or three weeks at the coast, when his wife was entrusted with it. Just two months after I opened the abscess he called to show me the limb, stating that the discharge had for at least two weeks been as little as it then was—a trifling moisture upon the paste, such as might be accounted for by the little sore caused by the incision. On applying a probe guarded with an antiseptic rag, I found that the sinus was soundly closed, while the limb was free from swelling or tenderness; and, although he had not attempted to exercise it much, the joint could already be moved through a considerable angle. Here the antiseptic principle had effected the restoration of a joint which on any other known system of treatment must have been excised.

Ordinary contused wounds are of course amenable to the same treatment as compound fractures, which are a complicated variety of them. I will content myself with mentioning a single instance of this class of cases. In April last a volunteer was discharging a rifle, when it burst, and blew back the thumb with its metacarpal bone, so that it could be bent back as on a hinge at the trapezial joint, which had evidently been opened, while all the soft parts between the

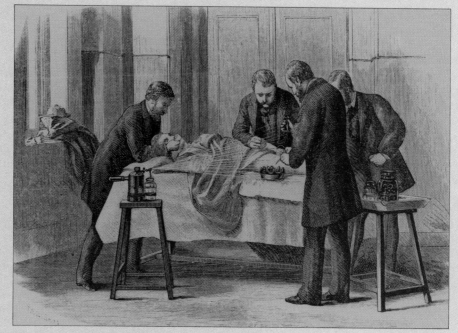

*Engraving in a book published in 1882 depicts surgeons operating on a patient while a mist of carbolic acid is sprayed into the area to provide an antiseptic environment.*

National Library of Medicine,
Bethesda, Maryland

metacarpal bones of the thumb and fore-finger were torn through. I need not insist before my present audience on the ugly character of such an injury. My house surgeon, Mr. Hector Cameron, applied carbolic acid to the whole raw surface, and completed the dressing as if for compound fracture. The hand remained free from pain, redness, or swelling, and, with the exception of a shallow groove, all the wound consolidated without a drop of matter, so that if it had been a clean cut, it would have been regarded as a good example of primary union. The small granulating surface soon healed, and at present a linear cicatrix alone tells of the injury he had sustained, while his thumb has all its movements and his hand a firm grasp.

If the severest forms of contused and lacerated wounds heal thus kindly under the antiseptic treatment, it is obvious that its application to simple incised wounds must be merely a matter of detail. I have devoted a good deal of attention to this class, but I have not as yet pleased myself altogether with any of the methods I have employed. I am, however, prepared to go so far as to say that a solution of carbolic acid in twenty parts of water, while a mild and cleanly application, may be relied on for destroying any septic germs that may fall upon the wound during the performance of an operation; and also that for preventing the subsequent introduction of others, the paste above described, applied as for compound fractures, gives excellent results. Thus I have a case of strangulated inguinal hernia, in which it was necessary to take away a half a pound of thickened omentum, heal without any deep-seated suppuration or any tenderness of the sac or any fever; and amputations, including one immediately below the knee, have remained absolutely free from constitutional symptoms.

Further, I have found that when the antiseptic treatment is efficiently conducted, ligatures may be safely cut short and left to be disposed of by absorption or otherwise. Should this particular branch of the subject yield all that it promises, should it turn out on further trial that when the knot is applied on the antiseptic principle, we may calculate as securely as if it were absent on the occurrence of healing without any deep-seated suppuration; the deligation of main arteries in their continuity will be deprived of the two dangers that now attend it—namely, those of secondary haemorrhage and an unhealthy state of the wound. Further, it seems not unlikely that the present objection to tying an artery in the immediate vicinity of a large branch may be done away with; and that even the innominate, which has lately been the subject of an ingenious experiment by one of the Dublin surgeons on account of its well-known fatality under the ligature from secondary haemorrhage, may cease to have this unhappy character,

when the tissues in the vicinity of the thread, instead of becoming softened through the influence of an irritating decomposing substance, are left at liberty to consolidate firmly near an unoffending though foreign body.

It would carry me far beyond the limited time which, by the rules of the Association, is alone at my disposal, were I to enter into the various applications of the antiseptic principle in the several special departments of surgery.

There is, however, one point more that I cannot but advert to—namely, the influence of this mode of treatment upon the general healthiness of a hospital. Previously to its introduction, the two large wards in which most of my cases of accident and of operation are treated were amongst the unhealthiest in the whole surgical division of the Glasgow Royal Infirmary, in consequence, apparently, of those wards being unfavourably placed with reference to the supply of fresh air; and I have felt ashamed, when recording the results of my practice, to have so often to allude to hospital gangrene or pyaemia. It was interesting, though melancholy, to observe that, whenever all, or nearly all, the beds contained cases with open sores, these grievous complications were pretty sure to show themselves; so that I came to welcome simple fractures, though in themselves of little interest either for myself or the students, because their presence diminished the proportion of open sores among the patients. But since the antiseptic treatment has been brought into full operation, and wounds and abscesses no longer poison the atmosphere with putrid exhalations, my wards, though in other respects under precisely the same circumstances as before, have completely changed their character; so that during the last nine months not a single instance of pyaemia, hospital gangrene, or erysipelas has occurred in them.

As there appears to be no doubt regarding the cause of this change, the importance of the fact can hardly be exaggerated.

---

[1] The addition of a few drops of water to a considerable quantity of the crystallized acid induces it to assume permanently the liquid form.

[2] In order to prevent evaporation of the acid, which passes readily through any organic tissue, such as oiled silk or gutta percha, it is well to cover the paste with a sheet of block-tin, or tinfoil strengthened with adhesive plaster. The thin sheet-lead for lining tea-chests will also answer the purpose, and may be obtained from any wholesale grocer.

[3] As an instance of one of these exceptional cases, I may mention that of an abscess in the vicinity of the colon, and afterwards proved by *post mortem* examination to have once communicated with it. Here the pus was extremely offensive when evacuated, and exhibited vibrios under the microscope.

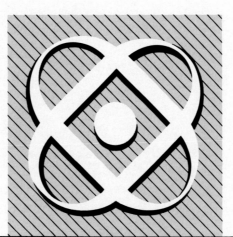

# Science
# for the
# Future

# Ships to the Stars

## by Robert L. Forward

New sources of energy and new designs for space vehicles are making it possible to envision journeys to the stars.

Not until a few centuries ago did people first realize that those points of light in the night sky were suns, like their own Sun. Later they decided that those other suns probably had worlds orbiting around them, some perhaps like the Earth. Since that time one of man's persistent dreams has been to visit those other worlds in ships that travel between the stars. But when astronomers began to realize the immensity of the vast distances that separate our Sun from the other stars, they despaired of ever building a craft that could travel so far. But now there is hope once again. Scientists have found new sources of energy and produced new ideas for making starships. This has made it possible to start planning for a trip to the stars instead of just wishing for it.

### Distances

It is difficult to comprehend the distances involved in interstellar travel. Of the billions of people living today, many have never traveled more than 40 kilometers from their place of birth. (One kilometer is about 0.62 mile.) Of these billions a few dozen have traveled to the Moon, which, at a distance of almost 400,000 kilometers, is 10,000 times farther away. Soon one of our interplanetary unmanned space probes will be passing the orbit of Neptune, 10,000 times farther out at more than four billion kilometers. However, the nearest star, at roughly 40 trillion kilometers, is 10,000 times farther from the Earth than that. The spacing between stars is so large that, even in terms of the distance between the Earth and the Sun (almost 150 million kilometers, described as one astronomical unit, or 1 AU), the nearest star is some 270,000 AU away. To cut interstellar distances down to size, astronomers use the light-year.

A light-year is the distance that light, traveling at nearly 300,000 kilometers per second (186,000 miles per second), travels in one year. It takes light from the Earth about one second to reach the Moon, eight minutes to reach the Sun, four hours to reach Neptune, and more than four years to arrive at the nearest star system.

*ROBERT L. FORWARD* is a Senior Scientist at the Hughes Research Laboratories, Malibu, California.

*Illustrations by Seichi Kiyohara*

510

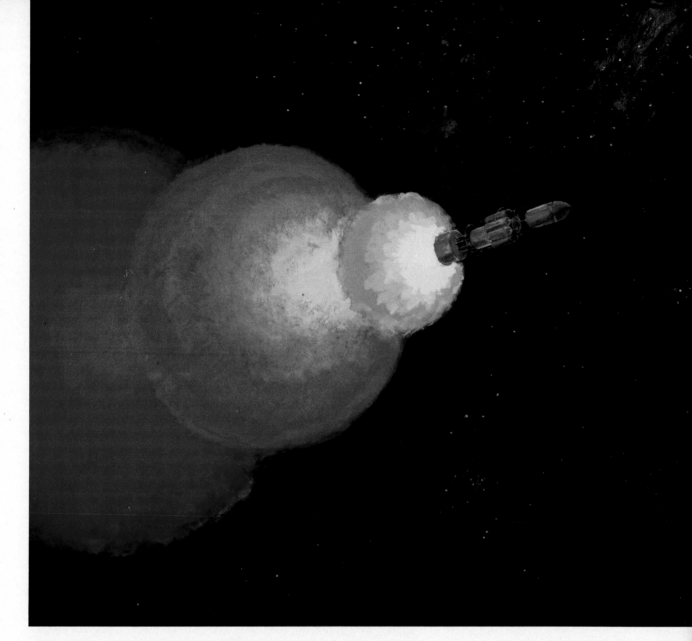

The nearest star system is called Alpha Centauri. Also known as "Rigil Kent," it is the brightest object in the southern constellation Centaurus and the third brightest object in the sky after Sirius and Canopus. Alpha Centauri is not a single star but a collection of three stars. The nearest to the Earth of the three is a small red dwarf called Proxima Centauri. The other two stars are one-tenth of a light-year farther from the Earth and are called Alpha Centauri A and B. Alpha Centauri A is similar to our Sun, while B is slightly redder. These two stars orbit around each other every 80 years, and Proxima circles the pair with a period of millions of years.

Farther away in the heavens are some single-star systems with stars that are also similar to our Sun. These are believed to be the best places for finding an Earthlike planet. They include Epsilon Eridani at 10.7 light-years and Tau Ceti at 11.9 light-years. Within 12 light-years of the Earth there are 18 star systems with 26 stars and, probably, hundreds of planets.

*The Orion interstellar vehicle, a ship with a payload of about 20,000 tons which could accommodate hundreds of crew members, would be propelled by 300,000 nuclear bombs weighing one ton each. The explosions of these bombs, one every three seconds, would produce an acceleration of 9.8 meters (32 feet) per second per second. After ten days the Orion starship would achieve a velocity of 3% of the speed of light.*

511

No matter how fast a starship can go, interstellar travel will always take a long time. Even if such a ship could travel at the speed of light, it would need more than four years to travel to the nearest star system and then an equal amount of time to return.

Why should we bother going to the stars if it is so difficult? One obvious reason is that in the future the Earth will be too small to support the increasing numbers of humans. If human beings are to survive, some small portion of them must leave this big blue egg and travel somewhere else to start a new settlement.

Another major reason for interstellar travel would be to find other intelligent life-forms. Some argue that if alien life-forms were intelligent, people could communicate with them by radio signals. Not all intelligent life-forms will have radio, however. For example, life could evolve on an ocean-covered world to produce intelligent whalelike or octopuslike creatures. Such beings could be highly advanced in music, mathematics, philosophy, hydrodynamics, acoustics, and biology, but they would have no technology based on fire or electricity.

## Nuclear-powered rockets

The most advanced propulsion system now available for a starship is based on electricity. Some source of energy is used to produce electricity, which is then employed to expel a propellant at high speed in order to provide thrust. Usually the energy is obtained from solar cells that convert sunlight into electricity. Unfortunately for interstellar missions, the sunlight rapidly becomes weaker as the spacecraft leaves the solar system; therefore, solar electric propulsion will not get us to the stars.

An alternate method is to use a nuclear reactor to supply the electric power. A nuclear electric rocket would be capable of reaching a velocity of $\frac{1}{2,000}$ of the speed of light after using up all the fuel in the nuclear reactor. Such a spacecraft would be useful for exploring space just beyond the solar system in order to search for planets beyond Pluto and for nearby "brown dwarf" stars. At that speed, however, a nuclear electric rocket would require almost 10,000 years to reach Alpha Centauri.

A faster nuclear-powered interstellar vehicle would be one propelled by nuclear bombs. Named the Orion spacecraft, it was proposed in the late 1950s at the Los Alamos National Laboratory. The original goal of the Orion Project was to send manned spacecraft to Mars and Venus by 1968. The Orion vehicle would be propelled by a series of small nuclear bomblets that explode after they are ejected from the rear of the spacecraft. The debris from the nuclear explosions would strike a "pusher plate," which absorbs the impulse from the explosion and transfers it through large "shock absorbers" to the spacecraft. Although it seems amazing that anything could survive a few dozen meters away from a nuclear explosion, a properly designed pusher plate can stand not only one but many thousands of such explosions.

Freeman Dyson took these ideas for an interplanetary spacecraft and extrapolated them to an interstellar vehicle. The ship would necessarily be large, with a payload of some 20,000 tons (enough to support a small town of many hundreds of crew members). The total mass would be 400,000 tons, including a fuel supply of 300,000 nuclear bombs weighing about one ton each. (This is approximately the world's supply of nuclear bombs.) The bombs would be exploded once every three seconds, pushing the spacecraft at an acceleration equal to that produced by the Earth's gravity (about 9.8 meters, or 32 feet, per second per second). After ten days the Orion starship would reach a velocity of 3% of the speed of light. To provide Orion with a deceleration capability at the target star, it would have to be redesigned to have two stages. Although Orion has minimal performance for a starship, it is one form that could have been sent on its way during the last decade.

At 3% of the speed of light Orion would need 140 years to reach Alpha Centauri, and it would take more than 300 years to get to the interesting star systems such as Tau Ceti and Epsilon Eridani. Because these travel times are longer than the present lifetime of a human being, the passengers on such nuclear starships would have to be long-lasting robots rather than humans, unless some technique could be found that would allow human crew members to live far longer than their usual lifetimes.

Biologists are presently studying the aging process in cells and multicellular organisms. They are finding that cells seem to be programmed to stop replicating after a given number of cycles. If they can find the right genetic switch, perhaps they can turn off the aging process and allow people to live the centuries that will be necessary to explore the stars in nuclear-powered rockets.

Even if biologic research does not produce a method to extend life, there is another method for carrying out such a mission. The original adult passengers would bring along their children, who would take over the ship when their parents died. As only the first generation would be true volunteers, such a starship should be a truly acceptable self-contained world with all of the amenities of life on Earth.

### Antimatter rockets

There is, however, a fundamental problem with any interstellar mission that would travel at speeds less than 10% the speed of light; even as such a spacecraft was launched onto its centuries-long journey, propulsion engineers back on the Earth would be dreaming about more advanced propulsion systems that could make starships travel faster than the ship that was leaving. Within 20 or 30 years those advanced systems would be a reality, and in another 10 to 20 years a faster starship would zip past the lumbering first spacecraft, arriving at and exploring the new star system first. Thus, until there were no more ideas for new propulsion systems, it would seem that no interstellar mission should be started if the flight would take more than 100 years. Instead, the money should be spent on research to build a faster propulsion system.

For example, research is just starting on a new propulsion energy source that is more than a hundred times more powerful than nuclear

The interstellar ramjet would carry a large scoop to collect hydrogen atoms that exist in space. The atoms would be used as fuel for the ship's nuclear fusion engine. Such a ship would never run out of fuel and thus could accelerate indefinitely. It would be the only starship that could reach such velocities that time aboard the spacecraft would be orders of magnitude longer than Earth time.

energy. This new source of energy is antimatter. For every elementary particle that makes up atoms, such as the proton, neutron, and electron, there exists a mirror-image particle, called, respectively, the antiproton, antineutron, and positron. The antiparticles have the same mass as the normal particles, but their electrical charge and magnetic field are reversed.

When a particle of antimatter, such as an antiproton, is put near a particle of normal matter, such as a proton, the two attract each other and almost instantly annihilate one another; this reaction converts all of the mass of both particles into energy. Thus, in effect, antimatter represents a highly concentrated form of energy with the ability to release "200%" of its mass as energy.

For propulsion the antimatter should be in the form of antiprotons (or antihydrogen) because, upon annihilation with the protons in normal hydrogen, most of the annihilation energy appears not as gamma rays

514

but as charged particles called pions. Moving at 94% of the speed of light when generated, the pions exist long enough to travel a distance of 21 meters (60 feet). This distance is long enough for the miniexplosion of pions to be redirected by a rocket nozzle made out of magnetic fields into a one-way stream that will provide thrust.

Antiprotons are being made and stored for days at a time in a high-energy particle physics facility at the European Organization for Nuclear Research (CERN) in Switzerland. The present production efficiencies are low, but techniques exist to improve them by orders of magnitude. Storing the antimatter fuel is relatively easy. Scientists working with atomic and molecular beams have already experimentally demonstrated methods for slowing, cooling, and storing atoms without letting them touch matter. They have built atom traps using lasers, electric fields, and magnetic fields. In the coming decades it is likely that a significant quantity of antimatter will be produced and stored. The first use for it will be for space travel within the solar system, but if no other propulsion system proves to be better, then one day people might ride to the stars on a jet of annihilated matter and antimatter.

### Interstellar ramjet

Although an antimatter rocket is the ultimate in rockets, it is not necessary to use the rocket principle to build a starship. A standard rocket consists of a payload, some structure, an energy source, some propellant (in chemical rockets the propellant and energy source are combined together into the "fuel"), and an engine. Because a standard rocket has to carry its fuel along with it, its performance is significantly limited. The more difficult the mission, the more fuel the rocket must carry. The extra fuel makes the rocket heavier, and so it must carry even more fuel to push that fuel. Soon the rocket is nearly all fuel and can carry only a minuscule payload. It is, however, possible to conceive of spacecraft designs that do not use the rocket principle. These are excellent candidates for starships. One example is the interstellar ramjet, invented by Robert Bussard in 1960.

The interstellar ramjet consists of a payload, a fusion engine, and a large scoop. It carries no fuel because it uses the scoop to collect the hydrogen atoms that are known to exist in space. The hydrogen atoms are used as fuel in the fusion reactor, where the fusion energy is released and the energy fed back in some manner into the reaction products (usually helium atoms) to provide the thrust for the vehicle.

If an interstellar ramjet could ever be built, it would have many advantages over other possible starships. Because it never runs out of fuel and never runs away from its source of power, it can accelerate indefinitely. The interstellar ramjet is the only starship design known that can reach the velocities where time aboard the spacecraft becomes orders of magnitude longer than Earth time. This would allow human crews to travel throughout the galaxy or even between galaxies in a single human lifetime.

515

The major difficulty with the ramjet starship is the design of the scoop, which must be ultralarge and ultralight. If the interstellar hydrogen is ionized, then a large, superstrong magnet might be sufficient to scoop up the charged protons. Although some stars are near clouds of ionized hydrogen, most of the hydrogen near the solar system is neutral. Thus, for now, in regions near the solar system the interstellar ramjet remains in the category of science fiction. The concept of picking up fuel along the journey through "empty" space is too valuable to be discarded lightly, however, and future scientists and engineers will almost certainly keep working on the remaining problems until this concept evolves into a real starship.

## Beamed power propulsion

There is another class of spacecraft that does not have to carry along any energy source or propellant or even an engine. Consisting only of payload and structure, these spacecraft work by beamed power propulsion. In a beamed power propulsion system the heavy parts of a rocket (the propellant, the energy source, and the engine) are all kept at home in the solar system near the Sun, where there is an unlimited amount of energy available. In addition, the engine can be maintained and upgraded by the people back home as the mission proceeds.

One form of beamed power propulsion would use beams of microwaves to drive the starship. An advantage of microwave energy is that it can be produced and transmitted at extremely high efficiencies. A disadvantage is that it is difficult to form into narrow beams that extend over long distances. Because of this short transmission range, the starship being pushed by the microwave beam must accelerate very rapidly to reach the high velocities needed for interstellar travel. The accelerations required are larger than a human being can stand, and so microwave-pushed starships seem to be limited to use by robots.

One design of such a starship, called Starwisp because of its extremely small mass, looks quite promising. Starwisp is a lightweight, high-speed, unmanned interstellar flyby probe pushed by beamed microwaves. The basic structure of the starship consists of a wire mesh sail with microcircuits at the intersections of the wires. The microwave energy to power the starship would be generated by a solar power station that would be orbiting the Earth. The microwaves from the solar power station are formed into a beam by a large segmented lens made of concentric rings of wire mesh separated by spaces.

The microwaves in the beam have a wavelength that is much larger than the openings in the wire mesh of the Starwisp. Thus, when the microwave beam strikes the wire mesh, the beam is reflected back. In this way the microwave energy gives a push to the wire mesh sail. The amount of push is not large, but if the sail is light and the power in the microwave beam is high, the resulting acceleration of the starship can exceed 100 times that of the Earth's gravity. Such an acceleration would allow Starwisp to reach a coasting velocity approaching that of light while

*Opposite page, Starwisp (right), an unmanned interstellar flyby probe, would weigh only 20 grams (0.7 ounce). Consisting of a wire mesh with microcircuits at each intersection of wires, it would be propelled by microwaves which would be generated by a solar power station in orbit around the Earth (left) and shaped into a beam by a large segmented orbiting lens (center). The microwave beam would accelerate the Starwisp to more than 100 times the gravity of the Earth, and the probe would arrive at Alpha Centauri in 21 years. There, Starwisp would use its light-sensitive microcircuits as an "eye" and send back to the Earth pictures of any planets near the star.*

516

the starship is still close to the transmitting lens in the solar system.

Prior to the arrival of Starwisp at the target star, the microwave transmitter back in the solar system is turned on again in order to flood the target star system with microwave energy. Using the wires in the mesh as microwave antennas, the microcircuits on Starwisp collect enough energy to power their optical detectors and logic circuits so as to form images of the planets in the system. The direction of the incoming microwaves is sensed at each point of the mesh, and that information is used by the microcircuits to transform the mesh wires into a microwave antenna that beams a signal back to Earth.

A minimal Starwisp would comprise a one-kilometer mesh sail weighing only 16 grams and carrying 4 grams of microcircuits. The entire spacecraft thus would weigh less than one ounce—it could be folded up and sent through the mail for the cost of first-class postage. This 20-gram starship would be accelerated at 115 times Earth's gravity by a ten billion-watt (ten-gigawatt) microwave beam; in a few days it would reach 20% of the speed of light. Upon arrival at Alpha Centauri some 21 years later, Starwisp would collect enough microwave power from the solar system to return a series of high-resolution color television pictures during its fly-through of the Alpha Centauri system.

The ten-gigawatt beamed power level needed to drive a Starwisp is approximately that planned for the microwave power output of a solar power Earth satellite. Thus, if such satellites are constructed during the next few decades, they could be used to launch a squadron of Starwisp probes to the nearby stars.

*The laser sail starship would be propelled by light from powerful orbiting lasers energized by sunlight. Achieving a velocity of half the speed of light in 1.6 years, the spacecraft would reach Epsilon Eridani in 21.6 years. Near the star the inner two portions of the sail, containing the crew, would separate from the large outer sail (right) and be used as a spacecraft to explore the area.*

## Laser sails

If and when the Starwisp probes find interesting planets, then those planets can be visited by means of another form of beamed power propulsion, called laser sail propulsion. Although microwave beams can be used only to "push" a robotic spacecraft away from the solar system, at laser wavelengths it is possible to design a propulsion system that can use laser beams from the solar system to send a spacecraft to the nearby stars and then bring the craft and its crew back home.

In laser sail propulsion, light from a powerful laser is bounced off a large reflective sail surrounding the payload. The pressure from the laser light pushes the sail and payload, providing the needed thrust. A laser sail starship is about as far from a rocket as is possible, consisting of nothing but the payload and the lightweight sail structure.

518

The thin aluminum film sails that the laser craft would use would be advanced versions of the Sun-pushed lightsails that have been designed by the Jet Propulsion Laboratory of the U.S. National Aeronautics and Space Administration (NASA) and by the World Space Foundation for comet missions and fast trips to the asteroid belt. The lasers would be advanced versions of the high-power laser arrays presently being studied for the Strategic Defense Initiative Organization of the U.S. Department of Defense. The important thing to realize is that no scientific break-throughs are needed to make the building of this starship possible. The basic physical principles of the lasers, the transmitter lens, and the sail are known. All that is required to make the laser sail starship a reality is a lot of engineering (and a lot of money).

The lasers would be orbiting in space and energized by sunlight collected by large reflectors. For pushing an interstellar starship the lasers would probably work best if they were in orbit around Mercury. There is more and stronger sunlight there than on the Earth, and the gravitational attraction of Mercury would keep the lasers from being "blown" away by the reaction from their light beams. Such lasers would use the abundant sunlight at Mercury's orbit to produce coherent laser light, which would then be combined into a single coherent laser beam and sent to a transmitter lens floating between Saturn and Uranus.

The transmitter lens would be a segmented ring lens 1,000 kilometers in diameter. It would consist of wide concentric rings of extremely thin plastic film alternating with empty spaces. The transmitter lens would be not in orbit about the Sun but either freely falling (very slowly at that distance from the Sun) or "levitated" in place by rockets or by the push from a portion of the laser light passing through it.

The goal is to design a starship that can carry out round-trip missions to stars as distant as Tau Ceti and Epsilon Eridani within a human lifetime. This will require a lightsail that is the same size as the transmitting lens. Such a sail would be built in three sections. The first would be an inner payload sail that is 100 kilometers in diameter. Surrounding that would be an inner ring-shaped sail 320 kilometers in diameter with a hole 100 kilometers in diameter. Surrounding that would be an outer ring-shaped sail 1,000 kilometers in diameter with a 320-kilometer-diameter hole. The total structure would have a mass of about 80,000 tons, including 3,000 tons of payload that would consist of the crew, their habitat, their supplies, and their exploration vehicles.

The entire structure would be accelerated at 30% of Earth gravity by 43,000 terrawatts of laser power. (Since the Earth produces only about one terrawatt of electrical power, it would be necessary to use the solar power in space instead of trying to get power from Earth.) At that acceleration the lightsail would reach a velocity of half the speed of light in 1.6 years. The expedition would reach Epsilon Eridani in 21.6 years of Earth time and 18.9 years of crew time, and it would be time to stop.

At 0.4 light-year from the target star the outer ring sail would be separated from the two inner portions. The inner portions would be allowed to lag behind while they were being turned to face the large outer ring sail. The laser light coming from the solar system would reflect from the outer ring sail. The reflected light would decelerate the two inner portions and bring them to a halt at Epsilon Eridani.

After the crew explored Epsilon Eridani for a few years (using the lightsail as a solar sail), it would be time to bring them back to the Earth. To do this, the smaller ring sail would be detached from the payload sail and turned so that the two sails faced one another. Provided that someone back in the solar system remembered to turn on the laser beam 10.5 years earlier, this beam would strike the ring-shaped sail and be reflected back onto the payload sail. The reflected beam would then accelerate the payload sail back toward the solar system. As the payload sail approached the solar system 20 Earth years later, it would be brought to a halt by a final burst of laser power. The members of the crew would have been away 51 years (including 5 years of exploring), would have aged 46 years, and would be ready to retire and write their memoirs.

It is difficult to go to the stars, but it is not impossible. There are not one but many future technologies under intensive development for other purposes. If suitably modified and redirected, they can give us a vehicle that will take us to the beckoning stars.

And go we will.

FOR ADDITIONAL READING

Robert W. Bussard, "Galactic Matter and Interstellar Flight," *Astronautical Acta* (April 1960, pp. 179–194).

Freeman J. Dyson, "Interstellar Transport," *Physics Today* (October 1968, pp. 41–45).

Robert L. Forward, "Roundtrip Interstellar Travel Using Laser-Pushed Lightsails," *Journal of Spacecraft and Rockets* (March–April 1984, pp. 187–195).

Robert L. Forward, "Starwisp: An Ultra-Light Interstellar Probe," *Journal of Spacecraft and Rockets* (May–June 1985, pp. 345–350).

Robert L. Forward, "Antiproton Annihilation Propulsion," *Journal of Propulsion and Power* (September–October 1985, pp. 370–374).

Eugene F. Mallove, Robert L. Forward, Zbigniew Paprotny, and Jurgen Lehmann, "Interstellar Travel and Communication: A Bibliography," *Journal of the British Interplanetary Society* (June 1980, pp. 201–248 [2,700 listings] ).

# Index

This is a three-year cumulative index. Index entries to feature and review articles in this and previous editions of the *Yearbook of Science and the Future* are set in boldface type, *e.g.,* **Astronomy**. Entries to other subjects are set in lightface type, *e.g.,* radiation. Additional information on any of these subjects is identified with a subheading and indented under the entry heading. The numbers following headings and subheadings indicate the year (boldface) of the edition and the page number (lightface) on which the information appears. The abbreviation "*il.*" indicates an illustration.

**Astronomy 88**–321; **87**–325; **86**–261
applied historical astronomy **87**–24
ground-based telescopes **87**–313
honors **88**–478; **87**–474; **86**–402
National Optical Astronomy Observatories **87**–260

All entry headings are alphabetized word by word. Hyphenated words and words separated by dashes or slashes are treated as two words. When one word differs from another only by the presence of additional characters at the end, the shorter precedes the longer. In inverted names, the words following the comma are considered only after the preceding part of the name has been alphabetized. Names beginning with "Mc" and "Mac" are alphabetized as "Mac"; "St." is alphabetized as "Saint." Examples:

Lake
Lake, Simon
Lake Placid
Lakeland

## a

A helix
fiber diffraction pattern **88**–406
A-spacer-B molecule
exothermicity **86**–276
A320
air transport **87**–457; **86**–384
AACR2: *see* Anglo American Cataloging Rules
Aalto, Alvar **86**–115
Aaronson, Marc **86**–265
abalone shell
cement research **88**–339
Abell 400 *il.* **87**–330
aberration
Bradley's discovery **87**–250
ABM: *see* antiballistic missile
Abrahamson, James A. **86**–280
abscess
antiseptic treatment **88**–506
absolute effect
synesthesia studies **88**–225
acacia
environmental concerns **88**–391
*Acanthaster planci: see* crown-of-thorns starfish
accelerator, particle: *see* particle accelerator
accelerator mass spectrometry, *or* AMS
Old Crow Basin finds **88**–315
radiocarbon dating **86**–254
accidents and safety
automobile brakes **87**–371
aviation **86**–385
materials inspection **86**–90
wind-change warning **87**–349
accretion disk
particle collision **87**–19
acetylcholine
neurobiology **86**–333
acetylene
toy chemistry **88**–174
Acheulian industry
*Homo erectus* **86**–251
achira *il.* **87**–50
acid rain
atmospheric sciences **87**–350; **86**–287
climatic cooling **88**–388
environmental pollution **86**–318
forestry **86**–327
lake management **86**–211
acoustic microscopy
nondestructive evaluation **86**–104
acquired immune deficiency syndrome: *see* AIDS
Active Magnetobarium Particle Tracer Explorers, *or* AMPTE
artificial comet creation **87**–453
acute equine diarrhea syndrome, *or* Potomac horse fever **86**–357
ADA: *see* American Dental Association
Adam, Waldemar **86**–273
Adams, Sir John Bertram **86**–414

Addra gazelle *il.* **88**–265
adenine
DNA nucleotide base **88**–406; **87**–311
adenosine triphosphate, *or* ATP
plant research **88**–399
protein manufacturing **86**–335
adiabatics
truck-engine technology **87**–459
Adler, Alan **87**–434
Adler, Dankmar **86**–111
adrenaline: *see* epinephrine
Advanced Land 1
European Space Program **88**–24
Advanced Orbital Test System, *or* AOTS
European Space Agency **88**–26
Advanced Tactical Fighter, *or* ATF
technological development **88**–345; **87**–344, *il.* 345
Advanced Technology Bomber, *or* ATB
stealth technology **87**–346
Advanced Train Control System, *or* ATCS
train design **88**–462
Advanced Turboprop transport, *or* ATP
aviation **87**–459; **86**–385
Advanced Very High Resolution Radiometer, *or* AVHRR
sea-surface research **87**–362
aeolian process
planetary gradation **88**–70
aerobie
aerodynamic principles **87**–435, *il.* 434
aerodynamics
flying disks **87**–434
kite research **87**–143
Aerosat
European space program **88**–10
aerosol
greenhouse effect **88**–348; **87**–352
stratospheric-tropospheric exchange **86**–286
aerospace plane
defense research **88**–342, *il.*
speed and takeoff *il.* **87**–457
African swine fever
outbreak **88**–430
*Afrotarsius: see* tarsier
AFT (Ire.): *see* National Agricultural Research Institute
Ageotropum
hydrotropism studies **87**–400
aging
interstellar travel **88**–513
psychological studies **87**–445
*see also* senior citizen
agoraphobia **86**–181
agricultural experiment station system (U.S.)
farm diversification **88**–393
agriculture: *see* Food and agriculture
Agriculture, U.S. Department of, *or* USDA
biotechnology lawsuit **86**–324
crop-price lowering **87**–392
herbicide research **86**–277
information services **88**–375
veterinary medicine **88**–428

**Agritechnology 88**–101
Agrivideotel
information services **88**–376
*Agrobacterium tumefaciens*
plant research **88**–399
AGS: *see* Alternating Gradient Synchrotron
AHA: *see* American Heart Association
AHA: *see* Applied historical astronomy
Ahlquist, Jon **86**–340
Ahmad, Saleem **86**–272
AI: *see* artificial intelligence
AIDS, *or* acquired immune deficiency syndrome
feline leukemia comparison **86**–357
medical research **88**–422; **87**–423; **86**–348
microbiological research **86**–330
oral lesion linkage **87**–426
AIDS-associated retrovirus, *or* ARV
medical research **86**–348
oral lesion linkage **87**–426
Aika, Ken-ichi **88**–337
Aimes, Andrew **88**–375
air
battery development **86**–137
Air Force (U.S.)
defense research **88**–342; **87**–344
electronic systems **88**–374
military transport **87**–457
air-launched miniature vehicle, *or* ALMV
kinetic-energy weapons **86**–283
air pollution: *see* pollution
air shower
astrophysics **87**–432
airfoil sail
kite development **87**–146
Airy, Sir George Biddell **87**–253
ajoene
chemical isolation **86**–272
ALA: *see* δ-aminolevulinic acid
Alanet
information system technology **86**–309
alcohol
catalytic production **88**–329
aldicarb
Colorado potato beetle control **87**–89
aldosterone
peptide secretion **87**–411
Aldridge, Bill G. **88**–468
alegría (food mix)
amaranth use **87**–49
Aleut-Eskimo languages
Americas colonization theory **88**–314
alewife
lake management **86**–209
"Alexandria Quartet, The" (Durrell)
scientists in literature **86**–229
algae
bacteria consumption **88**–405
hazardous-waste elimination **87**–341
oceanographic botany **87**–401
*Prochloron* nitrogen fixation **86**–332
reef growth and replacement **86**–339
*see also* blue-green algae; red algae
algorithm
computer science **86**–302
linear programming **86**–345
Ali ibn Ridwan **87**–36
alkaline cell **86**–132
alkaloid
bitter taste **88**–74
alkane
C—H bond activation **86**–269
alkene
catalytic hydration **88**–329
Allcock, Harry R. **86**–271
allograft
organ transplant **88**–166
"Almagest," *or* "He mathematike syntaxis" (Ptolemy)
astronomical records **87**–31
ALMV: *see* air-launched miniature vehicle
alpha-A interferon
leukemia research **88**–421
Alpha Centauri, *or* Rigil Kent
stellar distance **88**–511
alpha-2 interferon
disease treatment **88**–421
Alternating Gradient Synchrotron, *or* AGS
physics research **87**–439
aluminum
Hall-Héroult process **86**–344
lake pollution treatment **87**–387
soil acidity **86**–318
tenfold symmetry **87**–443
zeolite composition **87**–210
aluminum phosphate
crystalline structure **87**–223
Alvarez, Luis **88**–350; **86**–49, 288
Alvarez, Walter **86**–49, 288
"Alvin" (submersible) *il.* **88**–361
Alzheimer's disease
aluminum correlation **86**–318
medical research **86**–350
AMA: *see* American Medical Association
amaranth
Incan agriculture **87**–48, *il.* 51

Amazon River basin (Braz.)
deforestation problems **88**–346; *il.* **87**–389
*Amblyseus fallacis*
insect predation *il.* **87**–96
amenorrhea
medical research **86**–349
American Association of Zoological Parks and Aquariums
founding **88**–244
American chestnut
agricultural research **86**–323
American Cyanamid
herbicide production **88**–108
American Dental Association, *or* ADA
dentistry studies **86**–354
American Heart Association, *or* AHA
dietary recommendations **88**–397; **86**–349
medical advances **88**–422
American Indian
landscape management **86**–320
American Library Association
Alanet **86**–309
American Medical Association, *or* AMA
information services **86**–309
American President Lines
double-stack COFC **86**–389
American Psychological Association
membership statistics **86**–376
American Telephone & Telegraph (Co., U.S.): *see* AT&T
American Veterinary Medical Association, *or* AVMA
veterinary medicine **88**–428; **87**–426
Americas
earliest colonization **88**–313
Amerind languages
Americas colonization theory **88**–314
Amiga microcomputer *il.* **87**–368
amino acid
dissociation with lasers **87**–182
electron transfer research **88**–335
molecular biology **88**–407; **87**–405; **86**–334
Nobel Prize research **86**–395
amino-terminal
protein-chain synthesis **86**–334
δ-aminolevulinic acid, *or* ALA **86**–277
ammonia
electride salt synthesis **88**–329
nitrogen fixation **88**–337; **87**–341
amphibian
urban adaptation **87**–76
amphipathic segment
amino acids **86**–334
*Amphipithecus mogaungensis*
anthropological studies **87**–409
Amphitrite
Galileo probe **86**–380
AMPTE: *see* Active Magnetobarium Particle Tracer Explorers
AMS: *see* accelerator mass spectrometry
An Foras Talúntais (Ire.): *see* National Agricultural Research Institute
Anabaena
reduced-nitrogen supply **87**–405, *il.* 406
anaerobic bacteria
Gaia hypothesis **88**–39
analgesic
caffeine use **86**–353
analytic function
Bieberbach conjecture **86**–346
Anchorage International Airport (Alsk., U.S.)
volcanic disruption **88**–354
Andromeda Galaxy, *or* M31
IRAS observations **86**–42, *il.* 43
Milky Way comparison **87**–22
anesthesia
learning **86**–375
ANF: *see* atrial natriuretic factor
ANFO
tunneling **88**–142
Angel, Roger **86**–262
anger
heart disease linkage **88**–449
angiogenin
blood-vessel growth **87**–410
angle of attack
kite flying **87**–146
Anglo American Cataloging Rules, *or* AACR2
information services **88**–377
angular momentum
nuclear physics **88**–440; **87**–440
angular resolution
optical astronomy **87**–266
Anik
space shuttle launch **87**–448
animal behavior
captive environment breeding **88**–255
fear response **88**–477
Lincoln Park Zoo **88**–260
primate societies **87**–59
zoology **86**–338
animal breeding, *or* animal husbandry
San Diego Zoo **88**–244

# n

# Acknowledgments

58–59  (Top middle and bottom left) Alfred McEwen, Arizona State University and the U.S. Geological Survey, Flagstaff, Arizona; (others) NASA/JPL

72  Patrick Ward—Stock, Boston

158  Adapted from *Chemistry, Matter, and the Universe,* The Benjamin/Cummings Publishing Company, Menlo Park, California, 1976

181  Archivio Segreto Vaticano

198  Deutsche Staatsbibliothek, Berlin/DDR, Musikabteilung

209  © Filmteam

222  Adapted from *Daylight and Perception,* S. T. Henderson, reprinted by permission of John Wiley & Sons, Inc., copyright © 1986

260  Chicago Historical Society neg. no. ICHi-03463

325  Original plates taken by Ian Shelton using the Carnegie 10-inch refractor at the Las Campanas Observatory in Chile. Prints by Steve Padilla, Mount Wilson and Las Campanas Observatories. Ian Shelton is the University of Toronto's resident astronomer in Chile; the Las Campanas Observatory is operated by the Carnegie Institution of Washington

407  Adapted from "Structure of the DNA–Eco RI Endonuclease Recognition Complex at 3 Å Resolution," J. A. McClarin, C. A. Frederick, B. Wang, P. Greene, H. Boyer, J. Grable, J. M. Rosenberg, *Science,* vol. 234, no. 4873, pp. 1526–1541, December 19, 1986, © 1986 AAAS

502  Reproduced by kind permission of the President and Council of the Royal College of Surgeons of England

N ow there's a way to identify all your fine books with flair and style. As part of our continuing service to you, Britannica Home Library Service, Inc. is proud to be able to offer you the fine quality item shown on the next page.

B ooklovers will love the heavy-duty personalized embosser. Now you can personalize all your fine books with the mark of distinction, just the way all the fine libraries of the world do.

T o order this item, please type or print your name, address and zip code on a plain sheet of paper. (Note special instructions for ordering the embosser). Please send a check or money order only (your money will be refunded in full if you are not delighted) for the full amount of purchase, including postage and handling, to:

**Britannica Home Library Service, Inc.**
**Attn: Yearbook Department**
**Post Office Box 6137**
**Chicago, Illinois 60680**

# IN THE BRITANNICA TRADITION OF QUALITY...

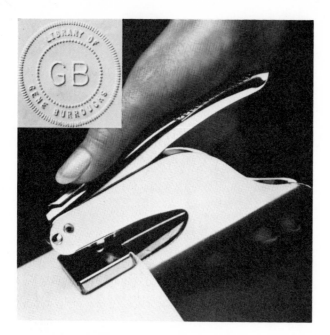

## PERSONAL EMBOSSER

A mark of distinction for your fine books. A book embosser just like the ones used in libraries. The 1½″ seal imprints "Library of _____" (with the name of your choice) and up to three centered initials. Please type or print clearly BOTH full name (up to 26 letters including spaces between names) and up to three initials.
Please allow six weeks for delivery.

Just **$20.00**

plus $2.00 shipping and handling

This offer available only in the United States.
Illinois residents please add sales tax

**Britannica Home Library Service, Inc.**